Gods, Goddesses,
and Images of God
in Ancient Israel

To the memory of
Pirḥiya Beck ז״ל

Gods, Goddesses, and Images of God in Ancient Israel

Othmar Keel

Christoph Uehlinger

Translated by
Thomas H. Trapp

FORTRESS PRESS   MINNEAPOLIS

GODS, GODDESSES, AND IMAGES OF GOD
In Ancient Israel

English translation copyright © 1998 Augsburg Fortress.
Translated by Thomas H. Trapp from the German *Göttinnen, Götter und Gottessymbole*
(QD 134), copyright © 1992 Herder Verlag, Fribourg.

Jacket design: Joseph Bonyata
Typesetting: Waverley Typesetters, Galashiels

In preparing this English-language edition, the publishers wish especially to thank
Dr Allan W. Mahnke for his preliminary translation work, the authors for their aid in
rendering some technical terminology, Peter Cousins for his skillful line editing,
and the Swiss funding agency Pro Helvetia for its generous financial assistance.

Library of Congress Cataloging-in-Publication Data

Keel, Othmar, 1937–
　　[Göttinnen, Götter und Gottessymbole. English]
　　Gods, goddesses, and images of God : in ancient Israel / Othmar Keel and
Christoph Uehlinger ; translated by Thomas H. Trapp.
　　　　p.　cm.
　　Material from a multi-session lecture for the annual meeting of the
Arbeitsgemeinschaft der Deutschsprachigen Katholischen Alttestamentler und
Alttestamentlerinnen, held Aug. 28, 1990, in Lucerne, Switzerland.
　　Includes bibliographical references and indexes.
　　ISBN 0-8006-2789-X (alk. paper)
　　1. Palestine—Religion.　2. Goddesses—Palestine.　3. Gods, Semitic—Palestine.
4. Idols and images—Palestine.　5. Jewish art and symbolism—Palestine.
6. Palestine—Antiquities.
I. Uehlinger, Christoph.　II. Arbeitsgemeinschaft der Deutschsprachigen Katholischen
Alttestamentler und Alttestamentlerinnen.　III. Title.
BL1640.K4413　1996
291.2'11'0933—dc21
　　　　　　　　　　　　　　　　　　　　　　　　　　　　96–37667
　　　　　　　　　　　　　　　　　　　　　　　　　　　　CIP

Printed in Great Britain　　　　　　　　　　　　　　　　　　AF 1-2789

02　　01　　00　　99　　98　　1　　2　　3　　4　　5　　6　　7　　8　　9　　10

Contents

❧

Preface to the English Edition

Awareness is growing among today's biblical scholars that conventional text-oriented approaches, whether focussing on epigraphical sources or on biblical texts, need to be supplemented by archaeological evidence and iconographical studies if a reasonably comprehensive and reliable picture of the historical realities involved is to emerge. This book is not a synthesis of the history of Syro-Palestinian religions, including the religion of Israel, but an attempt to give visual sources their due as a necessary element in any such undertaking.

Vigorous commitment to opening new vistas in scholarship against the inertia of conventional learning may at times lead authors to state opinions that, to themselves upon second reflection or to others looking from different viewpoints, might appear to be too bold or at least "unproven." We are grateful to a number of colleagues who have expressed their constructive, critical opinions in very substantial reviews of the first German edition of this book. Like all scholarship in the humanities, our argument rarely amounts to proof; although based upon primary evidence, it involves interpretation related to probabilities and plausibilities and allows for considerable disagreement in detail. We might also point out that we have written this book with a concern both for scholars *and* for a larger public interested in historical approaches to religion, theology, and feminism, a public who would not know what to do with too many "ifs" and "buts."

Göttinnen, Götter und Gottessymbole appeared six years ago and has already gone through four German printings. Since then, research on the history of the religions of Palestine/Israel has moved at a tremendous pace. New primary evidence has surfaced, such as a monumental stela from a definitely cultic context at the eighth-century city gate of Bethsaida/et-Tell, which shows a cultic pole topped by a bull's head relating to an Aramaean moon god, or a seventh-century building inscription mentioning the hitherto unknown goddess *Ptgyh* from a Philistine temple at Ekron. The finds from Ḥorvat Qitmit, the most astounding assemblage of late Iron Age cultic statuary and figurines found to date in Palestine/Israel (about which at the time of writing this book we knew only from summary descriptions in an exhibition catalogue) have since been published in an exemplary way by Pirḥiya Beck. As a necessary corollary to the ever-increasing stream of new finds, some much-needed corpus editions have

ix

appeared, e.g., Christian Herrman's *Ägyptische Amulette aus Palästina/Israel* (OBO 138, 1994), Raz Kletter's *Judean Pillar Figurines and the Archaeology of Asherah* (BAR International Series 636, 1996), or Naḥman Avigad's *Corpus of West Semitic Seals* (1997) thoroughly revised by Benjamin Sass. Our own *Corpus der Stempelsiegel aus Palästina/Israel von den Anfängen bis zue Perserzeit*, with an extensive introduction and the first volume of material, is now published, and we are assured that with the support of the Swiss National Fund for Scientific Research and the cooperation of the Department of Antiquities of Jordan and numerous excavators, it will also be possible to include in the *Corpus* a special volume with material from Transjordan. Consequently, our own thoughts on the subject, have not, of course, stood still during the past six years. Readers interested in some of these recent developments are invited to consult the fourth German printing (1998) of our book. It contains a substantial addendum that appeared too late to be incorporated into the English version.

We thank J. Michael West (Fortress Press) and Susan G. Nichol (T&T Clark) for all the care they took in going through the production process of this book. We are also indebted to Dr. Thomas H. Trapp for producing such a fine English translation of a text that must have contained numerous Swiss idiosyncrasies in addition to sometimes unusual technical terminology.

This English edition of *Gods, Goddesses, and Images of God in Ancient Israel* is dedicated with deeply felt emotion to Pirḥiya Beck, our much-esteemed colleague from Tel Aviv University. The sad news of her sudden death on August 28 reached us together with the final proofs for this book. Pirḥiya has been an outstanding scholar and teacher. She has done more than anybody else for the study of Syro-Palestinian iconography in the archaeology of Israel. Some of her publications, e.g., the edition of the drawings from Kuntilet ʿAjrud or the statuary and figurines from Ḥorvat Qitmit, will remain hallmarks of meticulous and intelligent scholarship forever. The months to come would have been her last term of teaching. We know that she was awaiting this English version of *Göttinnen* . . . on which, she had told us, she wanted to teach a seminar with her students. No doubt, she would have disagreed with one or another of our interpretations, and we would be so eager to know her opinion. Alas, we share the grief of many who shall miss her distinguished and insightful knowledge and understanding of ancient Canaan's and Israel's visual heritage.

Fribourg, Switzerland   OTHMAR KEEL
September 1998   CHRISTOPH UEHLINGER

Preface to the German Edition

The question of the origin of Israelite monotheism has been the subject of intensive study during the last decade, especially among those who work in the areas of feminist theology, biblical exegesis, and ancient Near Eastern religion. A related question deals with whether one or more female deities was worshiped along with the deity Yahweh in preexilic Israel and concerns the nature of their status. Diametrically opposite theories regarding the history of Canaanite and Israelite/Judahite religion(s) have provided an opportunity for intense scholarly discourse. It is quite obvious that these discussions have dealt almost exclusively with the interpretation of texts, whether biblical or extrabiblical, and inscriptions, whether Canaanite or Hebrew. Visual depictions, having been recovered recently by the thousands at archaeological excavations in Palestine/Israel, are seldom taken into account, even though they would expand the pool of raw data many times just by sheer volume. Since the biblical texts remain the same, and the inscriptional source material is not growing at the same rate as the scholarly essays and books that evaluate such evidence, the discussion has at times been reduced to a repetition of long-held opinions that do not seem to rise above the level of the term paper or beyond a wholesale recopying of the theses of others.

Anyone who systematically ignores the pictorial evidence that a culture has produced can hardly expect to recreate even a minimally adequate description of the culture itself. Such a person will certainly not be able to describe the nature of the religious symbols by which such a culture oriented itself. The following study proceeds from this conviction. It intentionally seeks to provide access to a new dimension in the discussion about the relationship between god and goddess in Canaan and Israel. In our opinion, the sadly neglected pictorial evidence from Canaan and Israel must be treated as being equally as important as textual evidence, offering its own unique type of information to assist in the investigation of Canaanite and biblical concepts of deity.

The material gathered together in this study was presented on 28 August 1990 in Lucerne as a multi-session slide lecture at the annual meeting of the Arbeitsgemeinschaft der deutschsprachigen katholischen Alttesta- mentler und Alttestamentlerinnen. The conference theme was entitled "The One God and the Goddess: Biblical Israel's Concepts about Deity as viewed by Feminist Theology." The exegetical lectures and joint reports of the conference have been published already in "Quaestiones disputatae" Vol. 135 (Wacker/Zenger 1991). Thanks to Dr Marie-Theres Wacker and Prof. Erich Zenger, the editors of the conference volume, we began the present study for that meeting. Since we quickly realized that our presentation would cover much more territory than could be appropriately included in that volume, it was determined that this volume would appear as a separate work within the same series. By his kind and friendly encouragement, Dr Peter Suchla, the editor of the series for the Herder Verlag, saw to it that the book was completed in a reasonable amount of time, in spite of many other projects. The pages of text and the illustrations were made available to the publisher in a camera-ready format.

It should go without saying that this volume does not replicate the lectures given in Lucerne down to minute details. We express our gratitude to Dr Judith M. Hadley (Cambridge), Ms Tallay Ornan (Jerusalem), Prof. Georg Braulik (Vienna), Prof. Norbert Lohfink (Frankfurt am Main), Prof. Oswald Loretz (Münster), Dr Robert Wenning (Münster), and Dr Wolfgang Zwickel (Kiel) who put unpublished manuscripts at our disposal that helped us to refine certain aspects of some theses. Dr Benjamin Sass (Haifa and Jerusalem), who is involved in a study of the iconography on Hebrew name seals, a project being funded by the Swiss National Fund for Scientific Research, was an especially skilled partner in dialogue and was an able interpreter of archaeological scholarly activity in Israel. We received help on as-yet-unpublished seals held in private collections from Mr Lenny Wolfe (Jerusalem) and Dr Wolfgang Zwickel (Kiel), among others.

During the course of the editorial process, as we considered, selected, and kept rearranging the 600 plus illustrations contained in this volume, we came to new insights that go beyond or correct what was presented at the Lucerne conference. The pictorial evidence provides the substance of what is argued in this study. References that identify the sources for this evidence are identified in detail at the back of this volume.

Many drawings are published here for the first time. We are grateful for the expert assistance of Ines Haselbach, Hildi Keel-Leu and Jürgen Rotner. Andrea Jäkle, Klaus Bieberstein, and Dr Arthur Uehlinger have supported us by giving great attention to the technical details that such a book demands (layout of the illustrations, indices, proof reading). We express our deepest thanks to all of them at this time.

In many respects this book is a cooperative venture. It could not have been written without the foundational work of Dr Urs Winter (*Frau und Göttin*, 1983, 1987) and Dr Silvia Schroer (*In Israel gab es Bilder*, 1987). The iconographic horizon of Dr Winter's pioneering study covers and evaluates evidence that has been gathered from Egypt to Elam, with emphasis on the Syrian cylinder seals of the second millennium, treating issues that frequently intersect our own interests. A different approach is taken in Dr Schroer's dissertation, which begins with biblical "information on pictorial art" and seeks to connect the references, primarily on a phenomenological level, with comparable iconographic evidence that admittedly comes from various time periods and geographical regions of the ancient Near East. Although her work was done as a way to provide a foundation for a book on the art history of ancient Israel, the author entered the field of the history of religions from a feminist perspective by her repeated assessment of biblical texts. Thus, both of these studies deserve special mention at this time.

If we follow our own path and disagree at certain points with these and other previous studies during the course of our interpretation, it will be due in part to advances in the scholarly discussion that have been made after they were completed, but more often it will be due to a different methodological point of departure. Unlike Dr Winter and Dr Schroer, in this study we evaluate only material remains that have been excavated in Palestine/Israel, or else finds whose origin can be traced to Palestine/Israel with confidence. Moreover, we differ from the two cited studies in that we pay careful attention to regional differences and diachronic changes. Our new methodological starting point is not merely due to theoretical differences. It has much to do with the fact that we who are at the Biblical Institute of the University of Fribourg (Switzerland) possess documented evidence for approximately 8500 stamp seals found in Palestine/Israel. This massive amount of evidence was gathered as part of a project initiated by Othmar Keel with the aid of the Swiss National Fund for Scientific Research, on which Prof. Karl Jaroš (Vienna) and Dr. Bertrand Jaeger (Basel), among others, have collaborated. The scholarly publication of the documentation is in progress (see authors' note at the end of this book) and will take years to complete.

As a joint work, this book is the fruit of many years of close cooperation between the two authors. Readers schooled in literary criticism will easily be able to tell that different hands contributed to the work. We wrote the introductory chapters I, II and the concluding chapter X more or less together. Othmar Keel wrote chapters III-V, dealing with the second millennium (Middle Bronze Age IIB – Iron Age I), and Christoph Uehlinger wrote chapters VI-IX, dealing with the first millennium (Iron Age II-III). The division of labor is by no means absolute. Each chapter contains unique insights from the co-author, occasioned by the different and supplementary interests and competencies of each. We both did editorial work to correct, critique, and expand on what the other author wrote. Each section was subject to intense discussion and consultation. For this reason we are mutually responsible for the entire text.*

Biblical Institute
University of Fribourg, Switzerland
March 1992

Othmar Keel
Christoph Uehlinger

* For abbreviations in the text see the list at the end of the book. Readers who would prefer a quick overview should begin by reading chapter X.

I

꧁

Starting Point

1. The Problem

§1.   Spectacular inscriptions discovered at Kuntillet ʿAjrud in the northeastern Sinai in 1978 have been published that deal with, among other issues, El and Baal and also "Yahweh . . . and his Asherah" (see below, §§129ff.). At the beginning of the 1980s, thanks to this revolutionary documentation, discussion about the appearance, origin, and significance of monotheism in ancient Israel started anew (see Keel 1980b, Lang 1981, Haag 1985). Stimulated by feminist theological research as well, the discussion has intensified concerning the question about whether Yahweh, the God of Israel and the God of the Hebrew Bible, might have had a divine consort in preexilic times, in the form of the ("Canaanite") goddess Asherah.

It is not just an historical interest that underlies the sharpened focus of this debate. The issue behind the question about whether Yahweh had a consort leads indirectly to a discussion about the role of women in the cult in preexilic Israel and moves into the realm of the status of women in both synagogue and church. With good reason, this topic has been very important in studies that are explicitly feminist, and rightly so in light of the patriarchal and androcentric aspects of the biblical heritage. Finally, and most importantly, one must deal with the question about the importance accorded feminine human experience and feminine personhood in discussions about the way God is conceptualized in the Judeo-Christian tradition.

As E. Gerstenberger has correctly emphasized, archaeological finds such as these certainly do not call for "us to direct all our energies exclusively to the analysis of ancient texts and to a study of the insights garnered from excavations," without at the same time "taking note of the questions from our own time, especially those concerning women who have been affected by patriarchal images of God and by church practices that have grown out of that viewpoint, continuing to discuss these matters and thus continually evaluating our own frames of reference" (Gerstenberger 1988, 15). And yet, if one does not want to be exhausted by theological reflection that is nothing but a sterile confrontation with myths of one's own making – whether it be the idea that monotheism was promulgated originally by Moses or that there was a "suppressed matriarchy in ancient Israel" – it is truly necessary to examine the relevant *sources* in order to *reconstruct the religious development of Canaan and Israel.*

Such sources offer something other than what one has available in the texts that have been transmitted in the Bible, texts that prove time and again to be difficult to interpret historically. Anyone who wants to study actual primary sources must focus on the treasure trove of iconographic and epigraphic documents provided by archaeological research in Palestine/Israel. In the present study, we will seek to use such sources to answer the following questions: What do these finds tell us about the significance of male and female deities? What roles do the deities perform? With what motifs and symbols are they connected? How do the deities interact with one another? Can one even go so far as to be able to speak about the relationship between the religious symbol system and the social symbol system? Can one identify a connection between conceptualizations of the deity and the way a society developed? Such a study ventures into territory that is new. Because the available evidence continues to be fragmentary, and due to the fact that space limitations are also a factor, it is impossible to do more than provide a basic sketch of the available data.

2. The Current State of the Question: Was Preexilic Israel Polytheistic? Did Yahweh Have a Partner?

§2.　Recent Old Testament research, at least so far as this is carried out by German-speaking scholars interested in religio-historical questions, generally assumes that the religion of preexilic Israel and Judah is to be characterized as thoroughly polytheistic. B. Lang can find relatively broad support today when he writes:

> In the four and a half centuries during which there were one or two Israelite monarchies (ca. 1020–586 B.C.), there was a dominant, polytheistic religion that was indistinguishable from that of neighboring peoples. Insofar as there were differences between the Ammonite, Moabite, Edomite, Tyrian, etc. versions of religion, these beliefs stayed within the framework of Near Eastern polytheism, and each should be interpreted as a local variant of the same basic pattern. The Israelites . . . venerated their own protector god who was there to provide for health and family. But they venerated Yahweh as well, the regional and national god, whose special domain dealt with war and peace issues. Finally, they worshiped gods who performed specific functions, those that were responsible for various special needs: weather, rain, women's fertility, etc. (Lang 1981, 53f.; see also 1983, 20).

E. A. Knauf operates from the position "that the ancient Israelites up to the time of Jeremiah (2:11) were without exception polytheistic and that the majority of them remained so for a long time after Jeremiah lived." He assumes that a different triad carried out these three functions in Bethel, in Jerusalem, and in Hebron respectively (1988b, 155–157). According to M. Weippert, biblical texts, such as Psalms 82, 89 and Deut 32:8f., indicate "that even the 'official' theology of the Jerusalem Temple itself was neither a monolatry nor a monotheism even in the late preexilic era, but was simply polytheistic" (1990, 152; see 1991, 178f., where Weippert suggests that Israelite religion remained polytheistic even as late as the Hasmonean Period[!]). According to Weippert, an essential element in this polytheistic religion was the existence and cultic venera- tion of a partner of Yahweh. "Yahweh, the national god of Israel (or later: Israel and Judah) did not stand alone in preexilic times; . . . he had a goddess next to himself" (1990, 156). B. Lang remarks carelessly, "The temple maidens of Jerusalem – and elsewhere – clearly offered them- selves as handmaids of a love goddess whose statue was in the sanctuary" (1981, 56; see 1983, 24). Are these and similar statements accurate assessments of the facts?

This conclusion regarding the polytheism of preexilic Israel is correct if it is limited to a strictly "theoretical level." The texts cited by Weippert (Psalms 82, 89; Deut 32:8f.) do in fact assume that other gods existed in addition to Yahweh. But the texts say nothing about whether these deities were venerated in any way in Israel and Judah – whether that be carried on in a public cultic setting or else in family or even in personal and private piety. The texts do not indicate whether these deities were merely concerned with and active on behalf of other peoples or groups. The answer to this question is of decisive importance for precisely that time period when scholars such as Lang, Weippert, and others posit a "Yahweh alone" movement that would have begun about the middle of the ninth century with Elijah and continued with Hosea and Deuteronomy, with a chief focus on establishing the practice that Yahweh alone would be worshiped.

Every attempt to reconstruct the religion of preexilic Israel and Judah must deal with a series of fundamental problems that are brought forth by the nature of the source material. "One ought not . . . to confuse the minority opinion expressed in the religious literature preserved in the Old Testament with the historic religion of Israel in the preexilic period" (M. Weippert 1990, 151), since the preexilic "Canaanite" religion of Israel is generally polemicized in the biblical writings. Exegetical discussion has been complicated still more during the last two decades by wide- spread uncertainty about how to date the biblical texts. It has become commonplace to date texts quite late, which means that such textual material is of little value for providing good evidence when one tries to reconstruct the religion of Israel and Judah for the period of the monarchy. And yet, unless one postulates the notion that monotheism appeared suddenly during the second half of the sixth century, like a *deus ex machina*,[1] some type of reconstruction is unavoidable.

No matter what decision is finally made in exegetical discussion about the appropriateness of assigning a late date to the texts, it is obvious that a reconstruction of the religious history of Palestine/Israel for the period covering the second and first millennia requires primary sources. Such sources are not provided by the biblical writings. Only finds that are provided as a result of archaeological activity can provide such primary data (see Knauf 1991, 46f., 51f.).

1 Studies by de Moor 1990; Smith 1990 use the same methodologies; see Lohfink 1985, 19–25; 1992.

3. Archaeology and the Religious History of Palestine/Israel

§3.　A careful study of archaeological evidence that can be dated with reasonable accuracy offers the surest path for reconstructing the religious history of Palestine/Israel during the second and first millennia. Some seventy years ago the Englishman Stanley A. Cook (1925) made an early attempt to pursue this line of questioning. Not only has much more evidence come to light since his study entitled *The Religion of Ancient Palestine in the Light of Archaeology* appeared, but his work is particularly weak in that it suffers from inadequate diachronic differentiation. Cook lumped evidence into just two periods, an "Old Oriental Period" and a "Graeco-Roman Age." Consequently, he did not even consider the developments that interest us in the study of what we now pursue.

　　H. Weippert's *Handbuch zur Archäologie Palästina/Israels in vorhellenistischer Zeit* (1988) provides access to most of the excavated material. It offers a splendid introduction to the architecture and small artifacts for the various periods. She does make some effort to include religio-historical observations about the material. But as one would expect in an archaeological handbook, such questions are not of central importance. Even though such artifacts provide the largest amount of material quantitatively, she makes only passing reference to glyptic art in her presentation of each period and says virtually nothing about what a detailed study of such material has to offer. North American researchers, such as G. W. Ahlström (1984), W. G. Dever (1983; 1987; 1990, 119–166), and J. S. Holladay (1987), have published archaeologically oriented studies about the religious history of Palestine/Israel during the Preexilic Period (Iron Age I-II). Their emphasis on the unique development of the religion of Israel and Judah is problematic because it gives too little consideration to the previous history of these peoples. For the relatively short time periods examined by these authors, one can hardly detect changes in patterns that are clearer when one considers the *moyenne* [Tr.: recent past] influences and especially *the longue durée* [Tr.: extended time period] shifts that can be detected in the material (F. Braudel). A shortcoming that these studies have in common is their lack of attention to one of the most important artifacts for Canaanite-Israelite religious history, the seal amulet (see below, §5). Using anthropological models and statistical methods, Holladay's study, *Religion in Israel and Judah under the Monarchy: An Explicitly Archaeological Approach*, uses an anthropological model and presents a carefully differentiated portrait of religious practices in Israel and Judah during the time of the monarchy. But his "explicitly archaeological approach" concentrates on a discussion of sacred architecture and objects connected with cultic activity. Iconographic ("artistic") documents, which are also proper subjects for archaeological research, are dealt with in a cursory way in his study. Holladay limits himself, by and large, to a discussion of figurines. He pays no attention to the seals, amulets, ivory carvings, etc., and ignores inscriptional evidence as well.

　　Jeffrey H. Tigay's book, *You Shall Have No Other Gods: Israelite Religion in the Light of Hebrew Inscriptions,* which appeared in 1986, deserves special mention. Tigay deals specifically with the question about monotheism and its relationship to the supposedly polytheistic practices within preexilic Israel that have been accepted recently as normative. He is right when he calls attention to the "notorious subjectivity" involved in dating biblical texts. He attempts to apply "external controls" to balance this subjectivity when he turns to archaeology for help (1986, 2f.). He is interested chiefly in previously ignored onomastic evidence and has thus studied Israelite and Judean personal names on inscriptions that can be dated to Iron Age II, to see if names of other deities besides Yahweh are in use. Tigay has investigated not only the personal names but also other Hebrew inscriptions. In addition – perhaps because he encountered so much onomastic evidence when he worked with the seals – he synthesizes the results of this aspect of his study by discussing the iconographic materials in an important appendix (1986, 91–96). Tigay produces a work that can be termed a pioneering effort, both in terms of his methodological premises, because he calls for supporting religio-historical theses with empirical data that take both chronology and geography into account, and in terms of his conclusions, because he raises serious doubts about the validity of the general consensus that Israel was supposedly polytheistic.

This book will seek to sketch out a general outline of the development of the religious history in Canaan and Israel (including Judah) that will stretch all the way from Middle Bronze Age IIB (from ca. 1800) to the end of Iron Age III (to just before 450). In certain ways, we recognize that what we offer is an expansion of Tigay's efforts and his conclusions are adopted and integrated at appropriate places in the study, even though his ideas will be critiqued at times, in an effort to sharpen the conclusions still further. Inscriptional evidence has dominated the discussion of the religious history of Palestine/Israel in recent years. By contrast, we will focus our attention on the generally overlooked iconographic data.

This study will be fundamentally different from others, particularly from those that seek to use only texts to reconstruct the religious history of Israel and Judah during the first millennium and that try to show that there was a gradual movement toward monotheism. That is because this work will focus on the "modest artifactual history of Palestine" (H. Weippert 1990, 187). The other approach has been most popular recently among English-speaking scholars (see de Moor 1990; Smith 1990; on this, see Lohfink 1992; see below, §5). One author has described the reconstructive work as "working with a puzzle that is missing many or most of its pieces" (Smith 1990, xxix). Only someone who chooses not to ignore an entire category of the puzzle pieces from the outset (and that the largest portion!; see Knauf 1991, 41f.), that category being the iconographic sources, will be able to hope to put together a more or less adequate picture of the puzzle as a whole.

II

Points of Departure

1. Symbols and Symbol Systems

§4.　Writing in an essay in a Festschrift for F. M. Cross and working from a definition of religion as a "set of symbolic thought forms and acts that relate human beings to the ultimate conditions of existence perceived as the Holy," the American archaeologist W. G. Dever has advanced the thesis that the study of the history of religions ought to aim "to reconstruct religion on the basis of its extant remains: belief through texts, cult through material culture" (1987, 210; cf. 220). This is not the place to discuss in great detail the problem of how to define religion (see Stolz 1988, 8–33). Dever's definition is grounded, by and large, in an anthropological approach that regards not only religion, but human culture as a whole, as a system of signs, usually termed a *"symbol system"* in English (Geertz 1973; Hofstee 1986). All realms of human existence – biological, economic, social, political, religious, etc. – when understood rightly, take shape within such symbol systems. Various cultures differentiate themselves from one another by their different symbol systems. If a culture has the time and opportunity to develop independently, it will construct a system whose various elements – economic, social, religious, etc. – form an interdependent and coherent whole. As a rule, whatever is created by such a culture is simultaneously relevant in the arenas of economy, the society and politics, religion, etc.

Compared to animals, human beings are not completely programmed upon arrival and their instincts are unfocused. For this reason, people must learn how to feed themselves, how to get along with other members of the group, even how to find a partner and how to propagate the species. Humans need a cultural system in order to endure. Because such a system is necessary and because it compensates for a deficit in natural instinct, individuals and societies regard their own specific system as natural and virtually necessary. The stronger the interdependence and coherence of the symbols from the various aspects of life, the more naturally and convincingly the system works. The following example illustrates this.

> In the village of Einsiedeln in central Switzerland, at a massive baroque monastery, one can see the famous Black Madonna. Until the 1960s this monastery, with its famous chapel dedicated to Mary and with its pilgrimages, shaped more than just the religious life of the village. The monks and the rest of the villagers existed together

within a rich and complex social and economic system, expressed in a complex symbol system that shaped the identity of the village.

The monastery sponsored the pilgrimages that were for the purpose of the veneration of Mary. Ownership and operation of the chapel, with its grace-giving image, bestowed a special social status on the monastery's inhabitants, one which the rest of the men and women in the village either respected or envied, but which was an important factor in the social life of the village nonetheless. The visits by pilgrims made it necessary to have guest accommodations, devotional items (prayer books, statues, pendants, rosaries), and offerings (gingerbread) and determined the economic life of the village as well. The interrelatedness of the various aspects of village life made the spiritual requirements of the system (the veneration of Mary) appear just as natural and necessary as the economic factors (such as the production and sale of statues of Mary).

Cultural change affected all aspects of life in the village after World War II. The partial replacement of the Marian pilgrimage by a tourism business that offered an aesthetically sensationalistic public performance affected the spiritual, social, and economic life of the village. Alongside veneration of sacred figures from Christianity and the desire to follow in their footsteps, some came on a quest for self-realization that was far removed from Christian salvation history. Still others came some time later on a quest to seek oneness with the cosmos. As a result of the appearance of these new activities, medallions of Mary and other saints, once the most popular and the most frequently sold pendants, were displaced to a certain extent by little hearts (symbols of personal love and friendship) and especially by star symbols (being at one with cosmic activity). Sport-related activities (self-realization) began to compete with the veneration of Mary. The social prestige and political influence of the monks diminished. The economy diversified.

In view of this kind of interdependence and coherence within widely diverse aspects of human culture, the dichotomy that Dever postulates between *belief* (faith, a conceptualization of the world) and *cult* appears to be quite problematic, particularly since *belief* and *cult* do not come from different arenas of activity, such as the economy, social structure, and politics, etc., but belong to the same arena, religion.[1] Perhaps there is a typically New Age experience behind this distinction: the idea that religious concepts and specifics about the faith can be regarded as true or meaningful apart from or even independent of established communities and institutions. In a certain sense, some people today regard themselves as believers even though they see no need to participate in cultic activity. This modern attitude could significantly hinder a modern person's ability to understand a traditional culture.

A widely held belief, such as that about Mary in her role as a model for all the faithful, as the Mother of God, and as intercessor, will be expressed in a corresponding cult (statues, altar paintings). These motifs will in turn

1 Dever does not consistently apply his theoretical distinction between *cult* and *belief* when he actually sets forth his study in detail (see Keel, et al., 1990, 396–404).

appear in private dwellings as statuettes and prints; individual believers might wear depictions of such beliefs as pendants or in some other way. It has been and continues to be common for the cultic products that give expression to a particular belief that originated at great shrines (Lourdes, Einsiedeln) to be taken great distances, resulting in the propagation of the unique aspects of the cult as practiced at each site. Already in the ancient Near East many temples used devotional objects to ensure the introduction and extension of the faith they promulgated far and wide (see e.g., Keel, et al., 1989, 281–323; Keel/Uehlinger 1990, 18–20, 27–30). By contrast, some cults could also exist without a central shrine, with activities taking place at many little cultic installations or even in private homes, and such influence could also extend to great distances. It is important to note as well that ancient cults, in rural areas for example, were able to survive for long periods of time (note the development from Latin *pagani,* meaning "villagers," through Italian *pagani* [French *païen,* English "pagan"], "heathen"). New cults can be making their appearance in the cities at the same time and can dominate the religious symbol system at those sites. One must assume that there will be considerable overlap in such a situation,[2] and one must take this into consideration in what follows. In this general survey which encompasses a period of some 1300 years, one cannot point out in detail everything that survives from one cultural epoch and remains an active force when some new influence arrives on the scene, whether this be during the Middle Bronze Age or the Late Bronze Age. Emphasis will be placed on what is new for each particular epoch, whether that is seen in the official art produced for royal palaces and shrines or what might instead be shown to have spread through a broad region. But we will not completely ignore the question about how what is new relates to that which continues to survive from the past.

2. The Sources: Texts and – More Importantly – Images

§5. One cannot distinguish radically between cultic and religious conceptualizations of the world for ancient time periods. But the other

---

2 The Christian symbol system dominated artistic works almost completely during the Middle Ages. Another symbol system entered into competition with it at the time of the Renaissance. In general, and somewhat vaguely, this can be described as secular and it produced portraits, nudes, historical paintings, still lifes, landscapes, etc. Both the old and the new symbol systems often appear in the same paintings and are brought together in the most different ways. Giotto places "The Flight into Egypt" (in the Palermo Cathedral) as the only theme in a landscape with a gold background. In a painting of the same subject by Claude Lorraine, the landscape is the most important part of the painting; the figures taking to flight appear very insignificantly at the edge of the painting. The impressionist painters who treated this subject let the figures disappear totally. This does not mean that the theme of "The Flight into Egypt" and the religious ideas connected with it – concerning God who entered human flesh, endured all humanity's suffering, and in whom the fate of all of Israel (whose God conquered all the gods of Egypt) is concentrated – had disappeared as well. Even today there are innumerable paintings made every year of "The Flight into Egypt." But, at least in Europe, this is no longer a theme for the artistic avant-garde. It is depicted today only by men and women on the artistic periphery, by wood carvers, and children's drawn pictures of this event.

half of Dever's dichotomy is too artificial as well, when he advocates that religious history is to be reconstructed by identifying "belief through *texts*, cult through *material culture*" (1987, 220); such a methodology is artificial and cannot stand the test. If one is to base a reconstruction of the cult exclusively on the articles used in the material culture, such as temple floor plans, podiums, altars, cultic pictures, and the objects used in the cult, one would be forced simply to ignore the many ritual texts found in excavations in Egypt, Syria, and Mesopotamia. There are, for example, hundreds of such ritual texts available for use in reconstructing the cult in Ugarit. Much of this material is unfortunately rather difficult to interpret, and religious and biblical scholars have been more hesitant to use these texts in the same way as the famous mythic and epic texts have been used. We must add immediately that we do not have such ritual texts for Palestinian contexts.

But when attempting to reconstruct the religious system (*belief*), which is the main point of this present study, we also reject emphatically the view that it is adequate to limit oneself to working with texts. Religious concepts are expressed not only in texts but can be given a pictorial form on items found in the material culture as well. Even those objects from a material culture that serve a purely functional role can be or at least might be an expression of certain religious concepts and elements of faith if they are found in contexts where they serve a specific religious function (a drinking cup for a libation of wine, a lamp in a grave, a tabernacle in a Catholic church . . .). Whenever possible, we will support our assertions in this book with the rather sparse epigraphic evidence that excavations in Palestine/Israel have provided to date and which are at the center of scholarly debate. But we will not limit ourselves to such data. We will concentrate on an evaluation of iconographic sources that now number in the thousands, even though this study is limited to the time span from Middle Bronze Age IIB through Iron Age III (see the overview in Keel/Schroer 1985, 9–25; for Iron Age II, see also Tigay 1986, 91–96).

Since 1981, the Biblical Institute of the University of Fribourg, Switzerland, has been involved in a project to document all the stamp seals recovered from legal excavations in Palestine/Israel that are dated from the earliest times to the end of the Iron Age and then to publish them in a catalog (see, most recently, Keel/Uehlinger 1990, 135–141). The corpus assembled within these parameters currently numbers about 8500 stamp seals. These provide the main source material for this present survey. Not only because of their sheer number but also because of their importance, seal amulets far outshine all other kinds of image-bearing artifacts in value, being even more valuable than inscriptional evidence. Since they are preserved in relatively comparable quantities for all periods, they can virtually serve as the standard by which religious history is documented, particularly because they are more or less public artifacts and can thus serve as a sensitive seismograph to detect subtle shifts in religious history (see Keel/Schroer 1985, 10f.).

The inclusion of the iconographic documentation expands the amount of source material and affords a significant methodological advantage. First, we can carry out this survey on a strictly *diachronic basis* and can illustrate the unique religio-historical profile for each period from Middle

Bronze Age IIB up to the end of the Iron Age.[3] Second, we can limit ourselves exclusively to material recovered from the geographic area known in earlier times as *Canaan* and later as *Palestine/Israel* (for the parameters of this territory, see Keel, et al., 1984, 239ff.). From the outset, this can ensure that one will avoid the danger of making pointless comparisons.

This danger has been noted recently in evaluations of U. Winter's important work *Frau und Göttin* (1983, ²1987), in which iconographic material from Bronze Age Syria predominates, even though it is not used exclusively (Lipiński 1986; H. Weippert 1990, 187). Such criticism must be more considerate of the limitations imposed on any scholarly endeavor that ventures into new territory. Methodologically, however, the critique is justified. Anyone who prefers to work exclusively with texts (e.g., to reconstruct "Canaanite" religion using nothing but textual sources from Ugarit) ought to get little or no hearing.[4] We obviously do not deny the relevance of the Syrian texts discovered rather recently at Ebla (Early Bronze Age III), as well as those from Mari (Middle Bronze Age IIA-B), Ugarit (Late Bronze Age IIA-B), or Meskene/Emar (Late Bronze Age IIB) that have stimulated research not only in Semitic studies but also in the religious history of Canaan and Israel and will continue to do so. But conclusions drawn from an interpretation of Bronze Age texts discovered in northern Syria, and the religio-historical hypotheses developed from such evidence, cannot be used uncritically to explain the religious history of Canaan during the second millennium and, though it has happened repeatedly, certainly not to clarify what happened in Israel during the first millennium. Such evidence ought to be compared initially with contemporary evidence from Canaan. When there is a positive correlation, that is, when specific iconographic or textual evidence is actually found or makes it at least probable that comparable religious concepts are at work in Bronze Age Canaan, only then can we take the second step and make a hypothetical correlation with Iron Age finds in Palestine. The primary context for *Palestine* is provided by iconographic and textual evidence recovered from those peoples who lived contemporaneously with and geographically close to Israel and Judah (i.e., documents from Syrian-Canaanite religions dating to the first millennium) and not by data from northern Syrian religious texts (or images) that date to the second millennium (thus, correctly, Niehr 1990, esp. 11f.). A religious history for Canaan and Israel must thus be constructed diachronically primarily by using whatever source material is available for each specific period (!) of Canaanite or Philistine/Israelite history. Seeking to establish links with Ebla, Mari, or Ugarit makes little sense when one tries to provide an accurate understanding of this history, particular for the first millennium. Such a connection is no more helpful than the distorted representation of

---

3 Only in exceptional cases will material from several periods be discussed together from a phenomenological viewpoint, for the sake of clarity. This will usually take place in the context of the time periods during which the material first appears or is found in significant quantities (see §§101f., 117).

4 One should remember that Ugarit lies far outside the borders of the province of Canaan, and that the Ugaritic lists *KTU* 4.96 (= *UT* 311) l.7 treat a Canaanite trader as a foreigner when he is registered (Rainey 1963).

the religious history of Israel and Judah that was provided by the deuteronomistic school – viewed by them as necessary in an effort to justify certain theological positions.

3. Methodology of the Iconographical Approach: Myth, Iconicity, Constellations

§6. When one interprets iconographic material, it is important to analyze not only the varied formats in which certain types of images are fashioned (figurines, cultic stands, seals, jewelry, ivory decoration on pieces of furniture, etc.) but also to note that different types of image-bearing artifacts each perform unique functions. A cylinder seal that is the same size as a stamp seal offers three to four times as much surface for the engraver as the corresponding stamp seal. This provides enough room to portray constellations of activities and roles that are sometimes quite complex. When one chooses to depict these interrelated themes on stamp seals, the scenes are generally greatly simplified. The possibility still remains, however, that different motifs can be combined there too. By contrast, bronze statues, so highly prized as archaeological finds and by museums, are not able to tell as much of a story, since the image that the figure represents (a divinity, a king, an animal, or something similar) is isolated, i.e., it does not appear in an iconographic context and is usually unaccompanied by the attributes that made it unique (see Keel, et al., 1990, 301, 400–403). The biggest problem is often that one cannot even determine the identity of the subject that is portrayed (see Moorey/Fleming 1984, 78–80).

The Heidelberg Egyptologist J. Assmann has made the point once again that mythological narratives are not always to be detected in the background of texts that seem to be using mythic language but that do not themselves retell the narrative. There may be some sort of "pre-mythic complex of ideas" that develop into a full-scale myth only over an extended period of time. Assmann has suggested that one use the term "constellation" for such a "complex of ideas" (1982, 13–61; see 1983, 54–95). He uses the term "mythic speech" to refer to the complex of ideas from different dimensions of reality, such as when one believes that there is a connection between the fertility of the earth and a divine couple copulating or associates a dispute that takes place in the setting of politics or in a military action with the battle against the chaos dragon. This complex of ideas from different dimensions of reality does not initially produce the myth itself (as narrative) but appears first at the stage where a constellation of ideas takes shape. This might happen when the relationship between husband and wife or god and goddess is first seen as symbolic of fertility or when serpent dragons are depicted in combat with military heroes.

"The myth owes its 'iconic constancy' to a few basic constellations" (Assmann 1982, 38). The constellations or "icons," as images, are "reference points" that can be detached from a narrative sequence. They provide a place where mythical expressions can take a crystalized form, being related to certain *relationships* and *basic situations* that contain their own meaning and need not derive their meaning from a particular story and from the way that story shapes the narrative. Significance and enduring character are not found in names that change and not in easily-forgotten narratives. Priority and the constancy of the motif is portrayed in the way icons depict these few basic constellations (themes that survive in the depiction of Mary with the child as the nursing mother of God and the way the resurrected one is shown as the victor, etc.).

Mythic texts are nothing other than icons (or else constellations) that have been presented in story form. Myths are able to retreat from the story line at any time and restate the real message depicted on the icon without losing their identity. The symbol of a battle against the dragon, to take one example, represents the "constellation" of the imminent destruction of whatever threat some evil force poses to that which is good, resolved by the savior who must intervene. The "constellation" appears repeatedly in many myths and stories that use a variety of different names (Baal and Yamm or Mot; Marduk and Tiamat; Yahweh and Rahab or Leviathan; Perseus and the sea monster that tries to swallow up Andromeda; St. George, who slays the dragon and frees the maiden, etc.). This same "constellation" has been used or misused by many different groups in the course of the millennia as a system of orientation and as a model for personal struggles (Uehlinger 1991b).

A culture, or one aspect of a culture such as its religion, is made up of a limited number of visible and audible signs that form a distinct framework or network. The first task of those who study a particular culture is to *describe* these signs as precisely and comprehensively as possible. The clearer this principle is, and the more carefully principles such as these are applied, the better job the researcher will do. One must search for what gives shape to the order and coherence in this network of concepts. One must determine the role played by individual signs, their relationship to one another, and the relative importance attached to each. Just as a language cannot be reconstructed from its vocabulary alone, the religious framework for a specific culture cannot be reconstructed from disconnected pictorial elements. Anyone wishing to understand a language must know the syntax and analyze the sentences. Anyone who wants to understand pictorial evidence must pay attention to complex constellations wherever they are to be found.

4. Periodization of the Archaeology of Palestine/Israel

§7. Without being able to go into great detail about the problems connected with the archaeological periodization of the history of Israel/ Palestine during the second and first millennia before Christ, we do need to make a few remarks at this time about the presuppositions with which we are working in this book. The archaeological model adopted in the *Encyclopedia of Archaeological Excavations in the Holy Land* (Avi-Yonah/ Stern 1975–1978), as well as by other scholars, has dominated the scene since the 1960s, but discussions have been reopened in recent years.

There are many reasons why this should happen. First, new archaeological evidence that can be dated fairly accurately has appeared. A letter from Ugarit (ca. 1230) has come to light in Aphek and a fragment from a bronze bolt for a gate, with the cartouche of Ramesses III, was found at

Lachish, suggesting that the Late Bronze Age Stratum VI at Lachish continued to exist during the rule of Ramesses III, a king whose rule is dated to the first half of the twelfth century. Second, and more importantly, because of surveys carried out by the Israelis in the occupied territories (Transjordan and the Golan) since 1967, a much more complex picture of the cultural-historical development of Palestine/Israel is being sketched, one that contrasts with the view that dominated discussion twenty years ago and that was based on excavations at the great tells situated on the plains and on the edge of the hill country. The new picture gives special emphasis to the regional differences and takes the occasional overlapping of epochs into account. Finally, the introduction of methods from the natural sciences into the study of excavated archaeological remains, and the possibility that one can achieve statistically more reliable results on the basis of the information that has been gathered, has opened completely new perspectives concerning how one can correlate the evidence recovered from excavations at different sites.

Unlike the earlier model, one that assumed that a sequence of periods with relatively clear boundaries could be achieved, one can currently place greater emphasis on the significance of developments that might have unfolded during periods of time that stretch for centuries. One must also take into account that there are many intermediate periods and situations for which time periods overlap. The sharp breaks in continuity that were assumed by the older models were based, for the most part, on correlating archaeological discoveries (e.g., "destruction layers") with events that could be dated from the historical sources. The ongoing effort to make such correlations is just as necessary for a study of cultural history today. But even when evidence of destruction shows that a conquest took place and *might* even indicate that there was a power shift in certain situations, with the resultant changes introduced by a new ruler and most clearly detected in changes to the material culture of the region, one must still recognize that one culture is replaced by a new, more dominant one only very gradually and that the process might take years or even decades. A change in the political power structure will cause the *history* of a region to go in a different direction. The *material culture* of that region will always be affected by those new influences as well. But a region does not suddenly reject its former practices. It adapts gradually to the new circumstances. "Rarely do political and cultural developments proceed synchronically: kings come and kings go, but the cooking pots remain" (H. Weippert 1988, 352). What applies to "cooking pots" is valid in many other areas of the material culture as well. The way in which each class of object must adjust to the new powers will vary according to whether the production of that type of object is placed under direct state control and whether changing that object makes sense in light of the political changes.

§8. For the purposes of our study, the points at which there is a difference of opinion concerning the periodization of the eras for Palestine/Israel include the transition from the Late Bronze Age to Iron Age I, the subdivisions within Iron Age II, and the end of Iron Age II, that is, the transition from Iron Age II/III to the Persian Period. Concerning the transition from the Late Bronze Age to the Iron Age[5] (see chaps. IV-V), the consensus opinion among scholars at present suggests that the deurbanization of Canaan at the end of Late Bronze Age IIB was a gradual process that lasted about a century. One of the earliest destructions would have occurred at the city of Hazor, preserved in the Stratum XIII level that dates to about 1250. By contrast, cities that were under more direct Egyptian authority such as Beth-Shean, Megiddo, or Lachish survived for a longer time, until about 1150. At the same time, the process of settlement in the central hill country that developed concurrently with the deurbanization process occurred in phases and took almost two hundred years. This resulted in a rather long coexistence between an urban culture that was dying out and a village culture that was gaining strength. Another way to characterize this would be to note that colonial Egyptian control diminished at the same time that the Philistines were immigrating and quickly assimilating and that the indigenous Canaanite culture was gaining in strength. It is therefore reasonable to think of the Late Bronze Age as lasting until ca. 1150 while, at the same time, dating the beginning of Iron Age I to ca. 1250.

When it comes to identifying subdivisions within the Iron Age II(/III) by coordinating them with certain dates that were important in political history, one must once again recognize that a certain unevenness is caused by some overlapping. The ceramic traditions of the coastal and interior regions lost their distinctive character during Iron Age IIA (tenth century; see chap. VI; Philistine ceramics, with their unique decorations, disappeared completely). This took place at the same time as a reurbanization movement, during which larger villages developed into cities while many small and some very small early Iron Age settlements in the central hill country were abandoned altogether. Both developments are symptomatic of a visibly changed political situation: massive construction projects that took place in the cities as they regained their strength (Jerusalem, Gezer, Megiddo, Hazor, et al., with palaces and governmental buildings) provide indicators that a territorial state was coming into existence and consolidating its power by constructing major buildings that served the central and regional power centers. Iron Age IIA is to be equated with the period of the so-called United Monarchy under David and Solomon. The breakup of this powerful kingdom, dated to the time of the destructive campaign waged by Sheshonq about 925, together with the abortive attempt to reestablish Egyptian control over Palestine, marks the end of this period.

During Iron Age IIB (chap. VII), the trend toward establishing regional governmental centers of power continued with the construction of "imposing and defensive monumental structures" (H. Weippert 1988, 511). This trend is most obvious in the early ninth century and makes sense because it was necessary to strengthen the power of the military and to establish lines of authority in both of the nation-states, Israel and Judah, that were formed after the death of Solomon about 925. H. Weippert uses only architectural evidence and consequently assumes

---

5 See, e.g., H. Weippert 1988; 340–343, 352–355; Finkelstein 1988, 315–321; Na'aman/ Finkelstein 1990).

that this period lasted only until ca. 850 (the end of the Omri dynasty). This concentration on just one type of evidence permits her to avoid having to explain why almost no small artifacts survive from this clearly demarcated Iron Age IIB period (1988, 510–517; see Frevel 1989, 45f.).[6] This approach also prevents her from attaching proper significance to a change of the magnitude of Assyria's conquest, with its concurrent political and administrative restructuring. Evidence for this shift in power can be detected clearly in the archaeological study of the settlements and in the remains of the material culture, right down to the types of pottery that appear (see, e.g., Zimhoni 1990). To be sure, she takes note of the shift and calls attention to the archaeological evidence that has been gathered from the settlements (1988; 587–594, 600–603), but she does not draw the necessary conclusions for how this affects the time period in question. If one considers the artistic works, as will be done here, it will seem not only plausible but unavoidable that the break between Iron Age IIB and C must be dated to the second half of the eighth century, when Palestine came increasingly under the direct political influence of the great Assyrian superpower. By contrast, up to that time, in spite of having paid tribute to Assyria since 841, Israel was clearly oriented toward Phoenicia while Judah was clearly more affected by forces within Palestine or else by Egypt.

It is hard even here to assign exact dates, since the Assyrian presence in the country caused changes gradually (key dates: 734–732, 722–720, 710, 701; see below §§166f.). In any case, Iron Age IIC (chapter VIII) gives evidence of definite Assyrian (and thus also Aramean) influence. Its character is shaped now by cultural contacts that are international in scope, brought about because of the new relationships with distant territories that were also part of this great empire. When compared with the preceding period, striking changes can be detected with ease.

After Judah, Ammon, and Moab lost their independent existence as states, and after a majority of their élite citizens were exiled, a new phase began both politically and culturally during the first half of the sixth century, designated as Iron Age III. One can detect a moderate impoverishment of the material culture in the interior part of the country. Like Iron Age I, this is a transitional period and it comes to an end about 450, when the region stabilized institutionally with the establishment of the locally autonomous Persian province of Yehud (chap. IX).

5. Why this Survey Begins with Middle Bronze Age IIB

§9.   At the end of the Early Bronze Age, about 2200, there was a decline in urban culture in Palestine. This does not mean that there were no cities, but they survived in just a few regions (in the northern coastal plain, at Megiddo and Beth-Shean in the great central plain), whereas a large part of the country was without urban settlements. During this transitional period, which should be dated roughly to 2200–2000 (Early Bronze Age

---

6 Small artifacts, such as the seals, amulets, or figurines that are used in our survey
  as a kind of "characteristic fossil," come frequently from graves. Such pieces are
  still being found and documented.

IV/Middle Bronze Age I, also called the "Intermediate Period"), corresponding approximately to the First Intermediate Period in Egypt, the inhabitants of Palestine appear to have lived as nomads who tended flocks of small animals. There was only minimal cultivation of field crops. Few material remains survive; what has been recovered comes almost exclusively from graves. Iconographic evidence is virtually nonexistent (H. Weippert 1988, 182–200).

Parallel to the beginning of the Middle Kingdom in Egypt, at the beginning of the second millennium, a general reurbanization began. Cities were established once again in the southern coastal plain and later in the interior of the country. The first phase (Middle Bronze Age IIA) runs roughly parallel to the Egyptian Twelfth Dynasty (ca. 2000–1750). The iconography of this period is limited generally to Egyptian imports. One finds statues of seated figures, discovered usually in secondary contexts, and seal amulets in the form of scarabs that are inscribed with non-pictorial elements such as ornamental designs, good luck hiero-glyphs, and the names of kings or officials.

But developments in Palestine at the end of the Middle Kingdom did not run parallel to those in Egypt in the same way as they had at the end of the Old Kingdom. Whereas Egypt grew noticeably weaker at the end of the Twelfth Dynasty, the Palestinian cities grew ever stronger during the eighteenth century, at the beginning of Middle Bronze Age IIB. Strong influences came from the north, specifically from Syria. The powerful Canaanite influence reached even as far as the Nile Delta and led there to the establishment of a Canaanite-dominated dynasty about 1650, the Fifteenth Dynasty that is often identified by using the term "Hyksos" (a hellenization of the Egyptian *ḥq3.w ḫ3š.wt*, "ruler from foreign lands").

One can justify beginning our survey at this point, when the urban culture in Palestine begins to flourish, because from this point on we can deal with a cultural continuum in Palestine that extends all the way to the time of the emergence of the Hebrew Bible. It is true that there will be a major gap once again when the Egyptians colonized Palestine during the time of the Egyptian New Kingdom that lasted from 1550 and 1150. But the effect is considerably minimized because both the Canaanite and the Egyptian cultures had begun to exert considerable influence *on each other* already during the Middle Bronze Age. It is also likely that the same ethnic groups continued to maintain their cultural system from the Middle Bronze Age right into the Iron Age. During Middle Bronze Age IIB, the Palestinian hill country was relatively thick with established settlements or at least with fortified encampments. Most of these were abandoned during the Late Bronze Age, probably due to pressure from Egyptian colonialism. The population from these settlements did not simply disappear. As I. Finkelstein (1988) has suggested, with good reason, they shifted to a nomadic lifestyle instead. As the Egyptians grew increasingly weak during Iron Age I, the tribes that had been forced into a nomadic way of life settled down once again. At any rate, there is a massive increase in the number of fortified, residential settlements in the hill country at this time.

III

⚜

Equality of the Sexes:
Middle Bronze Age IIB

§10. The scarabs that were typically produced during Middle Bronze Age IIA, with ornamental designs (spirals, concentric circles, etc.), Egyptian good luck hieroglyphs, and names of kings and officials, continued to be made in Middle Bronze Age IIB (1750–1550) and were manufactured in even greater numbers (Tufnell 1984, I 115–131; 140–148; II pls. 1–35; 49–64; Martin 1971). In addition, relatively new elements appear, some of which depict figures. Two of the most common are the caprid and the lion. They will be described more extensively at this point because they illustrate beautifully why a person studying Palestine must assume that influences came from both Egypt *and* the Near East, not only in regard to matters connected with form and style but also when dealing with semantic issues. For this reason, it is often difficult to determine from a particular symbol whether the figure is from a male or a female sphere.

1. Caprids and Lions

§11. The *caprid* is one of the few figurative motifs appearing on scarabs in the Levant already in Middle Bronze Age IIA (Ward 1978, pl. 6.174) that was used even more extensively during Middle Bronze Age IIB. It is usually portrayed lying down or striding (Tufnell 1984, I 132).[1] Artisans had portrayed ibexes and he-goats in Palestine since the Chalcolithic Age (Elliott 1977, 6–9; Bar-Adon 1980, 42–46, 100f.; Keel-Leu 1989, 17f. no. 20). Everything was eliminated from the scene, on occasion, except for the horns (e.g., Bar-Adon 1980, 24–28), showing clearly that these horns had originally been the most impressive aspect. These animals represent strength and power and are to be interpreted as symbols of virility. Caprids are depicted in the Early Bronze Age as well (Keel, et al., 1989, 28f. no. 35). Caprids thus provide evidence for an ancient Palestinian tradition, even though outside influences from Egypt and the Near East might have had an effect on how they were used during the Middle Bronze Age.

---

1 Tufnell identifies the caprids incorrectly as "antelopes" (see Keel, et al., 1990, 263–266).

Nearly half of the examples from Middle Bronze Age IIB (see Tufnell 1984, II pl. 36) combine a branch with the caprid (**illus. 1a**). As will be seen more clearly when the "Naked Goddess" is studied, this combination symbolizes prosperity and fertility. Approximately one fifth of the pieces include a *uraeus* with the caprid, most generally by depicting the caprid's tail in the shape of a *uraeus* (**illus. 1b**). The *uraeus* signifies defense and protection.[2] The figures in this combination are guaranteed to show the real purpose of each amulet: to accentuate positive, vital forces and to protect one from negative powers. The more frequently used combination, with the branch, shows that increasing the positive forces was foremost.

E. Hornung and E. Staehelin (1976, 138–140) group antelopes, ibexes, gazelles, and does together into one group and designate them "wild beasts of the desert." They think that these animals appear on scarabs because they are able to survive in the inhospitable, rocky world of the desert, where death reigns (though the doe does not inhabit that region), demonstrating that their special gifts would have made them stellar examples and wonderful symbols for depicting the forces of life and the ability to overcome death. This interpretation pays no attention to the gender of the animals, nor does it show any interest in identifying the specific powers that the animals might be representing.

It is certainly possible that other concepts might have been been more important in the Near East. But in the examples under discussion here, wild sheep, wild goats, ibexes, gazelles, and deer all belong in the sphere of the goddess. Reclining caprids, with their heads either facing forward or turned backward, often appear on Old Syrian cylinder seals in the same scene with a goddess.[3] A "Naked Goddess," with the snail-shaped horns of a ram, is depicted on a scarab from Jericho (**illus. 2**). She is the source of the power of life in the plants and animals. The vitality and powers of love in these animals can be seen in their agility, liveliness (cf. Hebrew *ḥayyāh* I "animals living in the wild" and *ḥayyāh* II "life"), and passion for survival (see Keel 1986, 57–61, 94–96). Even in as late a composition as the Song of Songs (2:7; 3:5), bystanders are adjured by the gazelles and the wild does of the wilderness not to disturb the lovers (see Keel 1986, 89–94).

§12. Like the caprid, the *lion* is one of the few figurative elements found on scarabs produced even before the time of the Twelfth Dynasty (Ward 1978, pl. 6.172f.). On the two known examples, the lion is represented as reclining. The lion is shown in the same position on a Twelfth-Dynasty scarab impression found at Kahun, situated near the entrance to Fayyum in Lower Egypt (Petrie/Brunton/Murray 1923, pl. 64.256). On another impression from Kahun, one sees a lion that is raised up on its hind legs (Petrie 1890, pl. 9.39). On the so-called "magic" knives of the Middle Kingdom Period, one finds lions in a variety of positions, some

---

2 Of the 53 scarabs we have assembled that include a caprid and that date to Middle Bronze Age IIB, 21 (39.6%) combine it with a branch; eight depictions (15%) connect the caprid with a *uraeus*; it is combined on three (5.6%) with both a branch and a *uraeus*. The remainder show the caprid with neither branch nor *uraeus*.

3 Winter 1983, illuss. 74, 82, 84, 93, 119, 200, 285, 366, 440.

1a

1b

2

3a

3b

3c

4

reclining, some raised up on their hind legs, some striding; (Altenmüller 1965, II 78f., illus. 13; Legge 1905, pls. 2.2; 3.3). These objects were made using hippopotamus' teeth, the pieces being flat yet curved. The decorations that were incised on these pieces showed scenes that had a primarily apotropaic function and served to protect both a mother and a toddler (Altenmüller 1965, I 148–152). Other types of evidence are also available to show that the decorations on the "magic" knives influenced the earliest types of decorations on scarabs (Keel, et al., 1989, 282–286). One finds reclining lions on the scarabs of Middle Bronze Age IIB more rarely (**illus. 3a**;[4] see Tufnell 1984, I 133f.; II pl. 40). The animals are usually shown striding or crouching on their hind legs (**illuss. 3b-c**). Of the 42 examples found in Palestine, 22 show the lion striding and it is crouching on the other 20 examples. On these 42 depictions of lions available to us, 24 (57%) are combined with the *uraeus* and only 6 (14%) with branches. The apotropaic character of the decoration is thus emphasized more strongly. The aggressiveness of the lions is brought out especially in the nine pieces on which the lion attacks a caprid from behind. In eight of these, the caprid's head is turned back toward the lion.[5] The lion appears on Old Syrian cylinder seals in all these positions as well: lying, striding, crouching on its hind legs, and attacking a caprid.[6]

In the Near East, the lion frequently embodies the aggressiveness of the goddess (Keel 1984, 39–45, 130–139). On a scarab found at Tell el-Ajjul, located south of Gaza (**illus. 4**), the goddess is depicted between a lion and a vulture as the "Mistress of the Animals." Three examples show a vulture perched on the lion's back (see Starkey/Harding 1932, pl. 43.37; Dumortier 1974, pl. 3.30; Giveon 1985, 118f. no. 24). This constellation of figures matches favorably with the epithet "Mistress of the Steppe" (*bēlet ṣēri*), a title assigned to the goddess Ashratum in Middle Bronze Age Akkadian texts. She is the precursor of the deity known as Atirat/Asherah in later times (see Day 1986, 386; Hadley 1989, 65–69).

---

4 Cf. Petrie 1931, pl. 14.169; Petrie 1934, pl. 9.272; Petrie, et al., 1952, pl. 10.110.
5 Tufnell 1984, II pl. 40; Petrie, et al., 1952, pl. 43.14; Tufnell 1958, pl. 39/40.345; Yadin 1960, pls. 137.16; 187.17; Giveon 1985, 118f. no. 23; Giveon 1988, 20f. no. 1.
6 *Lying*: Delaporte 1920–1923, A no. 918 = Winter 1983, illus. 200; Porada 1948, no. 967 = Winter 1983, illus. 269; *striding*: Porada 1948, no. 978. The front legs of crouching lions are often shown in a remarkable striding posture on scarabs (this is especially clear on a so far unpublished piece from Dan, IAA 68–1371). This peculiar posture could go back to images on cylinder seals on which two crouching lions face each other. One leg is placed firmly on the ground and the other is raised as if to engage playfully in contact with the opposite lion (Menant 1888, no. 395; Porada 1948, no. 945 = Winter 1983, illus. 298). We occasionally find single lions in this posture, but this does not seem to have any precursors (Porada 1948, no. 951.942 = Winter 1983, illus. 293). We occasionally find Old Syrian cylinder seals on which the lion assumes the unnatural posture of crouching on its hind legs, though the forelegs seem to be engaged in walking; this is typical of the lions on scarabs (Porada 1948, no. 998). We also rather frequently find a lion attacking a caprid from behind on Old Syrian cylinder seals. In six of the seven examples cited here, the caprid turns its head backward, as it does on the scarabs. There are also times when the caprids and the lions are shown in motion, as on the scarab found by Petrie 1933, pl. 3.35 = Tufnell 1984, II pl. 40.2651; see von der Osten 1957, no. 291; Winter 1983, illus. 248.) More often, the lion attacks from a kind of crouching posture (Delaporte 1910, no. 464; Speleers 1917, 215 no. 496; Porada 1948, nos. 986, 995; Winter 1983, illus. 98).

The numerous scarabs on which the lion is combined with one or two *uraei* make it more likely that one should assume that this motif was adapted from Egypt. It also seems to be an Egyptian motif when the lion strides over and away from a human figure[7] or attacks one (Petrie 1930, pl. 7.54) or more human beings (**illus. 5a**).[8] There is even a scarab from Jericho that shows both a caprid and a human underneath a lion (**illus. 5b**). Hardly any convincing parallels from the Near East match these triumphant Egyptian images.[9] A lion standing above a crocodile is completely without parallel in Old Syrian depictions (**illus. 6**).[10] Since the crocodile is portrayed hacked to pieces in three of the five examples, it should be interpreted as representing an evil power that the lion has conquered. The lion might represent the power of the king or could depict the king himself (Hornung/Staehelin 1976, 126), serving much the same function as the falcon that is depicted elsewhere above a crocodile that has been hacked to pieces (Keel, et al., 1989, 268–275). This conceptual background supports Tufnell's observation, offered with what seems to us to be mild astonishment: "The lion is always the victor, never the vanquished, and even *homo sapiens* is defeated" (1984, I 134).

We see a unique combination of influences from both the Near East and from Egypt on a scarab from Jericho (**illus. 7**). The scene includes a human figure and a lion that is raised up on its hind legs. The lions that are raised up on their hind legs on the "magic" knives attack the prisoners from behind (Legge 1905, pl. 2.47). The way the man and the lion face each other on our scarab is more reminiscent of Old Syrian compositions. On such Syrian scarabs, the man strikes the forepaw of an upraised lion and plunges a dagger into its body (Collon 1975, 129 no. 228), or else two men subdue an upraised lion as they attack it from both front and rear (Collon 1975, 131 no. 230; Porada 1948, no. 955). On our scarab, however, the upraised lion lays its forepaw on the man who is standing in front of it and the man raises his hand in veneration. A human figure with a hand raised in reverence and who stands by a lion that is attacking a caprid can also be seen on a scarab from Tell el-Ajjul (Petrie 1933, pl. 3.35). The lion is most likely to be treated as a metaphor for the king in both instances.

But the lion does not appear only as a conqueror or with the aggressive *uraeus*; though infrequently (six out of 42 examples), it is also shown with a branch (see illus. 3c). This fact and other evidence (Hornung/Staehelin 1976, 126f.) suggests that the lion, as an inhabitant of the desert and much like the desert itself, can represent not only aggressive powers to conquer but can also exemplify life forces and regenerative power as well. One piece connects a reclining lion with two humans who are holding a lotus blossom, the symbol *par excellence* for regeneration (Petrie 1934, pl. 9.272).

7 Petrie 1931, pl. 14.164; cf. Kenyon 1965, 653 fig. 303.16.
8 Cf. on this Rühlmann 1964, as well as the depiction of the lion that strides over and away from an enemy lying beneath it and strikes at another, as shown on a magic knife that is dated to about 1800 (Altenmüller 1965, II 78f. and illus. 13. See also Brunner-Traut 1974, pl. 16b).
9 The only example to which one might refer would be that of a lion that crouches on its hind legs and appears to be warding off a human figure, as seen on an Old Syrian cylinder seal (Moortgat 1940, pl. 64.535 = Keel, et al., 1989, 253 illus. 22).
10 Macalister 1912, III pl. 202a.9; see also Petrie 1934, pl. 7.259; 11.453; Rowe 1936, no. 319; Gophna/Sussmann 1969, 10, fig. 10.12.

Though not quite as common, the human-headed or falcon-headed *sphinx* is portrayed on Middle Bronze Age IIB scarabs in combinations that are similar to those in which the lion is depicted and with similar significance (Tufnell 1984, I 134; II pl. 41).

In summary, we can assert that lions on Middle Bronze Age IIB scarabs primarily symbolize male potency and aggressiveness. Like the caprids, lions occasionally appear in scenes that depict a goddess and characterize her then as the "Mistress of the Animals" in the widest sense. Whether the figure is to be assigned to the male or to the female sphere depends in each case on the overall classification of the motifs and the tradition history, in other words, on whether one detects stronger influences from Egypt or from the Near East.

2. The Hippopotamus Goddess and the Ω-Symbol

§13.   A number of Egyptian imports are clearly linked to experiences that are associated with the female. They depict a so-called *"Hippopotamus Goddess,"* given this name because her hybrid form includes aspects of both the crocodile and the lion. In the New Kingdom Period, this goddess is usually called Thoeris (*t3 wr.t* "the big one"). Her principal duty was to keep all types of evil from mothers and small children. She is depicted thus on a fragment of a "magic" knife from Tell el-Ajjul (**illus. 8a**). Iconographic reasons suggest to Altenmüller that this fragment is to be dated to the period about 1750 (1965, II 104f. no. 129). A larger fragment of this type of apotropaic device has been found at Megiddo and is dated to about 1900, though that piece does not include the Hippopotamus Goddess (Loud 1948, pl. 203.1). The Hippopotamus Goddess appears twice in this capacity among the fragments of bone inlay that decorate a small jewelry box that is dated roughly to the time between 1650 and 1550. These two specimens were found in a tomb 14 km south of Jaffa (Ory 1945, 38–41, pl. 14). The excavator incorrectly identified these images as Hyksos horses (see also H. Weippert 1988, 245). Comparison with an image depicted on a scarab that was found in the late Middle Bronze Age IIB necropolis at Azor, near Jaffa, makes it clear that we are dealing with the Hippopotamus Goddesses here as well (**illus. 8b**).

§14.   To this point, the image-bearing artifacts and their iconographical motifs that we have discussed are probably chiefly Egyptian imports. This is certainly true for images that portray the Hippopotamus Goddess. The scarabs that depict caprids and lions might just as likely have been produced in Palestine; there is no way to know this for certain. But a group of scarabs appears at the beginning of Middle Bronze Age IIB that was almost certainly produced in the Near East. A production facility was in operation about 1750 and it produced faience for export. The distribution pattern for its products suggests that it was located most likely either in northern Syria or in southeast Anatolia. Its products included very small seal amulets with decoration on the base that was primarily in raised relief and used an Ω-*shaped mark* as its principal motif (**illuss. 9a-b**). This rather unusual type of seal amulet was made in the form of an oval plaque with a ring-shaped handle in Anatolia and in the

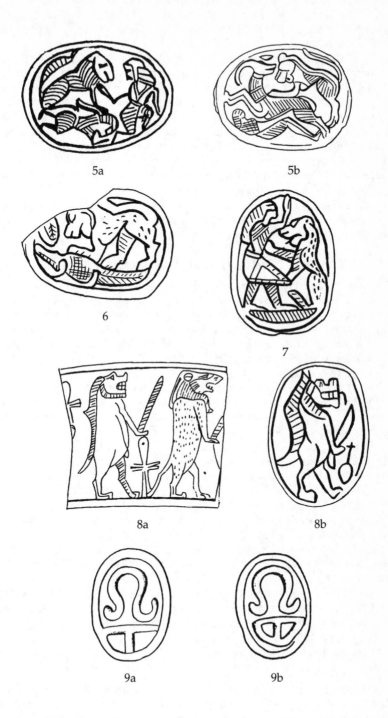

5a

5b

6

7

8a

8b

9a

9b

shape of a very rudimentary scarab in southern Palestine. The scarab shape must have been very popular already at that time throughout the Levant, and this popularity must have been known in northern Syria as well.

The Ω-shaped mark originated in Babylonia and may have symbolized a mother's womb. This sign was associated with ancient mother goddesses such as Ninḫursag or Nintu. An Old Babylonian terra-cotta plaquette depicts a mother goddess positioned between two miscarried infants. The Ω-shaped sign is placed above each one (Keel, et al., 1989, 59f. with illus. 32). Putting this sign above miscarried infants fits the pattern detected in the rather common practice of placing seal amulets with the Ω-shaped symbol in the graves of children. In any case, this symbol is still being used as a pendant around the neck of a mother goddess in the Late Bronze Age (see below, §44 and illus. 82) and even appears in Judean graves dating to Iron Age IIC, where its function might be to characterize the grave as a mother's womb (see below, illuss. 356f.; on the entire subject, see Keel, et al., 1989, 39–87).

3. Naked Goddess, Goddess Heads, and Trees

§15.   As has been noted already, depictions of figures that are somewhat realistic are largely absent from scarabs produced during the Egyptian Twelfth Dynasty, which is roughly coterminous with Middle Bronze Age IIA. But on one seal from the Ω-group that was found in Beth Shemesh, a realistic image of a *naked woman* is used instead of the Ω-shaped sign (**illus. 10**), with posture and hairstyle identical to that found on Old Syrian cylinder seals (Winter 1983, illuss. 130, 132).

The "Naked Goddess" which was adopted from Old Syrian cylinder seal glyptic art appears on 44 Middle Bronze Age IIB scarabs that have been recovered in Palestine (on this and what follows, see Schroer 1989, 92–138; Richards 1992, nos. 4–5). Twenty-two of the scarabs were recovered in controlled excavations or as surface finds in Palestine. The other half were purchased and a considerable number of these are known to have been bought in Jerusalem. Two of the scarabs were recovered in Petrie's excavations at Tell el-Yehudiyeh in the eastern Nile Delta (Petrie 1906, pl. 9, 137f.). These scarabs were either produced in Egypt for export to Canaan or were – more probably – manufactured in Canaan itself. The "Naked Goddess" is typical of the Near East. On cylinder seals she generally holds her arms across her abdomen in a bent position or else she holds her breasts. But neither posture is common on the scarabs (**illus. 11a**; see Petrie 1906, 97, nos. 3–5; 105 illus. 08). As a rule, on scarabs she lets her arms hang down alongside her body (**illus. 11b**). This posture is used on the cylinder seals as well, but such a pose is generally more typical of depictions of Egyptian maidservants (the so-called "concubines"; see Fechheimer 1921, 28f., 38f.).

There are two elements that distinguish the depictions of the goddess on the scarabs from her portrayal on the cylinder seals:

(1) On the cylinder seals, she is flanked by worshipers or she is shown opposite a partner, especially the weather god. But on the scarabs she appears in *splendid isolation*. This might be because only limited surface

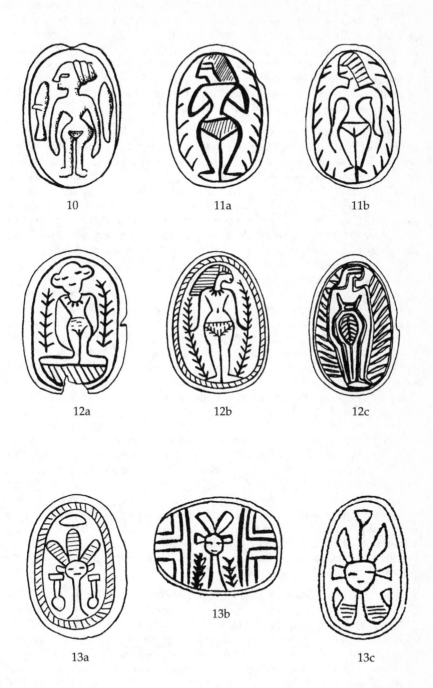

10   11a   11b

12a   12b   12c

13a   13b   13c

space was available. But the isolation of the figure, though forced by circumstance, is used in a positive way, since the goddess is portrayed frontally on two-thirds of the specimens and directly faces the male or female who looks to her (**illus. 12a**). The direct frontal view is extremely rare in the ancient Near East. She is depicted with overly large ears as well. Schroer interprets this – and is certainly correct in her assessment – as an expression of the willingness of the goddess to hear the worshipers who appeal to her and thus rejects the interpretation of some that this is a relic of Hathor's cow-shaped ears (Schroer 1989, 130–133).

(2) The figures that were originally part of the repertoire of cylinder seal glyptic art and that are depicted individually on the scarabs are unique in a second way as well. They are often accompanied by hieroglyphic good luck signs (see Keel/Schroer 1985, 76–81). Such signs are used but rarely with the "Naked Goddess." She is flanked instead by two branches (or little trees?) on 36 of the 44 specimens (82%) (**illuss. 12a-c**; cf. illuss. 11a-b). For this reason, Schroer assigns to these figures the name *"Branch Goddess."* In four examples, the goddess holds the branches; she is positioned between them on the remaining 32 specimens. Her central position between the branches, together with the frontal view, emphasizes that she is making an appearance. The accompanying object usually qualifies whatever it accompanies. In this case, the branches call attention to the deepest aspect of what is happening when the goddess appears, by accentuating the secrets connected with vegetation. On one piece, two branches sprout from her genitalia (illus. 12b); on another, her genitalia are covered by a leaf or a branch (illus. 12c). Whereas the breasts are not depicted in any way, the genitalia are frequently emphasized. Perhaps the real reason why the goddess lets her arms hang down and does not support her breasts is because of the effect caused by the exaggeratedly long arms as they provide a frame for her genitalia.

The genitalia are also shown clearly on the Old Syrian cylinder seals that depict the goddess disrobing or opening her clothing (see below, illuss. 30, 31b; cf. Winter 1983, 284–296). Nevertheless, she does this only in front of a male consort and primarily for copulation. By contrast, the genitalia of the goddess are associated with vegetation on the scarabs. Fertility and prosperity are accentuated on the scarabs, not the sexuality and eroticism of palace life. The goddess is more patently and directly associated with fertility on the scarabs, especially the fertility of the vegetation, than is the case on the Old Syrian cylinder seals. The "Naked Goddess" who is depicted during the Middle Bronze Age personifies the power of the earth to produce its fruits.

§16. On the scarabs dating to Middle Bronze Age IIB, in addition to the "Naked Goddess," one finds many examples that depict the *head of a goddess*, identified frequently in the past as a Hathor fetish (**illuss. 13a-c**). The way this is depicted is based on an Egyptian model that showed a human head with cow's ears and cow's horns. But on Palestinian seals this type of head undergoes certain changes as it is attached to the body of the "Naked Goddess." The cow's ears become huge human ears and the horns become palm leaves (?) that are combined occasionally with blossoms (Schroer 1989, 139–185).

§17. On a scarab purchased in Shechem, a *stylized tree* is flanked by two adoring figures and is positioned under the head of a goddess shown with a sign for gold; she herself is flanked by *uraei* and falcons (**illus. 14a**). On a similar scarab from Tell el-Ajjul, a single worshiping figure stands before a stylized tree (**illus. 14b**). The meaning of the motif is reinforced by the fact that it is found on different types of image-bearing artifacts. It appears not only on scarabs but also on a Middle Bronze Age IIB cylinder seal from Tell el-Farʿah (north) that may have been manufactured locally (**illus. 14c**). The combination of the "Naked Goddess" and the head of the goddess with leaves and branches or with a stylized tree makes it likely that the latter are to be seen as a symbol of the "Branch Goddess," irrespective of whether they are adored by accompanying figures or appear by themselves (**illus. 15a**; Schroer 1989, 106 illuss. 017–029). This probably holds true also for scenes in which the "tree" is flanked by those who guard it. The oldest evidence can be seen on a cylinder seal from Tell el-Ajjul that depicts a stylized tree, made using branches, that has two winged genii who have human bodies (**illus. 15b**). The piece was probably imported from northern Syria and should be dated to about 1750 (Collon 1985, 57; 62 no. 1). The lion that appears as a secondary motif on this cylinder seal also belongs to the sphere of the goddess (see above, §12). Two scarabs dating to late Middle Bronze Age IIB from Jericho portray a stylized tree that is flanked by and protected by two (in the second case, by four) *uraei*, a common Egyptian style (**illus. 15c**; Kenyon 1965, fig. 299.10). Finally, on one of the rare painted vessels from this period, found at Tell el-Farʿah (north), a stylized palm tree is flanked by birds (doves?) (**illus. 16**). The scene is reminiscent of the famous portrayal of the Ishtar temple at Mari, in which the sanctuary is flanked by two palm trees with a large white dove perched on each palm. The goddess shown in this temple has one foot placed on still another attribute animal, the lion (Keel [4]1984, 125 illus. 191). The doves give bodily form to the goddess as one who is tender and ready to act in loving ways, while the lion depicts her nature as one who is majestic and unapproachable (Keel 1986, 71–75; 144–150). As the following will demonstrate, the goddess, palms, doves, and lions will all appear in depictions of the goddess in Palestine as well.

4. The Iconography of the Cult Installations at Nahariyah and Gezer

§18. In far northern Palestine, at Nahariyah, near the sea, a cultic installation was discovered in 1947, close to a spring 800 m north of the tell. The site was established in Middle Bronze Age IIA and it remained in use on into the Late Bronze Age. The shrine peaked in importance during Middle Bronze Age IIB. At that time, a new round podium that measured about 14 m in diameter was constructed above an older, smaller building (6 × 6 m) that had a small podium in front of it, while a new rectangular building, measuring 10.7 × 6.2 m, was erected to the northwest of the new podium. The form of the podium, which served as an open-air altar, and that of the rectangular building itself, in which the temple workshops may have been located, suggests that it was built in

14a   14b   14c

15a   15b   15c

16

the Early Bronze Age (Dothan 1977, 908–912; Weippert 1988, 233–236; concerning this podium, one might compare it with the impressive round podium at Megiddo).

Iconographically, the most interesting piece from this site is a steatite mold 22 cm in height that was found on the platform, though it was probably used in the temple workshop. Metal statuettes could have been manufactured *en masse* using the open-sided mold and open sand casting, which would have served to promote the cultic activity practiced here. The statuettes depict a slender female figure whose hair hangs loosely about her shoulders. A high, pointed head covering, flanked by two horns (or rays?), rests on top of her head (but see illuss. 13a–14a as well). Her hands rest on her thighs, flanking her genitalia (**illus. 17**). The gender of the figure is emphasized in this way, similar to how this was shown on the "Naked Goddess" on the scarabs. Nineteen goddess figurines (or fragments thereof) that are quite typical of Middle Bronze Age Palestine were found in a vessel under the plaster pavement that begins about 4 m west of the platform. Some figurines were poured solid, of the type that one could produce by using the steatite mold, while others were cut out using sheet-silver or sheet-bronze (Negbi 1976, 177f. nos. 1525–1531, 1533–1534; 183f. nos. 1607–1612; 1620–1623). Concerning the way the figures were depicted, some have their hands resting on their thighs, while others hold a breast with one hand (**illus. 18a**) or even use both hands to hold both breasts. On some examples, the arms simply hang down along the sides of the body, much as is depicted on the "Naked Goddess" scarabs (**illus. 18b**). Except for a head covering, the figures are generally naked. The head covering is high and pointed on two examples, much like those produced in the mold, but otherwise they are made in a wide variety of shapes. The figures are 4–10 cm high; those cut from sheet metal often have a little hole cut into them near the top end, which shows that these figures of the goddess were worn as pendants.

§19. *Dove figures* made of clay have been discovered in Nahariyah in the same quantities as the goddess figures (Ben-Dor 1950, 27; pl. XII, 10–12; Dothan 1956, 22 pl. 4F). They are depicted generally with outstretched wings, which means they are shown in flight. Old Syrian cylinder seals from roughly the same time period show the goddess who reveals herself and from whom doves are flying toward her consort, the weather god or his cultic representative. The flying doves accentuate the love of the goddess; they are messengers of her love (Keel 1984, 58–62; 1986, 71–75). As votive gifts, the dove figures were to acknowledge her love or were to conjure it up. Dove figures that are nearly identical to those from Nahariyah have been found in the Middle Bronze Age shrine at Megiddo (**illus. 19**). One should also assume that the birds that are typically depicted on bone inlay during Middle Bronze Age IIB and that probably once decorated jewelry boxes are most likely to be identified as doves (**illus. 20**; see Liebowitz 1977; Ziffer 1990, 27f., 22f.*). The round head and the very prominent breast are typical of doves. An amulet pendant in the form of a dove was found at Tell el-Ajjul (**illus. 21**).

In addition to the dove figures, the Middle Bronze Age cultic site at Nahariyah yielded an amulet made from striped agate in the form of a

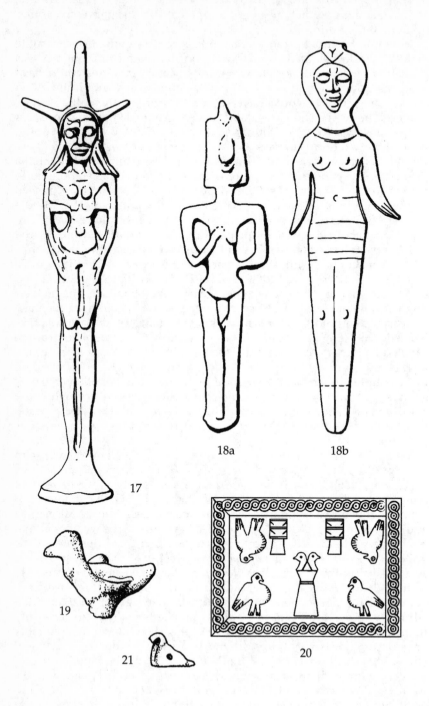

18a

18b

17

19

21

20

"humpbacked" bird – probably a vulture (Dothan 1956, 22 pl. 4C). A vulture appears with the lion on the scarab shown in illus. 4, the one on which the "Branch Goddess" appears as the "Mistress of the Animals." It is thus not surprising that an amulet in the shape of a reclining lion was found in Nahariyah along with the vulture amulet (Dothan 1956, 22, pl. 4A-B). The lion likely came from Egypt and was possibly made already at the time of the Twelfth Dynasty (ca. 2000–1750). But the lion would have taken on a new significance in a new setting when associated with the goddess to whom the sanctuary had been dedicated.

§20.   Another open-air shrine from the Middle Bronze Age was discovered at *Gezer* by R. A. S. Macalister at the beginning of our present century. Further American excavations during the 1960s revealed "that the ten monoliths measuring as much as 3.25 m in height (**illus. 22**), set up in a row arranged north to south, could not be identified as memorial stelae for rulers (as is the case with the stelae from Assyria to which they are often compared, *AOB* 414f., 417–421, 423) because they were contemporary with and clearly datable by ceramic evidence to Middle Bronze Age IIB (about 1600)" (A. Reichert in Galling ²1977, 207f., with bibliography).[11] These stelae may have functioned to make present those deities that were worshiped here. Such stelae have been thought by some in the past to be phallic symbols, but whoever followed that assumption sought to treat them exclusively as representations of male deities. A place for safekeeping treasures included a bronze figure that is iconographically very similar to those made from the steatite mold at Nahariyah and this piece suggests another interpretation. This naked female figure is wearing a tall head covering, in the form of a truncated cone that is flanked by two horns. Her hands are placed on the sides of her thighs (**illus. 23**). This suggests (and the discovery made at Tel Kitan, to be discussed shortly, will support further) the interpretation that the *maṣṣebah*s might also portray female deities.

A pair of figures, and a fragment of a third, that were cut from sheet-gold and were fashioned using the same style as those from the recently discovered hoard at Nahariyah, were found at Gezer as well, not at the cultic site but in a house from the same period that was built butted up against the inside wall of the city. The figures are typical of Middle Bronze Age Palestine (Seger 1976, 135; Ziffer 1990, 107). The largest and best preserved piece is 16 cm high (**illus. 24**). It portrays the goddess naked except for a high pointed head covering, a necklace having several strands, and a sash. Her genitalia are shown in larger scale and are accentuated even more by a continuous line that is drawn from the top of her body to the bottom. The figure comes to a point at both the top and the bottom but is wider in the middle of the body. The arms hang at the side and barely reach the hips. A gold ring around the neck probably served as a fastening device for the piece. That the figure comes to a point on the lower end makes one wonder whether the sheet-gold figures having this shape were

11   The attempt by A. Kempinski to date the installation to Middle Bronze Age IIA, on the basis of an Egyptian statuette found there (in Galling ²1977, 91), is hardly tenable, since such statuettes have been found frequently in contexts that date to a later time (see Giveon 1978, 28–30).

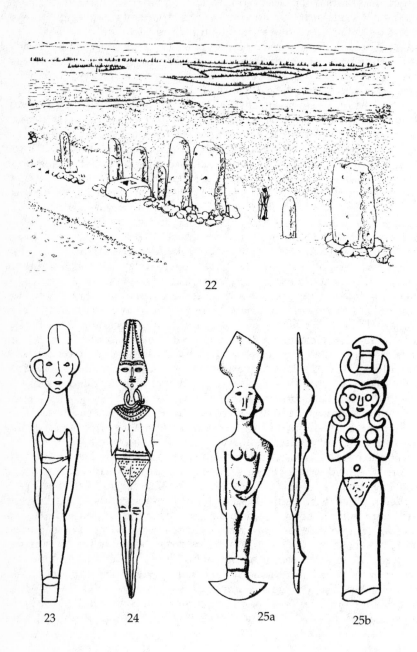

22

23   24   25a   25b

made to imitate the form of wooden or stone figures that were stuck into the ground.

Macalister himself found seven similar figures of naked females with a high head covering at Gezer (Negbi 1976, 179f. nos. 1547–1549; 184 nos. 1616–1619). One of these figures seems to depict a pregnant woman. While one arm hangs down alongside the body in typical fashion, the other supports a protruding abdomen (**illus. 25a**). This kind of emphasis on fertility is rare in Middle Bronze Age IIB. Emphasis on erotic sexuality is more customary.

Two lead figures from Tell el-Ajjul portray the goddess with her hands on her breasts. This gesture could be interpreted either as an expression of eroticism or as symbolic of fertility. On these figures as well, the goddess wears a high head covering that is flanked by two horns (**illus. 25b**).

5. The Iconography of the Middle Bronze Age Temples of Tel Kitan and Megiddo

§21. A village-sized settlement named *Tel Kitan* (Arabic: Tell Musa), located ca. 15 km south of the Sea of Gennesareth on the west bank of the Jordan, was excavated during the years 1975–1977 and is dated to the first phase of Middle Bronze Age IIB (i.e., ca. 1750–1650). There was a building in this village with outer measurements of 6.90 × 5.50 m. Five meters in front of the front side of this building, and parallel to it, there was a row of about ten small *maṣṣebah*s, made by using river stone and also having a stone foundation. Two somewhat larger *maṣṣebah*s were placed in front of this row (**illus. 26a**). One of the stelae in the main row was shaped, in very rough fashion, in the form of a naked woman (**illus. 26b**; Eisenberg 1977). This stele which was ca. 45 cm high, together with the other stelae, is now part of the collection at the Museum of Nir David in Beth-Shean.

What was suggested concerning the row of stelae at Gezer can be confirmed now at this site: stelae made of stone are not necessarily images of male deities. The characteristics depicted on the figure on this stele are clear. The gender is not identified by means of a triangle and a vertical line, like the Middle Bronze Age sheet-gold figures from Gezer, but is represented more realistically by means of sculpted genital lips. The breasts are hardly indicated at all, and the arms are little more than two small stumps. We are unable to determine whether the goddess held her breasts with her hands or not (Eisenberg 1977, 78).

§22. The sacral area (Area BB) at *Megiddo* at the end of Middle Bronze Age IIA (ca. 1800) was an open-air sanctuary. At the beginning of Middle Bronze Age IIB (Strata XII-XI) this was restructured. A broadroom temple (5.5 × 3 m) was constructed, open toward th᾽ west, with *maṣṣebah*s around the perimeter. To the east there was an altar podium. Near the end of Middle Bronze Age IIB (Stratum X) this installation was itself replaced by a rectangular temple with thick walls. Its entrance and vestibule opened toward the north and there was a niche in the wall on the south side (Dunayevsky/Kempinski 1973, 175–180; Kempinski 1989a, 178–181).

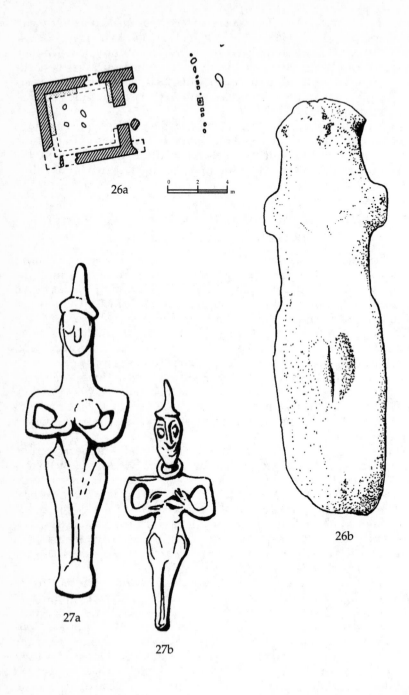

26a

26b

27a

27b

A mold and 21 metal figures of deities, characteristic of Middle Bronze Age Palestine, were found in the Middle Bronze Age levels of the sacral area. An additional piece was found in Area CC. Unlike at Nahariyah, Gezer, and the settlement of Tel Kitan, male deities are here as well, but they are by far in the minority. Of the 22 figures, 16 are female deities and only six are male (Negbi 1976, 131). Three naked female sheet-bronze figures that date to the time between 1800 and 1700 were found that are of a type very similar to those from Nahariyah and Gezer (Loud 1948 pl. 233.3, 9–10 = Negbi 1976, 184 nos. 1613–1615). For this early phase, one can also typically find figures of naked goddesses that are cast but that are almost flat, usually wearing a high, pointed head covering and generally holding their arms horizontally in a bent position in front of themselves (Loud 1948, pl. 233.4–8, 11 = Negbi 1976, 179 nos. 1536–1541). Not until the later phases of Middle Bronze Age IIB (1700–1500) do we find metal figures of naked goddesses at Megiddo that have a high head covering and that hold both breasts with both hands (**illuss. 27a-b**).

6. The Weather God and His Consort

§23. One of the naked goddesses, with arms held horizontally in front of her body (**illus. 28a**), may have formed a pair with a male figure found in the same room and from the same level (thus Negbi 1976, 62f.). Stratum XI, to which they belong, is dated 1700–1650. The male figure wears a short loincloth and holds his arms in front of his body (**illus. 28b**) in the same way as the female figure. Comparable pieces suggest that they once held weapons. Deities holding weapons in this so-called "Anatolian posture" have been discovered in Megiddo in contexts that date as far back as Middle Bronze Age IIA (Loud 1948, pl. 233.1 = Negbi 1976, 146 no. 39). A limestone casting mold from Stratum XIIIB (1800–1750; **illus. 29**) shows that gods with weapons were mass-produced. The figure produced in the mold appears to hold an axe with a hand that is stretched out horizontally, while the other hand is raised and is ready to strike. Their clothing consists of a high, pointed head covering and a loincloth.

§24. One of the figures displays certain similarities with a figure on an Old Syrian hematite cylinder seal from Megiddo, discovered apart from a clear stratigraphic context but belonging to this period (**illus. 30**). It is a god clothed in nothing but a loincloth and a high, pointed head covering. He holds a club in his raised left hand, while the right hand is extended forward and holds an axe. With his right hand he also holds a rope that is tied around the neck of a reclining bull. This is the weather god.[12] We see the weather god, with a reclining bull, who faces a worshiping figure on an Old Syrian hematite seal found at Tell el-Ajjul and on an Old Babylonian hematite seal from Beth-Shemesh (Petrie 1934, pls. 9.354; 12.2; Grant 1932, pl. 48.1020 = Parker 1949, nos. 2 and 8). On the seal from Megiddo, it is a goddess, not a worshiper, who faces the god

12 The silver-covered, bronze figure of a bull or a bull calf that was discovered recently in Ashkelon (Stager 1991, 24–28) should be related to the weather god in spite of a style that uses Egyptian techniques (on the bull and the weather god in the Late Bronze Age, see below, §31 with illus. 44, as well as §37, note 4; for a bronze bull from Iron Age I, see below, illus. 142).

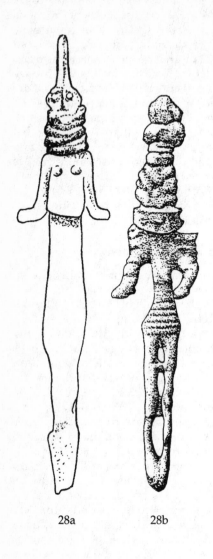

28a   28b

29

with one hand raised in greeting while pushing her clothing aside with the other (see Winter 1983, illuss. 296–306). We see three heads of bulls in front of her, probably to emphasize the close connection between the goddess and the weather god or his bull. The goddess occasionally actually stands on top of the bull (see Winter 1983, illuss. 269–271, 292f., 306). She is flanked in illus. 30 by two figures who are worshiping. One of the figures appears to be a ruler wearing a garment with thick fringes (see below, §26). The other figure has ram's horns on his head and carries an Egyptian symbol for life in his hand. The main theme portrayed by this cylinder seal decoration is the encounter between the weather god and the goddess, who demonstrates her readiness for engaging in love-making by pushing her clothing aside.

The identical theme that is depicted on the cylinder seal from Megiddo appears also on a fragment of a hematite cylinder seal from Hazor. It was discovered in Temple H in the Late Bronze Age Stratum I B (fourteenth century; **illus. 31a**; Beck 1989a, 310–312), but there is no question that it dates to the Middle Bronze Age. It shows the weather god who is approaching opposite the goddess. Unlike the seal from Megiddo, she does not push her clothing aside in this scene but pulls it up ostenta-tiously (see Winter 1983, illuss. 267–295). A secondary motif shows a cow with its head turned to the rear, as is typical of suckling cows. Thus the weather god appears in a context associated with both sexuality and fertility. Still another hematite cylinder seal from Tell el-Farʿah (north), from a stratum dated close to the end of Middle Bronze Age IIB **(illus. 31b)**, also portrays the goddess as she disrobes, which may be intended as a way, *pars pro toto*, to depict the entire constellation shown in illus. 31a. An second motif on this piece shows two worshipers under the winged disk. As seems likely on other Old Syrian cylinder seals as well (Winter 1983, illuss. 277, 285f., 293), they are probably supposed to represent worshipers of the goddess.

The weather god appears less frequently **(illuss. 32a-d)** on Middle Bronze Age IIB scarabs. Where he does appear, his relationship with fertility is accentuated, not his aggressive nature; that aspect will become more important during the Late Bronze Age. He does in fact raise his right hand but he holds no weapon, so that the gesture depicts more likely a victory rather than a battle. In his other hand, stretched out in front of himself, the deity holds a branch or a blossom. This suggests a natural link to the "Branch Goddess," who obviously must be his consort.

7. The Falcon-Headed Figure

§25. An anthropomorphic figure with a falcon head appears much more frequently than the weather god on Middle Bronze Age IIB scarabs. German scholars have generally tried to identify this as a Canaanite god, usually Horon; English-speaking scholars have identified it as the Egyptian sun god Re (Keel, et al., 1989, 244ff.). The one interpretation accentuates the non-Egyptian element (e.g., the branch in the hand of the deity) whereas the other emphasizes the Egyptian element (the falcon head). Neither side has tried to resolve the problem by means of the iconographic tradition. If one proceeds from this vantage point, one notes

30

31a

31b

that a falcon-headed figure appears on the Old Syrian cylinder seal glyptic art, wearing the Egyptian double crown. He is clearly shown as the royal god, which means he is probably Horus.

Not many years ago it became possible to isolate an assemblage of cylinder seals and scarabs that had been produced in Byblos or somewhere south of that city. The chief characteristics of this group include the material used to make them (green jasper, known by its geological name as green slate facies, along with other similar hard stone), the iconographic repertoire (males worshiping and being worshiped, rudimentary hieroglyphs), and a style that portrayed the figures as having exaggerated height that were also slender in form. This "jasper group" is to be dated 1720–1650 (Collon 1986; Keel, et al., 1989, 209–242). The falcon-headed figure with the double crown appears on one piece in this group (Collon 1986, 58 no. 4), on a fragment from an impression made by a cylinder seal that was found in the Stratum VII palace at Alalakh (1720–1650; Collon 1975, 78f. no. 144), and on a seal that belonged to Sumirapa of Tuba that belongs to the same period (Nougayrol/Amiet 1962). The elements that are brought together in the same scene on this and other Old Syrian seals, with a falcon-headed figure blessing a clearly human figure or else simply being worshiped by a human figure, are used on the scarabs as well, except that the falcon-headed figure appears without the double crown on the scarabs (**illus. 33a**; Keel, et al., 1989, 246–252). This seems to change his identity but little. We will see that the ruler who appears on scarabs dressed in the garment with thick fringes is also shown without the high head covering that he frequently wears when shown on the cylinder seals.

But how are we to interpret the very non-Egyptian theme of a branch or flower that is shown in the hand of the falcon-headed figure on numerous scarabs (**illuss. 33b-c**)? It is probably a branch scepter or a blossom scepter, adapted for the falcon-headed figure from the Canaanite weather god, who was a royal god as well. We are encountering a merging of attributes from the Egyptian royal god with those of the Canaanite royal god. The self-confident Canaanites who lived at the end of the eighteenth century and during the seventeenth and sixteenth centuries associated their royal god, their fertility god, with the chief Egyptian royal god, so they placed a branch or blossom scepter into the hand of their own royal god, their own fertility god (Keel, et al., 1989, 259–266). The Egyptians, who reacted to the foreign domination from the Canaanites under whom they lived during the sixteenth and fifteenth centuries, regarded this equating of deities as impudent and insolent, as we will see. But the idea that the deities could be equated did exist during the Hyksos era. Along with other types of evidence, one notes that a scarab found at Tell el-Dab'a, the Hyksos capital that was situated in the eastern Nile Delta, depicts a pharaoh wearing the crown of Lower Egypt. He holds a club in his right hand and in his left hand he holds a branch – quite unlike what the Egyptians would have included in such a scene (Keel, et al., 1989, 266 illus. 75).

A mixture of influences from both the Near East and Egypt might also be detected when the falcon-headed figure appears victorious over the crocodile (**illuss. 34a-b**; Keel, et al., 1989, 268–275). The crocodile is an Egyptian motif. But since it is thought of in Egypt not only as a dangerous

32a   32b   32c

32d

33a   33b   33c

34a   34b   34c

animal but also as a holy creature, there was great hesitancy about portraying it as conquered. In Canaan, however, Baal was acclaimed as victor over *lītānu*/Leviathan, the chaos monster depicted as a reptile. This motif may have encouraged portrayal (though discreet) of this victory.

The Horus falcon is depicted time and again with outstretched wings and talons on scarabs belonging to the jasper group (**illus. 34c**; Keel, et al., 1989, 232–239). This symbol of Egyptian royal might dominates the precious jewelry in the royal tombs of eighteenth-century Byblos. "The kings of Byblos fancied themselves, in their puny little territory, . . . as if they were in fact little pharaohs" (M. Chéhab, in Parrot/Chéhab/Moscati 1977, 39). Without reflecting much about the step they were taking, they appropriated for themselves the symbols of power that depicted pharaonic might. Pieces of jewelry that reflect this practice, such as five gold earrings in the form of a falcon with outstretched wings, have been found at Tell el-Ajjul as well (Petrie 1931, pl. 15 top row, in the middle and to the right; Petrie, et al., 1952, pl. 6 top row; Ziffer 1990, 64 fig. 67).

8. The Ruler with Male and Female Worshipers

§26. The dominant theme on the seals of the jasper group that was discussed in the last section can be characterized as clearly masculine. We find that the divine rulers and human rulers, together with their worshipers, are all depicted as males, on both the cylinder seals and the scarabs (Keel, et al., 1989, 209–242). As is so typical on the Old Syrian cylinder seal glyptic art, the *ruler who wears the garment with thick fringes* is once again right in the center of the picture on these cylinder seals (Collon 1986, illuss. 1–2, 5–6, 11; Keel/Schroer 1985, 49–115). On Old Syrian cylinder seals that date to the eighteenth century the garment with thick fringes is worn characteristically by both worshipers and the one being worshiped (cf. illuss. 30, 31a). They appear side by side on a piece from Hazor (**illus. 35**, though that piece was found in a much later context – in one of the thirteenth-century levels of Temple H; Beck 1989a, 312–315).

In the first phase of Middle Bronze Age IIB, the Syrian ruler who wears the garment with thick fringes appears quite often on the steatite scarabs that are typical of this period. On the oldest pieces, the relationship to the Old Syrian cylinder seal glyptic art is still especially clear. One scarab from a grave in Barqai (ca. 1650) provides us with the only piece on which the ruler who is wearing the garment with thick fringes also wears the tall Syrian cap (**illus. 36a**; see also Keel/Schroer 1985, 84 illuss. 45f.). Schroer has correctly determined that the depiction of the ruler who is wearing the garment with thick fringes and appears all alone provides an indication of the strong position that the Canaanite city-state kings assumed toward the end of the Thirteenth Dynasty (ca. 1700–1650). Politically, this led to the founding of the Hyksos Dynasty in Egypt. Religiously, the sovereigns appear as some sort of mediating figures who bridge the gap between the divine and earthly worlds. Perhaps they were deified after they died. The use of their images on seal amulets should thus come as no surprise (**illuss. 36b-c**; Keel/Schroer 1985, 101–106). An enemy lies prostrate under the throne of the sovereign on one unique piece (**illus. 36d**). This specimen reminds one of the enemies that are

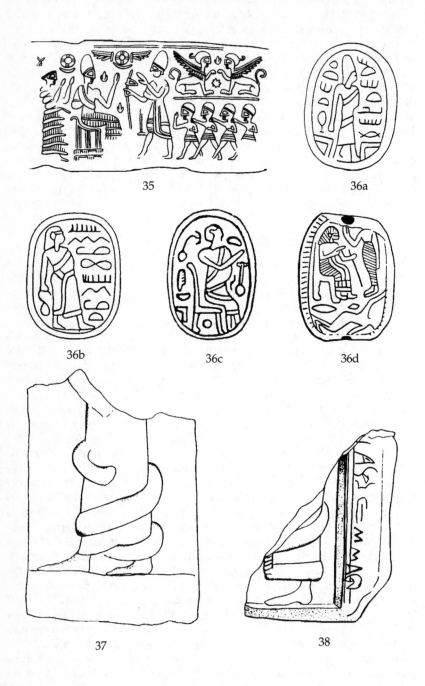

35

36a

36b

36c

36d

37

38

under the royal lion in illuss. 5a-b. Fragments of stelae found at Tell Beit Mirsim and at Shechem portray, in raised relief, the ruler who is wearing the garment with thick fringes (**illuss. 37, 38**; Merhav 1985). Perhaps these stelae were used in the cultic worship of the person who is depicted.

§27. On the scarabs of the jasper group, but also on many steatite scarabs, it is not the ruler who is wearing the garment with the thick fringes who himself holds a flower and/or raises his hand in greeting; it is the worshiper, who appears before the deity, who acts thus (**illuss. 39a-c**; Keel, et al., 1989, 217–221, 230f.). This may appear remarkable, but in the glyptic art we repeatedly detect a style in which many of the elements are eliminated from the scene. Some of the male and female worshipers who wore these images seem to have come to the conclusion that depicting their (own) piety and loyalty apparently would possibly guarantee them greater protection than if they wore images of the entities they were worshiping.[13] Based on evidence from contemporary or slightly older cylinder seal glyptic art and from information provided by a few scarabs that were executed with greater detail, it would appear that the common steatite scarabs from Middle Bronze Age IIB depict ordinary images of human beings, men who are standing or kneeling and women who are holding a branch or a flower in their hand, and are thus to be treated simply as *male or female worshipers* of the deity, unless further attributes are added in the scenes that would lead one to a different conclusion. This also seems to be the most likely interpretation in light of the fact that the same individuals who sometimes hold a branch or a flower can be portrayed standing before a deity, or holding a sacrificial offering, or dancing (**illuss. 40a-b**; see Smith/McNicoll/Hennessy 1981, 25f. figs. 24, 84; Tufnell 1984, I 135f.; II pls. 42, 47; Keel, et al., 1990, 172–181, 298–300). The enthusiastic activity taking place in the cult, expressed by scenes with dancers, is most likely to be attributed to worship of the weather god. A very interesting oval plaque shows the weather god on one side and three dancers with raised arms on the reverse. One of the dancers on the second side assumes the posture of the weather god and even holds a branch in his hand (see above, illus. 32d, and Keel, et al., 1990, 299f.).

9. Couples

§28. Perhaps we should treat a series of representations of couples that convey strongly erotic connotations as analogous to the encounter of the weather god with the "Naked Goddess." In any case, such representations are common for the Middle Bronze Age but disappear in the later periods. An Old Syrian hematite cylinder seal from Tell el-Ajjul shows a man and a woman using a tube with which they suck the liquid as they drink together from a vessel. The palms and the eight-rayed star are from the sphere of the Syrian goddess Ishtar/Astarte (**illus. 41**). A dove in flight replaces the star on an Old Syrian cylinder seal, now in Krakow, that likewise portrays a couple in a setting where intimate drinking takes place (Keel/Uehlinger 1990, 126 illus. 158). A number of scarabs from the

---

13 On this, see also illuss. 149a-c, 221, 234b, 271a-272d, 302a-d, 312.

39a   39b   39c

40a   40b

41

42   43

second half of Middle Bronze Age IIB depict a man and a woman being intimate with one another, sometimes showing this more graphically, sometimes less (**illus. 42**;[14] see Keel/Schroer 1985, 94f. illuss. 67–70). A scarab from Megiddo Stratum XII (ca. 1750–1700) shows a ruler wearing a garment with thick fringes together with a woman who has a long, thick braid of hair tightly wound; secondary motifs on that piece include a flower bud and a fully opened bloom (**illus. 43**).

Summary

§29.   The iconography that was typical of the period that preceded the material treated in this chapter was very strongly influenced by motifs borrowed from imported goods produced originally mostly in Egypt and to a lesser extent in the Near East. Some of these motifs were still used during Middle Bronze Age IIB. Images from the so-called "magic" knives from Egypt, as well as the scarabs that used the same iconography, and seal amulets with the Ω-symbol that originated in northern Syria or in southeastern Anatolia were used in the hope that such images would protect mother and child.

There was a creative merging, during Middle Bronze Age IIB, of themes that were at one time unique to Egypt or to the Near East. Older motifs, such as caprids and lions, fared well in an interplay with these outside influences. The Egyptians thought of the caprid as a symbol of regeneration and of the lion as a metaphor for the pharaoh, but both creatures could also be used to draw a person into the sphere of the *goddess*, in her role as "Mistress of the Animals." Typical items produced by this merging of concepts include the "Naked Goddess," depicted with branches, and the head of the goddess, now being shown with plant motifs.

The goddess was depicted not only on the seals that popularized and carried the message about her to the wider public, but also on precious metals – and she appears much more frequently than male deities. She even appears in one instance in a row of stelae – in a rudimentary style to be sure – as a stone sculpture. All these venues emphasized her gender as a woman, either by depicting her genital region proportionally too large and/or by identifying her female gender by depicting her physical body very realistically.

In addition to including caprids and lions in her sphere, as has been mentioned already, other creatures are linked with her, especially the dove as a messenger of love and the palm tree or its branches as symbols of life-giving vegetation.

The male consort of the goddess, the *weather god*, is represented with a fist raised victoriously. He occasionally holds a weapon in his hand, but he is most often portrayed holding a branch or a flower. When portrayed thus, he is shown to be responsible for producing vegetation as well. When the two partners draw close to one another, as depicted on cylinder

---

14 Scarab that was purchased, supposedly found ca. 6–7 km north of Jerusalem, now in the Biblical Institute of the University of Fribourg, Switzerland, no. SK 92; gray steatite, white slip, 17.8 × 12.1 × 9.2 mm.

seals imported from northern Syria, the goddess lifts up her clothing or pushes it aside, thus emphasizing the significance of her sexuality. When she is depicted on indigenous pieces, this pose accentuates the fact that she is a female. The Canaanite weather god and royal god is shown with the head of a falcon on numerous scarabs, which shows a conscious intention to identify him with the great Egyptian royal god Horus. In this form he does not appear as a warrior, but as one who has already been triumphant in battle with the crocodile.

On a *human level*, we find male and female worshipers who are professing their faith either in the female deity or in the male deity, as the one who provides vegetation, by means of their dancing and/or carrying branches and flowers in their hands. A couple portrayed on a cylinder seal while drinking together from the same vessel, and a couple shown on a scarab while wrapped in each other's arms, depict the intimacy between god and goddess on a human level. In addition to these erotic themes, we see the ruler wearing a garment with thick fringes depicted on objects large and small, most likely a portrayal of the person of the king who ruled the city-states that had sprung up in the newly established urban centers. The ruler is also never represented in battle, but is shown occasionally in triumph (illus. 36d). He is pictured most often as he receives homage from his subjects. Just as the weather god was portrayed as having certain aspects that originated in Egypt, the local ruler of the city-state is likened to the pharaoh at times when he is shown with a *uraeus* or when those who venerate him have an Egyptian look about them.

Assimilating Canaanite motifs to Egyptian motifs made it easier for the "Rulers of Foreign Lands" (the Hyksos) to acculturate themselves in Egypt. Egypt reacted to what had been done by these foreigners when it established Egyptian colonies, especially in southern Palestine, during the Late Bronze Age. The religious system of signs that used *maṣṣebahs*, sacred trees, deities and rituals that had a patently sexual character, regarded by many as typical of "the" Canaanite religion for the entire period from 1500 to 500, may in reality have played a decisive role only during Middle Bronze Age IIB and might have merely undergone radical modifications during the following periods, surviving only in a marginal way as the religion of the *pagani*, the villagers (see above, §4).

IV

꩜

Egyptian Colonialism and the Prevalence of Political and Warrior Deities: Late Bronze Age

§30. Much like the way the Early Bronze Age has been too neatly demarcated from the Middle Bronze Age, the traditional way of separating the Middle Bronze Age from the Late Bronze Age is too rigid. Destruction of the Middle Bronze Age cities and unwalled encampments in the hill country (Shechem, Shiloh) began gradually already in the sixteenth century. The Egyptians pressed forward into the Near East after expelling the "rulers from foreign lands" from Egypt. This period came to a closure of sorts only when Tuthmosis III was victorious over a coalition of Canaanite princes near Megiddo in 1457. There is thus a transitional period of 100–150 years (the so-called Late Bronze Age I) between the golden age of the Middle Bronze Age culture and the establishment of Egyptian rule in Palestine. This transition obviously did not take place in all parts of the country at the same time. Certain regions, such as the southern coastal plain, and cities, such as Beth-Shean, took on Egyptian characteristics both earlier and more intensively than did other parts of the country. By contrast, Hazor, to name one site, remained very much under northern influence (northern Syria, southeastern Anatolia) during the entire Late Bronze Age. In order to highlight the differences, determined largely by geographical location and by the different political circumstances in certain cities, we will discuss finds from four important cities within the country (Hazor, Megiddo, Lachish, and Beth-Shean) as representative of regional subsystems, supplementing the discussion from time to time by mentioning discoveries from other sites.

1. Hazor, or the Continuity of the Northern Syrian and Indigenous Traditions

§31. One notes a gentle and actually unbroken transition from the Middle Bronze Age to Late Bronze Age when observing the rich assemblage of finds from the four phases of the *temple in Area H,* located at the northwestern end of the large lower city of Hazor (Yadin 1972, 75–95; 1975, 79–119; 1989, 212–275; on the significance of Late Bronze Age Hazor in general, see Bienkowski 1987). From the time of its construction, about 1600, to that of its ultimate demise, when the city was destroyed in the

49

thirteenth century, the temple was rebuilt three times, with each new phase using almost the identical floor plan. Longroom temples of this type appear first in Syria – namely, at Ebla Str. IIIA (ca. 2000/1900) and then at Alalakh Str. VII (ca. 1720–1650) (Kempinski 1989a, 182; see also A. Kuschke in Galling ²1977, 336f.). Temples like this in Palestine were built not only at Hazor but also at Megiddo and Shechem.

Only a few image-bearing artifacts were found in the Middle Bronze Age and early Late Bronze Age strata of Temple H; nearly all discoveries were made in the topmost, latest stratum. It is clear, however, that the precious basalt orthostats that provided furnishings for the "Holy of Holies" located at the very back of that most recent temple, on which no images appear, were not the only items that survived from the fifteenth century temple of Str. II and that were used again in both of the succeeding structures. Other special equipment and votive offerings from earlier periods were also reused at a later time (e.g., carved goddess figures, one overlaid with silver and three with bronze, so typical of the Middle Bronze Age; see above, §§18, 20, 22). One bronze figure and the silver figure were found in Str. II (fifteenth century; Yadin 1961, pl. 339.3–4, 9–10). Two additional bronze figures were found in Str. IA (thirteenth century; Yadin 1961, pl. 339.5, 7–8; Negbi 1989, 348–354 nos. 5–8). The Middle Bronze Age cylinder seal shown above (illus. 31), that depicts the weather god and his consort who is disrobing, came from Str. IB (fourteenth century). In addition, a small basalt figure depicting a prince wearing a garment with thick fringes and a bronze figure of a princely individual, that may have been made in the seventeenth or sixteenth century, were discovered in Str. IB or possibly in Str. II (fourteenth or fifteenth century; Yadin 1961, pls. 330; 339, 1–2; see also Beck 1983, 1989b, 322–324; Keel/Schroer 1985, 74f., and illus. 30).

One detects northern influence not only on the basalt orthostats that served as ornamentation for the wall and that illustrate a typical Anatolian technique (Naumann 1955, 107f.); the influence is also apparent on the reclining lion (190 cm long) that, like the lion at Alaja Huyuk in central Anatolia (Bittel 1976, illus. 228; fourteenth century), served an architectural function as a cornerstone (Yadin 1961, pls. 120.2; 328 = Keel ⁴1984 illus. 166; Beck 1989b, 327f.). Since it was ceremonially buried, it is not clear to which stratum it belonged originally. From an iconographic perspective, a basalt block (170 cm in length) that was found in the center of the "Holy of Holies" in Str. IA (thirteenth century) suggests that it is from the same cultural context. It is decorated with beautifully worked relief, having the typical Old Assyrian-Anatolian or northern Syrian disk with a cross or four-pointed "star" in the center (Yadin 1961, pl. 331.1–3; Beck 1989b, 334f.). These symbols were first found in the northeastern part of the region, on Old Assyrian seals that date to about 2000 (Porada 1948, 108) and they appear later on a seal impression in the northwestern region, at Alalakh, dated to the fifteenth century (Collon 1975, no. 222).

A small fragment (barely 30 cm long) of a bull, with human feet on its back, was found lying in front of the entrance to Temple H in Str. IB (fourteenth century) (**illus. 44**; see Beck 1989b, 335–337). Only the torso of that bull has been found. It has the same Anatolian sun or moon symbol, the disk with a cross, on its chest. Since the *deity on a bull* is the weather god in northern Syrian-Anatolian cultural contexts (see above, §24 and illus. 30), we have here a most interesting combination of a weather god and a sun or moon god. Much like that large basalt block, a small bronze bull figure that was also found in the "Holy of Holies" of Temple H in Str. IA furnishes evidence for the existence of the cult of the weather god as well (thirteenth century) (**illus. 45**; Negbi 1989, 348ff. no. 10).

§32.   In the same archaeological context, 18 cylinder seals were found that were made using the so-called popular Mitannian style (Yadin 1961, pls. 319–322; Beck 1989a, 315–321. In addition to a series of animals depicting stags, caprids, and fish, one notes especially the *sacral tree*, flanked in three cases by a human worshiper and by an animal (e.g., a stag; Yadin 1961, pl. 320.2). Mitannian glyptic art is generally reserved when it comes to depicting deities anthropomorphically. The artists preferred to use a wide range of elements from the sphere of the goddess, such as the stylized tree, caprids, and birds. The palm, flanked by caprids and birds, is found on many painted vessels from the Late Bronze Age as well. Artifacts from Megiddo, and especially from Lachish, suggest that the tree should be considered as a way to represent the goddess (see above, §17). A fragment of one such vessel was found in the forecourt of the temple in Str. II (fifteenth century) (Yadin 1961, pls. 267.13; 310.6). Except for the three engraved figures with silver and bronze overlay, that are very likely from the Middle Bronze Age or from Late Bronze Age I, no anthropomorphic representations of female deities have been found in the later Late Bronze Age phases of Temple H.

Just as the deities are depicted mostly as male, worshipers are predominantly male as well. In addition to the two pieces that portray a prince in the garment with thick fringes, dated to the Middle Bronze Age, a basalt figure (20 cm high) of an enthroned male (probably also a prince) was found in Str. IA (thirteenth century; Yadin 1961, pls. 326f.; Beck 1989b, 324–327). Yadin and Beck interpret the statue of a seated person as evidence for a cult of dead kings or princes. This was probably an image of a praying figure at first; it is certainly possible that the enthroned prince could himself have later become a figure to be venerated. A very similar figure from the same period was found in Area F (Yadin 1960, pl. 197).

§33.   The *stelae temple in Area C*, built into the Middle Bronze Age wall at the southern end of the lower city (Yadin 1972, 67–74; 1975, 43–57), which was furnished with lion orthostats just like the temple in Area H (Yadin 1958, pl. 30.2), provides much the same picture. As was also true of the stelae grouped together at Tel Kitan (see §21), only the center stele in this grouping has an image on it. Whereas there was a female figure on the stele at Tel Kitan, here one sees a crescent moon with a disk above two outstretched arms (**illus. 46**). If two tassels are indeed supposed to be depicted under the crescent, then this is the symbol of the Moon God of Haran in northern Syria. The cultic symbol of this deity was a standard with a crescent moon ornament. This motif is common in Iron Age IIC glyptic art (see below, §§173–177), but it appears once or twice already on Late Bronze Age cylinder seals at Gezer (Parker 1949, no. 190; on the dating, see Courtois/Webb 1987, 39–41 no. 3) and at Tell Jemmeh (Petrie 1928, pl. 19.30, there without the tassels).

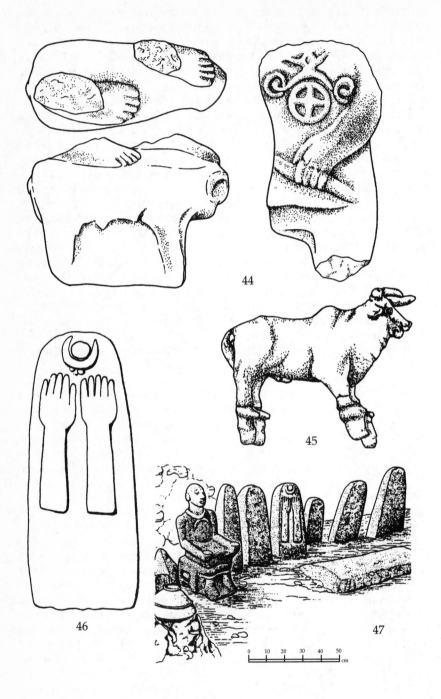

44

45

46   47

A basalt figure (40 cm high) of a seated man includes a large crescent moon as a breast pendant. This figure was found *in situ* at the southern end of the row of the stelae (**illus. 47**). It is not clear whether this is to be a portrayal of a god or of a deified ancestor. The crescent moon amulet on his chest does not indicate whether the figure is supposed to be human. The fragmentary remains of the god on a bull, found at the temple in Area H, also include an emblem on the deity's chest (Yadin 1972, 73 note 1). But it is obvious that such an amulet is just as appropriate for a human to wear. The cup in the right hand of the figure is also ambiguous, since cups are found in the hand of both gods and humans. The position of this piece at the south end of the row of the stelae, and not in the center of the group, would most likely argue against its being the image of a deity and in favor of its being an ancestor image. One would expect the image of a god to be placed right in the center, which is where we find a stele that is engraved in relief. P. Beck has interpreted three smaller, unfinished (?) statues of a seated individual from the same shrine as ancestor statues (Yadin 1958, pl. 162.5–7; Beck 1990c).

No one should dispute that this is a shrine to the moon god. A crescent moon is also visible on a silver-covered bronze standard that was found in another small shrine, also in Area C (Yadin 1960, pls. 181, 209). In addition to the crescent moon, two snakes are quite distinct, with two eyes and a nose positioned between them (in other words, a human face). Both above the crescent moon and also below the face there appears what seems to be a Ω-shaped symbol. The iconography which is so difficult to interpret, and which has not become much clearer even after recently published X-ray studies (Tadmor 1989), might depict a goddess, perhaps the consort of the moon god. At any rate, we can assert that the moon emblem and the combination that links the weather god with the sun or moon god furnish the first evidence of a piety in Palestine/Israel that is oriented toward heavenly beings, apparently having originated in northern Syria.

2. Megiddo: From the Gold Pendants of the Vegetation Goddess to the Dominance of Warriors

§34. Toward the end of the Middle Bronze Age, a large temple of the same type as Temple H at Hazor was erected at Megiddo on a platform in the old sacral precinct in Area BB. The imposing construction measured 21.50 m long and 16.50 m wide. Whereas the main room of the temple was constructed using the broadroom pattern at Hazor, the one at Megiddo used a longroom arrangement. A series of investigations has shown that this Temple 2048 should not be assigned to Str. VIII, as the excavators suggested in their publication, but clearly belonged to Str. X (1650–1550), thus to be dated to the end of the Middle Bronze Age (Kempinski 1989a, 181–186). In its first phase it would have been contemporaneous with both the Middle Bronze Age temple at Hazor and the so-called Fortified Temple at Shechem.

This temple, founded in Megiddo toward the end of the Middle Bronze Age, was renovated several times during the Late Bronze Age. Four phases can be isolated. As in Hazor, there are typical Middle Bronze Age female figures cast from metal or engraved on tin that survive in Late

Bronze Age strata in Megiddo (Loud 1948, pl. 236.25, 29; Negbi 1976, nos. 1670f.). Naked goddesses, holding their breasts with both hands, are particularly typical of the strata that date to the end of the Middle Bronze Age at Megiddo (see §22). New items, characteristic of the transitional period Middle Bronze Age/Late Bronze Age (also identified by some as Late Bronze Age I; ca. 1550–1450), include *pear-shaped pendants*. Three of these have been found at Megiddo, five have been discovered at Tell el-Ajjul, and one was recovered from the Fosse Temple at Lachish (Negbi 1976, nos. 1677–1684; McGovern 1985, 114, nos. 68–74). Unlike Middle Bronze Age IIB pendants, most of which were cut from silver-leaf or bronze-leaf (Tell el-Ajjul, Gezer, Megiddo, Nahariyah; see above), these are made from gold as a rule. They are different from the others since they do not show the silhouette of a slender female but rather have the shape of an inverted pear, for which the head, breasts, navel, and especially the female genitalia all have puncture holes (**illus. 48**). E. E. Platt (1976) also detects in the overall shape of the pendant a way to imitate the shape of the female genitalia, interpreting the design that runs along the outside edge as a way to depict the pubic hair. Individual finds suggest that this kind of jewelry might have been worn on a girdle wrapped around the hips (see Petrie 1930, pl. 26.103, pl. 27). Whereas Middle Bronze Age pendants were limited to Palestine as a rule, many pendants of the new variety have turned up in Ugarit as well (Negbi 1976, nos. 1685–1695). On some of these pieces, such as on one of the finds from Tell el-Ajjul (**illus. 49**), a branch grows from the navel or else from the genitalia of the goddess. Pendants that date to the emerging Late Bronze Age are now linked to the iconography of the "Branch Goddess" depicted on the scarabs of Middle Bronze Age IIB, on which a branch is depicted with the genitalia of the goddess at times (see illuss. 12b-c). The connection of the goddess with vegetation is emphasized additionally by the lotus flower, the Egyptian symbol of regeneration, that is on the pendant worn around the neck of the goddess in illus. 49. Much like the Middle Bronze Age IIB pendants, these Late Bronze Age pendants were passed on by inheritance over long periods of time, though none of these gold pendants survived beyond the Late Bronze Age to be found in an undisputed Iron Age context.

§35. In addition to the costly depictions of the goddess on metal, the Late Bronze Age witnessed the introduction of cheap, molded *clay figures* for the first time and these are found in great quantities. The metal figures that were recovered from Megiddo and that depict the goddess who presents her breasts with both hands show that this was an especially popular type of figure at the end of Middle Bronze Age IIB. This type (Winter 1983, 103–110 type 3) was also the most popular of the clay figures. The only complete piece from Megiddo comes from Grave 26B, which, on the basis of ceramics, is clearly to be dated to the end of the sixteenth or to the beginning of the fifteenth century (**illus. 50**). The figure wears a high head covering, like those frequently found on the metal figures from the Middle Bronze Age. May lists fragments of eight additional pieces and refers to parallels found in good condition at Gezer, Taanach, Shechem, and Tell Abu Hawam (May 1935, 30f.; pl. 31).

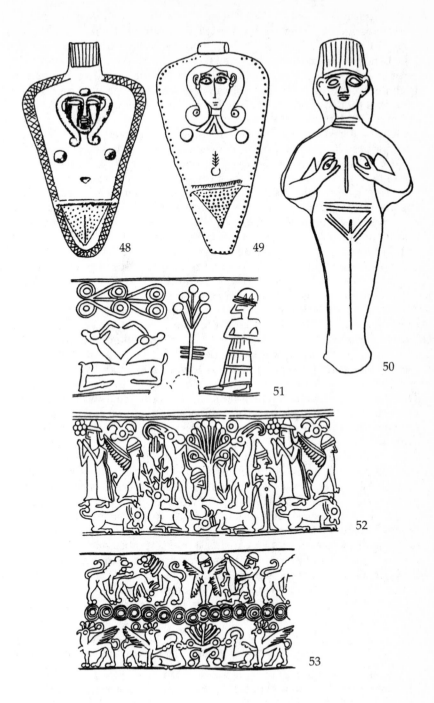

48

49

50

51

52

53

Cast glass or faience, at that time still rather expensive, provided a middle range between the very expensive metal figures and the less expensive figures made of clay. It was produced only during Late Bronze Age I and was used to make a small but full-figured female. Like the clay figures, these females hold out their breasts, but they do not wear any high head covering. For that reason, one is on less certain ground if one identifies them as goddesses.[1] The faience statuette from Megiddo Str. IX (1550–1479) that shows a naked woman with vividly depicted genitalia and arms placed close to her thighs could equally well portray a human or a goddess (Loud 1948, 241.5; concerning the entire issue, see §§57ff.).

§36.   The *sacral tree* that was depicted on the gold pendant in illus. 49 actually appears on a wide range of image-bearing objects from Late Bronze Age Megiddo. As at Hazor, numerous cylinder seals made using the popular Mitannian style were found at Megiddo. As at Hazor, they portray series of animals and the sacral tree flanked by human worshipers and by animals (**illus. 51**; see Guy 1938, 182–184; Loud 1948, pls. 160.9; 161.10–16). The "Naked Goddess" appears, along with the tree flanked by caprids, on a piece of above average beauty (**illus. 52**). Her counterpart is a stag flanked by both a lion and a bull, and the bull and lion simultaneously flank the goddess in her role as a "Mistress of the Animals." A male figure, with arms raised in worship, and a cherub, crouching on its hind legs, flank the tree as well, which is obviously closely connected with the goddess.[2] On a hematite cylinder seal from Acre that is carved in a similar fashion (**illus. 53**) we see a palmetto tree flanked by caprids and cherubs in the lower register, and we see a naked goddess who has four wings in the upper register, directly above the tree. The four wings are to be considered as attributes that indicate celestial elements. Celestial aspects of the goddess that are new to Palestine in the Late Bronze Age are also portrayed on pendants made in the shape of an eight-rayed star (see below, §44).

Individual examples of painted vessels, with a more or less highly stylized palm and flanked by animals, had been found already in Middle Bronze Age IIB contexts (see §17, with illus. 16). Whereas only one fragment of such a vessel survived from the fifteenth century at Hazor (see §32), a whole assemblage of such vessels survived at Megiddo, the majority from the fourteenth or thirteenth centuries. The palm is flanked on three of the pieces by two caprids (Loud 1948, pls. 48.4, 58.1–2, 72.3), once by four (Loud 1948, pl. 64.4), and once by four caprids and numerous birds (**illus. 54**).[3] Certain specimens of the vessels were also painted with nothing but palms and "wavy lines that depict water" (without animals; Loud 1948, pls. 63.3, 67.19). An especially interesting variation of this kind

1 Glass plaques have been found at Lachish and Beth-Shean (Tufnell 1958, 83 with pl. 27.2 = Winter 1983, 105 with illus. 27; Rowe 1940, pl. 68 A.7). Faience plaques or fragments have been found at Megiddo and Beth-Shean (Schumacher 1908, A 63f. with illus. 79a; Loud 1948, pl. 241.2, 4; Rowe 1940, pl. 35.12).
2 Winter (1983, 175), whose illus. 143 is a drawing of Parker's photograph (1948, no. 128), still refers to an "unstructured seal." The new analysis published here should make the highly organized nature of this design very apparent.
3 Parallels from throughout Palestine are found in May 1935, pl. 40; for the chronological sequence, see Amiran 1969, 161–165.

54

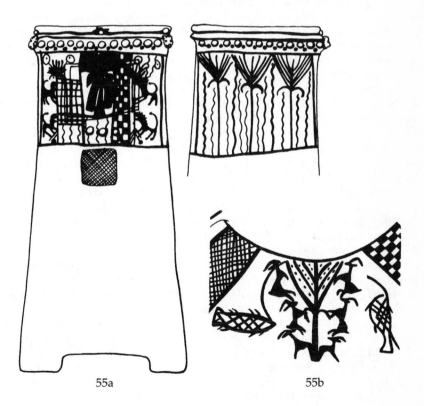

55a   55b

of painting can be seen on the upper third of a rectangular clay stand that was originally ca. 70 cm high (**illus. 55a**). We find three palms with "wavy lines that depict water" on each of two of the sides. It might seem unusual to see water streaming down out of a tree, but, on a painted vessel from Tell el-Far'ah (south), the wavy lines are clearly shown to be water by the presence of two fish (**illus. 55b**). On the front side of the cultic stand, which includes a window, there are two palms flanked by lions (concerning the lions, see also the bronze depictions in Loud 1948, pl. 240.3). Palms, caprids, lions, and doves are all part of the sphere in which the goddess exists (see §17). Artifacts from Lachish and Aphek will show unequivocally that the palms very clearly point to the vital forces possessed by the goddess (see §44). These vital forces are shown in the paintings but are never included on the figures that depict a female body. Kempinski (1989b) has proposed recently that one should think of the stand just described as a model for one of the temple towers. These towers flank the entrances of the so-called "Fortified Temples" at Megiddo, Hazor, and Shechem. If this hypothesis is correct, it is noteworthy that the lions would emphasize the aggressive side of the goddess.

§37.   The chief resident of the "Fortified Temple" may not have been a female, but a male divinity – indeed, the same figure that is shown standing on the bull at Hazor.[4] We see no reason to agree with Kempinski that a triad of divinities was worshiped in this temple, namely El, Baal, and a fertility goddess (Kempinski 1989a, 185f.). The finds seem to point in another direction.

As Kempinski himself asserts, hardly any of the precious metal figures of the goddess were still being manufactured in the Late Bronze Age. A small bronze figure (9.5 cm) of an enthroned individual was found south of the temple, wearing the garment with thick fringes that is typical of the Middle Bronze Age and the type of head covering that is also characteristic of that period, while holding up one hand either in blessing or in reverence (Loud 1948, pl. 235.23 = Negbi 1976, no. 1451; see also Loud 1948, pl. 236.24). Not only is it questionable whether the figure was ever part of the furnishings of the Late Bronze Age temple, but it is also doubtful whether it represented El. In contrast to the image on the famous stele from Ugarit (*ANEP* no. 493; see Wyatt 1983), the figure from Megiddo is beardless.

By contrast, there is an unusually large (a good 25 cm high) bronze figure that does come from the Late Bronze Age temple. It is covered by gold-leaf and portrays an enthroned youthful god who wears a knee-length garment and high head covering (**illus. 56**). This may be an actual cultic image. The god holds a blossom in one hand. It is too facile a solution to identify all enthroned gods as El and all striding gods as Baal. The battles and the defeat of Baal culminate eventually in his enthronement as well. The blossom in the one hand connects the figure iconographically with the weather god on Middle Bronze Age IIB scarabs (see above, illuss. 32a-d). The introductory formulas used in letters found at Taanach also provide supporting evidence to show that the weather god

---

4 A small bronze bull, of the kind from Hazor replicated in illus. 45, was found in
  Grave 912B (Late Bronze Age IIA, fourteenth century) (May 1934, pl. 34).

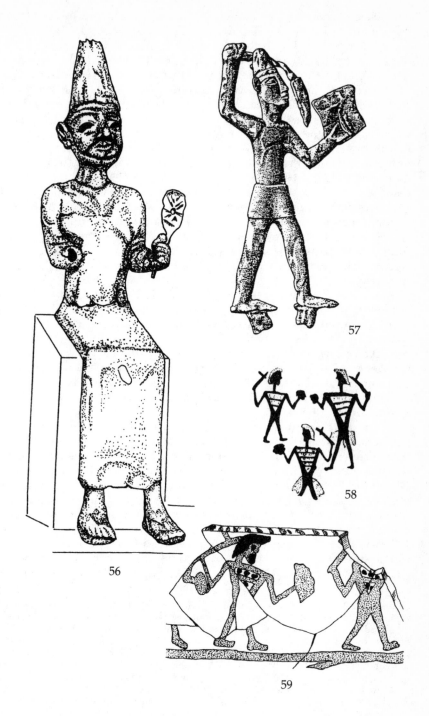

56

57

58

59

(Baal-Hadad) was the dominant deity in the area surrounding the broad central plain of Jezreel during the Late Bronze Age (Glock 1983, 60f.).[5]

Another bronze figure (barely 14 cm high) was found south of the temple. In contrast to the one just discussed, this individual is portrayed in a striding posture and wears only a loincloth and a high head covering, reminiscent of the white crown worn in Upper Egypt. The left arm is missing, as is the object held in his upraised (to strike?) right hand (Loud 1948, pl. 235.22 = Negbi 1976, no. 1360). This figure might be a depiction of the weather god, but it might also portray Reshef (Schulman 1985) or possibly even the pharaoh. A more assured conclusion could be drawn only if the attribute that had been in the hand had survived. The attributes that were held have been found with a figure (13 cm high) that was discovered in Grave 4 at Megiddo: a handheld weapon and a shield (**illus. 57**). This combination of attributes is typical of portrayals of Reshef, supported by the fact that it was found in a private setting.

There was a decisive change in what was depicted on metal figures during the transition from the Middle Bronze Age to the Late Bronze Age. Warrior gods, such as Baal and Reshef, virtually replace the naked goddesses.

§38. This change corresponds to a shift in the iconographic symbol system as it relates to what is depicted on the human level. Military themes replace those of loyalty and erotic contact between the sexes (§§26–28). *Warriors* with handheld weapons and small shields are portrayed on two painted sherds (perhaps from the same vessel) that date to the end of Late Bronze Age IIB. These are nearly identical to the warrior god depicted in the bronze figure from Megiddo Grave 4, except that the warriors lack the high head covering and, unlike the god, are wearing beards (**illuss. 58–59**).

In the Late Bronze Age the *chariot* is the new and most typical iconographic symbol for depicting battle and war. It came into Palestine from different directions. We find it, for example, on a Mycenaean vessel dated to the second half of the fourteenth century that was discovered at Dan (Biran 1975, 316, and color plate, 266). The most important source for this new iconography, however, is Egypt. A chariot scene appears in that country now for the first time on a scarab, on a seal amulet from the time of Tuthmosis I (about 1490; Desroches-Noblecourt 1950, pl. 9.8 = Keel 1975, 446 illus. 12; see also Hornung/Staehelin 1976, no. 662). Portrayals in Palestine show the pharaoh triumphing over his enemies from his chariot with his bow. The first examples known to date are from the

---

5 Letters 2.2, 5.3, 6.3. Glock (1983, 60 notes 18–19) observed that the reference in Letter 1.20f. (contra Albright) is *not* about a certain *um(m)ān Aširat* (thus observed already by Rainey 1977, 59; this has not been noted by Day 1986, 386; Smith 1990: 6.84; and many others)!

The West Semitic *personal names in the Amarna Letters* from Palestine indicate that the name Baal clearly dominated the scene in Canaan: Baʿlu-meḫir from Gath-Padalla, Addaya from Gaza, Pu-Baʿlu from Yurṣa, Adda-danu from Gezer, Šipṭi-Baʿlu from Lachish, Šamu-Addu from Shimron, possibly also Shubandu (cf. in addition ʿAbdi-Tirši from Hazor, Milki-Ilu from Gezer, Yabni-Ilu from Lachish). Names of goddesses among the personal names include ʿAbdi-Ḥepa from Jerusalem and ʿAbdi-Ashtarti from either Qiltu or Gath(?). Concerning the whole topic, see now Hess 1989; de Moor 1990, 104.

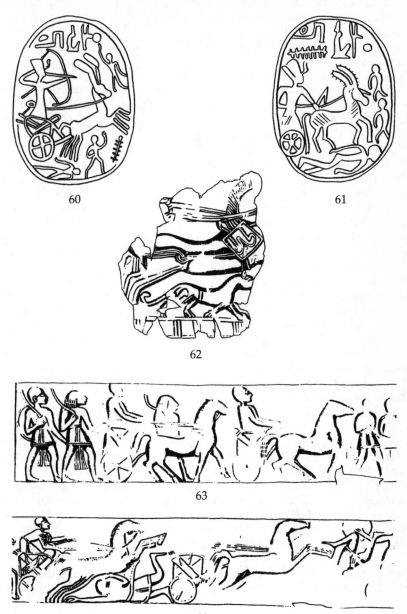

60

61

62

63

64

Nineteenth Dynasty (thirteenth century) (**illus. 60**; see Giveon/Kertesz 1986, no. 141). A scarab from Tell el-Far°ah (south), dating to the same time period, shows the pharaoh in his chariot without a bow but with captive enemies walking in front of him (**illus. 61**). The pharaoh is shown in his chariot, without any enemies in sight, on additional Egyptian seal amulets from Deir el-Balah, from Tell el-Far°ah (south), and from Gezer (see also Wiese 1990, 81–87).

There is an interesting ivory fragment in the Megiddo hoard, a collection that includes various finds dating to the time period that stretches from 1350 to 1150. On this particular piece, one can see a galloping horse that is apparently harnessed to a chariot. A lion trots alongside beneath it (**illus. 62**; concerning what follows, see Liebowitz 1980; 1987, 5f.). It is common to see a lion that was used in battle, positioned either beneath or next to chariot horses, on the large-scale reliefs found at Medinet Habu that show Ramesses III on the way to battle or else on the way back home (see Nelson 1930, pls. 17, 31; Nelson 1932, pls. 73, 77, 92; Schweitzer 1948, 51f.). One of the Megiddo ivories appears to show an actual battle scene. The very fact that such scenes were now being portrayed on seal amulets (see illuss. 60–61) shows that the pharaoh-in-battle has become an important motif within the religious system of Egypt. Two other ivories from the same Megiddo collection, unfortunately poorly preserved because of weathering, seem by contrast to show Canaanite princes, with none of the typical Egyptian attributes and without any religious symbolism, in a chariot on the way to battle and at the battle (**illuss. 63–64**). Such an important concept as war is portrayed on these latter finds without any visible religious interpretation.

§39.   On another very famous ivory, a prince returns in his chariot, victorious from battle (**illus. 65**). Two naked Shasu nomads walk in front of the chariot, tied to the horses (see Giveon 1971, 201f.; Staubli 1991, 64). The winged solar disk above the horses reminds one not only of the Egyptian origin of such scenes and their popularity under Ramesses III but also gives the impression that the victor was blessed by the deity. The left side of the scene on this ivory, separated from the right by three vertically arranged plants, portrays the victory celebration. Messenger birds carry forth the news of victory (Keel 1977b, 138–141; see also what is depicted on a roughly contemporaneous cylinder seal from Tell el-Ajjul, **illus. 66a**). The prince is seated on a cherub throne, the same type of throne as can be seen on a round, sculpted miniature relief from the same hoard from Megiddo (**illus. 66b**). The prince shown in illus. 65 holds a bowl similar to the ones that servants, standing to the left in the scene, are refilling from a large mixing vessel. There are two cups, shaped like animal heads (gazelle and lion), on a stand located just above the mixing vessel. A drinking cup shaped like a lion's head has been found at Tel Zeror, to name just one example (**illus. 66c**; see also Zevulun 1987). A princess hands a lotus blossom to the enthroned prince and serves him with a hand towel. A second woman is playing a lyre.

Like the war scene, the feast scene on this carved ivory piece has parallels on other ivories from Megiddo. On these pieces as well, the prince appears enthroned, with both a bowl and a lotus blossom (**illus. 67**). In these examples, instead of service being offered by a princess, the

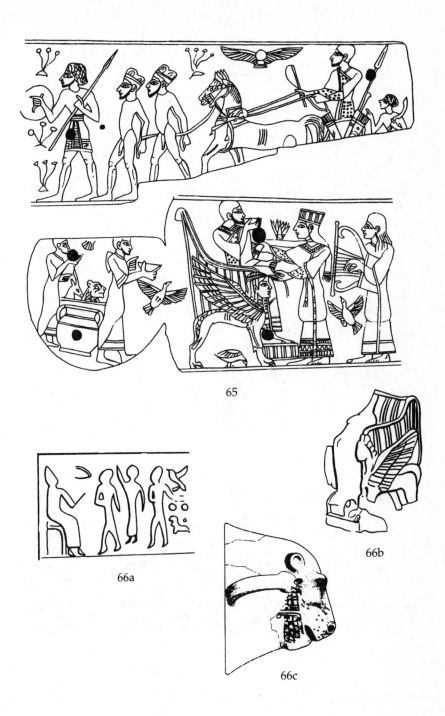

65

66a

66b

66c

67

68a

68b

prince is attended by a servant who holds a hand towel. All of the other celebrants at the feast are male as well. On still another ivory from the same assemblage, a man is shown bringing geese as tribute (Loud 1939, no. 162). Whereas women appear in depictions from the Middle Bronze Age both as sexual partners for men and with equal status, here they are shown either as servants who stand before the enthroned prince or are absent altogether. Analogous to the new way of showing the role that the gods play, the main concern of the prince is not his encounter with the goddess but rather a triumph over his enemies.

This new subordination of women is depicted on still another ivory from Megiddo. Using a purely Egyptian style, it portrays a woman bringing a bouquet of flowers to an enthroned king (?) (Loud 1939, no. 378). On another carved ivory piece, this one from Tell el-Farʿah (south), the same story is conveyed as at Megiddo – though this example is carved not in a pure Egyptian style but does show strong Egyptian influence (**illus. 68a**). Here a woman fills a bowl for the prince and hands him a lotus blossom. Liebowitz suggests interpreting this scene as analogous to the Megiddo victory celebration (1980, 165f.). But sufficient evidence to support this interpretation is lacking. The accompanying scenes (life in the marshes, catching ducks; **illus. 68b**), which Liebowitz interprets as showing how food is being procured, are not enough to justify this explanation. At most, some analogy to victory might be suggested if one interprets the hunt for ducks as depicting the ritual destruction of enemies, but this is not likely for fourteenth- or thirteenth-century Canaan (for the later period, see Alliot 1946; Keel ⁴1984, 78f. with illus. 111).

3. Lachish and Egyptian-Canaanite Syncretism in Southern Palestine

§40. Hazor, set in far northern Palestine, shows few traces of Egyptian iconography during the Late Bronze Age. We see considerably more Egyptian influence at Megiddo, in central Palestine. But Egyptian influence clearly predominates at Lachish and at other southern Palestinian sites.

The most important sites in Lachish are the so-called Fosse Temple at the base of the tell on the west, given this name because it was constructed in the moat or fosse that was part of the fortification of the earlier Middle Bronze Age IIB city, and the temple that was built on the top of the tell which shows Egyptian influence. The Fosse Temple went through three phases, dated to the fifteenth century (Phase I), the fourteenth century (Phase II), and the thirteenth century (Phase III) respectively (Tufnell 1940, pls. 66–73). Since the floor plan is not very characteristic of a temple, Ottosson suggests interpreting the installation as a pottery workshop, by analogy with similar buildings at Hazor and Zarephath (1980, 81–92). But the equally asymmetric shrines at Tel Mevorakh and Tell Qasile provide closer parallel structures for comparison and interpretation of the Fosse Temple. In addition to ceramic vessels typical of a Late Bronze Age cultic site, numerous other objects characteristic of these other temples have been found at the Fosse Temple site as well (see below).

Even the podium located by the south wall of the main structure, which was there during all three phases, supports the view that the installation was most likely a temple, even after the alternate evidence has been considered (see Mazar 1980, 61–73; Coogan 1987b, 4).

By contrast, the temple found in Str. VI (thirteenth century) that was situated on top of the site has a typical Late Bronze Age floor plan: vestibule, hall, and raised cella accessible by a staircase. The Egyptian character of this and comparable installations at Beth-Shean has been demonstrated by noting the common element of chapels that are constructed for the dead as well as similarities to the river temple at Tell el-Amarna. But it is also conceivable that the floor plans of those shrines that do not follow the pattern used in Amarna are related instead to the type of temple that developed in the Near East during the transition from the Middle Bronze Age to the Late Bronze Age. But at least some elements in the temple on top of the tell at Lachish are typically Egyptian: the octagonal pillars that support the ceiling of the hall and the low stone parapet by the staircase leading to the cella (Keel/Küchler 1982, 913–916; H. Weippert 1988, 284–293).

§41.   At the beginning of the Late Bronze Age, inexpensive terra-cotta figurines of the goddess holding her breasts were produced at Megiddo and at other sites north of Carmel. In the south, one finds a naked goddess as well, but with shoulder-length locks, holding her arms in a bent position and grasping a papyrus or lotus stem in each hand (Winter 1983, 110–114, type 4).[6] At least two such terra-cotta figures have been found at Lachish (**illus. 69**; see also Tufnell 1940, pl. 28.6). Iconographically, this is an Egyptian-style version of the Middle Bronze Age "Branch Goddess" (see §§15, 17). In place of the branches, one sees typically Egyptian plants, and instead of straight, shoulder-length hair, one detects a preference for shoulder-length locks that seem somewhat like the Hathor hairstyle (see Schroer 1989, 174–185). The term *"qudshu* type" has been applied to these images because we find the inscription *qdš* "holiness" on Egyptian stelae from the New Kingdom Period, the word being written close to a goddess who displayed these attributes.[7] As a rule, the goddess is shown standing on the back of a lion on Egyptian stelae (see illus. 4) and is flanked by two gods, usually Reshef and Min. The standing-on-a-lion posture is rarer in Palestine but does occur at times, as for example on a bronze pendant from Acre (**illus. 70**) and on two terra-cotta tablets found very recently at Tel Harashim.[7a]

An interesting variation of this type can be seen on a gold-leaf piece found in the temple on top of the tell. Instead of the goddess standing on a lion, wearing an *atef*-crown, she stands on a horse that is clothed with

---

6 About a half-century ago, Pritchard listed 37 pieces (1943, 6–10): three from Megiddo, and 34 from sites south of Carmel, especially Gezer, Beth Shemesh, and Tell Beit Mirsim. Since that time, the number has nearly doubled.

7 *Qdš* is probably not the name of the goddess but an epithet indicating the dominant aspect of her sexual and erotic powers that is shown in these images (on the whole topic, see Winter 1983, 112f.; Lipiński 1986, 89f.). For *qdš* as an epithet of the Atirat/ Asherah, and for the identification of the *qudshu* type goddess with Atirat/ Asherah, see Cross 1973, 33–35; Maier 1986, 81–96; Hadley 1989, 70–73, and many others.

7a See Sh. Giveon, Tel Ḥarashim: *Ḥadašot Arkeologiyot* 97 (1991) 76 fig. 110.

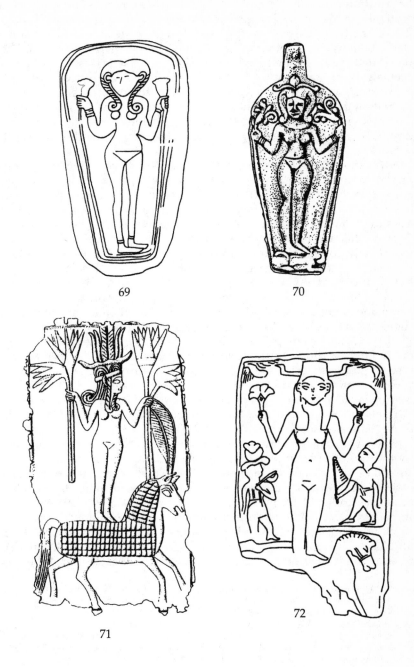

69

70

71

72

protective armor (?) (**illus. 71**; see Clamer 1980; Hadley 1989, 208–211). Both attributes, the *atef*-crown and the horse, are otherwise typically used with the warlike Anat.[8] The goddess stands on a horse here as well and is flanked by two male deities, typical of Egyptian stelae, as one sees on a clay model that was found at Tel Qarnayim near Beth-Shean (**illus. 72**; Ben-Arieh 1983).[9] In the Late Bronze Age the horse was used to convey exclusively military connotations. The goddess, whose role had been connected primarily with vegetation and, to some extent, with the animals of the wilderness, is now drawn into the arena of war as this new animal, the horse, takes center stage; war themes played an especially dominant role in the iconographic symbol system of the thirteenth century (see above, §§37–39).

§42. In addition to the *qudshu* type of goddess, which remains recognizable because of how she is depicted from a frontal view, is naked, and is associated with vegetation, having a Canaanite origin even though she has Egyptian elements, the purely Egyptian Hathor appears in her classical form in Late Bronze Age II as well. Six Hathor heads made of Egyptian faience, used as pendants and forming part of a necklace, were found in the topmost stratum (thirteenth century) of the Fosse Temple at Lachish. A Hathor head amulet with cow's horns and a solar disk were found in the same place (**illus. 73**; see McGovern 1985, 110 nos. 12f.; Tufnell 1940, pl. 14, top). A Hathor sistrum amulet, flanked by two *uraei* and made of gold, was found at Tell el-Ajjul. Based on its archaeological context, it is to be dated Late Bronze Age I or IIA (**illus. 74**; see also Petrie 1933, pl. 17, above left; pl. 28.9). On scarabs and similar seal amulets, the thoroughly Egyptian Hathor sistrum replaces the Middle Bronze Age type of goddess' head (see above, §16) and pushes aside the "Branch Goddess" on the seals, a theme that had been indigenous to the country (see above, §15). Of the 22 known examples, 18 come from sites south of Carmel. The objects in **illuss. 75a-c** were found at Lachish and the one in **illus. 75d** was discovered at Tell el-Ajjul.[10]

Female heads with Hathor locks appear in widely varying functional contexts and were manufactured using a wide variety of materials. They are found with some frequency north of Carmel as well. It is not always entirely clear whether the image is really supposed to be Hathor. Two heads made of gold, found at Megiddo in Str. VIII (1479–1350), served as stoppers for a double bottle that contained cosmetic oils. The circular bowls into which the oil flowed are reminiscent of solar disks (Loud 1948, pl. 232.5). A similar vessel stopper, made of ivory, was discovered recently in a Late Bronze Age I grave at Hazor (**illus. 76**). Since she was

---

8 See the image on the rectangular plaque in the Cairo Museum, where Anat appears wearing an *atef*-crown and stands on a horse next to Baal-Seth, who is on a lion. (Keel, et al., 1990, 408f. illus. 104.)

9 See Schulman 1984; Giveon 1986. It appears that these are a Canaanite weather god (to the right, with a plant [?]; see illuss. 32a-d) and an Egyptian war god of the Montu-Onuris type. See also the iconographic parallel on an ivory from Megiddo that has gone unnoticed until now (Loud 1939, no. 125).

10 The collection of artifacts listed by S. Schroer indicates six are from Tell el-Ajjul, five are from Gezer, four are from Lachish, three are from Acre, and one each from Tel Anafa, Ashdod, Beth Shemesh, and Tell el-Far'ah (south) (Schroer 1989, 143–146, 163–167, 185).

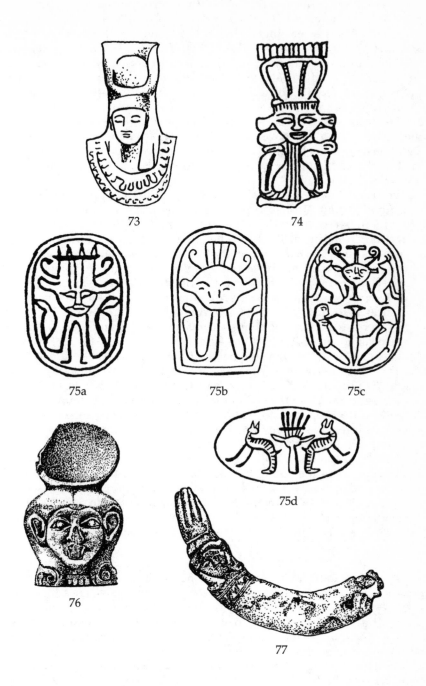

73

74

75a

75b

75c

76

75d

77

the goddess of beauty and love, Hathor certainly is in her rightful place in such a setting. The image on a fourteenth-century standard from Beth-Shean is certainly a Hathor head, since it shows the horns of a cow as well as the solar disk (Rowe 1940, pl. 47 A.3). An ivory clapper has been found at Shiqmona, near Haifa, decorated with a woman's head that has shoulder-length locks (**illus. 77**). A fragment of another clapper comes from a fourteenth-century stratum in Beth-Shean (Rowe 1940, pl. 47 A.4). Since Hathor is the goddess of music, this is probably her image as well (Giveon 1978, 68–72). One cannot be as certain about the identity of a series of appliqués, in the shape of a head with shoulder-length locks, that were found in the ivory hoard dating to the last phase of Late Bronze Age Megiddo (Loud 1939, pl. 44.190–193).

The clearest evidence for a cult in honor of the Egyptian goddess Hathor in Late Bronze Age Palestine comes from the extreme southern part of the region. The goddess had her own shrine there, at Timnah, north of Elath (Rothenberg 1988). Two capitals with Hathor heads and a relief from the time of Ramesses III, executed in the rock some 20 m above the temple, that shows the pharaoh sacrificing to the goddess, who is wearing the cow horns and a solar disk on her head (**illus. 78**), prove that this was a sacred shrine dedicated to this goddess (see Schulman 1988, 116, 143f.). Three fragments from large Hathor sistrums, made of glazed faience (or glazed clay), provide additional evidence (Schulman 1988, 118f.; see also fig. 27.2, 4). We find the name of the goddess or her title *nb.t mfk3.t* "Mistress of the Turquoise" on several faience fragments (see, e.g., Schulman 1988, 118 Egyptian Catalogue 21; 123 Egyptian Catalogue 55). From the end of the Old Kingdom/the beginning of the Middle Kingdom on, Hathor was known as the mistress of various foreign lands and of semi-precious stones (turquoise, lapis lazuli). She was probably given these titles being known as the "Goddess from Afar," having appeared as the eye of the sun that was sent far to the south, but also as the goddess of the treasure house and of beauty, whose valuables came from foreign lands (see Giveon 1978, 61–67). Reference will be made in §44 to a series of iconographic elements from the sphere of the goddess that appear in the Fosse Temple at Lachish as well as at Timnah and at other sites.

§43. An important artifact from House 6001 in Lachish, a gilded bronze ostrich feather that measures 14 cm (**illus. 79a**), shows that still other Egyptian goddesses were venerated alongside Hathor in Late Bronze Age Palestine. The ostrich feather is used primarily as an attribute of the goddess Ma'at, the goddess of the type of good order that ought to be at work in every area of life. If the feather was once part of a statue of the goddess, the original piece would have had to have been ca. 70–80 cm high. The god Ptah, who was rather widely known in Late Bronze Age Palestine (see below, §46), was celebrated at times as "Lord of Ma'at." It did not take long for Ma'at to be represented by the figure of a seated girl with an ostrich feather on her head. Not long after that, she was

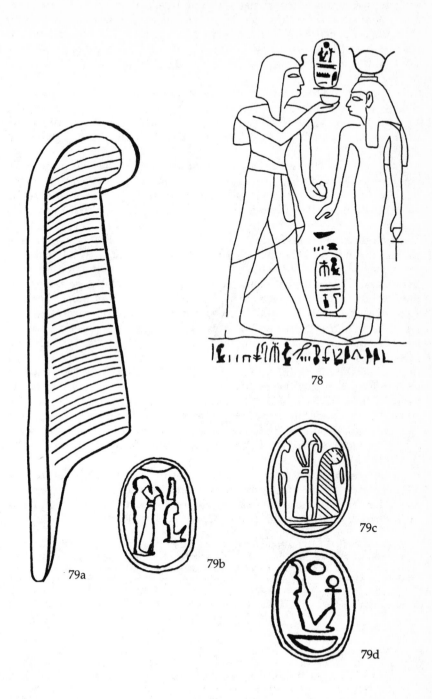

78

79a

79b

79c

79d

represented by the ostrich feather alone (**illuss. 79b-c**; see Keel, et al., 1989, 308f.). Ma'at was a frequent element in the names of kings in Palestine, especially on scarabs. Names include, for example, *Nb-m3ᶜt-rᶜ* (Amenophis III, **illus. 79d**; see Tufnell 1940, pl. 32.3–4; 1958, pl. 38.289– 294) or *Wsr-m3ᶜt-rᶜ* (Ramesses II, see illuss. 60–61; Tufnell 1958, pl. 39.380, 388).

In comparison to Hathor and Ma'at, other goddesses such as Sakhmet, Bastet, and the Hippopotamus Goddess, known already from the Middle Bronze Age (see above, §13), were portrayed only infrequently in the Late Bronze Age (see McGovern 1985, 110f.; Tufnell 1958, pl. 29.58f.).

§44. As in all Late Bronze Age temples, a considerable number of cylinder seals made in the popular Mitannian style were found in the Lachish Fosse Temple. The most frequent scene, once again, shows the *palmetto tree* flanked by caprids (Tufnell 1940, pl. 33.43, 49, 51). Numerous examples of the stylized palm tree, flanked by birds and caprids, were also found in the Fosse Temple on the painted pottery that is so typical of the Late Bronze Age (Tufnell 1940, pls. 48.249f., 60.1–2; 61.10). In a few of the depictions, the relationship between the goddess and the tree is clearer than usual. This is the case concerning a cup on which the palmetto tree flanked by caprids is replaced by a pubic triangle (?) (**illus. 80**; see Hestrin 1987a, 214–216; 1991, 53–66). It is clear that the stylized tree represents the fertile earth's procreative and nurturing power to bring blessing, having been personified already during the Middle Bronze Age by the depiction of the "Naked Goddess" (or the "Branch Goddess"; see above, §15). A pitcher has the inscription *mtn.šy [l'][rb]ty 'lt* "Mattan [or: gift]: a present for my lady Elat [or: the goddess].[11] The *'lt* is placed directly over the caprid-flanked tree (**illus. 81**; Hestrin 1987a, 212–214; 1991, 52–54; Hadley 1989, 202–208; see Maier 1986, 166). The venerated goddess is possibly to be identified as Asherah; in the mythological texts from Ugarit *rbt* "lady" and *ilt* "goddess"[12] are epithets of Atirat/Asherah (see Day 1986, 387f.; Smith 1990, 6).

In this connection, reference also ought to be made to a figure of a naked goddess manufactured from a pressed mold, one fragment of which has been found at Aphek and another nearly complete figure has been recovered at Revadim (**illus. 82**; see Beck 1986a; Kochavi 1990, 20,

11 See Sass 1988, 60f.; for a somewhat different view, see Puech 1986–1987, 17f. who would append the name of the deity *r[š]p* to the very end of the inscription (but see Hadley 1989, 204f.). For Reshef at Late Bronze Age Lachish, see below, illus. 85a. A sherd with writing that came from a fill stratum near the Iron Age fortification for the palace up on the tell, in other words, in the vicinity of the Late Bronze Age temple (Sass 1988, 61),Yadin (1959) and Puech (1986–1987, 13–15) would read . . .]*bᶜlt*[. . . "mistress," an epithet of Hathor (on this, see §42) or else of the goddess in illus. 71.

12 For *rbt* see *KTU* 1.1 (= *CTA* 1 = *UT* 'nt pl. X) IV 14; *KTU* 1.3 V 36f. (= *CTA* 3 = *UT* 'nt pl. VI E V 44f.); *KTU* 1.4 (= *CTA* 4 = *UT* 51) IV 49; *KTU* 1.6 (= *CTA* 6) I 40 (= *UT* 49. 12). For *ilt*, see *KTU* 1.14 IV 35f., 38f. (= *CTA* 14 = *UT Krt* IV 198f., 201f.); *KTU* 1.15 (= *CTA* 15 = *UT* 128) III 25f. At any rate, unlike *il* "El," *ilt* is not a personal name of the goddess; as a rule, the designation is used in parallel with a goddess' name – in the places discussed, with Atirat in *KTU* 1.3 (= *CTA* 3 = *UT* 'nt) but is parallel to Anat in II 18. *ilt* does not appear to be a designation for Atirat in the ritual texts either (especially *KTU* 1.39; 1.41; 1.50; 1.87).

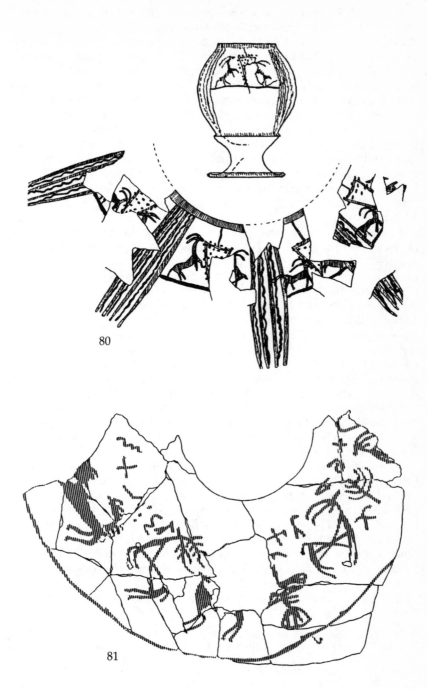

80

81

figs. 17 and 38). A palmetto tree flanked by caprids is shown on each thigh of this figure, positioned near the exposed genitalia. A nursing child is depicted on each breast of the goddess. The goddess wears a pendant around her neck in the form of a ring that opens downward, reminiscent of the Ω-shaped symbol that evokes the picture of a womb (see above, §14 and §34). Within one individual deity, this goddess combines the secret powers of mother earth, giving birth to humans and animals, nourishing them, and causing them to flourish. If one is inclined to seek literary support that will correlate well with this iconographic material, one notes that Atirat/Asherah is called *qnyt ilm* "creatrix of the gods" in the mythological texts from Ugarit.[13] She appears at times as the nurturing mother and functions in this role as the one who both gives birth and nourishes (*Dea nutrix*). She is apparently also called Rahmay (literally: "womb"; see also *šādayim wārāḥam* "breasts and womb" in Gen 49:25).[14]

In addition to the golden pendants that take the forms of goddesses (Tufnell 1940, pl. 26.4–5) and of stars **(illus. 83)**, two pendants in the shape of a stylized palm were found in the Fosse Temple as well (Tufnell 1940, pl. 26.6–7). Some would be inclined to regard stylized palms, frequently combined with lotus blossoms on various ivory carvings, as purely decorative (Tufnell 1940, pl. 19.16–17; see Loud 1939, nos. 13–15, 165–167). But this is not so likely in view of the recurrent clear relationship between the tree and the goddess (in addition, see below, illuss. 214, 219, and often elsewhere). One ought not forget that the cross, for example, has never completely lost its primary religious significance in western culture, even though it might be small in size, be made of gold, be decorated with precious stones, and be worn chiefly as jewelry. This suggests that the palm tree, as a symbol of life and of the goddess who provides life and beauty, is not as much out of place when it is used on cosmetic utensils as is the symbol of Christ's martyrdom when used in a context that is chiefly aesthetic or even erotic.

Along with the palm there are probably other small artifacts from the Fosse Temple that ought to be interpreted as belonging to the sphere of the goddess, such as the previously discussed doves and lions from the Middle Bronze Age temple in Nahariyah (§19; Tufnell 1940, pl. 28.3, 7; see also 21.44). The way the celestial aspect of the goddess is emphasized is new to the Late Bronze Age (but see already illus. 41). In addition to other ways, the theme is portrayed by use of star-shaped gold and silver pendants. The artifacts depicted in **illuss. 83a-b** were found at Tell el-

---

13 *KTU* 1.4 (= *CTA* 4 = *UT* 51) I 23; III 26, 30, 35; IV 32; and often elsewhere. See also *ům il[m]* "mother of the gods" in *KTU* 2.31 (= *PRU* II 2 = *UT* 1002) line 45 (see also Maier 1986, 211f.).

14 For earlier discussions, see Winter 1983, 397–403. In *KTU* 1.15 (= *CTA* 15 = *UT* 128) II 26–28, Atirat and Anat are called *mšnq[t ilm]* "Nursing Moth[ers of the Gods]." In *KTU* 1.23 (= *CTA* 23 = *UT* 52) Atirat and Rahmay are the mothers of both youthful gods, Shahar and Shalim, and they nurse them. The side-by-side quality of the two goddesses corresponds to the side-by-side quality of the two sons. In contrast, lines 60ff. of the text speak of *one* wife of El who gave birth to *both* gods and nurses them. Concerning the present discussion, note the iconographic relationship between the genitalia, the tree, and the goddess, and also the metaphoric mention of a "field" in lines 14ff.; 28ff.!

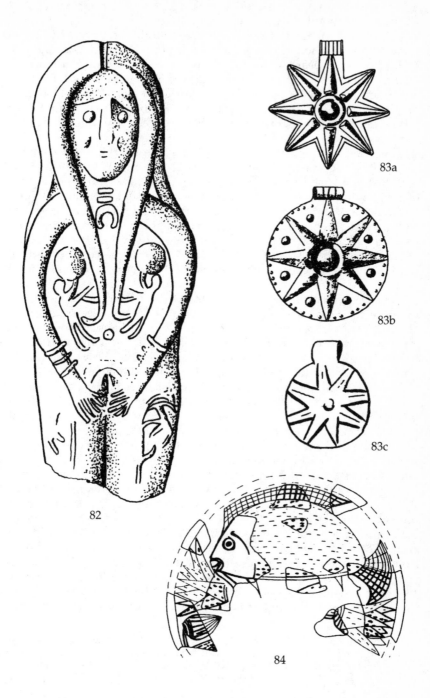

82

83a

83b

83c

84

Ajjul. Five such pendants were discovered in the Fosse Temple at Lachish (**illus. 83c**; Tufnell 1940, pl. 26.10–12, 14–15).[15]

Other small artifacts from the Fosse Temple, however, should be identified as Hathor, not as a goddess from the Near East. Since the Hathor fetish appears, flanked by cats, on a scarab from Lachish and on a gold finger ring from Tell el-Ajjul (see also illuss. 75c-d), the ivory cats from the Fosse Temple and the faience cats from Timnah, as from Serabit el-Khadem, probably represent Hathor rather than Bastet, who appears less frequently (Tufnell 1940, pl. 17.9; Schulman 1988, 125f., 131).[16]

The same identification should be made concerning the so-called *nun*-bowls: blue or green faience bowls, decorated with lotus buds and blossoms, fish (**illus. 84**), ducks flying upward, and other aquatic elements, and occasionally having the sign *nfr* "beautiful" or being decorated with *wedjat*-eyes (Tufnell 1940, pls. 22f.; Schulman 1988, 129, 131; see also Rowe 1940, pl. 49A.3). Images of the Hathor sistrum were used frequently in Egypt, along with the motifs just discussed, on the inside of these bowls (Strauss 1974, 20). The bowls were used to drink wine (see illus. 78), most likely in honor of the goddess who could fulfill every desire.

§45.   As for *male deities*, a bronze god with a high head covering was found in the Fosse Temple as well. One arm is raised to strike a blow (Tufnell 1940, pl. 26.31 = Seeden 1980, no. 1727). As happens so often, the attributes connected with the deity are lost. A cylinder seal in the popular Mitannian style that was found in the Fosse Temple shows a god in the typical pose, but with shield and hand weapon, which means it has the attributes typical of Reshef, **illus. 85a**; see also illus. 57). We also see this god on a scarab from the Ramesside Period, purchased in Jerusalem (**illus. 85b**; for more, see Parker 1949, no. 142; Seger, et al., 1988, 95f. with pls. 30.5; 75G, and often elsewhere).

The incised depiction of a god who holds a great lance over his head with both hands, from the Egyptian-Canaanite temple located up on the tell (**illus. 86**; see Ussishkin 1978, 18), should be interpreted as a figure that combines the Canaanite Baal (who defeats the sea serpent *lītānu*/ Leviathan) and the Egyptian Seth (who conquers the Apophis serpent; see Keel, et al., 1990, 233–236, 309–321). The sea serpent is not shown on the incised piece. But on an incised scarab, from the late Ramesside era Grave 120 at Lachish, Baal-Seth is shown adorned with two bull's horns, from which a long band hangs down (**illus. 87a**). With one hand he has struck a horned snake on the back of the neck, and with the other he is swinging a scimitar. The same Baal-Seth, this time furnished with wings (in the Egyptian style) and armed with a lance, overpowers the horned

---

15 Seven eight-rayed gold star-pendants, dating to the onset of the Late Bronze Age, appeared in two hoards at Tell el-Ajjul (Petrie 1934, pls. 13; 14.13–15; 36; see also 17.112; Petrie, et al., 1952, Frontispiece lower left; pl. 6 above; pl. 8.3, 5; Negbi 1970). Individual pieces came from Shechem, Megiddo, Beth-Shean and from Tel Kitan (see McGovern 1985, 134f.).

16 See also the reclining cats from Beth-Shean Str. VII (fourteenth century) in Rowe 1929, 65, and the cat scarabs from the Eighteenth Dynasty in Petrie 1932, pl. 7.13; Starkey/Harding 1932, pl. 53.232.

85a

85b

86

87a

87b

87c

snake on a Ramesside level scarab from Tell el-Far'ah (south) (**illus. 87b**). By means of the combination of Baal and Seth as serpent conquerors, the serpent, an Egyptian symbol of the danger in the dark of night and a Canaanite symbol of the stormy sea, became a symbol of danger in general. The god who could defeat such a creature is treated as a savior, pure and simple (see Keel, et al., 1990, 411f.).

Occasionally on Egyptian scarabs, the god who conquers the serpent is accorded the epithet *mry R'* "beloved of Re."[17] In illus. 87a and **in illus. 87c**, the warrior god who is close at hand is depicted with the solar disk located directly behind him or else above him, linking themes of the warrior god to those of the distant sun god (note, in illus. 44, the northern Syrian way to show the god who is both near and distant!).

A cylinder seal from Late Bronze Age IIA (fourteenth century) from Beth-Shean shows a god striking a blow as he nears two lions (**illus. 88a**). The connection between the god and the lions is not clear. By contrast, a cylinder seal from Acre shows the god lifting the lion up by the hind legs (**illus. 88b**). On another Late Bronze Age cylinder seal, from Tell es-Safi, we see Seth. In addition to playing his role as the one who stabs the horned snake, he has also taken over the role of the one who strikes the lion (**illus. 89**). This makes it quite likely that it is a Baal figure in each case who is striking a blow in illustrations 88a-b. By taking on a dual role (battle against the horned snake *and* against the lions), Baal-Seth's battle in this scene is also no longer against just *one* natural power but is rather a comprehensive war against everything that is inimical to life. In his role as savior, Baal-Seth, wearing a loincloth and with long locks of hair, also appears on a Late Bronze Age cylinder seal from Tell el-Ajjul. He holds, by the tail, a lion that, together with a winged daemon, is threatening a human who is lying on the ground (**illus. 90a**). On a cylinder seal from Beth-Shean, the god with the long locks of hair (or else wearing a band) defends a bull being threatened by a winged monster (**illus. 90b**). A comparison with the images from Middle Bronze Age IIB (§§22f.) makes it clear here as well that the god who guaranteed the earth's fertility, when combined with Seth, has become a champion against all evil.[18]

§46. In addition to the Egyptian-Canaanite gods Reshef and Baal-Seth,[19] a whole host of purely Egyptian male deities are present during the Late Bronze Age, particularly in southern Palestine, most noticeably

---

17 See Keel, et al., 1990, 313 fig. 88 and 311 fig. 84 (the crescent moon, mistakenly drawn here above the head of the crouching god, is not there on the original, as one can see by studying pl. XVII. 4; correspondingly, the inscription is not *mry Dḥwty*, but *mry R'*!).

18 The same function is carried out by Baal's fight with the dragon (or: serpent) in the Ugaritic ritual texts as well; see, e.g., *KTU* 1.82 (= *PRU* II 1 = *UT* 1001) lines 1–7 (de Moor 1987, 175f.; *TUAT* II/3 337f.), where Rashpu/Reshef appears as an enemy of Baal and not as a comrade in the battle (contra Smith 1990, 49; see below, §§65f. with illuss. 138a-b).

19 F. M. Cross has sought to demonstrate that a proto-Canaanite inscription on a fragment of a bowl found in 1983 in Lachish Str. VI (first half of the twelfth century) was evidence for interpreting *'l'b* as "father-god" or "divine ancestor" (1984, so also Puech 1986–1987, 20f.). This interpretation has been shown to be false in many respects (see Sass 1988, 62f.).

88a

88b

89

90a

90b

Amun (see below, §§51, 53 and 62–64). Tufnell suggests that scarabs with this god's name first appear at Lachish toward the end of the Eighteenth Dynasty and are very common during the Nineteenth Dynasty (thirteenth century) (1958, 108). This is also true of Re-harakhty, depicted with the head of a falcon, and for Ptah (Tufnell 1958, 109). As an analysis of the Ptah scarabs has shown, these small devotional items were products of temple workshops whose intent was highly propagandist, since the producers frequently tried thereby to suggest that their temple's god was superior to the gods worshiped at other shrines (Keel, et al., 1989, 281–323). Many other deities (e.g., the warlike Montu and Onuris) appear sporadically along with the principal deities previously discussed: Amun, Re-harakhty, Ptah, Baal-Seth, and Hathor.[20]

The divinities represented on Late Bronze Age Egyptian seal amulets are almost exclusively male. Insofar as there are females represented, they are generally depicted only in the form of a fetish (Hathor) or as part of a king's name (Maʿat). Thus they only rarely assume the role of an independent individual in the iconography, unlike the male deities. This is true not only for the actual Egyptian officials and their Canaanite counterparts, to whom these seal amulets most likely belonged, but is also true of the way the world beyond was depicted. Whether in the real world or in the world beyond, the goddesses play little more than a marginal role (but see below, §§57ff.). Four Egyptian funerary stelae from Deir el-Balah show Osiris, the ruler of the realm of the dead, as the only deity (Ventura 1987). On only one anthropomorphic sarcophagus from Lachish are Isis and Nephthys depicted as female mourners, next to an inscription written in hieroglyphics (Tufnell 1958, 131f.; pls. 45f.).

§47. The dominant human form on Egyptian seal amulets dating to Late Bronze Age II (fourteenth and thirteenth centuries), at least for southern Palestine (Tell el-Ajjul, Tell el-Farʿah [south], and Lachish, among others), is the *pharaoh*. One sees how, already as a child chosen by the gods, he sits victorious on the "nine bows," the traditional sign for enemy lands (**illus. 91**) and how he is taken by the hand and led by two gods, usually Amun and Re-harakhty (**illuss. 92a-b**).[21] An oval plaque from the time of Amenophis II (1426–1400) shows Re as he confers sovereignty on the king in the sun barque (**illus. 93**). The love shown by the gods for the pharaoh, and his role as son, correspond to the way he will carry out his loyal, filial duty. Numerous seal amulets show the king sacrificing to Ptah or simply standing in reverence before him (**illus. 94a**; see Keel, et al., 1989, 299–308). But other gods are also shown in this connection: the anthropomorphic Amun (**illus. 94b**), the falcon-headed sun god Re-harakhty (**illus. 94c**), the baboon-shaped Thoth (**illus. 94d**). As far as we can determine, Hathor (who appears along with the others in this constellation on the stone relief at Timnah; see above, illus. 78) is not accorded a special role in the royal cult on any scarabs.

---

20 See, e.g., Coogan 1975, 42f., fig. 6; Petrie 1932, pl. 7.50; Petrie 1933, pl. 3.45; 4.193; Starkey/Harding 1932, pl. 48.4 and the two gods, made from molds and found at Tel Qarnayim (illus. 72), that flank the *qudshu* type of goddess on either side.
21 See Tufnell 1958, pl. 39f., 365; Starkey/Harding 1932, pl. 55.284; Kochavi 1972, 239.

91   92a   92b

93

94a   94b   94c

94d   95

Internal harmony between the gods and the king corresponds to his godlike appearance in his own country. He is carried on a litter (**illus. 95**, on a cylinder seal from Megiddo) or travels in a cart (**illus. 96**). In foreign affairs, the victory of the king over the enemies who seek to destroy the order he maintains is portrayed in many ways. In addition to the chariot scenes (see §§38f.), we repeatedly see the icon depicting the "striking down of the enemies," which represented the triumph of the pharaoh over everything hostile to Egypt since the time the kingdom was established (**illuss. 97a-c**; see below, this chapter, note 32). Different pieces show variations, portraying the pharaoh binding his enemies or leading them away (**illuss. 98a-b**). His irresistible power is also shown when he is depicted as a bull or a lion that overpowers a human (**illus. 99**; Loud 1948, pl. 152.200) or as a lion that tears a man apart (**illus. 100**; Starkey/Harding 1932, pl. 52.169; Loud 1948, pl. 152.161; see above, illuss. 5a-b). It is only an apparent contradiction when the king's superiority is shown not by identifying him with the lion but rather when he is depicted overpowering a lion or an ibex (**illuss. 101a-b**). In these settings, the lion serves most likely as a metaphor for hostile foreigners and the ibex as a metaphor particularly used to depict hostile mountain dwellers (see Keel, et al., 1990, 27–65, 263–279).

4. Beth-Shean or the Egyptian State God and His Officials

§48.   Unlike Lachish, Tell el-Farʿah (south), Tell el-Ajjul, and Deir el-Balah, Beth-Shean does not lie in the southern part of the country or near Egypt. But the city controls the eastern entrance of the great central valley that separates the central hill country from the Galilee. It is at the crossroads where the east–west route from the Mediterranean to Transjordan meets the north–south route that runs along the Jordan valley. This important strategic location was probably what made Beth-Shean an important Egyptian center from the fifteenth century on and especially so during the thirteenth century.

Artifacts from Str. IX (fifteenth to early fourteenth centuries) and Str. VII (fourteenth century) portray a mixed Canaanite-Egyptian culture, similar to Lachish.[22] But the indigenous tradition survives in the later strata only on inexpensive terra-cotta images, contrasting with the monumental art and image-bearing artifacts made with precious materials. Such expensive articles could have been owned only by an urban élite and by the members of the Egyptian occupation force. The iconography is purely Egyptian, both in style and theme. Individual artifacts from Str. IX, such as the basalt relief of a lion, showing his teeth, and a dog (Rowe 1930, Frontispiece = *ANEP* no. 228), still show a clear northern influence, which is not surprising considering the location of Beth-Shean. But the stele from the same stratum that shows the enthroned "Mekal, the god of Beth-Shean" and depicts the Egyptian architect Amen-em-Opet, together with his family, standing in wait before the local city god (**illus. 102**), is

---

22 The temple from Str. VII (see Kempinski 1975, 212f.) is an installation that shows many similarities to the Egyptian-Canaanite temple at Lachish Str. VI.

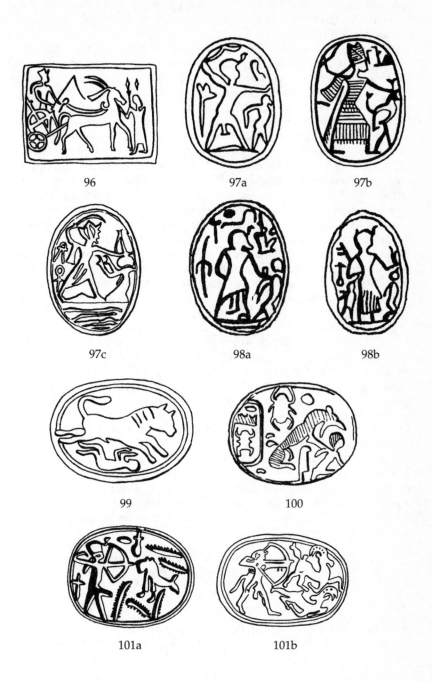

96

97a

97b

97c

98a

98b

99

100

101a

101b

fashioned in a pure Egyptian style.[23] Under pressure from the occupation forces, the city god's image apparently was made to adapt very quickly to the new circumstances.

§49.   Images of the *goddess*, however, show that Egyptian coloniza- tion did not immediately affect all the different types of artifacts that bore images. Terra-cotta was not as expensive to produce and was more popular, but was also more "conservative" than the metal pendants and larger pieces of artwork. As at Megiddo (see above, §35), typical domestically produced plaques and figurines of the goddess, made of clay or glass, have been found at Beth-Shean and in its environs.[24] The goddess holds her breasts or lays her arms on her thighs (see illuss. 121a-b and §§57ff.). In many of the earlier pieces, the genitalia, following the Middle Bronze Age tradition, are particularly emphasized (Rowe 1940, pl. 68A.1–2). A rare type of "Naked Goddess," in her role as mother, seems to have enjoyed special popularity in Beth- Shean. Clearly concerned about woman's fertility, the goddess holds a child in her arms (Winter 1983, 118f. type 7; for a special type of the goddess with *two* children, see above, illus. 82). Four examples of this type were found in Beth-Shean. The oldest was found in Str. IX (end of the fifteenth or beginning of the fourteenth century; Rowe 1940, pl. 68A.4), the most recent in Str. V A (tenth century; James 1966, fig. 112.7). An especially beautiful example from the late Ramesses Period, Str. V B, emphasizes the erotic nakedness of the goddess by using all sorts of decorations and jewelry (**illus. 103**).[25] Such images of the nursing goddess are functionally analogous to the Egyptian motif connected with Isis-Horus, as contemporary amulets imported from Egypt demonstrate (James 1966, figs. 109.5; 113.10), though on the imported items the goddess is always clothed. The nakedness of the goddess on the terra-cottas is a typically Canaanite feature. The Canaanite nursing goddess is an indigenous form, not just a local adaptation of an Egyptian theme.[26]

Two well-known objects, generally identified as cultic stands from the twelfth century, preserved only fragmentarily and found in side chambers of the south temple, document the continuing significance of the goddess and show that the manufacture of her image in terra-cotta continued to be influenced by Canaanite tradition. In **illus. 104**, she

---

23 The god of Beth-Shean (see Thompson 1970) also appears to have been portrayed on an Egyptian faience bowl, on a fragment of which we see legs and the tasselled loincloth of the god (?) and the remainder of an inscription ...]$k3r^{God}$ $b3$[... "[Me]kal, (God) of Be[th-Shean]." (Rowe 1940, pl. 67A.4–5).

24 Rowe 1940, pl. 42A.1 (mold [*qudshu* type?]); 45A.5; 64A.2; 68A.1–4, 6–7; Tzori 1958. See above, §35, note 1.

25 In addition, see James 1966, fig. 111.1; from Megiddo, May 1935, pl. 24 M 2653, probably also from Iron Age I. Images on the Egyptian pieces of the "concubine" type that include a child (Pritchard 1934, 22 nos. 187–188 (see below, §57 note 37!) do not belong to this type.

26 Two nearly identical terra-cotta fragments from Shechem and Tell Deir Alla demonstrate a variation on the mother-goddess-with-child theme. The child is not being nursed but is shown in a frontal presentation, sitting on the goddess' lap and with raised arms, i.e., in a position that assigns to him at least as much importance as is given to the mother (Beck 1990b, 89f. with illus. 11.)

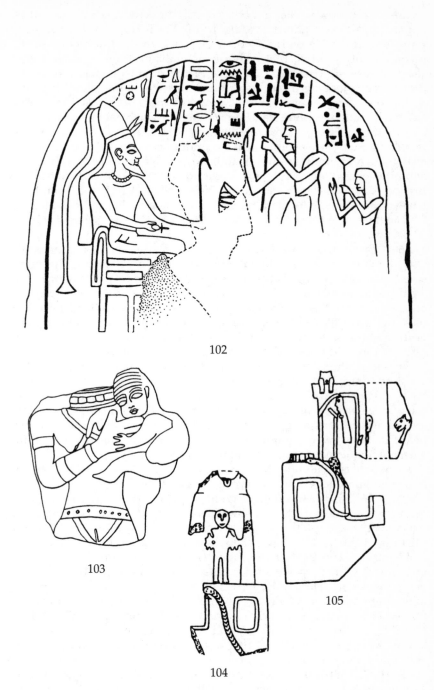

102

103

104

105

stands in a doorway that is now partially broken, holding two birds, apparently doves, under her arms. Below her is a snake that probably represents the underworld aspect of fertility. In the top section of the second example (**illus. 105**), only the genitalia and the legs of a naked seated figure are preserved. Because of the fragmentary nature of the piece, we cannot determine the gender of the two figures standing below in the doorways. The excavators commented about two gods (Rowe 1940, 62), but in light of the lion standing at the side, which belongs exclusively to the sphere of the goddess (see illuss. 4, 52, 55, 70, 184), these might be female figures. Once again, a snake is underneath. Snakes and doves are also found on cylindrical cultic stands (Rowe 1940, pls. 57A.3–4; 58A.1–3, and often elsewhere), while doves and lions, as noted already at Middle Bronze Age Nahariyah and in the Late Bronze Age Fosse Temple of Lachish, continue to be made as terra-cotta figures (Rowe 1940, pl. 20.4, 7–9; on the entire subject, see DeVries 1975: 141–145; Bretschneider 1991, 72–74 nos. 45–46).

§50. By contrast, images of the goddess made with costly materials and depicted on monumental art were made following Egyptian standards, much in the same way as the city god underwent changes. On a gold pendant that is typical of the early Late Bronze Age, she appears in an unusual form, as a mistress with a *was*-scepter and hand raised in blessing (**illus. 106**). Both her complete nakedness and the non-Egyptian gesture of blessing show that this is a native goddess. She is made very Egyptian in substance and style by the addition of the *was*-scepter and when she is shown from a side view. This Egyptian character of the goddess is emphasized even more on a stele from Str. VII (**illus. 107**). Here, in keeping with the way the Egyptian élite thought it appropriate, she wears a long garment and holds a blossom scepter in one hand while a symbol for life is held in the other. She wears the *atef*-crown on her head. In front of her stands a female worshiper, likewise in a long garment, who reaches out to hand her a lotus blossom.

If one wants to identify this goddess by name, Anat would probably first come to mind. On two Egyptian pictorial pieces from Tanis and on a stele in the British Museum, the goddess with the *atef*-crown is assigned the name Anat; in addition, she is assigned the epithets typical for Anat on these depictions: *nb.t p.t nb.t nṯr.w*, "Mistress of Heaven, Mistress of the Gods." Twice she is portrayed sitting next to Ramesses II, laying her arm protectively upon his shoulders. Once she appears enthroned with a shield and a raised lance (Montet 1933, pl. 47, below; 54.5 = Stadelmann 1967, 91f.; *ANEP* no. 473, below). Correspondingly, the goddess is identified as "Anat, Mistress of Heaven, Mistress of the Gods" in an inscription on another stele from Beth-Shean (**illus. 108**, detail). In spite of the inscription, Helck does not choose to identify her as Anat since she is holding a *was*-scepter and a symbol of life and holds no weapon. He identifies her as a local goddess from Beth-Shean (1962, 496). But it is not necessary to follow Helck in regarding this as completely contradictory, since the situation is not so simple. Especially when one is dealing with a warrior deity like Anat, one ought not say that she cannot function as a local deity because she has responsibilities over a wide geographic region (as Anat does). On the

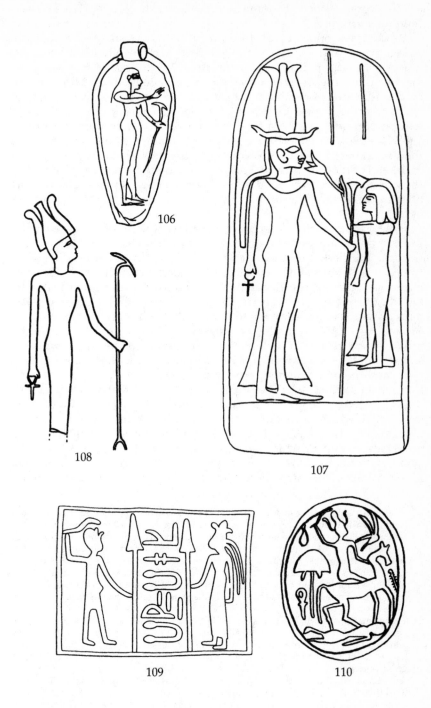

106

108

107

109

110

artwork commissioned by Ramesses II at Tanis, the goddess is also shown without weapons.[27]

By contrast, on a thirteenth-century cylinder seal from Bethel, she holds a lance and stands facing Baal-Seth, who also holds a lance and grasps a scimitar in his raised hand (**illus. 109**).[28] Anat also appears as a warrior deity on a scarab obtained in Jerusalem (**illus. 110**). She sits side-saddle on a horse that is striding over a fallen enemy. Once again, she is wearing the *atef*-crown and swings a scimitar in her raised right hand (additional evidence for a warrior Anat can be found in Winter 1983, 227–230). Whereas the *qudshu* images that were noted originally for their sexual-erotic features took on the functions of a warrior deity only at the end of the Late Bronze Age, when the goddess was associated with the war horse (see §41), Anat, who enjoyed a special popularity in Beth-Shean during the Late Bronze Age, was a warrior goddess from the outset.

§51.   Factors such as war, the occupation of the country, new elements in the population, settling on the one to whom an individual was to be loyal, etc. all led to greater emphasis on the male deities during the fifteenth and fourteenth centuries. This tendency increased still more noticeably during the thirteenth century, when Egyptian influence became even more pronounced. Egyptian *royal ideology,* shown in §47 to have provided one of the main themes of iconographic repertoire on Late Bronze Age IIB seal amulets, furnished to some extent the theme for monumental images in Beth-Shean during this time period. Two basalt stelae from the time of Sety I (1290–1279) are extant, one is intact (2.45 m high) and the other is only partially so (Rowe 1930, 23–31; pls. 41–45.1; Kempinski 1975, 214f.). The upper third of the intact stele (**illus. 111;** Kruchten 1982) was part of a sacrificial scene. Below the winged solar disk, Sety I, who surprisingly is shown striding in the direction from left to right (see also Keel, et al., 1989, 294, 304ff.), brings a ball-shaped *nw* vessel and a cup in which incense is being burnt. There is a slender stand, with a lotus blossom on it, between Sety I and the god. Because of the characteristic falcon head and solar disk, it is clear that this god is

---

27   A similarly unarmed goddess of the Anat type, wearing a long garment and high double feather crown, appears as a partner of a god who wears a loincloth on the famous stele of el-Balu' from southern Moab, reminding one of Mekal (illus. 102). The stele follows the pattern common to the Ramesses Period, and it must be dated to the twelfth century because of the way it depicts the local king by using the typical Shasu style (contra H. Weippert 1988, 666f.; see most recently Staubli 1991, 64–66). Whether a god or goddess appears with or without weapons depends on the context (in el-Balu' already to be identified as Chemosh and '*štrkmš*?; See Gese 1970, 140f.; H. and M. Weippert 1982, 101).

28   There are hieroglyphs that spell out the name '*strt* "Astarte" between the two vertically held lances. The name should probably not be interpreted as an additional marginal note that identifies the goddess depicted here, since the god has no similar identifying inscription; this points to the manifestation of a third great entity (so also H. Weippert 1988, 307). Compare this once again to the rectangular plaque in the Cairo Museum, discussed in §41 note 8. Anat is portrayed with Baal-Seth on this plaque and the name of Amun-Re appears in front of them. To be sure, the pair of gods in that scene move toward the name of the distant god, while here they guard the name of Astarte (as one would at the entrance to a shrine).

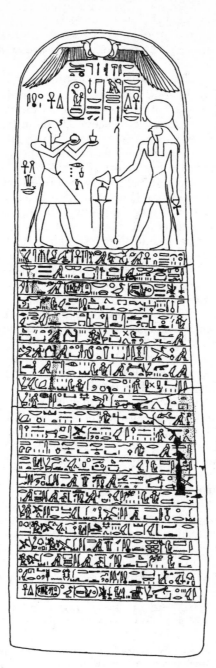

111

Re-harakhty. In one hand he holds the *was*-scepter and in the other the symbol for life. On the second, fragmentary stele, there appears to have been a similar scene, using a style in which the picture is symmetrically doubled (see the Merneptah Stele *ANEP* no. 342). Only the legs of the god being worshiped are extant. Their mummy-like appearance suggests that this was Ptah.

An additional large basalt stele (2.67 m high) was erected during the reign of Ramesses II (1279–1213) (**illus. 112**; see Černy 1958). The upper third of this stele does not show the usual veneration scene but portrays a whole campaign by using two scenes that function as a merism, representing the whole story. To the left, the royal god Amun faces toward the right and presents to the pharaoh the scimitar, signifying divinely bestowed power for victory (Keel 1974, 51–76). The campaign begins with the ceremonial transfer of the sword of victory (Nelson 1930, pl. 13 = Keel [4]1984, illus. 405a). The pharaoh holds a bow in one hand and the other is outstretched. This is probably to be interpreted in a double sense: it signifies simultaneously the taking of the sword of victory at the beginning of the campaign and the presentation of plunder at the end. The plunder here consists mainly of vessels of precious metal. The eight Asian prisoners, at the base of the stele, should probably also be considered as booty (no longer visible in illus. 112). Their bodies are replaced by walls formed into a circle, on which the names of cities are written. The consecration of the plunder portrays the final act of the comprehensive campaign cycles that tell the story of the pharaohs of the Nineteenth and Twentieth Dynasties.[29]

§52.   In a way that is similar to this monumental stele, the god-given victory of the pharaoh over the Asiatics is shown in condensed fashion on a cylinder seal of Ramesses II from Beth-Shean (**illus. 113**). Instead of Amun, it is an Asiatic god who presents the scimitar.[30] There appears to be a picture of the head of a gazelle or caprid on the god's forehead. The top half of the scimitar is possibly also shaped like the head of a caprid. This would allow the god to be identified as Reshef (see Keel, et al., 1990, 195–204, 302–304). It would be surprising to find Reshef in this role, because he is depicted in Egypt on private stelae almost exclusively as a god of plague and healing. Nevertheless, we still ought perhaps to identify Reshef with Mekal, as is suggested by a few, much more recent Phoenician inscriptions from Cyprus that date from the fourth through second centuries (see Keel 1990, 201, note 148). He would then appear as the city god of Beth-Shean on our cylinder seal, presenting the victory to Pharaoh Ramesses II. The victorious power of the pharaoh is represented by the drawn bow, with which he shoots arrows at a copper bar used as a target (cf. the bow in the pharaoh's hand on the monumental stele).[31] The actual targets in this incredible action are the two Asiatics who are tied to a

29 See the relief of Sety I on the outside of the north wall of the great pillar hall of the Amun temple in Karnak (Wreszinski 1934, pl. 37).
30 The Seth animal that Rowe (1936, pl. 28 no. S.61) sketched in front of the deity's face, and which was linked to Baal-Seth, does not exist on the original. Rowe identified a splintered spot as a Seth animal.
31 On this, see Decker 1971, 80–122; 1978, 74ff.; 1987, 42–54.

112

113

114a

114b

115

post. They represent the province of Canaan, which was conquered by the pharaoh.

A scarab from Beth-Shean, and a parallel to it that comes from Tell el-Ajjul, present another variation on the same theme and are probably also to be dated to the reign of Ramesses II (**illuss. 114a-b**). The royal god Amun presents the sword of victory to the pharaoh on both pieces. The pharaoh then either consecrates or kills a prisoner with this sword in front of the god who has given him the victory.[32]

§53. Whereas the monuments mentioned thus far present a complete campaign – from beginning to end – merismically, two other scarabs from Beth-Shean each symbolize the victorious power of the pharaoh by showing a unique action. On one scarab, Ramesses II, "the one who treads down foreign lands," is shown wearing the high double feather crown, identical with that worn by Amun, as the king puts an enemy into fetters (Rowe 1936, no. 672 = James 1966, fig. 109.4). It is probably also Ramesses II who is killing an enemy on the other scarab (Rowe 1936, no. 671 = James 1966, fig. 100.5; see above, illuss. 97–98). This classic scene probably decorated another monumental basalt stele, of which one fragment depicts a leg taking very long strides, on tiptoe, a typical element in a slaughter scene (**illus. 115**).

The monuments of Sety I from Beth-Shean portray the king peacefully worshiping the great gods. Without exception, by contrast, those of Ramesses II show the king engaged in military action, which he carries out by order of, and with the support of, Amun and, in one case (illus. 113), also with the support of a local Asiatic god. No goddess is to be seen on any of these royal monuments. It is equally remarkable how much the royal god *Amun* is emphasized at the time of Ramesses II. Already during the Eighteenth Dynasty, Amun and his name were quite prominent in Palestine. Thus, for example, of 38 typical Eighteenth-Dynasty plaques, engraved on both sides, that were recovered in excavations, 22 (58%) have the name of the god explicitly or cryptographically written on them.

Iconographically, however, Amun receives strong emphasis on seal amulets only during the Nineteenth Dynasty. He does indeed appear occasionally already during the Eighteenth Dynasty era in his classic, anthropomorphic form, with the high, double, falcon-feather crown (**illus. 116a**), but he is found more frequently during the Nineteenth Dynasty period (**illus. 116b**, seated; see also Lamon/Shipton 1939, pl. 73.1; Starkey/Harding 1932, pl. 52.121, standing).

The portrayal of the anthropomorphic god within a triad was especially popular, showing him flanked by two falcon-headed sun gods (**illus. 116c**).[33] For the most part, Amun is not portrayed anthropomorphically but rather with a ram's head or as a ram sphinx (**illus. 117a-b**). In the "hybrid form, made by using a lion and a ram, the apotropaic powers of the god – his ram shape and his nature as ruler, as 'king of the gods' – are

---

32 We can see the slaughter of an enemy in the presence of the god who had given the victory already on the famous Narmer Palette (ca. 2850 B.C.; *ANEP* no. 296 = Keel ⁴1984, 271ff. and illus. 397).

33 See Petrie 1930, pl. 31.305; Starkey/Harding 1932, pl. 52.138; 53.222; Rowe 1936, nos. 572, 711; Tufnell 1958, pls. 36.240; 39.339; Giveon 1988, no. 98.

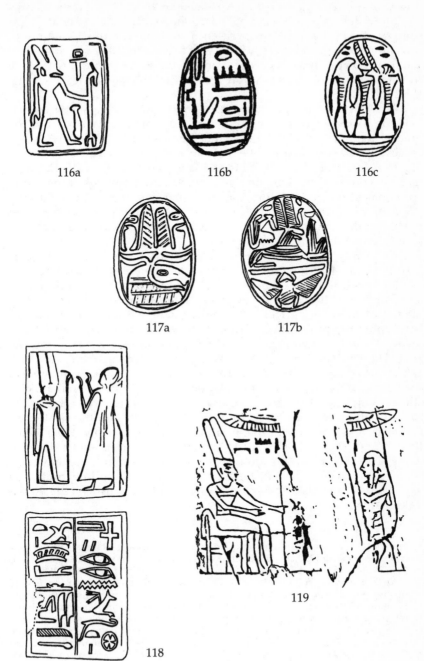

116a   116b   116c

117a   117b

118

119

united into one image" (Hornung/Staehelin 1976, 92).[34] When read as *nb* "lord," the ram sphinx forms, acrophonically, one element of the somewhat cryptographically written name *Ymn* "Amun." One might conclude from a clay model of a loaf of bread (ca. 10 cm in diameter), stamped several times with the name of the god (*Ymn-Rᶜ*), that there was a particularly strong Amun cult in Beth-Shean (James 1966, fig. 105.10).

§54.   This time period that put emphasis on males also manifested itself on a third group of monuments that come primarily from the time of Ramesses II (1279–1213) and Ramesses III (1187–1156), being especially well represented at Beth-Shean and Megiddo. These are images of *officials declaring their loyalty* to the king and to the royal god. Most representations of the king on seal amulets and a number of the representations of the gods are obviously, by their very nature, to be understood as an expression of the loyalty of the wearer. What is new and typical for the Ramesses Period, however, is that these officials included themselves in the portrayals.

One example of this type of monumental work, a rectangular plaque from Megiddo, shows a vizier of Ramesses II standing in a reverent posture before the anthropomorphic figure of Amun, who is also standing (**illus. 118**). An engraved ivory from Megiddo shows an official of Ramesses III kneeling in front of the enthroned anthropomorphic figure of Amun (**illus. 119**). But more often than posing reverently before the royal god, the officials are shown revering the king. The king appears, especially on seal amulets, in the form of his name cartouche.[35] As parallels from Egypt show, the king may have been portrayed anthropomorphically on two door lintels found at Beth-Shean, which unfortunately are only partially preserved. It is to be lamented that, in both cases, only the picture of the official offering reverence and a portion of the inscription are extant (**illus. 120a**; James 1966, 7; figs. 92.1; 93.1; 94.3; 95.3). A fragment of a statue and a statue of Ramesses III in a seated position, preserved almost completely, have also been found in Beth-Shean, both probably also to be interpreted as depictions of officials who are professing their loyalty (**illus. 120b**; Rowe 1930, 36ff.; pls. 50.1; 51).

---

34 From Tell el-Farᶜah (south) alone there at least ten known examples of the ram sphinx; see Petrie 1930, pl. 29.254; Starkey/Harding 1932, pls. 48.28; 49.967; 50.53; 52.143f., 146f.; 53.229; 55.278; 57.340. See also Petrie 1928, pl. 17.26; Rowe 1936, nos. 636.697; Tufnell 1958, pl. 39.343; Giveon/Kertesz 1986, no. 174. The reduction of this image to show only the ram's head with crown is more unusual (Starkey/Harding 1932, pls. 48.5; 53.192f.; 57.348, 383). In certain cases the ram's head sphinx, typical of Amun, is replaced by a composite sphinx that has a lion's body combined with a king's head (Starkey/Harding 1932, pl. 57.342), which then is read as *nb* or *n*, supplying an element of the god's name that is written cryptographically. The combination made using the sphinx, with Maᶜat in front and a winged *uraeus* above the back of the sphinx (Starkey/Harding 1932, pls. 50.52, 54f.; 52.141f.; 57.396) is to be read as *Ymn*; the *uraeus* (*yᶜr.t*) stands for *y*, Maᶜat for *m*, and the sphinx (*nb*) for *n* (on this, see Jaeger 1982, 294 note 218).

35 A rectangular plaque from Tell el-Ajjul shows, for example, an officer bowing before the name of Ramesses II. (Petrie 1932, pl. 6 lower left; see Hornung/Staehelin 1976, no. 554f.).

120b

120a

Summary

§55.   The picture sketched here, detailing the iconographic symbol system of Late Bronze Age Palestine, rests substantially on discoveries made in urban centers situated on the plains. During the Late Bronze Age, there were very few established settlements for permanent residents in the surrounding mountainous regions of the country. What has been found in such settings does not differ substantially from what has been discovered thus far in the large cities on the plains. Even in a settlement as tiny as that of Manahat, in the Valley of Rephaim, southwest of Jerusalem, a scarab was recovered with the name of Amenophis III, surrounded by four *uraei*, along with another scarab, typical of the Ramesses Period, with the combination of the sphinx, the winged *uraeus*, and a crouching figure, which are to be read together as a cryptogram for Amun (Edelstein/ Milevski 1990). The majority of the population in the hill country may have been nomadic during the Late Bronze Age (Finkelstein 1988, 341– 345) and thus may have left behind very little iconography.

The iconography of Late Bronze Age cities paints a completely different picture from that of Middle Bronze Age IIB. On monumental art and seal amulets alike, the major *male* deities such as Re-harakhty, Ptah, Seth-Baal, and especially the royal god Amun dominated the Egyptian- controlled centers such as Beth-Shean and Megiddo and the south as well. In the Late Bronze Age, warrior and political deities take over the role that was held during the Middle Bronze Age IIB by the weather god, who came together with his consort at a time when great impor- tance was attached to obtaining vegetation (the "Branch Goddess"). With very few exceptions (e.g., illuss. 72 and 109), male and female deities do not appear together in the same scenes and even when they do, they are not shown to be interacting in any significant way. The encounter of the sexes on a human level is clearly given less emphasis, being replaced by images depicting legitimation, war, domination, and loyalty. Women only play roles as servants at victory celebrations and at other festivals.

Costly metals are used to portray *goddesses* virtually only at the earliest stages of this epoch, after which time the precious metals were used to show warring, male deities. The "Naked Goddess" figure, with its relatively forceful public and confessional character, disappears from various types of glyptic art as well. The glyptic artwork that will be made during the subsequent Iron Age I will carry this tendency even further, at which time even the Egyptian Hathor fetish will appear no more. With the possible exception of objects imported from the north (e.g., illuss. 52, 53), the goddess is presented in the popular Mitannian style on cylinder seals, on painted vessels, and on other image-bearing artifacts only in the form of her attributes, especially the tree. Where she does survive on image-bearing artifacts in anthropomorphic form, Egyptian influence is clear. She is shown as the mistress of the city (Beth-Shean; illuss. 107–108) or as a warrior deity (illuss. 71–72), in other words, in a role that corresponds more closely to the "masculine" attributes that would be associated with a *power-woman* [Tr: The English words are used in the German original.].

§56. During this era, which witnessed the increasing suppression of the female god(s) within Late Bronze Age "official" religion, as represented in the great temples, in the Egyptian city-state and colonial power structure, and in products manufactured in the workshops that were to spread these ideas, there was concurrently a huge increase in the production of inexpensive terra-cotta plaques depicting a "naked goddess," clearly showing that the traditions connected with the Middle Bronze Age goddess continued to hold sway (see illus. 50; see Moorey/Fleming 1984, 77f.). Whether a costly *or* an inexpensive medium was being used, a certain Egyptian-Canaanite compromise was reached in the way the goddesses were portrayed in the use of the *qudshu* type of depiction, a compromise arrangement that disappeared at the end of the colonial period. It is very clear in Beth-Shean that there was a radical split between what was shown on the monumental art in comparison with themes that were shown on terra-cotta iconography (§§48f.). The unleashing of the cultural pressure, occasioned by Egyptian colonization, brought the production of metal figurines that portrayed the "Naked Goddess" to a halt and required that figures of warrior or enthroned male divinities be manufactured. The metal goddess figures were gradually replaced by others that were made using terra-cotta. Since terra-cotta images cost so little to produce, this seems to have been *the* material that worked the best for those who wanted to continue the indigenous veneration of the goddess. Surprisingly, male deities are hardly represented in terra-cotta. The change from expensive to easily affordable material carried with it the assumption that the goddess had now entered the realm of what some call a "private piety" and that the goddess was more approachable than ever before in the little cultic centers that were set up in each home (see H. Weippert 1990, 187; Uehlinger 1991a, 879–885).

Excursus: The Late Bronze and Early Iron Age So-Called "Astarte Plaques"

§57. On the *qudshu* type of terra-cotta plaques, discussed in §41 (see illus. 69), the naked female form is uniquely characterized as a goddess by means of various attributes: the hairstyle with shoulder-length locks and the plant stems that she holds in her arms that are depicted in a bent position. The high cylindrical headdress in illus. 50 suggests that the naked woman is to be identified as a goddess. It is more difficult to interpret the terra-cottas with images that are generally known among scholars as "Astarte plaques." Attributes like those just mentioned are absent here.[36] As regards the posture, different arm positions are represented (for the typology, see Winter 1983, 96–121): both arms hang down along the sides of the body and lie on the thigh (**illus. 121a**, from Tel Masad near Beth-Shean); the hands are folded tightly under the breasts or else they hold out or present the breasts (**illus. 121b**, from Tel Zeror); the hands lie on the often slightly bulging lower torso or near the genitalia (**illus. 121c** from Taanach; see also illus. 82). This last-mentioned

---

36 See Pritchard 1943; for reference to pieces found more recently, see, e.g., Tzori 1958; Winter 1983, 96ff. A new edition of the Pritchard corpus is urgently needed.

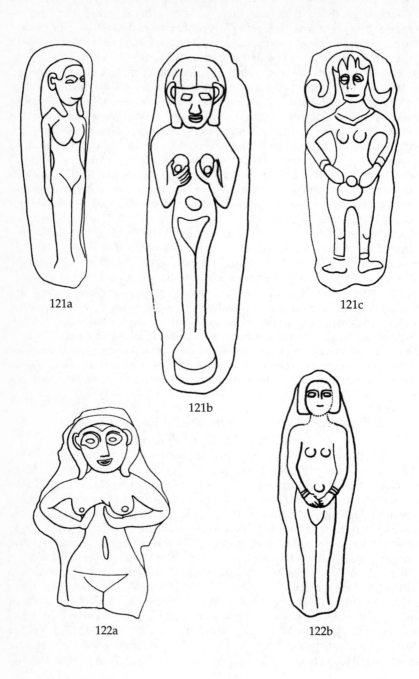

121a

121b

121c

122a

122b

positioning of the hands was one that Albright sought to interpret as a depiction of a woman shortly before childbirth (1937, 109, 119). There is a mixed form in which one hand is near the genitalia and the other is on a breast.

The feet in the *qudshu* type are usually pointing sideways to the right, but here they point straight forward in the scene, in a natural position. In contrast to the *qudshu* type, all these types of plaques appear to have been produced well into Iron Age I. Representative pieces come from sites such as Tel Zeror (**illus. 122a**) or Tell Beit Mirsim (**illus. 122b**). It is especially noteworthy that all the plaques that have been found to date come only from the cities and their environs; none have been found in the small, early Iron Age settlements in the hill country.

On the basis of two thirteenth-century limestone pieces found at the cemetery of Deir el-Balah (**illus. 123**), Miriam Tadmor seeks to show that the "Astarte plaques" do not represent goddesses but are analogous to the so-called Egyptian "concubine" figures. She says they represent a woman lying on a bed and are to be interpreted in the context of Egyptian-Canaanite funerary practice and the religious concepts or "mortuary beliefs" connected with it (Tadmor 1982). Helga Weippert (1988, 305) and others follow her in this opinion (see Lipiński 1986, 89; Hadley 1989, 224–233).

Tadmor has noted correctly that attributes are not shown, but does the lack of specific attributes conflict with the divine character of the form? We have encountered on scarabs the posture that shows the arms hanging, or lying on the thighs, or holding breasts, already during the Middle Bronze Age, on metal figurines as well as on images of the "Naked Goddess" (or else the "Branch Goddess"; see above, illuss. 10–12, 17–18, 23–25, 27). They have also been found for the Late Bronze Age on terra-cotta images, which can be assigned to the *qudshu* type because of hairstyle, foot position, and botanic attributes (e.g., Macalister 1909, II 415 fig. 500; III pls. 220.21, 221.4–5). As we have seen, however, this is nothing other than an Egyptian-style variation of the Middle Bronze Age vegetation goddess (see above, §41). In view of such traditio-historical evidence, a critical evaluation of Tadmor's thesis is needed. Three mutually complementary paths of argumentation, that can only be summarized here, suggest that the nude woman on the "Astarte plaques" is a goddess.

(a) *The typological* characterization of the plaques: The limestone plaques that provide the starting point for Tadmor's reflections are rectangular in shape, which supposedly suggests that it depicts a bed. But only a few of the terra-cottas are shaped in this way. In a few cases there are signs of cracks on the back side that might perhaps be interpreted as what remains from bed supports (see Tadmor 1982, pl. 5a). A few of the pieces that have been identified as "Astarte plaques" might actually be figures of women and of wet-nurses.[37] Most of the plaques have a long, extended oval shape; interpreting these as a bed

---

37 E.g., Rowe 1940, pl. 35.11 with *reclining child* (observe the projections on the back side of the plaque, probably the foot of the bed); Rowe 1940, pl. 35.16, with child and sandals (?; on this, see Bonnet 1952, 94 illus. 29!); see perhaps also Petrie 1928, pl. 35, 2–5; Tufnell 1958, pl. 49.5.

is improbable. Neither the back side, which has often been pressed flat, nor the lower end of the plaque, with its oval shape, prove conclusively that these did not originally stand on end, but must have lain flat. The *qudshu* plaques come in this same shape, which Tadmor and Weippert accept as representations of a goddess. Comparable representations of the goddess of the *qudshu* type on stelae and on other image-bearing artifacts (e.g., illuss. 70–71) show the goddess standing up. One might just as easily argue that the naked woman on the "Astarte plaques" is portrayed *standing*, not lying, and one might imagine that, as a rule, the plaque was originally set on the bottom edge, with the back side leaning against a wall.

(b) The older excavation reports do not mention at all or else give only a brief indication about the *archaeological context* in which the "Astarte plaques" were found. In spite of this, and in contrast to the data concerning where the Egyptian "concubines" are found, it can be said that these figures are *not* found in settings that would have a "consistent association with burials" (Tadmor 1982, 149). The vast majority of the published plaques were found in living quarters. As can be seen on examples found at Gezer, to take one example, there are at least 26 Late Bronze Age plaques but, at most, four of them were found in graves.[38] Approximately 80% of the Late Bronze Age graves contained *no* plaques at all. In the dozens of Late Bronze Age graves at Lachish, which were at times impressive family graves with multiple burials in each, only two plaques were found (Tufnell 1958, pls. 27.2; 49.1). The excavation levels that date to Iron Age I have yielded similar results. It is thus hardly in keeping with the facts to designate the plaques "chiefly as objects associated with mortuary beliefs and funerary practices," or even generally as "*ex voto* offerings for the dead" (Tadmor 1982, 170, 171). Even if the plaques *might* be used as burial gifts, this was in no way their primary function. Their main function, and the setting in which their use made sense, was in the family living quarters. It is easy to understand how one who served as protectress and mediatrix of blessing, who had accompanied a person throughout life, could also be placed in the cool darkness of the grave by the survivors of the deceased.

(c) The greatest difficulty in identifying these naked female figures that are depicted with no attributes is the fact that they appear on the terra-cotta plaques in isolation and cannot be related to other entities. Decisive help is provided by the *iconographic context* in which one finds similar images of the naked figures that are depicted on terra-cotta.[39] A few references will have to suffice here as well. A rectangular (36.6 × 25

---

38 From graves: Macalister 1912, III pls. 18.1; 19.7; 26.8 (those listed thus far came from pits that cannot be identified as graves with certainty); 78.47; from around the city: Macalister 1912, II figs. 496f.; pls. 220.3, 5–7, 11, 13, 15–19, 23; 221.1, 6, 11, 13–16; Dever 1974, 56, 133f. with pls. 40.15 and 74E. Plaques and fragments that might possibly belong to the *qudshu* type are not counted in.

39 U. Winter interpreted the "Naked Woman" in the context of Old Syrian glyptic art and came to the conclusion that the figure is intended to be a goddess ([2]1987, esp. 134, 192–199; on this, see Böhm 1990, 130–132). His argumentation makes use of completely different artifacts that are remote both in terms of place of origin and time period when compared with the Palestinian plaques.

cm) terra-cotta plaque was found at Tell Qasile on the floor of the temple, immediately in front of the cultic platform of Str. X (Iron Age IB, late eleventh century). It apparently imitated the facade of a shrine, with flanking pilasters and a slightly raised cornice (**illus. 124**; Mazar 1980, 82–84; pl. 30; Bretschneider 1991, 128f., 229 no. 79). Small holes placed at the top and bottom of each pilaster appear to have served to hold the fastenings for no longer extant doors on each side, which could have made it possible to close the shrine (for another view, see Zwickel 1990b, 58). This arrangement – though not it alone – could demonstrate that this might be a cultic image depicting the (Canaanite) shrine at Tell Qasile (Bunimovitz 1990, 213–215). Set back somewhat, in the flat background of the shrine, two *standing* female figures (of which only naked legs are extant) are positioned frontally, facing the male and female worshipers who were observing the scene. The figures appear to have been molded first and then affixed to the plaque. The feet of both figures, like the "Astarte plaques," are not turned to the side or outward but point toward the front in a natural position. In the area where the upper body would have been, fracture marks appear to show that both figures were of the same size (contra Bretschneider 1991, 129), and the hands would have been held close together and crossed under the breasts, or else both hands held the breasts. To represent naked female figures either in front of or actually inside a sanctuary shows clearly that they are to be interpreted as (twin?) *goddesses* associated with this shrine.

A large number of parallels to these shrine plaques have been found – most of which are more recent and are dated to the Iron Age II – with the majority coming from Egypt (especially the delta region) though some come even from southern Palestine (Mazar 1985b; see **illus. 125** from the Reuben Hecht Museum in Haifa). They show one or two naked women with arms laid upon their thighs and their feet pointed toward the front, in the very position that Tadmor would interpret as reclining ("supine position," 1982, 149), being positioned in front of what the pilasters and cornice would suggest is a shrine facade. Even though Petrie thought that he could identify these terra-cottas as showing a "woman on a couch" (1909, 16), the architectural elements clearly argue against his explanation. These figures are also portrayed in a *standing* pose. The large height of such women, stretching from the foundation all the way up to the cornice, again suggests the conclusion that this depicts *goddesses*.

The lack of specific attributes (hairstyle, crown, flower stem ...), that might connect these images to the "Astarte plaques," does not automatically mean that one cannot consider the figure to have divine status. Surprisingly, two *identical* goddesses of apparently equal size are portrayed side by side on the shrine plaque from Tell Qasile. A naked woman (goddess) appears in duplicate or in even more replications, with arms either hanging or holding her breasts, on Late Bronze Age and early Iron Age models of shrines[40] or temples (see illus.

40 Loud 1948, 147 with pl. 253.2 (Megiddo Str. VII[?], about 1200), Königsweg 1987, no. 128 (bought at Kerak); Seeden 1979, esp. pl. 4 (bought in Beirut; see Culican 1976, 53 and pl. 5B); Coulson 1986, 22f.; 28 fig. 5 (F–2 and F–3). See now Bretschneider 1991, esp. 127–134, 228ff. nos. 77f. and see below, §100.

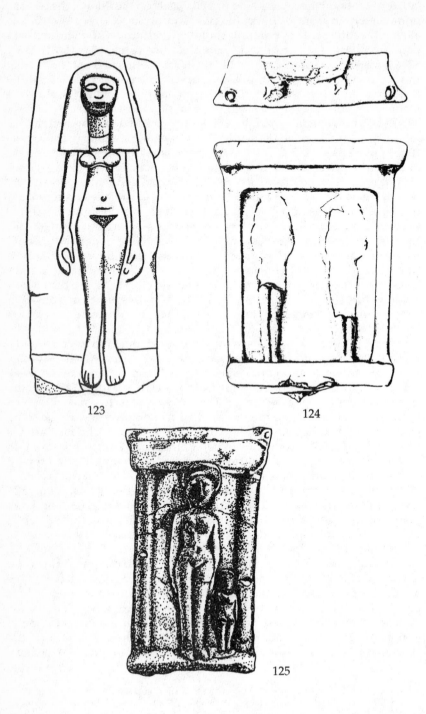

123

124

125

105),[41] on clay towers,[42] and on cultic stands[43] (see above, illus. 104) that have been found in both Syria and Palestine.[44] The female figures were commonly made in a mold at first and then placed in front of the pilasters on the model. This explains the close relation to the depictions of the plaque figures and it supports once more the interpretation that the figures on the plaques are to be viewed as *standing*. A cultic stand was found a few years ago in Pella, dated to the time of the transition from Iron Age I to Iron Age IIA (Potts, et al., 1985, 204 with pl. 42; Hadley 1989, 213–216; Bretschneider 1991, 80f., 214 no. 51). It displays two figures made in molds, having arms extended down along their sides and with a full, shoulder-length coiffure, standing on feline heads that were made by hand; they stand on either side of what looks to be an open window **(illus. 126)**.[45] The combination of a naked woman (or goddess) and the head of a lion shows that "Astarte plaques" and those of the *qudshu* type cannot be treated as completely separate entities. The "naked woman" on the "Astarte plaques" is a "naked goddess."[46]

Because the figure appears in duplicate (or even in multiples), the individuality of the form appears to have been made relative. Because they were placed on the outside of the model of the shrine, these statues have been interpreted by some as depictions of what has been termed "cult prostitutes" (recently, Böhm 1990, 138). But the plaques from Tell Qasile, the parallels collected by Mazar (on which the figure[s] appears *within* the shrine itself; 1985b), and the cultic stand from Pella with the lion heads all point clearly to the divine character of the portrayed individual.[47] The frequent use of the image on the *outside front* of the

---

41 On a temple model (or a two-stepped altar) from Emar that dates to the thirteenth century, the remains of three appliqués that were pressed in a mold have been found; there may have been at least five appliqués originally (Margueron 1976, 220–223 with pl. III.3; 1982, 90–93 = Bretschneider 1991, 52f., 205 no. 34).

42 Margueron 1976, 205–207, with pl. II.1 ("tower," Emar, thirteenth century). Bretschneider 1991, 53 (see 206 no. 36) questions whether these belong to a clay tower. But see illus. 126 for the tower-like stands from Pella.

43 May 1935, pl. 20 no. P 6055 = Amiran 1969, photo 343 (Megiddo Str. VI) = Bretschneider 1991, 84f., 217f. nos. 57f.

44 The recently discovered fragments of the "bassin aux femmes" from the sixteenth century B.C. site at Tall Muhammad Diyab in northeastern Syria offer, as far as we know, the oldest examples that depict the "Naked Goddess" in pairs in terra-cotta. The pairs of goddesses that were made by being pressed from molds alternate here with rectangular, counter-sunk metopes that are reminiscent of a shrine because they are crowned (Bachelot 1990).

45 On each of two fragments in the Museum of the University of Minnesota, Minneapolis, which are said to have come from Palestine, the "Naked Goddess" stands on a crouching feline (Coulson 1986, 22f., 28 fig. 5 [F–2 and F–3]; see also Weinberg 1978, 30ff. illus. 5 = Bretschneider 1991, 236 no. 92.

46 The "Naked Goddess" on the head or protome of a feline, which appears repeatedly in Iron Age II on Phoenician and northern Syrian specialty crafts (e.g., on bronze horse decoration plaques dating to the eighth century that come from Samos or Tall Tayinat [Röllig/Kyrieleis 1988; Kantor 1962; see Winter 1983, illus. 162]) and on ivory pieces from "Fort Shalmaneser" at Nimrud (Orchard 1967, pl. 28 no. 135; see pl. 31 no. 147) are in the tradition of the Late Bronze Age *qudshu*, shown on lions (see illus. 70 and Böhm 1990, 65–69).

47 In a shrine at Tall Munbaqa on the upper Euphrates, dated to about 1500, a fragment of a terra-cotta plaque was found with an upper torso and head leaning against the wall. It shows a woman who is naked except for the jewelry around her

126

shrine model identifies this shrine as belonging to the goddess (cf. the large number of crosses on some churches) and it also emphasizes her accessibility. The image in duplicate on the *inside* of the sanctuary (both of equal size) suggests divine sisters or twins (e.g., both Anat*and* Astarte). The fact that one cannot clearly differentiate the goddess and her worshipers in every case must be discussed next.

§58. The combination of variable iconography and the spread of this form by means of many inexpensive plaques gives one reason to think that this image is not of a great, distant, royal deity (note the lack of a crown and the fact that the nakedness contradicts a Late Bronze Age tendency to clothe deities). Instead, it portrays a goddess who takes care of the everyday needs of her worshipers and determines religious activity for significant numbers of people. The role played by the goddess in a pantheon remains a wide open question, since she – in contrast to the goddess of the *qudshu* type, and apart from paired images – never appears in relation to other identifiable deities.[48] For that reason, it is not possible to associate her with *any one* particular name (Anat, Astarte, Asherah; see Pritchard 1943, 83–87; Winter 1983, 194f., 466f.; Böhm 1990, 129). And yet, we cannot exclude the possibility of an identification with Asherah (see above, §44 on illuss. 81f.), Anat, or Astarte (or both of the latter two, in the case of doubled images).[49] Of course, one could group all these different goddess figures together to make one and the same individual and then relate this to the textual material that refers in the plural to "Astartes," as used both in Hebrew (ʿaštārôt) and Akkadian (ištarātu[m]).[50] Nevertheless, this correlation does not help much further, since this term is not to be understood as a plural proper name (analogous in English to "Marys"), but as a generic indicator and is to be translated as "(protecting) goddesses."[51]

More important than the name of the goddess, which can vary from one time and place to another, her meaning and function is significant.

---

neck and rings on her arms. She holds forth her breasts. Because of the size of the piece (21 cm high), the fragment could have been part of what was once a *cultic image of a goddess* (original height ca. 50 cm; Eichler 1984, 91f. with illus 24).

48 A late exception is a Phoenician(?)-Syrian silver bowl from Olympia, dated to the eighth century. The naked goddess who holds her breasts appears twice in a naiskos. Alternately, a bearded god appears twice in a naiskos as well (Winter 1983, illus. 412 = Markoe 1985, 204f. no. G 3; Böhm 1990, 48–51). The goddess here is most likely to be identified as Astarte.

49 "The goddesses ... merge together as one in the (only iconographically) comprehensible level of folk religion" (Knauf 1990a, 19). Even though the status and role of the goddesses is differentiated in texts from Ugarit and they are portrayed sociomorphically, these differentiations rarely correspond to a differentiation in the images, especially the terra-cottas. On the one hand, this is attributable to the characteristic dynamic of mythological-narrative literature, and on the other hand, this is because texts and terra-cottas belong to completely different functional spheres of religion.

50 Cf. *AHW* I 399f. *s.v. ištaru(m)* [2., 3.]; CAD I-J 271–274.

51 See a recently published eighth-century inscription from ʿAna on the middle Euphrates, which designates *Anat* as "the strongest of the *"Astartes"* (in other words, "goddesses," ᵈEŠ₄.DARᵐᵉˢ), ... whose heroic courage is identified as being without equal among the *Astartes* (i.e., goddesses)" (Cavigneaux/Ismail 1990, 380f. no. 17 lines 1 and 3f.). See also Müller 1989.

Neither the designation "fertility goddess" nor calling her a "mother goddess" adequately characterizes this individual. Neither aspect plays a role on the statues, and, as far as the plaques go, the functions are shown by using plants on the *qudshu* type (§41) and by the type that shows a nursing mother (illus. 82 and §49). One also does not find a goddess depicted in a role as ruler and at war, as is used when portraying Anat. Iconographically, *nakedness*, youthfulness, and erotic attractiveness are more prominent. These aspects are accentuated by the prominence given to hair and the eyes (Keel 1986, 71f., 132f.) as well as by use of jewelry (see Winter 1983, 302–311). The nakedness of the goddess is indicative of her emanating power, on the basis of which she is sought out as one who can bring a blessing to those who worship her in private.

§59.   Eroticism can hardly be separated completely from a woman's biological cycles (menstruation and pregnancy) and the mysteries and dangers connected with such events. Different hand and arm positions are shown on the plaques, noting especially the gesture of placing the hands by the lower stomach region and pressing (or massaging?) that part of the body. Such aspects are also to be noted on the so-called *Gravidae flasks* found in Palestine that date from Late Bronze Age II through Iron Age IIA (along with other similar vessels made in the shape of the female body). The flasks were small pitchers filled with oil that was to help prevent torn tissue and stretch marks during advanced pregnancy (Winter 1983, 372–374). An especially beautiful example was discovered in a Late Bronze Age grave at Gezer (**illus. 127a**; see Weippert 1977, 269f. no. 2). Cruder examples have been found, for example, in the temple of Beth-Shean, Str. VII (Rowe 1940, pl. 48 A.1–2) and in a Late Bronze Age IIB grave at Tell el-Farʿah (south) (**illus. 127b**; see M. Weippert 1977, 271f. nos. 4–5).

A medicinal vessel, similar to a *Gravidae flask*, was found in a *favissa* used in the early Iron Age temple at Tell Qasile Str. XI (eleventh century) (**illus. 128**; Mazar 1980, 78–81; Weippert 1977, 272f. no. 6). Both breasts have holes through which the liquid from the container may be poured. This renders more plausible the possibility, mentioned already by Pritchard (1934, 84; see Böhm 1990, 137), that the presentation of the breasts on the plaques could be understood as an offering of, or the pressing out of, the mother's milk.

§60.   The relationship of the "Astarte plaques" to the *Gravidae flasks*, with their emphasis on female sexuality leading up to motherhood, permits us to assume that the "Astarte plaques" played a special role in the piety of *women*.[52] On some of the parallels to the shrine plaques from Tell Qasile that were discussed above, (Mazar 1985b, nos. 1, 14–16), a *smaller* female figure was pictured at times along with the

---

52 Concerning this issue, about which more can be said only after a statistical examination of all the plaques found in graves – see the comments by Winter 1983, 199 (and the response of H. Weippert 1990, 186f.). According to W. Helck: "At those sites where observations were made about the circumstances of the finds, the dead individuals next to which the plaques were placed were female. Woolley noticed this in the excavations at Carchemish, but it is also true for Cyprus, Alaja Huyuk, Egypt, and Nubia." (1971, 61).

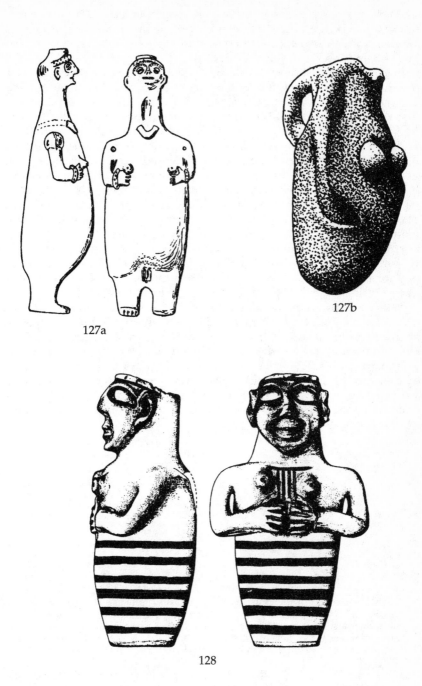

127a

127b

128

goddess, probably a worshiper or donor (Bonnet 1952, 94).[53] The small figure can in fact represent a miniature version of the goddess, as in illus. 125. But she can also appear in parallel to the goddess when a sacrificial gift is being offered (Mazar 1985b, no. 15) or might carry a sacrificial animal on her own shoulders (Mazar 1985b, no. 16). No evidence of males in this posture has been found, showing that the goddess was first and foremost an *identification figure for women*. In addition to the cultic image discussed in note 47, many molds and plaques with similar illustrations, made small in size, were found at Tall Munbaqa in northern Syria. These may have been produced for the local trade in religious items. One of the molds is inscribed on the back side with the cuneiform inscription m u n u s / m í = *sinništu(m)* "woman" (Kühne 1980, 214f. with illus. 13). If this inscription is to be taken as an annotation, then it is probably to be understood as identifying the *goddess as an exemplary woman*.[54] The modern question about whether a figure represents a goddess *or* a woman, posing strict alternatives, is too short-sighted. The plaques portray the goddess *as* a woman, and conversely they identify the female worshipers above the plaques with the goddess. It may be that the women pay for the cost of the plaque as a votive gift or they might keep this image in the home in hopes of a blessing (Winter 1983, 134).

Without getting into detail concerning the issues connected with so-called "sacral prostitution," most likely to be interpreted in the sense of an initiation rite at shrines in Canaan and Israel, one final question might still be raised about whether the plaques that depict the goddess as an exemplary woman could be understood in light of this very setting, as evidence for this rite of initiation, initially ensuring that the young woman would receive ongoing protection and blessing from the goddess and then that her family would receive the same as it grew and developed.[55]

53 Concerning the juxtaposition, see the image on an ancient Syrian cylinder seal in Winter 1983, illus. 300! Consistent with his interpretation of the "woman on a couch," Petrie goes further and identifies this little figure as a child (1909, 15), but anatomical details (massive hips, rounded abdomen, clearly breasts) plainly contradict this. The same observation, and the fact that the smaller figure can be found carrying a sacrificial animal on its shoulders (Mazar 1985b, no. 16), also argues against Bretschneider's interpretation that this is a "mother-daughter motif" (1991, 129).

54 *Sinništu(m)* "woman" is used in Akkadian texts as an epithet for Ishtar and other goddesses (Tallqvist 1938, 149f., 334).

55 Stadelmann 1967, 113 and Böhm 1990, 134 show that both the goddess and the so-called "cult prostitute" – probably a young woman set aside for the initiation rites – can be designated as *qdšt/h*. On the association between the production of cultic images and "prostitution," see Micah 1:7.

V

❧

The Hidden God, Victorious Gods,
and the Blessing of Fertility:
Iron Age I

§61. Iron Age I is a typical transitional period, marked by over-lapping trends. Many small, largely unfortified settlements were established in the hill country regions from about 1250 on. At the end of the thirteenth century and at the beginning of the twelfth century, the Philistines began to establish larger settlements at Ashdod and Ekron. Lachish, Megiddo, and Beth-Shean were still firmly under Egyptian control, at least under Ramesses III (1187–1156) (see above, §7; Singer 1990).

If we take a moment to update ourselves concerning the fortunes of the cities that provided for us the most important material for painting the picture of the religious history of the Late Bronze Age, the following circumstances emerge: At *Hazor*, Temple H and the temple in Area C fell out of use already during the thirteenth century; concerning Str. XIII, the last Late Bronze Age stratum, the settlement located in the lower city ceased to exist and from that point on people lived almost exclusively up on the tell. The next strata, XII and XI, preserve a few remains from poorer, unfortified settlements that were little more than villages. Yadin calls Str. XII simply "semi-nomadic" (1972, 131f.).

At *Megiddo*, the Late Bronze Age city of Str. VII A was destroyed in the mid-twelfth century, in fact in 1140 at the earliest, since a statue base dedicated to Ramesses VI (1145–1137) was found there in Str. VII B (Loud 1948, 135–138; see Davies 1986, 67f.; Singer 1989). Str. VI B, which follows, preserves the remains of a "small and poorly built village that covered mainly the northern part of the tell" (Kempinski 1989a, 78). The little village was built up about 1100 into a great center that had a marked Philistine character (Str. VI A). The old temple in Area BB had survived from the Late Bronze Age, or else it was put back into use in the Str. VI A period (Kempinski 1989a, 80–87). The settlement assigned to Str. VI A was destroyed toward the end of the eleventh century, and after this a rather poor, village-like settlement (Str. V B) followed. The development of this settlement into a city during the tenth century was part of a reurbanization typical of Iron Age II.

The Late Bronze Age city at *Lachish* lasted at least until the time when Ramesses III ruled (1187–1156; Giveon 1983; Tufnell 1958, pl. 39.388). A gap in settlements followed, lasting some two hundred years. Finally, to oversimplify, the Iron Age I period, politically speaking, did not take place in *Beth-Shean* at all (H. Weippert 1988, 365). In the level or levels that excavators have defined as Str. V, numerous examples of the Egyptian monuments described in §§48ff. were found together with cultic stands decorated with snakes and doves, as well as a city gate, all of which should be considered as part of the reurbanization that is typical of Iron Age IIA. There was apparently no typical Iron Age I village-like settlement at Beth-Shean that would correspond to those found at Hazor and Megiddo. James (1966, 151ff.) distinguished two levels within Str. V. Both temples from the older level show a continuation of the strong Egyptian influence. The Anat stele seen in illus. 108 was found in the temple that lies to the north (James 1966, 33f.); in the temple situated to the south, a stele was found that had been dedicated by a certain Amen-em-Opet, with bequests in honor of several male deities, among others: Atum, Re-Harmakhy, Horus, and Thoth (Rowe 1930, pl. 49.1; James 1966, 39). The gate, which resembles the tenth/ninth century gate at Megiddo, is in the more recent level of Str. V (Kempinski 1975, 215).

1. The Amun Temple in Gaza and the Widespread Presence of the Hidden God

§62.   By comparison with the repertoire of deities in the Late Bronze Age, that of Iron Age I is reduced markedly. Ptah, whose presence is noted at many different sites during the Late Bronze Age, disappears completely. But the two temples in Beth-Shean Str. V B, with the Egyptian stelae, show that Egyptian cults survived until well into the Iron Age in Palestine. These cults may have been located primarily in the Canaanite temples of those cities that were under the control of Egyptian government and guarded by Egyptian garrisons during the thirteenth and twelfth centuries (e.g., Beth-Shean, Megiddo, Aphek). But there was at least one uniquely *Egyptian* temple in Gaza, the capital of the province of Canaan (Wimmer 1990). On a list of temples supported by Ramesses III, compiled by order of his successor, mention is made of a "house that no one can enter," dedicated to Amun in the country *Ḏ3hy* (Palestine) in *p3 K³nʿn³*: "the foreigners from *Rtnw* [the Levant] come to him [to the cultic image of Amun] and present him with their gifts" (Pap. Harris I 9.1–3). This is the *Amun Temple in Gaza* (Uehlinger 1990a, 5–7). Three scarabs from Beth-Shemesh and Tell el-Farʿah (south) indicate that treasures from temples in the southern coastal plain and in the Shephelah defrayed the costs of this temple (Uehlinger 1990a, 8–14). Ostraca from Tel Sera and Tel Haror, written in hieratic Egyptian script (Uehlinger 1990a, 9; Goldwasser 1991), are probably also connected with the system of tribute for the Amun Temple at Gaza. An unusual scarab from Tell el-Farʿah (south) seems to depict a Philistine prince in front of a human form, but this form is clearly supposed to portray a god since it uses the head of a ram who wears two high feathers on that head, consequently reminding one of classic Amun iconography (**illus. 129**; Uehlinger 1990a, 14–19, pl. 1). As is often the case with unique finds, one cannot be completely certain about the interpretation of this piece.

§63. It is certain, however, that Amun played a dominant role on truncated *pyramid seals* that are new in Iron Age I and that have appeared thus far only in areas where the Philistines exercised control. On one such seal from Tel Qasile Str. X (late eleventh century), one side shows the winged sun with the explicit inscription *Ymn-r* "Amun-Re" (written with two reed stalks); a striding sphinx is on the side to the right of this; a human figure stands on a reclining horned animal on the side to the left (**illus. 130**). The side that is opposite this "Amun-Re" side of the seal is partially damaged and cannot be interpreted. The decoration on the base shows a striding, winged, bearded god with a horned cap, from which a long tassel hangs. He is flanked by two *uraei*. A very similar seal was found recently at Tel Gerisa, once again in a stratum dating to the end of Iron Age I (**illus. 131**). On the base, partly explicit, partly cryptographic, we read the name *Ymn* twice (reed stalk = *y* + *m3y* "lion" = *m* + *nb* "Lord" = *n*; *ytn* "sun disk" = *y* + *mn*). On the one slightly damaged side *Ymn-r* is written with two reed stalks; on the side next to it one reads *m3y* + *nb* + *mn*, which is to be understood as semi-cryptographic for *Ymn*. The other two sides are filled by a winged *uraeus* and a deity who holds one winged arm up as if to offer protection and in front of whom a rather degenerate form of a *uraeus* rears upward (see illus. 135). A third seal amulet of this type was purchased near Jaffa in 1889. On it also, two of the sides are filled with the writing of the name of Amun and another side has the winged god with horned cap and tassel, standing on a lion. Two very schematized human shapes fill the fourth side, and there is a rosetta on the base (Buchanan/Moorey 1988, no. 113; for other seals of this type, see Shuval 1990, 72–76, 124f.).

These motifs, especially that of the *cryptographically written name* "Amun-Re," and the crude, deeply scored style of these pyramid-base seals, appear frequently on scarabs and related seal amulets of what is known as late Ramesses Period mass-production goods. Because so many were manufactured, the glyptic art production for this era is known for being selective in its use of motifs and for much more crudely replicating the motifs, which date back to the time of Ramesses II.[1] The name *Ymn-R* "Amun-Re" recurs on numerous mass-produced pieces from the Ramesses Period (**illuss. 132a-b**; see, e.g., Petrie 1930, pls. 29.249–251, 255; 31.291, 321; 33.372; and often elsewhere). The name is frequently written cryptographically; for example, the sun disk instead of *y*, *mn* and the beetle (*ntry* "divine") for *n*, which can be read simultaneously as the throne name of Tuthmosis III, *Mn-ḫpr-r* (illus. 132a; Petrie 1930, pls. 29.247, 258; 31.292; and often elsewhere). Another cryptographic way to write the name reproduces the *y* with a red crown (*yns*) and the *r* by using the Horus falcon and flagellum (see Keel, et al., 1990, 347 illuss. 25–27; on the Amun cryptography, see Jaeger 1982, 294, note 218). Both explicit and cryptographic forms of the name Amun dominate not only the steatite seal amulets, but also the decoration on the

---

1 A. Wiese (1990, 90) suggests production began already at the time of Ramesses II and ended at the latest with Ramesses IV, thus lasting ca. 1250–1150. In view of the frequent presence of these pieces in strata dated between ca. 1150 and 900, we are inclined toward a somewhat later date for the beginning of this production (Keel, et al., 1990, 337–354).

129

a   b   c

d   e   130

a   b   c

d   e   131

132b

132a

133c   133e

133a   133b   133d   133f

oval faience seals with bundled handle that are typical of Iron Age I (Keel, et al., 1990, 355–367; see illus. 135).

§64.   The sphinx with a ram's head and the ram's head motif in general, found so frequently on scarabs during the Ramesses Period, appear no longer in Iron Age I. The cryptographic way of writing that uses the image of the royal sphinx is also absent. But just as on the truncated pyramid seals, one still commonly finds *m* written by using a depiction of a *lion*, which in this context (see above, §12) is to be understood as part of Egyptian royal iconography (**illuss. 133a-d**).[2] A hoard that Schumacher found during his excavations between 1903 and 1905 at Megiddo is especially interesting. In the level later designated as Str. VI A (eleventh century), he found a painted vessel, typical of Iron Age I, with seven handles, along with many pearls and amulets, including 32 seal amulets (Schumacher 1908, 88ff. with illuss. 123f.; pl. 28). Of the 32 pieces, 25 were published in such a way that the engraving on the base can be identified with some degree of certainty. Eighteen of the originals can be seen either in Berlin or Istanbul. Of these 25 pieces, five have the name of Amun in the cryptographic writing that uses a picture of the lion. On one piece, the *y* of *Ymn* is not written as a reed stalk, as it usually is, but with a *uraeus* (in other words, acrophonically from *yʿr.t*, "*uraeus*") (**illus. 133e**). Another piece is a lion scaraboid (**illus. 133f**). Four additional pieces bear the name in the form *Mn-ḫpr-rʿ*; one of these four is also a lion scaraboid. Appearing on 36% of the pieces, the name "Amun" dominates, by far, all other motifs in what was found in this hoard.

The Egyptian Wenamun, who undertook a trip to Byblos about 1075 to buy timber for Amun's divinely-owned country, represented the interests of Amun to the king of Byblos with the following words:

The sea is his, and Lebanon is his,
of which you say: "It belongs to me!" (. . .)
Truly, a lion loves his possessions. (II 24, 34; Goedicke 1975, 87)

The "king of the gods" was frequently praised also in other situations during this period as being a "lion." Amun's nature could be praised simultaneously in cryptographic writing by using the lion both to show him as the "hidden one" and as the one who had the power of a lion (on this whole topic, see Keel, et al., 1990, 405–410).

Mass-produced goods from the Ramesses Period that include Amun epigraphy and iconography could have been produced, among other places, in the workshops of the Amun Temple at Gaza, where the Philistines apparently continued to emphasize the cult of the god. The mass-produced goods associated with this worship are found concentrated on the plains and have been found especially in the southern coastal plain. But they also gained access into the Shephelah and into the hill country. The cult of this Egyptian deity figure could

---

2 From the evidence cited in Keel, et al., 1990, 349, illuss. 28–37, the piece in illus. 36 ought not be dated to Iron Age I but is later. But the examples noted there that are to be dated to the early Iron Age should now be supplemented by the piece shown in illus. 133 and by a piece from Tel Haror (Oren 1991, 12).

have influenced the cult of the Canaanite El, who was thought of in a similar way and then consequently might have had an impact on the way Yahweh was conceived of as well (for the early connection between El and Yahweh, see recently de Moor 1990, 30–34, 223–260; Smith 1990, 7–12).

2. Gods in Triumph and Domination: Seth-Baal, Reshef, and Horus

§65. The influence of the Egyptian deity Seth on the Canaanite Baal is certain. A winged deity with horned cap, occasionally standing on a lion, and a god standing on a horned animal, appear along with Amun on the truncated pyramid seals and on the finds in the hoard from Megiddo (see illuss. 130–131). The former is *Seth-Baal*, who is encountered regularly on the seal amulets that were mass-produced during the Ramesses Period (**illuss. 134a-c**; see Keel, et al., 1990, 133f., 304–308, 411f.). He appears occasionally already in the Late Bronze Age, not only as the one who defeats the serpent but also as the one who conquers lions (see illuss. 88a–90a). The lion on which he stands in such settings is not his attribute animal, but his opponent, known from Late Bronze Age glyptic art and probably to be identified as Mot, the Canaanite god of summer drought and death. Since the *qudshu* figure is virtually never depicted standing on a lion (see illus. 70) in the glyptic art of Iron Age I,[3] one might even wonder whether the new posture of this god, standing on a lion, has not been taken over from the *qudshu* type of figure. Baal-Seth appears to have taken over the role of the goddess, who at the end of the Late Bronze Age was shown occasionally as having military features (see illuss. 71, 72). It was shown in §45 that the weather and fertility aspects of Baal that had been emphasized in Middle Bronze Age IIB receded in importance, in deference to military themes, when Baal was associated with Seth in the Late Bronze Age.

Baal-Seth, who could be depicted already during the Late Bronze Age as a god who was in the foreground of the fight against disaster while the sun god carried out this role from the background, continued in this role as a close associate of the sun god during Iron Age I as well (as seen in **illus. 135**, on an oval seal with bundled handle found at Tell Keisan). But the sun god is replaced frequently by Amun (see illuss. 130, 131 and Buchanan/Moorey 1988, no. 113). The new relationship between these two gods appears also in a letter discovered recently at Ugarit (see de Moor 1990, 141, note 186), as well as in the Egyptian Wenamun story, where the prince of Byblos tells the Egyptian legate of the treacherous nature of a sea voyage with the following words:

> Behold, Amun can thunder in the heaven
> and send Seth at his time (II 19; Goedicke 1975, 76, 82f.)

---

3 There are questions about those pieces that are difficult to interpret, such as those in Petrie 1930, pl. 33.339; 35.391 from Tell el-Far'ah (south) and Shuval 1990, 138f., no. 33 from Tel Eitun (on no. 32, see illus. 164a in this volume); cf. Petrie 1925, pl. 15.1084; on the whole topic, see Keel, et al., 1990, 413 and 394f. The crude image on a clay conoid that was found in an early Iron Age context at Pella (Potts, et al., 1985, 203; pl. 40.3), should be mentioned here as well.

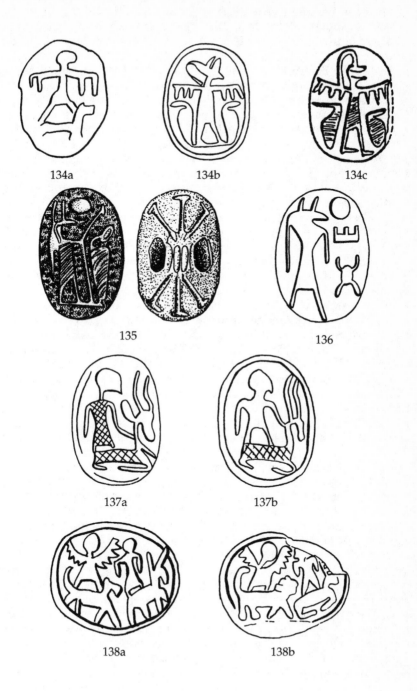

134a 134b 134c

135 136

137a 137b

138a 138b

The name of Amun, written cryptographically, appears alongside that of Seth on some seal amulets (**illus. 136**). The relationship between the two is reminiscent of that of Elyon to the gods of the individual peoples in Deut 32:8f.

§66. Like Baal-Seth, a second anthropomorphic god, who is shown on top of a horned animal, appears on the truncated pyramid seals. He is seen even more frequently by himself on scarabs and similar seal amulets. Carefully executed pieces permit us to identify the horned animal as a gazelle and the god as Reshef (**illuss. 137a-b**; Schumacher 1908, 86 illus. 124, 3rd row from the top, 2nd from the left; Keel, et al., 1990, 141–143, 195–201, 412f.). Baal-Seth and Reshef were portrayed together in their Egyptian-Canaanite form from time to time already in the Late Bronze Age (Keel, et al., 1990, 303 figs. 66f.). This is also the case on Iron Age I scarabs, where they appear in a dominant position as a winged god on a lion and as a god on a gazelle (**illuss. 138a-b**). One particular small bronze piece that was found in the vicinity of the shrine at Megiddo (Area BB Str. V B, ca. 1050-975) is most likely a depiction of Reshef, who, consistent with Late Bronze Age tradition, appears with a hand weapon in his raised hand and holds a shield (**illus. 139**). But when one examines these and other similar figures, one must wonder whether such artifacts were actually produced in Iron Age I or were rather pieces that had been handed down by inheritance from the Late Bronze Age. Even if they had been produced only recently, they were still following in the Late Bronze Age tradition nonetheless (see Negbi 1974). Images of Reshef wielding a weapon and Baal-Seth in battle are not typical of the Iron Age I. Images showing them in command and standing on animals become the norm (Keel, et al., 1990, 413). Baal-Seth on a lion and Reshef on a gazelle may have furnished the model for the majority of the indigenous seals, some perhaps Philistine, that show a deity that cannot be identified on an animal that cannot be identified either (Shuval 1990, 136–140, nos. 27–37).

§67. One variation on this theme that shows triumph and domination depicts *one or two crocodiles being lifted* by the tail. The god thus represented was originally the Egyptian royal god, Horus. On mass-produced goods from the late Ramesses Period he becomes a generic anthropomorphic figure without specifically Egyptian characteristics (**illus. 140a**; see Keel, et al., 1990, 341f., 410f.). One variation on the "master of crocodiles" theme is a figure who holds two scorpions up instead, by their tails (**illus. 140b**; see Macalister 1912, II 295 fig. 437.7). This goes back to an originally Egyptian figure as well, the Horus child as savior (Keel 1978, 148f.; see the Ramesses Period scarab, Matouk 1977, 377 no. 174). The early Iron Age I pieces are not only missing all of the clearly Egyptian characteristics; the image-bearing artifacts themselves are not Egyptian (two conoids from Megiddo, one conoid and one scaraboid from Gezer, and one scaraboid from Tell Jemmeh).[4] The motif has thus been claimed for the local repertoire and adapted.

---

4 Schumacher 1908, 86, illus. 124 , 2nd row from the top, 3rd from left (= illus. 142 in this volume); Lamon/Shipton 1939, pl. 72.13; Macalister 1912, III pl. 200.27; Petrie 1934, pl. 11.432 (= Giveon 1985, 58f. no. 7).

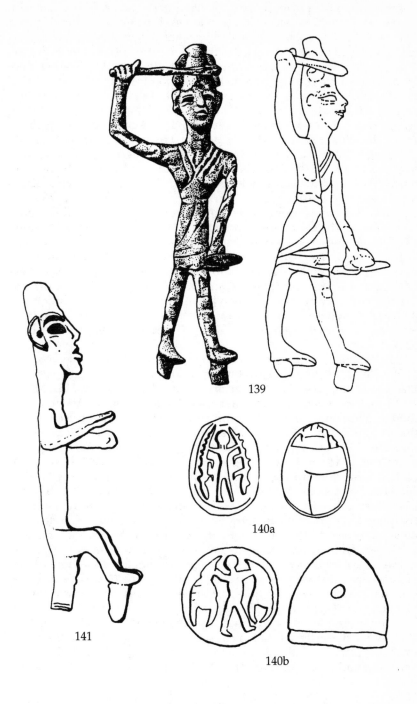

139

140a

141

140b

§68. A small bronze figure discovered in the hoard from Hazor Str. XI (eleventh century) also belongs to the assemblage of locally depicted deities, in the form of a *seated male figure* with a conic head covering and arms stretched out in front in a bent position (**illus. 141**; Yadin 1975, 255–257). One hand has a hole bored through it. Yadin regards this as evidence "that at one time it must have held a weapon" (Yadin 1975, 257). That conclusion is arbitrary; it is more likely that the hand held a cup or a scepter (H. Weippert 1988, 297–300, esp. 299). Another beardless bronze figure, shown in a seated position, from an Iron Age I level at Beth-Shean that also includes the conic head covering, apparently holds no weapon, grasping instead a *was* or comparable scepter (reserved for a divinity; Rowe 1940, pls. 35.9; 65A.2). Nor does the discovery of axe blades and lance tips among the items in the hoard found at Hazor and other places prove that the figurine was a "war deity" (Yadin 1975, 257). Since the figure's other hand appears to be shown in the act of blessing, this should be assumed to be El or the enthroned Baal (cf. illus. 56).[5] The fact that the figure is beardless could point toward identification with Baal. It has been suggested by O. Negbi that this might not be an image of a deity at all but that it depicts an enthroned prince instead, because the figure is beardless (1989, 358–362; see Moorey/Fleming 1984, 78f.), but the lack of a beard provides the only evidence that would argue in favor of this solution and proves nothing. An even more capricious assumption is that it might be an image of Yahweh (Ahlström 1970–1971; 1975; on this, see Keel 1973, 335f.).

§69. In view of the pictorial traditions from the Late Bronze Age (see above, illuss. 44f. and §37), the bronze figure of a *bull* dating to Iron Age I that was found east of Dothan at an open-air shrine (?) (**illus. 142**; Mazar 1982) may represent the weather god (Hadad-Baal, Yahweh?), even though, since this is in the hill country of Samaria, one might also identify this as El (Coogan 1987b, 1f.; Ahlström 1990; Curtis 1990, 27f.; note the mention of El-Berit at Shechem, Judges 8–9; for the metaphoric language describing El as a bull, see passages such as Num 23:22, 24:8). R. Wenning and E. Zenger jump to the conclusion that the depiction of a bull symbolically depicts its nature as a very fertile creature (1986, 82), but like every other important natural entity, the bull's significance is complex. Only context can show which of the possible meanings was most important in that particular culture (Keel, et al., 1990, 301f.; Curtis 1990, esp. 31f.). Such a context is not available when a bronze figure is found all by itself (see above, §6). Even the simplest two-dimensional picture generally furnishes more contextual elements. Warlike wild bulls, sometimes victorious over lions, are shown in thirteenth-century ivory carvings from Lachish and Megiddo. At least the piece from Lachish may be of northern Syrian provenance (**illuss. 143a-b**; see Hachmann 1983, 128). A northern Syrian hematite seal in the shape of a bull's head, found at Tell el-Farʿah (south), and a unique scarab from Tell Keisan, dated eleventh/tenth century (see below, illuss. 169a-b) both show a bull

---

5 Cf. also the depiction of a figure who is enthroned along with a worshiper on a bronze seal from Sahab in Transjordan (Ibrahim 1983, 52f. illus. 9 = Keel, et al., 1990, 419–421 with illus. 109).

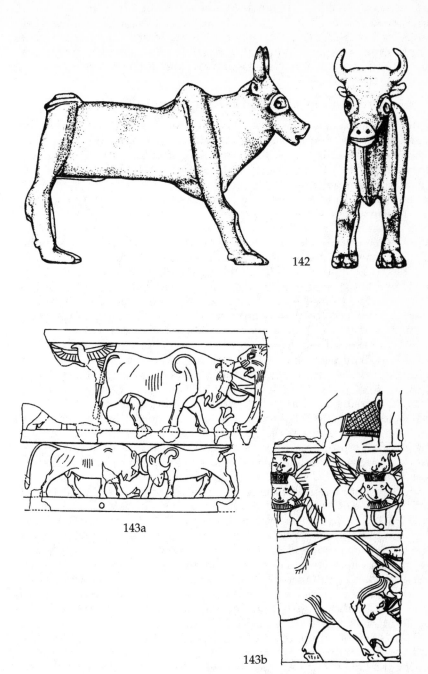

142

143a

143b

attacking or defeating a lion(ess). Wherever the bull does not appear as an isolated "vocable" during Late Bronze Age IIB and Iron Age I, II A, but is used in the context of "sentences," the animal's military prowess is emphasized, as is apparently appropriate for the demands of that age; his fertility is not the issue (see Deut 33:17, and often elsewhere).

3. The Conqueror, Who Triumphs over His Enemies

§70.   Dating back to Late Bronze Age Egyptian royal iconography on scarabs, a few examples survive that show the enthroned king, being attended by an official, and the coronation ritual showing the king in a kneeling position (Keel, et al., 1990, 337–341, 414), but none show the pharaoh sacrificing before Egyptian gods. By contrast, the theme of the king in triumph over his enemies and continuing to dominate them survives in a wide variety of formats.

The classic icon of the so-called *"striking down of the enemies"* is represented on only a few pieces, on which the pharaoh swings a scimitar above an enemy who has sunk down. There is one example from the oft-mentioned Megiddo hoard (**illus. 144a**), and others are among the finds recovered at Beth-Shean (§52) that come in part from occupation levels that even date to Iron Age I. One piece recovered from Tel Masos and another from Tell el-Farʿah (south) both show a worshiper in the background, though the pharaoh dominates the scene (**illuss. 144b-c**).

§71.   One motif, employed rather frequently during Iron Age I, shows the triumphant *pharaoh as a lion*, striding over and away from some individual or else attacking a caprid from behind (see above, §12 and illus. 99; Keel, et al., 1990, 344–346, 414; Schumacher 1908, 86 illus. 124, 3rd row from the top, 2nd and 3rd from the right). It is to be noted on one of the pieces from the Megiddo hoard but even more clearly on the scarab from Tel Masos, that was carved from bone, that this motif was used in the glyptic art produced by local artisans (**illuss. 145a-b**). It is probable that knowledge about the relationship with Egyptian royal iconography was lost gradually, so that this depiction became a popular motif associated with triumph in general (see the lions on seal amulets that bear the name of Amun; note also how the power of Yahweh is depicted in 1 Kgs 13:24 when a lion knocks down and slays the man of God). The theme might also simply be a way to show a high level of aggressiveness that the person owning the image wanted to possess. That is suggested by a composite picture showing a lion attacking a caprid, while itself being attacked simultaneously by an archer (Keel, et al., 1990, 340f., illuss. 9–10). Aggressiveness, as an attribute to be valued, is documented in relief on a sherd from early Iron Age Shiloh, where a panther(?) is shown assaulting a stag (Finkelstein 1988, 227 fig. 75).

§72.   Chariots are portrayed on a few of the Iron Age I scarabs; they had become an important element of the socio-political symbol system during the Late Bronze Age (see §38 with illuss. 60–65). An archer, now shown without any of the typical insignia of the pharaoh (*uraeus*, blue crown), rides in the chariot. The targets for his stretched bow, a caprid and a human being, are identical to the targets of the triumphant lion (**illuss. 146a-b**; see Keel, et al., 1990, 125–128, 285–294, 414f.). Those

144a   144b   144c

145a   145b

146a   146b

147a   147b

scarabs on which the chariot is no longer shown at all or are not needed for transporting the archer probably represent the next stage of development. The archer goes on foot, and the horse that had been harnessed to the chariot is now changed into a lion, so that the drawn bow is now the dominant power over caprids, human beings, and lions (**illuss. 147a-b**; see Keel, et al., 1990, 129–132, 290).

Baal-Seth and Reshef, two of the most important elements in the religious system of Iron Age I (§§64f.), are represented in a parallel manner in the socio-political symbol system by the archer who takes aim at caprids and lions (and human beings).

Iron Age I iconography, as it has been sketched thus far, shows continuity with the Egyptian tradition, though some of the uniquely Egyptian characteristics disappear, such as the ram sphinx in the Amun glyptic art, the falcon-head of Horus who conquers crocodiles, the *uraeus* and crown on the archer, and the like. Despite all the efforts to distance themselves from Egypt and their desire to be emancipated from this colonial power that had ruled in the previous age, the inhabitants in the southern coastal plain continue to use Egyptian-style glyptic art themes. Some pieces have been found in the Shephelah as well, but only a few have been discovered in the hill country. But in spite of the fact that Egyptian traditions survived, other forces were at work during Iron Age I as well.

4. Goddess Idols, Lyre Players, and Female Mourners: Elements of Philistine Iconography

§73. Even before the Philistines and other seafaring peoples entered forcibly into the country, there were imports from Mycenaean regions (see, e.g., the Mycenaean krater portraying a chariot that was found at Dan and was mentioned in §38). In addition to this piece, fragments of typical Mycenaean female idols should be considered here as well, such as have been discovered in a Late Bronze Age level at Beth-Shemesh and as a surface find at Hazor (Grant 1934, pl. B opposite p. 38 = Keel/Küchler 1982, 808f.; Yadin 1960, pl. 179.7). The famous idol of the goddess found at Ashdod (*Ashdoda*, **illus. 148**), made of one piece together with the chair on which she sits, illustrates a late provincial development of one such Mycenaean idol figure. Since, along with this complete piece, many fragments of similar figures have been found as well, it would appear that this type was quite popular during the twelfth century in Philistine Ashdod, but also in Ekron and in other Philistine cities along the coast all the way to Aphek (T. Dothan 1982, 234–238; Gitin/Dothan 1987, 202f.; Kochavi 1989, 89). The melding together of the figure and the chair (throne) as a symbol of rulership is reminiscent of the preference for depicting the "Mistress" in Late Bronze Age Beth-Shean (see above, §50). A fragment of one such Philistine mistress was found, holding a child at her breast, at Tell Qasile in Str. X, a level that dates to the end of the eleventh century (Mazar 1985a, 126; 1986, 12f. pl. 3A). After this time period the "Ashdoda" type disappears. It apparently did not survive the move to accommodate Philistine symbolism to the indigenous system (see Bunimovitz 1990, 215).

§74. Another element of Philistine iconography appears to be the male *lyre player* who is shown in a cultic setting. Female lyre players at the court were portrayed already during the Late Bronze Age (see illus. 65). A highly stylized lyre player can be seen on an anchor-shaped seal from the Philistine stratum (twelfth/eleventh century) at Tel Batash (Timnah) (Shuval 1990, 157 no. 78). This interpretation would have been less convincing were it not for another somewhat more realistic image on a seal amulet found in a late Iron Age II level at Ashdod, which for stylistic reasons is to be dated to Iron Age I. Only half of the seal is extant. The seated lyre player performed perhaps in front of a deity or was accompanied by a second (male or female) musician (**illus. 149a**).

A cultic stand was found recently at Ashdod in a level dating to the end of Iron Age I, on which five figures are portrayed in places that have been cut open as if to suggest they are windows. Four of these figures can be identified with certainty as musicians (**illus. 149b**; see T. Dothan 1982, 249–251; DeVries 1975, 26–28). Two of the players appear to play the double pipe (Heb. *ḥālîl*), one seems to play a tambourine (*top*, see below, §102), one most likely a lyre (*kinnôr*) (for this combination of instruments, see 1 Sam 10:5; Isa 5:12). A fifth figure is differentiated from the others by means of the headdress that she wears, reminiscent of the "Ashdoda" and the Mycenaean idol figures (see also Dothan, et al., 1971, fig. 62.5–6). This figure is usually identified as a musician as well, as if she holds cymbals, but what is thought to be "cymbals" probably shows the breasts of a female figure, possibly a singer. On the cultic stand, above the musicians, three four-legged creatures are portrayed in etchings and in flat relief.

A more recent clay figure, also from Ashdod but from a less certain stratigraphic context, pictures a single lyre player (Dothan, et al., 1971, 126f.; fig. 62.1; pl. 55.1). On a famous pitcher, the so-called "Orpheus jug," that was recovered from Str. VI A at Megiddo, a stratum which shows strong Philistine connections (first half of the eleventh century), a male lyre player is portrayed coming forth from a fairy-tale world that includes animals (fish, scorpions, crabs, swans, caprids, lions) and a giant lotus blossom (**illus. 149c**; see T. Dothan 1982, 150–153; Ahlström 1984, 119f.). The picture bears a striking resemblance to the middle, "terrestrial" world – between the heavenly/divine world and the underworld – that is shown on a Babylonian boundary stone dated to the twelfth century, on which one sees in procession: three four-legged animals (antelope?, goat, lion), a large bird (ostrich?), people making music, and a flower pot (Seidl 1989, 30f. no. 40, pl. 18a; Keel ⁴1984, 38 illus. 41). In Iron Age I – something new by contrast with the Late Bronze Age – cultic and/or palace music was performed exclusively by men (see 1 Sam 16:14–23; 18:10).

§75. An area or, one might say, a role that was reserved for women in the Philistine region, but not only there, is that of the *woman who mourns*. Men are willing to leave mourning rites to the women. A Mycenaean practice was adopted during the Iron Age I period, that of decorating the rim of vessels used for mourning and burial rites with small figures of mourning women, striking their hands together above their heads (**illus. 150**; see T. Dothan 1982, 237–249; Mazar 1986, 13f.).

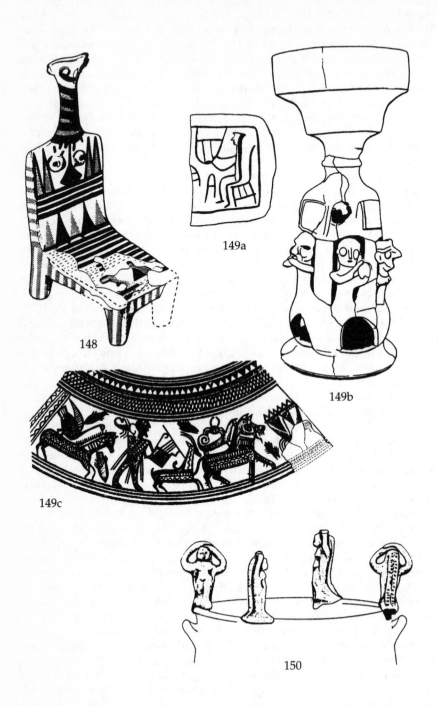

148

149a

149b

149c

150

5. The Prosperity of Plants and Animals

§76. A *cow* (?), *with her head turned backward as she suckles a calf,* was found portrayed on the base of a quartz piece made in the shape of a cone (**illus. 151a**) that was found at Megiddo in Str. VI (ca. 1140–1050). The conoid form became quite popular in Iron Age I Palestine, with a few early forerunners having appeared in the Middle Bronze Age and the Late Bronze Age (see H. Keel-Leu in Keel, et al., 1990, 378f.). Kempinski suggests tracing this form to Europe, from whence it was brought by the Sea Peoples (1989a, 87). The motif of the suckling mother animal is also new for Palestine, as is the use of the type of material on which it is now depicted, and it remained in widespread use from Iron Age I through Iron Age IIB – ca. 1150–750 (Shuval 1990, 105–111). The hard material, the related technique that allowed one to bore holes in the material, and especially the head of the suckling mother turned backward on the conoid from Megiddo all point to northern Syria as the place of origin. All of these aspects are found together in examples dating back as far as the Middle Bronze Age and the same grouping continues in the Late Bronze Age (Keel 1980a, 100f., 112f.).

A quartz conoid with the same motif has been found in Grave 134 at Tell el-Farʿah (south) (**illus. 151b**). The grave contained material typical of the end of Iron Age I. The suckling animal is accompanied by a scorpion. The scorpion appeared frequently already on Middle Bronze Age Syrian cylinder seal glyptic art with the goddess of love. The reason for this probably lies in the peculiarity of the mating behavior of scorpions, a kind of dance (Keel/Schroer 1985, 26).

The suckling *caprid* also appears already during Iron Age I on conoids made of brownish-black calcite, probably produced locally. In contrast to the pieces imported from Syria, the mother animal holds *her head straight forward* on these. A conoid from the oft-mentioned hoard from Megiddo Str. VI A (Schumacher 1908, 86 illus. 124, bottom row, 3rd from right) shows an unidentifiable image above the back of the mother animal that also appears on a limestone conoid recovered from Grave C1 at Tel Eitun (**illus. 152a**). A piece from Grave 601 at Tell el-Farʿah (south) is similar in every respect (Shuval 1990, 152 no. 66). On a fourth piece, this one from Beth-Shemesh Str. III, the image above the back is clearly a scorpion (**illus. 152b**). On all four of these pieces, which are generally carved quite crudely, the neck being turned to the front may represent nothing more than a simplification of the motif. But it might also show Egyptian influence. The suckling mother animal holds her head straight forward on *nun*-bowls (see above, §44), on Late Bronze Age scarabs, and on a rectangular plaque bearing the name of Ramesses III that was found at Gezer (Keel 1980a, 86–89). The frequent appearance of the suckling mother animal during Iron Age I and IIA ought not be ascribed simplistically either to northern Syrian or to Egyptian influence. Instead, after a period in which symbolic status was determined by affairs in the city-state and politics, men and women who owned seals showed a newly awakened, indigenous interest in the prosperity of the herds (Keel, et al., 1990, 415–417; see Knauf 1988b).

§77. Along with the classic suckling mother animal, shown with or without a scorpion, there are a whole series of variations on this theme, combining the suckling mother animal or a solitary caprid with a *small, stylized tree*. The prosperity of the plants and animals is evoked occasionally by a single element, such as a scorpion (Keel, et al., 1990, 103f., 149 nos. 46f.) or even more frequently by the solitary stylized tree shown on local limestone seals (**illus. 153**; see Keel, et al., 1990, 155 nos. 73, 380, 382f. illuss, 76–81), depicted in order to stimulate the animals and plants to be very productive. The *stylized tree flanked by caprids*, interpreted so often during the Late Bronze Age as showing the goddess and her activity (see illuss. 52–55, 80–82), can still be seen on conoids dating to Iron Age I that were found at Tell el-Far'ah (south) and at Taanach (**illuss. 154a-b**), and perhaps also on a conoid found at Megiddo (Lamon/ Shipton 1939, pl. 71.74). It is not entirely clear on a seal impression that comes from Megiddo, Str. VII A (Loud 1948, pl. 162.10; see Shuval 1990, 155 no. 74) whether the main figure shows a tree or depicts a tree god- dess who is "Mistress of the Caprids" and has anthropomorphic features. During Middle Bronze Age IIB (see illuss. 11–12), and even during the Late Bronze Age (see illuss. 49, 69–72), trees or branches or flowers were the preferred attributes that were used to depict the anthropomorphic "Naked Goddess." But in Iron Age I, the "Branch God- dess" and the *qudshu* type goddess disappeared from the iconography of Palestine.[6]

§78.   Two limestone conoids dated to the eleventh century or early tenth century deserve special mention. They portray an archer together with the suckling mother animal. On one of the pieces, from Gezer (**illus. 155a**), the archer seems to be shown taking direct aim at the mother animal that holds her head high (on this, see Giveon/Kertesz 1986, no. 147, on which no young animal appears). The second example, from Tell el-Far'ah (south), shows the archer positioned horizontally above the back of the suckling mother animal, which can be clearly identified here as a cow (**illus. 155b**). This suggests a paratactic combination of two pictorial themes.[7] The fact that the goddess Anat was described, on the one hand, in a Late Bronze Age Egyptian text as a suckling cow and was compared repeatedly to a suckling mother animal in Ugaritic texts (see Keel 1980a, 136f.; Winter 1983, 327, 404–413) and, on the other hand, that she is known as a warrior goddess and patroness of the soldier as well (see illuss. 109– 110), leads one to assume that these seals could be linked to the warrior class known as the Ben-Anat both in Late Bronze Age Ugarit and Egypt and in early Iron Age Canaan (see Judg 3:31, 5:6; Shupak 1989). About two dozen arrowheads from Lebanon and el-Hadr near Bethlehem, dated to the eleventh century, are inscribed with their owner's names (Sass 1988, 72–85). The pieces from el-Hadr apparently belonged to members of the warrior class Ben-Anat. On arrowhead no. 5 (**illus. 156**), we find the owner's name '*bdlb't* / *bn 'nt*; arrowheads nos. 1–4 carry the inscription *ḥṣ'bdlb't*, "arrow of '*Abdlabi'at.*" The personal name '*Abdlabi'at*, also found as the name of an archer at Ugarit (*KTU* 4.63 [= *UT* 321] III 38), means "servant of the 'lioness'," in which case *lb't* is to be understood as an

---

6 See §65, note 3.
7 On the combination of warrior and suckling mother animal, see, even now, Rowe 1936, no. SO. 9.

151a

151b

152a

152b

153

154a

154b

epithet of the goddess (Cross/Milik 1954, 8f.).[8] A recently published dagger blade found near the early Iron Age watch tower at Giloh can be added now to this group of arrowheads. It is stamped with a stylized little tree (**illus. 157**). Stampings of this type, just like the inscribed names, are to be regarded as ways to identify the owner (Mazar 1990b, 82; Tubb 1977; 1980; see the stylized little tree on the crude, locally produced limestone seals in Keel, et al., 1990, 380ff. nos. 8–14, 32; for archers, see Keel, et al., 1990, 380ff., nos. 30–31!). Whoever wants to use this evidence to show the continuing significance of one or more goddesses in early Iron Age Palestine must immediately narrow the focus and recognize that this evidence can be linked to traditions that are at home only within *specific social classes*. Even in such cases, the themes seem to be a carryover, by and large, from what has come down by inheritance from the Late Bronze Age (family names or personal names!).

Summary

§79. As the Egyptians departed, their goddesses, such as Hathor, and also the Egyptian versions of goddesses, such as the lady Anat, disappeared from Palestinian iconography. Images of female deities made using costly materials (metals) are entirely absent in Iron Age I. Even goddess depictions (reduced to being of one piece with a throne) that were introduced by the Philistines from Mycenaean contexts disappeared totally at the end of Iron Age I. As far as the glyptic art is concerned, the female aspect of fertility was no longer represented in anthropomorphic form, but only by means of symbols, substitute entities, and other entities from nature such as the suckling mother animal, the tree, or the scorpion, motifs that in some cases were imported from northern Syria and adapted for use on the locally produced, black calcite conoids. The crude, light-colored limestone seals that are typical of Iron Age I use, as an icon that is supposed to bring blessing, use only the stylized tree.

We now find images of the female deity only on inexpensive terracottas. Even on these, only the simplest forms of the "naked woman," without attributes, survive into the new period. *In the cities*, the plaques provide evidence that there was some continuity in the way the goddess was depicted anthropomorphically, but it seems that these images were used almost only in settings where "personal piety" was practiced and were used primarily for religious rites performed by women.

When one examines the role of male deities, it seems that the cult of Amun was initially simply taken over by the Philistines at the site of his temple in Gaza. The veneration of his name was propagated throughout the entire country by means of various kinds of seal amulets, though one notes that the typical Egyptian motifs, such as the ram sphinx, the ram head, and the royal sphinx, disappear. The cryptographic way of writing

---

8 The translation of *lbʾt* as "Lion Lady" (Dever 1984, 28; Maier 1986, 167, quoting F. M. Cross), is misleading; because of her aggressive character, the epithet calls the goddess a "lionness." She is not "Mistress of the Lion(s)" (on this, see illuss. 4, 52, 70, 126). On the Akkadian *labbatu* as an epithet for Ishtar, see *AHW* I 524b; CAD L 23a *s.v.*).

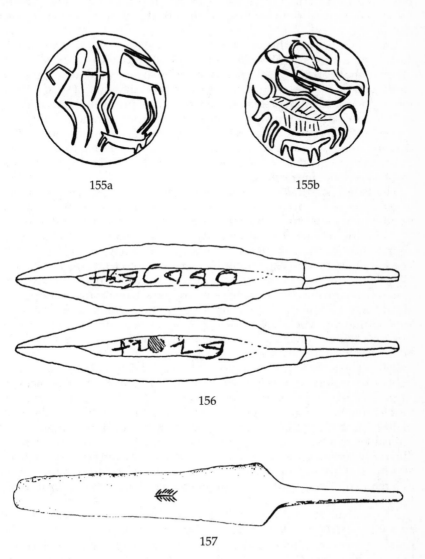

155a 155b

156

157

the name of the deity, by using a lion, adds an easily understandable accent on aggressivity to the mystery of it all. For Baal-Seth and Reshef, an emphasis on domination or authority was provided when they were shown standing on a lion and on a gazelle. The relative ranking of the deities that was apparent during the Late Bronze Age, with Baal-Seth in the foreground and the sun god as the more distant deity in the background, was lost in Iron Age I when Baal-Seth was associated with Amun.

The conquest of the enemy was also expressed in the purely anthropomorphic way that showed the "Lord of the Crocodiles" or the "Lord of the Scorpions," completely stripped of every uniquely Egyptian characteristic. Gods shown standing on animals that cannot be identified more exactly, when depicted on seals that were produced domestically, are also indicative of lordship. If one sets aside consideration of the terra-cottas for the moment, *anthropomorphic figures* in Iron Age I show *deities* that are exclusively *masculine, domineering, and triumphant*. Insofar as the bull is used as an attribute of the weather god, his combative character is emphasized, not his fertility.

The assessment that holds true for new ways to depict the gods holds true for the ways mortals are shown as well. The many portrayals of figures that show male and female worshipers in the Middle Bronze Age and the popular Late Bronze Age images that show a pharaoh in adoration before a deity disappear almost completely during Iron Age I. The only Late Bronze Age motif that survives into Iron Age I in its true Egyptian form is that of the king who "strikes down his enemies." The pharaoh portrayed in his war chariot during the Late Bronze Age appears in Iron Age I as an archer in a chariot or on foot, dominating people or animals, having been divested of all pharaonic insignia. The Late Bronze Age pharaoh-as-lion imagery is generalized now and becomes symbolic of deliberate aggressiveness.

§80.   The iconographic symbol system used during Iron Age I high-lights two factors that each take their own unique form. One factor is aggressiveness, oriented toward *superiority and domination*; it appears in the Hebrew Bible, roughly speaking, in the exodus narratives, in the book of Judges, and in the narratives describing the battles against the Philistines in 1 Samuel. The significance of the Baal-(Seth) tradition for the newly settled groups, who were colonizing the hill country, appears also in the names of the numerous newly established sites in the region that made up their names by using the pattern Baal-X (see Isserlin 1957; Rosen 1988).

The second factor is evident in a desire for human, animal, and agricultural *fertility*, as can be detected most clearly in the imagery of the suckling mother animal. This is shown most obviously in the Hebrew Bible in the patriarchal histories in Genesis (cf., e.g., the significance of fertility among the flocks in the Jacob cycle, Genesis 25–35). These two emphases are not mutually exclusive. This is shown, for example, in the Gideon traditions in the book of Judges (Judges 6–8), as well as in the evidence discussed in §78 for the existence of the Ben-Anat warrior class. In contrast to preceding periods, this second factor, with its emphasis on fertility, was expressed during Iron Age I primarily through the use of icons that depicted blessing but no longer used anthropomorphic figures, substituting a suckling mother animal, a scorpion, or a tree instead. When discussing the Middle Bronze Age "Branch Goddess" we asserted that this imagery could be interpreted as a personification of the mysterious power of fertility that was active in both the animal and the plant world. As the goddess disappeared, being represented only by the use of her attribute symbols, the personality of this power faded into the background as well. Blessing and fertility were no longer directly connected with a personal power who was acting consciously but was thought of increasingly as a numinous power and force. The disappearance of the depiction of the goddess in anthropomorphic form is an important precondition for what will have to be demonstrated in the succeeding chapters. During the Iron Age II, the icons that depict blessing will be assigned to a male deity (Yahweh), will be virtually taken over by him, and will finally be used as a way to express *his* blessings.

VI

❧

Anthropomorphic Deities Recede and Are Replaced by Their Attribute Animals and Entities: Iron Age IIA

§81. The transition from Iron Age I, with its village culture characterized by numerous small and very small settlements located in the hill country, to Iron Age II, a period that begins at the end of the eleventh century and continues on through the tenth century, brought with it a time that witnessed a noticeable shift in the settlement pattern. Many of the smallest settlements in the hill country were abandoned after only a few generations. The population became concentrated at the same time in larger villages, some of which developed into fortified cities. The process by which settlements became more concentrated and cities were rebuilt ran parallel to the establishment and consolidation of the Israelite/ Judahite state during the ascendancy and initial prosperity of the Israelite Kingdom in the period known as the "United Monarchy." The concentrated number of people living in the central hill country appears to have put pressure on the ability of that region to produce all the food that was needed, and this led to increased interaction between the hill country and the plain. At the same time, the development of orchards in areas less suited to produce grain and to graze animals required ongoing relationships for carrying on trade, which led to the expansion of permanent organizational structures that could deal with trade within regions and ultimately beyond individual regions (see Finkelstein 1989).

The development from a small-scale village culture into a territorial state could occur so quickly not only because of external political factors, such as the temporary weakness of the superpowers, but probably also because the concepts of reurbanization and kingship had never disappeared completely in some Late Bronze Age cities (e.g., Gezer, Megiddo, Beth-Shean). Development toward an Israelite state might have begun in the central hill country (Saul), but it moved quickly to gain control of the south and integrated itself with the Canaanite cities in the hill country and along the coast without giving up control (David in Jerusalem). Finally, during the second half of the tenth century, the state was able to establish for itself a commanding position in business and political dominance (Solomon; see 1 Kgs 9:15–19).

Even though the reurbanization of the plains and the hill country brought a new prosperity to Late Bronze Age cities, one ought not to think that the tenth century was simply a time for the restoration of Late Bronze Age urban culture. A system of city-states remained intact only in Philistine regions, supported by the larger cities such as Ashdod and Ekron. Iron Age cities in Israel/Judah were, as a rule, much smaller than their Late Bronze Age predecessors and, unlike those earlier cities, they found themselves being integrated into a state whose power extended over a wide area and that manifested clear tendencies toward centralization. This brought about a certain unified look to the country, standardizing not only the construction of monumental buildings, such as citadels, residential palaces, city walls, and city gates (see H. Weippert 1988, 425ff.), but also affecting the entire material culture.

In the context of our discussion, one notes particularly that Iron Age IIA urban temple sites are nowhere to be found. This is in sharp contrast to the situation during the Bronze Age, at which time the temple was the primary bearer of religious traditions for the various city-states. As a consequence of this new situation, one can expect only a very rough continuity of "Canaanite" religious traditions during the "Israelite" Iron Age II period. "One must understand the break in tradition" (which developed gradually, from the thirteenth century on, because of deurbanization, resulting in significant regional differences) "within the context of the city-states being replaced by nation-states. The construction of temples that the state found it necessary to build caused the society to concentrate on the establishment of and maintenance of national, not urban, sacral structures" (H. Weippert 1988, 447).

This means that from now on we will be able to discuss the iconography found at individual shrines only incidentally, even though this was the approach we used in the analysis of the Bronze Age that was covered in chapters III and IV of our study. When one considers the issue of polytheism and monolatry, one cannot conclude from the absence of a number of large cultic installations, equal in importance, or else from the concentration of a very few state-sponsored temples, that the deity who was worshiped at such central sites was therefore the only one being accorded such honor throughout the country. At most, one can conclude that he clearly held a dominant position within a possibly polytheistic symbol system.

The iconography of *the* Israelite sacred structure *par excellence*, the Jerusalem Temple, built (or at least thoroughly reconstructed) by Solomon, which would most closely show the continuity between "Canaanite and Israelite" ideologies, obviously cannot be studied archaeologically and can be evaluated only on the basis of biblical texts (see below, §§103–108). We encounter a paradox at this point, since we possess almost nothing but objects that were produced apart from the supervision of the state when we seek to interpret the religious history of a period that tradition says was that state's cultural highpoint and that has formative, if not paradigmatic, importance for the religious self-understanding of Judah at the very least. Texts such as 1 Kgs 9:26ff.; 10 describe Solomon as the great king of Israel who maintained trade relations literally with the whole world. But the material remains recovered from excavations correspond only minimally to this picture (concerning this discrepancy, see recent discussions by Miller 1991;

Millard 1991). Iron Age IIA looks much more like an experimental phase, in which the new state and its élite sought to establish a symbol system that was both coherent and plausible.

As is well known, the golden age of the "United Monarchy" was of short duration. The separation into Northern and Southern Kingdoms after the death of Solomon and the campaign of the Egyptian Pharaoh Sheshonq I about 925 marked the end of the period. The religio-historical profile remains incomplete in certain respects. Iron Age IIA made a continuation of Canaanite traditions possible, not least through trade and other cultural relations between Israel and northern Syria (see 1 Kgs 10:28f.) and with Phoenicia (see 1 Kgs 5:15ff.; 7:13ff.; 9:10ff.; 10:22). Phoenicia would have been able to play an especially decisive role in the culture, a fact that is also indicated in the texts that have been cited, when one recognizes that Solomon was somewhat of a vassal and client king for King Hiram (Ahiram) of Tyre (Donner 1982; Kuan 1990). But the adaptation of the Canaanite heritage was only partial. Some of this heritage, after a short *revival*, was abandoned once again. Other aspects survived only in a characteristically modified form. Certain developments that took place gradually over the entire second half of the second millennium, particularly the disappearance of the goddess(es) that was discussed in the previous chapter, seem in hindsight to have been irreversible. For that reason, the tenth century can be understood in some respects as a period that saw the process go still further, a period that simply gave further support to this trend.

1. The General Decline of
Anthropomorphic Representations of the Gods

§82. Anthropomorphic bronze figurines of deities of both genders provided characteristic evidence for cults in Middle Bronze Age II and for the Late Bronze Age (see above, illuss. 17–18, 23–25, 27–29, 56–57; see Uehlinger 1991a). The figurines found in levels assigned to Iron Age I, exclusively male deities (see above, illuss. 139, 142), may in large part have been manufactured during Late Bronze Age IIB. This holds true also for at least three of the four figurines or parts of figurines known to us from levels dated to Iron Age II.

A bronze clenched fist (4 cm in length), with a hole bored through it, has been found in the vicinity of the City of David in Jerusalem in Str. 14 (tenth century, according to Y. Shiloh). It probably held a weapon at one time and may have been part of a little statue of a warlike "striking god." On the basis of similar pieces, one can infer that this piece stood ca. 38 cm high originally, meaning that it probably was a cultic image (Shiloh 1984, 17; fig. 24; pl. 29.3).[1] Little statues that were assembled customarily by using several pieces would have had the arm cast as a single piece. That a separate fist would be attached is so rare (for examples from Megiddo and Kamid el-Loz, see Loud 1948, pl. 236.26; Hachmann, et al., 1980, 46

---

1 A statuette bought in Jerusalem, now in Los Angeles, that shows the deity as a pharaoh in a striking posture, might give some idea of how this figure looked originally (Seeden 1980, no. 1716).

no. 46 = 65 no. 12; see 72f.) that we must consider that it might have been used to repair the little statue (see also Seeden 1980, no. 17). The artifacts from Megiddo and Kamid el-Loz are from the Late Bronze Age. Just like these pieces, the bronze fist from Jerusalem ought to be dated to Late Bronze Age II. The fact that nothing else can be found from what once was a complete little statue suggests that the bronze fist had been separated from the statue a long time before this and that the piece had perhaps been used as an amulet for some time.

Like the hypothetical "Striking God" from Jerusalem, an enthroned figure, to be dated to the Late Bronze Age IIB period, shown giving a blessing, was found at Tell el-ʿOreme in Str. II (eighth century; Fritz 1986, 32–35; 1990, 113–115). It was found in a side room on the left side of the gate, which might be what is referred to in 2 Kgs 23:8 when it mentions the "cultic rooms in the gates" (*bāmôt ha=šeʿārîm*). Might we then also conclude, however, that this little statue that happened to survive by chance into Iron Age II (eighth century) – as an antique? – was still held in reverence? It is more important, when one assesses the piece religio-historically, to note that god-figurines of this type were *no longer being produced* in Iron Age II.

An additional little bronze statue, also found in an isolated context, was discovered in an eighth-century house at Tel Zeror. It cannot be classified with certainty, however, as belonging to the striking or enthroned types (Ohata 1970, 37; pl. 63.1). It might have originated, at the very latest, in Iron Age I. Finally, a figurine found at Hazor in Str. IX B (end of the tenth century) is ultimately useless because neither an interpretation nor a date for it are possible (Yadin, et al., 1961, pl. 176.23).

Anthropomorphic depictions of the chief deities are attested in literary texts that refer to neighboring states (Dagon in Philistia, 1 Sam 5:1–5; Milcom in Ammon, 2 Sam 12:30; see Schroer 1987a, 164–177), but they were apparently no longer produced in Israel during Iron Age IIA. Bronze images of goddesses had not been produced in Canaan since the end of the Middle Bronze Age. Their total absence from levels dated to Iron Age II[2] is thus not surprising and in itself provides no argument – if offered without other supporting evidence – to deny that one or more goddesses were venerated in Israel during Iron Age IIA.

§83.   Anthropomorphic depictions of a male deity that follow an *Egyptian* pattern are found quite commonly on just one particular group of steatite amulets that stands out from all other groups of seals produced in the country by having a characteristic square engraving pattern and by consciously using Egyptian motifs. Except for an as yet unpublished piece from Tel Tayinat in the Amuq region of northern Syria,[3] the artifacts whose provenance is known come from the southeastern Levant (Achzib,

2 In spite of the conflicting information from the excavators about the context in which they were found (Macalister 1912, II 335, "Third" or "Fourth" Semitic Period, in other words, Late Bronze II and Iron Age II), two figures from Gezer, which Galling (1977, 115 with illus. 31) thinks were made in Iron Age II (Macalister 1912, III pl. 211.2–3), should be dated to the end of Middle Bronze IIB (so also Negbi 1976, 66).

3 We thank Dr. Jan-Waalke Meyer of Saarbrücken, who dates the archaeological context to ca. 900–850, for calling our attention to this piece.

Megiddo, Taanach, Tel Zeror, Gezer, Tell el-Ajjul, and Tell el-Yehudiyeh). The distribution pattern and style seem to suggest that they were made in the Philistine region of southern Palestine in the tenth century (Keel 1982, 440–445, 467f.). The most important motif in the decorations is a male figure who sits above a *nbw* (gold) sign on a throne that has a high back and who usually raises an arm to greet someone with a blessing. A small (sun) disk is placed under the arm. This decoration is repeated four times on a four-sided prism from Megiddo, Str. V A (Loud 1948, pl. 163.22). Though one would ordinarily find a *uraeus* on the forehead on images that portray Egyptian kings, it is not positioned thus on this form, but comes instead right out of the mouth of the enthroned figure.[4] The majority of the scarabs portray an angular, stylized individual with one pair of wings arched above him (actually the winged solar disk) and surrounded by four falcons who provide protection, with wings spread out (**illuss. 158a-c** from Tel Zeror, Gezer, and Tell el-Ajjul). A simpler version portrays only a falcon but places a *nfr* sign in front of the enthroned figure (**illus. 159a** from Achzib). The simpler version appears as well on a rectangular plaque, engraved on both sides, from Taanach. The back side depicts a striding male figure with outstretched arms, from whose mouth a *uraeus* likewise comes forth (**illus. 159b**).

It is not quite clear whether this is an image of the deified king (the pharaoh who has achieved status as "perfect sun god" – thus Keel 1982, 466f.) or whether the sun god himself is being depicted. The throne is a clearly royal attribute but the sun god as a royal god can also be shown with this attribute (see above, illus. 119). The way the throne is shaped reminds one of the royal images that appear on the Ramesses Period mass-produced scarabs, though the king always holds a whip and a crooked staff in those depictions (see Wiese 1990, 27ff. type 3b; 89ff. type 1a; Keel, et al., 1990, 337–339). In other cases, when four falcons are depicted, they surround gods, or the throne name *Mn-ḫpr-rᶜ*, to be read as a cryptogram for the name of Amun or something similar (see Keel 1982, illuss. 36–38). The boat that serves as a throne for the figure on some of the scarabs that have been obtained by purchase (Keel 1982, illuss. 14–16) is just as important as the disk under the arm raised in blessing in providing evidence that this is more likely the sun god himself rather than the king with whom he is identified. Finally, the *uraeus* coming from the mouth is characteristic of the manifestation of the god who comes as a scorching breath.

One cannot determine unequivocally whether the striding figure in illus. 159b portrays the same deity in another posture, or whether this is a variation on the theme that depicts one deity in the background and the other in the foreground. The outstretched arms remind one of the royal gesture of supporting the heavens (Keel 1982, 471f.; Wiese 1990, 117ff.), but since the object being supported is not shown, the image probably depicts the restorative role of the air god. Both sides of the plaque may thus portray the activity of sunlight as both a scorching heat and as a reinvigorating breath of life (see Ps 104:29f.).

4 Concerning the very un-Egyptian nature of this detail, see the three Bes images on the Late Bronze Age ivories from Megiddo (Loud 1939, pl. 8.24–26)!

The seal amulets with the angular, stylized royal sun god were manufactured in Palestine; this type of scarab was unknown in Egypt. But they show a clear knowledge of Egyptian motifs and symbols, which we can assume were inherited by the Philistine cities when that region of Canaan was under the control of the Ramesses Period rulers. An early name seal from Revadim, which belonged to a certain *'b'* (**illus. 160**), appears to mark the next stage in the local development of the theme.[5] The enthroned figure is stylized, as on the earlier pieces that show Egyptian characteristics, but is now flanked by two or three worshipers; Egyptian motifs, such as the *nbw* and the falcon, are entirely absent.

§84. Even though the area in Canaan formerly under Egyptian rule was cut into small parcels of land as nation-states developed at the end of the second millennium, with each assigning a central role to that nation's own god who was now front and center – Yahweh in Israel and Judah, Milcom in Ammon, Chemosh in Moab, possibly Qaus in Edom (see §135), it would still seem that *Amun-Re* the Egyptian god who had been in the background and was involved in everything, did not lose his importance immediately and probably never lost it completely. Scarabs with his name or with the cryptogram of his name (see above, §§63f.) were still being made in Iron Age II.[6] Since they have not been studied systematically, we may only surmise that many of them came from Egyptian workshops and may have served as propaganda pieces to advocate Amun's Theban "theocracy."

Literary tradition suggests that the principal gods of the nations were warrior-military figures. As a rule, they have been associated with "weather gods" of the Baal-Hadad type (M. Weippert 1990, 157f.). Nevertheless, they must also be seen as showing continuity with Iron Age I Baal-Seth (see above, §§65f., 80). It would seem that the traditions about Baal-Seth and Reshef, known in Egypt and in areas that used Egyptian motifs, play no role in the imagery shown on seal amulets from Iron Age IIA.[7] This might indicate that the nation-state religions in Palestine/Israel during Iron Age IIA sought to distance themselves somewhat from Egyptian religious concepts.[8] On a faience conoid

5 See the seal from Sahab that was discussed above already, §68 note 5.
6 E.g., Tufnell 1953, pl. 43/43A.3–19; McCown 1947, pl. 54.3, 10f.,15f., 43; Dothan/ Porath 1982, fig. 27.7, pl. 24.11.
7 For examples from Iron Age IIA archaeological contexts, see, e.g., Shuval 1990, 141 no. 40; 144 no. 46; 146 no. 50; these are probably still items handed down by inherit- ance from Iron Age I. Dating to the transition point from Iron Age I to Iron Age IIA, the figure who fights a lion on a piece from Tell en-Nasbeh should probably be understood as Baal (McCown 1947, pl. 54.30). The stele of Rujm el-'Abd in Moab stands in a continuity with Baal-Seth images (Keel, et al., 1990, 320f. fig. 97).
8 Thus far, representations of the "Striking God" are known only from Gezer: one (perhaps two) etching(s) on a miniature limestone altar that stands only 9 cm high and can be assigned to Str. VIII (second half of the tenth century; Dever 1974, 67f., pl. 41.2) and also a scarab made of hard stone (agate?), with only a crudely carved decoration on the base, the original archaeological location not being known (Macalister 1912, III pl. 208.28). Posture, spear, and shield identify the god as Reshef. The affinity of the "Striking God" with the Egyptian royal image has been pointed out many times. The Canaanite free city of Gezer was an important point of support for Egypt at the end of the Late Bronze Age and it came under Philistine influence as time passed, without ever being integrated completely. The enigmatic

158a   158b   158c

159b   159b

160   161   162a

162b   162c   162d

recovered from Beth-Shemesh (**illus. 161**), a god is shown with a loincloth and with horizontally outstretched, winged arms. Two notched bows ("horns," possibly light beams; see Hab 3:4) jut out from his sides. Perhaps this is a local sun god.[9]

§85.   A clear break with Egyptian religious depictions is shown in the complete disappearance of the Egyptian "Lord of the Crocodiles," who lost all his specifically Egyptian attributes during Iron Age I and appeared as the "Lord of the Scorpions," a form that acculturated itself to Near Eastern depictions (see above, §67), being replaced completely now in Palestine by a depiction that shows the "Lord of the Ostriches," a thoroughly non-Egyptian concept (Keel 1978, 102–105). On a very crudely carved scaraboid from Tell el-Hama (ca. 15 km south of Beth-Shean), two anthropomorphic deities are shown together. One is portrayed with an ostrich and the other with a scorpion (Cahill, et al., 1987, pl. 35 C; 1989, 37, upper right). In light of the (generally) very crude way the earliest pieces were engraved, one might wonder whether the new type possibly developed as a mutation of the old type, as can be demonstrated by comparing two conoids from Megiddo (Lamon/Shipton 1939, pl. 72.13 scorpions; 73.8 ostriches). The handle on a vessel found in Str. VIIb (tenth century) at Tell el-Farʿah (north) bears the impression of a scaraboid with the "Lord of the Ostriches" motif (**illus. 162a**). Further evidence for the motif, which survived into Iron Age IIB, is found at Samaria, Gezer (**illus. 162b**), Tell en-Nasbeh, Beth-Shemesh (**illus. 162c**), Lachish, and Tell Beit Mirsim, in other words, scattered over the entire inland region of Israel/ Judah. On a piece that conforms to the pattern, found at Tell en-Nasbeh (**illus. 162d**), the neck of the ostrich on the right has a little disk on it. It is not clear whether this suggests some general, numinous presence or is supposed to depict a particular solar deity (see illuss. 164d, 175b, 176c).

As far as we can determine, the "Lord of the Ostriches" is not the only indigenous deity in the iconography of Iron Age IIA, but it is the dominant one. The connection with ostriches points to the fact that the inhabitants thought of this deity as at home in the steppe region of Palestine – just like the god Yahweh, who originally came from southeast Palestine (northwest Arabia), the region that served as home for the Shasu. Yahweh is connected with Seir, Paran, Edom, Teman, Midian, and the Sinai in ancient texts and those that speak about what took place in antiquity, such as Judg 5:4f., Deut 33:2 or Hab 3:3, 7 (see also Isa 63:1; Knauf 1988a, 50–53; concerning "Yahweh from Teman," see below, §§134f.).

---

remark in 1 Kgs 9:16 presupposes that the Egyptians still maintained their claim to this strategically positioned city in the tenth century (see Singer 1985, 116–118; 1990, 372–374). It is not surprising that this type of "Striking God" survived the longest here (see Seger 1972, no. 26 = Seger 1988, 95f. no. P8).

9 The "horns" may also represent wings; compare this with the kneeling god who has a wide "cap" and arms stretched straight out, from whose sides wings jut out, depicted on an unstratified, fist-shaped knob seal found at Tell Jemmeh (Petrie 1928, pl. 20.17); for an indigenous pattern, see the etchings on a gold pendant from Late Bronze Age Beth-Shean (Str. VIII; Rowe 1940, pl. 34.57 = McGovern 1985, 32f. no. 75 with fig. 26). See also Salje 1990, no. 344, an example from Late Bronze Age Ugarit.

2. Phoenician and Northern Syrian Influences in Glyptic Art: the Horse of Anat-Astarte; the "Mistress of the Mother Animals"; the Warrior Bull; and the Standard of the Moon God of Haran

§86.   We encountered the *war horse* in the Late Bronze Age as an attribute animal upon which the warrior goddess Anat stands (see above, illuss. 71–72, 110 and §41 note 8). The horse appears as the animal on which the goddess rides on Iron Age IIA seal amulets (**illus. 163a** from near Acre; Giveon 1978, 95f.). But consistent with the tendency to avoid using anthropomorphic images, the attribute animal replaces the goddess altogether. A calcite scaraboid from Tell Keisan (**illus. 163b**) shows this in a very beautiful way as it portrays the horse of the goddess along with a scorpion, a dove, and a tree (or branch), in other words, with three other elements that traditionally belong to the sphere of the goddess. These motifs, linked together in just this way, are typical of a group of stamp seals produced during the tenth and ninth centuries in the Amuq region of northern Syria (see Buchanan/Moorey 1988, nos. 155f.; Keel-Leu 1991, nos. 71f.; on the whole subject, see Keel, et al., 1990, 210–217, 309). In light of this background, some seal amulets from Iron Age I-IIA, with decoration that has been described as "horse-and-rider," or "horse that is led by a man" (Schroer 1987a, 294 with illuss. 112–113, 115–116), might actually be a veiled reference to Anat, using a much more abbreviated way to depict the theme (**illus. 164a** is from Tel Eitun,[10] **164b** is from Taanach, and **164c-d** are from Lachish; concerning a horse depicted on a cultic stand found at Taanach, see below, §98).

§87.   The goddess known throughout the Near East as the *"Mistress of the Animals"* never really had a presence in Palestine. Where the imagery did appear, the goddess was shown on a lion or on a war horse (see illus. 4, kneeling; illuss. 70–72, 126, standing); even where she is depicted, the attribute animal was not able to suppress her connection with vegetation completely, a theme that is dominant in the Middle Bronze Age with the "Branch Goddess" and in the Late Bronze Age with the *qudshu* type of goddess.[11] A surprising change takes place in Iron Age IIA. As had been noticed already during Iron Age I, anthropomorphic depictions of the deity, that could be interpreted as providing symbolic ways to portray the vegetation goddess, are no longer to be found. In an apparently irreversible process, the goddess has retreated behind or has been replaced by her symbol (the stylized tree; see below, §95). Whenever a goddess appears in anthropomorphic form in Iron Age IIA, she appears in the company of animals (nursing bovines or caprids, lions).

This sudden change in how such important things were portrayed could hardly have come about without outside pressure. On a very worn hematite scaraboid found at Acre, a city on the border between Israel and Phoenicia, an apparently female form uses bent, raised arms to hold up

10 Grey-black stone, probably calcite, 14.1 × 12.1 × 8.3 mm; now in Jerusalem, IAA inventory no. 69–1387. The information in Schroer 1987a, 294 note 178; 506 on illus. 115; Shuval 1990, 138 no. 32 are correspondingly to be corrected or supplemented.
11 See, however, §65 note 3.

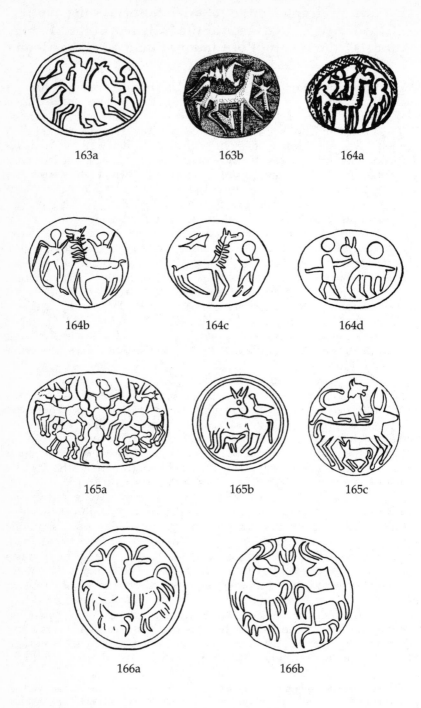

163a   163b   164a

164b   164c   164d

165a   165b   165c

166a   166b

two animals (?, perhaps lions; Giveon/Kertesz 1986, no. 139). An as yet unpublished, rectangular plaque from Tell el-Hama shows a human figure who is controlling two lions. It cannot be determined at this time whether this is a "mistress" or a "man" (see below, illus. 197c). The motif of the "Mistress of the Lions" is relatively uncommon in Palestine (see illuss. 4, 70, 126, 184). There is more evidence for the veneration of this goddess in Late Bronze Age Syria (see, e.g., Winter 1983, illus. 496, from Ugarit). She survived in Phoenician and northern Syrian artistic work until well into the first millennium (Winter 1983, illuss. 162f.; Böhm 1990, 64f.). One may thus conclude that an occasional appearance by the "Mistress of the Lions" in Iron Age IIA iconography is due to Phoenician influence.

§88.   A hematite scarab obtained in Jerusalem shows a goddess between two suckling *cows*, on whose backs doves are sitting (**illus. 165a**). The hard material, together with the round type of engraving technique and the shapes of the backs clearly identify this piece as belonging to a seal group of northern Syrian origin (Keel, et al., 1990, 367ff.; see Eisen 1940, no. 124). On an as yet unpublished hematite conoid in the Rockefeller Museum that was supposedly found at Shechem, a dove is shown as well, above the rump of the mother animal (**illus. 165b**).[12] A limestone conoid from Megiddo that was not recovered from a stratified context shows a suckling cow that looks very similar to the piece shown in illus. 165a, even though a different engraving technique had to be used because it is of a different material (notice the head facing forward, the flexed legs, and the rump). A reclining lion is shown above the mother animal (**illus. 165c**).[13] The suckling mother animal and the lion both belong to the sphere of the goddess, but she herself does not appear on the piece.

Another conoid that was also probably imported, from the former Clark Collection in Jerusalem, shows two suckling, horned animals facing each other, but without a goddess in between (**illus. 166a**). The goddess can be recognized in extremely rudimentary form (lower body, arms, and head) on a calcite conoid from Dor, which again shows two suckling mother animals (**illus. 166b**).[14] In contrast to the cattle shown in illuss. 165a-c, the horned animals shown in illuss. 166a-b are to be identified as *caprids*.

The pieces in illuss. 165–166, for which no contemporary parallels are known to us from Palestine, are clear evidence for the relatively fragile status of the anthropomorphic "Mistress of the Mother Animals" in Iron Age IIA Syro-Palestinian glyptic art. The fact that the figure between the mother animals is a goddess, or that the suckling mother animal with a

---

12 Diameter 12 mm, height 12 mm; inventory no. I. 751. We are grateful to the Israel Antiquities Authority for permission to publish.

13 Diameter 34 mm, height 27 mm; inventory no. I. 3558. We thank the Israel Antiquities Authority for permission to publish.

14 The description of this piece in Stern 1983, 261 (see H. Weippert 1988, 495) is to be corrected accordingly. On a stylistically nearly identical piece, bought in Jerusalem and now in the Biblical Institute in Fribourg, Switzerland, a little tree might be depicted in place of the goddess. But the piece is severely damaged at the decisive point and nothing but a vertical line remains (Keel-Leu 1991, no. 58).

lion and a bird points to the sphere of the goddess, is clearly supported by traditio-historical studies. It is obvious that the suckling mother can be identified sexually and thus transparently portrays a female deity (Knauf 1988b, 154–159). But even when the goddess herself appears, she is depicted with so few characteristics that her gender cannot be determined with certainty. Anthropomorphic representations of this deity or any other "Mistress of the Animals" did not survive in the long run.

§89. One particular group of seal amulets is characterized by the hardness of material from which it is made (mostly hematite, sometimes quartz) and by the extensive use of ball-point drill. The conoids in illuss. 151a-b and the scarab in illus. 165a belong to this group, most of which were imported into Palestine in the tenth century (see Keel, et al., 1990, 367–377, where the assemblage is dated a little too early). Bovines appear on pieces of this group remarkably often. They appear in pairs, facing each other (**illus. 167a** from Acre; Keel, et al., 1990, 368 no. 3; see also 370 no. 9) and alone, flanking a tree along with a human being (**illus. 167b** from Acre; Keel, et al., 1990, 368 no. 2), or else are completely alone in front of a tree (**illus. 167c** from Tell el-Farʿah [south]; Keel, et al., 1990, 372, no. 20). A tree, a scorpion (see illus. 151a-b, 163b) and/or a bird (**illus. 168a** from Tell en-Nasbeh; see also illuss. 165a-b) all point to the sphere of the goddess. There is a disk above the cow in illus. 165b, toward which the animal turns its head, and a disk is also above the animals in illuss. 167a-c. The disk may be interpreted as a degenerated star shape or more probably as a moon (see illuss. 151a-b; Keel, et al., 1990, 372 no. 17). We see a disk positioned within a crescent moon placed above a cow on two hematite conoids from Achzib and Lachish (**illuss. 168b-c**).[15] The crescent and disk are used to represent the heavens (comparable to the winged sun) in Anatolian and northern Syrian glyptic art from Middle Bronze Age IIA on. Besides the hardness of the material, the images suggest that these seals were imported from northern Syria. With the new alignment toward the religious symbol system of northern Syria, symbols that include astral imagery become more important on the stamp seals once again (see above, §33).

The bovine does not always appear so peacefully as on the seals just discussed. A hematite seal in the form of the head of a bull, found at Tell el-Farʿah (south) and recognized already by Petrie as a northern Syrian product, portrays a bull that appears to be attacking a feline. Above the bull there is a scorpion (**illus. 169a**). Placing a bull and lion together, as is done on a steatite scarab from Tell Keisan (**illus. 169b**), shows its combative nature clearly. As in illus. 168b, there is a crescent moon and a disk above the bull. The bull appears to have overpowered the lion, having thrown it on its back. This is an unusual motif in Palestine. The lion is usually the victor. This suggests that the image does not represent just any ordinary fight between two powerful animals but should be associated with a battle between two divine powers. The aggressive bull

---

15 The artifact shown in illus. 168c (diameter 13–13.6 mm, height 16.4 mm) was unpublished until now and is in the Municipal Museum of Nahariyah (Inventory no. 82–643, IAA 82–5548). We thank the Israel Antiquities Authority for permission to publish.

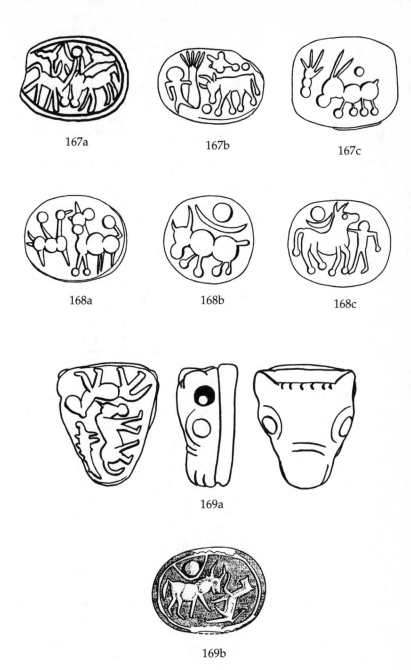

167a

167b

167c

168a

168b

168c

169a

169b

probably represents the weather god Baal and the lion that lies below is likely Mot, the god of summer drought. A bull attacking a lion is a typical northern Syrian motif (see above, §69); Keel, et al., 1990, 190–194, 301f.). It is surprising that the ball-point drill was used on such soft material; this might suggest that the motif was adapted locally from the northern Syrian hematite/quartz group of images that appeared in Palestine.

Once again we encounter a typical Iron Age IIA-B practice. Deities, male in the most recent case, are not portrayed anthropomorphically but in the form of their attribute animals (bull, lion, scorpion . . .) or else by means of their symbols (disk, crescent moon). When Jeroboam connected Yahweh as warrior and liberator with images of the bull in the Israelite state shrines at Bethel and Dan (see below, §119), it might be that he was acting in a way that was consistent with such a practice.[16]

§90.   Clear northern Syrian influence can be detected on a scaraboid, once again made of hematite, that was found at Tell el-Far'ah (south). Two crescent moon standards are shown adjacent to one another with some dots below (**illus. 170**). The two tassels that hang from the crescent moon clearly identify the standard as the symbol of the Moon God of Haran (Keel 1977a, 284ff.), whose image will be seen extensively in the upcoming Iron Age IIC period (see below, §§173ff.), but which apparently was known already in tenth-century Palestine. On two seal impressions, found on the handles of vessels from Hazor Str. X and Tell el-Far'ah (north) Str. VIIb, both of which are to be dated to the beginning of the tenth century (**illus. 171a-b**), the crescent moon standard is flanked by two worshipers. It is not clear whether the tassels are present on the impression made by the Hazor piece. They are clearly not there on the impression from Tell el-Far'ah. Perhaps a badly worn engraving on a limestone scaraboid from Tell Jemmeh might offer some additional help (Petrie 1928, pl. 20.19); a Late Bronze Age (?) cylinder seal from the same tenth-century stratum, depicting a crescent moon standard and flanked by worshipers, has no tassels (Petrie 1928, pl. 19.30).

The Late Bronze Age IIA stele shown in illus. 46 portrays the worship of the moon god at Hazor, a site that was always open to northern Syrian influences because of its location. The northern Syrian moon god was apparently known in tenth-century Palestine as well. But his significance must have remained marginal since there are only three or four examples from Iron Age IIA; they are geographically widely scattered and since two of them are from impressions made on pottery vessels, they could have entered the country through trade.

Portrayals of the deity by use of the crescent moon standards meant implictly that use of anthropomorphic forms was on the wane. There was a consequent increased use of symbols with astral connotations (disk,

---

16 When Baal-Seth is shown occasionally on Egyptian stelae of the New Kingdom Period with the head of a bull (see Keel, et al., 1990, 314f. with fig. 89), this is an Egyptian adaptation of a northern Syrian epithet or attribute of the weather god. This aspect of Baal-Seth is not employed on the scarabs of the Iron Age I Ramesses Period mass-produced scarabs. Consequently, the connection of Yahweh with the bull during Iron Age II could hardly have been the result of connections with the Egyptian-Canaanite Baal-Seth.

crescent and disk together). These two developments are either the result of northern Syrian influences or at least reinforce the complementary development of a process by which the deities were either removed to the heavenly spheres or else were "showcased" there. This development was compensated by frequent depictions of substitute entities related to mundane experience: expecially holy trees and animals, their reproduction being considered as tangible mediations of divine blessing.

3. Icons of Blessing and the Substitution of the Goddess by Entities through which She Worked

§91. Suckling mother animals depicted alone, with heads facing forward, have been seen already on locally produced conoids dating to Iron Age I (see illuss. 152a-b). In the domestic repertoire of Iron Age IIA(-B) they appear now more frequently also in pairs. In contrast to the (imported?) conoid from Dor (illus. 166b), no goddess stands between the mother animals in these pieces. The image on a conoid from Tell en-Nasbeh is particularly instructive. A worshiper with upraised arms is shown in a horizontal position beneath two suckling caprids that face one another (illus. 172). The goddess is missing, which means this collection of figures depicts an impersonal, numinous power that brings blessing and has, *as such,* itself become the object of worship.

With the disappearance of the central figure, the arrangement in pairs was no longer necessary either, so the two mother animals could be shown one above the other: this can be seen in the *tête-bêche* [Tr.: one figure inverted opposite the other] pattern on a conoid from Gezer that was not recovered in a stratified context (illus. 173). They can also face the same direction, as is seen on a piece bought in Jerusalem and currently owned by the Biblical Institute in Fribourg, Switzerland (Keel-Leu 1991, no. 59). In some cases a structured use of space is not seen as important. The liveliness and fertility of the herds can be shown as suckling animals and other creatures that stand alone are mixed together playfully (illus. 174, from Gezer; see Pritchard 1964, 128 fig. 50.3; Cahill, et al., 1987, pl. 35 D).

It seems possible to connect these icons of blessing with the deuteronomic formula, $š^eg$ar 'alāpekā $w^{e\langle}$ašt^erôt $ṣô'$nekā "the 'increase' of your cattle and the 'issue' of your flock," in the blessing and curse speeches of Deut 7:13; 28:4, 18, 51, in which the name of a northern Syrian deity (Shagar) and a Canaanite fertility deity (Astarte) survive,[17] similar to Text Combination I of Tell Deir Alla (end of the ninth century, see

---

17 Because of the deuteronomic formulation and the iconographically visible differences, one is tempted to identify the "Mistress of the Suckling Animals" with the northern Syrian deity Shagar and the "Mistress of the Suckling Caprids" with the Canaanite Astarte. If the suggested correlation between the nursing mother animal and Anat is correct (thus already Keel 1980a, 142), as noted in illuss. 155a-b above, where a caprid appears in one scene and a cow in the other, one would not be able to prove a connection between this type of mother animal and any particular goddess. For that reason, by contrast with the imports from northern Syria, it is more plausible to explain the rare appearance of bovines on locally

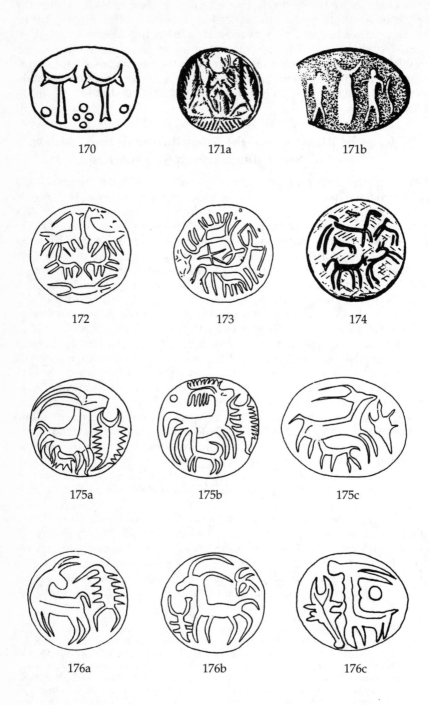

170   171a   171b

172   173   174

175a   175b   175c

176a   176b   176c

below, §§127f.), where *šgr.wʿštr* occur together (H. and M. Weippert 1982, 100f.; Müller 1989, 461f.).[18] In the "demythologized" language of Deuteronomy, fertility of the herds is a way to express the blessing of *Yahweh* (Delcor 1974; Loretz 1990, 86f.).[19] In Israel's early history, the association of verbal images with female deities, as well as the association with the pictorial icon(s), may have been more direct. But by the tenth century already, these deities would not have been conceptualized as being equal to and independent of Yahweh, but would have been viewed as entities and powers of blessing that functioned under his control.

§92.   Images showing a single suckling mother animal and a scorpion, a depiction that was common already in Iron Age I (see illuss. 152a-b), were depicted more frequently on locally produced conoids and scaraboids that date to the tenth and ninth centuries than were mother animals shown in pairs (Keel 1980a, 114–117; Keel/Schroer 1985, 34–38). The animals were most often caprids (domestic and wild goats), as one can see, for example, in **illus. 175a** from Taanach and in **illus. 175b** from Megiddo Str. V, which perhaps shows a stag (cf. the oath by the hind of the field, Cant 2:7; 3:5; 8:4; on this, see Keel 1986, 90–96). A small stylized tree appears as an additional motif, along with a scorpion, on a few conoids from the tenth century (Chambon 1984, pl. 80.3; Dever 1986, II pl. 62.17; Mackenzie 1912–1913, pl. 29.B2). It is not entirely clear on a bone scaraboid from Tell en-Nasbeh whether the image in front of the suckling mother animal is supposed to represent a scorpion or a little tree (**illus. 175c**; see Macalister 1912, III pl. 200.10; for the interpretation as a tree, cf. illus. 177c). We already know that the scorpion and the tree are traditional requisite items that are connected with the sphere of the goddess. To be sure, the little tree is not to be confused with those other images of a tree that include human worshipers (see below, §95).

§93.   In addition to the relatively complex images of the suckling mother animal, in which gender is quite clear and which, together with the scorpion, show that this is a goddess, we often find *single caprids* on locally produced limestone conoids and scaraboids whose gender we are unable to determine because no young animal is present. Only when a scorpion and a tree (or plant) are shown together is it possible to know for sure that such images are to be connected with a female deity who does not herself appear in the scene. Such portrayals seem to be a simple variation of the scene that showed the suckling mother animal and they begin to appear at the turn of the century between the eleventh and tenth

---

produced seals initially on a sociological level. Only a relatively few members of the upper level of society in Israel might have owned herds of cattle; goats, by contrast, represented a kind of "bad weather insurance" for families that were not as well off (see Knauf 1988b, 162f.).

18 It is disputed whether *šgr.wʿštr* refers to male or female deities at Tell Deir Alla (see below, §127). On *šeger*, see also Exod 13:12; Sir 40:19, and HAL IV 1316.

19 See also Braulik 1991, 125f., who suggests that the desemanticizing of the phrase was a "language-creative act" of Deuteronomy (see Müller 1982, 230 note 102: "*ad hoc* demythologizing of the divine name to become appellatives"; for a different view, also by Müller, see 1989, 462) but he attests that the "demythologizing" occurred essentially much earlier.

centuries (see Shuval 1990, 150 nos. 60–61). This is shown by the fact that a single male or female caprid often appears with a *scorpion* and, as a symbol for the love goddess, represents the arena where animal and human reproduction take place. On a conoid from Megiddo, Str. V, the caprid turns its head back toward a scorpion (**illus. 176a**); more frequently, this variant shows the head pointed straight ahead (**illus. 176b,** also from Megiddo, Str. V; see Tufnell 1953, pl. 43A/44.91). On a brownish calcite scaraboid from Beth-Shemesh, Str. IIA, a small disk is also inserted, being placed above the back of the caprid (**illus. 176c**).

More frequently than with a scorpion, a caprid is depicted in front of a *little tree*. In such cases, the point is not so much to emphasize fertility as to accentuate nourishment and prosperity. In the history of traditions, the combination linking a caprid and a tree, just like the combination linking a caprid and a scorpion, points to the presence of the goddess, but the imagery is even more clearly devoid of sexual characteristics. We have noted that a scene with these elements begins to appear already at the end of Iron Age I as, for example, on a steatite conoid from Tell el-Farʿah (north) (**illus. 177a**, made with exceptionally fine round tool engraving, despite the soft material). A hematite scaraboid from Tomb 521 at Lachish (dated about 1000) may have been a northern Syrian import (**illus. 177b**; see Keel, et al., 1990, 371). The popularity of this motif during Iron Age IIA(-B) can be seen by observing how frequently it is found: on an unpublished conoid from Achzib (**illus. 177c**);[20] on scaraboids from Grave 1 at Beth-Shemesh (Mackenzie 1912/1913, pl. 29.A1 and B2; Rowe 1936, nos. SO. 21, 31, 34); on another from Lachish (Tufnell 1953, pl. 43A/44.88, 90, 92; also pl. 43A/44.22, this time with two small trees), and at other sites (Keel, et al., 1990, 217f. no. 15), as well as on seal impressions from Beth-Shean and Tell el-Hama (Rowe 1930, pl. 39.14; Cahill, et al., 1987, 282, without illustration).

§94.   The aspect of fertility recedes completely into the background when we encounter a single striding caprid as the only motif, as, for example, on limestone conoids from Lachish (Tufnell 1953, pl. 44A/45.149) and Beth-Shemesh (Mackenzie 1912/1913, pl. 29.B2). The motif of a caprid standing alone picks up on a Middle Bronze Age indigenous tradition (see above, §11). This is the place to make mention of a whole group of seal amulets that were also produced locally, using limestone (less often, bone) to show a *human figure who stands in front of a caprid with arms raised in worship*. At Beth-Shemesh alone, five pieces of this type have been found, at least four in Tomb 1, which contains material from the end of Iron Age I through the beginning of Iron Age IIB. The conoid shown in **illus. 178a** may be one of the earliest examples of this group; the four scaraboids (Rowe 1936, nos. SO. 25, 27, 32, and an unpublished piece) were made later, as was a bone scaraboid from Tel Mevorakh (**illus. 178b**).[21] Human shapes appear behind the animal on the bases of other

20 A conoid of light brown, soft limestone, diameter 10.8–11.7 mm, height 9.5 mm; now in Jerusalem, Israel Antiquities Authority, to whom we are grateful for permission to publish (no inventory number, case no. 7211).

21 In addition, see McCown 1947, pl. 54.17 and 50(?); Tufnell 1953, pl. 43A/44.78; pl. 44A/45.151; Macalister 1912, III pl. 209.60; and an unpublished bone scaraboid from Tell el-Hama, mentioned by Cahill, et al., 1987, 282, but not accompanied by an illustration.

177a   177b   177c

178a   178b   178c

179a   179b   179c

180a   180b   181

seals (**illus. 178c,** on an unpublished bone conoid from Achzib)[22] or else are positioned above the animal's back (Yadin 1961, pl. 174.19; Lamon/ Shipton 1939, pls. 69f., 15, 29, 39; Herzog, et al., 1989, 333f., with fig. 28.1, 1).[23]

In contrast to illus. 172, the object of worship in these constellations is *not* the suckling mother animal but rather a single animal whose gender is not clearly shown. A scarab from Megiddo that shows a little tree between the legs of the animal being venerated and possibly shows a bird (?) above its back, elements that come from the sphere of the goddess, would suggest that these scenes were also connected at one time with the goddess (Lamon/Shipton 1939, pl. 69f.43; see also pl. 69f.13, 15, 39; see also Buchanan/Moorey 1988, no. 119).

The seal amulets discussed in §§91–94 have something in common: The female deity is represented no longer explicitly in bodily form but only by entities that indeed belong to the traditional sphere of the goddess but are now detached from her. These entities have themselves become icons of blessing or else have become objects of worship as some depersonalized, numinous entity.

§95.   Another group of scaraboids, typical of Iron Age IIA and made with locally available materials (bone and limestone), shows a stylized tree in the center of the decoration on the base of the piece, usually flanked by two human figures who are generally raising their arms in worship (**illus. 179a** was bought in Jerusalem; **illuss. 179b-c** are from Bethel and Beth-Shemesh). The sites where these seals were found (in addition to Megiddo, Tell el-Farʿah [north], el-Jib, and Lachish) lie in the heartland of Israel. These were produced locally and offer clear evidence that holy trees were venerated in Israel and Judah during the tenth and ninth centuries. S. Schroer has added to the assemblage that has been found in Palestine/Israel and for which a list was compliled by K. Jaroš in 1980. She has called attention to pieces from Samaria and Tel Halif that show that the motif was still being used in the ninth century, i.e., in early Iron Age IIB (1987a, 34).

In contrast to the stylized tree that looked more like branches on the local limestone stamps produced during Iron Age I (see above, §77, with illus. 153), and in contrast to the little tree or plant that was depicted with caprids on the conoids and scaraboids, this tree has a long trunk and a fully formed crown. Although there are variant forms, as the examples in illuss. 179–180 clearly show, it is always a depiction of a palm tree (see illuss. such as 16, 54–55). At the lower end of the tree trunk these representations depict a noticeable dot or knot. This could be a schematized way to depict a vessel and might possibly represent water that springs from the earth so that the tree can grow and be healthy (on this idea, see

---

22 Diameter 11.8–12.5 mm, height 12.7 mm; now in Jerusalem, Israel Antiquities Authority, to whom we are grateful for permission to publish (no inventory number, case no. 7211).

23 This type also makes its first appearance at the end of Iron Age I; see Petrie 1930, pl. 22.209A from Tell el-Farʿah (south) Grave 562; Chambon 1984, pl. 80.4 (intrusion!). To be excluded from this category are depictions of *bovines* such as the one included in Giveon/Kertesz 1986, no. 148 (human figure with an animal prod) and Crowfoot, et al., 1957, pl. 15.24.

Keel [4]1984, 23f., with illuss. 23 and 42). The scene emphasizes the ability of the earth to cause vegetation to grow.

On a related scene found at Beth-Shemesh, there is a schematized sign for a "mountain range" under the tree (**illus. 180a**). Here the earth is probably not shown simply as the location of the cosmic tree but the earth is represented as the underworld at the same time. There are two passages in the Hebrew Bible (Gen 35:8, 1 Sam 31:13) where one can assume that it was a practice of some to bury the dead under (holy) trees.[24] The idea behind this practice is connected with the notion that the earth is a fruit-producing mother's womb (see above, illuss. 49, 80, and 82) to which the deceased return. Biblical tradition connects various early Israelite shrines with holy trees, such as Kadesh in Naphtali (*'ēlôn*, Judg 4:11), Shechem (*'ēlôn môreh*, Gen 12:6; 35:4; Deut 11:30), Ophrah (*'ēlāh*, Judg 6:11, 19; in Judg 6:25f., 28, 30 it is called *'ªšērāh*), Mamre (*'ēṣ*, Gen 18:4, 8; *'ēlônîm* 18:1; 23:17f., probably an intensive plural), and Beer-sheba (*'ešel*, Gen 21:33). The graves of the ancestors (in other words, family and clan: Joseph's grave, Machpelah) were located in the vicinity of the tree sanctuaries at Shechem and Mamre. The depiction of the worshipers who flank the palm trees should probably be treated as relating to the cult that had holy trees such as these in the center of their worship.

Since the Middle Bronze Age and Late Bronze Age goddess was constantly shown with palm trees and palmetto trees (see §§16, 31, 35, 43), it would seem likely that these images, when depicted together, very probably related to the goddess (Asherah) or to the cult of the *asherah*s that is known to us from Old Testament texts (see Schroer 1987a, 21–23). Since the stylized tree was already being substituted for the goddess during the Late Bronze Age and since the process was completed by the time of Iron Age I, it is obviously questionable whether the trees would always have been consciously and exclusively considered to be a depiction of the goddess in Iron Age IIA-B, since the trees do not have characteristics that identify the entities as either male or female. The shift from the constellation that shows "caprids at the tree" to one that shows the "worshipers at the tree" is significant in any case. This tree no longer represents a *Dea nutrix* but appears by itself, with no sexual identity, as its own unique form of numinous power. On the seal in illus. 180a, on a bone scaraboid from Megiddo Str. V (**illus. 180b**), and on a limestone conoid from Acre from an unknown stratum (Keel, et al., 1989, 255, illus. 29), the two human figures no longer appear with their arms raised in worship. They seem to be touching the tree. This posture is shown on cylinder and stamp seals from the Middle Bronze Age on, as well as on Phoenician and northern Syrian reliefs and ivories from the Late Bronze Age on. The human figures are usually kings or genii, and their constellations show what they do to assure order in the cosmos.

Another scaraboid made from dark limestone, found at Tell en-Nasbeh, shows an enthroned figure to one side of a rather rudimentary

---

24 In these passages, mention is made of an "oak" (*'allôn*) or of a tamarisk (*'ešel*), but in the parallel passage for the second text, 1 Chr 10:12, speaks of an *'ēlāh*. The word can refer to any type of large tree that is connected with numinous powers and it is connected transparently with the isoglot *'ēlāh* "goddess" (see above, illus. 81, for the connection between *'lt* and tree!).

tree (see illus. 154a), with the usual worshiper on the other side (**illus. 181**; for an enthroned figure with a worshiper but without a tree, see above, §68, note 5 and illus. 160; see Tufnell 1953, pls. 43A/44, 76 [end of the tenth century]). The rudimentary style precludes a more extensive interpretation. Only on a more detailed and more recent eighth-century portrayal are we able to conclude that this constellation of figures depicts the deity El, Asherah, and a worshiper (see below, §181, on illus. 308).

4. The Iconography of the Cultic Stands from Taanach and other Terra-Cotta Image-Bearing Artifacts

§96.   We have referred already to a number of modifications to the image of the "Naked Goddess" that were necessary because of the medium that was being used (see §§49, 56ff., 79). We see a fundamentally "conservative" approach when terra-cottas serve as the medium. Various older ways to depict the subject matter are still visible on plaques and cultic stands long after such styles went out of fashion for those who used other media (seal amulets, metal figurines, and metal pendants) so that they could develop newer and more "modern" types. This "conservative" tendency makes sense sociologically, since most of these terra-cottas are associated with "private" or family piety.

This conclusion holds true once again for Iron Age IIA. We noted in §81 that urban areas did not generally have large cultic structures at this time. The official state cult in Israel and Judah seems to have been practiced in very few temples, initially in Jerusalem and then, after the so-called "division of the two kingdoms," also in Bethel and Dan(?), as well as still later in Samaria (see below, §135). At least within the central region of the country that was controlled by the Israelite state, the numerous temples that had existed in Bronze Age cities were no longer used during the Iron Age. The resulting vacuum in cultic matters was filled at least partially by the development of what has been termed "house cults." The existence of such cults has been documented by discoveries at Taanach (the so-called "cultic structure," Str. II B) and Megiddo ("sacred area"),[25] as well as at other sites. Stands, bowls, limestone altars, figurines, and other similar artifacts have come to light in areas of the city where none of the buildings look any different from private homes. In Lachish, which was just an insignificant village settlement during Iron Age IIA, aniconic stands, shells, and a limestone altar were found in a small cultic room. The little room was apparently associated with an open-air shrine that was furnished with several *maṣṣebah*s as well (Holladay 1987, 252–254; H. Weippert 1988, 447–449, 477–479).

§97.   Two famous cultic stands with relatively complex depictions, clearly connected with Late Bronze Age and early Iron Age traditions, were found at Taanach.[26] These towerlike objects are not incense stands,

---

25 For a discussion of the cultic nature of Buildings 1A, 10, and 338 in this area, see most recently Ussishkin 1989, 149–172; Stern 1990, 102–107.

26 Fragments of an additional stand that were found by Sellin at Taanach show what is left of decoration done in relief, but they cannot be reconstructed to form a coherent picture (Sellin 1904, 81f. with fig. 115). For an interpretation of the better

as interpreted previously, but serve as supports for bowls onto which small gifts were laid or into which libations could be poured. The stand that was found by E. Sellin at the turn of this century, reconstructed from 36 fragments (**illus. 182a**), has illustrations on the sides in five vertically arranged zones, alternating pairs of winged sphinxes (cherubs) with pairs of lions, the heads of the animals being formed three-dimensionally. The sphinx at the top appears to have worn an *atef*-crown. The stand makes use of a Syro-Phoenician tradition when it uses cherubs and lions together, as can be seen also on a small ivory box, found at nearby Megiddo, that dates to the end of the Late Bronze Age (Loud 1939, 13, no. 1, pls. 2–3; Barnett 1982, 26).

A volute is preserved on the left side of the top register, though it has to be reconstructed for the right side. A pair of volutes in this style, flanking such a piece, appear regularly on the corners of shrine models (e.g., May 1935, pl. 13; see illuss. 184, 188a-b) at the point of entrance into the holy place. We occasionally find images of the goddess in this same position on shrine models (see below, §100). The lions and cherubs arranged in pairs above one another on the cultic stand from Taanach should be interpreted as guardian animals. One might think of them as if they were actually standing one behind the other, horizontally positioned for the mind's eye, though shown vertically (see below for the discussion of the spatial sequence of the "floors" on the second stand). Unfortunately, only one of the decorations from the center of the piece has been preserved to offer help in determining which god(s) are being venerated. A stylized palmetto, flanked by two caprids, is recognizable between the cherubs in the lowest register (**illus. 182b**). We have already seen examples of this constellation of figures that function as substitute symbols for the goddess Asherah (see esp. illuss. 80–82). A stylized tree, flanked by two caprids facing the tree, is also portrayed on the second stand from Taanach (see below) and on a terra-cotta plaque done in relief that was recovered from Megiddo Str. V (**illus. 183**). It is significant in illus. 182b that the legs of the caprids point out away from the tree but that the animals keep their heads pointing toward the tree, nipping at the top volute. This apparently blends two different themes: the constellation of the "Mistress of the Caprids" with the caprids at the tree. The manner in which these motifs are combined in many different ways will be visible in the glyptic art from Iron Age I (Loud 1948, pl. 162.10) and well into Iron Age II (see below, illus. 222a; see Lamon/Shipton 1939, pl. 71.74).

The house cult in which this stand was used might thus have been dedicated to the worship of the goddess (Asherah). It might also have been for the god Baal, who is shown on the right side of the stand, below the middle sphinx. This scene, an appliqué created by use of a stamp seal impression, shows him as a youthful warrior who strangles a snake with both hands (*lītānu*/Leviathan: **illus. 182c**; see illuss. 87a-c, 89; see James 1966, fig. 117.1; Keel-Leu 1991, no. 103). But since the image is off to the side, Baal is not shown as the object of direct veneration by the cult; it

preserved stands, see esp. Lapp 1969, 42–44; De Vries 1975, 37–39; Hestrin 1987b; Schroer 1987a, 39; Taylor 1988; Hadley 1989, 216–222; Beck 1990a, 417–439; Bretschneider 1991, 81f., 215f. nos. 53f.

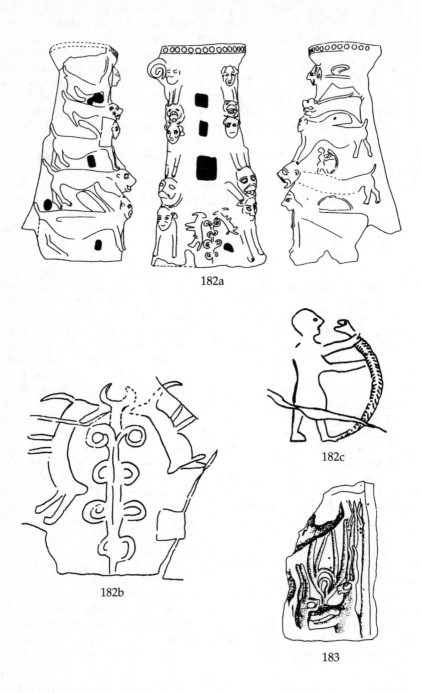

182a

182b

182c

183

suggests rather a certain subordination of that god. This partner of Ishtar/ Astarte assumes an analogous role as a bit player on an Old-Babylonian wall painting from Mari (Keel ⁴1984, 125 illus. 191). In contrast to that picture and to Middle Bronze Age iconography in general, illus. 182 does not show male and female deities in any relationship to one other.²⁷

§98. The second cultic stand, found at Taanach in 1968 by P. Lapp (illus. 184) in a much better preserved condition, also has several registers one above the other. Each register on this stand is separated by a small plinth. It has alternating lions and cherubs too, and the top register once again has two volutes turned outward. Next to each volute, there is also a small offering stand in each corner, which held a bowl in which a fire burned. This is another example of what is actually a model of a shrine. A naked "Mistress of the Lions" is in the lowest register (see illuss. 4, 70, 126 and §87). In the third register as well, flanked by lions, two caprids – facing the tree directly in this case – climb up and nibble at a stylized tree, certainly indicative of the goddess.

The second register and the topmost (fourth) register are more difficult to interpret. The second has only a pair of cherubs and a space and no depiction is missing between them (H. Weippert 1988, 472). The space appears to have been left empty intentionally. J. G. Taylor (1988, 560f.; see Hadley 1989, 220f.; Knauf 1990a, 20) suggests that the blank space depicts an "invisible deity," more precisely, indicates the existence of an aniconic cult of *yhwh ṣᵉbāʾôt yôšēb ha=kᵉrûbîm* (2 Kgs 19:14f. // Isa 37:16; Ps 99:1; see Ps 80:2; Ezek 9:3; 10:4). But *yôšēb ha=kᵉrûbîm* does not mean "who *dwells (between)* the cherubim," as Taylor would like it, but "who is *enthroned on* the cherubs" or "who sits on a cherub throne." That epithet is not depicted with this image. That epithet, characteristic of the Yahweh cult in Jerusalem (see below, §104), might have originated in Shiloh (see 1 Sam 4:4; 2 Sam 6:2), but there is no evidence for this term being used either in biblical texts that can be clearly shown to have come from northern Israel or in inscriptions that have been found in the Northern Kingdom.²⁸

R. Hestrin suggests that the blank space depicts the entrance to the shrine, which is guarded by cherubs. One could place an anthropomorphic figurine of a deity inside the stand and it would be visible through the opening (1987b, 71). Against this hypothesis, one must remember, among other points, that practically no such figurines were being produced in Iron Age IIA (see above, §82). There is another rectangular opening in both the second and the fourth registers on the back side of the stand. These kinds of openings are normal for cultic

27 To this point, no reference has been found in any Northwest Semitic inscriptions that describes a partner relationship between Asherah and Baal. The two deities are paired only in biblical texts that underwent deuteronomistic redaction (see below, §§122, 136).

28 Concerning *YHWH ṣᵉbāʾôt yôšēb ha=kᵉrûbîm*, see esp. Mettinger 1982; on the connection with Shiloh, see Mettinger 1982, 128–135. The story about the ark seems to suggest that its roots are in Jerusalem and not in Shiloh (see also 2 Sam 6:2).

For that reason, one must consider the possibility that the epithet applied to the deity in Jerusalem, *yôšēb ha=kᵉrûbîm,* is projected back into the beginning of the story intentionally and secondarily and that it was linked with the *YHWH ṣᵉbāʾôt* of Shiloh (thus now also Janowski 1991, 235–240).

stands and may have once had a functional purpose. But since only the front opening on the second register is flanked by two cherubs, the thesis is plausible that this shows an entrance that is being guarded.

The sequence of the four registers from the bottom to the top could be interpreted as a way of using a three-dimensional piece to portray graded sacredness that becomes more intense as one progresses from (a partial, then a restrained) chaos to an ordered cosmos. If the "Mistress of the Lions" reminds one of outlying desert regions (1), the cherubs then open up the entrance (2) to the holy place in which (3) the *asherah*, present in the form of a tree, bestows blessings. Finally, the topmost register portrays (4) the shrine itself with its inner sanctum, the cella. The winged solar disk expresses the idea that the earthly temple and the heavenly sphere come into contact with one another here.

The answer to the question about which cult actually used this stand depends upon the identification of the four-legged striding animal that represents the deity in the cella that is shown between the volutes in the top register. Since the animal was crudely made, it comes as no surprise that there are two irreconcilable opinions on this matter, both supported recently in opinions offered by zoologists. One group identifies the animal as a bull calf (among others, Lapp 1969, 44; Hestrin 1987b, 67; 1991, 57f.; H. Weippert 1988, 472; Bretschneider 1991, 82, 215), the other group calls it a horse (Glock 1978, 1147; Schroer 1987a, 39; Taylor 1988, 562f. with note 15; Hadley 1989, 219). In support of the first identification, in which Baal would be the main cultic figure being addressed, an iconographic parallel can be noted on a scaraboid found in Tomb 1 at Beth-Shemesh (**illus. 185a**) that shows a winged sun above a grazing cow.

But if one looks at the animal more closely, one becomes suspicious that the identification as a bull calf was influenced primarily by biblical associations (see below, §§119f.) and because of a traditional association of the (young) bull with the weather god Pate (see above, §§24, 31, 89). Not a single bit of zoological evidence identifies the animal clearly as a bovine. Since Iron Age terra-cottas of bulls are often shown without ears but not without horns, the absence of horns on this animal on the cultic stand would be quite remarkable. Hestrin resolves this by saying that it was a young animal, also arguing against identification as a horse by noting the absence of a mane. But manes are rarely depicted on Iron Age terra-cottas of horses (see below, illuss. 333–334). The animal's head does not help us one way or the other. In addition, neither hooves nor posture furnish firm evidence that this must be a horse, since ancient Near Eastern portrayals of bovines and equines are not differentiated clearly in this regard. But the hooves and posture and the relatively long snout might provide some supporting evidence if one thinks it is a horse. The rump and tail of a horse would help much with the interpretation, but they are unfortunately not clear on the scaraboid in illus. 185a.

Taylor, who interprets the second and fourth register "Yahwistically," wants to link this horse to a solar Yahweh cult on the basis of 2 Kgs 23:11 (1988, 563–566; see also Schroer 1987a, 39; Hadley 1989, 219f.). But in light of the way that the Assyrians typically used the combination of the horse and the sun god when they were divining, the "horses that

184

185a

185b

the kings of Judah had dedicated to the sun [or to the sun god]" in 2 Kgs 23:11 should not be thought of as cultic symbols representing the sun but should be assumed to be real chariot horses (see the contemporaneous reference to the "chariot of the sun god" below, §199). The words reflect a usage that probably first appeared in the Sargon Period (end of the eighth/beginning of the seventh century) in Jerusalem under Assyrian influence and cannot be used to furnish details about a requisite piece in a northern Israelite domestic cult that dates to the tenth century.

It is much more likely that the striding horse is to be interpreted, in light of the Late Bronze and early Iron Age iconographic tradition (see illuss. 71–72, 110, 163–164; see above, §86), as an attribute animal of Anat-Astarte. It would also make more sense in light of the observation that has been made many times already: Late Bronze Age and Early Iron Age terra-cottas with images on them were virtually all linked to worship of female deities. A two-story terra-cotta shrine from what was once the private collection of M. Dayan, of uncertain provenance but probably from northern Syria and most likely from the late second millennium, depicts the naked upper body of a goddess in what looks to be some kind of window and shows a horse in the lower story (Ornan 1986, 88f. no. 42). Finally, the winged sun disk above the horse on the stand from Taanach, is not to be interpreted as the symbol of a particular deity (be it the sun god, Baal, YHWH, or some similar figure) but as a way to portray the heavens that crown the shrine, this being depicted in the upper register in a pattern that follows the Phoenician iconographic tradition (Beck 1990a, 435–439; for the connection with the goddess, see, e.g., Winter 1983, illus. 412). Even from as late as Iron Age IIB, a scaraboid from Samaria depicts a striding horse with a disk below it and with a crescent and a disk above it (**illus. 185b**), i.e., using astral symbols that probably do not represent any particular deity but rather the heavenly realm in general.

§99. In addition to the two famous cultic stands from Taanach, fragments of stands that date to Iron Age I-IIA have been found at such sites as Pella (Tabaqat Fahil) and Jerusalem. The discoveries at Pella (Potts, et al., 1985, 204; pls. 41–42 = Bretschneider 1991, 80f., 214f. nos. 51f.) support what has now become quite clear: the goddess could either be shown anthropomorphically or by using her attribute symbols. Along with the fragments of the stand shown in illus. 126, on which two "Naked Goddesses," that were made with a mold and that have their arms on their thighs, are depicted standing on lion's heads; fragments of a second such stand were found that are decorated with trees incised on all four sides of both the upper and lower "stories" (**illus. 186**; see above, illus. 55a). Both stands may have been used in a domestic cult to hold offerings for the goddess, just as at Taanach (see Hadley 1989, 213–216).[29]

There is less certainty about the fragment of a stand that was discovered a few years ago during excavations of the City of David in

---

29 The crude, incised decoration on a clay conoid (Potts, et al., 1985, 203; pl. 40.3) is perhaps to be interpreted as a depiction of this goddess. See above, §65 note 3.

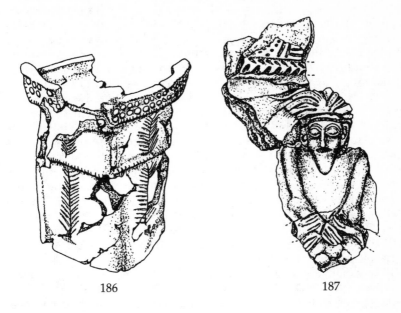

186

187

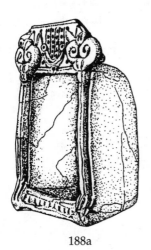

188a

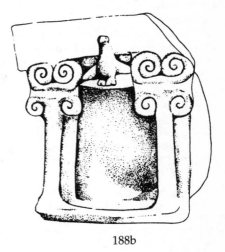

188b

Jerusalem (**illus. 187**; Shiloh 1984, 17). It portrays a man, viewed frontally, with his hair combed very high and with a pointed beard, a typical hairstyle for a Palestinian who was one of the Shasu (see illus. 65).[30] The interpretation of the figure depends on how one interprets the group of what appears to be four hands, visible in the lower part of the fragment, and the two bulges that extend downward at an angle from the man's shoulders. The fragment is damaged above both of the man's shoulders. The man appears to be carrying a sacrificial animal on his shoulders, holding the front and back leg(s) of the animal with both of his hands. The body of the animal, which one could only try to restore hypothetically, has obviously been broken off. Musicians are shown on a slightly older cultic stand from Ashdod (see illus. 149b), and it would be just as plausible to portray the bearer of sacrificial offering on a cultic stand.[31] This is more likely than the suggestion that this is a "Lord of the Animals" (H. Weippert 1988, 471f.; the animal's legs seem to be shown at too much of an angle and the joints point in the wrong direction). It is also probably not a Philistine prisoner (T. and K. Small 1986), nor is it an image of Humbaba, who was killed by Gilgamesh and Enkidu (Beck 1989c, 147f.). If the interpretation of the fragment is itself disputed, it is impossible to say with certainty for whom the sacrificial animal is intended.

§100.   Finally, when discussing these large terra-cottas, a number of *shrine models* that might have been related to house cults devoted to the goddess deserve attention. Unfortunately, the majority of these have been obtained by purchase and have appeared as a result of grave robbing. Their original archaeological context cannot thus be known. Two intact examples were found in official excavations, but only one has been published with an explicit description of exactly where it was found.[32] It comes from Tell el-Farʿah (north) and was found in a pit in the courtyard of a residence in Str. VIIb (end of the tenth century; **illus. 188a**; Chambon 1984, 77f.). The facade of the shrine is flanked by two pilasters which are capped by palmette volutes that curve inward. A crescent moon between the volutes suggests celestial connections for the deity worshiped here (the dots that are above it, being patterned after a northern Syrian iconographic tradition, could represent rain). Other models from southern Syria and Palestine suggest that the deity might have been a goddess.

---

30 We see the same general hairstyle in a somewhat different form on a terra-cotta figurine from Megiddo Str. V (May 1935, pl. 28 no. M 5402). It is thus more likely that we should interpret this as a Canaanite individual rather than that we consider this to be a representative of the "Sea Peoples" on the basis of depictions of warriors found at Enkomi (thus T. and K. Small 1986; see H. Weippert 1988, 471). The Philistines in the "Sea Peoples" relief of Ramesses III at Medinet Habu (see also illus. 129), unlike the way they are depicted at Enkomi, do not have beards.

31 See also the very unsatisfactorily published (alabaster?) fragment from Gezer, that shows an individual who carries a sacrificial offering, in Macalister 1912, II 342f.; III pl. 213.19.

32 The Phoenician model of a shrine that was found by I. Ben-Dor in 1944 in the southern cemetery at Achzib, discussed by W. Culican (1976, 47, 49; pl. 1B = 1986, 481, 483, 488) ought to be dated to Iron Age IIC. Nothing else is known even now about the precise archaeological context in which it was found (see Weinberg 1978, 47 note 10).

Early Iron Age examples from Jordan and Lebanon use images of the "Naked Goddess" that are made from molds, instead of using voluted pilasters (Königsweg 1987, no. 128; Seeden 1979).[33] Another fragment, said to have come from Mount Nebo and dated to the ninth or eighth century, shows the torso of a goddess on each side of a metope that is positioned between the pilasters (Weinberg 1978). This kind of anthropomorphic representation of the goddess has not been found on models in central Palestine.[34] The model that is most similar to the one found at Tell el-Farʿah is roughly contemporary or else dates to the early ninth century and comes from Transjordan, now to be found in the Rockefeller Museum (**illus. 188b**). The dove in the pediment between the palmette pilasters shows clearly that the shrine belongs to a goddess (just like the model in Hachlili/Meshorer 1986, 42; on the connection between the dove and the goddess, see §§17, 48 and below, illuss. 319–320).

§101.   In spite of the "conservative" tendency that has been discussed concerning the images used in this genre, some significant new elements appear during Iron Age IIA in the *small terra-cottas*. The plaque form that was commonly used in the Late Bronze Age and in Iron Age I goes out of vogue now; the background – which M. Tadmor erroneously thought was a bed – is used no longer. The sides of the figurines are also shown three-dimensionally now, even though the back side is still left flat; only the front side was supposed to be viewed. More significant than these stylistic innovations is the fact that only a select number of the types known to this point continue in use. Images depicting the goddess completely naked, with her genitalia emphasized, are less common (Winter 1983, illus. 47 from Aphek; May 1935, pl. 24 M 2653 from Megiddo). A few finds of this type depict the suckling goddess once again (see illus. 82; for the goddess with child, see also illus. 103). A roughly made piece from Beth-Shean (James 1966, fig. 112.7) shows the goddess naked, with the genitalia accentuated, as was typical during the Late Bronze Age. By contrast, she appears on a plaque from Tell el-Farʿah (north) (**illus. 189**) on a throne and with a garment that covers her lower body from her hips to just above her ankles. So that she could nurse, her upper body was still exposed, covered only by bracelet and necklace decorations. The clothing and throne now replicate much more closely the Egyptian pattern that shows Isis as she nurses, always clothed and usually on a throne (see below, illuss. 327–328). After this time, the "Canaanite" type

33 Nothing is known about the site at which two supposedly "Palestinian" fragments from a single (?) model of a shrine, nor where they were purchased; each shows a "Naked Goddess" above a crouching feline (Coulson 1986, 22f., 28 fig. 5 [F-2 and F-3]; see above, §57 note 45).
34 Concerning other models of shrines from Iron Age IIB-C, see Weinberg 1978, 41–44 with figs. 16–18. On the entire group, see now Bretschneider 1991, esp. 129–135; on the connection with the goddess, see also Zwickel 1990b, 58–61.
    The two seated figures who are positioned in front of the pilasters on the fragment of a terra-cotta shrine from Gezer (Macalister 1912, II 437–439 with figs. 517–519) can hardly be identified as female figures. Could these be priests who guard the entrance to the shrine (thus Keel ⁴1984, 110f.)? Macalister's dating to the "Second Semitic Period" (i.e., Middle Bronze Age IIB) hardly fits; for a suggestion that it should be dated to Iron Age IIA, see, e.g., May 1935, pl. 28 M 5403.

of naked suckling figure, with emphasis on the genitalia, will be seen no more. Other types of the "Naked Goddess" also appear much less frequently in Israel when compared with previous periods, with production seeming to have continued only in the region of southern Palestine and Philistia (see below, illuss. 216–217, 330). There is no recent study of these figurines that would allow us to identify chronological or regional differences more exactly within Iron Age IIA-B.[35]

§102.   By contrast, figurines that portray a female holding a round disk in front of her upper body are typical of Iron Age IIA-B (Hillers 1970; Winter 1983, 119–121; Beck 1990b lists 22 examples). Naked and clothed variants of this type exist side by side as well. Because of the fragmentary state of most of the figurines, further classification is generally not possible (**illus. 190a** from Hazor; see Yadin, et al., 1960, pl. 76.12–13; Levy/Edelstein 1972, 364f. fig. 17.7; Chambon 1984, pl. 63.1). The naked style of female with accentuated genitalia, of which one example was made with a press-mold and found at Taanach (**illus. 190b**; see McCown 1947, pl. 87.3), was out of step with the times (see May 1935, pl. 27 M 810; pl. 28 M 5418; Macalister 1912, pl. 221.2; Beck 1990b, 87 illus. 1, 89 illus. 7). The women who are portrayed now are shown more commonly wearing at least a veil but can also wear a skirt wrapped around the hips (**illus. 190c** from Tell el-Farʿah [north]; see Schumacher 1908, 61 fig. 71) or else they wear a dress that covers the entire body (**illus. 190d,** from Megiddo Str. V). This tendency toward clothing the individual will be even more prevalent during Iron Age IIB-C, as can be seen on two examples, one from Samaria (**illus. 190e**) and one from Gezer (**illus. 190f**), that date to the late eighth century (see May 1935, pl. 27 M 787, 4365, 4495).

To understand these figurines, which according to evidence from excavations at Taanach and Megiddo are clearly associated with house cults, one must first try to determine the significance of the round disk and then clarify the status of the figure (human female or goddess?). Some scholars have suggested that the disk might be a tambourine, others a sacrificial cake (or loaf), and still others maybe even a solar disk. One need not take much time to refute this last suggestion.[36] One cannot with certainty, however, eliminate the possibility that it shows a cake or a sacrificial loaf of bread (most recently Schroer 1987a, 277–281) but this interpretation places more weight on evidence from texts that were written later and that might have occasioned a prejudicial analysis of the iconography for this earlier time period (cakes for the "Queen of

---

35 T. A. Holland's dissertation, "A Typological and Archaeological Study of Human and Animal Representations in the Plastic Art of Palestine During the Iron Age," 2 vols., Faculty of Anthropology and Geography, University of Oxford, 1975, has un-fortunately not been published and was unavailable to us. But see Holland 1977 and the review by Hadley 1989, 30–32; *passim* 224–248.

36 Amiran 1958 connects the (double) grooved border decoration on the disk that is on a figurine from Gezer (here, illus. 190e) with a (simple) "pearl-ring" border that is on a winged solar disk on northern Syrian ivories. That connection suggests to her that the woman with the disk is a Canaanite solar goddess. But an isolated iconographic detail that serves an exclusively decorative function does not permit that kind of expansive, substantive conclusion.

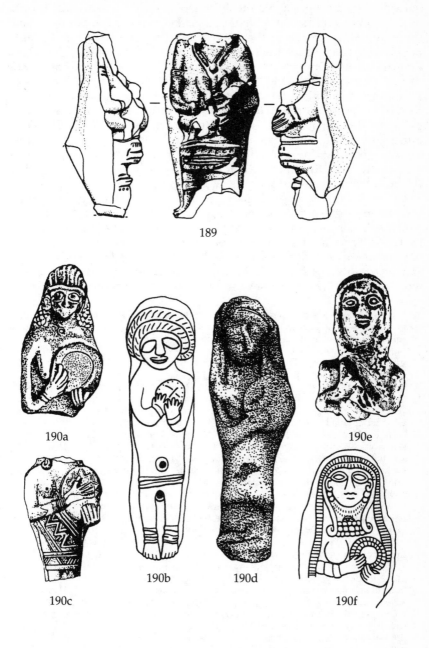

189

190a

190b 190d

190c

190e

190f

Heaven" Jer 7:18; 44:19; see below, §171 and §197).[37] If one seeks a larger iconographic context for the figurines, it is most probably to be found in Syro-Phoenician portrayals of processions shown on ivories, bronze bowls, etc. In addition to female musicians playing double pipes and other female musicians, there is usually a woman who strikes a tambourine (see, e.g., Winter 1983, illus. 259, 412; see below, illus. 229). Figurines from Iron Age IIC – III (Meyers 1987; 1991) hold the handmade disk at a right angle to the upper body, in other words, as one would hold a tambourine, with one hand holding the edge and the other beating the membrane. If the Iron Age IIA-B figurines shown on plaques appear to press the disk against their breasts, that might be explained by taking into account the technical problems connected with producing them from a mold. In addition to the figurines that hold a tambourine, other – admittedly rare – figurines are made showing a double pipe being played (Hebrew *ḥālîl*) (James 1966, fig. 115.2; see Schumacher 1908, 84 illus. 117) and these also show a female participating in the cult and playing (both instruments appear together on the cultic stand shown in illus. 149b).

If the disk is interpreted as a tambourine (Hebrew *top*), an instrument that Old Testament texts describe primarily as being in the hands of women and girls at victory celebrations (see Exod 15:20, Judg 11:34, 1 Sam 18:6, Jer 31:4, Pss 68:26f.; 149:3), then it would seem that the female who is depicted is probably not a goddess but is a cult participant instead.[38]

---

37 Sacrificial cakes are, of course, older than Jeremiah 7 and 44. For early iconographic evidence, see the portrayal of a procession on a fragment of an Akkadian Period relief from Halawa on the middle Euphrates (twenty-third century). A female who participates in cultic activity hold a round disk with both hands at waist level (not in front of the chest!; Orthmann 1989, 75 illus. 44; 78 illus. 47a). Concerning the baking of ash cakes, see Winter 1983, illus. 520).

38 Terra-cotta plaques with naked women who hold a disk in front of the breast or by the side of the body are found in Mesopotamia already during the Old Babylonian Period (Opificius 1961, 54–58). There too the interpretation is in dispute about whether this is to be identified as a goddess or a woman. There are exceptional cases in glyptic art that also depict a goddess with a tambourine: thus, on a cylinder seal from Alalakh Str. IV (fifteenth century), one sees a "suppliant goddess" and a small dancer(?), as well as a "Naked Goddess" (?) depicted frontally, all next to an enthroned goddess, being accompanied by a female harp player who plays a tambourine to provide accompaniment (Collon 1982, no. 47; 1987, no. 664; Salje 1990, no. 6). On a Neo-Assyrian cylinder seal from the ninth or eighth century, now in the Biblical Institute of the University of Fribourg, Switzerland, we see Ishtar rejoicing by playing a tambourine as she receives the weather god, who holds an axe and ears of grain (Keel/Uehlinger 1990: 24 illus. 13). On other Neo-Assyrian cylinder seals, playing the tambourine seems rather to get the weather god fired up for his battle with the sea monster (see Keel ⁴1984 , 43 illus. 48; Glock/Bailey 1988, no. 98). In spite of such portrayals, we cannot regard the tambourine as an attribute of the goddess. This instrument would take on a ritual or cultic function as a rule only when used by humans (see, e.g., Teissier 1984, no. 218). The passage from Lucian's *De dea Syria*, cited by Hillers (1970, 103f.), that characterizes Atargatis/Rheas as a goddess who is carried by lions, with a tambourine and a tower on her head, does not provide sufficient evidence to suggest that the tambourine is clearly an attribute of the goddess in Iron Age II Palestine. The same holds true for the Punic type of image that shows a goddess standing in a temple while holding a tambourine (see, most recently, Pisano 1991, 1146 fig. 2.a-b). In this last example, the woman (or goddess) holds the disk in a manner analogous to the terra-cotta figures that were made in molds, flat against the upper body. This may also have been depicted in this fashion due to technical requirements.

These plaques continue a tradition that began already in Iron Age I with Philistine production of terra-cottas, depicting men and women who are participating in the cult (cultic stands from Ashdod, female mourners; see above, §§74f.). Hesitations about representing the goddess anthropomorphically had apparently influenced the "conservative" local production of terra-cotta figurines in Iron Age IIA in Israel as well. Just as Judges 4–5 describe Deborah as a "mother in Israel," replacing the warrior goddess, perhaps Anat who was associated traditionally with war and battle (Winter 1983, 644–648), so also the portrayal of the female tambourine player replaces the iconographic representations of the goddess in Israel as well.

5. The Iconography of the Jerusalem Temple

§103. The examination of the iconography of Iron Age IIA calls for a few observations about decorative elements connected with the Jerusalem Temple. To be sure, all we know about the temple comes from biblical texts (esp. 1 Kings 6–7 // 2 Chronicles 3–4; cf. Ezekiel 40–41), but some details can become clearer by using some iconographic material for comparison. It is almost impossible even to keep up with the scholarly discussion of this issue (see Keel [4]1984, esp. 99–150; Schroer 1987a; 46–66, 75f., 82–84, 121–133; H. Weippert 1988, 465–474, and many others), so we will limit ourselves, in this study that is dedicated to making use of archaeological source material, to taking note of a few basic points of correspondence.

When one considers the structure as a whole, one notes that the Jerusalem Temple was built in the tradition of the Syrian long-room style, with a porch or vestibule (see A. Kuschke in Galling [2]1977, 338–341; Fritz 1980). Such northern influence is not surprising in light of Solomon's privileged trade relations and technological ties with the Syro-Phoenicians. Buildings having three parts, porch, antecella, and cella, were built already in Middle Bronze Age and Late Bronze Age Palestine, buildings known now as "Fortress Temples." K. Rupprecht (1976) has set forth a thesis that uses a traditio-historical approach – based on a proposed reconstruction of a pre-Israelite legend about the establishment of the cult in 2 Samuel 24* – to suggest that Solomon, contrary to the description recorded in the Bible, did not build the first Jerusalem Temple but rather restored an already existing Canaanite temple that had been taken over by David. Such a conclusion cannot be refuted here merely on the basis of temple typology.

By contrast, the Holy of Holies (*dᵉbîr*), which one imagines to have been an enclosed, windowless (see 1 Kings 8:12) cube made of wood, with sides that each measured about 10 m, appears to have been an adaptation of an Egyptian tradition about a chapel of the gods (Keel [4]1984, 139–144). Taken as a whole, the structure combines indigenous elements with Syro-Phoenician and Egyptian influences. No matter how the temple was decorated in detail iconographically, certain elements dominate the structure as a whole at this site that were common in the iconography of Palestine, particularly during the Late Bronze Age, being passed on then primarily by Phoenician artisans.

§104.   A pair of gold-covered wooden *cherubs* stood in the Holy of Holies with inner wings that were held horizontally to form the throne for Yahweh who was present invisibly – the so-called "one who was enthroned on the cherubs" (*yôšēb ha=kᵉrûbîm*) (1 Kgs 6:23–28; see Keel 1977a, 15–45; Schroer 1987a, 121–130). The cherub throne, not the ancient Israelite ark that was placed under the inner wings of the cherubs, became "the new symbol for the presence of God that functioned architecturally to depict the sacred nature of the temple (. . .). As a symbol that correlated the heavenly and earthly presence of God, it took the cosmic aspects of the temple into account and yet integrated these with the aniconic worship of YHWH by taking over the function of the ark. They now conveyed a theology that asserted that God was present there" (Janowski 1991, 256, 258f.).

Cherubs that are depicted as bearers of the throne on Late Bronze Age ivories have been found in Megiddo (see illuss. 65, 66b; see also the Late Bronze Age griffin throne from Beth-Shean in Rowe 1940, pl. 48A; Metzger 1985, 257–259). Early Iron Age terra-cotta fragments from Megiddo appear to have been part of cherub- (or sphinx-) thrones as well (May 1935, pl. 25 M 5400; pl. 28 M 5403). They provide the only evidence that can support the idea that there was a continuity, right within the country, for cherub thrones, one that stretched from the Late Bronze Age to Iron Age IIA.[39] It is more probable that the impulse for the use of the throne came from Phoenicia, where (sometimes empty) cherub thrones appear in widespread and fairly continuous use from the end of the second millennium all the way into the Hellenistic/Roman Period, being used on Iron Age IIC seals, for example, as the throne for the god Melqart of Tyre (Keel 1978, 32 illuss. 15–17; Gubel 1987, 37–75). A depiction of King Ahiram of Byblos, shown sitting on a cherub throne on a sarcophagus dated to about 1000 and thus approximately contemporary with the Solomonic temple, is well known (*ANEP* nos. 456, 458).

The most magnificent powers in the creaturely world are combined in the cherubs, which are a composite of a lion (the body), a bird (eagle or vulture wings), and a human being (the face). As those who carry the throne, these hybrid creatures reflect the nature of the figure who is enthroned above them, with such figures being primarily though not exclusively kings or male deities (see Metzger 1985, pls. 113–118; Gubel 1987, pls. 4–12) – depicted either as an all-powerful king or as the "Most High God" (see Niehr 1990, 82f.).[40]

§105.   In addition to carrying the throne, the throne cherubs functioned as guards as well, as is shown very clearly by the outer wings

39 On the question about the connection between the epithet "enthroned on the cherubs" and the temple at Shiloh, see above, §98 note 28.

40 On the reconstruction and meaning of the cherubs as the throne of the deity, see Keel 1977a, 15–45; Mettinger 1982, 113–117. Metzger's attempt to explain the throne of the cherubs and the epithet of God by suggesting that the cherubs stand upright on their hind legs and are attribute animals of the Syrian weather god (1985, 309–351), rather than on the basis of the Syro-Phoenician traditions about the throne of the cherubs (1985, 259–279), is based on a comparison of material (both literary and iconographic) that basically shares nothing in common: The concept of "one who is *enthroned* on cherubs" is in no way related to the cherub as a (*single* [in the singular]) animal that carries or pulls the weather god in Ps 18:11.

that were held vertically (Janowski 1991, 250f.). The cherubs certainly appeared as guards that flanked palm trees in the golden, incised depictions that were on the walls and gates of the temple (1 Kgs 6:29, 32, 35; see Ezek 41:17–20, 25) and on the side decorations of cultic stands, on which lions and bulls were also portrayed (1 Kgs 7:29, 35; see Schroer 1987a, 50–54). We have already encountered cherubs and lions that serve as guards on the clay stands at Taanach (illuss. 182 and 184), though that iconography generally points to a goddess being worshiped there. In that context, the cherubs emphasized the numinous power of the entity for which they were standing guard, while the lions underscored the aggressive aspect of the goddess (see also illuss. 52, 55a).

Even though *lions* had belonged to the sphere of the goddess since the Middle Bronze Age, they were brought into the sphere of the male chief gods in Iron Age I as well, becoming attribute animals for Baal-Seth and being included in cryptograms of the name of Amun (see above, §§63–64). In the Solomonic Temple, depictions of lions appear only on the cultic stands.

The lions are much more important in the palace, where they appear by the royal throne, flanking the six steps on each side and being positioned on each side of the seat as well (1 Kgs 10:18–20; see Schroer 1987a, 78–81). As with nearly all Palestinian Iron Age II depictions of lions, the Solomonic lions clearly also function chiefly as aggressive guards (see, in addition, §118) and/or in a specific connection with royalty (see §158), following the Egyptian tradition. The only qualified exception to this observation comes in regard to the lion shown with a caprid by a tree on a painted vessel from Kuntillet ʿAjrud; see below, illus. 219). Taken alone, neither the presence of the cherubs nor that of the lions suggests that they serve a female deity. The cultic stands can thus hardly be linked unilaterally to the cult of the goddess Asherah, as Zwickel (1987) has suggested, especially since the *cattle* (or bulls) that are portrayed on them would suggest links with the sphere of the weather god instead (see illuss. 30, 44f., 142–143, 169a-b; §§89 and 119f.). A scaraboid from Tell el-Farʿah (south), from a tomb dated to about 900, shows a palm tree that is flanked by a lion and a bull (**illus. 191**), thus linking the same three elements that appear together on the stands. Cattle (or bulls) also bear the weight of the "bronze sea," a mighty bronze caldron in the shape of a lotus blossom, symbolic of the waters of the primal sea that have been restrained (1 Kgs 7:23–26). Here as well, the cattle are to be interpreted as attribute animals of the weather god who triumphs over the sea. The link between the Egyptian lotus symbolism and the northern Syrian bull symbolism once again betrays Phoenician inspiration (see Keel ⁴1984, 120–124; Schroer 1987a, 60, 82–85).

§106. Taking traditio-historical considerations into account, the decorative elements on the cultic stands could suggest a connection to both female *and* male deities and are thus quite ambiguous. Their gender is not specifically identified in tenth-century Jerusalem. They are rather a paratactic collection of substitute entities, displayed as a way to express different aspects of the numinous power that resided in the Holy of

Holies as the "Most High God."[41] This presence is shown also by the *palms* that are portrayed on the temple walls, the gates, and the cultic stands. The palms are not flanked by grazing caprids, as in images that show a clear connection with the goddess, as has been seen in illuss. 52–55, 80–82 and 182–184, but they are guarded instead by cherubs. Thus they no longer represent a *Dea nutrix*, an entity that nourishes and that can produce fruit and create life. The palms simply suggest the presence of a numinous power whose gender plays no special role, though they are admittedly placed within the framework of a symbol system that tends to use symbols that point to the "male" system of kingship and order.

§107.   The two bronze or bronze-covered pillars, *Jachin and Boaz*, stood each to one side of the entrance to the temple structure and were either free-standing within or were placed in front of the vestibule or else served as support beams for this vestibule (1 Kgs 7:15–22; see Jer 52:21–23). The description of the lotus-shaped capitals, which is so hard to understand clearly, is probably to be interpreted in the sense of a crown of leaves of the kind known from a more recent Phoenician ivory piece that was made as a furniture inlay (Keel [4]1984, 144f.; Schroer 1987a, 57–60). A painted clay candelabrum from Megiddo might give us some idea of how the "lotus work" with a crown of leaves looked (**illus. 192**). Bronze pomegranates were also hung from the capitals. This pairing brings the Egyptian symbol for regeneration together with a Near Eastern symbol for fertility (Keel 1986, 79–84, 107–109, 134–136; cf., recently, Görg 1991).

In the Late Bronze Age iconography of Canaan, lotus blossoms are to be found in the hands of the *qudshu* type of "Naked Goddess" (see illus. 71), but they are also a symbol of life in the hand of an enthroned figure (see illuss. 65, 67–68). We find different varieties of pilasters with volute "capitals" that flank the edges of clay stands (illuss. 182 and 184) and appear on shrine models (illuss. 188a-b) that are linked to the goddess. Last, but not least, it has been suggested at times that Jachin and Boaz are monumental "stylized trees" or else *asherahs* (Keel [4]1984, 144f.; Schroer 1987a, 59; Zwickel 1990b, 60–62). The two names – masculine in form no matter what they mean – do not support such an interpretation (see now Görg 1991, esp. 92–96). Comparable monumental pillars are mentioned in literary texts that describe the Melqart Temple at Tyre (Herodotus 2.44) as well as the Astarte Temple at Heliopolis (Lucian, *De dea Syria* 28). Jachin and Boaz may have been constructed following a Phoenician tradition of sacral architectural decoration that is not gender specific.

An Assyrian relief from the Southwest Palace of Sennacherib in Nineveh (ca. 690; Barnett 1969, 6f. with pl. I), that depicts the Melqart Temple of Tyre, shows what has been called a Proto-aeolian volute capital. Many examples of this have been found on Israelite monumental structures from Iron Age II (**illus. 193**; see Weippert 1988, 444–447). This decoration stylizes the palm tree geometrically and makes it shorter. These capitals were not used just in temple structures but were used predominantly in palaces, where they characterize the residence and surroundings of the king as the place where the forces of life are at work.

---

41 The openness about the substitutionary entities implies that there could be certain historical situations when circumstances would permit them to be associated with still other entities besides Yahweh.

191

192

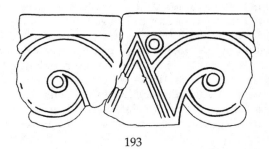

193

These highly stylized palms or volutes, when used in the context of monumental architecture, no longer function as a symbolic substitutionary entity to replace a female deity and do not depict Asherah in stone. They are to be treated as symbols of life and regeneration, without being differentiated in terms of gender.

The ornamental colocynths and open blossoms also belong to the *botanical motifs* depicted on the tendrils that decorated the walls and gates of the temple, along with the palms guarded by the cherubs (1 Kgs 6:29, 32, 34f.; see Schroer 1987a, 47–54). They can be regarded in the same way as many of the previous symbols, as gender-neutral ways to depict regeneration and are still another element inspired by Phoenicia. It goes beyond the evidence to treat them, along with lotus blossoms, cherubs, and the palmettes, as elements that symbolize "afterlife and resurrection" as J. Strange (1985) suggests.

§108.   What remains now is to show in *conclusion*, by way of summary, that the individual elements that were used to decorate the Jerusalem Temple are also to be found in the iconography of Late Bronze Age Canaan or else at least in Syro-Phoenician artistic work that dates to the first millennium. Against this background, the relevant information in 1 Kings 6–7 seems generally plausible. There is no compelling reason to think that the Solomonic Temple was dedicated to another (or possibly even to several other) god(s) besides Yahweh (against Mulder 1989).

In the Holy of Holies – and thus in the very center of the national and religious symbol system of the "United Monarchy" – the cherub throne depicts the presence of a kingly deity. The resident of the temple who was enthroned there was characterized as an all-powerful ruler, next to whom all other numinous entities functioned in servant roles at best. The cattle (or bulls) under the primordial sea and on the cultic stands can only be connected with a male deity of the Baal-Hadad type. It is noteworthy, however, that the lordly power of this deity apparently did not have to be shown by the use of depictions that portrayed his right to rule as being earned in battle. Cherubs and bulls appear only as resting beasts of burden. In the Late Bronze Age, warrior iconography showed Baal-Seth conquering the serpent (§44), succeeded by the iconography in Iron Age I that showed Baal-Seth triumphantly standing upon a lion (§65). Something that would correspond to this is represented only marginally in the iconography of Iron Age IIA (see illuss. 169a-b, 182c, and §84 note 7). In the tenth century and the succeeding time periods, symbolism that would depict the battle against chaos would once again play a relatively important role in both text and ritual. But this paradigm apparently was treated as obsolete when it came to providing iconographic themes to decorate the Jerusalem Temple.

Cherubs and lions could be associated equally with male and female deities during Iron Age II. Their connection with Yahweh thus causes no problem. Motifs and pictorial elements from the flora and fauna that were linked inseparably with female deities, such as doves, caprids by a tree, or the suckling mother animal, seem to be absent entirely from the plans for how the Solomonic temple was to be decorated. Finally, elements from the plant world had become interchangeable pieces within a common iconographic repertoire during Iron Age IIA, no longer differentiated as belonging uniquely with either male or female figures.

Neither the literary sources, nor an iconographic interpretation of the elements that were used, supply any reason to think that there was a partner for Yahweh, even in the background, in the Solomonic temple. It is possible, of course, that evidence for such a being was eliminated as the literary material was chosen and redacted. In the context of our religio-historical reconstruction, possible guesses made *from silence* cannot carry more weight than the effort to interpret the *available* material fairly.

Summary

§109. After goddesses disappeared generally from the iconography of Iron Age I, there was a growing reluctance to depict deities of either gender anthropomorphically during Iron Age IIA. Metal figurines that had been characteristic of the Bronze Age were no longer produced at all. Only a few other media were used and only a few ways to represent the deities anthropomorphically were employed. The most significant were the "stylized, angular Sun God" and the "Lord of the Ostriches." The former has its roots in an Egyptian iconographic tradition and the latter is indigenous. Since, by contrast, the approach that portrayed the deities by using attribute animals, such as the bull, horse, and caprid, or by depicting natural entities (the tree) or by using symbols (the crescent moon, disk) is a typically Syrian phenomenon, the tendency to substitute other images for anthropomorphic depictions of a deity is consistent with the decisive termination of Egypt's hegemony in Palestine and Israel's reorientation culturally and economically toward Phoenicia and northern Syria. The diminished use of anthropomorphic portrayals of deities and the beginning of a tendency to use symbols with astral connotations – still very discreet at this point when compared with what will happen in Iron Age IIC – signals a process of positioning the gods far away or else "showcasing" them in the heavenly sphere. These deities were shown now through the use of images that depicted mediating natural entities that were visible in the realm of human experience, but through which the activity of the distant deities could be detected: trees, plants, animals, and their propagation and prosperity, entities that could now become objects to be worshiped respectfully in their own right.

§110. With respect to *male* deities, it is very apparent that the bull – as the attribute animal of the weather god – is represented prominently (§89), whereas the lion that was so clearly associated with Amun and Baal-Seth in Iron Age I plays a marginal role at best in Iron Age IIA. It should be noted, however, that symbols depicting the bull are found primarily on seals of northern Syria provenance and they appear only occasionally in the local repertoire. Themes of war and domination that were portrayed chiefly during Late Bronze Age II and Iron Age I by the use of images of Baal-Seth and Reshef, with the serpent slayer shown in illus. 182c still part of this tradition, are now depicted using indigenous forms, chiefly the figure of the "Lord of the Ostriches" (§85). The ostriches indicate that this god came from the remote steppe and they also emphasize his aggressive character. These two aspects are shared with this deity by Yahweh, which is why the ostrich is also significant for the Israelite-Judean concept of the deity.

Warrior and military portrayals of a deity serve a legitimating function. A deity deserves to be worshiped because it has shown superior strength in a confrontation with an inimical entity. Yahweh, shown in the Jerusalem Temple as the "Most High God," is depicted in a very different way from what could be seen in the Phoenician iconography that was being used at that time. Here even bulls no longer have their aggressive characteristics, appearing as mere beasts of burden, supporting the "brazen sea," whose waters have now been becalmed (§105). Does the Yahweh of the Jerusalem Temple require no special legitimation? The "angular, stylized figure" (§83) is shown in much the same demeanor, neither fighting nor in triumph, but unarmed and *enthroned* as a royal figure who has no enemies (see also illus. 181).

Perhaps there is a connection between this way to depict the deity peacefully and the generally quiet political climate throughout the region during Iron Age IIA. In contrast to the following periods, military buildings did not yet play a very important part in the monumental architecture of Palestine during Iron Age IIA. The emphasis was much more on palaces and governmental buildings, i.e., on an ostentatious display of great royal power.

§111.   With regard to *female deities*, a few examples of the "Mistress of the Lions" and the "Mistress of the (Mother) Animals" do appear in Iron Age IIA. Do they signal a "return" to depicting the goddess anthropomorphically? Anyone who notes that a "Mistress of the Mother Animals" had never appeared indigenously in Palestine before that time and who recognizes that only a few examples were found even for this time period (§88) would be inclined, at the very least, to regard this phenomenon as evidence for a northern Syrian influence and not as indicative of an indigenous movement. By contrast, the "Mistress of the Lions" that had appeared in Palestine previously, though infrequently (see above, illuss. 4, 70), must be dealt with somewhat differently. She had made an appearance in the northern part of the country in the tenth century, in local terra-cotta production (illuss. 126 and 184) and perhaps even made inroads into production on seals (§87). But this representation of the deity could not survive for very long either. The glyptic art that showed the deity during Iron Age IIA demonstrated an increasing use of images of substitute entities and natural entities when compared with previous periods. In addition to the suckling mother animal, which is obviously identified as female, other images are by and large not identified sexually at all (animals without their young, trees, plants) or are generic symbols of regeneration.

All of this points to a general loss of status for the goddess. The large terra-cottas linked to house cults in Taanach and Pella do show that goddess worship continued to receive attention in Israel during the tenth century, apparently especially in the cities as a part of the local piety. One ought not to write off these large terra-cottas as irrelevant for Israel's religious history just because they might have come originally from the Canaanite element of the population (see Smith 1990, 20). But even the "conservative" terra-cotta production did not simply replicate the traditions of the Late Bronze Age, having come up instead with its own innovations during Iron Age IIA. Naked goddesses pass increasingly from the scene. In their place, we see new types, especially the *female worshipers* who strike their tambourines, by and large replacing the anthropomorphic portrayals of the goddess in Israel at the latest during the course of the ninth century.

VII

Baal, El, Yahweh, and "His Asherah" in the Context of Egyptian Solar and Royal Imagery: Iron Age IIB

§112.   What is known as the "United Monarchy," an era that was at times celebrated and held up as the ideal age for Israel in the biblical historiography written extensively from a Judean perspective, came to an abrupt end with the death of Solomon (ca. 925). From the vantage point of cultural history, Iron Age IIA thus encompasses a relatively brief episode in the history of the region. Iron Age IIB, that now follows, extends from ca. 925 to the last third of the eighth century, lasting thus for about two hundred years, during which time Israel and Judah existed next to one another as separate states, surrounded by other nation-states that were themselves also independent: Moab, Ammon, Aram-Damascus, the southern Phoenician city-states of Tyre and Sidon, and the Philistine league of cities.

In addition to numerous points of continuity in residential architecture, burial customs, handicraft, etc., archaeological research has shown that a particularly noteworthy innovation and unique contribution during Iron Age IIB was an obvious tendency to construct monumental buildings in the cities. Each of the monarchies took great pains to show off its wealth, especially in the regional and district capitals. In addition to the predominant palaces, which supported the necessary functions of administration and representation, military fortifications appear now in greater numbers as well. Garrisons and barracks were built for permanent military forces in the larger centers. Massive fortifications and measures taken to secure the water supply in case of siege (e.g., at Hazor, Megiddo, Gezer, and el-Jib) show a need for taking defensive measures to ensure security. Furnished with the background provided by numerous narratives in the books of Kings that tell of wars with Aram and Moab, as well as about the animosity between Israel and Judah, it is not hard to imagine that defensive measures must have been a priority, especially at the beginning of Iron Age IIB.

The reasons for the loss of the vassal regions that had been subjugated by David and for the breakup of the larger state of Israel into two smaller states, a trend that began already during Solomon's lifetime, are too

194

complex to be discussed here in detail. According to 1 Kings 12, the un-
equal way in which taxes were assessed and the compulsory service that
had to be provided for the Davidic kings who resided in Jerusalem both
played a decisive role. Despite their seemingly archaic slogan, "To your
tents, O Israel!" (1 Kgs 12:16; cf. 2 Sam 20:1), the northern tribes did not
question the appropriateness of a monarchical form of government in
principle and even constituted their own state as a monarchy. This can be
explained against the background of the reurbanization of the entire
country that had been taking place ever since the end of the eleventh
century and was already quite far along. It also shows the leading role
taken by the urban élite in the Israelite independence movement. If the
description in 1 Kings 11–12 is correct, then Egypt itself played an
important role in the events that led to the ultimate separation of the
Northern and Southern Kingdoms.

The presence of the "angularly stylized" group of seals (see above,
§83), an ongoing use of Amun scarabs (§84), and the presence of the
"striking god" in Gezer (§84, note 9) all show clearly that the cultural
influence of Egypt remained considerable during Iron Age IIA, at least
along the southern Palestinian coastal plain. The first pharaoh of the
Twenty-second Dynasty, Sheshonq I (944–923), apparently took great
pains to undermine the concentration of power in Jerusalem and to regain
a foothold in Palestine politically during the second half of the tenth
century. Rebels pursued by Solomon, such as the "Edomite" (or
Aramean?) leader Hadad (1 Kgs 11:14–25) and the Ephraimite Jeroboam,
found political asylum initially in the court of Sheshonq (1 Kgs 11:40,
12:2). Just a few years after Solomon's death, Sheshonq undertook a
campaign, not only against Judah (1 Kgs 14:25f.) but against Jeroboam as
well. Even though it did not last for long, he met with some success, as is
demonstrated by a fragment of a victory stele with the cartouche of that
pharaoh that was found at Megiddo and was originally from Str. IV A
(**illus. 194**; Lamon/Shipton 1939, 60f.; see Ussishkin 1990, 71–74).[1]

One wonders whether this might have been a punitive action against
someone who had once been under his protection. The assumption makes

---

1 A list in the Temple of Amun at Karnak mentions settlements in the Negev and in
central Palestine that had been conquered, but refers to no sites in the Judean hill
country and none in the Judean Shephelah. See Aharoni 1984, 332–340.

sense when one considers that, according to 1 Kgs 12:28, when Jeroboam announced his plan for autonomy as it was explained to those gathered before the bull calf images in Bethel and Dan (see below, §119), he tied it to an exodus tradition that was very critical of Egypt. No matter what was actually behind those events, Sheshonq died shortly afterward and his successors did not continue his aggressive policies. What followed was a time period that lasted about two hundred years, during which time a relatively stable system of small states could be maintained.

§113. The following survey of documents that are relevant from a religio-historical perspective will need to pursue not only the question about continuity with previous developments (esp. §§114ff.) but will also have to ask whether the iconography and epigraphy show any particularly unique religious elements that can be detected in the various small states that now existed next to one another as independent entities. Egypt, as in previous times, clearly remained the cultural center of the entire region. Everywhere one looks, there are clear traces of a fascination with that great power situated on the Nile. And yet, the two states that are our primary focus, Israel and Judah, each went their own way in carving out a relationship with Egypt. After the kingdoms were split, Judah was relegated to the role of being a rather insignificant minor state situated off the beaten path of the main trade routes and was clearly dominated at times by Israel as under Jehoash ben Jehoahaz and Jeroboam II (see 2 Kings 13f. and below, §146), going through a period of cultural stagnation that lasted into the middle of the eighth century. By contrast, because of its close political and economic ties with its northern neighbors, especially the Phoenician cities of Tyre and Sidon and Aramean Damascus, Israel kept control of the major trade routes that passed through its country. From the middle of the ninth century, it regularly joined with the Phoenician cities and with the Arameans in anti-Assyrian coalitions, a clear indication that they shared common political and economic interests.

It comes as no surprise that the differing geopolitical ties maintained by each of the two states show up in different iconography as well. In Judah, iconography was generally limited at first to the continued use of indigenous motifs (see below, §§114ff.) and to provincial adaptations of Egyptian royal symbols (§§156ff.). Specific "religious" themes were brought into the land only late in the eighth century, influenced perhaps by craftsmen who resettled there from the north (§§160f.). By contrast, Israelite/Phoenician speciality crafts that were produced in very significant quantities in the north, from the beginning of the ninth century on, show much greater independence and a greater self-confidence in how the religious symbols that were inherited from Egypt were used (§§148ff.). Syrian-"Canaanite" traditions and motifs that also appear in the north at this same time are generally absent in Judah (§§122ff.).

Adaptations of Egyptian motifs, as well as Syrian-"Canaanite" motifs, are found very prominently and characteristically during Iron Age IIB in the glyptic art (both anepigraphic and on name seals) and on carved ivory pieces. Ivories had enjoyed great popularity already during the Late Bronze Age in Canaan (see above, §§37f.). Production of such pieces had been interrupted, however, by the decline of urban culture and the crisis in international trade. Phoenician-Israelite craftsmanship gave it new impetus during Iron Age IIB. It has been common for such wares to be described simply as "Phoenician." In fact, during the first half of the first millennium, Phoenicia was one of the most active centers for the production and trade of luxury goods that were made using a clearly Egyptian style, such as metal bowls, ivory carving, and similar precious goods. At least some of these specialty items that have been found in Israel, such as a decorated bronze bowl from Megiddo Str. IV A (Lamon/ Shipton 1939, pl. 115.12), may have been imported from Phoenicia. But there seem to have been workshops in the Northern Kingdom of Israel in which such specialty items, especially ivories and seals, were produced.[2] For that reason, it is probably more correct, rather than speaking of a Phoenician "influence" on the Northern Kingdom of Israel, to refer to a "relationship between the cultures of the two regions" (Parayre 1990, 289). This relationship can be seen clearly in the realm of linguistics and epigraphy. The Israelite language was closer to Phoenician (both of them being major Canaanite "dialects") than to the Judahite language (a "peripheral," conservative dialect of Canaanite, comparable to Ammonite and Moabite). Conversely, emphasis on this relationship should not be pressed to the point that one no longer wishes to seek out differences between the Phoenician and Israelite cultures.[3]

When it comes to dating the Phoenician/Israelite specialty crafts, there is uncertainty about whether *ivory carving* began to flourish again already in the ninth century (Barnett 1982, 46–55) or only after the Syrian elephant population became extinct in the eighth century. That would have been the period when those who lived in central Syria (e.g., in Damascus) would have found it difficult to obtain raw material, whereas the coastal regions would have still been able to get ivory from Egypt (I. Winter 1976,

---

2 By contrast, only marginal representation of hand-crafted ivory is available for Judah, even up to the end of Iron Age IIB. One notes that there is only sparse evidence from Lachish, the second most important city in Judah (Tufnell 1953, pl. 63; Ussishkin 1978, pl. 16.2), when compared with what has been found in Samaria, Hazor, Megiddo, and Gezer, which will be discussed in what follows. Among the lesser-known ivory carvings from Judah, which date at the earliest to the end of Iron Age IIB or even to Iron Age IIC, a plaque with a flute player and sheep was found at Khirbet Kirmil. (The exact findspot is unknown; it is currently on display in the Archaeological Museum in Amman. As far as we know, it is unpublished.) An additional piece is a three-dimensional woman's head "from the area around Hebron" (Beit Aula?; Chouraqui 1983, III 475). It is currently exhibited in the R. and E. Hecht Museum in Haifa (Hachlili/Meshorer 1986, 35).

3 It is obviously very hard to differentiate between relationships that presuppose indigenous productive forces and influences that come from the outside the region. Should not one have already had to mention this "relationship between the cultures" for Iron Age IIA, where we spoke repeatedly about a "Phoenician influence" on the artifacts that had been recovered in northern Israel (see esp. §§87 and 111 concerning the "Mistress of the Lions"). The admittedly vague line between influence and relationship can be drawn only by one who pays very careful attention to the history of the traditions (motifs and constellations) and to the geographical distribution of artifacts, to the diffusion of particular motifs and their presence on one or several types of artifacts. Only then can we determine where the centers of production are to be located. This approach allowed us to distinguish, in §111 above, between the group that portrays the "Mistress of the Mother Animals" and that which depicts the "Mistress of the Lions."

15f.). The only fairly large collection of Iron Age IIB ivory and bone carvings from Palestine was found in Samaria. The stratigraphic context of this assemblage does not permit sure dating either to the ninth or to the eighth century. Even literary references to the luxurious aspect of Samaria's ivories are of little help. Relevant biblical materials include references to ivory in that city in the ninth century (1 Kgs 22:39 is probably a reference taken from annals that relate events that took place during the time of Ahab, who was married to the daughter of a king of Tyre) as well as in the eighth century (Amos 3:12–15; 6:4, ca. 750; on the whole topic, see I. Winter 1981, 109–115, 123–127; H. Weippert 1988, 652–660).

Phoenician/Israelite *anepigraphic seal amulets*, mostly scaraboids, were being produced already in the ninth century. The engraving is shallow, and they include individual drawings within a larger scene, identifiable by their use of schematic, parallel lines. With few exceptions, the decorations on their bases are organized vertically; several registers are arranged one above the other, being separated by horizontal lines, or else the impression of registers is created by motifs that are placed one above another without any lines of demarcation. Egyptian solar motifs are the chief decorative elements on these seals (§§148ff.).

Inscribed *name seals* represent a genre that appears for the first time in the Levant at the end of the ninth century and at the beginning of the eighth century. The seal amulets have a characteristic marking: the name of the male or female owner, usually preceded by the *lamed* that identifies ownership, is included along with the iconographic motif. The name of the owner's father is frequently included, generally but not always with *bn* "son of" or *bt* "daughter of" as well. Sometimes a title or an indication of occupation is provided also (for a general overview, see Lemaire 1988; Sass 1993).[4]

The material that follows will be grouped according to unique aspects within the iconography. The discussion of religio-historical issues can be supplemented from now on by epigraphic sources which become more common already at this time and will begin to be available in rich supply by the second half of the ninth century (§§125ff.). But since the inscriptional materials are generally much better known and are discussed in scholarly literature again and again, usually without any attention being paid to non-literary documentation, we will highlight what can be learned from the iconography, which is after all the primary reason for this book. After some observations about the religious concepts that Israel and Judah held in common, based on the iconographical record, (§§114–118), the individual characteristics unique to each will be sketched out.

---

4 As a rule, we will start by using name seals that are on objects whose archaeological context can be known with certainty. But only 10 per cent, at most, of the known Northwest Semitic inscribed seals have been recovered in scientific excavations. All the rest have been purchased through trade in antiquities. Of these, the Hebrew (i.e., the Israelite or Judean) seals make up far more than half of all the Northwest Semitic seals. The difficult question concerning authenticity cannot be discussed here in any great detail (but see Garbini 1982, 163f.; more recently Hübner 1993; Sass 1993).

1. "Lord of the Animals" and Animal Images
in the Near Eastern Tradition

§114.   Now, as well as in earlier eras, the *"Lord of the Ostriches"* appears among the indigenous anthropomorphic figures that are used in both Israel and Judah (see above, §85). The majority of the finds that use this image come from Megiddo, Gezer, Lachish, and from graves that were used over a long period of time, such as no. 32 at Tell en-Nasbeh (end of Iron Age I – Iron Age IIC) or no. 1 at Beth-Shemesh (Iron Age IIA – end of Iron Age IIB). Time and again, the frequently incomplete documentation concerning the archaeological context in which these were found unfortunately does not permit one to differentiate these pieces so as to find out what is unique in Iron Age IIA and in IIB. This is a fundamental problem that repeatedly frustrates every attempt to use the finds from archaeological contexts to sketch the main lines of the development of the religious history.

Nevertheless, it seems that a new type of image, portraying a single ostrich, appeared at the time of transition from the tenth to the ninth century. We find it, among other places, on scaraboids from el-Jib and Tell en-Nasbeh (Dajani 1953, pl. 10.65; McCown 1947, pl. 54.7) as well as on a somewhat more recent piece from Megiddo (Lamon/Shipton 1939, pl. 67.38). This form no longer depicts the anthropomorphic figure frontally and in the center of the composition, but shows him to one side, facing the single ostrich. The raised arms identify him as the "Lord of the Ostriches." But since this gesture could also signify veneration on local scaraboids of similar design, and since the figure does not clearly seem to be seizing the creature by its neck, one cannot say with certainty that this always shows the "lord," since it might more likely be portraying a human worshiper. This last interpretation could mean that the "Lord of the Ostriches" was being replaced at times by his attribute animal (see below, illus. 379). The likelihood that this substitution did occur is shown, for example, on two scaraboids made at the same workshop in Lachish. One shows the traditional constellation while the other shows two ostriches, arranged in *tête-bêche* fashion, without any human figure in the scene (**illuss. 195a-b**; see Tufnell 1953, pl. 43A/44.86; pl. 44A/45.143). It is common to see an ostrich and a caprid, without any accompanying human or divine figure, on scaraboids from the tenth and ninth centuries (Lamon/Shipton 1939, pl. 69f.40; Loud 1948, 153.238).

The ostrich, whose relation to humans is not always easy to figure out and that is tamed only with great difficulty, represents not only a deserted, dangerous and sinister world (see Job 39:13–18; Keel 1978, 64–68; Keel, et al., 1984, 161f.) but also a numinous power that commands respect and honor because it can survive mysteriously at the edge of habitable land (cf. the same ambivalent relationship one has to the crocodile, the scorpion, the lion, etc.). Fear and respect for numinous powers that are demonic is not far distant from fascination with such beings.

§115.   In addition to the typically Palestinian "Lord of the Ostriches," a *"Lord of the Caprids"* also appears during Iron Age IIB. Four fragments of clay vessels have been found in Dan, each showing the identical

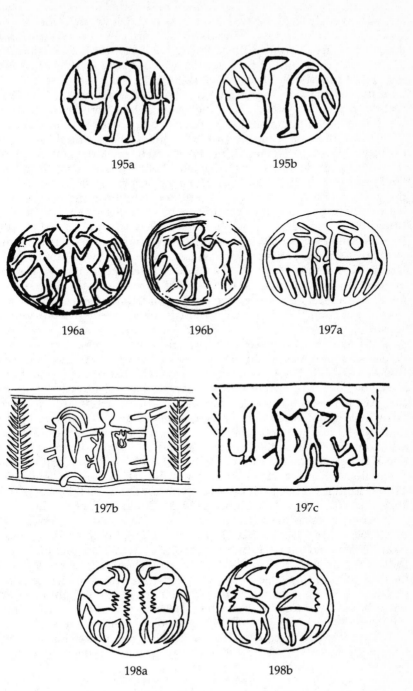

195a

195b

196a

196b

197a

197b

197c

198a

198b

impression of a stamp seal. Two were found in the area of the temenos [Tr.: sacred enclosure] and two in the gate area. They show a male figure wearing a short loincloth who holds, by the horns, two caprids (probably ibexes) that face outward (**illuss. 196a-b**; see Biran 1982, 27, 42 note 25). The motif of the "Lord of the Caprids" was used in Palestine already at the end of the Middle Bronze Age (Keel 1978, 92f. with illus. 19b). To date, only a few pieces from Iron Age IIB have been found,[5] which means that not much can be said about the status of this "lord" and where he was influential. A human figure is positioned between two caprids facing each other, both on a locally produced limestone scaraboid from the countryside around Samaria (**illus. 197a**)[6] and on one from Beth-Shemesh (Rowe 1936, no. SO. 19). One cannot tell whether this shows a "lord" or a "mistress" (see illuss. 165a, 166b). The same problem of trying to identify the gender of a human figure is repeated when the figure is shown between two caprids on a roughly made cylinder seal from Taanach (**illus. 197b)** and between two lions on a piece of similar quality from Hazor (**illus. 197c**; Str. IX, end of the tenth century), as well as in regard to a figure shown between lions on a scaraboid that was purchased in Jericho (Keel-Leu 1991, no. 79). The stylized little trees that serve as scene dividers on both cylinder seals, depicted by using just bare branches, might suggest that this is a goddess who would have been shown naked as well, as in illus. 184. But since no female deities are depicted in glyptic art during Iron Age IIB, it is still probably more likely that this is a "lord."

§116.   The shift toward avoiding anthropomorphic depictions of deities iconographically, on any one of a wide variety of media during Iron Age IIA, held true by and large for Iron Age IIB (for a few exceptions, see below, §§121ff.). Continuing a trend we have observed already for Iron Age IIA (see above, §94), animals, especially *caprids*, are shown repeatedly without any accompanying humans and without any figures that even have a human shape in Iron Age IIB. Whenever these animals stand opposite one another as a pair, as on two scaraboids from Lachish, one of bone and one of limestone (**illuss. 198a-b**), it is very striking that no numinous element is in the middle, whether it be a "lord," a "mistress," a tree (see illuss. 222a-b), or even a small tree (for more on this, see Reisner 1924, II pl. 57a.7; Rowe 1936, no. SO. 29; McCown 1947, pl. 54.22).

Whenever the animals are arranged in *tête-bêche* fashion (Petrie 1930, pl. 48.560; Rowe 1936, no. SO. 36; see illus. 195b), the composition has a more ornamental tone to it, as for example when they are pictured back-to-back (Yadin 1961, pl. 216.13–14; pl. 253.10). They are frequently shown all alone in a striding pose and from time to time near some type of plant (see illuss. 269a-c and, as a representative group from eighth-century Lachish, the three scaraboids in **illuss. 199a-c**; for Megiddo, see Lamon/ Shipton 1939, pl. 67.35; pl. 69/70.17, 34, and often elsewhere).

When compared to Iron Age IIA – with only tentative conclusions being possible because of problems with identifying where the items were found

5 A conoid of "blue glass" found in Gezer (?; Macalister 1912, II 347; III pl. 214.29) may be Assyrian and may date to Iron Age IIC (see Macalister 1912, I 359 with fig. 186).
6 Unpublished, 17.4 × 14 × 9.3 cm; formerly in the Clark Collection, YMCA, Jerusalem, no. 201; present whereabouts unknown.

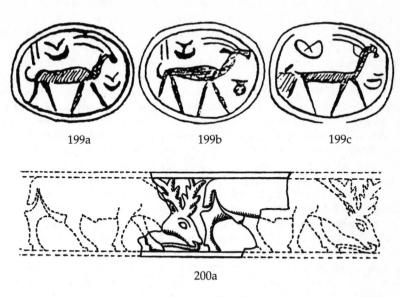

199a   199b   199c

200a

200b

200c   200d

– some differences can still be noted. In the first place, one notices that human worshipers are rarely shown with the caprids (see §94). The scorpion that had been shown so regularly with the caprids (see §93) was portrayed less often in Iron Age IIB (if correct, Grant 1934, fig. 3.16; McCown 1947, pl. 54.19; these could have come from Iron Age IIA). Nursing mother animals (see above, §§88, 92) remain a prominent motif for Phoenician and Syrian specialty crafts (Keel 1981, 128–136) during Iron Age IIB, but they are not shown on the ivories found at Samaria (Crowfoot, et al., 1938, pl. 10.7 can hardly be restored to include them) and the same holds true for the glyptic art produced locally in Israel and Judah during the ninth and eighth centuries (see Shuval 1990, 105–111). Portraying caprids with a little tree seems to have continued for a while right after the beginning of Iron Age IIB (see, e.g., Tufnell 1953, pl. 43A/44.90, 92) but this motif disappears soon after, at least in the glyptic art that was produced locally (for two caprids by a tree, see below, illuss. 222a-c).

The great majority of the caprids depicted on stamp seals that are dated to Iron Age IIB give no indication that they were connected originally with a female deity. As had been happening, to a certain extent, already in Middle Bronze Age IIB (see above, §11), animals are now shown without their gender identified or else they even become important in their own right, as they evoke ideas that they can grant life and prosperity. These four iconographic changes that differentiate this period from Iron Age I-IIA fit together as aspects of one single, clearly identifiable development. Motifs that were connected in a special way to the female deity, or could perhaps even be used as a way to portray this deity, are found very infrequently in the repertoire used by the individuals who made *seals in Israel and Judah* during the ninth and eighth centuries.

§117.   Depictions of "neutral" animals, which had not been used as attribute animals for deities, caused no big problem in either Israel or Judah during the eighth century and not during the seventh century either. Striding male *deer* are shown on an ivory from Samaria, done in the southern Syrian style (**illus. 200a**; I. Winter 1981, 113; see Stern 1978b, 12–15), just as they are also depicted on contemporary pieces from Arslan Tash and Nimrud. There was an apparent preference for *does* in Judah. A doe on the move, apparently seeking food or water, appears on at least a half dozen name seals and bullae from Judah that date to the eighth century and especially to the seventh century (**illuss. 200b-d**; Avigad 1979, 126 no. 9; Bordreuil 1986a, no. 42). The preference by Judean seal carvers for does can hardly be because of the animal's traditional historical connection to the goddess (Keel 1986, 92ff.), but may be explained indirectly by referring to Ps 42:2, where the doe that seeks water serves as a metaphor for the *nepeš* of the praying individual that "craves for life" (*nepeš* is feminine; the *taw* in *'ylt* "doe" has disappeared through haplography). The seal owner uses the doe to represent himself or herself as the person praying and worshiping. The practice of representing oneself directly as the worshiper on a seal amulet, is also to be noted on southern Palestinian bone seals (see below, §§157ff.).

§118.   *Lions* which, along with caprids and does, also belonged to the sphere of the goddess in the Bronze Age and still appeared during Iron Age IIA in the background on the cultic stands found at Taanach and

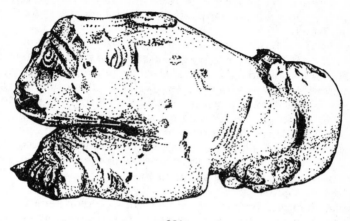

201

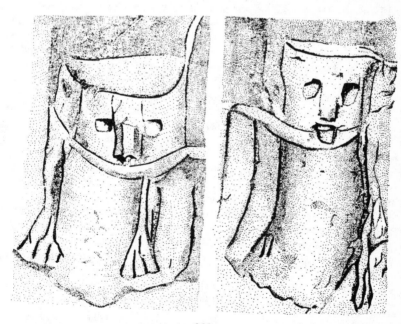

202

Pella (see above, illuss. 126, 182, and 184) have a completely different role to play in the iconography of Iron Age IIB. They either represent or embody the pharaoh on Judahite bone seals (see below, §158) or else they are aggressive guard animals, presented as such already next to Solomon's throne (see above, §105). Their importance can be seen in the fact that they appear on so many different media and are found in both Judah and Israel.

Guard lions are represented in Iron Age Judah on a limestone statue from Tell Beit Mirsim (50 cm long) that was at least partially painted red (**illus. 201**). Since one side (the right side) of the lion is cut flat, R. Amiran (1975) thinks that this was originally one of a pair, the second lion being lost, that together flanked a central object. A ninth-century date for the lion has been disputed.[7] Two crude etchings in a ninth-century tomb from near Tel Eitun (**illus. 202**) appear to show lion-daemons portrayed frontally.[8] The figures flank the entrance to the tomb and look into the grave. Their function was not to secure the grave and the repose of the deceased, but to keep the spirits of the dead away from the living (H. Weippert 1988, 488f.).

In Israel, lions are shown primarily on ivories and on name seals. The theme of the aggressive lion attacking a bull, depicted twice in the Samaria ivories (**illus. 203**; Crowfoot, et al., 1938, pl. 10.2), follows a pattern known from Late Bronze Age ivories produced in northern Syria (see illus. 143a; Loud 1948, pl. 204.3). Indications of Syrian style are also noticeable on two round, three-dimensional depictions of reclining guard lions (**illus. 204**). The holes for fasteners on their sides and the square opening in their backs indicate that these must have been moveable pieces that could be used on furniture, such as a throne or a bed (Schroer 1987a, 382–385). We see reclining lions serving this very purpose on Ashurbanipal's bed on a famous relief from his palace in Nineveh (*ANEP* no. 451 = Keel 1986, illus. 38). Even though this bed, which was probably acquired as plunder and was definitely an import from Syria, also has ivory decorations showing the "woman at the window" (in a scene that also depicts springing lions by the window supports; see below, §123), these animals still do not have any connection to the Syrian goddess, neither in Nineveh nor Samaria. They have now been assigned a new function, that of guard animal, which cannot be linked with any known deity.

S. Mittmann has suggested that the use of extravagant beds, decorated with lions that perform an apotropaic function, helps to explain Amos 3:12, as the prophet attacks the ruthless way the upper class of Samaria exploit others and suggests that they will finally come up empty.

7 See Holladay (1987, 293f. note 125), the most recent scholar to suggest a date in Late Bronze Age IIB for the monumental reclining lions at the gate of Hazor (see above, §31).

8 Wenning proposes that they be identified as Bes depictions (1991a, 945; Wenning/ Zenger 1990, 292 with note 13, were more cautious). The unusual frontal way to present lions could argue in favor of this proposal. But individual details, such as the straight legs and paws (instead of bent human legs and feet) contradict it. In addition, six other heads of animals that cannot be identified as Bes-heads were found in the same grave. Typical Bes attributes, such as feather decorations, beard, and tail, clearly recognizable on a scaraboid from the same grave (see below, illus. 226c), are missing from all of the sculptures.

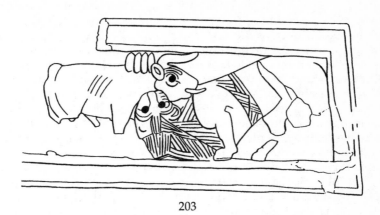

203

204

205a   205b   205c

Mittmann thinks that the lion shown on the beds in Samaria functions as an enduring symbol that "obviously represents Yahweh's power" (1976, 166). Somewhat more cautiously, H. Weippert does "not want to eliminate the possibility that the inhabitants of Samaria thought of Yahweh's power in a *bona fide* way when they thought of the lion's apotropaic role and that, when all was said and done, they were really worshiping Yahweh as the one who promised them the security in the protective presence of the lion" (1985, 17). In fact, Phoenician and southern Syrian art dated to Iron Age IIC offers isolated examples of male deities who stand upon striding lions (see *ANEP* no. 486; Ornan 1992, fig. 35). It is possible that Yahweh was worshiped as such an apotropaic, protective deity in Samaria as well, but images of lions on furniture that was in daily use should hardly be interpreted as a way to *venerate* a particular deity. Such pieces do illustrate, however, that people thought of the lion as a creature that offered powerful protection. When the prophet *compares* Yahweh to a roaring lion (see such passages as Amos 3:8, Hos 5:14; 13:7) that appears now to *attack* Israel, this must have been especially dramatic and shocking for the men and women of Israel in light of this background (but see below, §§223f.).

The original northern Syrian motif of the roaring lion, with its jaws wide open, appears repeatedly on southern Syrian glyptic art dated to the first millennium. Reclining, roaring lions are found on Phoenician as well as Aramean seals (Bordreuil 1986a, no. 1, 88f.). Striding or attacking lions, the latter in a slightly crouching position and with both forepaws held in parallel and somewhat raised, are characteristic of Aramean and northern Israelite glyptic art in the eighth century. There are a few Phoenician examples of this type as well (Buchanan/Moorey 1988, no. 276; Culican 1986, 390 pl. 36.c-d). These are always expensive seals, made of hard stone (jasper, agate, carnelian) or lapis lazuli. The most famous piece of this group, of which over a dozen with the Hebrew or Aramaic names of the owners are known to date (Lemaire 1990a; *Archäologie zur Bibel* 1981, 311 no. 268), is the seal found at Megiddo that belonged to *šmˁ ˁbd yrbˁm*, a high official of Jeroboam II, perhaps the provincial governor of Megiddo (**illus. 205a**). The motif appears also on private seals that do not identify what office the person holds, such as on the seal of *šˁybb* (**illus. 205b**), of unknown provenance, and that of *ˁšnʾl* (**illus. 205c**), a seal impression from Hazor Str. V A that gives no other information about the owner at all (second half of the eighth century; Yadin, et al., 1960, pls. 89.5; 102.23; 162.5). Unlike the horizontal arrangement that is common on the other seals, the seal in illus. 205c is divided, "Phoenician" style, into vertically arranged registers. A winged scarab, shown moving away from the solar disk that is in front of it, is shown below the lion. This motif comes from Egypt and was very popular on specialty crafts made in Phoenicia and Israel (see below, §151). Even though the symbols had a completely different provenance and significance, lion symbolism and sun symbolism could be used in tandem and interpreted in a complementary manner in the Israelite symbol system (see, even now, McCown 1947, pl. 58.74; see also a most extraordinary Phoenician seal, Bordreuil 1986a, no. 5; for Iron Age III, see below, §224). Women's names have not been found to date on lion seals. Clearly Yahwistic names are absent as well but this might be by chance. In any case, it appears that the roaring lions of Iron Age IIB – holding their tails high above their heads in contrast to the more peaceful *qudshu* lions – have no connection with a goddess but are used instead as a way to depict a sphere of power that is dominated by males.

This same may be true for the aggressive, roaring lions that are found in the Southern Kingdom of Judah on other types of Iron Age IIB-C image-bearing artifacts. One is a terra-cotta roaring lion that dates to the eighth or seventh century, supposedly found near Hebron at Beit Aula (**illus. 206a**). Its posture reminds one very much of the animal shown in illus. 205a. Less helpful is an animal that, along with the first letters of the Hebrew alphabet and other scratched figures, is scratched into one of the steps on a staircase that led to the governor's palace in eighth-century Lachish (**illus. 206b**; Tufnell 1953, 85, 118; pl. 48.3). As in the Northern Kingdom, Yahweh could also be depicted in Judah by means of the image of a roaring lion (see Amos 1:2; Joel 4:16; see below, §§222f.). But these images can hardly be interpreted as symbols or attribute animals of Yahweh. Instead, they are a way to express the respect that humans have for this powerful animal (see Gen 49:9; Deut 33:22; for striding lions on bone seals, see below, §138; for lions on official Judean seal impressions dating to Iron Age III, see below, illuss. 268a-c).

2. Israel: God and Bull and Other Baal Figures

§119.　According to the Old Testament, worship of Yahweh that included the use of one or more bull calf images (*'egel, 'ªgālîm*)[9] was the most distinctive element of the state cult in northern Israel that was established by Jeroboam after the "division of the kingdoms" (see Hahn 1981; Schroer 1987, 84–104; Smith 1990, 51, and many others). If one pays careful attention to the message that was proclaimed at the sanctuaries in Bethel and Dan at the same time that the images of the bulls were set up ("Here are your gods, Israel, who brought you up from the land of Egypt . . ."), then one can see that such activities were part of a program that was to give expression to an emancipation intended to free them concurrently from subjection both to Egypt and Jerusalem.

---

9 Tradition vacillates on the number. The Deuteronomistic History counts *two* images of bulls at Bethel, one of which remained in Bethel while the other was placed in Dan, i.e., at the northern and southern centers of power in the kingdom (1 Kgs 12:28–30, 32; 2 Kgs 10:29; 17:16). The book of Hosea generally speaks of only *one* bull calf (image), located according to 10:5f. in Beth-Aven/Bethel, although it is called the "calf of Samaria" in 8:5f. Only in 13:2 is the plural used ("men kiss calves!"). The narratives about the "golden calf" that was worshiped in the wilderness (Exodus 32: Deut 9:16f.; Ps 106:19f.; Neh 9:18) refer to just one bull image; this may be because of the paradigmatic theme of the narrative.

　This literary evidence has caused some to deny that a shrine ever existed at Dan. They suggest that the idea of a bull calf image at Dan was a deuteronomistic fiction. Others suggest that Hosea's reference to just one image means that Dan had been separated from Israel along with Megiddo after 734/733. But there is no question that Bethel had priority over Dan, as is clear already when 1 Kings 12 reports about Bethel's opposition to Jerusalem and its temple. It is highly likely that Jeroboam's measures could have tied in with an older, local, bull image tradition (see above, §69).

Jeroboam's bull images are normally interpreted as being analogous to or in opposition to the cherub throne in Jerusalem that served as a pedestal on which the invisible Yahweh took his place (Hahn 1981, 332–334; see illus. 44) or else as analogous to or in opposition to the ark that was interpreted theologically as a way to show that Yahweh was present (Hahn 1981, 359–362; Schroer 1987a, 100f.). Both interpretations raise the question about whether contemporary iconography shows any parallels.

Images showing an anthropomorphic deity on an animal carrying the deity, so popular in the Late Bronze Age and in Iron Age I (see above, illuss. 44, 70–72, 134a, 137–138), are extremely rare in Iron Age IIB. The animals shown carrying the deity, on two scaraboids from Samaria, can be identified as clearly bovine because of their long tails (**illuss. 207a-b**); on another, from Lachish, the animal is more probably a caprid (Tufnell 1953, pl. 43A/44.80). That a deity is so rarely shown on a bull might be because there was no developed iconography that showed Yahweh and because the type of portrayal that showed the "deity, on an animal that was carrying the deity," had gone out of fashion already at the end of Iron Age I, though this theme was still very popular both in northern Syria and in Mesopotamia right through to the end of the Iron Age.

What is more surprising, however, is that the striding, leaping, or, with head lowered, attacking bovine that appears on the seals of the northern Syrian hematite group and is found rather frequently during the tenth century in local adaptations of the theme (see above, §89) appears, at most, only sporadically in Israelite glyptic art dated to Iron Age IIB; this can be explained at least in part by the fact that Israel's trade relations with northern Syria were more marginal at that time when compared with the cooperative arrangement Israel had with the Phoenicians.[10] A rather tall seal from Samaria, with a square base, shows a worshiper positioned horizontally above a bull (**illus. 208**). The same arrangement appears on a conoid from Acre as well (Giveon/Kertesz 1986, no. 148) and on a scaraboid belonging to a Judean named *gdyhw* (though its authenticity is very much in doubt; Avigad 1989a, no. 2). It reminds one of the seal discussed above in §94 that shows a worshiper behind a caprid.[11] A charging bull is also shown on a bone handle from Tell en-Nasbeh (**illus. 209**). The charging bull furnishes a stock element

10 This finding is in marked contrast to the Ammonite glyptic art that dates to Iron Age IIB-C, in which one sees the leaping or striding bull quite frequently; this is probably a depiction of the god Milcom (e.g., Aufrecht 1989, nos. 1, 3, 5, 11, 13a, 30, 52, 91f., 132f., 135f.; cf. Hübner 1993). The bull protome is just as uncommon as striding and leaping bulls on Palestinian seals during Iron Age II. It also can be associated with Milcom in Ammonite glyptic art (e.g., Aufrecht 1989, no. 79). It is possible that a relationship between the "Weather God" and the bull might be indicated on an unpublished scarab from Achzib that shows a bovine head in front of a "Striking God" (Jerusalem, IAA no. 48–630) and on a cylinder seal from Hazor Str. V A (end of Iron Age IIB) that shows a bovine with a blossom(!) behind a "Striking God"; this motif clearly makes use of Late Bronze Age traditions (Yadin, et al., 1960, pl. 162.2).

11 In addition, this constellation is depicted in two parts on the two flat surfaces of a rectangular plaque that was found in Str. IIIa (ca. 950–850) at Tell Abu Hawam (Hamilton 1935, 27 no. 142). The form of the seal indicates of course that it was manufactured during Late Bronze Age II.

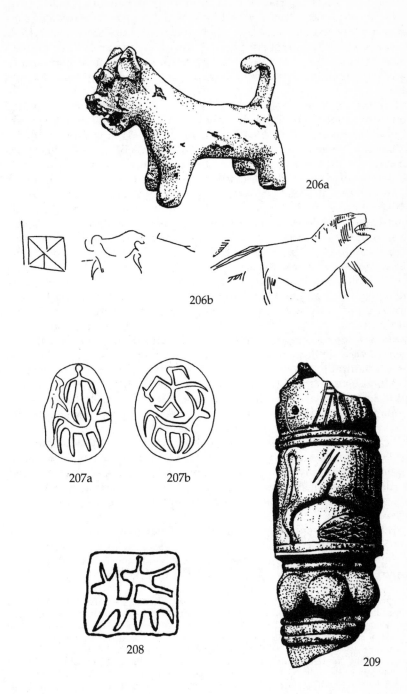

206a

206b

207a 207b

208

209

for the repertoire of Syrian ivory carvings (see above, illuss. 143a-b). But it is just as doubtful that the bull represents a deity there, which is the same conclusion that was drawn about the guard lions discussed in §118. Nevertheless, one cannot simply treat this motif as purely "decorative," since deities are portrayed anthropomorphically on two comparable handles, one of bone and the other of ivory (see below, illuss. 210 and 214).

Other evidence that shows striding bovines on seals comes from the Southern Kingdom of Judah (see above, illus. 185a, from Beth Shemesh) or else belonged to Judahites (Galling 1941, no. 31, a seal belonging to *šmᶜyhw bn ᶜzryhw*) and these could hardly have been connected with Jeroboam's bull images. Most of the relatively common terra-cotta depictions of bovines that date to Iron Age II have been found in Judah (or southern Palestine). Holland (1977, 126f.) counts 143 examples, of which 75 are from Tell Jemmeh and 32 are from Jerusalem, while only three come from Bethel and five from Samaria.[12] Most of these terra-cottas date from the later Iron Age IIC period. For that reason, they are of no help in understanding a specifically Israelite worship of Yahweh that incorporates bull calf images.

When all the evidence is considered, the conclusion is clear: images of bulls play no dominant role in the specialty crafts of Iron Age IIB Israel, which is certainly not what one would expect in light of the literary traditions concerning the significance attached to the cultic images of Jeroboam. Interpreting the presence of the bull from a religio-historical point of view, in the sense of something that is *longue durée* [Tr.: survives for a long time], this seems to favor supporting the thesis advanced by H. Motzki, among others (1975; cf. Ahlström 1984, 11), that Jeroboam's cultic activities started nothing new – nothing that had to be spread by propaganda and that thus would have called for appropriate small items to be produced – but simply attached new significance to a traditional cultic image that was at Bethel, probably a *leftover* from the Late Bronze Age or from Iron Age I (see illuss. 44f., 142), which was probably connected originally with El rather than Baal (cf. the place name Bethel, "house/temple of El," as well as 2 Kgs 23:15, according to which an *asherah* was in this sanctuary in the seventh century as well; on this, see below, §137).

§120. E. A. Knauf suggests that the existence of more than one bull image, according to 1 Kgs 12:28 and other passages, indicates that a triad of deities was worshiped at Bethel, citing evidence from fifth-century papyri from the Jewish military colony at Elephantine that mention in

---

12 The personal name ᶜglyw that is recorded on Samaria Ostracon no. 41 should probably be translated "Bull calf of YW" instead of "YW is a bull calf" (as suggested once again by Ahlström 1984, 11). ᶜgl is connected to the one who has this name and not to the cultic image (Fowler 1988, 120, 235, 254). In addition, see a (so far) unique lapis lazuli scaraboid in the shape of a resting calf that was found in the area of the citadel at Samaria (Crowfoot, et al., 1957, 88 no. 27, pl. 26.8). It is to be noted that 83 zoomorphic vessels in the shape of bovines were found near the cultic site E207 at Samaria, dating to the end of the eighth century (Crowfoot, et al., 1957, 78f., 81f.; Holland 1977, Type J). It is not clear what relationship such vessels, which had some specific functional use, would have had to the deity or deities that were worshiped there.

addition to Yahweh, among others, two deities with the names '*ntyhw*, "'Anat-Yaho" and '*šmbyt'l* "Ishim(-Bethel)" (1988b, 155f.). But beside the fact that it is completely hypothetical to posit specifically the existence of a triad, since in addition to the other named deities, Bethel, 'Anat-Bethel, and Herem-Bethel are mentioned in those texts as well (on the texts and their interpretation, see Winter 1983, 494–508; see below, §217) and since one never finds a written reference to three bull images, the second bull image of Jeroboam might, at most, be connected to the god '*šmbyt'l*, "Ishim(-Bethel)."[13] But the image of the bull calf ('*egel*) cannot in any way, shape, or form depict Anat as a (hypothetical) partner for Yahweh. A nursing mother animal (see above, §78) or a horse (see above, §§40, 98) could have been used to portray Anat, but neither of these is mentioned in the sources that describe the temple at Bethel.

§121. On Iron Age IIB specialty items produced by Phoenicia and Israel during the eighth century one sometimes sees a youthful four-winged god with no beard, most often shown striding, who wears a short loincloth. Portrayals of this god seem to be found far and wide in Phoenicia and Israel, but none have turned up in Judah to date. The best preserved example is on a bone carving from the southern Syrian group, recovered from a private home in the upper city at Hazor. Str. VI (first half of the eighth century). The youthful god shown in this piece holds in each hand a bough from a little stylized tree (**illus. 210**). Bone handles with the same or at least very similar decorative elements have been found at Gezer (Macalister 1912, II 343f.; III pl. 214.32), and the same figure is probably portrayed on an anepigraphic scarab found at the same site (**illus. 211a**; on the crude iconography, see Bordreuil 1986a, no. 20). Though the god appears bareheaded here, on Northwest Semitic name seals from the eighth and seventh centuries he generally wears a head covering, modeled after the double crown of Egypt (Galling 1941, nos. 91–93; Giveon 1978, 112–116; Hestrin/Dayagi-Mendels 1979, no. 30.99; Bordreuil 1986a, nos. 19, 61, 105; Avigad 1990a). Instead of the little tree shown in illus. 210, he holds a blossom in each hand on the name seals.

The four wings indicate that the god is a celestial figure, so it makes sense that the image of the crown on the name seals is altered so extensively at times that the crown looks more like a "pair of horns" with a solar disk or even just like a disk by itself (e.g., Hestrin/Dayagi-Mendels 1979, no. 99; see illuss. 241b-c). Youthfulness and a pair of wings were characteristics of the god Baal already during the Late Bronze Age; doubling the pairs of wings in Iron Age IIB heightens the celestial aspect by emphasizing the omnipresence of this god. The blossoms (or the tree) indicate that the god is very closely associated with vegetation. Blossoms or branches appeared in the hand of the weather god already in Middle Bronze Age IIB (see above, illuss. 32, 33b-c). The youthful god with four wings is most likely to be identified as Baal or as one of the mediating entities that served the "Lord of Heaven" (Keel 1977a, 200–204).[14]

13 At Ugarit, the god Ishim is linked with Shagar in a "molecular-like" relationship in the name *šgrwitm* (*KTU* 1,148.30f.).
14 Two owners of seals of this group had names that included the theophoric element *b'l* (Giveon 1978, 114f.). The element *'l* is used once (Bordreuil 1986a, no. 20) and

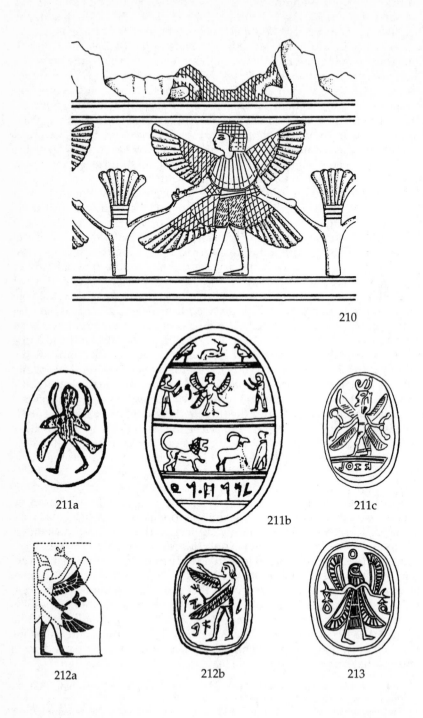

210

211a

211b

211c

212a   212b   213

Four closely related name seals have been found that each have four pictorial registers. It is not yet known exactly where they come from. It could be that they were made in a Phoenician, an Aramean, or an Israelite workshop. The owners' names (*š'l, mnḥm, mqn, ṣdqy*) and the iconography certainly make it at least possible that they are Israelite.[15] Three of these seals portray a four-winged scarab, flanked by worshipers, in the middle one of the three registers that have images. On one piece, belonging to a certain Menahem (**illus. 211b**), the two worshipers flank a youthful god who has four wings, a figure that is apparently inter-changeable with the scarab beetle as a way to portray the sun god (see below, §151; see Gubel 1991b, 919f.). The god's short loincloth is quite typical of images dated to the eighth century. On similar images that date to Iron Age IIC, such as on a seal found near Dan that belonged to ʿz̧ (**illus. 211c**), the god is portrayed in the Assyrian manner instead, bearded and wearing a long robe (concerning Iron Age IIC anepigraphic scaraboids, see Petrie 1930, pl. 48.566; Lamon/Shipton 1939, pl. 67.27).[16]

Perhaps it is also Baal, or a subordinate genius attached to his entourage, who is shown on a scarab from Megiddo as the male figure with two wings offering a blessing (?) (Lamon/Shipton 1939, pl. 67f.1). This figure has no beard either, wears a short loincloth, and also appears with blossoms in his hand, just like those figures in the Egyptian-style "silhouette-inlay" (also known as the *champ-levé*) group of Samaria ivories (**illus. 212a** and Crowfoot, et al., 1938, pl. 14.8–11; see I. Winter 1981, 110f.). Baal can also be shown wearing a long garment, open in the front, which is how he appears on the ivories from the eighth century (Crowfoot, et al., 1938, pl. 4.1, 3). Female figures are portrayed in the same location on Syro-Phoenician ivories from Nimrud (e.g., Barnett ²1975, pls. 44f S 69, 68 S 160, and often elsewhere). But they are not represented in the repertoire of Samaria. An eighth-century seal that once belonged to an Israelite by the name of *yw'b* and that shows this same figure (**illus.**

---

kmš is used once (Galling 1941, no. 92 = Timm 1989, 171f. no. 4). A passage that goes back to Sanchuniathon in the "Phoenician History" of Philo of Byblos identifies the four wings as signs of the leadership of Kronos = Ilos/El (*Praep. Ev.* I 10.36f.). The images of El and Baal are not always distinguishable during the first millennium; both are heavenly deities that have solar connotations during Iron Age IIB (see below, §144). Chemosh (as also, in certain ways, Yahweh), belongs to the national gods of the Baal type and might be recognizable in this image as the young, four-winged deity. But the theophoric element in the personal name only rarely corresponds to the deity portrayed on a seal. The decoration of the seal would have been selected on the basis of the preferences of the male or female owner of the seal. That individual's parents would have been responsible for their given name (see below, §125 note 23).

15 See below, §151 note 141.

16 A good photograph of the piece from Tell el-Farʿah (south) permits one to see that the depicted deity is not female (Keel 1977a, 196, 199 illus. 144) but is rather a bearded male deity. The same seems to be true of the piece from Megiddo (Keel 1977a, 199 illus. 145). The original is missing, so an autopsy is not possible. A female deity might be portrayed on the Moabite seal belonging to *kmšṣdq* (Galling 1941, no. 92; so also Keel 1977a, 196, 199 illus. 143; see especially the Syrian ivory depiction in Keel 1977a, 199 illus. 142); Timm, nevertheless, has raised questions about this identification (1989, 171f. note 24).

212b) has been found in a tomb at Carthage, one that dates centuries later (Galling 1941, no. 97).

Youthful gods and youthful genii of this and similar types, depicted along with attributes from the plant world, appear commonly on anepigraphic scarabs and scaraboids that date to Iron Age IIB(-C) (James 1966, fig. 117.1; Giveon 1985, 132f. no. 67; Petrie 1930, pl. 35.426). A youthful god, without wings but apparently armed, appears on a scaraboid from Tell el-Far'ah (south) (Petrie 1930, pl. 39.435). A figure with two wings, on an unpublished seal belonging to *pdh*, differs from the one shown in illus. 212b only in that it has a falcon head (Sass 1992, fig. 208). A four-winged god depicted on a seal from Tell el-Far'ah (south) with a solar disk above his head (**illus. 213**) has the head of a falcon as well. In addition to the way youthful Baal is depicted in illuss. 210–212, this particular piece shows a variation that uses Egyptian as well as solar elements, most clearly the four wings and the blossoms in his hands, to suggest that the youthful, four-winged Baal and the sun god were related, if not one and the same. All these items just mentioned allow celestial aspects to take center stage and document Baal's development into a solar-connoted "Lord of Heaven" (see below, §153). As regards how this god's influence spread geographically, he shows up in the Northern Kingdom, as well as on Phoenician, Aramean, and Moabite name seals. Variant forms of the same imagery appear on anepigraphic seals from Philistine areas. No examples of this type of depiction have been found to date in Judah (concerning sun symbolism in Judah, not apparently connected with Baal, see below, §§160–162).

3. Isolated Anthropomorphic Images of a Goddess

§122. Scholarly discussion concerning the religion of preexilic Israel and Judah has been dominated in recent years, because of discoveries of texts at Kuntillet 'Ajrud and Khirbet el-Qom, by the question about whether Yahweh had a female partner (see below, §§134ff.). The discussion has not given adequate consideration to the fact that the dominant aspects of a symbol system show up in different geographic regions and on different media (see above, §4). In the book of Hosea, which achieved its present form substantially already about 740/730, thus at the end of Iron Age IIB, and which serves as the chief witness to the conflict between "Canaanite" and "Israelite" religion in eighth-century Israel, the polemic against Baal, or against cultic practices connected with Baal, is reiterated repeatedly (Hosea 2:10, 15, 18f.; 9:10; 11:2; 13:1).[17] A comparable, explicit polemic against a female

17 Passages that criticize cultic activity at the high places in Israel never refer by name to the central male or female figure addressed in this cult. Scholars thus disagree about whether the supposed cultic practices should be thought of as relating to the Canaanite/Phoenician Baal, to a "Canaanized" Yahweh, whose image may not have looked all that different from the image of Baal during the eighth century (see below §§125, 153), or to a goddess (Astarte or Asherah; thus, most recently, Braulik 1991, 119ff.).

deity[18] is never delivered by Hosea. There may possibly be a few implicit allusions to a goddess (Hosea 4:18; 14:9).[19] This matches the fact that the iconography, which has appeared to date in Palestine/Israel on the specialty craft items that are typical of Iron Age IIB in Phoenicia and Israel, has produced only two or three depictions of *female* deities depicted in a style typical of the Near East. We dare not ignore this fact as we investigate the possible position and significance of a (hypothetical) partner of Yahweh.

Two of these specimens come from controlled excavations and were found in the area around the acropolis in royal cities of the Northern Kingdom of Israel. One is an ivory ointment spoon from Hazor Str. VI (first half of the eighth century) that, like the contemporary bone carving shown in illus. 210, is a product of southern Syrian specialty crafts (**illus. 214**). The handle is in the form of a stylized palmetto tree, while the underside of the spoon shows a female face, with hair parted, and a dove can be recognized in the locks on either side of her head. Tradition history connects the iconography shown on the underside with the Bronze Age motif that linked the goddess and the dove (see above, illuss. 16, 19–21). The artistic rendering allows *each* side of the spoon to show unique aspects of the same goddess, as if depicting the two sides of her body. When the spoon would be in use, the stylized palmettos on the front (top) would show the visible aspect of the goddess in the foreground, her body as it were, while the back side or underside would depict the hidden aspect of the goddess that remained in the background. One ought not to describe this unique configuration as nothing more than a "random arrangement of unconnected elements" (H. Weippert 1988, 659).[20]

Since the goddess shown on the ointment spoon can be interpreted as a late manifestation of the Late Bronze Age Tree Goddess (see esp. §44, with illuss. 81–82), it is possible to identify the figure as Asherah (on Asherah iconography, see also below, §§130, 137ff., 181). The object is transparent in its portrayal of the goddess, but yet it does not depict her anthropomorphically in the foreground. The iconographic element that shows a figure transparently rather than openly will be encountered once again below (illus. 219, with §142) and matches the literary evidence in the book of Hosea when it makes a veiled allusion (or allusions) to a goddess. It ought to be emphasized that this technique of using a

---

18 One or even two such deities have been posited conjecturally by Ackroyd (1983, 252), Weinfeld (1984, 122f.), Loretz (1989) and others, following a conjectured reading for Hos 14:9b suggested by J. Wellhausen: *ʾanî ʿanātô wᵉʾašērātô*. For those who reject such a reading, see Olyan 1988, 19–22; Hadley 1989, 109–111; Braulik 1991, 121–123, and others.

19 N. Lohfink (cf. also recently Braulik 1991, 118–123) suggests translating the text-critically difficult passage in Hosea 4:18b *āhᵃbû hēbû qalôn māginnehā* as "they love the (goddess) whose shield is shame" and is of the opinion that she is an antagonist who opposes Yahweh. But there is no evidence for "a type of image . . . in which the goddess is adorned with a shield" (Braulik 1991, 119f. note 68) for Iron Age IIB(-C) Israel.

20 On the link between the dove and cosmetics, see also a much more crudely carved ivory ointment bowl from Beer-sheba that might date to the same period (Aharoni 1975b, 170, pl. 17B).

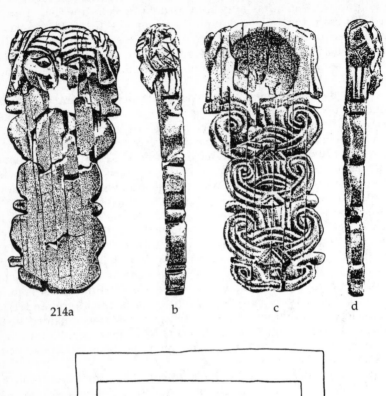

214a   b   c   d

215

transparent way to portray images is clearest in depictions that are of Phoenician origin or inspiration (illuss. 214 and 219; see also illus. 215).

Is the Asherah in illus. 214 perhaps the consort of the four-winged Baal, shown in illus. 210, which was recovered from a neighboring house? We cannot answer the question because the two figures never appear together in the same picture (see, however, above, illus. 182). The fact that Baal and Asherah are never paired in Northwest Semitic inscriptions, appearing together only in biblical texts of deuteronomistic redaction, suggests that it is more likely that this pair had no such relationship. But even if these two figures could be placed together, this would not show two deities interacting sexually with one another, as we encountered in the iconography of Middle Bronze Age IIB (see above, §§23f.).

§123.   The second image of a woman that might be a portrayal of a goddess is found on an ivory plaque from Samaria and uses the well-known motif of the "woman at the window" (**illus. 215**; for other fragments of the same motif, see Crowfoot, et al., 1938, 29; I. Winter 1981, 111), "in any case the work of a student, not an imported piece" (H. Weippert 1988, 660 note 49) – but clearly a student work that attempts to replicate a Phoenician pattern. It features the full face visage of a woman who appears in a window above a balustrade. There is disagreement about whether the woman is a goddess herself or – imitating the role of the goddess in any case – is to be identified as a priestess or cult prostitute (Winter 1983, 296–301). In contrast to the detailed execution of parallel pieces found at Arslan Tash and Nimrud, the figure on the Samaria ivory wears no jewelry on her forehead, which O. Keel thinks would be the characteristic element that would identify her as a temple slave (1981, 193–212; see illuss. 190e, 325). Three frames, with each one that is closer to the center being depicted smaller than the one that is farther outside, as if to show distance, must be understood as a way to portray a temple (see a similarly enthroned goddess, around whom the same type of "frame" is shown, on a Phoenician ivory in Barnett [2]1975, pl. 65 no. S 149).

It is noteworthy that when the viewer looks at the "woman at the window" and at the goddess on the ointment spoon from Hazor, the viewer's attention is drawn to the *face* of the woman that appears in the window or the shrine. In contrast to Bronze Age images of the "Naked Goddess," with their accentuated genitalia and breasts, these pictures signal an important shift in how images were designed, an issue that we will have to consider again in the next chapter (§§190ff.).

§124.   Images of the *"Naked Goddess,"* shown with a variety of attributes (wings, flowers, lions, etc.), are quite widespread in the Syro-Phoenician ivory repertoire during Iron Age IIB (see Barnett [2]1975, 100f., pls. 43, 72–77, 89f., and often elsewhere; Winter 1983, 181–186). But they are apparently absent from the material known to us from Israel and Judah. *Bone amulets* portraying a naked woman, with no accompanying attributes, in what has been called the "concubine" posture with arms on her thighs (**illus. 216** from Tell el-Farʿah [south] = Petrie 1930, pl. 40.482–497; see pls. 27 above left; 35.419f.; 38.226; 1928, pls. 21.3, 3A; 33.27; 1937, pl. 28.1; Bliss/Macalister 1902, pl. 83.1 = Winter 1983, illus. 389),[21] probably analogous to images of the goddess on the small terra-cottas, are known thus far from Iron Age IIB levels in the Philistine territory, but seem not to have been accepted into the repertoire in Israel or Judah.[22]

Contrary to what is often thought to be the case, *terra-cottas* from Iron Age IIB with images of a "naked goddess" have not been found "by the hundreds," but are relatively rare by comparison with the so-called pillar figurines that appear in the following periods. Besides this, these figurines also seem to have been limited in use to the Philistine coastal region. A beautiful example comes from Ashdod Str. VIII (**illus. 217a**; Dothan, et al., 1967, 162f. fig. 43.4; cf. figs. 43.6; 46.3; Dothan 1971, 138f. fig. 64.2). Two molds for the production of such plaques have been found at Tel Batash (Timnah), in the border region between Philistia and Judah (**illuss. 217b-c** show the positives pressed from these molds). They were found in the Str. III city destroyed in 701, dating thus to the very end of Iron Age IIB, the same dating as for a plaque from Samaria (Crowfoot, et al., 1957, pl. 11.6). In general, the "Naked Goddess" seems to be represented only marginally in Israel and Judah during Iron Age IIB. This is especially true for 850–735, from which time period come the inscriptions that are so critical in answering the question about a partner, specifically about Asherah as a female partner. By contrast, plaques continued to be produced in Israel with depictions of the woman with a disk (see above, §102, esp. illuss. 190d-e) that we interpreted not as a goddess but as a female tambourine player.

Finally, the so-called pillar figurines came into Palestine in great numbers only toward the end of the eighth century. If Holladay's thesis is valid, the list he assembled (1987, 280) showing that the (few) figurines found in the north begin to appear barely one generation earlier than they begin to show up in the south, as well as the fact that the pillar figurines are found everywhere during the seventh century, may indicate that their appearance is part of a phenomenon connected indirectly with the advance of the Assyrians, with the resultant changed territorial boundaries and alterations in the market structure, a phenomenon that is characteristic of the next period and will be discussed in the next chapter in the context of Iron Age IIC (see below, §§190ff.).

In the *glyptic art* of Iron Age IIB from Israel and Judah, there is not a single seal known to us on which a goddess might have been depicted anthropomorphically. The absence of the goddess from Hebrew name seals is especially significant. One single Hebrew name seal, dated at the earliest to the end of the eighth century, shows a "naked goddess" (see below, illus. 331). Even if it was supposedly found in Israel, it is highly likely that it was an imported piece, to which an inscription was added later. This one seal cannot alter the overall impression that no significant role was played by a particular goddess, or by any goddess at all for that matter, in the symbol system of Israel during Iron Age IIB. Since the seal

---

21 It is noteworthy that the artifacts were often found near Bes-head amulets (see below, illus. 224).

22 Other "parallels" from Samaria, Gezer, and Beer-sheba (Macalister 1912, III pl. 221.17f.; cf. II 416; Crowfoot, et al., 1957, pl. 26.9; Aharoni 1974a, pl. 59B = Winter 1983, 100 with illus. 16) are dated to the Hellenistic Period.

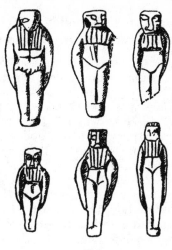

216

217a

217b

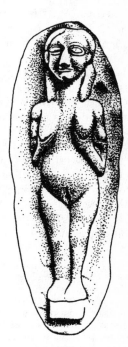

217c

belongs to the very end of Iron Age IIB at the earliest and was not made using a local, long-standing tradition, it is rendered of no significance in the discussion about Asherah.

4. Theophoric Personal Names with Inscriptional Documentation

§125.   In 1986 J. H. Tigay published a study that concentrated on, and provided detailed documentation for, an examination of the question about whether there was polytheism or monolatry in the religion of preexilic Israel, a study in which he used the "external evidence" of Iron Age Hebrew inscriptions (see above, §3). The first part of his study examines the more than 1200 personal names documented in inscriptions from Israel and Judah that date to Iron Age II-III, by means of which he seeks to identify which deities are mentioned and also tries to determine the relationships between Yahwistic and non-Yahwistic personal names. Tigay correctly begins with the presupposition that the religious concepts of preexilic Israel and Judah should be, at least to some extent, reflected in the proper names recorded in the onomasticon. Conversely, he maintains that the proper names in the onomasticon may provide an important source for reconstructing the religious symbol system of Israel and Judah.[23] In this part of the study, Hebrew name seals and ostraca from Samaria (Iron Age IIB), Arad, and Lachish (Iron Age IIC, see below, §209) are naturally the principal sources. The second part of the study investigates non-onomastic aspects of these and other inscriptions from the same perspective.

The most important source of onomastic evidence dating to Iron Age IIB is a group of over 100 ostraca – clay sherds inscribed with ink – found in 1910 in debris that had been leveled out to make a floor for two long rooms of a storage house in the immediate neighborhood of the palace of Omri, in the citadel area of Samaria (Reisner 1924, I 227–246; Lemaire 1977, 21–81; cf. Davies 1991, 39–57). The ostraca are significantly older than these two storage buildings that were destroyed in 722. They may have come from (or at least from near) a previous building on the same site that would have dated to the first half of the eighth century. As one would expect at such a site, the ostraca are of a purely administrative nature. They include stereotypically formulated information about wine and oil shipments that were sent in the ninth, the tenth, and the fifteenth

---

23 Note Tigay's fundamental observations: "1) Names express the views of those who choose them, normally parents, and not necessarily of those who bear the names. 2) In Northwest Semitic personal names, even members of polytheistic groups rarely invoke more than one deity in a single name. (. . .) 3) The beliefs and attitudes expressed in Northwest Semitic personal names are simple and elemental. They express thanks for the god's beneficence, hope for his blessing and protection, submission to his authority, and the like. They are not theoretical, theological statements. Thus even if the names of a particular society should reflect the predominance of a single deity to the total exclusion of all others, this would tell us only that the members of that society did not expect from other gods the kind of actions that are mentioned in personal names, and perhaps that they did not worship other gods. The absence of other gods from the onomasticon would not by itself tell us whether that society denied the existence or divinity of those gods" (1986, 6f.).

years of an unnamed king[24] to those who lived in the palace in the capital city and came from localities that were all in the vicinity of Samaria and that were probably part of the royal estate. Since, as a rule, one or more senders (estate managers?) and a recipient of the shipment are mentioned, these ostraca offer rich documentation for the onomasticon of the Israelite upper and middle class. Among the 50 different personal names, a significant number use the short forms, without a theophoric element. These are not helpful in answering the question of which deities were worshiped in Israel during the eighth century. Seven names with the theophoric elements *'ḥ, 'l,* or *'m* cannot be connected unequivocally with any *specific* deity (see Pardee 1988, 129–131).[25] Eleven names contain the theophoric element *yw* and a half dozen have the element *b'l* or some rudimentary form of it (see Smith 1990, 41, 65 note 3). We encounter *'byw* and *'byb'l* alongside each other, and the verbs used with names that include the element *yw-* or *b'l* are generally typical of the piety that was expressed when personal names were given, so that no different impression is left when either *yw-* or *b'l* was used. One can no longer assume that an "ethnic" distinction is being made, in the sense that Israelite men had names that included the element *yw-* and that Canaanite men were given names that included the element *b'l.* It is probable that both elements, *yw-* and *b'l,* refer to the same deity, namely Yahweh, who was worshiped also as Baal in Iron Age IIB Israel (cf., in the Old Testament's Yahwistic transmission of tradition, the names *'îšba'al, y'rûbba'al, m'rî(b)ba'al,* and *b''alyāh*).[26] Toward the end of the period, the two names for the deity were apparently no longer interchangeable. The three ostraca that were found in the excavations of the Joint Expedition of 1931–1935, dated to just before 722 (Lemaire 1977, 245–250), contain no *b'l* names.

§126. In addition, three Egyptian names appear on the ostraca from Samaria: *qdbš* "Bes has created" (?; for the significance of the god Bes, see below, §131),[27] *'šḥr* "belonging to Horus,"[28] and *'nmš* "the beautiful one is on the pool(?)." The last name might be connected with the god

---

24 Lemaire (1977, 39–43, 79–81) follows the lead of Aharoni and divides the entire collection into two groups, dating one group to the ninth and tenth years of Joash (i.e., 794–793) and the other to the fifteenth year of Jeroboam II (i.e., 773).
25 The theophoric element *'l* is no longer connected as a personal name with *one particular* deity, but apparently was used in both Israel and Ammon as an appellative for the respective national god of the land (see Smith 1990, 24; Tigay 1986, 19 with note 60; see below, §126, note 31). *'l* is far and away the most frequently occurring theophoric element in personal names in Ammon (Jackson 1983, 518; Israel 1990, 325–335). See also below, §§238, 179f.
26 A reference to the cultic worship of Yahweh might be provided by a fragment of a votive pitcher that includes the incised inscription *lyw* (May 1933–1934), but the inscription [. . . ?]*lyh* on the rim of a bowl from Samaria can hardly be interpreted in the same way because the spelling is unusual; one would expect *-yw* in Samaria (Reisner 1924, I 238, 243; II pl. 55b; concerning the entire topic, see Tigay 1986, 24f.).
27 No. 1.5, following the reading of Lemaire 1977, 29 and 54; this is doubted by Tigay 1986, 75 with note 1.
28 No. 13.3f., following the reading of Lemaire 1977, 31 and 49f.; this is doubted by Tigay 1986, 76 with note 12, who would derive the name from the Hebrew *šḥr* "black." The same name, with the Yahwistic patronym (*'šyhw*), is on a bulla from Judah that dates to about 600 (Avigad 1986, no. 32; Tigay 1986, 66 with note 9).

Nefertem, who is often found in the iconography of Iron Age II Palestine (see below, §202), or possibly in the depiction of that deity as a sun-child in a blossom.[29] The iconographical motif that shows the deity on a flower represents, to be sure, primarily the youthful sun god or Harpocrates (on the youthful Horus, see below, illuss. 240–241), and the name '*nmš* could certainly refer to this god. It is especially doubtful whether these two gods, who were both associated with the lotus, were clearly differentiated in eighth-century Israel. The presence of Horus in the Iron Age IIB Israelite onomasticon should not be surprising in view of the significance of this and many other concepts that were connected with the solar deity (or with Horus) in Israelite/Phoenician iconography (see below, §§141ff.).[30]

Other deities are not represented in personal names on the ostraca from Samaria. Keeping the object of our study in mind, it is very important to point out that neither personal names on the ostraca nor Iron Age IIB Hebrew seal inscriptions provide so much as a hint about worship of a *goddess* in Israel (Tigay 1986, 14f.). The only evidence for a goddess is found in an Egyptian name with the theophoric element '*s* "Isis" on a (clearly Phoenician) name seal from Samaria (see below, illus. 252). The giving of clearly Yahwistic names and the absence of goddesses in personal names are indications that, at least in one sense during Iron Age IIB, "personal piety" in Israel (and Judah) was shaped by Yahwistic thinking and had aligned itself in a significant way with the "official religion" of the Israelite state.

One must take into account the limitations of onomastic documentation: the absence of the name of a goddess or of goddesses among the personal names that were used during Iron Age II cannot, in and of itself, convince someone that female deities played no important role in Israel during the eighth century. H. Weippert has noticed the contrast, during the Middle Bronze Age, between the theophoric personal names (a majority referring to male deities) and the iconographic images (a majority depicting female deities; 1988, 240). Tigay has pointed out, for example, that the goddesses Atirat and Anat are important figures in mythological texts in Late Bronze Age Ugarit, but that they play only a marginal role in the onomasticon (1986, 20). Among Phoenician/Punic personal names, there is a great discrepancy – especially significant for the *asherah*-problem – between the very few names that include the element "tinnit" and the thousands of dedicatory inscriptions in honor of this goddess. The lack of names of a goddess or of goddesses in Israelite personal names dating to Iron Age II could simply be related to the rules that were followed when names were given (Pardee 1988). And yet, the evidence in Israel and Judah is quite remarkable when compared with the hundreds of Phoenician/Punic personal names that contain the element '*štrt* (the name of the goddess Astarte, partner of the Phoenician Baal; see Olyan 1988, 36f.).

---

29 The popular view that Nefertem could be represented as a god on a flower is disputed by Schlögl (1977, 30ff.).

30 Horus is the best-documented foreign god in the onomasticon of Israel and Judah from Iron Age II, being mentioned seven or eight times. But, with the exception of one example from Samaria, all the others come from the southern part of the country and date to Iron Age IIC (see below, §202 with note 94).

In any case, seal inscriptions and ostraca give nothing more than a quick impression of the names used by the Israelite establishment (Tigay 1986, 10),[31] and the names represented in the onomasticon are almost exclusively male. But even if the glance into the world of the religious concepts that were at work in preexilic Israel obtained in this way is very limited in scope – as Tigay emphasizes continually in his methodical, very careful and reflective study – he still relies on empirically verifiable data that must be taken into consideration. As supporting evidence, his work can give additional plausibility to the diagnosis that has been set forth in this book, here chiefly through the use of iconographic evidence, showing that female deities played almost no role at all in the symbol system of Israel (and Judah) during Iron Age IIB.

At this point in our study, we will examine the famous and frequently discussed inscriptions from Tell Deir Alla, Kuntillet ʿAjrud, and Khirbet el-Qom that seem to be diametrically opposed to our own thesis that there was a dominant Yahwistic religion in Israel during the eighth century and that Yahweh had no consort.

5. Tell Deir Alla: El, Shagar, Ashtar, and Shaddayin

§127. At *Tell Deir Alla*, in the central Jordan Valley and not far from the mouth of the Jabbok – at a site often identified as the biblical Succoth (Gen 33:17; Josh 13:27; 1 Kgs 7:46, and often elsewhere), excavators working in 1967 in a room whose function was unknown came upon an inscription that was written with ink on a plastered surface. The room belonged to a phase of the settlement, identified as M = IX, that was partially destroyed in an earthquake and that can rather assuredly be dated to the end of the ninth century (Ibrahim/van der Kooij 1991; Wenning/Zenger 1991, 182–187). The inscriptions must therefore also date to this time. Alternate dates suggested by paleographic analysis have not been convincing.

The excavators were able to arrange 119 fragments from this plastered wall to form 12 so-called combinations, though only two of these provide a longer, coherent text (Hoftijzer/van der Kooij 1976). *Combination I*[32] bears the superscription *spr [b]lʿm[.br bʿ]r.ʾš.ḥzh ʾlhn*, "the writing of

---

31 De Moor has carried out a religio-historical investigation of the Israelite and Judean personal names that are found in the *Bible* up to the time of David. He accentuates particularly the differentiation between El and Yahweh names (1990, 10–34). He asserts that Yahweh and El would have been identified with one another already during Iron Age I. He notes a marked decrease in the use of ʾl names over time, seeing this trend as a development from a Yahweh/El religion to a pure Yahweh religion. His assessment is that the dominant Yahwistic onomasticon shows "that people could not afford to admit their sympathy for polytheism openly. They could not name their children after pagan gods and had to be careful not to introduce elements of polytheism in the personal names they chose" (1990, 11). This view assumes that there were elements of social pressure and censure at work that simply cannot be validated in the sources that date to Iron Age I-IIB.

32 The most important editions and translations in the German language are: Müller 1982; H. and M. Weippert 1982; Hoftijzer 1986, 139–144; on the whole topic, see now the articles published in the symposium volume, edited by Hoftijzer/van der Kooij 1991.

Balaam, the son of Beor, who sees the gods," thus recording a message that goes back to the same seer who is the central figure in Numbers 22–24. Combination I from Tell Deir Alla contains what is currently the oldest evidence for the genre of prophetic narrative found so frequently in the Bible (Lemaire 1991, 44f.; M. Weippert 1991, 164–174, 177). In this text, one can confidently say that mention is made of the deities Shagar and Ashtar (see above, §91), who are connected with the fertility of animals, of "divinities" in general (*'lhn*), and of *šdyn* "Shadday deities." It is possible that the last two groups of deities may be one and the same.[33] The god El[34] may also be named here indirectly.[35] In any case, this clearly polytheistic text deals with a number of deities of both genders that have come together for a meeting, possibly with El in the role of the head deity. This text does not permit one to deduce that El had a female partner; Asherah, a possible candidate, is not mentioned. But based on the "profile" of the deities named, one can say with confidence that a female goddess (probably Shagar) was acknowledged to have the skill and competence to cause disaster and to disturb the overall order of the world.

If Combination I seems to be beset with numerous problems of interpretation, *Combination II*[36] is that much more difficult to understand. This is apparently a prophetic text as well, but Balaam is not mentioned on the extant fragments. Commentators vacillate between a "positive" and a "negative" evaluation of the importance of this text.[37] Unlike Combination I, it can at least be said here with confidence that the deity identified as El plays an active role, though no other deities make an appearance.

The contents of these two combinations provide no hint that they are related. But both of them suggest that they are presenting portions of the content of one or more written scrolls in graphic form (see *spr* in I 1, II 17?). In their present form, they seem to record traditions that had already undergone a process of transmission (see Lemaire 1991, 50–52). In fact, the function that the texts served at the place where they were found is

---

33 Concerning chiasmus and parallelism in Lines 5f., see esp. H. and M. Weippert 1982, 92; M. Weippert 1991, 156.

34 In the combination: *kmš*ʾ.*'l* "according to the utterance of El," at the beginning of Line 2 (thus H. and M. Weippert 1982, 84; M. Weippert 1991, 155). The reading of the name of the god *Šmš* in Line 6 is less sure (most recently, also M. Weippert 1991, 154, 156; Sentence XX, 170), which would also imply the mention of a *female* sun goddess.

35 The narrative reports that *'lhn* appeared to the seer and gave him a message (from El?). Balaam passes the following morning with fasting and weeping. He shares some type of report about the vision with his family: a catastrophe was going to occur that would be caused by the goddess Shagar(?). The *šdyn* had in fact besought the angry goddess, within the assembly of the gods (*mwʿd*), for restraint; they perhaps had even sought a change of heart, but they appear to have been unsuccessful. For this reason, the seer called upon his people, perhaps identified as the opponents of "Sha[gar?]," to change their behavior. The text ends with a stereotypical threat of a "world turned upside down."

36 See at least Müller 1982, 231–238; Lemaire 1985, 275–277; Hoftijzer 1986, 145–148.

37 The discrepancy can be illustrated by the difficulty in translating *byt.ʿlmn* in Line 6, which can mean either "house of young people" or "house of eternity," i.e., the grave (on this, see Müller 1982, 231.)

not known.[38] In any case, one can assume that the men and women who passed these traditions on and who lived in the valley of Succoth did not assume on a merely "theoretical" level that a variety of deities of both genders really existed. Those that are presented as the most active among them (El, Shagar) are depicted as being able to interfere directly in the world of humans and were venerated in the cult, as were also the Shaddayin that were tied more closely to family piety.

§128. The texts from Tell Deir Alla make it clear that local worship of El was taking place in the central region of the land east of the Jordan at the end of the ninth century, as one can ascertain from the Bible as well (see Gen 32:31; Num 23:8, 19, 22, 24; 24:3f.), a worship that was probably not Yahwistic and that certainly was not monolatrous. Apparently at least one female deity was worshiped along with El, but the texts do not give any indication that Shagar is to be considered El's partner.[39] Within the framework of this particular study, one must ask about what importance should be attached to these texts for the religious history of *Israel* proper during Iron Age IIB. Are those who pass these texts down to others to be considered in any way as belonging to Israel?

Paleographically and linguistically, the texts show themselves to be related to the Aramaic script and language, possibly peripherally Canaanite, but they certainly do not preserve Israelite or Phoenician inscriptions (on the disputes concerning linguistic classifications, see the various positions summarized in Hoftijzer/van der Kooij 1991; Müller 1991). The language in the texts is probably just as indigenous as the religious concepts that are described therein (see Knauf 1990b, 16f.; M. Weippert 1991, 159–164, 178f.). Viewed historically, it is very doubtful whether the Tell Deir Alla settlement was under Israelite control at the time that the inscriptions were recorded there. Transjordan was ruled by Damascus from 841 on (2 Kgs 10:32f.), which means that religious developments in the region during the space of about a hundred years would have been separated completely, or at least to a great extent, from a Yahwism that was certainly never deeply rooted there anyway. Only toward the end of the reign of Jeroboam II (in other words, a long time *after* the destruction of Tell Deir Alla Str. M/IX) did the Northern Kingdom of Israel apparently attempt to recover Gilead (Lemaire 1991, 36–41). One cannot know how these historical events affected the religious development of the region.

38 Is this a sacred inscription written here because it was a pilgrimage site or a memorial place associated with the seer Balaam (see H. Weippert 1988, 626f.; M. Dijkstra in Hoftijzer/van der Kooij 1991, 217)? As at Kuntillet ʿAjrud, there was absolutely nothing in this empty room, on whose walls these inscriptions were found, to indicate that it had any sacral function (see also Wenning/Zenger 1991, 189). The conjecture that the room served as a place for sleeping in order to receive visions (Ibrahim/van der Kooij 1991, 21) is just as speculative as Lemaire's hypothesis that this was a school room (1991a, 52ff.). Wenning/Zenger expand on Lemaire's thesis and think that this was a "'gathering place' for a local prophetic society (. . .) that considered the famous seer Balaam to be their 'patron' and prophetic 'teacher.'" They would in essence have gone about learning the "basic forms of prophetic speech" by using the wall inscriptions (1991, 192; cf. 2 Kgs 4:38; 6:1f.).

39 Winter (1983, 491–494) has still not changed his mind about the existence of such a relationship.

The inscriptions from Tell Deir Alla shed a most instructive light on the presence and significance of El, Shagar, and Shaddayin on the periphery of the Transjordanian countryside. Similar religious concepts may have been current in the incipient Yahwistic piety of the clans in the culturally similar periphery in southern Judah (Mamre, Hebron, Negev) and in the Samarian hill country (note particularly the El and Shadday traditions in the patriarchal narratives of Genesis, evaluated critically by Köckert 1991). But since the discoveries at Tell Deir Alla Str. M/IX are not simply witnesses to a merely "personal" or "clan" piety but rather offer written (and pictorial[40]) documentation for an "official religion," that was passed down by those who were educated, shows that here – in contrast to the caravanserai of Kuntillet ʿAjrud, which was under Israelite control, and in spite of much more epigraphic evidence than is available at that site – there is absolutely no reference to Yahweh, which means that one cannot assume an Israelite presence for Tell Deir Alla Str. M/IX. The Tell Deir Alla inscriptions are therefore not directly useful as primary sources for reconstructing the religio-historical developments in Israel.

6. Kuntillet ʿAjrud, Khirbet el-Qom and *"Yahweh's Asherah"*

§129. About 50 km south of Kadesh Barnea, not far from Darb el Ghazza, the old overland route from Gaza to Elath, University of Tel Aviv excavations at *Kuntillet ʿAjrud* in 1975–1976 uncovered the remains of a caravanserai that can be dated to the first half of the eighth century (**illus. 218**; for a more precise historical classification, see below, §146). The finds remain published, now as then, in only a brief summary fashion and in a preliminary form (see esp. Meshel 1978; Weinfeld 1984). Paintings and inscriptions on two large storage jars (pithoi) have created a sensation in the scholarly world and have dominated the discussion. Other discoveries that are at least as important for the interpretation of the site have been practically ignored. At this point, we can hardly document completely the wide range of views concerning Kuntillet ʿAjrud, so will limit ourselves to a selective critical analysis and discussion of the most important points. For methodological reasons, we will interpret the pictorial evidence first, completely separate from a study of the inscriptions.[41]

Both pithoi were found in the gate area of the well-preserved, fortress-like main building. There are two rooms in the building and both have low benches in them. Pithos A came from the north room that was right next to the passage leading from the gate to the courtyard.

---

40 Take note of the stylistically perfect image of a cherub on a limestone plaster fragment that was found at the same site: Hoftijzer/van der Kooij 1976, pl. 15; 1991, 243 fig. 2.

41 It is to P. Beck's credit that the paintings were discussed separately at first (1982) and that there was no premature effort to correlate the depictions and the inscriptions. Dever (1984, 31f. note 4) and Margalit (1990, 288f.) are wrong to criticize this approach and to fault it. As Dever suggests, it might in fact be true that "this purely art-historical approach confines itself to description." But his own work shows that we cannot gain an adequate understanding of the depictions without serious preliminary work.

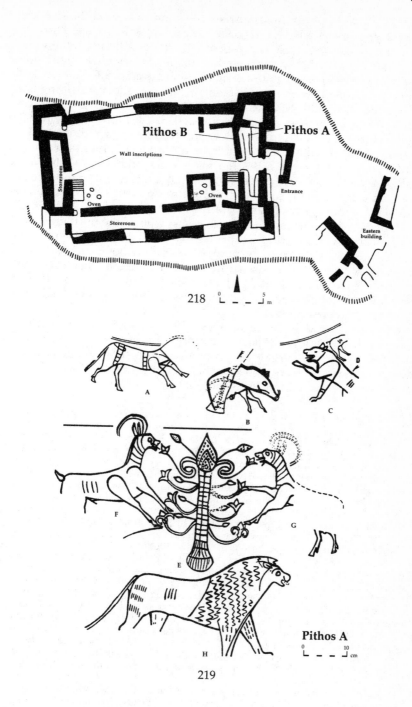

218

Pithos B   Pithos A

Wall inscriptions

Storeroom

Oven   Oven   Entrance

Storeroom   Eastern building

0 ___ 5 m

A

B

C

F   G

E

H   Pithos A   0 ___ 10 cm

219

On one side of this pithos, between the handles and on the shoulder (**illus. 219**), one sees what is left of a scene painted with a brush, showing a leaping, harnessed horse (**A**), a boar (**B**), an erect lion (**C**), the hindquarters of a caprid drawn considerably smaller (**D**), a stylized tree below it with lotus blossoms (**E**), with caprids flanking it, associated with it, and eating from it (**F-G**), with the tree being positioned above a striding lion (**H**). On the other side of Pithos A (**illus. 220**), from left to right, one sees another harnessed horse, perhaps striding (**I**)[42], a suckling cow with calf (**J**), and above it, situated in relation to and feeding from a lotus tree (**K**), an erect caprid (**L**), that one would have to turn 90 degrees to see in its correct position,[43] then two Bes figures, viewed frontally (**M, N**), and finally a seated female lyre player (**O**). The paintings on this pithos are all done using a red color, in contrast to those on Pithos B, where black drawings are found as well. The paintings on Pithos B (**illus. 221**), which was found in the courtyard next to the west wall of the northern room with benches, depict a striding caprid (**P**), the raised tail of a lion (**Q**), an incompletely preserved nursing cow (**R**), a striding bovine (**S**), and two representations of humans, one of an archer (**T**) and the other a series of five men with arms upraised (**U-Y**). On two additional sherds, neither of which has any connection with either of the pithoi, a bear and a seated male figure can be recognized.

§130. Even a quick glance at illuss. 219–221 shows that the various paintings on each side of the jars do not form a coherent composition, but are rather made up largely of a set of motifs that are positioned paratactically either next to one another or above one another,[44] motifs that will be discussed briefly in what follows.[45]

---

42 The alphabetical markings that are assigned to the individual motifs in this treatment of the depictions are somewhat different from the way each item was identified by P. Beck (Pithos A: A-H, S-X; Pithos B: J-R), since that approach seemed too confusing. The raised letters in the paragraphs that follow (^A or ^B) indicate the pithos on which an image was found.

43 The interpretation that these two motifs are part of a constellation is more probable than that the motifs ^AJ-K depict a "chasse au bouquetin" and are thus part of one group (Puech 1988, 191 note 6). P. Beck regards ^AK-L as a variation on the constellation that shows caprids grazing in a lotus thicket (1982, 20; on this topic, see Keel 1984, 86–88 with illuss. 82–93; 1986, 108, 110f., 140f.,). But take note of the fact that Pithos A(!) "must have been lying on its side at some stage, since the inscriptions were written in various directions" (Beck 1982, 43).

44 This observation can be verified by taking note of the stylistic differences, the different thicknesses of the lines, the different colors, and an inconsistency in terms of the content (cf., e.g., ^AA/B, ^AC/D, ^AJ/M, ^BY/S). Only a few of the motifs can be thought to form a group (^AE-G and H; ^AK-L; ^BU-Y; possibly ^AM, N; ^AB,C?). The very penetrating analyses of every feature that were carried out by P. Beck have established the probability that the individual motifs were painted by different hands. A significant time period must have elapsed between the time when ^AK-L were painted (by the same hand as ^AE-G?) and when ^AM was later added to the vessel. During this time period, some of the older drawings would have faded. ^AN was done shortly before ^AM (see below). Beck identifies three different artists (1982, 43).

45 Since P. Beck's publication, the best discussion that analyzes the pithoi at Kuntillet 'Ajrud was written by J. M. Hadley (1987b; 1989, 143-201). She, as well, has tried to keep the inscriptions, which she treats first, separate from the pictures. Unfortunately, she discusses only the paintings of the Bes figures (^AM-N), the (female) lyre player (^AO), and the stylized tree above the lion (^AE-H).

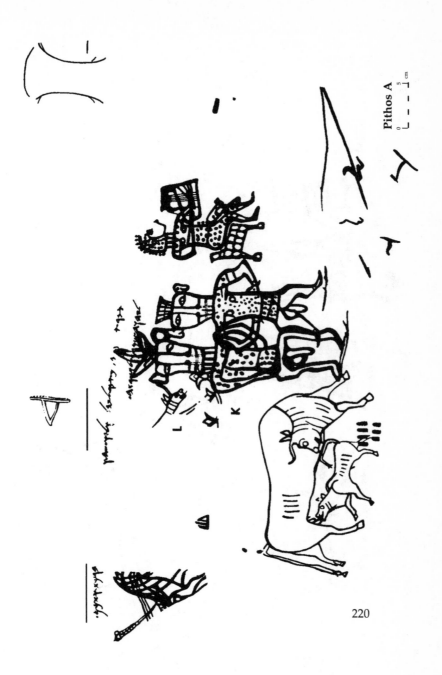

Pithos A

220

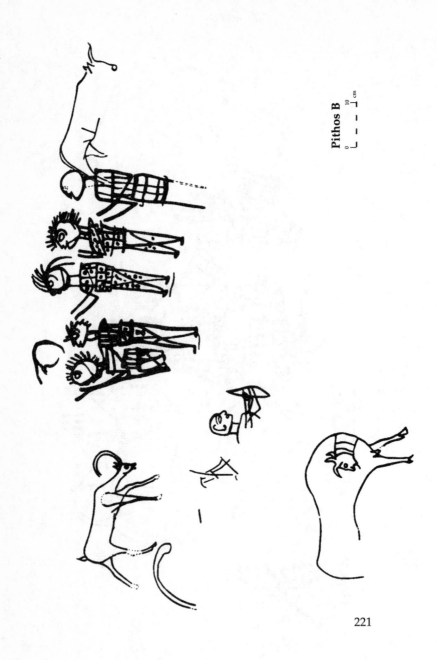

Pithos B

221

The two harnessed *chariot horses* (^A^A, ^A^I; Beck 1982, 19–22) belong, like the *archer* (^B^T; Beck 1982, 40f.),[46] to the repertoire of royal prestige iconography, as documented from the mid-ninth century particularly on the Assyrian palace reliefs and related media, such as ivory, that are used to portray such pictorial themes. This imperial iconography originated in northern Syria, from which point it also spread to Phoenician workshops that made small artifacts. These pieces were from movable sets depicting scenes of the hunt or battle that only indirectly – because they were transmitted via the royal ideology – had a "religious" character as well. At least one picture of a horse, painted on the outer wall of the east building and very poorly preserved, must also have been visible (Beck 1982, 52f. no. 8). Since this same facade also shows a picture of a (besieged?) city (see below, illus. 237), a military context is probable, such as is shown on Phoenician metal bowls (see Markoe 1985, no. Cy4). Because this context is depicted on the wall so near to where the jars were found, the asssumption makes sense that these could be "preliminary sketches by the artist who was assigned to paint the wall" (H. Weippert 1988, 671). Of course, the reverse is also conceivable; perhaps the wall paintings made a special impression on those who traveled through and on those who were stationed there in the desolate surroundings and inspired someone on the spur of the moment to paint a copy of the motifs depicted thereon onto a jar (see Beck 1982, 43, 60–62).

Images depicting a single striding *animal* (^A^D, ^B^P, ^B^S) are also part of the repertoire of both Phoenician and Israelite artisans (Beck 1982, 18f., 41; see above, §§116ff.). The raised lion's tail in ^B^Q reminds one of the way the guard lions were depicted in illuss. 205f. The boar, found so far only in northern Syrian art (^A^B; Beck 1982, 20f.), and the attacking lioness, which stands opposite him (^A^C; Beck 1982, 18f., also with northern Syrian parallels), are perhaps to be interpreted together as portraying an animal battle scene. In favor of this interpretation is the fact that, in contrast to all the other animals, the lioness is turned to the left and her posture calls for a figure to be shown opposite her.

Drawn by two different individuals, both images of a *suckling cow* (^A^J, ^B^R; Beck 1982, 4–13) and the two representations of *caprids at the lotus tree* (^A^E-G, fragmentary ^A^K-L; Beck 1982, 13–16, 20) are specifically religious depictions of blessing and both are connected in the historical traditions with the goddess. The suckling mother animal (see above, §91) is absent from the Samaria ivories as well as from Israelite glyptic art during Iron Age IIB. A tree flanked by caprids – in a different artistic style, to be sure – is shown on the Samaria ivories (Crowfoot, et al., 1938, pl. 13.6). The engraving on the base of a recently published Phoenician-Aramean name seal is more closely related to the images at Kuntillet ʿAjrud (Lemaire 1991b, no. 24). Palestinian glyptic art usually shows the tree flanked by caprids as a stylized palm, such as is seen on a seal impression from Tell Jemmeh (**illus. 222a**), on an obsidian scaraboid from Tell el-Farʿah (south) (**illus. 222b**), and on an almost identical seal impression from Jericho

---

46 On this, see the fragmentary drawing of an archer (or lyre player[?] or worshiper[?, Stern 1978b, 21]) that was incised on a sherd from Hazor Str. V (Yadin 1961, pl. 189.28; 356.6).

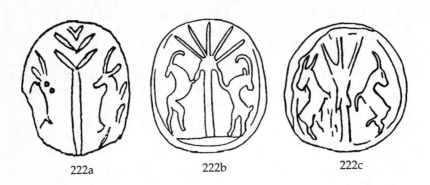

222a   222b   222c

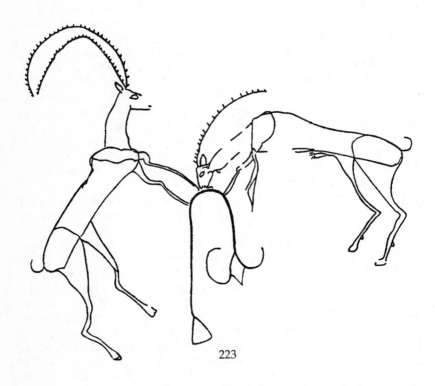

223

(**illus. 222c**). The imprecise documentation about where these pieces were found permits only a rough dating to somewhere during Iron Age II-III. Caprids are also shown by a lotus "tree" etched in a very rudimentary fashion on a pithos from Lachish that is dated to the late seventh century (**illus. 223**; see Stern 1978b, 19f.).

Iron Age IIA terra-cottas from Taanach and Megiddo (see above, illuss. 182–184) that were discussed in §§97–98 furnish more significant parallels for understanding the composition. Their stylized trees, flanked by caprids, were clearly connected with the goddess. R. Hestrin, referring to the second cultic stand from Taanach, makes a good case when she suggests that the *lion* (^AH) under the tree in illus. 220 is not a separate motif (thus Beck 1982, 17f.) but that ^AE-H are to be understood as one complex composition (1987a, 222; see Schroer 1987a, 38; Hadley 1987b, 204f.). ^AE-H, taken as one complex composition, is by far the largest and most prominent depiction on the pithos. In contrast to ^BQ, the lion's tail hangs in this picture, so this animal should not be associated with the roaring guard lions. As is also true of other Late Bronze Age depictions, it functions as an animal that carries someone, with the tree in this painting serving as a replacement for the *qudshu* type of goddess (see above, illuss. 70–72; see *ANEP* nos. 470–474). In spite of the great gap in time and the lack of clear lines that would show any connection between the *qudshu* stelae and this composition, the similarity is striking. As with illus. 214, even though this image is not anthropomorphic, it still provides a *transparent* reference to the goddess.

Based on the evidence at hand, it is hard to say whether the "animal painter" to whom Beck ascribes these last-mentioned compositions and most of the animal portrayals (Beck 1982, 22–27) is of northern Syrian or Phoenician origin. It is improbable, though not impossible, that the artist was an Israelite. P. Beck emphasizes correctly that the animals and hybrid creatures (sphinxes, griffins, falcons, *uraei*, etc.; see below, §§141ff.) that appear so frequently in the glyptic art of Iron Age IIB Israel and that are connected with sun symbolism that has its roots in Egypt, are completely absent from both the pithoi and the wall paintings at Kuntillet ʿAjrud (Beck 1982, 44).

§131. The two frontal figures ^AM and N have occasioned great debate and have caused much confusion, especially because one of the two inscriptions, the one referring to "Yahweh . . . and his *asherah*" (see below, §134) runs right across the head ornamentation on the figure on the far left. Methodologically, the inscriptions and depictions are to treated as completely separate and are each to be interpreted independently. Only after this is done can the question about their possible relationship be examined (see below, §142).

As regards the effort to identify figures ^AM and N, the iconographic features (the head ornamentation that is probably a blossom and/or feather crown; the grotesque, lion-like, grimacing face with protruding ears;[47] the beard or collar; the arms akimbo, turned outward and resting

---

47 Gilula (1979, 130–133) wants to interpret the head portion of the two figures as frontal portrayals of bovines. Meshel (1979, 30f.) and Margalit (1990, 275, 288f.) recognize the similarity to Bes, but they agree with Gilula's interpretation of the head portion. Even Koch speaks of "human-bovine figures" (1988, 100). The fact

on the hips; the crooked legs that are relatively short by comparison with the upper body; the tail) and the formal characteristics (frontal representation) leave no doubt that these are representations of *Bes-type figures* (see above, illus. 143b; concerning the iconographic characteristics of this type, see esp. Altenmüller 1975a; concerning the extant examples, see Wilson 1975; Hermary 1986; Tran Tam Tinh 1986a). The great majority of the commentators who have written about these paintings agree with this interpretation (see esp. Keel 1980b, 171–186; Beck 1982, 27–31; Hadley 1987b, 189–196; 1989, 175–185).

The only question is whether the two figures belong together and possibly form a pair. On the Bes figure on the right, one can see two circular marks representing female breasts, an interpretation supported by the fact that the female lyre player is depicted the same way. Is the figure thus female (thus, e.g., Gilula 1979, 129ff.; H. Weippert 1988, 673; Margalit 1990, 277) and can she be identified, under certain circumstances, as *Beset* (for this, see Bonnet 1952, 116–118; Altenmüller 1975b; Tran Tam Tinh 1986b; Malaise 1989, 56–62)?

Iconographically, one can distinguish (a) clearly male Bes figures, (b) clearly female Beset figures (mostly beardless, with a female face, female breasts, *and* more or less clearly represented genitalia) and (c) so-called bisexual or "androgynous" Bes images (a figure that "tends" to be the male Bes, with beard and lion tail, but with breasts that under certain circumstances are used for nursing).

With reference to the last category, it is significant from an Egyptian point of view that the concept of androgynous gods was unknown in Egypt before the Hellenistic Period. Female breasts and nursing always indicated the presence of a goddess during earlier times (Ward 1972; Malaise 1989, 59f.). This does not seem to hold true, however, for Bes iconography in the Levant, where images of androgynous Bes figures make their appearance already during Iron Age IIB (see Homès-Frédéricq 1987, 93 with fig. 4, from an eighth-century grave at Amman).

The image ᴬN, at any rate, belongs to group (c), with problematic indicators of gender. Since the beard is not shown in as much detail as in ᴬM, and since the breasts are not the hanging breasts typical of Bes – an attribute of fertility deities – but are round (see the female lyre player ᴬO)[48] one is inclined to consider this to be a female figure. It is not of

---

that bovines, so far as we can determine, are almost never portrayed frontally on ancient Near Eastern two-dimensional artistic works contradicts this idea. The ornamentation on the head of the left Bes figure (contra Gilula and Margalit) does not show horns that are bent or curved since they would have to be positioned on the sides of the head and not in the middle; this ornamentation must therefore depict a blossom or else a feather crown (see, e.g., illuss. 225 and 227). Bes figures have human or lion-like heads or faces but never have bovine heads or faces.

48 Hadley's reference (1987b, 191f.; 1989, 178f.) to Bes images on two Achaemenian cylinder seals and to the bearer of the heavens on an Aramean scaraboid (Hestrin/ Dayagi-Mendels 1979, no. 130) is therefore misleading because these depictions are of a developed, muscular chest of a male hero and not of a female breast. Pieces that are more comparable show the Bes image (illus. 143c) on an ostracon from Deir el-Medineh (Vandier d'Abbadie 1937, pl. 81.2622) and on a Phoenician bronze bowl from Nimrud (Barnett 1935, 203 fig. 7).

particular help that the tail might be missing from the figure to the right,[49] since that is not necessarily always portrayed on male Bes figures either. Conversely, the primary indicators that identify a Beset figure (genitalia, noted already in Altenmüller 1965, II 116 illus. 8, from the Middle Bronze Age) and the shoulder-lock hairstyle that is usually shown on Beset are absent. Since there is no clear evidence that Bes and Beset appeared together as a pair in Egypt before the Ptolemaic Period (see Tran Tam Tinh 1986b, 113 sub D), and since Beset can be clearly distinguished from her partner in those later depictions, unlike in illus. 220, the two figures from Kuntillet ʿAjrud are not to be treated as a heterosexual pair, in the sense of Bes and Beset, but it is rather more likely that they are two Bes variants, one masculine and one bisexual-feminized (so also Beck 1982, 30f.; Hadley 1987b, 190–192; cf.1989, 179f.).

The overlapping of the two figures (hardly "arm in arm together," as H. Weippert 1988, 673 suggests) and the different positions, depthwise, in which they stand – if that is even so intended – argues not only against interpreting the two as a pair but even more so against the idea that the two are shown together in the sense of a coherent group. The two Bes figures are placed together paratactically and perhaps were even drawn by different individuals (see Beck 1982, 36, 43; Hadley 1987b, 194f.)[50]

Bes does not belong to the group of the most significant deities of the Egyptian pantheon, but rather to the group of daemons that were especially popular in the area of "personal piety" and on small artistic pieces. During the Middle Bronze Age, he was initially the protector of pregnancy, birth, and a child's bed, but then later he became a protector

49 The drawings that were made of the two figures (Meshel 1978, fig. 12; Beck 1982, 9 fig. 5 and 28 fig. 13) show both of them with a hanging tail; published photographs, both in color and in black and white (Meshel 1978, fig. 12; 1979, 35; Beck 1982, pl. 5.2; Lemaire 1984b, 45) raise doubt about the existence of a tail on the smaller figure to the right. For that reason, it was left off the drawings that were provided in Keel/Uehlinger 1990, 115 illus. 147; only a very detailed examination of the original piece will resolve the problem. If the tail is really missing from the right figure, it could provide further evidence for that figure being a female, if one suggests that the tail might really be a phallus (Keel 1980b, 180; Korpel 1990, 218 "exaggerated genitals"; for a different view, see Hadley 1987b, 192).

50 One must reject, as completely misguided, an interpretation by Margalit, following the views of Gilula and supported by the art historian H. Künzl but which completely ignores the stylistic conventions of ancient Near Eastern iconography. Margalit suggests that the smaller figure on the right is shown in perspective(!), either standing behind or moving behind the figure on the left (1989, 378 note 19; 1990, 277, 295; cf. already Coogan 1987a, 119; McCarter 1987, 146f.). The problem posed by the fact that the image ᴬN is smaller cannot be resolved by suggesting that it is shown in perspective. As a whole separate issue, this certainly offers no argument that the figure can be identified as a female. That this might be a "traditional 'man-and-wife' posture" (Margalit 1990, 275) is just a grasping for straws (for portrayals of such a pose from the Middle Bronze Age, see illuss. 30–31, 41–43; for the Late Bronze Age, see illuss. 65, 68a). It is not possible to interpret the U-shaped "loop" under the right foot of ᴬN as a "footprint" left by the taller Bes figure, into which the right Bes figure now sets its own foot (Margalit 1990, 277 note 22) since the comparable "loop" that is visible under the lower portion of the lyre player's body is simply part of non-figurative skips of the brush work and does not relate to any specific figure. Margalit's discussion is based entirely on the equation 'šrh = "she who follows (her husband)." It mixes analysis of the images with textual analysis and operates with a semantic approach that seeks to propose etymologies that disregard the co-text and that employs a highly questionable methodology.

who defended from disasters in general. His importance in Palestine[51] during Iron Age II is shown not only by his appearance in the personal name *qdbš* (see above, §126) but primarily by the dozens of amulets that turn up again and again in excavations throughout the entire country (e.g., **illuss. 224a-b** from Lachish; illus. 224c from Tell es-Safi).[52]

The emphasis on the feather crown is typical for Iron Age II Bes amulets (McGovern 1985, 16, with note 22). It would seem that people hoped for special protection when showing the head of this god with its characteristic feather crown and lion face or grimacing face, since many reproductions seemed to be satisfied just to reproduce the image of the face (e.g., **illuss. 225a-c** from Tell el-Far'ah (south), **illus. 225d** from Gezer).[53] Molds found in Palestine (**illus. 225e** from Gezer; Petrie 1928, pl. 45.59) show that Bes-head amulets were produced within the country as well, and that these little faiences do not always have to be treated as imports from Egypt, as most have thought in the past.[54]

There are also images of this god on seal amulets from Iron Age IIB,[55] but in smaller numbers. In connection with our study, we would especially call attention first to a scarab from Achzib (**illus. 226a**),[56] on which a bareheaded man, who is turned to the right and wears a short loincloth, holds in each hand a Bes figure that is shown frontally, as is usual, and additionally to a scarab from Beer-sheba Str. V (end of the tenth century) that shows Bes as "Lord of the Serpents" (**illus. 226b**,[57] compare the way the nose is drawn with that in illus. 220; on this whole topic, see Keel/Uehlinger 1990, 72 illus. 90d), and finally to a very worn scaraboid from Tomb 1 near Tel Eitun that dates to the ninth century

---

51 For amulets from the Late Bronze Age, see McGovern 1985, 16f. and 109f. nos. 5–11 (Type I.B.); 20f. and 111f. nos. 27–40 (Type I.G.2); Giveon 1988, no. 88. The Bes figures that appear to dance sideways (or to beat a tambourine) seem to be limited to Late Bronze Age II (McGovern 1985, 17); for ivory carvings, see Loud 1939, pls. 8, 24, 26; 1948, pl. 204.3 (= above, illus. 143b).

52 See, e.g., Lamon/Shipton 1939, pl. 74.1–2, 4–10; Lapp 1967, 37 fig. 25.6; Crowfoot, et al., 1957, fig. 91.8; McCown 1947, pl. 55.77; Kenyon, et al., 1965, 512f. with fig. 261.1; Macalister 1912, II 331f.; III pl. 210.1–3, 5, 7–8, 10–11; Mackenzie 1912–1913, 60 pl. 28B.21, 24; Tufnell 1953, pls. 34.12–14; 35.45f.; 36.48; Giveon 1988: no. 108; Dever 1969–1970, 188; Bliss 1894, 153, pl. 33: Bliss/Macalister 1902, pls. 83.2–3 (= Rowe 1936, no. A 12); 84.3; Petrie 1928, pl. 45.31f., 40, 53; 1930, pls. 33.362 = 37.222 (Iron Age I); 35.414; 40.493–495; 41.258; 42.342; 1937, pl. 30.32–40; Rowe 1936, no. A.14, etc.

53 See §123 and §§190ff. (esp. illuss. 322a-b and 331) for emphasis on the face in the image of the *goddess!*

54 The same holds true for the Late Bronze Age faience amulets with Bes images; see the molds in Petrie 1933, pl. 16.42.

55 For a general interpretation of Bes on seal amulets, see Hornung/Staehelin 1976, 94, 124–126; Jaeger 1982, §§1388–1470. Late Bronze Age Bes images have been found, for example, at Acre (Ben-Arieh/Edelstein 1977, 71, 28 fig. 14.2, pl. 11.10) and at Achzib (Giveon 1988, no. 22 and an unpublished piece). The figures that flank what is either a tree or a blossom on a scarab from Shiqmona are not Bes figures (Schroer 1987a, 38 with illus. 9); they are fertility deities of the "Hapi" type from the Persian Period.

56 Unpublished; steatite, white coating, ochre-colored in places, 16.2 × 11.5 × 7.3 mm, from Tomb 36 in the east cemetery (er-Ras or Gešer Achzib); now in Jerusalem, Israel Antiquities Authority (Inv. no. IAA 48–624), to whom we express our thanks for permission to publish.

57 Unpublished; blue impression, 11.5 × 8.4 × 6 mm; presently in Tel Aviv, Institute of Archaeology, find no. 19790/50. We thank Prof. Z. Herzog for permission to publish.

224a

224b

224c

225a   225b   225c   225d

225e

226a   226b   226c

227   228

229

(**illus. 226c**),[58] on which Bes seems to hold a flower stalk or a knife in each hand, instead of the snakes. Bes appears flanked by four flying falcons (**illus. 227**), like the sun god (see §83, with illuss. 158a-c) on a cylinder seal found in Tomb 116 in Lachish, a tomb that was in use primarily during the ninth century. This same entity appears in the center, and is flanked by human worshipers, on a limestone scaraboid with three registers from Hazor Str. VI (**illus. 228**) that was most likely imported from Phoenicia. It comes from the same area of the site as the bone carvings shown in illuss. 210 (winged Baal) and 214 (the ointment spoon with the tree and the head of the goddess).

Even the few images assembled here illustrate clearly the complex associative possibilities that the Bes figure had offered ever since the end of the Late Bronze Age. A very broad spectrum of ideas can be depicted, ranging from showing a daemon that is more on the dangerous side and must be restrained (illus. 226a) to that of a deity with solar features, accorded honor in depictions on small artifacts as a "commoner's form of the solar deity" (Altenmüller 1975a, 721; cf. Malaise 1990). His special roles included protection for pregnant women and small children as well as prevention against snakebite. Only the iconography and the context of a particular portrayal can determine which image of such a polyvalent daemon or deity is being emphasized. The iconographic context of the two Bes figures in illus. 220 clearly points to a Syro-Phoenician setting. But as has already been mentioned, the vessels and wall paintings at Kuntillet ʿAjrud show a complete absence of motifs that were inspired by Egyptian symbols. There are no winged sphinxes, griffins, *uraei*, or falcons, all elements that play a prominent role on ivory and in the glyptic art from Israel dating to Iron Age IIB. These motifs play a prominent role in portraying the sphere of the "Most High God" in solar categories (see below, §§141ff.; combined with Bes in illus. 228!). Because these elements are not present – and contrary to what we suggested earlier (Keel/Uehlinger 1990, 72, 114–116) – it is most unlikely that the two Bes figures on Pithos A have specific associations with the solar deity or with the "Great (or Most High) God" (Egyptian *nṯr* ʿ3), especially since neither figure is shown with any attributes that are attached to that pantheon.[59] Since no other major deities are shown in the paintings on the two pithoi, it is much more likely that these simply represent two apotropaic daemons whose powers were to be mobilized, by these depictions, to afford protection for those who were threatened

58 See §118 note 8!
59 The dots that are scattered about on the upper bodies of the Bes figures should not be understood as *wedjat*-eyes. They appear to have no apotropaic significance (see Hadley 1987b, 192–195; 1989, 180–182) and are to be understood as purely decorative. They probably do show which portions of the body in this painting were to be thought of as clothed (in addition to the garments on the female lyre player ᴬO and on the worshipers ᴮV-X, see the Bes-image on the ostracon recovered by Vandier d'Abbadie 1937, pl. 81.2622). Since they were painted rather carelessly, being placed outside the outlines of the figures at some points (e.g., between the "left" arm and the upper body of ᴬM or in front of the abdomen on the female lyre player) or else in places that apparently were first intended to be naked (e.g., on the "right" hand and the upper body of ᴬN and on the upper body of the female lyre player), one should assume that these were done by a second hand, perhaps by an unskilled, provincial "sketch artist," like the one who painted ᴮV-X (on this

with many types of dangers as they sojourned in the northern Sinai Desert (see Hadley 1987b, 196).[60]

§132. With regard to the seated human *figure that holds the lyre* (^O), the first question to be resolved is whether the figure is male or female and then, if female, whether it might possibly depict a goddess. Neither the hairstyle nor the clothing is of any help in assisting with the identity of the gender; in our opinion, the two small, but clearly drawn, breasts favor an interpretation of the figure as female (cf. Stern 1978, 18f. with pl. 3; for the opposite view, Hadley 1987b, 198f.; 1989, 187–192).

Dever (1984, 22–25; 1990, 144f.) used three Late Bronze Age images of an enthroned goddess found in Ugarit, one a statuette of a sitting person and two gold pendants done using a *repoussé* technique (see Winter 1983, 447 with illuss. 480–482) to identify the sitting lyre player painted at Kuntillet ʿAjrud as a goddess and her chair as a schematic depiction of a cherub throne (see above, illuss. 65, 66b and §104). But the goddesses from Ugarit in those three depictions – as is proper for those who are enthroned – wear garments that are appreciably longer than that worn by the woman at Kuntillet ʿAjrud. Furthermore, none of the three is shown holding a lyre.[61] We have no clear evidence that ever shows a goddess playing a lyre. The gender of a seated figure shown with a lyre, on a bronze seal of unknown origin that is now in the R. and E. Hecht Museum in Haifa (**illus. 229**), is uncertain. Because of the table for offerings that is shown between this figure and the female tambourine player (see above, §102), this might show a deity, but this portrayal would not constitute sufficient evidence to postulate an iconographic type known as the "Enthroned Goddess with a Lyre," certainly not enough for the lyre player at Kuntillet ʿAjrud to be identified as a goddess.

One might be tempted to accord this figure divine status solely because she is seated or enthroned. One glance at contemporary representations shows that this is not permissible. Royal and courtly figures are also shown seated (e.g., illuss. 238–239). Whatever the importance of the female lyre player's seat, it is not a cherub throne (Dever 1984, 24f. seems

---

question, see also Beck 1982, 29, 33f.; Hadley 1987b, 195, 197). It is not possible to determine whether the dots in the hairdo of the female lyre player, which seem to indicate locks (cf. a similar face on a wall painting, Beck 1982, 59 no. 12 with pl. 14), were original or were added later by a second hand.

60 Against the notion that the two Bes figures might be shown dancing, perhaps even to the music of the female lyre player (Beck 1982, 35f.; Lemaire 1984b, 46; Schroer 1987a, 36f.; Olyan 1988, 31), one might note the stereotypical posture of the figures (dancing figures would raise their arms) and also their disposition: dancers would be portrayed *in front* of the female who is playing the music and would be about the same size (see illuss. 68a, 229) and not behind her back.

61 Dever (1984, 24) and Hadley (1987b, 202), when discussing the female lyre player, also refer to a Syrian ivory pyx from eighth-century Nimrud, on which one can supposedly see a female lyre player in a procession of female musicians who are behind an enthroned goddess (Barnett 1935, pl. 26.1; 1975, pl. 16. p. 3). They are certainly referring to the two(!) (male?) figures who appear on this very fragmentary piece in the fourth and fifth positions, who hold what appears to be some "washboard"-like instruments that Barnett (²1975, 191) called a "psaltery" and that certainly are not lyres in any case. For a representation of a lyre on a stylistically related pyx, see *ANEP* Suppl. no. 796!

to be unaware of portrayals of cherub thrones in the first millennium).[62] The schematically drawn lion's feet are are not enough to make this a cherub throne since they are included on all kinds of furniture during the first millennium. The grill work on the box portion of the seat ought to be interpreted as panelling and not as a stylized way to portray cherub wings. The best parallels to the lyre player's seat are found on Phoenician images of the first millennium. This is a type of armchair, characterized by a back angled slightly to the rear and by the absence of a footrest (Gubel 1987, Type II-g; see esp. pl. 22.57, 59f.; similarly 20.52; 38.143, 146). It is indeed true that deities are always seated on such chairs in Phoenician representations, but this may have more to do with the pictorial genre (primarily scarabs) that normally only portrays seated deities. A woman or goddess is seated on a chair very similar to the one from Kuntillet ʿAjrud, for example, on a Phoenician scarab from Acre (Giveon/Kertesz 1986, no. 76).[63]

This furniture does not necessarily have to evoke royal associations. In spite of the backrest, it is not an actual throne, but is more likely a courtly armchair (similarly, Hadley 1987b, 205–207; 1989, 195–198). A lyre player sits on a chair with very similar grill work, for example, on a scaraboid from Nippur, whose music is probably being played for the moon god, who is represented by a crescent moon (Giveon 1978, 119, with fig. 67). Playing the lyre in the cult is represented widely in both texts and iconography dating to Iron Age I-II Palestine/Israel (Keel [4]1984, 323–326; see above, §74). The bronze seal shown in illus. 229, which we have discussed already, portrays a woman who stands holding a tambourine (see above, §102) and a seated figure that holds a lyre. For whom the music is being played and whether this picture represents cultic activity must remain undecided, since the male or female addressee is not portrayed either in person or by a symbol.[64] In the case of the female lyre player at Kuntillet ʿAjrud, the same holds true; it is only with a measured degree of confidence that one can say that this is more likely a human figure rather than a divine one. But since she appears in isolation, apart from a constellation,[65] it is not possible to assume that her playing involves cultic activity.

62 On this, see Metzger 1985, pls. 113–118; Gubel 1987, pls. 4–12. If one were to be restricted to comparable pieces from the second millennium, the depictions of chairs with lions legs, such as have been collected by Metzger (1985, pls. 109–111), would provide closer parallels (see also Metzger 1985, pl. 32.226).

63 But unlike what has just been described here, this particular scarab does not depict a lyre player; the woman or goddess holds her arm or arms upraised, in worship or in blessing.

64 This would not be the case if the food on the table was placed there for the seated figure with the lyre, who could then be a deity. On a scarab from the Matouk Collection, now in the Biblical Institute in Fribourg, Switzerland (M. 5982 = Matouk 1977, 400 no. 1569), a female figure with a harp is seated on a throne; one can see a dancing double flute player opposite her. A drinking vessel on a high stand is between the two of them. In this case as well, there is no way to determine whether the two figures have the same status or not.

65 As shown above, there is no direct relationship between the Bes figures and the female lyre player. It would therefore hardly be permissible to assume that the apotropaic function of the Bes figures would suggest a similar function when the lyre was being played (thus Görg 1981, 8f.).

§133. The interpretation of the five striding figures (illus. 221), with arms raised in front of their chests, presents fewer problems for inter- preting the scene as a portrayal of a group of *worshipers* (ᴮU-Y; Beck 1982, 36–40). The representations are stylistically quite different from the rest of the painting on the vessel, even different from the archers that have been painted just below them, so that one can identify them readily as a group. These figures, the only human figures on the pithoi that are arranged facing left, were done by a very unpracticed hand. The details on each of these five individuals are rendered quite differently (hair, arm position, clothing), so that it seems that these were painted "spon- taneously," unlike the other images that adhere clearly to a (Syro- Phoenician) artistic "canon."[66]

It light of this relative "spontaneity," it is probably justified to speak of this as a procession of worshipers, in spite of the irregular arrangement and the fact that they do not all seem to be standing on the same level. In the context of our study, it is particularly important to emphasize here that this procession is of men only. The same holds true of the *inscriptions* from Kuntillet ʿAjrud that will be discussed next, in that they also mention only masculine personal names.

§134. On the shoulder of Pithos A we find the following Hebrew inscription, moving from above the right Bes image (ᴬN) toward the chariot horse (ᴬI) (see above, illus. 220):[67]

P. ᴬ1 Line 1 *ʾmr. ʾ[. . . .]h[. .] k*[68]*. ʾmr. lyhl[. .] wlywʿš. w . . . brkt. ʾtkm*

       Line 2 *lyhwh.šmrn.wlʾšrth.*

       Line 1 "Thus says ʾ[. . .] (PN 1) . . . :

           Say to Yehalle[lel?[69]] (PN 2), Yoʿasa (PN 3) and . . . (PN4?):

           I bless you (herewith – or: have blessed you)[70]

---

66 Concerning the dots that decorate the clothing (which, surprisingly, are missing from the detailed drawing in Beck 1982, 37 fig. 16 = Dever 1984, 27 fig. 9), see §131 note 59!

67 The inscriptions are marked as follows: using the same pattern as used for the paintings, the superscript ᴬ or ᴮ identifies the vessel. The transcription, including the line breaks, follows the information that has been published provisionally to date (esp. Meshel 1978; Chase 1982; Weinfeld 1984; Puech 1985, 359; Hadley 1987b; 1989, Davies 1991, 80f.) and makes use of photographs; the translation is divided according to the syntax and the sense of the material.

68 The expansion that results in ʾ[*šyw*] *h[ml]k* "King Ashyo (= Joash?; Meshel 1978, fig. 12, adopted by Davies 1991, 81 no. 8.017; but cf. Hadley 1987b, 182f.) is attractive. But the question about the well-being of a person of equal or higher rank, which one would expect to follow the name of the person being addressed, is missing.

69 The expansion to read *yhl[lʾl]* was suggested by Hadley 1987b, 182; 1989, 160f.; it has been adopted by Davies 1991, 81. The gap seems a little too small for three characters to fit in and traces of the two *l* marks should have still been there above the break.

70 On *BRK . . . lyhwh*: "If a human being is the subject, then the 'blessing' is at most an ascription of praise that encourages the deity to bless another person, or else it is simply a formula of greeting," as in "praise before YHWH in the sense of an ascription of praise concerning the person who is being mentioned" (Scharbert 1973, 813, 818). In each case, an indirect blessing is intended: "you are commended to the deity for blessing" or, using a corresponding intercession, "may you become one who is blessed by the deity." Whether *brkt* is to be translated as a performative

Line 2   to/before[71] Yahweh of Samaria[72] and his *asherah*."

In a narrow column, marked by a vertical line on the right, to the right of worshiper [B]Y, there is a similar sounding, but more detailed, inscription over the shoulder and on the main rounded portion of Pithos B:

P. [B]2   Line 1'   [']*mr̃*
　　　　 Line 2'   '*mryw*
　　　　 Line 3'   '*mr l.'dn*[*y*]
　　　　 Line 4'   *hšlm. 't*[73]
　　　　 Line 5'   *brktk.l*[*y*]
　　　　 Line 6'   *hwh tm̃n*
　　　　 Line 7'   *wl'šrth. yb*
　　　　 Line 8'   *rk.wyšmrk*
　　　　 Line 9'   *wyhy 'm. 'd*[*n*]
　　　　 Line 10'   *y* [. . .
　　　　 Line 11'   *k* [. . .

　　　　 Line 1'   "Thus says Amaryau:
　　　　 Line 3'   Say to my lord:
　　　　 Line 4'   Is it well with you?
　　　　 Line 5'   I bless you (herewith – or: have blessed you)
　　　　　　　　　　　 to/before Yahweh of Teman[74] and his *asherah*.
　　　　　　　　　　　 May He [i.e., Yahweh] bless (you)[75]
　　　　　　　　　　　 and keep you
　　　　 Line 9'   and be with my lord . . ."

There are three fragmentary abecedaries written partially above and partially alongside Inscription [B]2, together with single words that apparently have no context (see Lemaire 1981, 25–27; Puech 1985, 363; 1988, 191; Davies 1991, 81). There is another more important inscription on the shoulder of this same pithos, somewhat overlapping the first two lines of [B]2. It seems to give more specificity to the contents of the blessing

---

or as a preterite cannot be determined for sure. The use of a formula that is employed when writing letters (see below) assumes spatial separation between the sender/speaker and PN 2–4.

71 On translating *l* = with "before," following Couroyer 1978, see Puech 1988, 192 note 10.

72 Meshel (1978; 1979, 31) and Naveh (1979, 28 with note 9) would read a participle with a pronominal suffix here ("our protector"), as has been suggested most recently once again by Scagliarini 1989, 206f. (without any new argumentation). The interpretation of *šmrn* as a toponym was first proposed by Gilula (1979, 130–133. XV).

73 See Chase 1982, 63–67.

74 On this, see esp. Emerton 1982, 3; Weinfeld 1982, 237; 1984, 125; Hadley 1987b, 183, and many others. Scagliarini (1989, 208) treats *tm̃n* in line 6' as "purely conjectural."

75 This should be understood substantially in this way, even though the suffix =*k* is missing (on Num 6:24a and the silver amulets found in Jerusalem, see below, §210).

requested from "Yahweh ... and his *asherah*" in Teman (and probably similarly in Samaria):[76]

P. ᴮ3   ... [*brkt* = ...] *lyhwh htṁn wl'šrth*
             ... *kl 'šr yš'l m'š ḥnn ... wntn lh yhw klbbh*
             ". . . by/before Yahweh of Teman[77] and his *asherah* . . .
             Whatever he shall request of anyone,
             may he [i.e., Yahweh] grant it[78] . . .
             and may Yahweh give him according to his intention . . ."

It has been correctly pointed out that these inscriptions include formal features that follow the rules of letter writing (Naveh 1979, 29; Lemaire 1981, 26–28; Chase 1982, 65f.):

	P. ᴬ1	**P. ᴮ2**	**P. ᴮ3**
A. Introduction of letter with indication of writer	*'mr* *'[. . ..]h[..]k*	[']ṁṙ *'mryw*	
B. Introduction of content with indication of addressee	*'mr l=* *yhl[l'l']* *wlyw'šh.* *w . . .*	*'mr l=* *'dny*	
C. Question regarding welfare		*hšlm. 't*	
D. Blessing or greeting formula The blessing deity Assisting entity	*brkt. 'tkm.* *lyhwh.šmrn.* *wl'šrth.*	*brktk.* *lyhwh tmn* *wl'šrth.*	[*brkt* = ...] *lyhwh htmn* *wl'šrth*
E. Desire for continued blessing		*ybrk.wyšmrk wyhy 'm. 'dny*	(. . .*wntn lh yhw klbbh*)

We find the closest parallels to this formula on an Edomite ostracon from Horvat Uza (end of the seventh/beginning of the sixth century),[79]

---

76 This was described by Weinfeld 1982, 237 without the lines being numbered or the words divided (see also Weinfeld 1984, 125f.; Hadley 1987b, 187f.; 1989, 171f.). Davies treats the two lines reproduced here as two different inscriptions (1991, 80f. no. 8.016 and 8.022. Tigay 1986, 26 note 30, refers to a sketch – not available to us – in the *Jerusalem Post* dated March 13, 1979, p. 3.

77 The *h*= in *htmn* is perhaps a dittography of the =*h* on the end of *lyhwh* (M. Weippert 1990, 171 note 40; for another view, see Conrad 1988, 563 note 5a). Scagliarini (1989: 208f.) disputes reading *htṁn* here as well, but offers no better alternative.

78 Scagliarini understands *ḥnn* as a PN: "Whatever is sought for Hanun by anyone ... Yahweh will grant it according to his intention" (1989, 208f.).

79 Beit-Arieh/Cresson 1985, 97f.; see Hadley 1989, 166f. The text reads (A) *'ṁṙ. lmlk.* (B) *'mr. lblbl.* (C) *hšlm. 't.* (D) *whbrktk lqws. w't* (. . .). "Thus says *Lmlk*: Say to *Blbl*: Are you well? I bless you (herewith – or: have blessed you) by/before Qaus. And now: . . ." Then follows the actual body of the letter with the substance of the message.

in a Phoenician letter from Saqqara (sixth century),[80] on an Ammonite ostracon from Tel el-Mazar (sixth century)[81] 3 km north of Tell Deir Alla, and perhaps also in a seventh-century Judean letter with a severely damaged prescript that was found at Wadi Murabbaʿat.[82] These are private letters with contents related to business.[83] The letter found on a fourth-century Phoenician pithos from Zarephath is related to the epigraphic artifacts from Kuntillet ʿAjrud. It contains a portion of a letter prescript along with an incomplete alphabet.[84] Concerning the function of the letter prescript and the alphabets on the pithoi from Kuntillet ʿAjrud, see below, §143.

§135.   There is currently a general consensus regarding the meaning of the two syntagma *yhwh šmrn* and *yhwh (h)tmn*. The name of a god is linked to a place name, comparable to "Ishtar of Nineveh" and the like. These two particular names are indicative of the local manifestations of the Israelite national god, who had a shrine in Samaria (the capital city) and in the southeast Negev or in the region (or city) of Teman, located in Edom, just as many other localities had a shrine, where he could be approached when seeking a blessing (see Emerton 1982, 9–13; McCarter 1987, 139–142, and many others; for the connection of Yahweh with Teman, see Hab 3:3). If this interpretation is correct (for another view, see Scagliarini 1989, 208f., 212), then the first inscription would make it clear, once and for all, that Yahweh had a temple in the capital of the Northern Kingdom (Olyan 1988, 34f.; Hadley 1989, 163f.), whereas the mention of the name of a "Yahweh of Teman" reintroduces the question about the relation of that deity to the Edomite national god Qaus (for a discussion of this, see Knauf 1988a, 55f.; Bartlett 1989, 194–204; and see below, §221 for Qaus at Hurvat Qitmit).

§136.   What is of greatest interest to us in this study, however, is the interpretation of the phrase "Yahweh ... *and his asherah*," since it is a stereotypical refrain in the blessing formulas (C.) in all three cited inscriptions; in particular, what is meant by *ʾšrth* "his *asherah*," in other

---

80 *KAI* no. 50 = Pardee 1982, 165–168. By contrast to the inscriptions from Kuntillet ʿAjrud, the addressee is named here first, and then the woman who sent it: (B) *ʾmr. lʾḥty. ʾršt.* (A) *ʾmr. ʾḥtk. bšʾ.* (C) *wšlm ʾt. ʾp ʾnk. šlm.* (D) *brktyk. lbʾl ṣpn. wlkl ʾl tḥpnḥs.* (E) *ypʿlk. šlm* (...). "Say to my sister Arišut: Thus says your sister Baša: Are you well? I am well also. I bless you (herewith – or: have blessed you) by/before Baal-Zaphon and all the gods of Tahpanhes. May they bring you health!" etc.

81 Yassine/Teixidor 1986, 47f. no. 3: (A) *ʾmr plty* (B) *ʾmr lʾḥh lʾbdʾl* (C) *šlm ʾt wʿt* (...). "Thus says Palti: Say to his brother, to ʿAbdiel: How are you? And now: ..." etc.

82 DJD II no. 17 = Davies 1991, 111 no. 33.001: [(B) *ʾmr l=PN 1]ʾ* (A) *ʾmr* [...]*yhw* (PN 2) *lk* (C) *šlḥ šlḥt ʾt šlm bytk wʿt* (...). "[Say to PN 1:]ʾ Thus says ... -yahu to you: I wish for your family all good things. And now: ..." etc. See Dion 1979, 554f.; Pardee 1982, 120–122.

83 The differences in both genre and context could provide the reason why the prescripts in the "business" letters from both Arad and Lachish (seventh/sixth centuries; see Pardee 1982, 145–150) are formulated completely differently, with one exception. On Arad 16.2f.; 21.2; 40.3, see below, §141 note 110.

84 Pritchard 1988, 8f. no.2: (B) *ʾmr lʾdnn grmlqr[t]* "Say to our lord Germelqart [...]" By contrast to the inscriptions from Kuntillet ʿAjrud, this sentence and the alphabet were not written on the pithos with ink, but were scratched onto the pot before it was fired.

words, *$*šrt$ yhwh* "Yahweh's *asherah.*"[85] The debate[86] has continued for over a decade, and we highlight the following hypotheses[87]:

(a) *'šrth* refers to the *goddess* Asherah, who is known in Ugaritic texts as the consort of El and is mentioned in the Hebrew Bible in conjunction with Baal, and she is the female *partner* of Yahweh (thus, e.g., Coogan 1987a, 118; M. Weippert 1990, 156f.). Authors adopting this point of view face the problem that there is no clear evidence for the goddess Asherah in Canaanite/Phoenician inscriptions that date to the first millennium (recent discoveries or interpretations in the last few years could bolster this position and provide a better foundation for this view).[88] They rely on the fact that *^{7a}šērāh* clearly refers to a goddess in certain passages in the Hebrew Bible, with the "clearest" texts being 1 Kgs 15:13 // 2 Chr 15:16; 1 Kgs 18:19, gloss; 2 Kgs 21:7; 23:4, 6f. (plural in Judg 3:7; see Gesenius[18]I, 112f.). But in all those cases it reads *hā=^{7a}šērāh* (1 Kgs 18:19; 2 Kgs 21:7; 23:6) or else *lā=^{7a}šērāh* (1 Kgs 15:13 // 2 Chr 15:16; 2 Kgs 23: 4, 7), with the article. Since Hebrew never uses double determination (article + proper name), *^{7a}šērāh* cannot strictly be treated as a proper name. But the determination, with the article, that gives the *nomen* its quality as a proper

---

85 What if we were theoretically to treat the suffix =*h* in the cited inscriptions from Kuntillet ʿAjrud as a third *feminine* singular suffix and connect it to the toponym that is linked with the divine name (^1 *šmrn*, ^B2 and ^B3 *(h)tmn*), which would mean that this could read "the *asherah* of Samaria" (see Amos 8:14 conj., 2 Kgs 13:6; 16:33) or "the *asherah* of Teman" (see Tigay 1986, 26f., Olyan 1988, 33; Smith 1990, 86)? The inscription from Khirbet el-Qom, to be discussed in §141, shows that this is not possible. The divine name appears in that text without mention of a toponym, which means the suffix =*h* must apply to the deity (thus also Hadley 1989, 164).

86 Nearly every new contribution tries to rework the literature. See, e.g., Emerton 1982, 13–18: Schroer 1987a, 21–45; Olyan 1988; Hadley 1989; Smith 1990, 85–88, 106–109. The following comment is symptomatic not only of the interpretation itself but also of what each scholar hopes to achieve when studying the inscriptions: ". . . this find corrects the picture of the religious history of Judah as advocated by the later biblical writers. Their censorship has been broken" (Ahlström 1982, 43).

87 A detailed critical analysis of these and other suggestions concerning the interpretation must be postponed because of space limitations. Against interpreting *'šrth* as the name of a goddess "Ashirta" (A. Angerstorfer) or "Asherata" (Z. Zevit; thus also Conrad 1988, 557f., 563f.), see, e.g., Day 1986, 392 note 21; Maier 1986, 173; Hadley 1987a, 58f.; Olyan 1988, 25; against the inter-pretation of *$*šrt$ yhwh* as a hypostasized "trace of Yahweh" (McCarter 1987, esp. 145–149), see Smith 1990, 87f.

88 *New discoveries*: Excavations in 1990 at Tel Miqne/Ekron, under the direction of T. Dothan and S. Gitin, produced fragments of large olive oil vessels (from a seventh-century context) that include writing. According to the initial reports (Gitin 1990, 41, 59 note 18; *BA* 53 [1990] 232), one can read "sanctified to Asherat" (= *qdš l'šrt?*; on the photograph in the same article, one can see only *l'šrt*), "for the shrine" (= *lbyt?*), and "oil" (= *šmn?*). By contrast to Kuntillet ʿAjrud, and not surprisingly, given the "elite zone" status of the city of Ekron, these inscriptions are connected with a shrine. The question about whether *'šrt* refers to a goddess or a cultic symbol (see illuss. 222a-b from Tell Jemmeh and Tell el-Farʿah [south]) must remain unresolved. See also Braulik 1991, 114.

New Interpretations: I. Kottsieper, referring to the end of a list of deities mentioned in the Aramean Pap. Amherst 63 (first half of the fourth century) col. VIII, which is written in demotic script, suggests reading ʿ*hr** ʿ*w*ʿ*s*ʿ*r*$_2$ʿ° as referring to El and Asherah (1988, 58, 72; cf. Hadley 1989, 23), according to which Asherah would be a partner of El here as well as at Ugarit. But one must wait for a critical edition of the text and for further philological discussion.

name, is perhaps to be understood as the deuteronomistic technique for slandering "Canaanite" deities (analogous to *ha=baʿal*).[89] But even if *asherah* is supposed to refer to a goddess in the cited passages, which is by no means certain,[90] the texts are not particularly helpful for interpreting *ʾšrth* "his [i.e., Yahweh's] *asherah*" in the texts of Kuntillet ʿAjrud because, without exception, these are essentially later, deuteronomistically redacted texts. Even if the deuteronomists made use of information from historically reputable sources,[91] these texts still make no mention of Yahweh's *asherah* in Samaria or Teman. Wherever a cultic image of the *asherah* is mentioned (1 Kgs 15:13 // 2 Chr 15:16; 2 Kgs 21:7), or might be (2 Kgs 23:7), that text refers to an *asherah* in Jerusalem. The issue concerning "Yahweh's *asherah*" in Samaria and Teman in the early eighth century is independent of the question about a cultic image in seventh-century Jerusalem (on this, see below, §195).

The grammatical rule just mentioned, that double determination is excluded and therefore that a proper name cannot also be furnished with a possessive suffix,[92] argues as well against the assumption that *ʾšrth* "his [Yahweh's] *asherah*" might refer to a personal, independent goddess and partner of Yahweh in the inscriptions found at Kuntillet ʿAjrud.[93]

---

89 Hadley interprets the fact that this is made definite by use of the article as evidence for the semantic shift of the term *ʾašērāh* from "(goddess) Asherah" to "(cultic symbol) *asherah*" (1989, 93–108, esp. 92f.).

90 This is most probably the case in 1 Kgs 15:13 (see the following note) and in 2 Kgs 23:4, 7. The last passage refers to cultic vessels or garments for (the) *asherah*s at the time of Josiah (or else for the baldachin [Tr.: cloth canopy]; see Schroer 1987a, 41f.; for a depiction of a baldachin above a goddess, see Barnett 1935, 203 fig. 7). Even here a direct connection to the goddess cannot be demonstrated, since the text gives no information regarding the function of the listed requisite items. But see below, §195.

91 On 1 Kgs 15:9–14, see Spieckermann 1982, 184–187; Wacker 1991b, 143. Asa's measures against the cultic *asherah*-image of Maacah are very clearly described, being a retrojection of how Josiah went about his reform. Even if the deuteronomists did record a historically accurate remembrance of a cultic *asherah*-image that was in Jerusalem in the early ninth century, this remained an isolated episode, cult-historically speaking. Nothing is mentioned about the exact appearance of the "abominable image of the *asherah*" (*mipleṣet lā=ʾašērāh*).

92 M. Weippert 1990, 171f. note 40, questions this and refers to composite names of deities such as *ʿntbytʾl*, *ʾšmbytʾl*, *ḥrmbytʾl* (see above, §120) or *ʿštrkmš* (see above, §50, note 27). But, in the first place, such names, which do indeed represent proper names *in their composite form*, cannot be merely converted to a shortened form of the DN + possessive suffix; the names that have been mentioned, which are found in this textual corpus, do not include a short form of the name alongside the long form of the name. (The only exception known to us is the Ugaritic name *ʿnt.gṭr* (*gṭrt*) in *KTU* 1:108.6, which is used along with *ʿnth* in *KTU* 1:43.13; see the following note!) In the second place, discussion continues about whether these composite names are always to be resolved by translating them as if a genitive relationship must be assumed, or whether there are times when at least some of them suggest rather a "molecular-like" associative connection with the deities.

93 There are a few examples in Ugaritic that have the combination DN + possessive suffix: *ilîbh* "his deified ancestor" *KTU* 1:17 I 26, 44; *ilîby KTU* 1:17 II 16 and possibly *l àṭrty* "forʾ my Atirat" (?) in the badly damaged letter *KTU* 2:31 (= *PRU* II 2 = *UT* 1002) line 41, possibly also line 62. The most interesting example for our interests is *ʿnth* in *KTU* 1:43.13 along with *ʿnt.gṭr* (*gṭrt*) in *KTU* 1:108.6. Concerning these passages, see Maier 1986, 211f.; de Moor 1987, 188 with note 5; Smith 1990, 86 with

(b) This frequently cited grammatical objection[94] has led to other interpretations, treating *ʾšrh* as a generic indicator for "goddess" or as an appellative meaning *"consort"* (Meshel 1979, 31; Margalit 1990). Neither translation is convincingly based in fact.[95]

(c) The same argument can be raised against the thesis that *ʾšrth* refers to Yahweh's *"shrine"* (Meshel 1979, 31; see Lipiński 1986, 93f.; McCarter 1987, 145). Already in 1972, E. Lipiński had tried to show that the biblical term *ʾᵃšērāh* (or the plural *ʾᵃšērîm* referred to "holy places" or "shrines." Such an interpretation is probably correct for Akkadian *aširtu(m)* (and other similar terms), for Phoenician *ʾšr(t)*,[96] and for Aramaic *ʾšrt / ʾtr(t')*, but there seems to be no evidence to back up such a use for the Hebrew term under discussion (Emerton 1982, 16–18). The lexical evidence is indeed rather irritating,[97] but it cannot be dismissed out of hand.

(d) In the Old Testament the term *ʾᵃšērāh* (plural *ʾᵃšērîm*) refers to a *cultic object* as a rule. The biblical texts never actually describe this object, except to say that it was made of wood, that it was "made" or "set up," which suggests that it is an artifact ("[to] plant" in Deut 16:21 might be understood as using this verb in its transferred meaning); conversely, it could be "torn out," "chopped down," and "burned." For this reason, this cultic object is usually conceived of as being in the shape of a stylized

---

note 52. M. Dietrich and O. Loretz plan to engage in a thorough discussion of KTU 1:43 in one of their upcoming monographs (in the meantime, see *TUAT* II/3 [1988] 326f.), a text that does not mention Anat; more recent discussions can be found in de Moor 1987, 168–171 [Ritual III]; de Tarragon 1989, 161–163). Concern-ing the *asherah* issue at Kuntillet ʿAjrud, Khirbet el-Qom, and in the Old Testament, nothing can be *directly* gained from *KTU* 1:43 (see §§5, 230).

94 See, e.g., Lemaire 1977, 607; Winter 1983, 490; Lemaire 1984b, 47; Day 1986, 392; Maier 1986, 169; Miller 1986, 247; Tigay 1986, 27f. with note 34; Schroer 1987a, 58; McCarter 1987, 143; Olyan 1988, 33f.; Hadley 1989, 136f., and often elsewhere; Koch 1991, 33, and many others; for a more restrained treatment, see Smith 1990, 86.

The most well-balanced position, now as before, is very likely that of J. A. Emerton: ". . . we should perhaps hesitate to be too dogmatic in stating what was not possible in Hebrew, and we must be prepared to modify our opinions in the light of new evidence. Nevertheless, the use of a suffix with a personal name is not in accordance with Hebrew idiom as far as we know it, and it is unwise to interpret the newly-found inscriptions in such a way unless there is no satisfactory alternative (1982, 14f.).

It would be even more problematic to use a conjectural reading for Hosea 14:9b (conj. *ʾᵃnî ʿᵃnātô wᵉʾᵃšērātô*) as the starting point for the discussion (see above, §122 note 18).

95 In a parallelism that occurs only once in Ugaritic texts that includes *àtt* // *àtrt KTU* 1:3 (= *CTA* 3 = *UT* ʿnt) I 15 (see Margalit 1990, 272f.), *àtrt* is, as usual, to be under-stood as the name of the goddess Atirat. One must raise serious doubts about Margalit's linking of the term *àtr*, which according to his explanation means "follow in the traces of," with the notion that this is a reference to a "consort"-concept (1990, 273f.; see above, §131 note 50).

96 See the new passage that was published a few years ago from an inscription from Acre that dates to Iron Age III (early Persian Period, fifth century), in which an *ʾš ʾl ʾšrt* "elder of the shrine" is mentioned (Dothan 1985, esp. 83 Line 2 and 85f.).

97 Concerning the factual possibility that a shrine might be understood to be a medium for blessing, see the Akkadian evidence cited by Tigay (1986, 28) (and see also Jeremiah 7 on this issue). On the parallel terms "Yahweh // his temple," see, e.g., Ps 132:8; 2 Chr 6:41.

tree (Day 1986, 402; Olyan 1988, 1–3; Smith 1990, 81–85), just as it is pictured, among other places, on Pithos A from Kuntillet 'Ajrud (illus. 219f., motif ᴬE, ᴬK; see below, §142). The frequently discussed connection between the goddess and the stylized tree in the history of the traditions supports this idea (see above, §§36, 44, 97ff.).

The controversial reference to *'šrth* in the inscription from Kuntillet 'Ajrud thus most likely refers to such a cultic object.[98] Among other passages, Deut 16:21 and 2 Kgs 23: 4, 6, 15 make it clear that *asherahs* could be found very close to Yahweh or to his altar. So far, the *asherah* of Yahweh in Teman is known only from the two inscriptions on Pithos B from Kuntillet 'Ajrud. The *asherah* of Yahweh in Samaria, by contrast, is also known in the Bible: According to 1 Kgs 16:33, it was erected by Ahab (ca. 871–852), and 2 Kgs 13:6 reports that it was still standing at the time of Jehoahaz (814–798) and was thus not affected by reform measures instituted under Jehu (2 Kgs 10:28f.) that date to about 840. Since nothing was ever reported about the removal of the *asherah* of Samaria during any time that led up to the fall of the city in 720,[99] the inscription on Pithos A that is dated to the first half of the eighth century refers to this particular item (Olyan 1988, 32f., see also 6f.; see the same study for possible suggestions about how it appeared).

§137. The question remains about how closely this cultic object in Samaria, along with the corresponding objects in Teman, Bethel (2 Kgs 23:15), Jerusalem, and other Yahweh temples, was *related* to the *goddess* Asherah? Some scholars, who on philological grounds accept the thesis that the *'šrth* mentioned in the inscriptions at Kuntillet 'Ajrud refers to the cultic symbol, in the form of a stylized tree, rather than to the goddess, nevertheless interpret these *asherahs* as representing the partner of Yahweh (see, e.g., Day 1986, 392: Olyan 1988, 29, 31–34). The three pithos inscriptions themselves offer no indication of this, since nothing is mentioned in these examples about the function of the cult object and nothing is said about the goddess herself. That "the goddess and her cult object are inseparable" (Winter 1983, 555) is correct according to *the tradition history*. It is also quite probable that, through being identified with the god El, Yahweh had become associated with the cultic symbol of the *asherah*. What is questionable, however, is how directly *Iron Age IIB Israel* related this cultic symbol to the *goddess* Asherah and, as a related issue, how explicitly this relationship was depicted in the religious symbol system of Israel during the ninth and eighth centuries. Do the sources permit one to describe the role and status of the *asherah* as one who is depicted as a personal, female partner/deity? Or – as with the phrase *šᵉgar 'alāpekā wᵉʿaštᵉrôt ṣōʾnekā* "offspring" of your cattle and the "increase" (*astartes*) of your small animals" (see above, §91) – are we dealing with the recasting of the former name of a deity to signify a particular manifestation (an aspect) of Yahweh's blessing?

98 See Emerton 1982, 15, 19; Lemaire 1984b; Olyan 1988, 31–34; Smith 1990, 16, 85–94, and many others.

99 The *asherah* of Samaria could have been among those items named in an inscription of Sargon II at Nimrud as having been captured as booty and taken away by the Assyrians: *ilāni tiklīšun*, "the gods in whom they trusted" (Spieckermann 1982, 348–350; Tigay 1986, 35).

In our opinion, when discussing this question one cannot ignore the fact that, already since Iron Age I, the goddess was no longer simply being *represented* by her symbol(s), as had previously been the case, but that these symbols increasingly became important in their own right and could virtually almost become *substitutes* for her. This is true specifically of the link between the goddess and the tree, a shift that became more and more explicit from Iron Age I on. The iconographic evidence for Iron Age IIB can best be characterized by the word *"transparency"* when one seeks to characterize the relationship between the goddess and the stylized tree. The ointment spoon from Hazor (illus. 214) is one example of this and the depiction of the stylized tree above the lion on Pithos A from Kuntillet ʿAjrud (motifs ᴬE-H in illus. 219, see above, §130) is another instance of the same trend. The head shown in illus. 214 and the positioning of the tree above the lion, as shown in illus. 219, make it possible for the tree to seem to be associated with the goddess in both images, without the goddess having to make an actual appearance as a personal power. It is particularly noteworthy that the stylized tree that is shown in both images functions as a power that bestows or mediates blessing (specifically: perfume or nourishment for the animals). The word "transparency" seeks to take the polysemy of the word *ʾšrh* into account and does not eliminate the possibility that the goddess, under certain circumstances, could be imagined at times as more of a personal entity; this is very possibly the case already on the ivory shown in illus. 215 and is certainly more true for the Iron Age IIC period that follows (see below, §§190ff.). It should be emphasized once again that the iconographic evidence that shows this transparency during Iron Age IIB is clearest in images that come from or were inspired by Phoenicia (illuss. 214, 215, 219). During the ninth and eighth centuries, this type of representation may have been more the exception rather than the rule *in Israel*, as the following images show.[100]

§138. In addition to images containing these "transparent" depictions of the goddess, there are some on which the palm-like, stylized tree does not appear primarily in the role of bestowing blessing, but as a completely undifferentiated *numinous symbol of power* that is not characterized as having gender connections at all. It appears either in isolation or else flanked, guarded, or worshiped by winged hybrid creatures and/or by humans. The tree can be shown in a more or less stylized form. The spectrum of ways it can be depicted varies from one atelier to the next, from a stylized image simply utilizing branches all the way to elaborate combinations of palmetto and lotus trees, as on the seal of a certain *šbnyhw* reportedly found in Gezer (**illus. 230**; see also below, illus. 258b). Two eighth-century seal amulets from Megiddo portray the sacred tree in the middle register, guarded and protected by two-winged sphinxes with heads of falcons (**illuss. 231a-b**). In illus. 231a, the upper register shows a vulture attacking a rabbit and the lower register portrays

---

100 With the depictions that we have shown already and with those that are to follow, we hope to be able to refute the notion that the iconography of Iron Age Palestine/ Israel provides "no worthwhile iconographic evidence for the cultic object described in the texts as an *asherah*" (thus Koch 1988, 113).

a lion attacking a caprid (see above, §12, note 5), images that contrast strongly with the carefully guarded tree in the middle.

The motif that shows the tree flanked by hybrid creatures appears frequently on Samaria ivories. Examples there use both the style common in inland Syria (**illus. 232a**) and the variation that was typical of coastal Phoenicia (**illus. 232b**; see Crowfoot, et al., 1938, pls. 5.2–3; 14.5). The inland Syrian style seems more naive, crowded, less well-proportioned, and less elegant (H. Weippert, 1988, 655–657), but there is little iconographic difference between the two versions. In both cases, whether it be the winged sphinx or the cherub, the creature has a human head, not a falcon head, and – although this seems a little strange on the Syrian version – wears the Egyptian double crown. The royal ceremonial beard is missing on the Syrian version, and the Phoenician palmetto tree is replaced by some type of bouquet of lotus blossoms (see illuss. 219 ᴬE, 230). On a typically Egyptian version, that unfortunately is only partially preserved, the sphinxes are portrayed with rams' heads (Crowfoot, et al., 1938, pl. 6.2).

The stylized tree, as a symbol of numinous power, guarded or protected by the hybrid creatures (note the cherubs in §§39, 97f., 104 that carry the royal or divine throne and watch over the holy place; for the connection between these protecting powers and concepts about kingship, see Ezek 28:12–15)[101] symbolizes mythologically the garden of the deity, concretely the temple and palace area, and, more abstractly, the ordered earthly cosmos and the life that has been made possible by this order. Here the tree no longer fulfills the former "feminine" function, derived originally from a link with the goddess, to provide nurture and sustenance for life. Though he does not appear in the portrayal itself, it is in the service of a royal god that the tree appears and represents this deity's power to bring blessing.

These images lend additional plausibility to the thesis that, during Iron Age IIB, the stylized tree can be a sexually undifferentiated cultic symbol that can be assigned also to a male deity. It is possible that "Yahweh's *asherah*" ought not be explained in any way other than in connection with this tree. A stylized tree that is shaped rather differently, but still looks like a palm tree, appears both on a scaraboid from Tell en-Nasbeh dating from the end of the eighth century (**illus. 233a**) and on a seal from Judah that belonged to a certain *ḥlqyhw bn pdy*, a piece on which the tree is flanked by two human worshipers, approximately contemporary or else just a little younger (**illus. 233b** shows the side of the seal with the iconography; the piece is engraved on both sides). This tree is also

---

101 On this, see Barnett 1969; it is true that this is a text from the sixth century; nevertheless, it makes use of an apparently older Phoenician mythology. Williams (1976) disputes whether there is a mythological background for Ezek 28:12–19 and suggests that the text refers to the king of Tyre only with respect to his "hybris in commercial activities and his participation in the local sanctuary rites of sacral kingship." He mistakenly assumes that a sacred rite and a mythology can be strictly separated. As a rule, a ritual constellation recognizes that a (mythological) narrative has been told, so that the ritual is then based on some aspect of its meaning. Where this is not the case, it can also achieve mythological significance on its own.

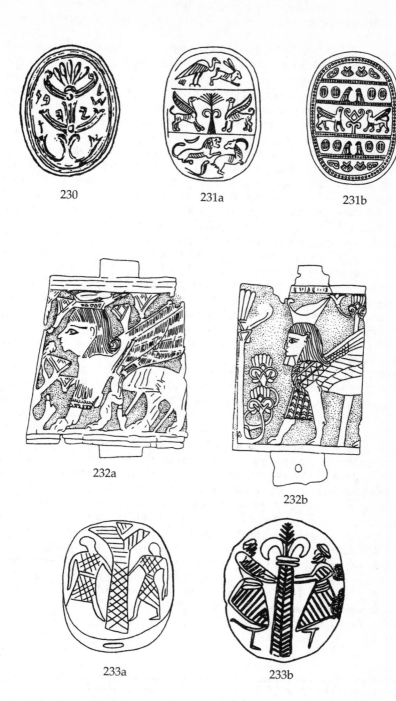

230

231a

231b

232a

232b

233a

233b

to be identified as depicting this central entity in the state symbol system in both Israel and Judah during Iron Age IIB-C (see above, illuss. 179–181).[102]

§139.   In addition to the blessing formulas from Kuntillet ʿAjrud and the formula from Khirbet el-Qom that we are about to discuss, pictorial depictions also show that this entity signified a means of blessing for an individual. The motif of guarding the sacred tree is combined with that of a human being at worship (**illus. 234a**) on an ivory pyx that dates to the second half of the eighth century, found near the citadel of Hazor in Str. V A. The portrayal shows that the piece is clearly a product of the southern Syrian school. Perhaps it is just a piece of local carving (concerning the palmetto tree, see illus. 214 from Hazor Str. VI); in any case, specifically Egyptian features are absent from the extant portions. The kneeling man, with his short loincloth, is reminiscent of the youthful god shown in illus. 210, and his posture recalls that of the sun-"child" on the seal shown in illus. 241c; nevertheless, the gesture shown here is connected with an act of veneration, and the man is a human being at prayer (see Bordreuil 1986a, no. 5). A similar figure appears on a seal impression from Hazor Str. VI (first half of the eighth century) and resembles a "quotation" taken out of context, because the object of worship is not shown (**illus. 234b**). In just the same way, the stylized tree can be represented as an isolated symbol during the eighth century as, for example, in a painting on an everyday ceramic piece from Rosh Zayit in lower Galilee (**illuss. 235a-b**) and as an incised drawing on a storage vessel from Beer-sheba Str. IV (**illus. 235c**).

§140.   The iconographically important evidence, referring transparently to the goddess by means of a stylized tree, but which even more frequently represents a gender-neutral symbol of numinous power, can best be understood if we interpret the Iron Age IIB *asherah* as a *mediating entity* associated with Yahweh, rather than as a personal, independently active, female deity (see Koch 1988, 99). To be sure, what B. Margalit has emphasized is correct: in the inscriptions recording Northwest Semitic blessing formulas from the first millennium and using the form *brktk l=* . . . , the entity that bestows the blessing is otherwise always a deity (Margalit 1990, 276; see Braulik 1991, 111f.). This would lead one to expect that the *asherah* named at Kuntillet ʿAjrud also ought to be treated as a "separate identity" (Miller 1986, 246). But only two of the parallels cited by Margalit are really relevant to our investigation. They are the only ones that – like the inscriptions of Kuntillet ʿAjrud – mention more than one deity as being involved in providing the blessings (*KAI* 50.3 [see above, §134 note 78]: "Baal Zaphon and all the gods of Tahpanhes"; Dupont-Sommer 1945, 20 line 3: "Yaho and Khnum"). Neither of these two cases furnishes an example that mentions partner deities.

---

102 In terms of the subject matter, this is essentially comparable to the Egyptianized-Phoenician variation of this constellation, as can be seen on a seal that was supposed to have been found in Palestine, whose owner had the Aramaic name *brkʾ* (Horn 1962, 17). The men who are shown here on either side wear short loincloths and double crowns.

Neither of these two letters concludes with a wish for a blessing (E), as do Inscriptions ^B2 and ^B3 from Kuntillet ʿAjrud. In our opinion, one must start by examining the context of the inscriptions on the pithoi themselves before comparing them with supposed "parallels." Such very careful observation will help to show very precisely which concepts the original writer of the inscriptions tried to connect with granting the blessings: if "Yahweh . . . and his *asherah*" occur side by side in the blessing formula (D) in the pithos inscriptions in each of the three examples, but the concluding wish for blessing (E) is stated in ^B2 (Lines 7ʹ–9ʹ: *ybrk wyšmrk wyhy ʿm ʾdny*)[103] and also in ^B3 (*wntn lh yhw klbbh*) in the *singular*. It is accordingly *Yahweh alone* who is to be understood as the power that effects or produces the blessing.

In a votive inscription found on the edge of a stone bowl (approximately 200 kg) that was found in the north "benchroom" near Pithos A,[104] Yahweh alone is mentioned as the deity who causes or produces blessing.

lʿbdyw[105] *bn ʿdnh brk hʾ lyhw*[106]
"From ʿObadyau b. ʿAdnah. Blessed is/be he of/to Yahweh."

Neither the iconography nor the texts force us to interpret the relationship between "Yahweh . . . and his *asherah*" in Iron Age IIB in the sense of a (sexually-determined) relationship of two forces that are paired and thus compel us to assume that the *asherah* has the status of a partner. "Yahweh's *asherah*" does not have equal rank with Yahweh but is rather a *mediating entity* that brings *his* blessing and is conceived in the mind in the shape of a stylized tree that was thus subordinate to Yahweh.

§141. A slightly more recent Judahite inscription (second half of the eighth century), scratched on bedrock in a tomb at *Khirbet el-Qom*, about 13 km west of Hebron, apparently confirms the understanding of "Yahweh and his *asherah*" in the sense of a deity and an entity that is subordinate (Dever 1969/1970, 158–169, 201f. Tomb II, Inscription no. 3).[107] It was written above a drawing of a large hand pointing downward. The hand should perhaps be interpreted apotropaically (**illus. 236**; Keel 1980b, 172; Schroer 1984):

Line 1   *ʾryhw. hˤšr. ktbh*
Line 2   *brk. ʾryhw. lyhwh.*

---

103 The verbs in this sentence could also be understood theoretically as defectively written forms of the third *plural* prefix conjugation. The clearly singular form in ^B3 and in the inscription from Khirbet el-Qom (§141) counsel against accepting this reading.

104 Meshel 1978, fig. 10; 1979, 32f.; Weinfeld 1984, 127 note 5; Davies 1991, 80 no. 8.001; cf. Conrad 1988, 562.

105 Scagliarini (1989, 204f.) reads only *ʿbyw* "ʿObyau."

106 Because this spelling of the divine name is unusual among the passages at Kuntillet ʿAjrud, Lemaire (1984a, 134f.) proposes that the writer made a mistake when copying from an original that had two lines (*lʿbdyw bn ʿdn¹ / brk hʾ lyhwh¹*).

107 On this inscription, see esp. Lemaire 1977, 597–603; Miller 1981, 315–320; Zevit 1984; Tigay 1986, 26, 29f.; Hadley 1987a; Olyan 1988, 23f.; Hadley 1989, 121–142; Scagliarini 1989, 202 with note 20 (and further literature citations). The text has been studied most recently by Davies 1991, 106 no. 25.003.

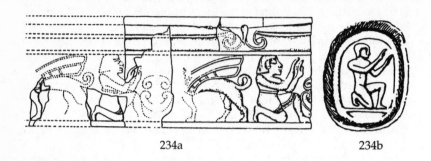

234a   234b

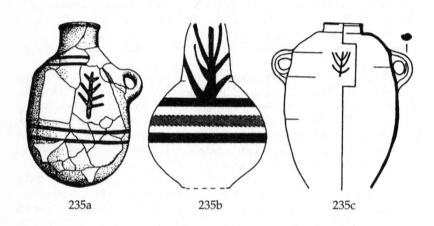

235a   235b   235c

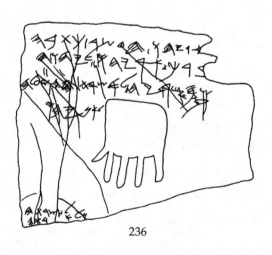

236

Line 3   *wmṣryh l'šrth hwš' lh*
Line 4   *l'ṅyhw*
Line i   *l'šrth*
Line ii   *wl'[š]rth*
Line 1   "Uriyahu, the honorable, has written [this]
          (or: "this is his inscription)
Line 2   Blessed is/be Uriyahu by Yahweh
Line 3   And [because?] from his oppressors,
          by his *asherah*, he has saved him
Line 4   [written?] by Oniyahu."
Line i   ". . . by his *asherah* . . .
Line ii   . . . and by his *asherah* . . ."

The interpretive difficulties for this inscription arise from the fact that, among other things, it is often almost impossible to distinguish written lines from cracks in the rock. In addition, it appears that the writer rewrote several characters, especially in Line 3 and from time to time curiously shifted these letters slightly in so doing. For this reason, S. Mittmann has disputed Lemaire's reading of *l'šrth* and would read in its place the "bold, compressed word-combination" *l'l šrth* "God of his service."[108] But this usage is completely without analogy, and furthermore, the reading is probably *l'šrth* in Lines i and ii as well, though Mittmann has not addressed this fact. Lemaire's thesis (1977, 602) is just as bold as what Mittmann proposed: *l'šrth* has been positioned incorrectly in Line 3 – and ought to to be read along with the end of Line 2 (*brk. 'ryhw. lyhwh. <w> l'šrth*). Even though Lemaire wants to use the blessing formulas from Kuntillet 'Ajrud to support his thesis (1984b, 44), this reading is still improbable (note that even the conjunction needs to be supplied). In any case, the inscription does not need to be reconstructed in order to make sense, as is shown in the translation above that follows Miller (1981, 317), Hadley (1987a, 51; 1989, 123), and others.[109]

For our purposes, two aspects of the inscription are particularly important: First, the Judean Uriyahu does not say that he is blessed by **yhwh yršlm* "Yahweh of Jerusalem" or the like, but simply by Yahweh. By contrast to letter prescripts, it was perhaps not customary to combine the divine name with a toponym in formulas of the type *br(w)k* PN (note the votive inscription of 'Obadyau just cited). If the inscription were made after the fall of Samaria, the use of a toponym would have been superfluous since Yahweh would then have been the national god of one state only.[110] Second, it is interesting that Line 3 of the inscription is formulated in the singular, not the plural. Only one divine

108 *wmmṣr ydh l'l šrth hwš' lh* "and in the midst of oppression he praises the god whom he serves, who helps him" (1981, 144).
109 To the bold hypotheses that have already been proposed, Margalit has added a few more, among which is a less than convincing suggestion that a line that runs across the entire inscription should be treated as a rudimentary drawing of a tree (1989, 371).
110 See ostraca 16.2f.; 21.2; 40.3 from Arad, which date to the early sixth century. At the point that is analogous to the blessing formulas from Kuntillet 'Ajrud, these read *brktk lyhwh* "I bless you by/to Yahweh." On this, see M. Weippert 1975, 208–211; Tigay 1986, 22; see below, §209.

power, namely Yahweh, is considered as the active agent who provides freedom from enemies, whereas Yahweh's *asherah* is the medium or entity through which it happens (Miller 1981, 319, note 18; Tigay 1986, 30; Koch 1989, 99f.).

The evidence corresponds exactly with the pithos inscriptions from Kuntillet ʿAjrud. In summary, we can assert: the *asherah*s in eighth-century Israel *and* Judah were thought of not as partners of Yahweh but as cult objects in the form of a tree – and thus as a medium that delivered *his* blessing (see below, §181, for more on the relationship of Yahweh/El and Asherah).

§142.   If we look once more at the two pithoi from Kuntillet ʿAjrud, it remains for us to discuss the *relationship between the drawings and the inscriptions*, which we postponed for methodological reasons. There are opposing views about the connection between the two as well.[111] Time and again it has been supposed or suggested that Inscription [A]1, that runs horizontally across the head ornamentation of the left Bes figure in illus. 220, should be interpreted as an annotation for motifs [A]M-N or - [A]O. This has led to an identification of the two Bes figures as "Yahweh and his Asherah" (Gilula 1979; Coogan 1987a, 119; McCarter 1987, 147; Margalit 1990, 277;[112] Korpel 1990, 218; cf. H. Weippert 1988, 673) or else to the identification of the female lyre player as Asherah (Dever 1984, 22–25).

An identification of the two *Bes images* [A]**M-N** (see above, §131) with "Yahweh . . . and his Asherah" is impossible.[113] The iconography and inscriptional evidence known thus far offer no evidence for a connection between Yahweh and Bes, though this has often assumed, especially not for Yahweh being depicted in the shape of a Bes figure. If this identification is abandoned, the question of the gender of the right figure [A]N (Bes or Beset) is no longer as crucial. There is no evidence for a connection between Beset and Asherah, and for Bes and Asherah there are at most a few very hypothetical references.[114]

---

111 One cannot *a priori* either argue in favor of or exclude a connection between drawings and inscriptions – and can definitely not suggest from the outset that we are dealing with just *one* drawing and *one* inscription (contra Margalit 1990, 289).

112 Margalit (1990, 298) goes so far as to speak of a "graphic commentary on the word **ʾšrh*" and thus perpetuates a typically Judaeo-Christian tradition (see Keel/ Uehlinger 1990, 127–130) that gives priority to the word and treats pictorial evidence as merely illustrative of – sometimes no longer extent – texts.

113 More than for any other reason, the fact that the Bes figures do not have the heads of bulls shows that they have absolutely no connection with the bull images at Bethel (Gilula 1979; Margalit 1990), nor with any "'bull of Jacob' and his lady" (Coogan 1987a; see above, §131 note 47).

114 See the portrayal on the Phoenician bronze bowl from Nimrud mentioned in §131 note 48, which shows an enthroned goddess (a kind of Queen of Heaven!) whose star-covered baldachin is carried by two Bes figures (Barnett 1935, 203 fig. 7; cf. Dever 1984, 26). Dever points out (1984, 25) that Bes figures are often found in connection with "'Astarte' figurines" (he is probably referring to the pillar figurines), but the relationship between the amulets and the figurines remains completely unclear.

  S. Schroer has suggested that Maacah's "abominable image for the *asherah*" (1 Kgs 15:13) was a "larger-sized Bes figure that the queen mother had set up as a votive gift" (1987a, 38; Lipiński 1986, 93f. had made the same suggestion, with reference to the way it is rendered in the Vulgate; but see Day 1986, 401; Frevel 1989, 79 note 87).

There is equally little reason to identify the *female lyre player* ^A^O with Asherah, since this is hardly a depiction of a goddess (see above, §132). There is simply no evidence, textual or iconographic, to identify Asherah as a lyre player.[115] The inscriptional evidence for *'šrth* suggests an impersonal interpretation of the *asherah* as a cultic symbol. There is evidence for lyre-playing as a cultic activity that is connected with a whole variety of deities (among others, Yahweh; see *HAL* 461a), so that the female lyre player, interpreted as a human being and appearing without any other motif being placed opposite, cannot be convincingly linked either to a cult of Asherah or to a cultic symbol called an *asherah* (see Schroer 1987a, 34f.).

The motif of *"cow and calf"* (^A^J, compare ^B^R) is associated in the history of the traditions more strongly with Anat or Astarte than with Asherah. On Israelite ivory carvings and on other glyptic art that dates to Iron Age IIB, the suckling mother animal never seems to have been depicted (see above, §116). This would discourage us from making a connection with the *asherah*. If one looks for any single motif in the paintings with which to associate the *asherah* that is mentioned in inscriptions, based on what has been said to this point it would have to be the image(s) of the *stylized tree* above the lion (^A^E-H, and possibly ^A^K; see above, §130; Hestrin 1987a, 222; 1991, 56f.; Hadley 1987b, 204f.; 1989, 199f.; cf. Schroer 1987a, 38). The correspondence between the painting and inscriptions extends only to the point that the *asherah*s are not shown anthropomorphically in either medium but rather in the shape of their symbol, appearing as the one who produces or else mediates blessings (see also illuss. 222, 308). The inscription from Khirbet el-Qom, the seal images in illuss. 230 and 233a, and the image in illus. 223, which is possibly from a more recent time, all show that the *asherah* was known in this form not only in Israel but also in Judah.

As regards the drawings on Pithos A (especially on the basis of the images just discussed), one might speak of a kind of *"asherah* atmosphere" about the scene, taking care not to overemphasize this aspect, since motifs ^A^A-D and ^A^I (compare ^B^Q, S, and T) cannot be correlated with the *asherah* topic anyway.

§143. An appropriate answer to the question about the relationship of images and inscriptions must be based on a comprehensive examination of *all* the drawings and inscriptions on the pithoi, rather than by singling out just one inscription or just one iconographic motif (or constellation of motifs).[116] The key to understanding the entire assemblage

---

115 Concerning *Anat* with a lyre in Ugaritic texts, see *KTU* 1:101 (= Ug. V 3 = UT 603) Rs. 15–18 (Caquot, et al., 1989, 50); for additional evidence, one can then also consult *KTU* 1:3 (= V AB = *CTA* 3 = *UT 'nt*) III 3–8 (see de Moor 1987, 8). We are unaware of any corresponding *iconographical* depictions.

116 It is remarkable that no suggestion has as yet been offered that would link "Yahweh . . . and his *asherah*" (mentioned twice on Pithos B) with the drawings on this same pithos (such as with the procession of worshipers ^B^U-Y, the striding bull ^B^S, or the cow ^B^R that are shown in illus. 221). Methodologically, such a suggestion would rank on the same level with those that have been discussed already. Inscription ^B^3 is placed almost right above the procession of worshipers. The lack of a published text of the original unfortunately means that this cannot be shown in illus. 221.

may be found in the procession of worshipers on Pithos B (illus. 221; see above, §133). This scene, which is the only one not drawn according to the Syro-Phoenician artistic canon, offers the most instructive *functional* analogy to the blessing formulas and wishes for blessing among the drawings of both pithoi (see Beck 1982, 46). In both cases, men (!) walk in a prayerful pose in front of a deity (who is not portrayed in the scene); in both cases, one can see that there is a need to *show* others one's piety and one's loyalty to the deity (whether in word or with a picture). "Is not your piety (fear of God) your confidence?" (Job 4:6).[117]

From this we can understand why people copied onto the pithoi letter prescripts that followed the pattern used in private or business correspondence.[118] One either anticipated that others would read these prescripts and take note of the blessing that was asked from the deity for those being addressed or else that the reproduction of formulas of blessing and wishes for blessing could cause the blessing of Yahweh to be present at this far away place as well – or even do both. In any case, it is not by accident that these inscriptions preserve excerpts.[119] What was required here was not to inform someone about some business matter but rather to obtain a blessing from those contact persons in Samaria and Teman for officials[120] who were stationed in Kuntillet ʿAjrud or for those who were traveling. The prescripts state in

117 In the psalms of individual lament and petition and in the psalms of individual trust, the one who prays often suggests that the mere offering of the petition should provide a reason for why the prayer should be heard and why that individual can have confidence (see, e.g., Pss 27:7f.; 28:1ff.; 57:2f.).

118 We assume that the prescripts are excerpts from actual letters that were sent from Samaria to Kuntillet ʿAjrud. It is true that no ostraca have been recovered from the excavations that preserve entire letters. One might imagine that the prescripts are to be understood as short letters written to travelers whose acquaintances knew in advance that they would be stopping there and who wanted to send to them these short greetings and wishes for blessing (thus, e.g.: PN 1 sends best wishes to PN 2 as he goes on his trip). The introduction, which would be ponderous if used in direct communication, would be phrased thus because it would be following the genre that provided the pattern for how one would convey a "written greeting."

119 That these might be student exercises (sample letters), as Lemaire (1981, 28) has suggested, seems improbable to us, since there is no evidence that a school existed there. ". . . One did not go to Kuntillet ʿAjrud in order to learn how to write or to paint, but the scribes who were passing had learnt that elsewhere" (Puech 1988, 192; 1985, 363) – especially since the handwriting and the personal names show that the pithos inscriptions came from scribes from northern Israel. The architecture of the "benchrooms" is not enough by itself to designate these rooms as a place where instruction took place. As the plan in illus. 218 shows, identical low benches were also found along the east wall of the caravanserai and in the small adjacent gate entryway. The "benchrooms" serve no different purpose than do the two rooms that are in the entryway by the gate (thus also Holladay 1987, 259).

120 It has been suggested at times that the "lord" (*ʾdny*) who is addressed in ᴮ2 may be the "city commandant" (*l =šrʿr*, Meshel 1978, fig. 21*)* who is mentioned in four inscriptions incised on clay vessels (Meshel 1979, 33; Chase 1982, 66, among others). In spite of the fact that Hebrew script is being used, the lack of the article points to an affinity with Phoenicia or with northern Israel (for a different situation elsewhere, cf. below, illus. 345). In place of *šrʿr*, Catastini (1982, 128f.) reads the Phoenician *šr dr* "president of the congregation (of prophets)" (thus

the formula of greeting ([D] *brkt . . . lyhwh. wl'šrth*) *that* the persons being addressed had been commended to the deity.[121] The wish for continued blessing (E) makes the *details* of this blessing more specific. Copying the prescripts onto the pithoi finally places this blessing in public view, stating that it was "*appropriate* that the deity provide the blessing as suggested."[122]

If one reflects on the enormous social prestige that a literate person had, and still has, in a society where most did not even know the alphabet, one can understand why partially incomplete *alphabets* are written right next to highly formalized prescripts for letters. To suggest that the alphabet may virtually have had a "magical-religious" significance (Naveh 1979, 30 note 13; Puech 1988, 192) may be somewhat of an exaggeration (see Millard 1985). These additional letters are more likely a form of documentation written by someone who was showing off to gain social prestige (comparable to someone drawing a picture of a chariot or an archer), but which that individual might construe as a concrete way to address the deity that had given a blessing. It is precisely at this point, where civil prestige, religious ostentation, and the petition for a guarantee of constant blessing from Yahweh come together, that one can make sense of the presence of the stone vessel discussed in §140, with its votive inscription from 'Obadyau ben 'Adnah, which must have cost the owner or his servant a great deal to transport to Kuntillet 'Ajrud.

Clearly, there must have been an especially great need for communication such as this in the bleak desert of the northern Sinai. J. Naveh has correctly pointed out the commonality of subject matter between the pithos paintings and inscriptions and the rock paintings and inscriptions from widely differing periods in the Sinai (see Beck 1982, 46).

§144.   In addition to the ancient Hebrew inscriptions already mentioned, the remains of *ink inscriptions in ancient Phoenician script* have been found on fragments of wall plaster. Because we still await publication of these inscriptions, we can make only a few summary references. In addition to a completely undecipherable fragment found *in situ* in the passageway that led from the north "benchroom" to the inner court, the following inscription that was found in debris in the room could be deciphered (Meshel 1978; 1979, 30; cf. Davies 1991, 80 no. 8.015):

Wall 1   Line 1   . . .]*brk* (or '*rk*''). *ymm. wyšb'w*[. . .
            Line 2   . . .]*hytb. yhwh*[. . .

---

also Scagliarini 1989, 203f.). This interpretation is improbable on paleographical grounds and is based on a questionable identification of the function of the entire site at Kuntillet 'Ajrud that suggests that it is a center for a prophetic guild (see §127 note 38 concerning Tell Deir Alla).

121 This means that here, as well as in the Hebrew Bible, *BRK* pi. refers to "celebratory words that are uttered, that proclaim to those for whom they are meant the recognition, the thanks, the reverence, the solidarity of the relationship, or the best wishes of the speaker, in hopes that the reputation of that other person might increase . . . and with wishes being expressed for his good fortune, success, and for a multiplication of his possessions" (Scharbert 1973, 825).

122 Scharbert 1973, 814 (not related at this point to the inscriptions from Kuntillet 'Ajrud). The emphasis is ours.

Line ?   . . .]*ytnw. l*[. . .]*'šrt*[*h* . . .
Line 1   ". . .] Blessed (or long[?]) be your[123] days,
              and they ought to be made abundant[?] [. . .
Line 2   . . .] Yahweh will do good things [. . .
Line ?   . . .] may they give . . . his[?] *asherah* . . ."

Additional fragments of this inscription add at least one more reference to the divine name *yhwh*. It is remarkable that this is the only
example at Kuntillet 'Ajrud for a *plene* writing of the divine name. In spite
of the old Phoenician characters, this is apparently a Hebrew inscription.
Davies reconstructs the text so that the words *ytnw. l*[. . .] and *'šrt* [. . . are
a continuation of Line 2. If the fragmentary conclusion has been reconstructed correctly, it shows that the blessing, given by Yahweh and
mediated by his *asherah*, was sought or reciprocated by means of (votive)
gifts that were not for Yahweh alone, but for Yahweh and his *asherah*.[124]
Another somewhat better-preserved wall inscription appears to have
come from the entrance to the long storage room at the west end of the
site.[125] According to Meshel's preliminary report (1978; 1979, 30; cf.
Conrad 1988, 563, who arranges the sequence of the lines differently) we
read there:

Wall 2   Line 1   . . .] *wb'rḥ. 'l. b*[. . .
              Line 2   . . .] *brk. bʿl. bym. ml*[. . .
              Line 3   . . .] *šm. 'l. bym. ml*[. . .

              Line 1   ". . .] and when El bursts forth on [the
                            day of["] . . .
              Line 2   . . .] blessed be Baal on the day of the [. . .
              Line 3   . . .] the name[?] of El on the day of the [. . ."

In a different treatment of this text, M. Weinfeld produced an appreciably
longer text (esp. for Line 1) in a brief note (1984, 126):

Wall 2   Line 1   . . .] *wbzrḥ. . . .*[?] *'l. wymsw¹ hrm*[. . .
              Line 2   . . .] *brk. bʿl. bym. ml*[*ḥmt*[?]
              Line 3   . . .] *lšm. 'l. bym. ml*[*ḥmt*[?]

              Line 1   ". . .] and when El beams forth, the mountains
                            melt [. . .
              Line 2   . . .] blessed be Baal on the day of the b[attle . . .
              Line 3   . . .] the name[?] of El on the day of the b[attle . . ."

Apparently because of the reference to theophanies using language
clearly comparable to what is found in the Bible (cf. Line 1a with Deut
33:2 "Yahweh of Seir"; Isa 58:8; 60: 1–3; for Line 1b see Mic 1:3f., Ps 97:5;
on the whole subject, see Hab 3:3–6), the longer version has, under-

---

123 The suffix (and possibly the entire utterance of blessing) could apply to those
    who go in and out of the gate. On this, see Deut 11:18–21 (with the promise of a
    blessing) and 6:4–9. On this subject, see Keel 1981, 183–192.
124 See above, §136 note 88.
125 Meshel's accounts of the findspots of the three inscriptions are contradictory (cf.
    Meshel 1978 with 1979, 29f.; Beck 1982, 4).

standably, essentially been adopted in the most recent *Ancient Hebrew Inscriptions: Corpus and Concordance* (Davies 1991, 82 no. 8.023). It is obvious that this longer textual reading needs to be corroborated. No matter which way the text is read, it should be noted that both the divine name El – apparently a solar El[126] – and Baal are mentioned explicitly. What remains unclear is whether the text is of Phoenician or Israelite provenance and what relation the two deities or identifications of deities have to each other and to Yahweh, who is not mentioned on the fragment. Other isolated fragments of wall inscriptions appear to use the names *yhwh* and *b'l* for the deity frequently (Meshel 1978).

Wall Text 1, with its theme of blessing and the mention of Yahweh (and possibly also the *asherah*), is more like the pithos inscriptions that are written in ancient Hebrew than like Wall Text 2. Because the context is unclear, the two inscriptions cannot be used as clear indicators that there was a Phoenician/Israelite syncretism.

§145.   The main difference between these inscriptions and those on the pithoi lies in the fact that these, unlike those on the pithoi, are not seeking a private blessing. On the contrary, much like the *wall paintings* that are intentionally there as a part of the architectural decor, these texts seem to have an official character about them. Olyan (1988, 34), Koch (1989, 99) and others have emphasized correctly that the discoveries at Kuntillet 'Ajrud cannot be interpreted as peripheral evidence for a heterodox syncretism that was in full bloom in the desert, far from state control. The letter prescript on Pithos ᴬ1 connects itself expressly with the "Yahweh of Samaria." The wall paintings show especially, with all the clarity one could desire, that the caravanserai was a royal/state outpost on a trade route that was under government control. The decorations, using designs featuring ornamental boxes and lotuses in series, indicate the official character of the site (Beck 1982, 50–52 no. 6; 56–58 no. 10; cf. the lotus garlands on the Samaria ivories, Crowfoot, et al., 1938, pl. 16.1–2), but this is made even more clear in the portrayal of a (besieged?) city. On the battlements, one can see a man with a helmet, with a bareheaded man right behind him (**illus. 237**). The picture is thematically reminiscent of Assyrian palace reliefs and paintings on bricks and walls that were done in the period from the ninth to the the seventh centuries. The representation of an enthroned prince with lotus blossom also has an official character about it (**illus. 238a**; compare this to the very worn image on the base of a faience scarab from the ninth or eighth century from Beth Shemesh, **illus. 238b**). Behind the prince shown in illus. 238a we can see the remains of a second enthroned or standing figure. There is a comparable scene on an approximately contemporary ivory carving from Samaria that is unfortunately equally fragmentary (**illus. 239**). On this piece, the seated figure in the front is a woman (queen?) and the figure to the rear is a man (servant?; see Stern 1989a, 106f.). One can see a lotus stalk between the two figures.

§146.   The "parallels" we have just discussed allow us to draw conclusions about how to determine the significance of the artifacts at

---

126 *ZRH* is used most often to describe the sunrise (HAL I 270; Stähli 1985, 40–42; Smith 1990, 115f.); on solar symbolism during Iron Age IIB, see below, §§148ff.

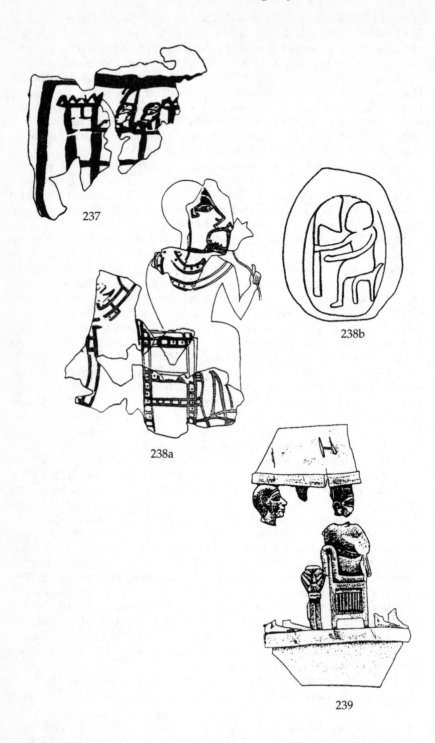

237

238b

238a

239

Kuntillet 'Ajrud for religious history. Ever since Meshel's first detailed report (1978), these discoveries have been used repeatedly, because of the geographic location of the site, as evidence for the dominant religious situation in *Judah* during the monarchy. But incorrectly! The mention of "Yahweh of Samaria" (Pithos ^A1 Line 2); the fact that the theophoric personal names found at Kuntillet 'Ajrud are formed without exception using the element -*yw* (not -*yhw*)[127] (Lemaire 1984a, 133); the paleographic commonalities that link the pithos inscriptions and the ostraca from Samaria (Lemaire 1984a, 134–136; Olyan 1988, 32; see above, §125 note 24), as well as the iconographically and epigraphically demonstrable combination of elements of (Syro-) Phoenician and Israelite culture all demonstrate clearly that the caravanserai at Kuntillet 'Ajrud was not Judahite. It was set up using Phoenician "know-how"[128] but was controlled by *Israelites* and had no local roots.[129] It was probably in use no longer than one generation.

We ought to abandon the notion, once and for all, that the site was a pilgrimage shrine or some other kind of religious center (Meshel 1978; Dever 1984, 29f.; H. Weippert 1988, 619, 625f., among others). The architecture and decoration at the site both characterize it much more clearly as a state-run caravanserai (see Beck 1982, 61f.; Hadley 1987b, 207f.; 1989, 145–158).[130]

The historical context for this Phoenician/Israelite *joint venture* is most likely the time of the Israelite King Jehoash[131] (ca. 802–787; McCarter 1987, 138f.) or that of Jeroboam II (ca. 787–747; Lemaire 1984a, 136–139). Jehoash had freed Israel not only from the threat of the Arameans (2 Kgs 13:24f.) but also from Amaziah of Judah, whom Jehoash defeated shortly after Amaziah's successful campaign against Edom (2 Kgs 14:8–14). The

127 In addition to *yw'šh* (also found on a name seal from the seventh century, Avigad 1954a, 150f. no. 5), which has been discussed already, *'mryw* and *'bdyw* (also found on Samaria Ostracon 50.2; see Lemaire 1977, 36, 53), one must also include the personal names that were scratched onto the stone vessels: *ḥlyw* and *šm'yw bn 'zr* (Meshel 1978; 1979, 32). Late evidence from Judah (1 Chr 4:16; 2 Chr 29:12) is not sufficient by itself to designate the restored name on Pithos ^A1 *yhl['l]* as Judean (contra Hadley 1987b, 184f.).

128 In addition to the Syro-Phoenician background of the majority of the drawings that are on the pithoi, the Phoenician script that is used on the wall inscriptions supports this as well.

129 The fact that the two pithoi on which the writing and drawings are found and the other "hole mouth" pithoi must have been produced in the vicinity of Jerusalem, as has been demonstrated by neutron-activation analysis, does not contradict this. They must have reached the caravanserai by means of the overland trade route. Note that pithoi from the same source have also been found in Beer-sheba and Arad. Other storage vessels at Kuntillet 'Ajrud came from the Philistine coastal plain. Only a pair of weights and a stopper for a jug were "made" using local clay. It should be carefully noted that, among the finer ceramic pieces, two examples of the so-called "Samaria ware" from northern Israel were recovered (Gunneweg, et al., 1985, esp. 273, 280–283; for a discusssion of these finds, see also Hadley 1989, 150f.).

130 On Lemaire's thesis that a school was here, see above, §143 note 119. Hadley (1989, 152) makes reference to the institution of the *mālôn* "inn, lodging for the night" that is mentioned in the Bible (see Exod 4:24 [Midian]; Jer 9:1 [in the desert]).

131 See above, §134 note 68.

king could then have controlled the entire trade route from Samaria to Teman; in addition, 2 Kgs 14:22 implies that Judah lost the port of Elath under Amaziah. This same verse dates the return of Elath to Judean control to the time of Uzziah/Azariah, which means after the death of Amaziah (ca. 773). It is said of Jeroboam II in 2 Kgs 14:25 that Israel's territory extended under his rule from Lebo-hamath in the north to the Sea of the Arabah in the south. If we gather all this information together, it gives us as a more probable context for the establishment and use of the caravanserai at Kuntillet ʿAjrud: the time span of ca. 800–775, which agrees with the suggested dating of the ceramics[132] as well as the paleographic assessment of the inscriptions on the pithoi when based on connections with the ostraca from Samaria.

§147. Many hypotheses from recent years that have sought to describe the religious history of Israel have begun with individual pieces of evidence, usually considered without taking cognizance of their context (a single word or even the etymology of that word or else a single picture such as the female lyre player on Pithos A), from which a mighty leap has been taken to construct a comprehensive generalization (discussion of partner deities; polytheism in preexilic Israel). Our account of the relevant discoveries at Kuntillet ʿAjrud, set forth in somewhat greater detail in spite of this book's character as a survey, seeks to find some middle ground between the extremes. Each piece of evidence ought to be examined – including material that so far has been given scant attention in the scholarly discussion – though not in isolation from its context. Semantics alone, apart from supporting evidence and context, will not do. This seems to us to be the only methodologically responsible way to develop a religious history that understands reconstructing symbol *systems* as its task.

We have attempted to interpret the discoveries at Kuntillet ʿAjrud as elements within such a symbol system, avoiding drawing narrow conclusions by using as much material as possible to justify an interpretation, avoiding the use of just half an inscription or a single figure. As a *result*, it can be stated with confidence that none of the evidence from Kuntillet ʿAjrud (nor from Khirbet el-Qom) offers any compelling reason to argue against the thesis that adoration of Yahweh in Israel during Iron Age IIB was largely monolatrous. There is evidence that speaks *against* the notion that Yahweh was thought of as having a female partner during this time period.

The next section will show that the micro-system of Kuntillet ʿAjrud is only a part of an extensive macro-system, and that important aspects of the religious symbol system of Iron Age IIB Israel were not expressed at Kuntillet ʿAjrud.

7. Solar Symbolism and Winged Protective Powers in Phoenician/Israelite Specialty Crafts

§148. Near Eastern gods are not completely absent from artifacts included among the specialty crafts of Phoenician/Israelite origin that have

132 See Beck 1982, 63 note 22.

been found in the Northern Kingdom of Israel, but deities, hybrid creatures, and other protective powers of *Egyptian* origin predominate. Among the *anthropomorphic* Egyptian deities on the Samaria ivories, the *sun god* shown as a child *in a lotus blossom* is seen most frequently (**illus. 240**; see Crowfoot, et al., 1938, pl. 1.2–3). The motif appeared first in Egypt in the New Kingdom (Schlögl 1977) and it quickly came to enjoy great popularity. It combined the lotus, the symbol of regeneration that had been so common already in the Old Kingdom, with the sun god, who achieved a dominant role in the New Kingdom (Assmann 1983).

The motif appears in Israel during the eighth century not only on ivories but also on name seals, as on a seal belonging to a certain ʿšyw bn ywqm and engraved on both sides (**illus. 241a**),[133] and also on another belonging to ʾbyw ʿbd ʿzyw (**illus. 241b**), whose owner, as his title (ʿbd, i.e., "servant, minister") reveals, was a high official, perhaps an official of the Judean king Azariah/Uzziah (ca. 773–735; this king's name appears in Isa 6:1 and 2 Chr 26:1 as ʿzyhw). On a third Hebrew name seal (**illus. 241c**), the sun god is shown kneeling on a papyrus plant and is flanked by two falcon-headed gods who crouch among lotus blossoms.

Shown in a typical Egyptian posture, the child depicted on the ivories holds a finger of one of his hands to his mouth, as children do, while in the other hand he holds a royal "whip." On the name seals, either one hand is held on his chest while the other is raised in the gesture of greeting or blessing, as is found frequently on the Phoenician seals (illuss. 241a-b), or else the sun god raises both hands in the gesture of blessing (illus. 241c; cf. illuss. 234a-b). It also diverges from Egyptian style when the god is shown kneeling and not sitting, as in illuss. 241b-c. On illus. 241b, the child additionally has completely un-Egyptian cow horns on his head, with the solar disk between the horns. These are characteristic of Hathor and Isis in Egypt, but on our seal they are intended to clarify the solar character of the god shown in illus. 241c who sits among the blossoms. The child is depicted also on one of the Samaria ivories wearing the solar disk on his head (Crowfoot, et al., 1938, pl. 1.2). In a way that is very similar to illus. 241c, his solar character is emphasized by an anthropomorphic, falcon-headed figure with a solar disk on his head, who kneels before the sun child and to whom he presents a figure depicting Maʿat above a nb basket (representing "everything connected with justice and order"; see §43).

In addition to the lotus, the sphere of the sun god also includes his role as the god of endless space and especially of endless time (*Ḥḥw*). In this role, the deity is shown as a kneeling human figure, holding two palm branches (palm branches: *rnpt* = "year"); a solar disk is depicted above the god's head, interrupting a palmetto frieze pattern (**illus. 242**). The falcon-headed god with the solar disk above his head, shown in illus. 213, also belongs to the same sphere (see below, illuss. 252–253).

Another composition appears to belong to the Osiris cycle. A *Djed* pillar, a symbol of Osiris at this time, is flanked by two winged female figures, Isis and Nephthys. Solar disks appear not just on their heads but are also above the *Djed* pillar (**illus. 243**). The clear integration of solar

133 It was still possible for a Judean by the name of ʿšyhw to give his son the theophoric name ʾšḥr "belonging to Horus" (Avigad 1986, no. 32; see below, §202).

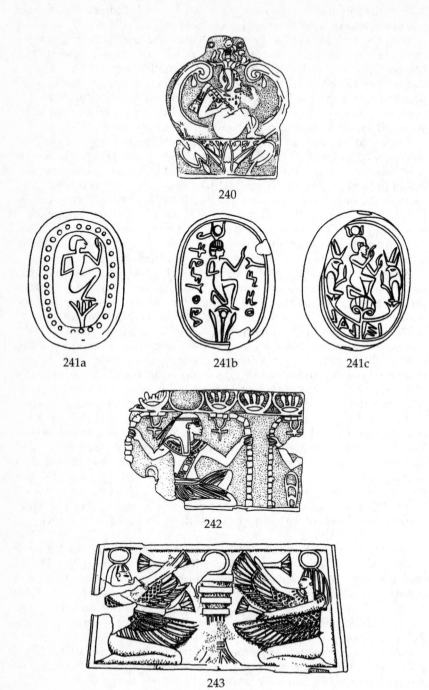

240

241a   241b   241c

242

243

elements makes our depiction a variant way to show the union of Re and Osiris, as it is impressively represented already in the thirteenth century at the grave of Nefertiry, the consort of Ramesses II (Hornung 1971, pl. V). As we saw above, in illus. 227, Bes could also approximate the sun god when shown in association with the four falcons. It is primarily this central focus on the sun god, and what belongs to his spheres of influence, that attracts one's attention in the Iron Age IIB portrayals of anthropomorphic deities of Egyptian provenance. It is true that male deities appear more frequently, but gender plays no special role and opposition between male and female deities is not an issue. Far more important is the connection with the sun observed for both Isis and Nephthys as well as for the male deities.

§149. The second element that is characteristic of this art is the portrayal of protecting *wings*, like those that the goddesses shown in illus. 243 are extending over the *Djed* pillar. As the following examples will show, winged creatures of every kind, falcons, *uraei*, scarabs, etc., are the most important iconographic symbols during the ninth and eighth centuries that help one to identify this Phoenician/Israelite monument group. The wings stress the celestial aspect (see above, illuss. 210–213) as well as the idea of protection. In combination with the sun god, they convey the idea of a mysterious connection between unapproachable distance and effective protection.

A *falcon* with outstretched wings appears in the lower half of a depiction on a scaraboid from Megiddo and on two scarabs from Tell en-Nasbeh; in the upper half, the Megiddo example shows the sign for life, flanked by two worshipers (Lamon/Shipton 1939, pl. 69.49), while the upper half of one of the two scarabs shows the scarab with spread wings (illus. 244) and the other shows a winged *uraeus* between two winged griffins (McCown 1947, pl. 54.12). Two impressions of a seal have been found in Hazor Str. VI (first half of the eighth century). This seal may also have had a falcon with spread wings on the lower part and a winged solar disk in the upper section (Yadin 1960, pls. 67.13; 162.6). A unique combination of a falcon with wings spread and a winged solar figure is shown on the base of a conoid made of green stone that was recovered at Samaria (Crowfoot, et al., 1957, 393 fig. 92.81). Falcons with spread wings supplied a principal motif already in the Middle Bronze Age for the jasper group and appear regularly on southern Palestinian bone seals (see below, §158 with illuss. 267a-b) and here, as there, are associated with a royal ideology (see Giveon/Kertesz 1986, no. 118).

We have encountered *uraei*, with two wings spread forward in a protective manner, above the cartouche with the king's name, above the royal sphinx and the ram sphinx of Amun, and above other numinous beings already from the time of the Eighteenth Dynasty on (Keel 1977a, 101–103, illuss. 77–83; Jaeger 1982, §446). *Uraei* like these are found, dating to the eighth century, on Phoenician name seals (Hestrin/Dayagi-Mendels 1979, no. 118; Bordreuil 1986a, no. 22). *Uraei*, with two wings spread out and held forward in a protective manner, were depicted on the Samaria ivory carvings that were found in the area around the palace (**illus. 245**; see Crowfoot, et al., 1938, pl. 13.4–5). Two mirror-image winged *uraei*, shown in just this posture, fill the middle register of a scaraboid from Beth-Shean Str. IV (eighth century) and are also in the same register on a seal impression on the handle of a vessel from Shechem that dates to the same period (James 1966, fig. 117.3; Horn 1966, fig. 1.54). On a name seal from Megiddo that was recovered from a level dating to the sixth century, two winged *uraei*, which face each other and have two short, pointed horns on their heads, are shown beneath the name *'l'mr*; for paleographic reasons this is dated to the eighth century. The lower register shows a reclining, winged sphinx (**illus. 246**). Each of two Hebrew name seals that might have come from the Northern Kingdom depict a *uraeus* with spread wings that are not stretched out to the front but are turned out to the sides. The one that belonged to *'byw* was supposedly found in the Galilee (**illus. 247a**); the other belonged to a certain . . .]*kryw khn d'r*, to the (high) priest of Dor (**illus. 247b**).[134]

§150. In addition to protective powers with wings, such as falcons and winged *uraei*, *winged hybrid creatures* appear frequently, such as cherubs and falcon-headed sphinxes, in Phoenician-Israelite artistic work that is inspired by Egyptian themes, such as are shown flanking a sacred tree in illuss. 231–232 and 234a. A carefully carved scarab from Tel Dan shows a *uraeus* in the center scene, flanked by two sphinxes with wings and heads of falcons along with two other falcons that face outward, with the top and bottom registers containing two rows of good luck signs reminiscent of the scarabs of Middle Bronze Age IIB (**illus. 248**).[135] The object being worshiped or else guarded is often not even shown, as in illus. 234b, or is just hinted at. Often – especially in name seals – only a *single hybrid creature* is depicted, such as the striding, winged sphinx with a human face (cherub) shown on the seal found in the vicinity of Lachish that belonged to a woman named *ḥnh* (**illus. 249**). The falcon-headed sphinxes are also more numerous than the human-headed versions on seals having only a single image; e.g., an anepigraphic scaraboid from the former Clark Collection in Jerusalem (**illus. 250a**),[136] two pieces from Megiddo, one belonging to *'sp* (**illus. 250b**) and the other to *ḥmn* (Lamon/Shipton 1939, pl. 67.10), and the seal belonging to *rm'* from Ashkelon (Galling 1941, no. 4). On a bulla from Samaria, the seal impression is only partially preserved and the name is illegible (Crowfoot, et al., 1957, pl. 15.38; see Gubel 1985, 93–95, 105–109).

A previously unpublished scaraboid from Tell el-Far'ah (south) offers an interesting variation on the pieces just discussed (**illus. 251**).[137] The striding falcon-headed sphinx (or else having the head of some similar

---

134 The title of the priest, which provides the name of the place where he serves and not, as is otherwise common in Northwest Semitic inscriptions, the name of the deity he served, has raised questions about the authenticity of this seal (Garbini 1982, 171f.). But the combination *khn* + toponym is found frequently in the Hebrew Bible (Amos 7:10; cf. Gen 41:45; Exod 3:1), and it is entirely plausible in the context of a state monolatry.

135 Unpublished until now; steatite; 21.3 × 15.7 × 8.3 mm. We are grateful to Prof. A. Biran, Hebrew Union College, Jerusalem, for permission to publish.

136 Bluish stone, perhaps a somewhat faded lapis lazuli; 14.2 × 10.8 × 7.7 mm. We are grateful to the Directors of the YMCA, Jerusalem, for permission to publish.

137 The piece was discovered in Area F8 on Level 381" and can probably be dated to the eighth century. Made of glass, the base being partially broken off, it measures 17.1 × 13 × 7.4 mm; it is presently in the Institute of Archaeology, London (no inventory number). We are grateful to Prof. P. J. Parr for permission to publish.

244 245 246

247a 247b 248

249 250a 250b

251

type of predatory bird) does not hold its wings parallel but rather in a half-frontal position, so that we see the back of one wing and the front of the other (cf. illuss. 246, 254b). This hybrid creature wears a solar disk on its head rather than the Egyptian double crown that has been shown on all of the other examples that have been discussed (cf. illus. 213).

Along with the striding, winged sphinx, we also see a sphinx crouching on its hind legs, with its forelegs straight out or shown almost in a striding position; this type is especially common on examples found in Cyprus (Gubel 1985, 101–105). Of the three specimens known to us to have been found in Palestine/Israel, one was purchased in Jericho and belonged to a certain *'hz (bn) pqhy* (Jakob-Rost 1975, no. 180). The falcon-headed sphinx wears nothing on its head; the remains of a sign, probably the sign for life, is in front of it (see illuss. 249–250). The second specimen, a surface find from Samaria, belonged to someone named *pt's*, probably an Egyptian name (**illus. 252**; see Tigay 1986, 13,65).[138] The hybrid creature wears a solar disk on its head and a *uraeus* snake rises in front of it. The third example is a seal impression on a vessel handle from Samaria Str. VI (before 720; Ben-Dor 1946, 81f., pl. 25c).

A third type depicts a reclining, falcon-headed, winged sphinx (see Gubel 1985, 97–100). An earlier and more famous example is on the seal of *yzbl* (see 1 Kgs 16:31; Hestrin/Dayagi-Mendels 1979, no. 31 = Keel 1977a, 96 illus. 63). On an example from Shechem that belonged to a certain *yhzq*, there is a solar disk above the falcon-head, with a stylized life sign or flower visible in front of the creature (Galling 1941, no. 11). The hybrid creature on the seal of *hym* from Tell el-Far'ah (south) should also be considered to be one of the reposing, falcon-headed sphinxes. There is an Egyptian double crown on its head and a sign for life is positioned in front of it (**illus. 253**). Reclining, falcon-headed, winged sphinxes wearing the Egyptian double crown also appear on two anepigraphic scarabs from Megiddo Str. III (end of the eighth century). An oval, with rudimentary hieroglyphics, is in front of one of them (**illus. 254a**), perhaps a reference to *mn-hpr-r'*; a Horus eye (see below, illus. 260), flanked by two *uraei* and the hieroglyph *h'* ("hill of the sunrise"), is beneath it. The other falcon-headed sphinx (**illus. 254b**; for the position of the wing, cf. illus. 251) holds a forepaw, which looks like a human hand, raised to signify blessing and protection; four collars are shown in the middle register; two falcons, flanked by the god sign (*ntr*), are shown in the lowest register. On an unfortunately badly damaged scarab or scaraboid from Samaria Str. VI (before 720), a *uraeus* rises directly up in front of a reclining, falcon-headed, winged sphinx (**illus. 255**); above it is the sign for life and below it is a flying scarab that holds a solar disk. These latter forms, as the following paragraph will show, are also among the chief motifs on North-Israelite glyptic art during the ninth and eighth centuries.

In spite of the double crown or the solar disk, which as a rule they wear on their heads, the winged hybrid creatures in illuss. 231–232 and 248–255 are hardly to be regarded as embodiments of any of the deities.

---

138 For epigraphic reasons, Lemaire considers this to be a Phoenician name seal and not a Hebrew seal (1986a, 93f.).

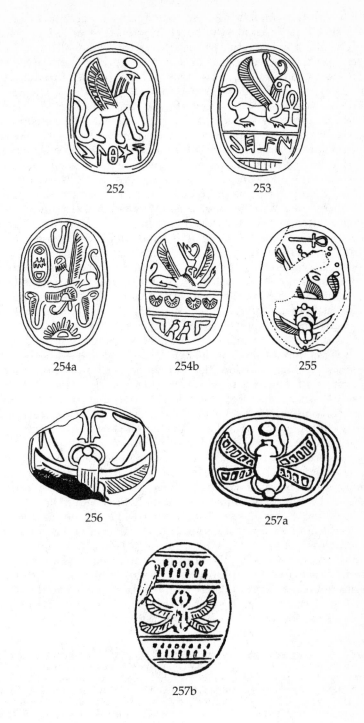

252 253

254a 254b 255

256 257a

257b

But the attribute on their heads confers on them a royal or solar character. These hybrid creatures are thus probably to be regarded as guarding and protecting powers in the service of a "Most High God" or a "Lord of Heaven" who is conceived of in solar categories. Their presence on private seals may mean there was a certain individualizing and "democratizing" of the ideas connected with such a deity. The Egyptian sign for life, which we see in front of the hybrid creatures in illuss. 249– 250 and 253, probably replaces the sacred tree that is depicted in illuss. 231–233a. These powers, whose chief role is probably to serve the "Most High God" and to actualize his rule and ability to bring order on earth, were used by the male and female owners of these seals to claim for themselves protection and certain guarantees for their own personal lives. Here again, "personal piety" and official religion can flow back and forth from one realm to the other, as shown in illus. 250b, where the sign for life is shown in a royal cartouche, and in illus. 254a, where one can also see a cartouche that is being guarded by hybrid creatures.

§151.   In addition to the protecting creatures linked to the sun god, two symbols of the sun god himself are found regularly in the Iron Age IIB glyptic art in the Northern Kingdom of Israel: the two- or four-winged scarab, generally pushing the ball of the sun before himself (see illus. 255), and the winged solar disk. The *two-winged scarab* appears not just as one element among others (illuss. 244, 255) but rather as the main element on a scarab from the former Clark Collection, purchased in Samaria in 1907, thus far unpublished (**illus. 256**).[139] Above the head of the scarab, two ostrich feathers function like a crown; this grouping is flanked by two falcons with outstretched, protecting wings. The same constellation is found both on a scarab from Megiddo Str. III (Lamon/Shipton 1939, pl. 72.1) and on one from Ashkelon (Dothan/Porath 1982, 166f. with fig. 33.7; for early examples from the Ramesses Period, see Petrie 1928, pl. 6.33; 1932, pl. 7.18). On the seal owned by a certain *yw'r* that supposedly came from the Northern Kingdom, we see a two-winged scarab alongside the name (Avigad 1969, 6 no. 15). It appears that the *four-winged scarab*, holding a small solar ball with its front feet and another with its rear feet, was especially typical of Samaria (see illus. 255). It should be interpreted as representing the rising sun.[140] In the palace area of Samaria, nine bullae have been found with impressions of a seal that uses this motif (**illus. 257a**; Crowfoot, et al., 1957, 88). In the early 1950s, Tushingham (1970) acquired a scaraboid with this motif that supposedly came from somewhere near Samaria. In conjunction with the publication of this piece, and with reference to the bullae from the palace area, he argued that the four-winged scarab was a symbol for royal power and rule in the Northern Kingdom. With good reason, Millard (1972) questioned this

---

139 Gray steatite, a piece of the base is broken off; 17.6 × *13 × 8.8 mm. We are grateful to the Directors of the YMCA, Jerusalem, for permission to publish.

140 Tushingham suggests that this motif entered Israel from Phoenicia at the time of Omri (886–875) when he inititated intensive Phoenician contacts (1970, 76). But it actually appears already on one of the oldest known Phoenician seal amulets that was recovered from a level dated to the ninth century at Khalde, near the airport at Beirut. A four-winged scarab is shown above and a two-winged scarab appears below (Culican 1986, 385–390).

interpretation. Another scaraboid from Gezer provides evidence that would argue against Tushingham's interpretation that this is indicative of royalty, a piece on which a four-winged scarab is framed by friezes that depict *uraei* above and below (**illus. 257b**). Three seals with four registers (one belonging to *š'l*, another to *mqn,* and the third to *ṣdqy*), possibly made in an Israelite atelier,[141] also all depict a four-winged scarab in the main register, with the scarab flanked in this case by worshipers (Lemaire 1986b, 307 fig. 2a-b; Zuckerman 1987, 25–27).

The *winged solar disk* is found frequently on Phoenician as well as on Israelite seal amulets. Wings bent at a sharp angle form a frame around the upper register (Parayre 1990, 274, 289). The winged solar disk is combined with a four-winged scarab on a very beautiful scarab from Samaria (**illus. 258a**) and it hovers above a stylized palmetto tree on a scaraboid from Shechem (**illus. 258b**). On still another scaraboid from the same site, it is even shown twice, protecting the royal, falcon-headed sphinx, with the sun disk positioned above the sphinx's head (**illus. 258c**). The engraver of both the Shechem pieces made conspicuous use of the drill, which seems to be characteristic of a particular, local workshop (on a third example from Shechem, see Horn 1966, fig. 1.54).

In addition to the solar disk that has wings that are very bent and that are positioned at the upper edge and occasionally at the lower edge of the picture, other examples show the wings pointed straight out. They serve generally as dividers between two registers. A scarab from Megiddo (of which barely half remains) places this type of solar disk between a falcon shown with a "whip" in the upper register and a winged hybrid creature positioned in the lower register (**illus. 259a**). On a badly damaged piece from Samaria, this sign separates a winged *uraeus* and a winged hybrid creature in the top portion from an oval in the lower portion that is flanked (?) by *uraei* (**illus. 259b**).[142] The winged sun also appears in the same position in the middle on the famous seal of *yzbl* (Keel 1977a, 96 illus. 63 = Hestrin/Dayagi-Mendels 1979, no. 31).

One final symbol for the sun or moon (see Müller-Winkler 1987, 93) is the *wedjat* or *eye of Horus* that appeared already in illus. 254a. On a seal belonging to a certain *qnyw*, the winged solar disk is above and the eye of Horus is below (Jakob-Rost 1975, no. 183). A rather fantastic combination can be seen on a Samaria ivory that shows an eye of Horus, a falcon claw, and a *uraeus* with a solar disk (**illus. 260**). Taken together, this shows how clearly this symbol of the eye of Horus was associated with the sun god in the Phoenician/Israelite symbol system. The eye of Horus is the motif most frequently encountered among the Iron Age II amulets found in

---

141 See above, §121. Lemaire hesitates to be any more precise about the location of the workshop (1986b, 309). In any case, the iconography does not argue against this being an Israelite atelier. On the winged hybrid creatures that belong to the sphere of the solar "Most High God," which can be seen in the upper registers of the seals belonging to *mqn* and *ṣdqy*, see §150; on the lion that chases a caprid in the lower register on all four seals (see above, illus. 211b), see illus. 231a (but see also Gubel 1986, no. 248).

142 Black steatite, heavily damaged; 15.5 × 12 × 6.7 mm; presently in the Office of the Palestine Exploration Fund, London, to whom we are grateful for permission to publish.

258a   258b   258c

259a   259b

260

261a   261b   261c

Palestine that portray some object on them.[143] It appears regularly in connection with Bes amulets (see above, illuss. 224–225). Two such examples from Megiddo Str. IV are seen in **illuss. 261a-b; illus. 261c** from Lachish shows the eye of Horus four times. A shaped Samaria ivory fragment shows, analogous to Maʿat being given as a present (Crowfoot 1938, pl. 1. 2), an eye of Horus being offered (Crowfoot 1938, pl. 13.13).

§152.   The coherence within the symbol system belonging to this monument group is amazing. It accentuates solar motifs that almost all come from Egypt (sun-child in the blossom, winged solar disk, scarab, eye of Horus) and uses winged creatures that belong in the sphere of the sun god, such as the falcon-headed, winged sphinx, which often wears the solar disk on its head, the Horus-falcon, and the winged *uraei*. As in Egypt, these symbols are closely connected with the monarchy, the same is true here, as can be seen very clearly by the use of the double crown on the head of the falcon-headed sphinx and by the occasional presence of a cartouche or oval.

In view of this coherence and the meaning generally assigned to religious symbols in the ancient Near East, it is rather misleading when archaeologists such as A. Mazar (1990a, 507) or religious historians such as J. H. Tigay (1986, 94f.) join so many others in reiterating the old refrain that foreign symbols were used on ivories and seals merely as decorations and had no religious significance. As G. Dalman correctly emphasized already in 1906(!), it is "in fact hard to believe that the sacred symbols that the Israelites wore as seals on their fingers or on their breasts ... were just decorative items and had no meaning for them" (1906, 44). The purely aesthetic use of figurative elements is recent, and the notion that such a use existed in the ninth and eighth centuries is anachronistic. Even if part of the charm was that these motifs came from Egypt, that country was much too close geographically and its religion was far too well-known along the eastern coast of the Mediterranean, from the second millennium on, for us to think that a half-way intelligent Israelite would not know the significance of what he was wearing on his seal amulet as he went about his daily business. It is cavalier of W. G. Dever to assert that these symbols never really lost their "pagan connotations," and that their use was to be attributed to a "popular religion ... where un-sophisticated folk did not draw fine distinctions and so were always inclined to syncretism" (1990, 162). On the contrary, seals and ivories document a symbol system that was highly "sophisticated," one that did not express the religious preferences of the common masses, but rather of the Israelite élite. G. Hölbl (1989) has shown that Phoenician culture was thoroughly acquainted with Egyptian religious ideas, and there is no reason to assume that the Israelites did not have at least a modest acquaintance with them.

143 See Yadin 1961, pl. 176.26; James 1966, fig. 113.14f.; Lamon/Shipton 1939, pl. 75.1–
      30; Kenyon, et al., 1965, 512f. with fig. 261.2; Macalister 1912, III pl. 210.20–32, 34f.;
      Mackenzie 1912–1913, 60, pl. 28A; Bliss/Macalister 1902, pl. 84, 5–8; Tufnell 1953,
      pls. 34.8–10; 35.37, 41–43; 36.52; Dever 1969–1970, 188; Petrie 1928, pl. 45.21, 27,
      30, 43–45, 47–50, 54–56, 58, 64; 1930, pls. 33.369f.; 35.410–413; 41.260–263; 43.516;
      1937, pl. 30.58–79; Rowe 1936, no. A. 58, etc. For examples from the Late Bronze
      Age, see McGovern 1985, 60–62 and 127 nos. 240–250 (Type V.E.).

Naturally, one must investigate thoroughly the possibility that supply and demand played a role in the inflationary growth of Egyptian and Phoenician motifs during the eighth century. Not all the ivories and seals of Iron Age IIB found in Israel were necessarily produced in the Northern Kingdom itself. Did the Israelite upper class, interested in acquiring ivory and similar luxury items from Phoenicia, have to accept whatever iconographic repertoire came their way, even if the religious ideas that were presented therein were not congruent with their own beliefs?

One glance at the enormous treasures of ivory from Nimrud will clarify a few points here: northern Syrian, Phoenician, and Egyptian ivories, along with other imported pieces of miniature art, are found mixed together indiscriminately. The products acquired by trade and plunder did not influence the religious concepts of the Assyrians in any substantive way, if the products that can be traced to local Assyrian production are any indicator. Israelite discoveries show a completely different picture. The Phoenician/Israelite symbiosis went so deep that we are not always even able to tell which specialty items were produced locally and which were imported. At the same time, it is remarkable that not *all* the motifs and symbols represented in the Phoenician repertoire have been documented in Phoenician/Israelite crafts, only a limited selection. On the one hand, we note a clear preference for a symbol system that accentuates solar themes, in which the questions dealing with how to differentiate male from female are completely in the background. On the other hand, selectivity can also be observed: anthropomorphic images of goddesses and motifs from the sphere of the goddess such as are typical on pieces produced throughout Phoenicia are almost completely absent from Israel.

To be sure, arguments from silence prove nothing. We do not know whether the collection of Samaria ivories is representative of the entire repertoire that existed in the capital of Israel before 720. The most valuable and best pieces may have found their way to Assyria as plunder. Inscribed ivory fragments from Israel have been found in the storehouses of Nimrud (Millard 1962, 45–49; cf. Davies 1991, 112; Conrad 1988, 564). Since these fragments have not proved helpful in matters of iconography, future research will be necessary to determine whether any – or possibly, which – of the ivories from the storehouses in Nimrud can be linked to Israelite ivory pro-duction and whether the description of Samaria's repertoire, based on what has been preserved in the country itself, will have to be modified substantively.

§153.   The religious scene that emerges from what appears on the Phoenician/Israelite specialty crafts found in Palestine may at first glance be surprising, but the biblical traditions reflect much the same picture. For a long time already, the Baal against whom polemics were uttered by someone like Elijah in 1 Kgs 18:17–40 had not been that same weather god who had been known in Late Bronze Age IIB for his interaction with the sexually attractive goddess (see illuss. 30–31a). Nor is he any longer the Baal from the end of the Late Bronze Age and the beginning of the Iron Age who is represented as a warrior in the service of some other distant god in the heavens or on behalf of the sun god (see illuss. 86–89). The Baal of the ninth and eighth centuries, as O. Eissfeldt demonstrated as long ago as 1939, is actually a kind of Baalshamem, the "Lord of Heaven" himself. This god, whom we encounter for the first time in Byblos in the tenth century, was really an elevated version of the old weather god of the type seen in Hadad (Clifford 1990, 60), converging in function with the distant god of the type, seen in El, to form a kind of Zeus figure (Gese 1970, 182–185; Olyan 1988, 62–64; Smith 1990, 41–45; Niehr 1990, 22–24, and often elsewhere). As "Lord of Heaven," following as well as before this shift, this god was still responsible for rain. Yet he now expressed his majesty and the increasing range of territory over which he ruled by using celestial and solar categories.

We would have to say the same about *Yahweh*, who, according to the evidence of personal names and inscriptions, must have been the dominant deity in Israel. The correlation of the iconographic symbols for the sun and the heavens with epigraphic documentation that gives evidence for a contemporary context, in which Yahwism was dominant, leads one inevitably to formulate a hypothesis that the movement in which the Phoenician Baal took on celestial and solar attributes and became Baalshamem is to be seen as part of a larger shift in religion concerning the entire Levant, a shift that affected Israel as well. Like the Phoenician Baal, the Israelite Yahweh took on the characteristics of a celestial/solar "Most High God" during Iron Age IIB as well. Some biblical texts also show Yahweh in the role of Baalshamem. In Ps 104:1–4, Yahweh has characteristics strongly associated with the sun and is surrounded by winged servants. As more recent works have shown, central motifs in this psalm are inspired by Phoenician themes. Aspects of a weather god and a sun god converge with images depicting a creator god that result in a Baalshamem type of figure (Uehlinger 1990b; Dion 1991).

In connection with what we note here, Hos 6:3 is very significant. Yahweh's appearance is connected directly with sunrise and rain, which means that Yahweh is portrayed in the same role in which Baalshamem is depicted, against whom or against whose local representations the book of Hosea directs so vigorous a polemic. Hosea 6:5 also adds to this picture the idea of the sun god as judge. The conflict between Yahweh and Baal has nothing to do with a genetic incompatibility between worship of the "Canaanite" Baal and the Israelite Yahweh proceeding from diametrically opposed ideas about the nature of deity. Ultimately, the reason appears to have had much more to do with the fact that the two gods were nearly indistinguishable in eighth-century Israel, fulfilling the same functions and roles and being conceived of using the same categories. As is clear in passages such as Hos 2:4-15, Hosea primarily addresses the fact that Yahweh and Baal had been permanently switched within the cultic practices in Israel.

A significant difference between these two gods, one that is centrally important in this study, is the fact that Yahweh (El) does not seem to have had any consort at all, in contrast to the Phoenician Baal, who seems to have had a different consort in each city – Baalat in Byblos; Astarte in Tyre and Sidon.

8. Symbols of Royal/Courtly Rule

§154. The symbols of royal or courtly rule shown on Israelite/Phoenician specialty crafts during the eighth century were clearly oriented primarily toward Egypt. A group of flat ivories from Samaria, executed without relief in the "silhouette inlay" ("*champ levé*") style, illustrate this. In this group, the *king* appears in the form of a sphinx who strides over a enemy who is lying on the ground (**illus. 262a**; for examples that shows this theme that are made in molds, see Crowfoot, et al., 1938, pl. 10.3–5), and the king is depicted in another example wearing a double crown and holding a club in the canonical posture of "striking down the enemy" (**illus. 262b**; see above, illuss. 97 and 144). At first glance, the images seem purely Egyptian, but still they may be Levantine pieces (see I. Winter 1981, 110f.). Egyptian portrayals would not combine a stylized tree with the striking motif (note the blossom behind the pharaoh on illus. 262b). Once more, the stylized tree is used here as well to portray a power associated with the monarchy.

§155. The wall paintings in illuss. 237–238 and the ivory in illus. 239 show clearly that Egyptian royal symbolism was adopted but used creatively, so that Near Eastern elements could be included as well. This is especially true of a group of name seals that show the engraved image of a clothed, striding man of high rank on their bases, holding a scepter or a staff in one hand and raising the other hand in an act of reverence or blessing. Most of these men are wearing the double crown of Egypt, shown in a more or less rudimentary way. As a rule, the inscription gives only the personal name of the owner. Remarkably, these private seals omit the name of the owner's father, commonly included elsewhere. Some of the names listed on these seals are found among the names of the Syrian/Palestinian kings who ruled during the eighth and seventh centuries. Thus Bordreuil (1985; 1991) and Gubel (1991b) identify the pieces belonging to this group, all obtained by purchase, as seals of kings (with crowns) or officials (without crowns), whose clothing and attributes (with or without scepter, weapon) allow one to detect certain differences of status.

Kings of Israel and Judah have not appeared as yet in this group of seals. Thus we do not know whether these kings, like their neighbors, had themselves portrayed wearing Egyptian double crowns.[144] A few *seals belonging to officials* that date to the end of Iron Age IIB are especially important for our purposes. A seal engraved on both sides (**illuss.**

---

144 An anepigraphic scarab that is engraved on both sides comes from a tomb located in the vicinity of Bethlehem; on its reverse side it has a striding, royal figure with a *uraeus* on the forehead; another *uraeus* comes out from its long loincloth. A falcon is seated behind the figure on a blossom scepter. The base decoration is divided into two registers, showing a winged griffin with a *uraeus* above and a two-winged *uraeus* below. We are grateful to Dr. W. Zwickel (Kiel) for calling our attention to this piece.

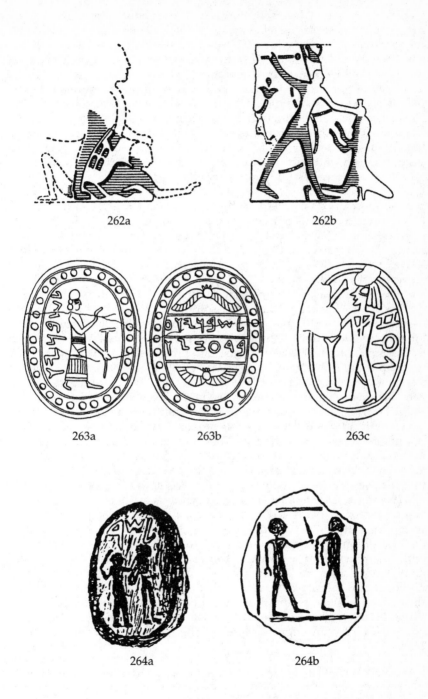

262a

262b

263a

263b

263c

264a

264b

263a-b) portrays, on one side, an aristocratically dressed official with a scepter, identified in the inscription as *šbnyw* (without patronym!). A two-register inscription on the reverse side reads *šbnyw ʿbd ʿzyw* (again without the paternal name, for which the title and name of the royal patron are substituted) and this name is framed above by a solar disk with bent wings and below by a solar disk with wings extended (see below, §160). *ʿzyw* may be the same King Uzziah/Azariah who is mentioned on the seal of *ʾbyw* (see above, illus. 241b) and who ruled as king of Judah 773–735. Since the names (including the king's name!) on both seals are written with the theophoric ending *-yw* (not *-yhw*), as is typical in Israel, these may be the work of a northern Israelite seal engraver. The decoration on both sides allows one to suppose that side a, with its graphic that expresses both authority and loyalty, may have been used for purposes connected to the palace or to the capital, while the more precise inscription on side b, with its exact and precise indication of function, may have been used for outside business.

Another comparable juxtaposition is seen on two different seals (not two sides of *one single* seal) in the case of *ʾšnʾ*, perhaps a minister to King Ahaz of Judah (742–726). Here, above the inscription *lʾšnʾ ʿbd ʾḥz*, a crowned solar disk is shown, flanked by two *uraei* (see below, illus. 273). Another seal, bearing the person's name without patronym or title, depicts a striding man with a blossom-like scepter (Hestrin/Dayagi-Mendels 1979, no. 40). Both pieces were obtained by purchase. It is no longer possible to demonstrate whether they might both have belonged to the same man, as Bordreuil (1985, 23f.) proposes. Equally hypothetical for the present is Bordreuil's suggestion (1985, 27f.; 1986c) that the seal of a certain *pqḥ*, purchased shortly before the turn of the century in Nablus and showing a striding official with a lance(?) or club in front of a cultic stand(?) (**illus. 263c**), may have belonged to (the future) king Pekah of Israel while he was still a weapon-bearer and confidant of Pekahiah, that is, until Pekah overthrew him (ca. 740) and became king in his place (see 2 Kgs 15:25). In any case, a seal impression found at Shechem that was made by a very similar seal of an official (Galling 1941, no. 133) shows that such seals were actually used in the Northern Kingdom.

§156.   Seal impressions showing a striding prisoner with arms tied behind his back, being led or driven by a warrior, also belong to the sphere of state power symbolism. A bulla found in Samaria carries the inscription *lšr* "to the commander" (**illus. 264a**).[145] On another bulla with a similar picture, Lemaire thinks it could be read *lmlk* "to the king" (1986b, 313f. no. 7). An impression of a seal from Tell esh-Shekh Zuweyid and a bulla(?) from a seventh-century level at Ashdod both show that the same pictorial constellation was used in Philistia as well (**illus. 264b**; Dothan/Porath 1982, pl. 26.8).[146] It is impossible to be sure how far this striking figure resembles the man in the *pqḥ* seal in illus. 263c.

145 Another seal with the inscription *lšr* that is supposed to have come from Hebron shows an official without any attributes, who (like the men in illus. 221) raises both arms in worship (Lemaire 1986b, 314f. no. 8).
146 Lemaire knows of yet another unpublished Aramean bulla with the same depiction (1986b, 314).

In contrast to illuss. 262a-b, this constellation does not have roots in Egypt alone. The striking figure in Egypt is always the king, who is taking long strides, and the enemy is usually represented kneeling opposite the king. Striking warriors who drive prisoners in front of them appear frequently on Assyrian palace reliefs and on related image-bearing artifacts. But comparable images are missing altogether from Assyrian glyptic art. Since especially illus. 264b follows its own stylistic path and because there are simply no other better parallels available, we may tentatively classify this (in conjunction with the previously discussed officials' seals) as a local Palestinian pictorial constellation from the late eighth century.

9. Judah: From the Provincial Reception of Egyptian Royal Iconography to the Integration of Religious Solar Symbolism

§157. If one were to ask about specifically *Judahite* production of specialty crafts during Iron Age IIB, a group of *bone seals* that is equally representative and typical is a good place to begin. These seals can be clearly defined as a homogenous group on the basis of their material (bone), their form (from rectangular to square, with clearly rounded corners and a slightly bulging back), and their decoration and style (surface engraving with cross-hatching).[147]

Among the approximately 120 documented pieces known to us, individual pieces have been found from throughout the country: in the north, for example, at Tell el-ʿOreme (Hübner 1986, 260–263; Hübner in Fritz 1990, 128, pl. 117.6) and at Acre (Giveon/Kertesz 1986, no. 132 and an unpublished piece). There are several examples from Megiddo (six pieces) and Gezer (five), and single pieces from Shechem, from Tell en-Nasbeh, and from Jerusalem; the central hill country is also represented. The principal sites where they have been found, however, are Tell el-Farʿah (south), with ten pieces, and Lachish, with twelve pieces that certainly belong to the same group. In addition, there are finds in the area of the southern coastal plain (Ashdod, Tell Jemmeh, Tell esh-Sheh Zuweyid) and in southern Judah (Tell Beit Mirsim, Arad), so it is clear that this group originated in southern Palestine, and the idea that they were produced in Judah (Lachish?) has at least some plausibility.[148] Where the context of the find at the site can be determined with some probability, the origin of the group seems to be chiefly in the ninth century, with continued use of the seals from this group on into the eighth century.

---

147 H. Keel-Leu has done important preliminary work for the understanding of this group in her work on the catalog of the stamp seals in the collection at the Biblical Institute in Fribourg (Keel-Leu 1991, 75–78). We are grateful to Lenny Wolfe of Jerusalem for calling our attention to approximately 60 additional pieces that have been purchased and that are now in private collections.

148 The majority of the bone seals in this group that have been bought in recent years have supposedly come from the area around Hebron. Though information regarding the origin of such seals should be treated with caution, this information also points to the Judean Shephelah as the center for the production of these seals.

The iconography on these bone seals gives evidence of an intense fascination with Egyptian power symbols. Most significant is the royal *cartouche*, portrayed on about 20 pieces in the simplified form of an oval. In most cases, there is a male figure positioned next to it, wearing a short loincloth and raising one arm in worship (**illuss. 265a-b** from Tell el-Farʿah [south]; **illus. 265c** from Gezer; see Hübner 1986, 260–263; Keel-Leu 1991, nos. 92f.). Various attempts to read the signs written in the oval and to connect them to particular pharaohs must be regarded as failures.[149] If one were to place the "cartouches" of the entire group together, one would note that there are always one or more wide "signs" in the middle, at least one of which shows a faint resemblance to a *mn*, and each has a disk at either end (see also illus. 254a). Correspondingly, it is not advisable to read the middle sign in illus. 265b as a *š3*. These might be variants of the same theme – most probably a simplified form of *Mn-ḫpr-rʿ*, which can be taken as either a "pseudonymous name of the king" or else as an Amun cryptogram. This is also clear on a contemporary faience scaraboid from Beth-Shemesh that is iconographically closely related to the bone seal group, but which shows even more pronounced Egyptian influence. The signs *mn* and *rʿ* alternate twice each in the "cartouche" on this scaraboid (Rowe 1936, no. SO. 45). It is hard to say which of the two forces – the Egyptian royalty itself or the royal power of the god Amun that was the subject of much propaganda during the reign of the Twenty-second Dynasty (see above, §84) – exercised greater fascination for ninth-century seal production in southern Palestine.

As a whole, the motifs of the group lean toward depicting royal ideology.[150] There is clear biblical attestation for the continuation of Egyptian royal ideology in this former province. The issues related to the royal name play a direct, important role in Judah (see 2 Sam 7:9; Keel [4]1984, 238–246). Ps 72:17 is written with the king's name in mind:

His name will be forever blessed,
　　his name will sprout before the sun.
All nations should bless themselves through him;
　　may they praise him.

Important themes in the bone seal group include the blessing of and praising of the royal name (see illus. 265), the growth of the name before

149　Rowe (1936, S. 108), read the lowest sign on the piece that is shown in illus. 265c as a sign that resembles an Egyptian *yb* and reads this as "*W3ḥ-yb-rʿ*, the throne name of Psammetichus I (664–610); Hübner (1986, 261) reads the name as *Nfr-yb-rʿ* (Psammetichus II, 595–589), while Tufnell (1953, 363) considered the possibility that this is Amasis, *Ḫnm-yb-rʿ* (570–526). All three thus choose to identify this as the name of a king because they expect one here. But the middle sign in illus. 265c admits none of the three possibilities, not *w3ḥ*, not *nfr*, and not *ḫnmw*. This is completely independent of the fact that the names of these kings do not fit here chronologically. A very good photograph shows that the lower and the upper signs are quite similar. In other words, a disk may have been intended both times, possibly to be read as *rʿ*.

150　The traditio-historical derivation of the motif of the "worship of the cartouche" from Ramesses Period rectangular plaques (Keel-Leu 1991, 74; cf. Petrie 1932, pl. VI, at the very bottom) could also support this interpretation of a royal ideology. But no plausible connecting links have been found to date that would lend support to this view.

265a   265b   265c

266a   266b

267a   267b

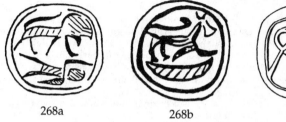

268a   268b   268c

the sun (see illus. 266), and mutual blessing of the king and the sun by one another (see illus. 272).

Both elements in this constellation shown in illus. 265, the "cartouche" and the worshiper, can be isolated as individual units that can be substituted, one for the other, so that they can appear alone or together with other pictorial elements on other pieces of the group. **Illustration 266a** from Acre[151] portrays two identical "cartouches" side by side (see Starkey/Harding 1932, pl. 73.49), divided by a long, vertical element, the meaning of which is unclear. It is probably a widely accepted sign for *nb* "lord," but it may also be a radically altered depiction of a pair of wings (see illus. 272a). In any case, a carefully executed pair of wings appears above the "cartouche" on a piece from Gezer (**illus. 266b**). On another piece from Samaria, the "cartouche" is flanked or else guarded by two such pairs of wings (Reisner 1924, II pl. 56.e3), and a third piece from Lachish shows a *nb* sign between two very stylized pairs of wings (Tufnell 1953, pl. 43A/44.108).[152] All of these images give expression to divine protection for the monarchy, which picks up on an important iconographical theme from Egypt during the New Kingdom Period.

§158.   The linkage between the "cartouche" and a *falcon* or a vulture, represented frontally with wings spread wide and tail fanned (**illus. 267a** from Lachish;[153] see above, §149), is also clearly associated with depictions of the royal ideology. On many of the examples, the bird appears in the same posture, as the only motif (**illus. 267b** on a seal of black stone from Tell en-Nasbeh; for bone seals, see Macalister 1912, III pl. 203a.11; Tufnell 1953, pl. 44/44a.107; Toombs/Wright 1963, 41 fig. 18.2; Rowe 1936, no. S. 110; an unpublished piece from Beth-Shean as well as Keel-Leu 1991, no. 90;[154] a seal impression from Tel Amal, Levy/Edelstein 1972, 345 fig. 7.19). A piece from Beth-Shean shows the falcon in a side view, in a somewhat different posture (Rowe 1936, no. S. 88). The royal falcon with spread wings is found on another Judean name seal from the eighth century as well, which belonged to a certain . . .]*yhw bn ʿmlyhw* (Avigad 1979, 121f. no. 4). This same bird is also seen, in the same pose, on Middle Bronze Age scarabs of the jasper group, an indication that, already during that era, Syrian/Palestinian princes were fascinated with Egyptian royalty (see above, §25).

Royal associations are shown on the seal amulets as well, and a striding *lion* is the chief element. The lion is represented here in an entirely different way than it was on the Israelite lion seals, discussed above in

151 Unpublished, 14.2 × 11.2 × 5.1 mm; formerly in Lefkovitz Collection in Acre; it is currently held in Jerusalem by the Israel Antiquities Authority, to whom we are grateful for permission to publish (IAA no. 73–155, case no. L.93). R. Reich recently found an identical piece in Tomb No. 5 in the Mamilla Street in Jerusalem. We thank Dr. B. Sass (Jerusalem) for calling this to our attention. Two further examples with the same motif are in private collections (information: L. Wolfe, Jerusalem).

152 Two pieces in private collections show a human figure between two cartouches (information: L. Wolfe, Jerusalem).

153 A seal impression on the handle of a vessel, on a bulla, and on an additional seal that have the same motif are in a private collections (information: L. Wolfe, Jerusalem).

154 We are grateful to L. Wolfe for calling our attention to four additional pieces in private collections that have this same motif.

§118, and, like the other motifs of the group, must be understood as having come from Egypt. Two examples show the lion striding in triumph over a man who is in the pose reserved otherwise in this group for worshipers (**illus. 268a** from Lachish; Keel-Leu 1991: no. 91; cf. Lamon/Shipton 1939, pl. 67.40). We have seen the lion in triumph over a man, as a way to depict the king, already on Bronze Age scarabs (see above, illuss. 5, 99–100). An additional piece from Lachish (**illus. 268b**)[155] and a seal impression from Jericho (Sellin/Watzinger 1913, sheet 42.d 1) show the striding lion above a *nb*. The lion is shown alone on the remaining pieces (**illus. 268c**; Rowe 1936, no. SO. 35; cf. Tufnell 1953, pl. 45.129; Petrie 1930, pl. 35.409).[156] A striking feature is the tail that curls over the entire back of the animal, shaped clearly like a *uraeus* in illus. 268c, and thus reminiscent of the *uraei* tails shown in many depictions of the lion on Middle Bronze Age scarabs (see illuss. 3a and c; Tufnell 1984, II pls. 40f.).

A striding *caprid* that generally has very long horns, held almost horizontally, appears even more frequently than the lion on the seal amulets of this group. Lions and caprids were the most commonly portrayed animals in Middle Bronze Age IIB glyptic art (see above, §§11f.), and a somewhat indigenous motif comes to the fore with the use of the caprid (see above, §116). Nevertheless, this does not permit us to connect the caprid images on Iron Age IIB bone seals with the traditions concerning the goddess and her sphere. In **illuss. 269a-b**, from Ashdod, the animal is placed once above the "cartouche" and once above a *nb*, and is thus connected with the sign of royal power. Perhaps the surprising association connecting a caprid with power becomes plausible when we note that the male goat (*ʿattūd*) can be used metaphorically in Hebrew for a concept such as "leader" (e.g., Isa 14:9; Zech 10:3; see Miller 1970, 184). The striding caprid – much like the lion – appears alone on most of the pieces (**illus. 269c** from Lachish; Petrie 1930 pl. 43.515; 1937, pl. 6.20; Tufnell 1953, pl. 44/44A.114; Rowe 1936, no. SO. 20; Reisner 1924, II pl. 56.e1, and an unpublished piece from Beth-Shean.)[157] In contrast to analogous depictions from the Bronze Age, there is a complete absence of all vegetal elements (little trees, plants, branches, etc.). We see a stylized tree flanked by *uraei* only on one isolated piece of unknown provenance, now in the Rockefeller Museum (**illus. 270**), and on an unpublished seal in the R. and E. Hecht Museum in Haifa. The tree also has iconographic links with earlier depictions of the same element during the Bronze Age, in which the stylized tree, flanked by *uraei*, much like the goddess' head, was connected with the goddess (Schroer 1989, 186f., 140ff. nos. 71, 81–83, 98–110, 121; see above, §16). The royal cartouche, similarly flanked by two *uraei* that face outward, appears on still another unpublished seal from the Hecht Collection. Since these *uraei* are primarily protective powers who serve the king, perhaps the tree in illus.

---

155 An additional seal with this motif is in a private collection (information: L. Wolfe, Jerusalem).
156 Two additional seals with this motif are found in a private collections (information: L. Wolfe, Jerusalem).
157 Four additional seals with this motif are in private collections (information: L. Wolfe, Jerusalem).

270 should also be linked to kingship. This would mean that, here as well, we are dealing with an issue that has been addressed so often, that the tree symbol was de-semanticized or re-semanticized, with the result that the symbol of the goddess has become a symbol of kingship.

§159.   Much like the "cartouche," the *worshiper* with a raised arm can be separated from this grouping of images, seen together in illus. 265, and used alone, a kind of reapplication of a Middle Bronze Age theme that was especially prominent in the jasper group (see above, §27). The worshiper can appear before the long, vertical element (**illus. 271a** from Lachish;[158] see illus. 266a) or between two such elements (**illus. 271b** from Megiddo; the positioning of the arm precludes us from thinking that this is the "Lord of the Crocodile" or something similar; cf. also Macalister 1912, III pl. 208.54; Albright 1938, pl. 32.16; in front of a disk, Petrie 1932, pl. 7.66; alone, Tufnell 1953, pl. 43A/44.62). As a rule, the person is shown twice when the object of worship is missing or else two worshipers are shown facing each other (**illus. 272a** from Acre; see Schumacher 1908, 124, pl. 39d; Lamon/Shipton 1939, pl. 67.51),[159] either in a pose where the two "inner arms," the upraised right arm of the one and left arm of the other, are shown by the use of a single line (**illus. 272b** from Tell en-Nasbeh; see Petrie 1930, pl. 40.458; Tufnell 1953, pl. 43A/44.66; an unpublished piece from Arad; Lamon/Shipton 1939, pl. 69.68) or in a pose where they are shown symmetrically as exact opposites (**illus. 272c** from Tell el-Farʿah [south]; Tufnell 1953, pl. 43A/44.65; McCown 1947, pl. 54.38; possibly also Petrie 1930, pls. 35.424 and 39.444). In this last portrayal, on which neither the top or bottom is shown, the act of worship or mutual blessing of one another is enhanced. Occasionally, three figures who are worshiping or in the act of blessing are portrayed together, a variation that serves the same purpose, as shown in **illus. 272d** from Tell el-Farʿah (south) (see Macalister 1912, pl. 206.5).[160]

In summary, the group of southern Palestinian bone seals suggests a strong fascination with Egyptian symbols of royalty and loyalty. The monarchy was represented by the falcon with spread wings, by the lion that strides over an enemy in its path, by the "cartouche" with the king's name, and perhaps also by the tree flanked by *uraei*. The worshiper in front of the "cartouche," or the worshiper simply shown once, twice, or even three times, is typical of a symbolism that declares one's loyalty. Only the caprid seems to have a less clear relationship to this theme.

§160.   In contrast to what was discussed above concerning Iron Age IIB Phoenician/Israelite specialty crafts, contemporary Judahite iconography shows itself to have been relatively provincial and conservative. Apart from the bone seals, local stamp seal production was limited to

158 Three additional seals with this motif are in private collections (information: L. Wolfe, Jerusalem).

159 For an impression on a bulla that was bought in Jerusalem, see Keel-Leu 1991, no. 94. Five additional seals with this motif are in private collections (information: L. Wolfe, Jerusalem).

160 This background might also suggest that one ought to identify the very stylized human figures that appear in groups of two or three on locally produced limestone scaraboids of Iron Age IIA-B as worshipers. See, for example, Starkey/Harding 1932, pl. 73.45; van Beek 1986, 55 fig. 24 left (bulla); Tufnell 1953, pl. 43A/44.71–75; Lamon/Shipton 1939, pl. 67.53, 56 (cf. 67.21), etc.

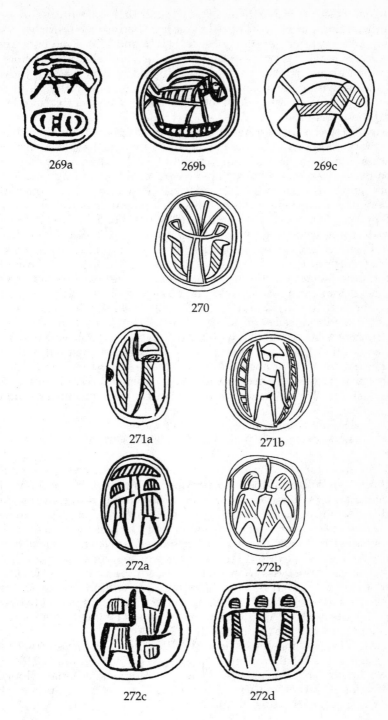

269a   269b   269c

270

271a   271b

272a   272b

272c   272d

indigenous motifs and to themes that were already widespread throughout the region during Iron Age IIA (on the "Lord of the Ostriches," see
§114; on the caprids and the lions, see §§116 and 118). Even bone seals
frequently make use of these motifs. Exclusively religious symbols of
Egyptian origin or inspiration were adopted in Iron Age IIB Judean
glyptic art with greater hesitation than were the previously discussed
symbols of royal power, which took root more easily because of related
indigenous traditions.

Toward the end of Iron Age IIB, one notes an apparent shift in Judahite
seal production as well, at a somewhat different time than when this took
place in the north. This is seen, first of all, on Judahite name seals and
then more clearly on royal stamps, where Egyptian and Egyptianizing
motifs appear now in a way that had been seen a little earlier in the north.
Among the earliest examples of this development, in addition to a seal
belonging to *šbnyw* (see above, illus. 263b) that is dated to about 750, we
have a scarab belonging to a certain *'šn'*, a minister of King Ahaz (742–
726), on which one can see a solar disk with a massive *atef*-crown, flanked
by two *uraei* turned outward (**illus. 273**; see above, §155). The way the
theophoric element in the name has been written on this *šbnyw* seal
suggests that both seals could have come from northern Israelite
workshops. A remarkable note in 2 Kgs 20:11 // Isa 38:8 reports that
King Ahaz introduced some kind of "sun dial" in Jerusalem.

The new solar orientation within the Judahite symbol system toward
the end of the eighth century may have had deeper causes. It probably
relates indirectly to the encroachment of the Assyrians and to the related
fact that Judah established considerably closer ties with Egypt under
Hezekiah (ca. 725–697) when it faced the threat from the north, as Judah:

"sought to feel strong in the power of Pharaoh
and to seek shelter in the shadow of Egypt (Isa 30:2)."

If ninth-century bone seals provided evidence for a strong fascination
with the symbolism of the Egyptian monarchy (oval, falcon, lion), the
documentation which follows will show how Judah also came increasingly under the influence of the Egyptian *religious* symbol system toward
the end of the eighth century. The motifs and concepts (winged *uraei* and
sun symbolism) that will now be discussed relate *in terms of content* to the
concepts discussed in §§141ff. There seems as yet to be no critical
positioning against Assyrian themes, as will be characteristic of the
seventh century. That is why these concepts will be discussed here.
Viewed chronologically, they belong to the transitional period between
Iron Age IIB and Iron Age IIC; in terms of subject matter, they are clearly
developments that are an outgrowth of Iron Age IIB.

§161.   Toward the end of Iron Age IIB, the *winged uraeus* that had
appeared in the Northern Kingdom of Israel (§149, with illuss. 246–247)
shows up now in Judah as well.[161] On a seal from Lachish that belonged
to a certain *šptyhw* (*bn*) *'šyhw*, a *uraeus* with two wings guards a very
stylized sign for life (**illus. 274a**).

161 See above, §155 note 144.

More characteristic than the *uraeus* with two wings is a *uraeus with four wings* that has two wings spread out on either side. This is common on seals produced in Judah toward the end of the eighth century and is the characteristic form of the Egyptian *uraeus* that dominated the entire Levant. In contrast to the two-winged *uraei*, usually portrayed as if guarding some object, the four-winged variety of the *uraeus* guards the name of the seal owner. The increase in the number of wings from two to four would supposedly increase their protective powers. O. Keel assembled six name seals and three impressions from two additional seals with this motif in 1977 (1977a, 106–110). The names on these seals are either typically Judean (for example *yḥmlyhw (bn) mʿšyhw*, **illus. 274b**) or at least nothing would speak against Judean provenance (such as when the short form *špṭ* or the name *mlkrm* is used). Since 1977, seven additional name seals or impressions with a four-winged *uraeus* have come to light. Thus the number has nearly doubled. Two impressions of a seal with this motif, which belonged to the son of a certain *ṣpnyhw*, were discovered at Lachish already during the 1930s (**illus. 274c**). An impression of the same seal, as yet unpublished, is on the handle of a vessel that was recovered not long ago in Y. Shiloh's excavation on Ophel.[162] Two bullae with four-winged *uraei* are among the remains of an archive from late Iron Age IIC that was published by Avigad in 1986 (see below, illus. 342). The name seals with four-winged *uraei* were obtained by purchase. One bears the name of a woman named *sʿdh*, probably a short form of *sʿdyh* (Avigad 1989b, 91). Another belonged to someone named *yrmyhw bn ʿš* (**illus. 274d**). There is a seal belonging to *dlyhw bn gmlyhw* in the R. Hecht Museum in Haifa (Avigad 1979, 122 no. 5), as well as the still unpublished impression of a seal that belonged to a certain *šbnyhw*, thus also a Judahite. Even if not all of the commercially acquired seals are genuine, the new evidence that has appeared since 1977 demonstrates clearly that the four-winged *uraeus* is a typical Judahite motif.

Zoologically, the *uraeus* in these images is the black-necked cobra (*Naja nigricollis* Reinhardt). This creature applies its poison not only by biting but also by spitting (see Keel, et al., 1984, 165f.). The Hebrew name for both the zoological variety and the mythological variant with wings is *śārāf* "the one that burns" (Num 21:6–9; Deut 8:15; Isa 14:29, 30:6). The famous *seraphim* of Isa 6:2, 6 are not to be understood in any other way. Only theriomorphic or hybrid creatures could be conceived of as "standing" *above* Yahweh. To imagine creatures in human form above the enthroned, anthropomorphically depicted king Yahweh would have been gross and an unpardonable breach of ancient Near Eastern court etiquette. The hands and feet of the seraphim in Isaiah 6 are not proof that they had a human shape, since cobras shown in the numinous realm could appear not only with wings but also with hands, feet, and even with a human voice (see Keel 1977a, 77f. illuss. 28–35). The adoption of the winged *uraei* at the end of the eighth century shows that a clearly Egyptian religious protection symbol is now being used. The six wings in Isaiah 6 signify an increase in potency even by comparison with the four wings that the *uraei* have on the Judean name seals. But the point may be

162 We are grateful to Dr. B. Sass (Jerusalem) for this information.

that the seraphim that are seen by Isaiah use none of their pairs of wings to protect their lord; instead – apart from the one pair used for flight – the wings function as a way to protect themselves against the rays of the holiness that were coming from their lord and spreading out everywhere. By this approach, the numinous, protecting power of the *uraei* is made relative in relation to the God who is enthroned on Zion.

The *copper/bronze snake* (Nehushtan) that Moses had made and that, according to 2 Kgs 18:4a, King Hezekiah destroyed, is identified as a seraph in Num 21:6–9. In contrast to the other cultic reforms of King Hezekiah mentioned in 2 Kgs 18:4, which may be deuteronomistic retrojections, this particular action is quite concrete and can be treated as accurate historically (Hoffmann 1980, 146–155; Spieckermann 1982, 172f.). We can no longer determine with any confidence whether the copper snake was a genuinely Canaanite element or was Egyptian instead (Schroer 1987a, 104–115). The first option is more likely, since Hezekiah, as we will see shortly, was quite receptive to uniquely Egyptian symbols of the day. His readiness to stop the use of the copper snake is probably to be understood as an expression of his thorough aversion to theriomorphic images of the deity that were made in the Canaanite tradition.[163]

§162.   Since the end of the last century there have been professional excavations in the area once covered by the Kingdom of Judah; more than 1000 seal impressions have been found on the handles of storage vessels with a capacity of 40–45 liters each. On these impressions, *lmlk* "(belonging) to the king" is written above; one of four place names (Hebron, *mmšt*, Sochoh, or Ziph) is written below (Welten 1969; Garfinkel 1988, 70). Between the two parts of the inscription, aligned vertically, one sees either a four-winged scarab, with detail shown (**illus. 275a**) or just in outline (**illus. 275b**) or else a winged solar disk aligned horizontally, once again shown with detail (**illuss. 276a-b**) or just in outline (**illus. 276c**). Overall, there are more impressions with the winged solar disk than with the scarab. Welten (1969, 114) had thought that the royal stamp with the scarab could be dated to the time of Hezekiah (725–697) and that those with the winged sun disk belonged to the time of Josiah (640–609). More recent discoveries, especially at Lachish, have shown that both types were in use at the same time and that they both date to the time of Hezekiah (Ussishkin 1977, 28–60; 1983, 160–164; Mommsen, et al., 1984, 89–113).

Numerous two- and four-winged scarabs pushing the solar disk ahead of them with their front legs have been found in the Northern Kingdom (see above, §151) and they also appear on private seals in the Southern Kingdom. A two-winged scarab with a sun disk is shown on a

---

163 It is pure speculation to try to interpret the destruction of the copper snake as an anti-Assyrian measure (Spieckermann 1982, 172f., note 33; Dohmen 1985, 264–266; Camp 1990, 285f., who refers to a war ritual from the time of Ashurbanipal). The pre-deuteronomistic text in 2 Kgs 18:4a gives no indication of this and neither literary nor iconographic evidence would indicate that the copper snake might have had any negative associations with the Assyrian supremacy or religion. The connection that links Nehushtan with Asherah, suggested once again most recently by Olyan (1988, 70f.), is just as baseless.

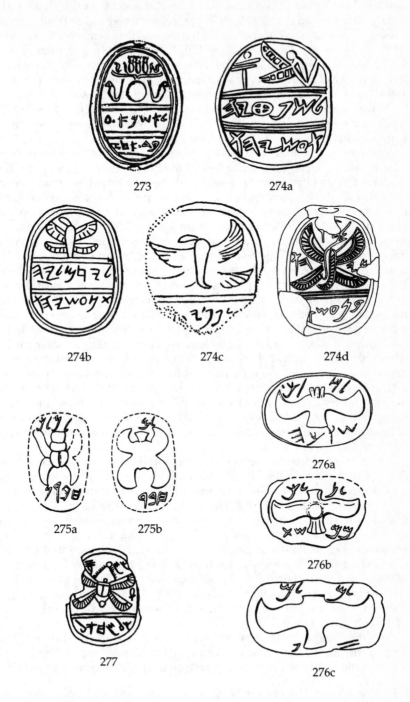

273

274a

274b

274c

274d

276a

275a

275b

276b

277

276c

seal that belonged to a certain *mnšh bn hmlk*, dated by Avigad (1987, 200, 202 fig. 7) to the time of Hezekiah. A carefully carved scarab from Lachish shows a four-winged scarab depicted above the name *'ḥmlk (bn) smk* (**illus. 277**; see also Sass 1992, figs. 120–121).[164] The winged solar disk is found less frequently on Judahite seals when compared with those from the Northern Kingdom, where such an image is less common (Parayre 1990, 291f.; Avigad 1989b, 91). It appears twice on the seal of *šbnyw 'bd 'zyw*, with very bent wings in the upper scene and with straight wings in the lower scene (see above, illus. 263b). The way the name was written suggests that this was a northern Israelite product.

Welten thought that both the winged solar disk and the four-winged scarab showed strong influence from Syro-Phoenician culture. From this he drew the conclusion that it might no longer be possible "to use one or the other of the two symbols . . . to determine with which of the great powers of the day, Egypt or Assyria, the Judean king sought to associate himself" (1969, 30). Viewed from purely stylistic grounds, this assessment might be accurate. But if we look at the material discussed in the previous sections all together, we see how the broad spectrum of both Israelite and Judahite society, especially the upper strata (name seals) and thus also royalty, were deeply fascinated by the power of Egypt during the ninth and eighth centuries. The close contacts that existed with neighboring Egypt, particularly at the end of the eighth century, make it quite improbable that the people of Judah, just like the people of Israel (see above, §152), would not have known what the winged solar disk, a scarab, or a *uraei* meant. This does not necessarily mean that they were knowledgeable about the intricacies of Egyptian solar theology. But the vision described in Isaiah 6 betrays the fact that people in Judah and Israel had some very definite notions about what was at the root of the use of winged *uraei* as guarding powers and of the scarab as a mysterious embodiment of or metaphor for the sun that rose victoriously anew each day (see Stähli 1986, 10f.).

There was a close connection between scarabs and winged solar disks and the monarchy in the Levant during Iron Age IIB. The winged solar disk was a picture of the sun god, first in Egypt but in due course also in the Near East, whose earthly representative was the king. We can, for that reason, support the views of D. Parayre completely when she says of the winged disk on royal stamps: ". . . the choice of decoration on the seals is explicable . . . in part because of the extraordinary symbolic power of the winged disk, which by itself evokes the idea of the king and his domain in Egypt, Hittite Anatolia, and Assyrian Mesopotamia. This confers on this motif a clear symbolic merit. Finally, it is associated, as the image of anonymous power, with the palace in general and its administration" (1990, 293f.).

Younker suggests that this symbol reached Judah for the first time when refugees came from the Northern Kingdom about 720 (1985, 175). The adoption of the four-winged scarab on the Judean royal stamps might

---

164 The excavator thinks he can recognize a four-winged scarab, flanked by two human figures, found along with a two-line Judean inscription on a large bulla from Beer-sheba Str. II, though the piece is preserved only fragmentarily (Aharoni 1973, 75f., pl. 32.1).

be an expression of Hezekiah's claim to have inherited (at least ideologically) the land of Israel. But, in any case, the Judahite repertoire is not simply a facsimile of Israelite motifs. In the north, for example, we never find the four-winged *uraeus* that is so typical in the south. Winged hybrid creatures, such as cherubs(!) and sphinxes, appear on Judean seals much less frequently than on those in the Northern Kingdom (see illus. 249). For that reason, the solarization of the religious symbol system in Judah at the end of the eighth century could not have occurred just because of the flood of refugees from the north. It was fed by its own streams (including Jerusalem; see 3 Kgs 8:53 LXX) and was nourished directly by springs from Egypt.

In more recent times, various exegetes have directed their attention once again to the question of the solar aspects connected with faith in Yahweh (see Stähli 1986; Janowski 1989; Smith 1990, 115–124). There is indirect attestation that solar concepts, as found on the royal stamps, supplied a common element in the worship of Yahweh in Judah, such as is noted in the name *yhwzrḥ* "Yaho has shown forth" that appears on a bulla dating to about 700 and that was owned by the son of a minister of Hezekiah[165] (Hestrin/Dayagi-Mendels 1979, no. 4). We encounter the same name about a century later as a patronymic on a Jerusalem bulla (Avigad 1986, 81 no. 118; for recent examples, see Stähli 1985, 40f.). We find biblical evidence for *zeraḥ* as a Judahite and as an Edomite personal name (*HAL* I 270). Judahite/Temanite descriptions of theophanies in Deut 33:2 and Hab 3:3ff. (see also §144, Wall Inscription 2 Line 1') show some common strands in Judahite and Edomite concepts of deity. The metaphor of Yahweh as the sun god, noted in the use of *ZRḤ* "shining forth," corresponds semantically to the representation of the rising sun in the picture of the winged scarab or the solar disk. When compared with Israel, Yahweh appears somewhat differently in Judah at the end of the eighth century. He is not primarily the "Lord of Heaven" (Baalshamem, see above, §153), but he is conceived of as the actual sun god. Judahite texts depict him as a punishing, saving, or healing sun god (see Pss 46:6; 84:12, 91:4, 101:8; Zeph 3:5; Mal 3:20, etc.; see Niehr 1990, 150–161; on Genesis 19, see Keel 1979) and he seems to be more of a real presence here than in the Northern Kingdom.

Summary

§163. In view of the different geopolitical relationships for both Israel and Judah during the ninth and eighth centuries, as was sketched out in the introduction, it is hardly surprising that the iconographically documented symbol systems of the Northern and Southern Kingdoms do not coincide totally during Iron Age IIB. The indigenous "Lord of the Ostriches" appears in both regions, but is found more frequently in the more provincial and peripheral Southern Kingdom. By contrast, we encounter other *"Lords of the Animals,"* with caprids and lions in the

---

165 The name of the son of one of Hezekiah's ministers can hardly be taken as indicative of the beginning of the solarization of Yahweh in either the "personal piety" or the "folk piety" (contra Niehr 1990, 151).

Northern Kingdom. Indigenous traditions were also still in use in the realm of *animal images* (caprids, deer, and lions), but not without a significant modification of their unique aspects. As hallmarks of Iron Age IIB, one can mention the continuing move to depict animal motifs without identifying gender and in the distancing of animal motifs from the traditional sphere of the goddess, observed in the products of the glyptic art, which no longer depict suckling mother animals, use the caprid tree motif less often, and, conversely, increase in importance the northern Syrian guard-lion symbolism. When, in remarkable contrast to what is found in the local glyptic art, all three aspects (a nursing mother animal, a caprid at a stylized tree, a lion in the *qudshu* tradition) are represented prominently in the vessel paintings at Kuntillet ʿAjrud, this supports the thesis advanced by P. Beck, on the basis of iconographic and stylistic observations, that those paintings derive largely from Syro-Phoenician hands. Only the procession of worshipers and possibly also the archer on the pithoi, both on Pithos B, can be considered to be actual local motifs.

In view of the Old Testament references to the use of bull images in Yahweh worship, it is noteworthy that bovines seem to play no special role in Iron Age IIB Israelite iconography. We have referred in passing to evidence that Jeroboam's bull image was not an innovation (that would thereby cause one to expect a corresponding spate of propaganda), but was rather a cultic image (of El) from Bethel that dates to the Late Bronze Age, worship of which was revived by Jeroboam.

One notable characteristic of Iron Age IIB Israelite iconography, shown predominantly on seals and ivories, is its close relationship with Phoenician specialty crafts. When compared to finds that have been made outside of Palestine, it is still to be noted that Israel did not duplicate or even import the entire spectrum of the Phoenician repertoire of motifs on its products. Most notable is the almost total *absence of anthropomorphic images showing a female deity*. By contrast, we do find images of a *stylized tree*, flanked (or watched over) by animals or hybrid creatures or else venerated by a human worshiper. These two findings relate to each other reciprocally; they form an iconographic backdrop for the written evidence of an *"asherah" of Yahweh*. This *asherah* can most likely be understood in the sense of a cultic symbol assigned to Yahweh, by which his blessing is mediated to the people. The exact relationship between the cultic symbol and the female deity must be determined for each co-text (or co-icontext). Even if (Phoenician or Phoenician-inspired?) images, such as illus. 214 or illus. 219 ᴬE-H, allow one to detect a certain "transparency" that suggests according to the history of the traditions that the goddess is somewhat present when the stylized tree is shown, this does not preclude the fact that this numinous symbol of power has been completely disconnected from the concept of a female deity and has been transposed into a royal power structure, portrayed when a tree is shown being guarded by cherubs. Taken as a whole, neither the iconographic nor the epigraphic documentation allows us to regard Yahweh's *asherah* as an autonomous divine partner.

§164. But the iconography also documents the great significance of *sun and celestial symbolism* in the religious symbol system that comes to Israel from Egypt during the ninth and eighth centuries. In the Northern

Kingdom this was seemingly transmitted through specialty crafts of Phoenician origin, arriving there somewhat earlier than in Judah, where we first see it, in a somewhat different form, toward the end of the eighth century. But we detect a great fascination in the south with Egyptian symbols for power on the bone seals already during the ninth century.

If we disregard for now the little-studied amulets that were wide-spread already in Iron Age IIB, primarily showing depictions of anthropomorphic Egyptian deities (see §202), we see that the Palestinian specialty crafts during the ninth and eighth centuries, in contrast to those of the Late Bronze Age and Iron Age I, do not emphasize personal Egyptian deities but rather accentuate the mysterious protective and healing powers, like the winged solar disk, the two- or four-winged scarab, winged hybrid creatures, *uraei*, etc. The question of gender (male or female) with respect to these powers is not particularly relevant. Their celestial and protective character appears to be more important, especially as one detects this by the presence of their wings. These various entities and powers appear therefore, specifically in light of their relationship to the sun, as elements of a coherent, celestial, and solar-oriented symbol system. The closest one gets to an anthropomorphic depiction of the sun god is that of the winged, youthful god shown in illuss. 210–213, whom we have identified as Baal or a subordinate figure who serves the "Lord of Heaven."

According to the evidence from the personal names and from the inscriptions, Yahweh continues to be the sovereign god in Israel. The correlation of this conclusion with the iconographically documented sun and celestial symbolism has led us to formulate the hypothesis that Yahweh was conceived of in Iron Age IIB Israel, with solar and celestial connotations, to be the "Most High God" and the "Lord of Heaven," like the Phoenician Baalshamem. It must be emphasized in the context of this study that one sees the trend toward accentuating solar and celestial depictions of the deity much earlier and much more unequivocally in the iconography than in the very sparse number of relevant texts.[166]

With little delay, solar motifs appeared also in Judah toward the end of the eighth century. In comparison to Israel, we find relatively few hybrid creatures in Judah, apart from the four-winged *uraei*. By contrast, a remarkably large number of images represent the sun god himself, such as the scarab pushing the ball of the sun and the winged or crowned solar disk. If Yahweh was represented in eighth-century Israel more often as the "Lord of Heaven" (Baalshamem), was he seen in Judah more in the role of a solar El? The hypothesis sketched out in §162 is presented here for the moment only as a question; more research is still needed.

§165. In general, the images and texts discussed in this chapter represent a differentiated and coherent picture of the religious symbol

---

166 Niehr thinks that the solarization of the "Most High God" concept could have occurred during the Assyrian Period at the earliest (1990, 141f. but see 148). In our opinion, this process began earlier. The "most productive phase" of this solarization would have occurred during the eighth century, even though solar concepts were still very much alive at a later time. The main accent during the following period was on concepts connected with astralization (stars of the night; concerning this, see the next chapter).

system of Israel and Judah during the ninth and eighth centuries. The evidence for an Israelite religion generally oriented toward Yahweh, which has been assembled by Tigay in his study of personal names, is not contradicted by the extra-onomastic epigraphic or the iconographic documentation.

The evidence would indeed be misunderstood if we were to impute strictly monolatrous or directly monotheistic tendencies to the male and female inhabitants of Israel and Judah during the ninth and eighth centuries. The discoveries at Kuntillet ʿAjrud and the products from the Phoenician/Israelite specialty crafts both show that there were no strict boundaries between the Israelite/Judahite religion and that of its neighbors, especially the Phoenicians (but probably also the Arameans and Gileadites, according to the evidence found at Tell Deir Alla) at the end of the ninth century and during the eighth century. This is shown, not least of all, in the fact that both the Israelite and Judahite forms of Yahwism, though different in the ways they were manifested, participated in the general Levantine tendency toward the celestialization and solarization of the religious symbols.

There is no doubt that both Israel and Judah took for granted that other deities besides Yahweh existed, both assumed also that they were active, and both thought that there were other daemons, hybrid creatures, powers, and forces in addition to Yahweh. The selection of images shown on seals and ivories gives us lively insight into the many ways that the beings that surrounded the "Lord of Heaven" could be depicted. The only question that remains concerns how they conceived the relation of these powers and forces to Yahweh. Iconography, epigraphy, and biblical texts all point in the same direction: these powers and authorities, *asherahs*, Bes figures, *šaddāyim*, cherubs, *uraei*, etc., were not of the same order as Yahweh, but were rather subordinate to him, *mediating* the protection and blessing of Yahweh. During Iron Age IIB, the *asherah*, the cultic symbol in the form of a stylized tree, appears to have been the most important mediating entity through which Yahweh was seen as functioning. This is the only one of the mediating entities that is mentioned in inscriptions. We see that winged hybrid creatures were subordinate to the *asherah* in depictions. The flanking creatures indicate, by their position, the hierarchical priority of the power that they flank and guard.

The amulets that appear with great frequency during Iron Age IIB, and that are, to a large extent, as yet unpublished, have been discussed in this chapter only in terms of selected categories (Bes, the eye of Horus; see above, illuss. 224–225 together with §131 note 51; illuss. 260–261 together with §151 note 143). These depictions may also be categorized as showing beings that mediate blessing and protection. These beings, and the winged powers that appear on the seals, were apparently not perceived in the eighth century as forces in competition with Yahweh. The iconographic evidence fits well with K. Koch's recently formulated thesis that the claim that worship had to be exclusively of Yahweh meant, first of all, that El (or Baal) was to be eliminated and only later did the same occur in connection with references to Elohim (1991, 28–33; see above, §127 for the juxtaposition of *ʾlhyn* and *šdyn* deities in Combination I at Tell Deir Alla).

In the texts, whether they be biblical or epigraphical, the high deities, on the "level of El," especially Yahweh and his rival Baal(shamem) but also El, are the chief characters. But there are only a few images in the iconography that can be connected to these deities with confidence (four-winged Baal, sun-child on a blossom). As regards the iconography, the portrayal of the subordinate powers and authorities is much clearer than that of the distant god of heaven who is shielded to a certain extent within his sphere and is represented only in a symbolic way (winged solar disk, scarabs, and the like). The *asherah* alone, as the most important intermediate entity, assumes a similarly important place in both media. It is necessary, therefore, to point out once again that the literary, epigraphical, and iconographical sources must all be consulted in order to have a complementary picture that can help to reconstruct a religious symbol system.

VIII

The Astralization of the Heavenly Powers, the Revival of the Goddess, and the Orthodox Reaction: Iron Age IIC

§166. Iron Age IIC, which began in the final third of the eighth century and lasted until the beginning of the sixth century (for how the periods are delineated, see above, §8), was shaped politically and culturally by Assyrian conquests, the foreign imperial control that resulted, and the collapse of the Syrian/Palestinian system of small territorial states. To some extent, allied Syrian/Phoenician states were able to keep Assyrian attempts at expansion in check during the ninth century, in spite of isolated Assyrian incursions as far as Damascus or even all the way to the Phoenician coast. During the first half of the eighth century, Assyria went through a phase in which it consolidated its rule internally and stabilized relationships with its possessions that were situated between the Tigris and the Euphrates. But then, within a single generation, during the last third of the eighth century, the Assyrians attacked first northern Palestine, then the Samarian heartland, and after that the southern Palestinian coastal plain all the way to the Egyptian border (for more on what is now to be discussed, see, e.g., Weippert 1980, 202–208; 1982; Donner 1986, 297–329).

In contrast to his predecessors, who were satisfied with assigning vassal status and with pledges of tribute from conquered kings in the Trans-Euphrates region, Tiglath Pileser III (745–727) carried out a systematic policy of conquering the subdued regions and then, with the exception of the Phoenician states, integrating them into an ever more powerful territorial empire according them the status of provinces that were ruled by representatives from the Assyrian bureaucracy. Tiglath Pileser III also introduced the policy of mass deportation as a way to consolidate this territorial expansion. In this connection, especially the élite and skilled workers were resettled in Assyria proper or in other provinces. This consequently forced an extensive mixing of cultures and a dilution of national identities.

Several important dates relating to the Assyrian conquest of Palestine deserve at least brief mention. Tiglath Pileser's inscriptions from 738 mention "Menahem, the Samarian" as one of the vassals who was obligated to pay tribute. He is the king of the Northern Kingdom who is mentioned in 2 Kings 15. A Palestinian campaign in 734, directed primarily against Hanun of Gaza, brought Tiglath Pileser as far as the southern coastal plain, where he established a military and trade outpost "at the Brook of Egypt." Campaigns against Rezin of Damascus in 733 and 732 led to the subjugation of Aram. As a result of these three campaigns, territory that belonged to Israel – Gilead and Galilee (Hazor) in the northern region, the Jezreel Valley (Megiddo), and the northern coastal plain (Dor) – was annexed and converted into Assyrian provinces. Israel was reduced in size, being left with nothing but the territory of Ephraim and Manasseh. Pekah of Israel (see above, illus. 263c), who had allied himself with the Arameans, lost his throne to Hoshea.

Less than a decade later, Hoshea's refusal to pay tribute led to a three-year siege and to the ultimate capitulation of Samaria to the troops of Shalmaneser V (726–722). This brought the independent existence of the Northern Kingdom of Israel as a nation-state to an end. From then on, the Israelite heartland was an Assyrian province as well, being called Samerina. Sargon II (721–705), who also celebrated the conquest of Samaria in his Display Inscriptions, maybe in connection with the suppression of a subsequent Samarian rebellion, exiled the élite from the former capital of Israel to northern Mesopotamia and Media in 720. At the same time, he resettled in Samaria deportees from Babylon and from some of the Arab clans (Na'aman/Zadok 1988; see 2 Kgs 17:5, 24; for two additional relocations of colonists during the seventh century, see Ezra 4:2, 10). Additional campaigns by Sargon or his generals into southern Palestine led to the consolidation of control over the Philistine city-states and to the (re)establishment of the Assyrian trade colony in or near Gaza. Fragments of Sargon's victory stelae have been discovered at Samaria itself, about 20 km west-northwest of Samaria on the coastal road at Qaqun, and at Ashdod (Crowfoot, et al., 1957, 35, pl. 4.2; *Hadašot Arkeologiyot* 51–52 [1974] 16; H. Tadmor in Dothan, et al., 1971, 192–197, pl. 96f. = **illus. 278a**). Along with a bulla from Samaria made with Sargon's royal seal (**illus. 278b**; Reisner 1924, pl. 56.a), the stelae provide evidence to demonstrate that Assyrian rule had been established in Palestine. The seal impression shows the Assyrian king in battle against a lion, possibly symbolizing all the peoples and forces that might possibly threaten this newly established political cosmos. This is precisely the opposite of the legendary depiction of a state of anarchy that is described in 2 Kgs 17:25–28. But archaeological discoveries suggest that the picture sketched in 2 Kings 17 might not be entirely inaccurate: Assyrian control concentrated itself in provincial capitals such as Dor, Megiddo, and probably also Samaria, which had been rebuilt or restructured. On top of the ruins of other cities, such as Hazor or Beth-Shean, nothing but short-lived settlements are to be found. Instead of what had once been cities, there were small palaces and fortifications, built in the Assyrian style, that served as communication outposts for the officials of the kingdom. The deurbanization of the northern parts of the country, which can be clearly demonstrated in the archaeological record (H. Weippert 1988, 587–594, 600–603), having resulted from conquest, destruction, flight, and partially from deportation of the people – and, one can assume, having been accompanied also by a renewed renomadization in regional districts – will force us to concentrate more on the coastal plain and Judah in this chapter.

278a

278b

279

Sennacherib's (705–681) Western Campaign in 701 brought with it even more intense Assyrian control of the petty kings of southern Palestine after still another revolt, this one led by Hezekiah of Judah. For Judah, which lay off the beaten path of the major trade routes and had thus been spared the troubles that had come upon the Northern Kingdom in the past, this direct act of rebellion had drastic consequences. Hezekiah was able to resist the Assyrian occupation of Jerusalem itself, but only at the price of large payments of tribute and the amputation of western and southern districts in the Shephelah and Negev, which now came under Assyrian/Philistine control. Several of the cities destroyed by Sennacherib, such as Beth-Shemesh, and settlements at Tel Eitun and Tel Beit Mirsim, were not rebuilt.

In several campaigns, in which Manasseh of Judah (696–642) would have participated as a vassal, the Assyrians under Esarhaddon and Ashurbanipal (669–630) successfully advanced all the way to Egypt, where they held their ground until ca. 655. But it was increasingly apparent that they had overextended themselves and that the gigantic, cosmopolitan kingdom was increasingly beset with inner weaknesses. From the middle of the seventh century, Ashurbanipal struggled against serious domestic and foreign revolts and threats and yet he was able to settle Babylonian and Elamite colonists in Samaria during the 640s (Ezra 4:9–10). But by the time of his death at the latest, the peripheral Assyrian territory of Palestine quickly slipped away from Assyrian control. The reign of Manasseh, which was as quiet as it was long, later demonized by the deuteronomists, was marked by pragmatic cooperation with the overlords. Judah was now able to extend itself into the Negev once again, where massive efforts to reurbanize and secure the borders clearly took place during the second half of the seventh century (Tatum 1991) under Josiah (640–609), being followed by similar efforts in the districts of the former Northern Kingdom (for particulars, see Na'aman 1991). Under Josiah, forces seeking the reestablishment of the nation achieved the upper hand in Judah. With the political-military "Renaissance," there seem to have been intentional efforts to integrate the religious traditions of the Northern Kingdom, including those linked to the exodus and to the covenant traditions, by which Judah clearly staked its claim to be the heir of northern Israel in ideological matters as well. A civil war in Assyria ultimately enabled Josiah, in the eighteenth year of his reign (622), to separate his kingdom from the former super-power. One notes particularly that, in the reform described in 2 Kings 23, the cult of the national god Yahweh was concentrated in Jerusalem and that in the districts claimed by Josiah (and Yahweh) cults that were not dedicated to the worship of Yahweh were eliminated by military action.

Viewed in the light of political history, the national "renaissance" remained at first an interlude, coming to an abrupt end with Josiah's death at Megiddo in an enigmatic battle against the Egyptian Pharaoh Neco. Egypt's renewed claims upon Palestine, played out contrapuntally over against those of Judah, are reflected in an image on a seal (**illus. 279**), discovered at Megiddo in Str. II (end of the seventh century), that shows the Egyptian king in the traditional "striking down the enemy" posture, in front of an emaciated, crouching Asian(?). But Egyptian claims upon Palestine had no future either. The heirs to Assyrian power in the Near East were the Babylonians, led by Nebuchadnezzar II (605–561). Two Judahite revolts against the new world ruler were unsuccessful and they led, in 598 and 586, to the siege of Jerusalem and to the deportation of the Judahite élite. With the second conquest and the destruction of the temple, the independent state of Judah ceased to exist. Shortly afterward, Ammon (582), Moab, and Edom (553–552) were conquered as well.

§167.   This historical sketch merely helps to set the stage for the religio-historical developments to be discussed in this chapter. It is obvious that such a profound political upheaval must have produced cultural-historical and religio-historical consequences as well. The local religious symbol system that dates to Iron Age IIC was pushed into the background by the symbol system of a foreign conqueror in a way that had not happened since the Late Bronze Age. It is precisely in the glyptic art that the stamp seals and the cylinder seals, which appear for a while in great numbers, show clear Assyrian or Assyrian-Babylonian themes on which one can detect no local influence. Nevertheless, we should not jump to the conclusion that the Assyrian conquerors exercised a repressive policy also with respect to religion by compelling subjugated people to worship their own Assyrian state deities.

The familiar thesis that suggests that there was an Assyrian infiltration of Palestinian religions, especially as regards the religion of Israel and Judah (see, e.g., Donner 1986, 329–338), must be refined in many respects, no matter how one might evaluate the issue regarding religio-political coercion. First, since the end of the ninth century, Assyrian culture had itself been influenced strongly by the Arameans, during a time when the northern Syrian and Aramean territories situated between the Tigris and the Euphrates were being integrated into this larger configuration. These lands were administered initially by loyal local potentates who were able to make careers for themselves within the Assyrian governmental system. By the end of the eighth century, the Assyrian government apparatus had taken on a significantly Aramean character. The Aramean language itself achieved an increasingly greater significance, along with the Assyrian language, as a governmental language in the Trans-Euphrates region (see 2 Kgs 18:26). One must thus consider an impact on Palestine that came not only from the Assyrians but, even more, one that originated with the Arameans.

Second, the policy of deportation, concentrated especially on the upper classes of the subjugated regions who were the "prime bearers of culture," led to an "international" cultural mixing, to a relativizing (partially due to the loss of national identity), and to a certain unsureness about the competence of divine powers whose claims had been defined clearly in the past by observing national borders that were under each particular deity's control.

Third, one must bear in mind that there was a progressive collapse of the network of trade and cultural exchange that had been established among the smaller states. Such relationships had to be reconstituted as well. In terms of the material culture, it can be demonstrated that imports, from luxury items to ceramics for everyday use, were available during the seventh century from many distant lands; especially noteworthy are the wares from eastern Greece that now make their first appearance (Wenning 1981; Zimhoni 1990). The foreign traders who had settled in the Palestinian cities but who respected local practices by following the principle of what has been called *"enoikismos"* now brought along their own religious practices in the seventh century, no longer hindered in a world that was increasingly international and open, even though it became increasingly complex, too. In the light of the political and cultural situation that has just been described, it seems quite plausible that one could have seen in Jerusalem a colorful array of indigenous and foreign cults, of Aramean, Phoenician-Canaanite, Ammonite, and Moabite provenance, during the late Assyrian period (the second half of the seventh century), as described in 2 Kings 23. As the dominant political power, the Assyrians played a decisive role in this development. Nevertheless, for what concerns the religious history of Iron Age IIC Palestine, internationalization and permeability by the foreign cults from the closest neighboring states are more significant factors in this development. What some have assumed – that every change was caused monolithically by an imposition of the Assyrian yoke – is probably not a sufficient explanation for this situation (see below, §214).

1. Assyria, Aram and the
Astralization of the Heavenly Powers

§168.   As has been mentioned, the presence of the Assyrians in Palestine during Iron Age IIC, in contrast to the preceding periods, can be detected by the rapidly increasing number of cylinder seals, which had generally been out of use since Late Bronze Age IIB. To be sure, this phenomenon must be assessed proportionally. In contrast to the Late Bronze Age, when inexpensive faience seals were mass-produced from molds for use as votive gifts and amulets (see above, §§32, 36 and 44), there is no general use of cylinder seals in Iron Age IIC; not even three dozen such seals from the eighth and seventh centuries have been found to date in Palestine.[1] These come almost exclusively from the urban centers that were under direct Assyrian control (such as Megiddo, Dor, Samaria, and Gezer) or else from the smaller communication outposts occupied by the Assyrians (such as Beth-Shean, Shechem, and Dothan). The renewed appearance of cylinder seals is directly connected with the presence of Assyrian officials in the Palestinian provinces. Their iconography and style indicate that the majority of Iron Age IIC cylinder seals are Assyrian imports, likely brought to Palestine by their owners. Three cylinder seals include a cuneiform inscription. One of these is dated to the mid-seventh century and comes from Samaria, having belonged to an official by the name of Nabu-zabil. It bears a single, fairly long cuneiform inscription addressed to the Babylonian divine couples Nabu and Tashmetu and also to Marduk and Sarpanitu, seeking a blessing for the owner of the seal (Crowfoot, et al., 1957, 87, pl. 15.18).

In view of the close connection with the Assyrian authorities, it should not be surprising to find that the most frequently occurring motif (on six of the cylinder seals) is a cultic scene, in the center of which the Assyrian *king* stands as a loyal servant of the heavenly powers. Four seals of this group are well preserved, but three of them are either unpublished (Ornan 1990, nos. 16 and 19 from Acre and Palmahim respectively) or inadequately published (James 1966, 348 fig. 117.6). Only the bottom two-thirds remains from a seal found at Shechem (**illus. 280a**; Ornan 1990, no. 15) but, thanks to the many known parallels from Mesopotamia and northern Syria, the rest of the picture can be restored easily, as can a badly worn seal from Megiddo Str. II (**illus. 280b**; Ornan 1990, no. 14). The best preserved piece that has been published (**illus. 281**; cf. Keel 1977a, 291–295, with numerous parallels from outside of Palestine) was supposedly found at Tell Dothan and may have come into the country as early as the eighth century, perhaps during the time of Sargon II.

The main scene on all the seals in this group is the same. The king is always shown standing before a ceremonial setup, with a sword in his belt though he is bareheaded, while he rests his bow on the ground. Across from him stands an unarmed official with a hand towel thrown over his shoulders and a raised fan. In the space that is either in front of the king or behind him one sees either an eight-rayed star or else a crescent moon. In illus. 281, the crescent moon appears as a standard with two tassels, the cultic emblem of the Moon God of Haran (see below, §173). It is flanked by a hoe and a stylus, the cultic symbols of the Babylonian gods

---

1 There is a pressing need for documentation of all of the cylinder seals found in Palestine. Older works by J. Nougayrol (1939) and B. Parker (1949) are out of date, not only as regards which materials have been evaluated, but also in respect of an archaeological and iconographical evaluation of their importance (see Keel/Uehlinger 1990, 56). An unpublished master's thesis by T. Ornan (1990) discusses Assyrian, Babylonian and Persian seals from first-millennium Palestine, but does not claim to be comprehensive.

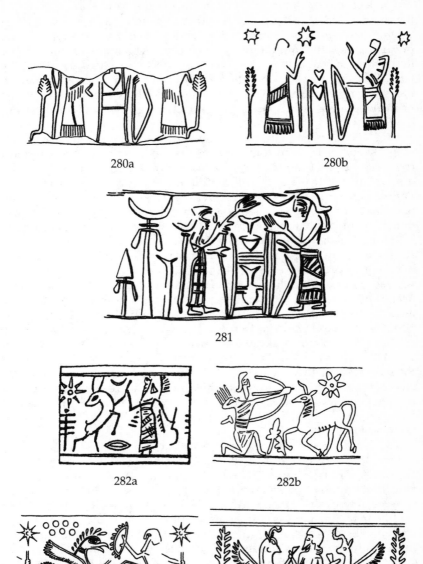

280a

280b

281

282a

282b

282c

283

Marduk and Nabu (on the unpublished seal from Acre only the crescent moon standard is shown).

The fact that the king wears no head covering, and additionally that the cultic emblem is present, demonstrates that this is a depiction of ritual activity. This cult is dedicated to the worship of heavenly powers that are present only in the form of their emblems or, even more discretely, only in the form of heavenly bodies. The emphasis in the illustration is on the king. The "grain stalks" or "little trees" that are used as scene dividers in illuss. 280a-b express the fact that the loyalty shown by the king to the heavenly powers effects, or ought to effect, the growth and prosperity of the fertile land.

§169.　The image of the Assyrian king, as it is shown on the cylinder seals, is characterized by this cultic loyalty. The more dynamic aspects of royal rule (e.g., heroism in war or the hunt, as celebrated on Assyrian monumental art; see above, illus. 278b) are entirely absent from the Palestinian cylinder seals. But these themes are generally of only marginal importance in Neo-Assyrian cylinder seal glyptic art. The military conflicts that are shown on the cylinder seals take place primarily in the mythological realms and are intended to show ways to secure cosmic order.[2] Correspondingly, the protagonists are hybrid creatures, heroes, genii, and deities. To take one example: on a piece from Gezer, a winged genius with a scimitar fights a bovine creature (**illus. 282a**; Reich/ Brandl 1985, 46f. no. 2 = Ornan 1990, no. 21). On seals from Megiddo, one hero can be seen shooting an arrow at a falling bull (**illus. 282b**; Ornan 1990, no. 19); another can be seen holding an unidentifiable weapon while confronting two griffin-like hybrid creatures (**illus. 282c**; Ornan 1990, no. 28). All three of these seals also have astral symbols in the upper part of the scene, especially the eight-rayed Venus star, the Pleiades, and/or the crescent moon; the significance of the rhombus that can be seen directly between the battling protagonists in illuss. 282a and c is still unexplained (see Uehlinger 1990b, 328; see below, illuss. 286, 297b, and often elsewhere).

The astral symbols are absent on a seal from Dor, on which a hero, in the role of "Lord of the Animals," appears between two winged cattle (**illus. 283**; Ornan 1990, no. 23). Even though this seal may not have come from the "imperial" production in the center of Assyria, but rather from a provincial workshop, it still ought to be considered to be an import. We find neither the "Lord of the Animals" nor winged bulls in any works attributable to local stamp seal production (for a "Lord of the Animals" on a locally produced cylinder seal, see below, illus. 308).

§170.　Only four of the more important Assyrian deities are shown in anthropomorphic form on Iron Age IIC cylinder seals from Palestine. The warrior god *Ninurta* is depicted in battle against the winged Anzu dragon (**illus. 284a**; in the Rockefeller Museum, but of unknown provenance; Ornan 1990, no. 20) and one can also find depictions of the weather god

---

2　A seal from Gezer represents the only exception (Macalister 1912, III pl. 214.24 = Reich/Brandl 1985, 46f. no. 4 = Ornan 1990, no. 29). Themes of war and the hunt seem to be linked in a meristic fashion; a riding archer pursues a fleeing animal and a human being simultaneously. The eight-rayed star, the crescent moon, and perhaps also the Pleiades are in the upper pictorial field.

Adad (or his son) and the goddess Ishtar; see below, §171. A seal from Gezer shows Adad with drawn bow in front of a horned snake (Akkadian: *bašmu*, **illus. 284b**; Reich/Brandl 1985, 46 no. 1 = Ornan 1990, no. 27). The piece is published incompletely and there is no description of the material from which it is made, though it may be made of frit and may have been mass-produced in Assyria or in northern Syria. Such products may have reached all the regions under the control of this world power during the seventh century, as can be seen by comparing exact or nearly identical parallels from Khorsabad, Nineveh, Nimrud, and Asshur, but also those found at Karmir Blur in Urartu or Tell Halaf, al-Mina, or Tell Abu Danne in Syria (Reich/Brandl 1985, 46; see also Keel/Uehlinger 1990, 47 illus. 53, purchased in Damascus).

Literary sources enable us to assign names to the two deities and to their opponents. Both Ninurta and Adad are personalizations of the weather god and were practically regarded as twin deities in Assyria (for their relationship, see, most recently, Moortgat-Correns 1988). Representations from the center of Assyria itself, rich in detail, show both gods with lightning in their hands; the arrows that they shoot in the depictions on the seals that we are discussing here may represent the lightning that the weather god uses to drive away the chaotic sea monster that threatens the fertile land (see Pss 18:15; 144:6). The deity who, according to Gen 9:12ff., places his bow in the clouds as a sign of his victory and to show his reliable control after the ominous flood reflects this same idea (Uehlinger 1989). Since Canaan already knew of a tradition about this battle between the weather god and the horned snake (see above, §45, where the weather god fights with a lance or a scimitar rather than with a bow), it is not surprising that this widespread theme from the Neo-Assyrian cylinder seal glyptic art struck a cord in local Palestinian production (the name of the Edomite national god Qaus shows that the bow of the weather god had practically assumed hypostatic form).

On other cylinder seals, the weather god appears in the form of his cultic image, as he is shown standing above an attribute animal. A surface find from the area around Netanya (**illus. 285a**; Ornan 1990, no. 3) shows him standing, armed with club, sword, and bow, on his reclining attribute animal, the bull. Two bareheaded, beardless officials stand before him in the typical Assyrian worship posture. Astral symbols are once again visible at the top of the scene; here, they have the form of the crescent moon and the Pleiades. The cuneiform inscription identifies the owner as "Bel-asharedu, chief administrator over the palace (*rab ekalli*)," showing that this seal too had belonged to an Assyrian official. In place of Adad himself, the less well-known Aramean god Apladad ("son of Adad") appears on a votive seal that turned up not too long ago at Beer-sheba and belonged to a certain "Rimut-ilani, son of Hadad-idri" (Aharoni, et al., 1973, 56–70; Ornan 1990, no. 1). The names of the deity and the seal owner, as well as the provincial linear engraving technique, point to northern or central Syria as a place of origin for this seal. The owner apparently did not dedicate and hand over his seal to the god that is named here, as the cuneiform inscription implies (or possibly did so only in passing?), but brought it along as an amulet as he carried out his duties in remote Beer-sheba.

§171.   There are only two *female* deities of Assyrian origin shown in the iconography of Iron Age IIC Palestine, namely the healing goddess Gula and *Ishtar*. Gula is depicted with her scalpel on a surface find from Beth-Shean (**illus. 285b**; Ornan 1990, no. 4; cf. Ornan 1990, no. 5, a seal from Tyre). Ishtar appears, for example, on a scaraboid from Shechem Str. VII (**illus. 286**), which must have arrived there before the Assyrian conquest of the city. The scaraboid shows the warrior goddess with a sword at her side, standing in front of a worshiper. Between the two figures there is a cultic stand(?), shaped like the stylus of Nabu. The Venus star, Ishtar's special astral symbol, shines above it. The Pleiades and the rhombus are also present.

The privileged connection between Ishtar and the stars is emphasized especially by the motif of the goddess as she is shown *in a shining wreath* or in a nimbus of stars. This is shown on a cylinder seal from Shechem, of uncertain stratigraphic context (**illus. 287**; Ornan 1990, no. 2). We see the Assyrian king opposite her once again, bringing a burnt offering while making the typical Assyrian pointing gesture that shows that he is making an oath. As in illus. 281, the spade that is behind him is indicative of the presence of the god Marduk. In the upper half of the scene we see the eight-rayed star and the Pleiades. Astral symbols and the shining wreath (cf. illuss. 288a-c) indicate that this is a power in an astral form that can be recognized as ruling over the night (or ruling the time of transition between day and night, in the form of the morning and evening star); the incense emphasizes the celestial character of the deity.

Ishtar is the only one of the Assyrian deities who appears in anthropomorphic form on Iron Age IIC Palestinian stamp seals as well.[3] At first glance, this appears to support the idea that there was a more general acquaintance with (or sphere of influence for) this deity. S. Schroer has correctly linked the cylinder seal shown in illus. 287 to a stamp seal from Ashdod (**illus. 288a**) on which Ishtar appears alone within a shining wreath, using these pieces to show that Ishtar was known in Iron Age IIC Palestine (1987a, 276). Two additional representations of Ishtar have been found in Palestine, showing her in the nimbus of stars, and these can now be added to the examples already mentioned (**illuss. 288b-c,** one from the area around Beth-Shean[4] and the other from Dor). A scaraboid from Megiddo engraved on both sides (**illus. 289**) can also be considered here. This last piece does not show the goddess herself, but it divides an adoration scene of the type shown in illus. 287 into two parts, so that what appears to be a female worshiper is shown on one side of the seal amulet and an eight-rayed star, the symbol of the goddess, is depicted on the other side (cf. illus. 311a; Lamon/Shipton 1939, pl. 67.9).

Schroer, following the lead of Weinfeld and Winter, suggested (1987a, 273–276; see Koch 1988, 112f.) that this deity should be identified with the Assyrian Ishtar and that it is this deity that was worshiped during the early part of the sixth century in Judah and Jerusalem as the "Queen of

---

3 Note as well, however, the very extraordinary seal in Bordreuil 1986a, no. 58 = illus. 331b below!

4 An unpublished, surface find; limestone, 22.5 × 18 × 10.7 mm. It is presently in the collection of M. Reschef, Kibbutz Bet-Alfa, to whom we are grateful for permission to publish.

284a

284b

285a

285b

286

287

288a

288b

288c

Heaven" (*malkat ha=šāmayim*) (see Jer 7:16–20; 44:15–19, 25). In point of fact, the cult of the "Queen of Heaven" evinces unmistakable Assyrian features: incense, drink offerings, and especially the offering of "ash cakes," which may be identified as what is meant by the Akkadian word *kawwānîm* (see Weinfeld 1972; Winter 1983, 561–576). Titles such as *šarrat šamê* "Queen of Heaven," and *bēlet šamê* "Mistress of Heaven,"[5] and other similar names are applied to Ishtar in Akkadian texts. The special connection with the stars, recognizable in the motif of the goddess in the shining wreath, is expressed verbally in the epithet *šarrat šamê u kakkabāni* "Queen of the Heavens and the Stars" (Tallqvist 1938, 64, 239f., 276, 333f. 462). Ishtar's astral character and her frightening appearance as a warrior are also in the background of Cant 6:10, where the beloved is portrayed as shining with the radiance of the goddess who is associated with the dawn and the full moon (see Keel 1986, 204–206; Müller 1988). The seals portrayed in illuss. 287–289 show that the Assyrian goddess was known in Iron Age IIC Palestine primarily in her astral connotations: within a shining wreath or else in a nimbus of stars. But these particular seals, taken alone, can hardly be used to provide the link to the "Queen of Heaven," since they were found primarily in areas that were close to the centers of Assyrian power or else at Assyrian outposts (illus. 286 is indeed older, but it is certainly an import) and they permit no conclusion regarding how the goddess was accepted locally. To date, such seals have not been found in Judah, which means that to identify the "Queen of Heaven" *exclusively* with the Assyrian deity Ishtar, *and no other possible deity*, cannot be the last word on the subject (see further below, §197).

§172. It is typical of nearly all the seals shown in illuss. 280–289 to find *astral symbols* (especially the eight-rayed Venus star, the Pleiades, and the crescent moon), in the middle or upper pictorial field as a rule. As we will see repeatedly in what follows, Assyrian and Aramean influence during Iron Age IIC caused the heavenly powers to be accepted and worshiped, primarily in their astral manifestations (the moon, Venus, the Pleiades . . .), as *deities of the night*. On a cylinder seal found at Megiddo (**illus. 290**; Ornan 1990, no. 8), we see the king(?) worshiping before a whole group of such powers that have primarily astral connotations. Besides the symbols already mentioned – the marks in front of the king are perhaps to be filled out to form the Marduk spade – even Scorpio and Pisces appear here, constellations that we still identify today by the same names.[6] A conic limestone seal from Tell Keisan Str. V (end of the eighth century),[7] on which not only the base is decorated but also the top (**illuss. 291a-c**; see Keel, et al., 1990, 238–242), displays a similar kind of survey of all the deities that appear together in Iron Age IIC glyptic art. On one side

---

5 Also: *malkat šamāmi u qaqqari* (Tallqvist 1938, 129). Nevertheless, these and similar meristic epithets (*šarrat / bēlet / etellet samê u erṣeti*, Tallqvist 1938, 64, 239f., 333) are not directly relevant for the comparison with *malkat ha=šāmayim*.

6 Parker 1949, 28 no. 122 would identify the archer in illus. 308 (cf. illus. 282b) with Sagittarius ("archer").

7 Both the dating and the fact that this must be an Assyrian import are confirmed by a stylistically nearly identical cylinder seal from Khorsabad/Dur-Sharrukin (see Keel, et al., 1990, 240–242 with fig. 59).

are both of the great Babylonian gods, Marduk and Nabu, whose symbols in the upper portion (a) are on top of the back of a *mušḫuššu* dragon. On the base (b), by contrast, they are shown standing on the flat earth (see illuss. 281, 285b). On the back side of the upper portion (c) we see the moon god, Sin of Haran, whose cultic emblem is flanked by two branches. Sin also appears in the form of a crescent moon on the base, next to the Venus star (Ishtar) and two dots that might represent the Pleiades (*sebettu*). The incense stand was especially popular during Iron Age IIC as a requisite piece in the cult of a wide variety of deities (cf. illuss. 285b, 287). The branch behind the worshiper, a very common motif on stamp seals of Iron Age IIC (see Giveon 1978, fig. 66b; Keel-Leu 1991, no. 138; see below, illuss. 312a and 317c), indicates that heavenly powers, for all their astral and celestial characteristics, were still seen as responsible for the flourishing of the vegetation.

The contrast between these symbols and the artifacts of Iron Age IIB is remarkable. The earlier era used a symbol system that was oriented almost exclusively toward solar themes. This shift is accentuated by the observation that the winged solar disk previously located above the winged hybrid creatures, which we connected to the sphere of the "Lord of Heaven" in Iron Age IIB (see above, §150), is replaced now by a crescent moon and a lunar disk (**illus. 292** from Samaria;[8] see Keel, et al., 1990, 229 no. 19 from Tell Keisan). This shift is further emphasized by the fact that there are fewer images of the sun on Iron Age IIC glyptic art from Palestine, whether these were produced locally or imported. The *winged disk* appears only periodically and then in combinations that often suggest it was used as an image to depict heaven itself, rather than being an exclusive representation of the sun or a symbol of the sun god Shamash (e.g., above a stylized tree on a cylinder seal from Shechem, Roos/Toombs 1962, 13). This does not mean that it could not have been known as a symbol of Shamash. A carnelian conoid from Gezer with an oval base shows the winged solar disk above a single worshiper. The worshiper is standing in front of a winged hybrid creature, above which a crescent moon has been inserted as well (**illus. 293a**; see *Archäologie zur Bibel* 1981, 147f. no. 94). Though the piece was found in a tomb that dates to the early fifth century, the Assyrian iconography particularly shows that it is an older piece from Iron Age IIC that had been passed down by inheritance (on the worshiper, see illus. 291b; on the form of the winged disk, see also Macalister 1912, III pl. 205a.19). On two impressions of a stamp seal, found on a single cuneiform plaque that can be dated to 651(Becking 1983, 80–86), we see the winged sun above two worshipers who stand to the two sides of what is either an angular, stylized *ankh* sign(?) or else a cultic stand (cf. illus. 286; **illus. 293b**; on this particular constellation of figures, see below, §174).

Similarly, on a seal that is engraved on both sides and that belonged to *mnḥmt ᵓšt ǧdmlk* (**illus. 294**), we find a winged disk above two (human or semi-divine?) worshipers standing to either side of a crescent moon and star

---

8 An unpublished, surface find; brownish-red limestone, 17 × 14.6 × 9.4 mm. Formerly at the YMCA, Jerusalem, Clark Collection no. 214.

(cf. illuss. 298a, 305a-b).[9] In contrast to the images previously mentioned, the upper body of a god who is bringing a blessing is shown coming out of the nimbus in this scene. Assyrian representations of this form were commonly identified as Asshur, Urarturian images as Khaldi, Achaemenian versions as Ahuramazda, in other words, as being each country's respective supreme, state deity (see Galling 1941, 151). But the identification of the god being shown by means of the winged sun has been called into question and with good reason. It is more likely that the god who is always shown in conjunction with the king on Assyrian and Achaemenian monumental works ought generally to be connected with the sun god (Mayer-Opificius 1984). Calmeyer interprets the sun god as a hypostasis of the kingdom or as the personal protective deity of the ruler (Calmeyer 1979, 352–359; 1984; Calmeyer/Seidl 1983, 107–114). In view of later connections with Gad and the royal Tyche (Calmeyer 1979, 347–352), one might identify the god in the winged sun in illus. 294 as Gad, especially since the name of the husband (*gdmlk*) of the owner of the seal would support this identification.[10] In spite of the alleged place of discovery (Jerusalem), this piece cannot be of Judean provenance.[11] Nevertheless, together with the representations of a deity shown in the act of blessing in a lotus nimbus (see below, illuss. 337a-b) on tridacna bowls that have also been found in Judah, it presents an analogous picture to that of the Yahweh vision in Ezek 1:26b–27 and is connected with the concept of *kābôd*. In Ezekiel, the figure has a mixed form, being only partially anthropomorphic, with a human upper body and a "radiant" lower body (see Keel 1977a, 260–263).

§173.   The cylinder seal from Dothan shown in illus. 281 depicts three cultic symbols behind the Assyrian official on the left side of the scene. The *crescent moon standard* with its two tassels juts out from the image more prominently than the two symbols that flank it, the spade and the stylus. Clear priority is given thereby to the Moon God of Haran over against Marduk and Nabu – the chief gods of Babylon and the deities whose names appear most frequently in the onomasticon. The standard is assigned approximately the same status as the other two cultic emblems on the decoration on the top part of the conoid in illus. 291. The Assyrians adopted the Moon God of Haran when they conquered the Aramean regions of northern Syria, worshiping him under the Akkadian name Sin. Even though not an indigenous Assyrian god, Sin was among the most important deities of the Neo-Assyrian Empire, both in the official state cult and in "personal piety."

An interesting piece of evidence showing that the Assyrians practiced cultic veneration of this god as far away as the Palestinian provinces is provided by the bronze ornament atop a standard, 17 cm wide and,

9 The seal was supposedly found in Jerusalem by a missionary during the last century (see Timm 1989, 247f. no. 39, with literature). It is now in the British Museum, London; BM 136202 (information from Dr. B. Sass, Jerusalem).

10 Lemaire (1993) thinks the reading *p̄dmlk* is more probable.

11 The paleography points to Edom as the most probable source (Lemaire 1993). For both paleographic and iconographic reasons (Assyrian clothing of the worshiper and the angular, stylized *ankh* sign at the end of l. 1 on the written side of the seal, which is not shown here) a date in Iron Age IIC (seventh century to the early sixth century) is more likely than the Persian Period, as suggested by Galling (1941, 151), Timm (1989, 247), and others.

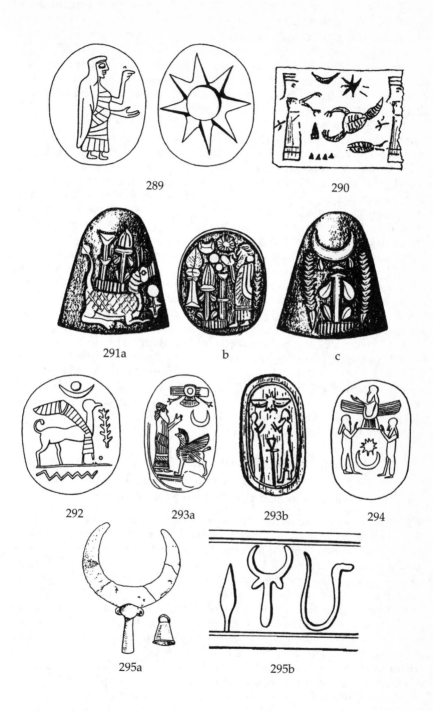

289   290

291a   b   c

292   293a   293b   294

295a   295b

including the socket, 21 cm high, found at Tel Sera' Str. VI (**illus. 295a;**
see H. Weippert 1988, 627f.) on the brick floor of a fortress occupied by
Assyrian/Aramean officials, judging by evidence provided by an Aramean
ostracon, Assyrian palace ware, and other small artifacts (Oren 1978, 1062).
The two little holes at the upper end of the socket probably served as a
place to tie on the upper end of each of its two tassels. These are typical of
cultic standards from Haran (see above, illus. 46 and §90) and are rarely
absent from the representations of these emblems in glyptic art.

They also allow us to connect the crescent moon standard that is
portrayed on a cylinder seal to the Moon God of Haran. It shows Egyptian
influence, is made of frit, and was found at Tell Jemmeh (**illus. 295b**).
Similar images, made using the same inexpensive material, have been
found at Nimrud and in northern Syria. The motif, as can be seen in illus.
284b, was produced in this fashion in great quantities during the seventh
century and was widely disseminated. Like illus. 284b, it places a deity in
a central position, according to a profile assigned to it by this new world
power, but it associates the deity with Egyptianizing and/or Levantine
elements. The *uraeus* (from the Egyptian symbol system), positioned to
the right of the symbol and shown turning away, thus links it to Egypt.
The *uraeus* expresses the great power of the god and keeps all hostile
forces at a distance. The little tree to the left of the standard shaped like a
lancet is, as we will see shortly, a rather constant requisite piece that
accompanies the moon standard in southern Syrian glyptic art.

Both the ornamental top for the standard, depicted in illus. 295a, and
its archaeological context, show clearly that the worship of the Moon God
of Haran was brought to Palestine by Assyrian/Aramean officials (see
also illuss. 281 and 291). The cylinder seal shown in illus. 295b furnishes
evidence for a local, southern Palestinian reception of the crescent moon
emblem. We will examine shortly the issue surrounding the adaptation
of this emblem in a more detailed fashion.

2. The Local Reception of Astralization Tendencies:
The Crescent Moon Emblem of Haran, the Moon God
in a Boat and the *Asherah* Once Again

§174.   Used to certify the sale of a piece of real estate, a stamp seal has
been impressed three times on a cuneiform plaque from Gezer – datable to
the year 649 (**illus. 296**; see Becking 1983, 86–89). The text on the plaque
identifies the seller and seal owner as *na-tan-ia-u*, in other words, as an
Israelite or Judahite with the Yahwistic personal name *nᵉtanyā(h)û*. By contrast, the witnesses to the transaction have foreign names. Four are preserved: one is Egyptian or Aramean, two are Akkadian, and one is unclear,
but certainly not Semitic). On a second plaque, found at Gezer and dated
to 651, one reads one Egyptian name along with several Aramean and
Akkadian names (Becking 1983; Zadok 1985, 568f.). In a mixed population,
with a substantial proportion being Assyrian/Aramean, the moon emblem
of Haran apparently found ready access also into Yahwistic circles.

This finding is supported by two bullae discovered a few years ago.
One (**illus. 297a**; see Shiloh 1985, 78, 80) comes from a Jerusalem archive
of the seventh century – from the so-called City of David. The emblem is

296   297a   297b

298a   298b

299a   b   c   d   e

300

unique in its iconographic form and could have come from a local workshop. In place of the standard pole, there is a thick, cross-hatched pillar that is vaguely reminiscent of contemporary portrayals of a pillar with a volute capital (see below, illus. 353a; see Keel-Leu 1991, no. 132). The two diagonal lines jutting out from where the crescent and pillar come together, remind one of the tassels on the emblem from Haran, and show that this is an adaptation of that emblem (see another way this is adapted in illus. 171b). Another anepigraphic bulla from about the same time, with the depiction of the crescent moon emblem, comes from Horvat Uza in the northeastern Negev, which would have belonged to Judah at that time (Beck 1986, 40f.).

Two dots and a rhomboid are placed alongside the emblem on a scaraboid found near Nahshonim in the southern Sharon plain (**illus. 297b**). The rhomboid is a motif that was adopted from Assyrian glyptic art (see above, illuss. 282a, c; 286), but this seal must have come from a local, southern Syrian/Palestinian workshop: the square pattern on the post and pedestal are never found on northern Syrian or Assyrian portrayals, but this is quite common on seals from Palestine and Trans-jordan. The shaping of the pedestal, with the middle bent downward (resembling a triangle that is balanced on its point), is characteristic of seals from this region (see the illustrations that follow).

Right next to the crescent moon emblem, a scaraboid from Gezer also depicts a so-called "cross with ball" that resembles the Egyptian *ankh* sign (Macalister 1912, III pl. 207.48 = Reich/Brandl 1985, 48 no. 5). The fact that what is, in the final analysis, an Egyptian motif appears on a seal that was apparently imported from northern Syria, while an Assyrian symbol (the rhomboid) is used on the piece shown in illus. 297b, which certainly comes from a southern Syrian and perhaps even from a Palestinian workshop, shows clearly how problematic it is to assume confidently that dependency and influence can come from only one direction at a time in an era when "international" contacts and cultural blending characterized the entire region.

§175.   Images that depict the crescent moon emblem along with *cypress-like trees* are known from only Palestine and Transjordan, as we perhaps already see on the tenth-century seal impression from Hazor shown in illus. 171a. **Illustration 298a** shows the design on the base of a stamp seal found in the Edomite city of Tawilan. The excavator dates this excavation level roughly to the ninth or eighth century. The seal itself can have come only from the end of the eighth century. An eight-rayed star has been added within the crescent (see illuss. 294, 305a-b). To the right of the standard one sees a cypress-like stylized tree. The pendant on the left side is perhaps likewise to be understood as a "tree" (Spycket 1973, 384; Keel 1977a, 286). It is clearly different from the tree on the right (three horizontal lines instead of two on the "trunk"; the triangular form instead of the rhomboid form of the "crown"; a different grid pattern) and is more likely a provincial way to depict the spade of Marduk (see above, illuss. 281, 287, 291). The two or three horizontal lines and both of the two little lines on an angle that are shown on each image at the juncture of the "trunk" and the "crown," and that are found repeatedly along with the cypress-like trees on these seals, are not there for any botanical reason. It would make the most sense if there was a development of the motif that started with the spade of Marduk and that evolved until it became a cypress-like stylized tree. On two unstratified scaraboids, one from Tell Keisan (**illus. 298b**) and one from Tell en-Nasbeh (McCown 1947, pl. 54.51 = Keel 1977a, 292 illus. 215), the crescent moon standard is flanked by what one might identify as two identically drawn "trees."[12]

A four-sided prism from the former collection of M. Dayan (**illuss. 299a-e**) represents the emblem and both trees in a complex constellation of images. It offers much more material for interpretation than does the limited surface of a stamp seal: the four sides of the prism show, in a sequence from left to right, a lyre player, a double-pipe player, the two cypress-like trees, above which is a winged disk, and finally the crescent moon standard with the characteristic cross-hatching and bent pedestal. Next to the standard there are three dots as well, probably stars, while a crescent moon inserted above each of the two musicians also emphasizes that the cult represented here is primarily dedicated to the moon god. The signs in front of the musicians are probably not items that are needed for the cultic activity but are rather *ankh* signs with triangular, stylized loops. They call attention to the numinous nature of the area through which the worshipers move during the cultic activity, pointing this out as a realm of life (Uehlinger 1990b; see below, illuss. 300, 302).

Cypress-like, stylized trees appear frequently on Phoenician metal bowls that date to the eighth and seventh centuries (see Markoe 1985, 244f., 266f., 289–293, 296f., 306–309, and often elsewhere). In marked contrast to the palmetto-like stylized trees (Markoe 1985, 254–257, 259), these depictions make it clear that (unlike the artificial cultic symbol) these are supposed to represent natural or at least "somewhat natural" trees. But these trees appear on the metal bowls in a cultic context only as exceptions to the rule (Markoe 1985, 348f.), and they never have the straight horizontal lines or diagonal lines that are used characteristically on the seals.

When A. Spycket (1973, 384) and H. Weippert (1978, 51f.; 1988, 627f.) attempt to interpret these trees as ways to depict a little forest or an open-air shrine, as they are identified in the biblical texts, the connection seems quite plausible at first, especially since the idea of a cult under the open night sky would make sense for those who were worshiping the moon god or his emblem. But their thesis is contradicted by the relevant biblical texts that polemicize against such cultic activities "on heights and hills and under every green tree" (cf. 1 Kgs 14:23f.; 2 Kgs 16:4; 2 Kgs 17:9f.; Jer 17:2; and often elsewhere). The cultic inventories include "*maṣṣebah*(s)" and "*asherah*(s)," and the passages refer to sacrifices and incense, but they never link these activities to an astral cult (Keel 1978, 53). Conversely, texts that mention astral cults and date to Iron Age IIC (see 2 Kgs 21:3–5; 23:5, 12; Deut 4:19; Jer 7:17f.; 19:13; 44:17; Zeph 1:5; see below, §184) do not connect them with open air shrines and green trees. When such

---

12 These are badly damaged but still recognizable. Non-vegetal rhomboids are represented very rarely as a pair (Braun 1991, 21 fig. 7) and are apparently never in the flanking position shown in illus. 298b.

activities take place out-of-doors, they are carried out in the streets and on rooftops.[13]

Seal amulets are not picture postcards. The trees in illuss. 298–300 and 301b cannot be used in a purely "naturalistic" way to show what a "forest" or a "sanctuary on a high place" looked like; they must be interpreted in light of the context of the entire constellation of figures that are shown together (Keel 1978, 44–54). When two trees or branches flank a third subject, they call attention to and emphasize that central entity's ability to bless (see above, §15, for what was said about the "Branch Goddess"). This general statement can be made still more precise by what is seen in illus. 299: here the two trees appear "between" the worshiper and the crescent moon emblem and a winged disk appears above them as well. We have an analogous situation to that shown in the topmost register in illus. 184 (see Keel 1977a, 300f.). The two "trees" mark the entrance to a shrine and the crescent moon standard is in the Holy of Holies in that shrine. The trees identify this as a place of blessing (see also illuss. 188a-b). Perhaps we may go further yet and relate the trees to the gate of heaven, as the place where the (rising) moon god appears (thus Keel 1977a, 296–303, with pictures of the gate of heaven through which, in that scene, it is admittedly the *sun god* who is striding forth), especially if one includes illus. 304 as well. The earthly and heavenly dwelling places of the deity (see the *zᵉbul* of the moon in Hab 3:11a) cannot always be separated neatly in the ancient Near East. Admittedly, the moon god in illuss. 304 (–307) appears alone in his anthropomorphic, heavenly form as a person, whereas, by contrast, in illus. 299 and in the depictions that will be discussed shortly (illuss. 300–301), the portrayal of human worshipers with the cultic symbol of the god leads one more readily to think of the context of an earthly shrine. Here the trees mark the entrance to the shrine. In this earthly shrine – and this is the main theme in illuss. 298–301 – the god who bestows blessings *appears* in the form of his cultic symbol and is thus present to be worshiped.

§176. A cylinder seal from a tomb on Mount Nebo, east of the Jordan, dated to the end of the eighth century or the beginning of the seventh century, portrays a scene nearly identical to the illustration just considered (**illus. 300**), showing a lyre player and a double-pipe player, before each of whom we see angular, stylized *ankh* signs. They are approaching a crescent moon emblem. To the right of the emblem is a cypress-like, stylized tree; this one tree serves the same function as the two trees in illus. 299c. It acts simultaneously as a scene divider and would frame the whole scene if the seal were rolled several times in succession. In the background, we see dots (or stars), the eight-rayed Venus star, and the rhomboid. The close resemblance between the images

---

13 The only possible exception, 2 Kgs 23:5, does not contradict this evidence. This text does not try to differentiate these items but is intent on summarizing everything that was there. It mentions the *bāmôt* in the first half-verse and the incense stands for astrally-defined heavenly powers, including moon and stars ("Host of Heaven"), in the second half-verse. The two halves are thus juxtaposed paratactically *next to* one another; in addition to this, the literary-critical analysis of the verse separates the mention of the *bāmôt* and the astral cults completely (see, e.g., Spieckermann 1982, 83–88).

301a   301b   301c

302a   302b

302c   302d

303   304

in illus. 299 and illus. 300 is striking. There are only slight stylistic differences, perhaps because the two seals are from different workshops. The worshipers in illus. 299 are bearded and are dressed in more of an Assyrian style than are those in illus. 300. The tassels on the moon emblem in illus. 299 are doubled, as in illuss. 297b and 298b (and as also on the bulla from Hurvat Uza mentioned in §174; Beck 1986, 40f.).

A scaraboid from Tell Jemmeh (**illus. 301a**) is also very similar to what is shown in illus. 299 in these and other details (e.g., the angular shape of the pedestal box). Since stamp seals do not have much surface, there must be some selectivity about which elements to include when the scenes are designed, as can be seen in illuss. 299–300 (see above, §6). In this connection, the selection could depend upon the preference of the workshops and the customers. For example, a scaraboid from Shiqmona (**illus. 301b**) depicts only one little tree and one worshiper and no musical instrument. Another piece from the same site shows a Nabu-stylus(?) next to the moon emblem instead of a little tree being there (**illus. 301c**). Reducing the number of elements on the seals can go even further, to the point at which the crescent moon emblem itself is omitted completely and only the worshiper is portrayed. On an unpublished scaraboid, which is supposed to have been found in a grave in the vicinity of Bethlehem,[14] almost as if it could be a quotation taken from the more complex constellation shown in illus. 300, one sees a double-pipe player in front of an angular, stylized *ankh* sign, above which is a crescent moon. Behind(!) the musician is a cypress-like, stylized tree (in the same position as on a conoid purchased in Bethel that shows a worshiper who holds no instrument [Kelso 1968, 91 §379, pl. 121.1] as well as on an unpublished surface find from Beth Susin). On other seals, the tree is missing as well and sometimes only the lyre player is shown (**illuss. 302a-b;** the first is from Tell Keisan and the other was bought in Jerusalem; see Braun 1991, no. 7); elsewhere a worshiper is shown without an instrument (on an unpublished scaraboid from a seventh-century tomb in Mamilla, Jerusalem).[15] The astral-cultic connotations in these depictions are usually shown in the scenes by means of a crescent moon, the eight-rayed star (**illus. 302c** from Acre), and/or dot-stars placed in front of the worshiper. When the worshiper appears between two *ankh* signs, as in **illus. 302d** from Acre, only knowledge about the way this scene can be depicted in a more complete way, and an awareness of the complex nature of the motif, can make it possible to see that a particular image functions like a quotation from what is connected with the astral cult in the seventh century.

Smaller and larger iconographic differences and stylistically distinctive elements (among others: orientation of the scene, clothing and hairstyle of the worshiper, shape of the crescent moon emblem) allow one to surmise that the seals discussed here did not all come from the same workshop, but yet probably form a single coherent group thematically. Since it seems that there are no close parallels to these seals in northern

---

14   We are grateful to Dr. Wolfgang Zwickel (Kiel) for information about this and other seals from the same grave; he is preparing the publication that will describe these pieces fully.

15   We are grateful to Ms. Tallay Ornan (Jerusalem) for the information. She will publish the piece shortly.

Syria, it would appear that this is probably a specifically southern Syrian/ Palestinian theme. The artifacts in this pattern that have been found to date are concentrated at sites located on the plain of Acre (along with Shiqmona and Tell Keisan), though some examples have been found in the southern coastal plain, in Judah, and in Transjordan.

§177. Some individual pieces that date as far back as Iron Age IIA have been discovered showing the crescent moon standard of Haran *flanked by two worshipers* (see above, §90). This constellation has not so far been found on Iron Age IIC Palestinian seals recovered in controlled excavations. But a scaraboid of unknown provenance in the Bibliothèque Nationale in Paris (**illus. 303**) shows not only a square pedestal in the typical southern Syrian/Palestinian style, but also the doubled tassels that are just as characteristic, as one can see in the examples shown in illuss. 297b, 299 and 301a-b. These seals come from the Palestinian coastal area (from Tell Keisan to Tell Jemmeh). A piece that shows only one worshiper, very similar to illus. 303, was purchased at the end of the last century in Tartus (Buchanan/Moorey 1988, no. 316). The Parisian scaraboid surely comes from the Levant and can be placed with confidence in the group described in §§173–176.

As we have seen, *symmetrical representations* that emphasize the crescent moon emblem, by placing it in the center, can be flanked by two branches resembling ears of grain (illus. 291c), by two trees stylized to resemble cypresses (illus. 298b; see 299c), by two worshipers (illus. 303), and by a single worshiper and a single tree (illus. 301b). On the seal impression shown in illus. 171a, from Hazor, the drawing of which (taken from the excavation report) may leave something to be desired, the emblem appears to be flanked by two worshipers *and* two cypress-like stylized trees at the same time. O. Keel postulates that this combination shows the basic constellation and that the other representations are variations and he believes that, in view of the symmetrical nature of the representations, tree and worshiper are interchangeable (Keel 1978, 45f.).

The emphasis being placed on the central image, the interchangeability of trees and human worshipers, and various other details permit us to interpret the fifth vision of Zechariah (Zechariah 4: A gold *lampstand between two olive trees*) against the background of the pictorial constellation of the "crescent moon between two trees" (Keel 1977a, 274–320). In contrast to Isaiah, who at the end of the eighth century could still see Yahweh in human form (Isaiah 6; see above, §161), Ezekiel, at the beginning of the sixth century, describes the appearance of "the likeness of the glory (*kābôd*) of Yahweh" only partially by use of anthropomorphic figures (Ezekiel 1 and 10; Keel 1977a, 125–273; cf. illuss. 294 and 337a-b). By the time one comes to Zechariah, ca. 520, in contrast to the older prophets, this prophet no longer deals with Yahweh directly but communicates through the mediation of a "messenger" or "angel"; nor does he see Yahweh himself but sees only the lampstand as a cultic symbol. It is the angel who first gives him the interpretation of the vision and connects the lampstand with Yahweh.

The representation of the deity by means of a cultic symbol, whose primary connotation is light, plus the presence of the flanking trees, identified as symbols of the deity's human "officials" (cf. illus. 298b with illuss. 303 and 308), provide important background elements for suggesting how one can correlate images and texts. The lampstands seen by Zechariah represent Yahweh, who is identified as "Lord of the Whole Earth" (4:14), as a brightly shining deity, present where there is light (cf. the personal name *nērîyāhû*, "my light/my lamp is Yahu," and see below, §210). The interpretation of the two trees as the "sons of oil," seemingly a reference to Zerubbabel and the high priest Joshua, reminds one of the two figures on either side of the enthroned god shown in illus. 308 (one is armed and comes from "somewhere else" on some important executive business and the other is occupied with carrying out ritual functions at the cultic table). To be sure, there is a certain looseness about the relationship between iconography and literature. Particular facts (e.g., the nature of the trees) are defined more explicitly in texts (that are written in more recent times). Texts furnish details that could have been left unclarified in the pictures that had been in use already in earlier times. Zechariah's vision is thus not simply an exact description that explains what is seen in the images. The time gap also argues against such an idea: the use of the constellation that includes the emblem shown between two trees can be dated to the end of the eighth century and perhaps also to the seventh century; it does not appear in use any longer, however, on sixth-century Palestinian seals. Under King Nabonidus of Babylon, whose mother was active for a long time as a priestess in the temple of the Moon God of Haran, the cult of this god once again achieved great significance during the last half of the sixth century. But Nabonidus' efforts to favor the shrine of the Moon God of Haran does not appear to have had any effect in the glyptic art anywhere, certainly not in Palestine, at least not in the form of the constellation of figures that shows the crescent moon between two trees, as discussed here.

We must assume that there was quite a long "incubation period" for the transfer of this constellation from picture form to the verbal formulation as described in Zechariah's vision. In spite of the temporal distance, it remains certain that some features of the vision would have made sense only when understood against the backdrop of the images on the seals (such as the two pipes that came out from the lamp according to Zech 4:12b being equivalent to the double tassels shown in illuss. 297b, 298b, 299d, 301a-b, 303).

§178. On one seventh-century group of scaraboids, the moon god takes a very specific local form that must have been related to the one just discussed, because of the characteristic, cypress-like stylized trees and other similarities in material and engraving technique. These pieces show the *moon god in anthropomorphic form*, enthroned on a low stool, as in **illus. 304** from Shechem, or in illus. 305a, which reminds one of the cross-hatched box on which one could sit and that served as the pedestal for the crescent moon emblem. The enthroned deity raises both arms at the same level as his head, which is to be understood as a gesture of blessing. The two flanking trees emphasize his manifestation (see above, §175).[16]

On most of the pieces of this group, the moon god is enthroned *in a boat*, as on a seal belonging to a certain *šlmʾl* (**illus. 305a**), on which a tree, an angular stylized *ankh*, and a crescent moon with a star enable one to include this with the previous group and to securely identify the enthroned figure as the moon god. The little tree is absent from **illus. 305b**, but one can clearly see behind the god an angular, stylized *ankh* symbol and an incense stand. The exact provenance of the seal shown in illus. 305a is unknown;[17] the anepigraphic seal in illus. 305b, and a third piece with an image of an enthroned figure in a boat (Keel-Leu 1991, no. 133), were both bought in Jerusalem.

On the anepigraphic side of another seal that belonged to a Judean by the name of *ʾšyhw (bn) mšmš* (**illus. 305c**), engraved on both sides and now in the Rockefeller Museum, one sees the image of a bearded deity in the act of blessing, seated on a throne with a high backrest, with a stylized *ankh* sign in front of him, as in illuss. 305a-b. Since there is a crescent moon positioned above the figure, this may be a depiction of the same deity that has lunar connotations.[18]

The deity appears in a boat in at least three other seals. **Illustration 306a** shows the iconic side of a scaraboid that was engraved on both sides and that was acquired at the turn of this century in Jerusalem. The aniconic back side offers the two-line Judahite name inscription *ʾlšmʿ bn gdlyhw*. A very similar, anepigraphic seal (**illus. 306b**), now in the National Maritime Museum in Haifa, was supposedly found in the vicinity of Jerusalem (Barnett 1969–1971, 48 no. 5; pl. 14.5).[19] The scaraboid in **illus. 306c** was obtained in Irbid about 1970. Whereas the god in this depiction is enthroned between *two* burning incense stands, another anepigraphic piece from Yokneam (**illus. 307**; see Ben-Tor/Rosenthal 1978, 81 with note 50) has three such devices placed in front of him. We

---

16 For an anthropomorphic depiction of the enthroned moon god of Haran, from the northern Syrian border area, see a rectangular plaque from Nimrud, dated to the late seventh century (Spycket 1973, 387 fig. 13, 391; see below, §182 note 37).

17 In spite of paleographic considerations, Avigad thought that it was from Moab (1989a, 16f.). But not a single piece from this group, nor from the group of seals discussed in §176, has been recovered from excavations in Moab. An Ammonite provenance is also more likely paleographically.

18 Other enthroned deities, on seals of unknown provenance, belong to the same iconographic tradition – as, for example, on a four-sided prism with the inscription *ʾbgd* (Rahmani 1964, pl. 41.C) and on an Aramean(?) scaraboid (*NAAG* 1991, 19 no. 39). See also the Ammonite seal of another *ʾlšmʿ*, which shows a seated human figure in the act of blessing, above whom there is a star (Hestrin/Dayagi-Mendels 1979, no. 111). The figure is usually identified as Harpocrates, and he does appear to be seated above a (damaged) blossom. But this individual is quite similar to the enthroned figure shown in illus. 304.

19 Barnett, who had not seen the original and who knew of no parallels, thought that he could detect in this a depiction of "Isis suckling Horus" (1969–1971, 48). Gubel, who likewise does not seem to have seen the original, agreed with Barnett, even though he noted, "the child's paraphernalia are either inexistent or completely eroded" (1987, 110 no. 48).

305a   305b

305c   306a

306b   306c

307

find three stylized incense stands by themselves in a boat (the moon god is not portrayed) on still another scaraboid in the National Maritime Museum (Barnett 1969–1971, 48 no. 6; pl. 14.6).

That someone would choose to depict an enthroned god in a boat calls for explanation. The boat is probably intended as a way to symbolize the movement of the god through the heavens and represents the crescent moon metaphorically. In the Assyrian and northern Syrian/Aramean regions, already from the end of the ninth century on and right into the sixth and fifth centuries, Sin, always dressed in typical Assyrian or Babylonian fashion, is shown standing in the crescent moon (for relevant Aramaic name seals, see Bordreuil 1986a, 95, 99, 109, 111, 113–115; see below, illus. 358c). Palestinian images of the enthroned moon god in a boat cannot be linked closely with these images. It may be that Phoenician models were used that suggested replacing the crescent moon with a boat. Phoenician stamp seals show Egyptian deities such as Isis and characteristic high gods such as Eshmun enthroned in a barque, and representations of boats on which both ends of the boat are shown as heads of birds are – except for our group of seals – typical of Phoenician iconography (see Gubel 1987, 111–113).

§179. When he first published the seal of Elishama (illus. 306a), G. Dalman advanced the thesis that, since the seal belonged to a man with a Yahwist patronym, the god enthroned in the boat might be identified exclusively with Yahweh, who was enthroned in the Jerusalem Temple as the Lord of Heaven.[20] He expressly emphasized that this meant "there was no hint of a female partner" (1906, 49; but see below for a discussion of illus. 308). L.-H. Vincent immediately and vigorously disputed this thesis and argued, based on the incomprehensible iconography, that the "pseudo-figure de Iahvé" was a forgery (1909, 121–127; cf. Diringer 1934, 257f.). In more recent times, scholars have attempted to evade the question about the identification of the deity by suggesting that the figure might be a worshiper (e.g., Avigad 1989a, 16). If one examines the individual depictions, not in an isolated manner but rather on the basis of as many comparable pieces as possible, this latter suggestion can be confidently rejected.

Was Yahweh worshiped during the seventh century as the moon god? Vincent's idea that the seal shown in illus. 306a might have been a forgery is no longer tenable, since a great number of comparable pieces, available not only from commercial sources but also from excavations, are now known, and there is no difficulty in matching the inscription paleographically with Hebrew inscriptions from the seventh century (see Herr 1978, 144f. no. 152). The seals shown in illuss. 304–307, by contrast, no longer leave any doubt, when compared with those discussed in §176, that this must be a representation of the moon god. He is imagined both

---

20 "The god who makes thick clouds his vehicle according to Ps 104:3 and who travels to Egypt on swift clouds according to Isa 19:1 is enthroned on his cloud-ship here, between trees of life, as if borne upon the wings of a stork" (Dalman 1906, 49). One might criticize the appropriateness of the identification of certain pictorial elements (trees and storks). But if one is not hindered by such problems, one can admire the skill with which Dalman interprets the scene by turning a static picture into a dynamic event.

to be majestically enthroned, moving powerfully above the expanse of the heavens, and as a gracious, beneficent deity. The evidence from Shechem, Beth-Shean (see below, illus. 308), Yokneam, and Transjordan also shows that the image of this god was not known only in the Judahite capital during the seventh century. That fact alone would place into jeopardy the suggestion that the enthroned figure can represent none other except the (chief) god of Jerusalem, as Dalman had suggested. Against the view that these images were used to represent Yahweh, an observation about the iconography might be made as well. A central element in the iconographic setting of this deity – the cherub throne (see above, §104) – is missing here,[21] even though use of the throne is common in Phoenician iconography of Iron Age IIC.[22] It would be equally as unjustifiable to argue for an *exclusive* identification of the enthroned moon god in a boat in the seventh century with Yahweh as it would be to call for the exclusive association of Yahweh with the familiar four-winged, youthful god known to us from the eighth century (see above, §121). The conception that the female and male worshipers had of *each of* these two deities, during the eighth century in Israel concerning the one and during the seventh century in Judah concerning the other, certainly influenced the way they thought of Yahweh, but the images on the seals cannot simply be equated with portrayals of Yahweh.

Since 1906, the number of Northwest Semitic inscribed seals has easily come to exceed a thousand. We know today that the theophoric element in the name of a male or female seal owner, especially in the patronymic, is very rarely correlated with the decoration on the seal.[23] And yet, when it comes to the appearance of what is apparently a brand new type of image that appears for the first time about 700 and that cannot be linked to any older traditional type of representation, the name might nevertheless offer evidence to help identify by name the particular deity in this case. On the one hand, of the eight seals known to us from this group, three have name inscriptions. That one seal owner had a Yahwistic name and that two had *El* names (*'lšm'* and *šlm'l*; one also had a Yahwistic patronym) cannot be an accident. On the other hand, one must also remember that, to date, only seals with the crescent moon emblem (and no name seals) have been found in the coastal regions. The inscribed seals with the image of the enthroned figure and the anepigraphic seals of the same group have been found only in Jerusalem, in what had once been Israel, and in northern Transjordan. The texts from Tell Deir Alla (see above, §§127f.), however, document Ammonite personal names (Jackson 1983, 518; Israel 1990, 325–335) and Iron Age IIB-C Judean inscriptions from right in the Jordan Valley, from Transjordan, and from Judah (i.e., from the more peripheral regions of Palestine), that will be discussed

---

21 Isa 6:1 does not actually mention the cherubs, and the seat on which Yahweh sits is described only as a "high and lofty throne".

22 See particularly a portrayal of an enthroned(!) god in the barque of heaven, in Gubel 1987, pl. 20.51. (Gubel does not classify the throne as a cherub throne, but wings are clearly visible on the sides; Culican is also imprecise; see 1986, 282 fig. Ib.) For terra-cotta depictions from Zarephath, see Pritchard 1988, 265 fig. 10.10; 266 fig. 11.21.

23 See above, §121note 14 and §125 note 23.

next, all document the continuing veneration of the god El, whether he be identified as an independent deity or linked to the principal local deity (Yahweh, Milcom?).

Based on that information, it is but a short step to assume that the enthroned figure is an El figure. Not least important in favor of this interpretation is the fact that the figure could be venerated in southern Aramean or in Ammonite areas just as easily as in the region of what had once been the Northern Kingdom or even in the context of the Judahite capital where Yahweh was dominant. In contrast to the tense relationship between Yahweh and Baal according to the biblical sources – as is seen again and again – there is no reference to a comparable conflict between Yahweh and El. The two deities are identified with each other already in Iron Age I or, at the latest, by Iron Age IIA. "El" was, so to speak, the common appellative by which the women and men who lived in central Palestine each worshiped their own principal deity during the first millennium.

The way the moon god was depicted, not only in the form of his emblem but also anthropomorphically as an enthroned figure and as a figure who was bestowing a blessing, being the "Most High God" in the west during the Assyrian Period, approximates the role played by El in Palestine. Conversely, the ideas connected with this deity bestowed lunar features on the local El (and, implicitly, on Yahweh as well; see below, §210).

§180. By contrast to Iron Age IIB, with its *"Baal"*-symbolism revolving around the solar "Lord of Heaven," *El*-aspects advance into the foreground of the Palestinian religious symbol system during Iron Age IIC, especially in the central parts of the country. The ascent of El 'Elyon (identified not long afterward in Jerusalem with Yahweh) may fit into this context. In Deut 32:8, this El 'Elyon assumes the role of the "Most High God." A sherd found in excavations in the Jewish Quarter offers an explicit indicator of the importance of an El deity in Jerusalem during the seventh century. It contains a fragmentary inscription that, along with two or three Yahwistic personal names, also includes the words ʼ]*l qn* *ʼrṣ* "El, creator of the earth" (P. D. Miller 1980; Avigad 1983, 41; cf. Gese 1971, 113–115; Gen 14:19; and below, §200).[24] The sherd probably comes from a votive vessel. The personal names belong to those making the offering and the deity named is the one who receives the offering. The inscription says nothing precisely about the relation of the creator god *ʼl qn ʼrṣ* to Yahweh. El and Yahweh were most probably not regarded as two separate deities in Judah and Jerusalem during Iron Age IIC; instead, Yahweh was known there also *as El*; in this respect, he was worshiped in his capacity as the creator god.

An inscription dated to about 700 from *Khirbet Beit Lei* (Inscription B) assumes that Yahweh is identical with El:[25]

---

24 Cf. the inscription *ʼl* on a bowl from Khirbet el-Qom (Dever 1969–1970, 172–174; P. D. Miller 1981, 45).

25 See also esp. Naveh 1963, 85f.; Cross 1970, 302; Lemaire 1976, 560f.; P. D. Miller 1981, 328–332; Davies 1991, 89 no. 15.007. The German translation is in Conrad 1988, 560.

p̂qd yh ʾl ḥnn nqh yh yhwh

"Come in, Yah,[26] gracious God/El,
speak free, Yah, Yahweh."

ʾl appears to be connected here with an indeterminate adjective, and is thus to be understood as an appellative, "God" (see *yhwh ʾēl raḥûm wᵉ=ḥannûn* in Exod 34:6f.). The concept of Yahweh as a gracious El deity is at least implicit though not stated, as the parallelism ʾl ḥnn // yhwh shows.[27] Inscription A, dated to the same time period, assigns Yahweh the title *ʾlhy kl hʾrṣ* "God of the Whole Earth"[28] (cf. *ᵃdôn kol-hā=ʾāreṣ* in Zech 4:14), but not without emphasizing simultaneously his special relationship to (Judah and) Jerusalem.[29]

In view of the fact that, in the traditions connected specifically with the inland region of Palestinian during the seventh century, the moon god was *portrayed* anthropomorphically in the form of an El deity and Yahweh was *conceived* of at the same time as an El deity in inscriptions, we ought not exclude the *possibility* that the enthroned god in the boat – as one can assume in a clearly Yahwistic context on the seals of Ashyahu (illus. 305c) and Elishama (illus. 306a), and as is probable on other "Jerusalem" seals, such as those shown in illuss. 305b and 306c – could represent *Yahweh as the celestial/lunar El.*

§181. A cylinder seal from Beth-Shean may give additional plausibility to the suggested interpretation that the enthroned figure is El. It was found in a stratigraphic context that cannot be identified exactly (James 1966, 104f., 348f.) and for that reason can be attributed only with caution to Str. IV.[30] Iconographic and stylistic considerations permit one to attribute the piece to Palestinian local production without question, to include it with the group discussed in the preceding section, and finally to date it to the end of the eighth century or early in the seventh century.

The seal appears to offer a selection from an iconographic anthology of deities and other numinous beings (**illus. 308**). In the upper register,

---

26 For the interpretation of *yh* as a short form of the divine name or as an interjection, see P. D. Miller 1981, 329.
27 In Inscription A, by contrast, the appellative *ʾlhy* "god" appears once or twice.
28 Thus according to the interpretation of Naveh 1963, 82–84; Lemaire 1976, 558f.; Mittmann 1989, 18–20; for another view, Cross 1970, 301; P. D. Miller 1981, 320–323; cf. Davies 1991, 89 nos. 15.005f.; Conrad 1988, 560.
29 The latter point is valid no matter which of the two competing interpretations of the second part of the inscription is accepted: *hry yhwdh lʾlhy yršlm* "the mountains of Judah (belong) to the god of Jerusalem" (Lemaire, similarly Naveh and Mittmann; on the epithet, see 2 Chr 32:19) or *ʾrṣh ʿry yhdh wgʾlty yršlm* "I want to deal graciously with the cities of Judah and want to redeem Jerusalem" (Cross, Miller). On the epithets *ᵉlohê kol-hā=ʾāreṣ* (Isa 54:5), *ᵃdôn kol-hā=ʾāreṣ* (Zech 4:14; 6:5; Mic 4:13; Josh 3:11, 13; Ps 97:5) and *melek kol-hā=ʾāreṣ* (Zech 14:9; Ps 47:3) and the like, see Mittmann 1989, 23–29.
30 Rowe, who treated Str. IV as generally from the Ramesses Period, dated the seal accordingly, to the twelfth century, and compared it stylistically to Kassite seals (1940, 87; pl. 40.22). B. Parker dated it "c. 1200–800" and also considered it to be Kassite, but noted that it had late Middle-Assyrian and Neo-Assyrian hallmarks as well (Parker 1949, 28 no. 122). There are no comparable pieces in the periphery of the region to which one can point for cylinder seal glyptic art from the thirteenth and twelfth centuries. Ornan, 1990, does not include this particular seal in her study.

one can see a winged, anthropomorphic figure, holding two caprids up by their hind legs; the gender of this figure cannot be known for sure. It is remarkable that, by comparison with the male and female figures shown holding caprids in an earlier era, as seen in illuss. 196–197, this being has now sprouted wings. In the Neo-Assyrian glyptic art dating to the eighth and seventh centuries, there are indeed two-winged goddesses, but no such winged "Mistresses of the Animals." By contrast, there are winged "Lords of the Animals." But these "Lords" always have four wings, which means that the question of the gender in this case must remain open.[31] To the right of this figure stands a caprid with head turned – appearing here like a quotation taken out of its proper context. Alongside it are four dot-stars (the Pleiades?). The archer reminds one remotely of illus. 282b, but a bull is being hunted there, rather than a caprid.[32] A winged, possibly falcon-headed, hybrid creature reclines in front of the archer. Taken together, the items in the upper register give the impression of paratactically combined elements that can be interpreted to some extent as portraying an astral scene, even though the individual details are not clearly understandable to us. Perhaps this is a representation of various star signs, which would offer an explanation for the parataxis.

The lower register, in remarkable contrast to the relationship among the various pictorial elements in the upper register, is very clearly assembled in such a way that *one* complex constellation is portrayed. It is of greater interest to us, because here, once again, we find the enthroned god that we encountered above in illuss. 304–307. That we are dealing with the same figure can be determined by noting the characteristic, stylized tree behind him (cf. illuss. 298a-b, 300, 301b, 304, 305a) and by other details (on the beard, see illuss. 305a, c; 306b-c; on the long garment, see illuss. 305c, 306c, 307). "Behind"(!) the god, moving closer to greet him, is an armed(!) man, who is probably to be thought of as merely standing next to him.[33] In front of the deity stands a servant with fan or brush. A comparable figure never appears in front of a god in contemporary glyptic art (cf. esp. illus. 181); one does appear, however, in the Neo-Assyrian cultic scenes in front of a standing or seated king, as was discussed in §168. Aspects that are connected with a king's display of his royalty that appear frequently in Neo-Assyrian cylinder seal glyptic

---

31 Late-Kassite (Keel 1978, 121 illus. 68), Middle-Assyrian or Mitannian (Porada 1948, no. 1031) two-winged "Lords of the Caprids" were made so much before this time that they cannot offer any reliable help here. It is of course conceivable that the author of the little "anthology" shown in illus. 308 was inspired by a piece that was passed down by inheritance and that was originally Mitannian or Kassite, which dated to the thirteenth or twelfth century.

32 See also §172 note 6.

33 The man's weapon cannot be identified with certainty. It is clear that the man belongs in the scene, along with the weapons that surround the enthroned figure. He is possibly being addressed as the leader of the "Host of Heaven" (see below, §200) and might be depicted here as representative of that whole group. One might compare this with the heavenly "Leader of the Host of Yahweh" who appears before Joshua in Josh 5:13–15. Concerning *both* the men who flank God as he sits enthroned, see also the "sons of oil" in Zech 4:14.

art (a servant with a brush, a cup being raised) appear here as well, in the royal imagery that portrays a local deity.[34]

That it is possible to identify this deity with El (and then by extension with a national deity such as Milcom – or maybe even Yahweh?) can be demonstrated indirectly by the constellation of figures immediately to the left: a palm-like, stylized tree is flanked by a caprid with its head turned back (cf. illuss. 182b, 222a) and by a winged griffin. It is a conflation of two pictorial constellations that are both connected with the *asherah*: the one shows the tree flanked by caprids and emphasizes the blessing aspect of the cultic symbol (see illuss. 80–82, 182–184, 219, 222–223); the other shows the cultic symbol as a numinous entity that guarantees order, being guarded by cherubs and/or winged griffins (see illuss. 231–232; on the combination of the two aspects, see Galling 1941, no. 149). The function of the tall vessel between the griffin and the tree is not completely clear; perhaps it emphasizes the power of blessing that proceeds from the cultic symbol, whereas the rhomboid (see illuss. 284a, 286, 300, and elsewhere) identifies the sacred sphere above the griffin.

The juxtaposition of the anthropomorphically represented, enthroned male figure and the non-anthropomorphic cultic symbol, which mediates the blessing of the god in the form of a stylized tree, points clearly to the fact that this is a *representation of El and "his asherah."* The cylinder seal from Beth-Shean allows us, in retrospect, to have a better understanding of the Iron Age IIA portrayal in illus. 181. And finally, it hardly needs mentioning that illus. 308 presents itself as an additional and completely independent confirmation for the interpretation of the meaning of "Yahweh . . . and his *asherah*" in the inscriptions dating to Iron Age IIB, as this was explained above in §§136–141 (on the proximity of Yahweh's altar and the *asherah*, see Deut 16: 21; 2 Kgs 23:4, 6, 15).

§182. As we have seen, the god portrayed in illus. 308 is an El figure. Pieces like those discussed in §178 show that this El could assume celestial/lunar features. He appears repeatedly in the same surroundings as the cultic symbol of the Moon God of Haran (see esp. illuss. 304, 305a, 307). Anthropomorphic representations and cultic symbols appear to be interchangeable entities, used according to regional preference (see esp. illuss. 298–300 along with illus. 304). From this evidence, one can draw the conclusion that in Palestine, during Iron Age IIC, the Moon God of Haran (who was also venerated by the Assyrians as the highest god in the western provinces) and the local El were identified with each other, at least in certain circles of the population, as two manifestations of the same "Most High God."[35]

34 Contemporary provincial cylinder seals from Tell es Saʿidiyeh suggest that this transfer to the local deity was not made directly, but may have been adapted from a depiction of the local king's image (Pritchard 1985, 87 and figs. 173.1–2). The seated king, shown at a table set with food and accompanied by a figure who holds a fan, has a Syro-Phoenician prehistory as well (e.g., the Ahiram sarcophagus from Byblos, early tenth century, and a northern Syrian ivory pyx from Nimrud, eighth century; cf. Muyldermans 1989).

35 S. Dalley (1990) has recently been able to make a good case for worship of the deity Yahweh among the leading circles in Syrian Hamath during the second half of the eighth century. Deported Israelites were resettled in 720 in the area near the city of

308

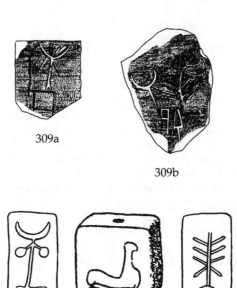

309a

309b

310

It is thus not surprising that we see a crude representation of a branch-like, stylized "tree" next to a crescent moon standard on each of two etchings on clay amulets(?) from Tell Keisan (**illuss. 309a-b**; for the specifics, see E. Puech in Briend/Humbert 1980, 297–299; see Spycket 1973, 385 fig. 6 for parallels from Sultantepe near Haran). A branch or "tree" also appears near the crescent moon emblem on an unpublished conoid, dated roughly to about 750–600, from the Amuq region.[36] The "tree" not only picks up the theme of the twin branches shown in illus. 291c, but is apparently equally as important as the crescent moon emblem and is grouped with it. An emblem and a stylized tree also decorate two sides of a squared stone, probably imported from northern Syria, that was found in Beth Zur and is dated to the seventh or sixth century (**illus. 310**; see Jakob-Rost 1975 no. 368; on reclining hybrid creatures, see above, illus. 308). The Moon God of Haran is thus associated with the cultic symbol of the stylized tree as well. One need not decide at this point whether this is an impersonal symbol, subordinate to the god, or whether the tree is supposed to represent a cultic symbol of an actual personal partner.[37] A scaraboid from Samaria shows a typical Assyrian worshiper, before whom there is a single object of worship – a branch (Reisner 1924, II pl. 57.a2). Local northern Syrian/Aramean and Assyrian/Babylonian symbol systems (note the Nabu-stylus and Marduk-spade in illus. 309b) flow back and forth among one another on these and similar representations.

3. Distant and Close Heavenly Powers and the Significance of the Cult

§183.   In their own unique way, both the imported Aramean and the locally produced glyptic art provide evidence for the strong astral influence on the symbol system of Iron Age IIC Palestine. This is without doubt the greatest hallmark of the period. In comparison to the preceding epoch, however, we should not only emphasize how solar symbolism was replaced by astral motifs, but we should also note the fact that the astralization tendencies could be expressed by means of the *juxtaposition of astral, emblematic, and anthropomorphic representations* of the moon god as the "Most High God," each of which could be shown in different ways. During Iron Age IIB, there was no comparable juxtaposition in the way the solar "Lord of Heaven" was depicted.

These tendencies toward astralization and the concentration upon nocturnal deities during Iron Age IIC may appear at first glance to be

Guzana, close to the source of the Khabur river and thus very close to Haran (2 Kgs 17:6). It is unclear what role was played in this process by the élite who had been deported there, how they communicated with the motherland, and their exact contribution to the identification of the gods discussed here.

36 We are grateful to Dr. Jan-Waalke Meyer (Saarbrücken) for this information; he will publish this piece and other glyptic art from the Amuq region in the near future.

37 See the enthroned moon god next to his emblem, with a branch in his right hand, on a seventh-century rectangular plaque from Nimrud (Spycket 1973, 387 fig. 13.391; see above, §178 note 16).

something novel, but when one looks more closely, one might say that a long-lost "Canaanite" tradition, inherited from earlier time periods, was now reactivated. After centuries of great reticence about portraying deities anthropomorphically, we see a surprising phenomenon occurring: an anthropomorphic, enthroned deity reappears. This could hardly have happened without outside influence. Considering the Melqart tradition from Tyre and the Baal/Hamon tradition, Phoenician influence seems very likely to us. This influence led to the revival of *indigenous "Canaanite" traditions* whose roots reach down into the Bronze Age. We will see later the reactivated "Canaanite" traditions expressed in Iron Age IIC terracotta production (see below, §§189ff.).

§184. The astrally connoted heavenly powers appear at first to be *distant powers*. Their distance manifests itself in the fact that, among other things, *cultic symbols* such as the crescent moon emblem, together with the Nabu-stylus and Marduk-spade, become very important. The solar symbol world of Iron Age IIB did not use such artificially abstract cultic symbols to represent the deity (or deities). The Iron Age IIB stylized tree, the only entity that appears in both periods, was not actually so much the representation of a deity as a channel for mediation and a numinous type of entity that brought order. But the emblems used in Iron Age IIC are more or less abstract representations intended to transport remote deities directly into the cultic activity and make it possible to address them.

By contrast, during Iron Age IIB we saw an abundance of numinous channels for mediation and protective powers, such as the falcon-headed sphinx, cherubs, seraphs, and other similar numinous entities from the sphere of the solar god of heaven (see above, §§150f.). We do not find *such* instances of mediating beings nearly as frequently in Iron Age IIC. Those who wanted to show the venerated deity to be really present by means of cultic symbols no longer needed other mediating channels – particularly since the most important powers of that period (above all, moon and stars) were already present and visible (in their astral form) in the night sky. To that extent, the deities of the night during Iron Age IIC are not just distant divinities but also deities that are *closer* than the Iron Age IIB "Lord of Heaven." The dialectic between distant and near will become particularly clear whenever the cultic standard and the astral symbol appear together in one and the same pictorial representation.

The growing awareness of this tension between distant and close aspects of the deity is nowhere so well documented as in the very center of Assyria, especially in the Assyrian state archive in Ashurbanipal's library at Nineveh. The religious insecurity that gripped the chief authorities of the Assyrian kingdom in the seventh century was connected largely with the increasingly complex political situation; many problems were left unresolved in the different parts of the empire and this led to a growing uncertainty for the rulers "between existential anxiety and political propaganda" (H. Spieckermann). The popularity of "observation of the stars" – whether astronomy or astrology, and the astral cults connected with them – under Esarhaddon and Ashurbanipal, unparalleled in times past, was a direct consequence of these developments (see the overview in Spieckermann 1982, 257–273). The "Handbook for Omen-Specialists" asserts "that all mantic omens occurring on earth are only valid when they correlate with omens in the heavens" (Koch 1988, 116). Stars and constellations were seen to be both "locations" (*manzāzu*) of the deities in the heavens and also "replicas" (*tamšīlu*) of the same (Spieckermann 1982, 259). Although these deities were distant and remote, they allowed their intentions to be ascertained by scientifically regulated observation of the stars and by divination. Eclipses that could be anticipated in advance were regarded as especially important events, for which people performed appropriate apotropaic rituals. Hemerological factors (Spieckermann 1982, 273–281) conferred special importance upon lunar observation. The moon regulated the calendar and the sequence of "good" and "bad" days that went with it.

The documentation that is provided here in summary fashion points to similar, though not quite so refined, developments on the southwestern periphery of this vast empire. The prominence of the crescent moon emblem and the accompanying worship of the Moon God of Haran can be understood within this context. The appearance of the new moon seems to have been celebrated with cultic activity already in earlier times (see 1 Sam 20:18ff.; 2 Kgs 4:23; Amos 8:5; Isa 1:13f.); nevertheless, the Deuteronomists knows that there had been a massive increase in astral cults in Judah at the end of the eighth century and at the beginning of the seventh century (2 Kgs 21:3–5; 23:5, 12; Deut 4:19; cf. Jer 7:17f.; 19:13; 44:17; Zeph 1:5). The glyptic art during this period shows a strong astralization of the religious symbol system throughout Palestine. As in Assyria, the heavenly bodies of the night, especially the moon but also Venus and others that make up the "Host of Heaven," come to the fore now.[38] Though entities with solar connotations are still present,[39] they have less significance.

The heavens, along with the heavenly bodies that are essential parts of the eternal order (see the "ordinances of the heavens" in Job 38:31–33), are able to transmit feelings of stability and permanence in the midst of a world that is becoming international and multicultural (see Pss 8:4; 89:30, 38; and often elsewhere). The predominance of astral symbolism, accompanied by the decline in importance of the mediating, numinous protective powers, is probably connected to a growing need for a more direct relationship with the eternal orders, a need that was in conflict with the concurrent revival of the old, "Canaanite" traditions.

But simultaneously with this need, many representations on artifacts from Iron Age IIC show an *awareness of a new problem*. Portrayals that

---

38 The "Host of Heaven" may refer primarily to the stars (see Deut 17:3; Jer 8:2; and *ndglwt* in Cant 6:10; in addition, see Keel 1984, 46f.; Müller 1988, 118–120). Occasionally, the expression ṣᵉbāʾ ha=šāmayim appears to have referred to the moon and the sun as well (see Deut 4:19; 2 Kgs 23:5).

39 The two-winged scarab and the four-winged *uraeus*, above a blossom, are still in use in the late seventh century (see below, §203). But it must be admitted that they play only a marginal role in the iconographically documented symbol system of Palestine during Iron Age IIC.

show the enthroned moon god anthropomorphically include no worshipers. This is not by accident. The juxtaposition of the cultic emblem and the astral symbol signal in a new way that there was tension between the *believed real presence* of the heavenly powers in the cultic symbol and their *actual astral presence* in the heavens (see esp. illuss. 291, 299–301). Earthly reality and heavenly metahistorical reality (the reality characteristic of the gods) begin to diverge.[40] The experience of this tension may be related to the fact that *depictions of the cult* in Iron Age IIC, supposedly a way to mediate between the two realities, are a clear indicator of the need to be reassured and these cults played a prominent role (see above, illuss. 280–281 with the king; illuss. 285–287, 288c, 289–291, 293, 299–303 with non-royal persons).[41] We will return to these depictions in the paragraphs that follow.

§185. A scaraboid from Samaria that dates to the seventh century shows two *worshipers* facing each other. Between them is a cultic stand (?, cf. illuss. 285b, 287, 293b), not a crescent moon emblem, as in illus. 303. The deity they worship is shown only in an astral manifestation as a crescent moon (**illus. 311a**). Two astral symbols, the crescent moon and a disk, can be seen above two men on a scaraboid bought at the beginning of this century in Ashkelon (**illus. 311b**). On the basis of comparable pictures, the disk should probably be understood as a very schematic representation of a star (see, e.g., Ornan 1993, figs. 50, 52, 57, 59, and esp. 65).

This pictorial constellation is found on at least nine other Northwest Semitic inscribed seals (Ornan 1993, figs. 50, 56–65). But the two pieces mentioned are the only ones known to have been found for certain in Palestine/Israel. Stylistic and paleographic differences show that these eleven pieces must have come from several different workshops. This scene was apparently quite popular and was widely used. The approximate provenance is known in only three cases: the two pictured here and a seal which was purchased in Kerak that can be classified paleographically as Moabite (Ornan 1993, fig. 62 = Timm 1989, 185f. no. 8). This last piece is not typical of the series because it positions the winged solar disk in the center of the composition. Paleographic study suggests that at least one more piece, belonging to a certain *ḥkš*, was of Moabite provenance (Ornan 1993, fig. 57 = Timm 1989, 197f. no. 13; perhaps also Ornan 1993, figs. 49f. = Avigad 1989, nos. 17–18). On the seal from Samaria shown in illus. 311a, we might be able to complete

---

40 An awareness of this problem is also expressed when one sees the weather god appearing clearly in the *form of his cultic image* in the worship scene in illus. 285. Ishtar is the only deity who continues to be actually shown in scenes with worshipers for some time yet, which emphasizes the idea of the nearness of this goddess.

41 A comparable phenomenon, illustrating a new awareness of the problem and the resulting separation of divine and mortal spheres, with consequences for the cult, is observable in the Neo-Assyrian palace reliefs. In the ninth century, King Ashurnasirpal II was portrayed being accompanied in battle by a deity that was partially anthropomorphic. By the time of Tiglath Pileser III, one sees only the divine symbol in battle. Sargon II goes into battle with just the emblems of the gods. Then Sennacherib is pictured with little more to convey the divine legitimation of his Assyrian campaigns than the cultic activity in which his diviners engage in a tent in his camp before the battle.

the extant consonants *kṁ*[. . . by using the theophoric element *kmš* "Chemosh," which would make it a Moabite personal name. But since the name is scratched out and even the second letter is damaged, this remains nothing more than a slim possibility (see Timm 1989, 240f. no. 35).

The evidence provided by these pieces is hardly adequate to assume a Moabite provenance for the entire group of pieces. The inscription on the seal from Ashkelon (illus. 311b) lists an owner by the name of *'ḥ'*, i.e., a man with an Aramaic name. Aramaic names appear on at least five seals of the group and thus dominate the "Moabite" series. The iconography of the group generally shows evidence of Aramean influence, even though it was adopted in greater numbers in Moab.

§186.   A scaraboid from Acre shows a *worshiper* in front of a sacrificial table(?). A crescent moon and an eight-rayed star are above him (**illus. 312a**; for the branch behind the worshiper, see illuss. 291b and 317c). A name seal with the inscription *lstmk* (**illus. 312b**) also shows a worshiper. Paleographically, this could be a Hebrew seal as well, but the iconography causes one to be cautious (Avigad 1989a, 18; cf. Aufrecht 1989, nos. 24, 82). A solitary worshiper without any astral symbols is shown on a bulla (certainly Judahite) that belonged to Yeqamyahu, found in a Jerusalem archive dating to the end of the seventh century or to the beginning of the sixth century (**illus. 312c**; for parallels classified as Ammonite, see Aufrecht 1989, nos. 96, 105). The gesture could be interpreted in several ways and might be depicting either a greeting (see below, illus. 344) or a blessing (see above, illus. 263a).

On a seal that belonged to a certain *ḥnn* (**illus. 313**), we see a striding man with one hand raised in blessing while the other holds an angular, stylized *ankh* sign. In the area in front of the man there is a crescent moon rotated 90 degrees, with a disk inserted within it, and above that an eight-rayed star. It is not completely clear whether the man is worshiping the astral symbols, as in illuss. 312a-b, or whether the images of the symbols serve to depict him as a prince who has been legitimized by the distant deities who are represented by these signs. The latter is probably the case, if Bordreuil (1985, 25 no. 2) and Gubel (1991b, 914f. fig. 1.5) are correct in their conjecture that the piece should be interpreted along with the kings' and officials' seals mentioned above in §155 and that the person portrayed is the same Hanun who is mentioned in inscriptions of Tiglath Pileser III and Sargon II (thus ca. 730–ca. 720) as being the king of Gaza.[42]

§187.   On other Iron Age IIC seal amulets we see only *astral symbols* and the signs associated with them (*ankh* or rhomboid); no worshiper is present. A scaraboid from Tell es-Saʿidiyeh uses a crescent moon, a ray-star, a dot-star, and three(!) angular, stylized *ankh* signs as a design on the

---

42 One can clearly see engraving lines above the head of the man, described as depictions of some sort of a crown (Hestrin/Dayagi-Mendels 1979, no. 123; Bordreuil 1985, no. 2: "une sorte de couronne"). Gubel suggests that this is actually an Egyptian double crown (1991b, 914 fig. 1.5). The latter view is probably over-confident, as shown in the drawing reproduced here, which was checked against the original. But even if this were supposed to be an Egyptian double crown, the astral symbols clearly document the near total reorientation of the symbol system in contrast to what is shown in illus. 263.

311a 311b 312a

312b 312c 313

314a 314b

315a 315b 316

base (Pritchard 1985, fig. 171.10). A circular piece, engraved on both sides and found at Tell Keisan, shows on the reverse side an eight-rayed star (**illus. 314a**; cf. illus. 289). On the base there is a crescent moon, an eight-rayed star, and an angular, stylized *ankh* sign (**illus. 314b**; cf. Uehlinger 1990b).[43] A scaraboid from Tell el-Ajjul, which came from the same workshop, has a rhomboid in addition to the three pictorial elements shown in illus. 314b (**illus. 315a**). A surface find from Tel Terumot near Beth-Shean (**illus. 315b**; see Buchanan/Moorey 1988, no. 257) is comparable to this, even though it is shaped differently stylistically. Astral symbols, *ankh*, and rhomboid appear here in an adapted form, in which one notes that there are many dot-stars (nine instead of the seven that are normal for the Pleiades) and that the rays of the Venus-star are shown in a special way (see illus. 317b). A limestone scaraboid, bought in Jerusalem, originally belonging to a man with the Aramean name *yl'*, shows the crescent moon(?) and at least sixteen dot-stars (**illus. 316**; see Keel, et al., 1990, 222–224). The multiplicity of the stars is probably intended to show not just one constellation, the Pleiades, but the entire "Host of Heaven," whose protective power was supposed to be mobilized on behalf of the female or male who wore the seal amulet.

No representations of this kind have yet been seen on seals discovered in excavations in Judah. The combination of a crescent moon and a single star, usually six-rayed, appears more frequently on Moabite name seals (see Timm 1989, nos. 2, 6, 17, 22–24; as a secondary motif on no. 9; unclear on nos. 28, 33). The seal belonging to *mnšh bn hmlk* "Manasseh, the king's son," of unknown provenance, has been classified by scholars in more recent times as Moabite (Timm 1989, 207–210 no. 18). A crescent moon and a rhomboid are found side by side on two Judahite inscribed seals of unknown provenance (Hestrin/Dayagi-Mendels 1979, no. 70; Bordreuil 1986a, no. 46), and there is perhaps a semicircle, to be identified likewise as a crescent moon, on another Judahite name seal that was purchased (Aharoni 1974b, 157 no. 1 thinks this functions like an abbreviation). On the lack of astral symbols on Judahite bullae from the seventh and sixth centuries, see below, §207.

§188. Remarkably, astral symbols appear on a few seals from Judah whose base carvings use traditional themes that were connected with the goddess during the Bronze Age. Star and rhomboid symbols appear in front of a plant or a branch (see above, illuss. 1a-b), together with a striding *caprid*, on the seal belonging to *ṣpn <bn> nryhw* (**illus. 317a**; see Lamon/Shipton 1939, pl. 67.4). A leaping caprid appears, accompanied by a many-rayed star and an angular, stylized *ankh* sign, on a scaraboid found in Tomb 106 at Lachish that may date to the second half of the seventh century (**illus. 317b**). A scaraboid bought in Jerusalem shows a leaping caprid, with its head turned backward, in front of a worshiper. Behind the worshiper is a branch, and in the upper part of the scene one sees a crescent moon (**illus. 317c**). The constellation is perhaps to be

---

43 A scaraboid that is presently in the holdings of the Musée Bible et Terre Sainte in Paris (Bordreuil 1986a, no. 60) has not only the same decoration on the base but is also nearly identical in size and in regard to the material used to make the piece from Tell Keisan. No one knows where it was found, but it was purchased in Jerusalem before 1967 (see most recently Puech 1991, 604).

interpreted as showing that worship of the caprid ultimately becomes worship of the moon god, with the caprid and the branch expressing the visible power of the god to bless. Even the suckling mother animal, which had fallen into disuse in the local stamp seal production during Iron Age IIB (see above, §116), reappears and is associated now with astral symbols (see Keel 1980, 113 illus. 86 from Rabat Moab [Iron Age IIC!]; Stern 1978, 14 fig. 3 from Buseirah; Reifenberg 1938, 115 no. 8; Rahmani 1964, 180f. no. 1, pl. 41A was purchased). No examples have been found to date in Judah.[44] But a scaraboid from Megiddo shows a leaping caprid with a young nursing animal (**illus. 318a**), combined here with a flying bird and vegetal pictorial elements (leaves?).[45] A very similar leaping caprid, shown in an astral context, can be seen on a very worn scaraboid from Acre (**illus. 318b**). The parallels from Megiddo suggest that the engraving marks under the belly of the caprid should be interpreted as what is left of a representation of a young suckling animal.

We also find a crescent moon and a moon disk above a *dove* on a scarab from Lachish (**illus. 319**; see above, illus. 299e). The dove is still another attribute creature linked to the goddess (see above, illuss. 19–21, 188b, 214, and often elsewhere). These indications of the revival of Bronze Age traditions are sufficient reason for reconsidering the status of the goddess in Judah during Iron Age IIC.

4. Terra-Cottas of Doves, Goddesses and Riders

§189. Representations of doves have also been found at Lachish in Tomb 1002, which was used during the entire seventh century. Two three-dimensional *terra-cottas* that were molded by hand depict this bird with outspread wings and positioned above a cylinder-shaped pedestal (**illus. 320**). The two figurines come from the middle or upper levels of the tomb (Tufnell 1953, 374, 376). They are thus to be dated roughly to the middle or to the second half of the seventh century, approximately contemporary with the scarab shown in illus. 319. Comparable figurines have been found in Jerusalem (Holland 1977, 142f., 152; Franken/Steiner 1990, 128) and in widely diverse places, predominantly in Judah (see Holland 1977, 126f. Type E).[46]

---

44 S. Schroer has proposed that the "cultic image of jealousy," which was located according to Ezek 8:3–5 by the north gate of the temple during the sixth century, should be interpreted as a representation of a nursing mother animal (1987a, 26–30; for a somewhat different view, see Koch 1988, 111f.).

45 The piece is registered as IAA 34.1483 in the Rockefeller Museum in Jerusalem, and it was probably found in excavations conducted by the Oriental Institute of Chicago. The piece can no longer be located in the museum, and it is known to us only from a photograph.

46 See, e.g., Tell en-Nasbeh (McCown 1947, pl. 90, esp. nos. 6f.); Gezer (Macalister 1912, III pls. 73.14; 126.10); Tel Goded (Bliss/Macalister 1902, 137 fig. 50; cf. pl. 69.10); Tell Beit Mirsim (Albright 1943, pl. 32.3, pl. 32.17: a woman with a bird?). Holland's published diagram (1977, 126f.) unfortunately does not distinguish between doves with a pedestal and those without. Twelve bird terra-cottas from Ashdod have been listed, a comparatively high number, but these are all doves without a pedestal (cf. Holland 1977, 133). The type in the shape shown in illus. 320 is very typical, at least for Judah, even though the pieces were not produced there (see, e.g., Yadin 1961, pl. 66.33 for an example from Hazor). No dove figurines with pedestal bases were found in the sacral area(?) E 207 in Samaria (see below, §201).

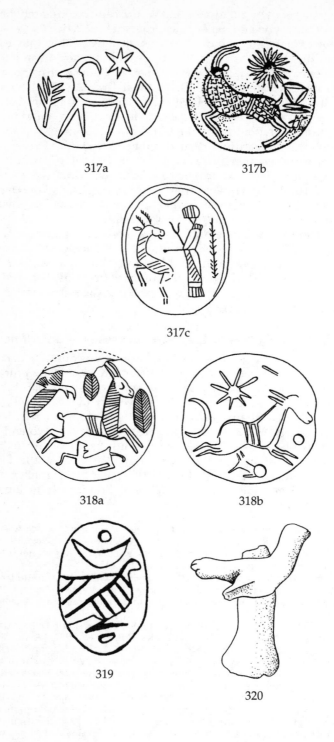

317a

317b

317c

318a

318b

319

320

The isolated representation of a dove, not being pictured with any other entity, naturally complicates the interpretation. But an examination of the tradition history can prove helpful here. Middle Bronze Age votive doves from the shrines at Nahariyah and Megiddo were connected with doves that served as messengers of love between the goddess and god (see §19), as they appear on Old Syrian cylinder seals. The doves could be understood by analogy in Iron Age IIC tombs as "a final proclamation of love to the one who died" (Keel 1984, 62). In fact, such doves are found not only in tombs but also singly in private homes. But they *never* appear in such settings *together* with goddess figurines of the pillar type (§§190ff.). We might deduce from this that the dove, as an attribute creature of the goddess (see above, illuss. 188b and 214), appears *in place* of the goddess. As a messenger, the dove would transmit messages of the goddess' blessing or love to the buried in any case (not – or only very indirectly – bringing a message from the survivors to the deceased).

§190. We find many more – hundreds in fact – of the so-called *pillar figurines* that date to the end of the eighth century and to the entire seventh century (Winter 1983, 107–109). The upper bodies of these figurines have anthropomorphic breasts, arms, and a female head (Holland 1977, Type A).[47] These figurines appear in different versions, most frequently having a hand-formed pedestal (rarely turned on a wheel and hollow). Above the pedestal, the female upper torso was always shaped by hand and a molded head was then inserted at the very top (**illus. 321a** from Lachish, **illus. 321b** from Jerusalem; for the relation of the body to the head, see below, illus. 325). Even though various types of heads made from molds can be differentiated, they are alike in certain very significant respects, since it is characteristic of all of them that they usually have large, almond-shaped eyes and a hairstyle with tightly twisted "tear drop" curls. In addition, at least a third of the pieces are of a variety made completely by hand, on which the nose and eyes are indicated only by crude pinch marks. This gives them a rather "birdhead"-like appearance (**illus. 321c** from Beersheba). The various types are similar in their emphasis on full breasts, often hanging down, as on illus. 321b, supported by thick arms (on this gesture, see above, illuss. 11a, 25b, 27a-b, 50, 52, 121b, 122a, 127a, 217c). Some of the examples (illus. 321c from among those pictured here) show traces of paint, which may be understood either as marking especially the eyes or hair or might be a way to show some decoration (jewelry?). (For jewelry in relief, see illus. 325.)

There is no question that the cruder and probably less expensive type[48] with pinched faces was *produced locally*, based on the location where the pieces have been found. This is probably also the case for the examples that are of higher quality. By contrast to the number of figurines or

47 T. A. Holland's dissertation, which lists in a catalog all the Iron Age terra-cottas known up to 1975, including the pillar figurines, unfortunately remains unpublished and it was unavailable to us (see above, §101 note 35). His 1977 essay summarizes some of the results, with special emphasis on Cave 1 in Jerusalem (see below, §201). See Hadley's review and comments as well (1989, 30–32, 232f., 237–248).

48 "It is possible that the 'pinched-nose' heads were made by or for people who had no access to the moulded heads" (Hadley 1989, 236).

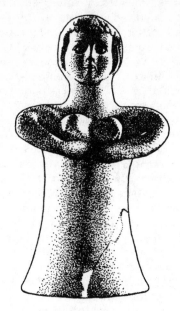

321a

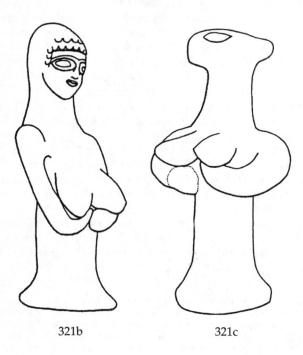

321b   321c

fragments of figurines that have been excavated, very few of the molds that would have been used in the production of the heads have been discovered. While more than eight hundred pillar figurines from Judah have been found, only two molds have been recovered, one each from Lachish and Beth-Shemesh (Grant 1934, pl. 22.5; Tufnell 1953, pl. 31.14; purchased, Deutsch 1989, no. 273). But four such molds were found just at Megiddo (**illus. 322a**, dated about 600); this suggests that production was on a larger scale there and that the pieces were then perhaps even exported.[49] The discrepancy between figurines and molds may be due mainly to the fact that molds were only in the potter's atelier, and archaeologists only rarely come upon such ateliers. It might also be due to the fact that some of these little heads might have been imported and were then inserted into the locally produced figurine bodies (see Albright 1943, 140). Many molded heads have been found in excavations without their corresponding bodies. The reason might be, at least in part, that the little heads were not only made separately from the bodies but were also sold without the bodies. A unique discovery at Hazor shows that one such head could be used, in a way somewhat different from its original purpose, as a pendant or amulet (**illus. 322b**).

Even if we were not really able to determine the exact provenance of the little heads (to our knowledge, neutron-activation analysis of the figurines has not been conducted), we may nevertheless confidently assume that production of the bodies, as well as the assembly of the pillar figurines, was carried out in Palestine, also, and most specifically, in Judah itself. Along with the sheer number of the pieces, this is important for the interpretation of the figurines in the context of Israelite/Judean religious history.

§191. The pillar figurines are a characteristic expression of *Judahite* piety during Iron Age IIC. Engle (1979, 9, 16f., 126ff.) goes so far as to suggest that this is an exclusively Judahite phenomenon. He arrived at this idea, however, only on the basis of a very selective typology, limited to standard types such as those in illuss. 321a-b (for a critique, see Hadley 1979, 37–41, 234ff.). Pillar figurines shaped slightly differently have been found, although less frequently than in Judah, in Phoenician, northern Israelite, Philistine, and Transjordanian areas as well (see Holland 1977, 126f. Types A and B).[50] According to Holladay, who limits himself to brief comments (1987, 280), they appear in the north even a little earlier than in the south. The publication of a catalog of all these artifacts is urgently needed.[51] So long as such a survey is not available, observations such as those that follow can be formulated only with reservation and with an awareness of their preliminary nature.

The commonly held general impression that the pillar figurines were in wide use throughout Iron Age II (from the tenth through the sixth

49 See the observation by Holland (1977, 131), who suggests that the mold that was copied for use here probably goes back to original molds for heads that were from the Philistine region (Tell Jemmeh, among others). For a mold from Tell Jemmeh, see Petrie 1928 pl. 36.6.
50 In what follows, we will concentrate on the Israelite/Judean discoveries, ignoring in particular the Cypro-Phoenician examples.
51 See above, §101 note 35.

centuries) is incorrect. Engle's more refined assertion, that they were produced for the first time in the ninth century, flourished during the eighth century, and fell increasingly out of use after the middle of the seventh century (1979, 18–26), needs correction as well. The pieces cited to support an early dating are either atypical (Grant/Wright 1938, pl. 51.28; cf. 1939, 156 from Beth-Shemesh Str. III; cf. Hadley 1979, 232f.),[52] incorrectly dated by Engle (Mackenzie 1912–1913, pl. 22.8f. from Beth-Shemesh Grave 1), or cannot be clearly assigned stratigraphically (Aharoni 1975a, pls. 12.2; 33.2 from Lachish).[53] Pillar figurines, or fragments of such, are first found in contexts that can be dated with confidence and/or in significant numbers, in the north as well as the south, toward the end of the eighth century (Beth-Shemesh, Samaria E 207, Jerusalem Cave 1, and elsewhere), but are clearly still in use in the second half of the seventh century. Engle starts too early with his dating and overestimates the frequency with which the artifacts appear and his views must be adjusted so that the onset comes one or two generations later.

§192.   Apart from scattered finds, the pillar figurines have been found most frequently in *private homes* and then, also in significant numbers, in *tombs*. Close to half the houses that have been excavated at Tell Beit-Mirsim and at Beer-sheba have had terra-cottas that might have served a function in a house cult. Not always, but very often, these have been pillar figurines. As far as the often inadequate classification and publication of the sites allow us to determine, no more than one figurine was found per house in the Judahite private homes (Holladay 1987, 276f.). It also appears that burial sites have no more than one figurine deposited per person (Wenning 1991b, 90; for extraordinary concentrations of these finds at cultic sites in Samaria and Jerusalem, see below, §201). The figurines represent a kind of "household icon" (Winter 1983, 131). In a way that is comparable to the biblical teraphim, they belong to the household effects (*keʿlê bayit*; see Gen 31:37) and they assume the same role in personal and

---

52 The atypical little head from Hazor, shown in illus. 322b, was found in Str. VI, and thus, like the bone handle in illus. 210 and the ointment spoon in illus. 214, is dated to the first half of the eighth century. Apart from this isolated find, if we are correct, there is not a single fragment of a typical pillar figurine in this stratum or in the succeeding strata from Iron Age II. The marked increase in the number of "religiously significant artifacts," which was noted by Holladay to have begun about 750 (1987, 278f.), applies first of all to animal figurines (among others, horses; see below, §199). Four rough, hand-molded, anthropomorphic figurines were found in Str. V. (Yadin, et al., 1960, pl. 103.2–5). What appears to be a breast identifies one as female. Isolated examples of such figurines with solid pillar bases continue to appear. Among the earliest is one from Lachish Str. VI (Late Bronze Age II); see Aharoni 1975a, pls. 12.4; 33.1. These pieces have no connection with the pillar figurines being discussed here.
  As an early precursor of the hollow pillar figurine, one might consider an example from Megiddo Str. IV (ninth century) that has a bell-shaped body and stubby arms (May 1935, pl. 28 M 5401). The gender of the figure cannot be determined with certainty. There is no indication of breasts and continuity between this and the actual pillar figurines is highly questionable.

53 It supposedly came from Str. IV, Locus 41 (Aharoni 1975a, 107); nevertheless, this could be an intrusion or could have come as fill from Str. III (see Aharoni 1975a, pls. 59 and 63).

family piety[54] during Iron Age IIC that was played by the plaques with the representations of the goddess during the Late Bronze Age and Iron Age I (see above, §§57ff.).[55]

Notwithstanding this "continuity of intent" (Hadley 1989, 234), the hiatus in the local production of small terra-cottas with representations of the goddess – addressed above in §§101f. and 124[56] – is too clear for one to assume an unbroken transition from one type to another *in Israel or Judah* (see Tadmor 1982, 172; Holladay 1987, 279f.). Intervening transitional forms are as rare as the examples that show the simultaneous appearance of both forms. Presently, more can be said in favor of this revival of the "Canaanite" tradition being a harmonization linking indigenous forces with a new impulse that came "from the outside." To be sure, one is unsure about how this development began and what shape it took. It might be at least indirectly related to the Assyrian invasions, to the new territorial divisions, and to the related changes in market forces. The change is often perceived to have been *influenced by Phoenicia* (Tadmor 1982, 172; Holladay 1987, 279; and often elsewhere). Archaeological discoveries in Cyprus are similar for the same period (Gubel 1991a). Discoveries from Shrine 1 at Zarephath, dedicated to Tinnit-Astarte, seem to support this idea (Pritchard 1988, 31–55). But that shrine is dated roughly between the seventh and fifth centuries (Pritchard 1988, 54f.; 1975, 39f.), so it cannot claim a temporal priority that would assist in the evaluation of the Palestinian finds. The gesture shown in illuss. 321a-c, with the arms placed under the breasts, is very rare on the terra-cottas from Zarephath (see Pritchard 1975, fig. 46.3 = 1988, fig. 13.53 from Shrine 2). Whatever the case, even if the Phoenician hypothesis were to prove correct, the question remains: If there was a Phoenician influence, why did it find an echo specifically in Judah, one that so quickly led to the pillar figurines becoming a typical requisite of Judean personal piety?

§193. An unstratified scaraboid from Lachish, a piece imported from Phoenicia or from the northern coastal plain and dated to the seventh century, might likewise offer evidence that there was a new period of popularity for anthropomorphic representations of the goddess, stimulated by those who lived farther up the Levantine coast. The scaraboid shows a woman represented *en face* in a tight-fitting dress.[57]

54 One should not speak of the practice of a "folk piety" limited to the lower classes of the population. Pillar figurines were also found in the palace installations at Ramat Rahel (Aharoni 1962, 14, 41 and pl. 24.3–4; 1964, pls. 35.1; 36.1–3). But it is just as incorrect to identify these figurines as "expressions of the official, national cult" (Ahlström 1984, 22).

55 There is no evidence that pillar figurines served any primary function at funerals, nor is there any reason to believe that they were particularly concentrated in women's graves (see Wenning 1991b, 92 with note 11).

56 We do not consider the figurines with the tambourine to be depictions of goddesses (see above, §102). From time to time, one finds isolated portrayals of women with tambourines among the pillar figurines that date to Iron Age IIC (Saller 1965–1966, 260f. no. 1; Meyers 1987; 1991; Deutsch 1989, no. 276). The figurines that depict a woman holding a dove are probably likewise to be understood as votive statuettes (see, e.g., Keel 1977b; 54f. illus. 14; Briend/Humbert 1980, pl. 103.16f.; see also Albright 1943, pl. 32.17 from Tell Beit Mirsim) and such figurines are found concentrated in the (Cypro-) Phoenician region, where the woman holding a dove is also portrayed on ivory (Barnett ²1975, pl. 150, suppl. 72).

57 Not in a Baubo-position (Schroer 1987b, 214)!

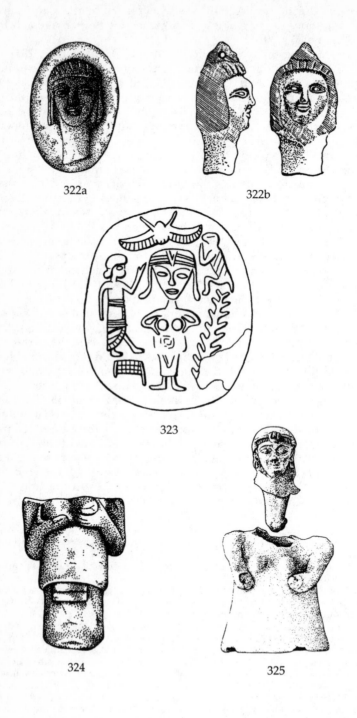

322a

322b

323

324

325

She supports her breasts with arms that are bent (**illus. 323**). Whether the upper body is clothed or not cannot be discerned on this piece. The dimensions of her face and her parted hairstyle appear too large relative to the lower body (cf. illuss. 214f.). To the left, there is a worshiper above a pedestal, with arms raised. This clearly demonstrates that the woman is a goddess. To her right is a branch, above which a monkey is crouching.[58] A winged solar disk hovers above the entire composition.

This piece has no immediate prototypes or contemporary analogies in local Judahite glyptic art (see, however, an Aramaic seal, Bordreuil 1986a, no. 92). Nevertheless, the gesture and the branch suggest a late form of the Middle Bronze Age "Branch Goddess" (see Schroer 1987b, 213f.; 1989, 100, 123). A small, fragmentary limestone sculpture from Megiddo Str. III (**illus. 324**) shows that this figure was known in her anthropomorphic form during Iron Age IIC in what had once been the Northern Kingdom. This piece also portrays the goddess clothed and presenting her breasts. Two contemporary Ammonite round sculptures belong to this same pictorial tradition (Abou Assaf 1980, 21f. no. II, pl. II; Ornan 1986, 36f. no. 12). On these pieces and in illus. 324 the upper body is unmistakably clothed. Thus the gesture of supporting (or offering) the breasts, as shown in illus. 323 and on the pillar figurines (see illuss. 321a-c), does not necessarily accentuate the nakedness of the upper body or an "aspect of exposure" (Wenning 1991b, 91). One pillar figurine of unknown provenance – unusual in its great detail – shows ornaments on the forehead, ears, and nose and may also present the goddess dressed as an upper-class woman or princess (**illus. 325**). As in illus. 321a, and in contrast to the popular variations shown in illuss. 321b-c, the breasts here are more proportional to the rest of the body.

§194. The identification of the pillar figurines as representations of the goddess Asherah (see below), the demonstrable interchangeability of the tree and the goddess during the Late Bronze Age, and the fact that the *ʾašērāh* is primarily a cultic symbol, shown in the form of a stylized tree in the Hebrew Bible (see above, §136, end), has led time and again to the thesis that the hollow body-pedestal of the figurines imitates a tree trunk in a schematic fashion, which means that the goddess might appear in the hybrid form with a tree trunk base and a female upper body (see most recently Hestrin 1987a, 222; 1991, 57).[59] Hybrid forms that combine a tree and the goddess have been found in Egyptian paintings (see Keel [4]1984, 165f. with illuss. 253f.; Winter 1983, 438–440 with illuss. 460–465), but those are primarily from the Late Bronze Age and are limited exclusively to funerary contexts (tombs, sarcophagi, papyri). A correlation between this iconographic tradition and the Judahite pillar figurines of Iron Age IIC is highly improbable. The hollow pedestals of the

---

58 For the playful-erotic meaning of the monkey, see Schroer 1989, 189–195. Contra Winter 1983, 181, this monkey has no connections with the monkey that stands and greets the rising sun in Egyptian depictions.

59 This thesis has recently been taken even one more remarkable step further, since it has been suggested concerning the pillar figurines with depictions of doves (see above, illus. 320) that the hollow body is to be interpreted as a "wooden pole" (Franken/Steiner 1990, 128) even when it supports a depiction of a dove (see above, illus. 320).

figurines do not really provide evidence that anyone understood them to be trees, tree trunks, or cultic poles. Viewed purely functionally, this style represents a technical development of the solid pillar body or bell-shaped body that provides the figurines with greater stability.[60] From a semantic perspective, the hollow pillar for the goddess figurines is most probably to be understood as a schematic representation of a long robe (thus also Wenning 1991b, 91).[61] Whether the upper body of the figure was imagined as clothed or not is in general hard to determine (but yet, see §193).

The emphasis on the face and breasts, mentioned several times already, is much more important in any case for an understanding of the pillar figurines than is an imaginary symbolism linked to a tree. Most generally, the back side is executed very carelessly, which shows that the figurines – corresponding to the *en face* representation in illus. 323 – were intended to be viewed from the front. The face personalizes the goddess and allows her to appear close and approachable to the females and males who drew near to worship her. The fact that her face alone is represented at times (compare illuss. 322b and 332 with illuss. 214f.) suggests that we should not underestimate the aspect of closeness over against that of the *Dea nutrix*.[62] The full breasts emphasize the *nutrix* aspect as an expression of blessing (compare Gen 49:25 with Hos 9:14).The pillar figurines, at least the ones that are shown half-clothed, are not without erotic character (Wenning 1991b, 91f.),[63] but this aspect plays a clearly subordinate role (Engle 1979, 114).

When we compare the figurines with the "Naked Goddess," we see a definite alteration in the image. On Middle Bronze Age images, the goddess' face and features that identify her gender are especially emphasized, but the breasts might be omitted entirely (see above, illuss. 2, 10–12, 24, 26b, and often elsewhere). During the Late Bronze Age, one line of development clearly continues this tradition (see above, illuss. 48–49, 55b, 80) while another line tends to depict more realistic images (see above, illuss. 69–72). Terra-cotta production generally followed the latter path and continued to do so on into the Iron Age (see above, illuss. 121–122; for Iron Age IIC, see below, §196). During Iron Age IIA, a tendency can be seen to depict the goddess as clothed (§101). For the pillar figurines from Iron Age IIC, the pillar or robe prevents one from seeing the lower

60 For the same reason it makes sense to use the hollow pillar to support the body of a dove or a lamp (see illus. 320; Albright 1943, pl. 32.2–3).

61 This is quite clear on those examples where the lower end of the coat does not reach all the way down to the circular stand, but comes down only to a little above it, as, for example, on two figurines from Nebo (Saller 1965–1966, 261 fig. 28). Only secondarily might we consider that there is a connection with the so-called Tinnit sign (Holladay 1987, 278, 293 note 120).

62 In the Phoenician/Punic religion, Tinnit is identified as the *pn b'l* "the face of Baal" (Baal Hamon = El?), i.e., as a hypostasis of his gracious presence and approachability (found in inscriptions from the fifth century on; see Maier 1986, 96–121; Olyan 1988, 56–60). H. Weippert (1988, 631) has pointed out correctly that the little heads on the pillar figurines from Tel Sera' appear so similar to the "women at the window" on the ivories that one could mistake the one for the other (see above, illus. 215).

63 In biblical texts, the breasts themselves (or pressing on the breasts) often have a pronounced erotic connotation (see Ezek 16:7; 23:3, 21; Prov 5:19; Cant 4:5; 7:8f.; 8:10; cf. Keel 1986, 226, 230).

body of the goddess. The face and nurturing breasts are emphasized instead.

An extraordinary variant from Tell Beit Mirsim, on which the figure carries a child like a pack on her back (**illus. 326**), suggests that the figurines are supposed to show the goddess as a nursing *mother*. Already during Iron Age IIC we find the beginning of the idealization of the goddess as mother which, during the Persian and Hellenistic Periods, received greater emphasis in depictions that, in addition to some other types, show the so-called "*Isis lactans*" (see below, illuss. 363–364). Terracotta molds also provide evidence for this, showing an enthroned goddess with a child on her lap (**illuss. 327a-b** from Samaria; see above, illus. 189); they are probably to be understood as a local adaptation of the Isis-Horus motif, found elsewhere on Egyptian faience amulets (**illus. 328** from Tomb 1002 at Lachish; cf. Rowe 1936, no. A. 26). Since there is only one solitary example of a Judahite "pillar goddess" with a child (illus. 326), this may not simply be because the mothering closeness of the goddess is first of all supposed to bring benefit to the female and male worshipers, but is more likely – except for the king being the child of God (Ps 2:7; see Psalm 45) – because there is no indigenous tradition concerning a divine child in Judah during the Iron Age that is comparable to the Isis-Horus constellation.

The pillar figurines are often found in houses and graves along with small model beds, little lamps, and rattles (**illus. 329**). These groupings permit various interpretations; the function and meaning of the rattles is most unclear. The overall purpose is apparently to mediate blessings, such as motherly closeness, peaceful rest, light and warmth. In a very significant way, the pillar figurines represent the protective deity of a family. She offered everyday blessing and protection to the family and bestowed her motherly closeness even when the deceased was lying in the grave.[64]

§195. Can a name be assigned to the goddess represented by the pillar figurines? The goddess worshiped at the shrine in Zarephath that was mentioned above is identified by an inscription as Tinnit-Astarte (Pritchard 1982; 1988, 7f.). As for seventh-century *Judah*, the goddess might rather be identified as *Asherah*.[65] The dove associated with the goddess might suggest Astarte, but one cannot decide conclusively. First of all, the relation of the dove to the pillar goddess is not entirely clear. In

---

64 This applied as long as those who had died were in the personal time of transition even after they died, when their bones were still intact. The personality of a female or male corpse ceased once the bones were separated one from another – at the latest when the grave site was reused – when the bones were pushed back from the main burial spot.

65 Thus, correctly, Ahlström 1984, 22; Hestrin 1987a, 222; 1991, 57, and others. Holladay (1987, 279), followed by Braulik (1991, 109f., 116), considers the possibility that a syncretistic connection was made linking Asherah and Anat/Astarte, but there is no evidence for this. Wenning speaks in general terms of "the goddess" but favors an identification with Asherah (1991b, 91–94).

Olyan (1987b) has recently thought he could detect a – polemically criss-crossed – reference to Asherah's function as mother in Judah during the seventh century in Jer 2:27a, in which a stone (probably a *maṣṣebah*) is identified as "the one who gave me birth" and a tree (the *asherahs*?) is called "father" (cf. Smith 1990, 92).

326

327a   327b   328

329

the second place, the dove could be connected with Asherah as well (see above, illus. 214). There are no literary references to any worship of Astarte in Judah, and they are extremely rare in conjunction with Jerusalem. The cultic site for Astarte of Sidon, supposedly built by Solomon (1 Kgs 11:5, 33), is assumed to still be in existence on the Mount of Olives at the time of Josiah according to 2 Kgs 23:13. But beyond that, we hear nothing else about Astarte in Judah, which means that this was most likely a cult with restricted access and under royal protection, one which had no impact on the general religious practices of the country. Significant in this context is illus. 323, with its recognizable tradition of the "Branch Goddess" and her motherly features, which we have just discussed; possibly also her popularity and dissemination throughout the regions where the El deities were also worshiped (Judah and Ammon); these furnish good grounds for identifying this figure in Judah as Asherah.[66]

This does not mean, conversely, that the pillar figurines can simply be equated with the biblical *ʾăšērîm* "asherahs," as suggested first by Patai (1967, 29–52, esp. 35), and later supported by Engle (1979, esp. 52f., 71, 102).[67] Asherahs are often mentioned together with altars and *maṣṣebahs* (Exod 34:13; Deut 7:5; 12:3; 16:21f.; and often elsewhere) and they belong with the furnishings at open-air shrines and at other local sanctuaries (Judg 6:25–30) and may normally be identified as a cultic symbol in the form of a stylized tree (see above, §136). The usual verbs for the destruction of *asherahs* (chop down, cut down, tear out, burn up, etc.) could not apply to the pillar figurines that would have to be broken up.

The cultic symbol that was associated with Yahweh, subordinate to him to mediate his blessing, and present as a numinous symbol of power within the Israelite cult for centuries, "offered ... a constant means of access to the fertility cults and goddess cults from which it had evolved" (Schroer 1987a, 43f.). To consider just one narrative, this may be what is meant when reference is made to Maacah's cultic image in Jerusalem in the ninth century (1 Kgs 15:13). The worship of an anthropomorphic *asherah* in the seventh century was of greater significance. For several centuries, the Israelite or Judahite *asherah* was present almost exclusively in the form of the stylized tree, and its relation to a female deity remained in the background (see, however, §§122, 130, 137, 142 concerning the

---

66 This example makes it clear once again that pictures are different from names and points out just exactly what knowledge about one or the other can mean for religious history (see §228): for the *pictorial-semantic* interpretation of the pillar figurines, it is enough to identify the figurine as *the goddess* (though it is important to distinguish her from her contemporary, the "Naked Goddess"; see below, §196). "The goddess" and her image have an importance that transcends an individual culture. Her *identification* by name is of significance for the religious history of a particular region, or ethnic group, or some smaller group. The pillar figurines, as an iconic type, may have come from Phoenicia; nevertheless, this goddess certainly would not have been called Asherah there, since this name was not used in Phoenician religion during the first millennium. The identification of the "pillar goddess" as Asherah applies only to Judah, just as the name Tinnit applies to the goddess in the Phoenician/Punic area. On the relationship between Tinnit and Asherah, see Maier 1986, 96–121; Olyan 1988, 53–61.

67 See also Braulik (1991, 110 with note 14). For a critique, see Winter 1983, 557; Hadley 1989, 240–243.

transparency aspect of the symbol). After a long period, during which representations of the goddess were almost exclusively not anthropomorphic, there was a shift toward an anthropomorphic, personalized image for depicting the goddess during Iron Age IIC. We can observe this same tendency toward anthropomorphic representation in portrayals of the moon god (or lunar El) (see above, §§178ff., 183). In light of this tendency, it is probable that the cultic image of the *asherah* constructed by Manasseh in the seventh century (2 Kgs 21:7), which stood in the Jerusalem Temple until the time of Josiah's reforms (2 Kgs 23:6f.), may have had a female shape. The "linen clothing" that was woven by the female temple personnel for the *asherah*, previous to Josiah's reforms, according to 2 Kgs 23:7, fits precisely with the thesis that Manasseh's *asherah* had a female form and with the iconographic evidence that during Iron Age IIC there was a preference for, if not an exclusive practice of, depicting the goddess as clothed. Manasseh would have thus given a type of official sanction to the revival of a "Canaanite" tradition within family piety. If this notion is correct, it would be further evidence for a close interdependence between official, state religion and personal or familial piety, which could hardly have existed alongside each other as completely distinct religious spheres. The problem discussed above (§192), why the pillar figurines were so uncommonly popular in seventh-century Judah, may find a partial answer in connection with the state cult that called for an *asherah* to be depicted in female form.

§196.   Other portrayals have been found in non-funerary contexts in the neighboring regions of Judah and along its borders that feature a more or less realistic depiction of the *"Naked Goddess,"* one that emphasizes her erotic charms and thus continues a Late Bronze Age tradition (see above, illuss. 121–122). One example of this is a fragmentary terra-cotta plaque from Ashdod in Philistia (**illus. 330**; see Dothan 1971, 138f. fig. 64), where this tradition of the "Naked Goddess" was never completely interrupted (see illus. 217a). The goddess also appears naked on a plaque from the cultic site E 207 at Samaria (Crowfoot, et al., 1953, pl. 11.6). Two examples from Tel Batash, in the Judahite–Philistine border region (see above, illuss. 217b-c), show that the "Naked Goddess" was likewise known and wor-shiped there at the end of the eighth century. But we no longer find that kind of image in the seventh century in Judah, in contrast to Ammon where the "Naked Goddess" still appears on two name seals (Avigad 1977). This suggests that the "Naked Goddess" found in Iron Age IIC is to be identified as Astarte, by contrast with the clothed Asherah. The absence of naked images being depicted in Judah agrees with the literary evidence, which shows that Astarte was widely worshiped, particularly in the coastal regions, but was of little importance in Judah.

The iconography of Hebrew name seals during Iron Age IIB provided an "argument from silence" for the lack of importance of anthropomorphic goddess images, especially the "Naked Goddess," in Israel or Judah during the ninth and eighth centuries. The picture on a sardonyx scaraboid belonging to a certain ... *']gʾl bn šʾl* (for the name inscription, see Lemaire 1990b) and dating to the end of the eighth century or to the early seventh century is therefore surprising. The seal depicts a naked

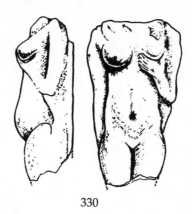

330

331a

331b

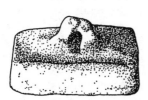

332

goddess, presented *en face* with horns and four wings, holding star-shaped "flowers" in her hands (**illus. 331a**). Like the deity in illus. 323, this goddess is without parallel in local Israelite or Judahite glyptic art. During the eighth and seventh centuries, there was a preference for four-winged goddesses, portrayed frontally on seals that are clearly Assyrian or use Assyrian techniques (Winter 1983, 187–191 with illuss. 172–181). On those portrayals the goddess usually wears a horned helmet and turns her head to the side (for the history of the tradition, see illus. 53). There is no parallel to the pair of horns in illus. 331a; it has been transferred here from the Egyptian Isis to the naked goddess.

As is often the case with these seals, the provenance is unknown; the piece has been classified as a "Hebrew" seal for paleographical reasons. Even if it had been found in Israel, it would still be questionable whether it had been manufactured there. It is more likely an expensive, imported piece from a workshop in the northern Levant. The individual characters of the name inscription are scattered about the seal surface, so we must conclude that this was initially an anepigraphic pictorial seal, to which the owner's name was added at a later time (see Bordreuil 1986a, 47).

§197. The astral connotations suggested for this goddess by the star-flowers pose the question whether she might perhaps be the *"Queen of Heaven"* (**malkat ha=šāmayim*) who was worshiped in Judah and Jerusalem during the early sixth century (see Jer 7:16–20; 44:15–19, 25). We noted above, in §171, that there was a relationship with the Assyrian Ishtar and we pointed to evidence for an acquaintance with her in Iron Age IIC Palestine. At the same time, we must assert that the Assyrian goddess can hardly be the *only* possible deity that could be meant by references to the "Queen of Heaven," since iconographic evidence does not support her being accepted in Judah or Jerusalem. The goddess in illus. 331a, probably Astarte, shown by using a combination of Assyrian, Phoenician, and "Canaanite" aspects on a Hebrew name seal, would provide a more likely candidate for the "Queen of Heaven" in Jerusalem, but the image is so unusual that we cannot claim with confidence that she would have been as popular a figure as was the "Queen of Heaven."

But then who was the Judahite "Queen of Heaven"? In recent times S. Olyan has been at the forefront of an effort to identify this goddess with Astarte (1987a), whereas K. Koch has advocated the view that this refers to Asherah (1988, esp. 107–109). Identifying the "Queen of Heaven" is especially problematic since, on the one hand, the epithet is very general and allows her to be compared to the Assyrian *šarrat šamê* (for Ishtar, see above, §171), to the Egyptian *nb.t p.t* "Mistress of the Heavens" (for Hathor, Anat,[68] Astarte, "*Qudshu*," Ishtar),[69] and also to the Aramean *mlkt šmyn* of Hermopolis (Anat?). On the other hand, up to the present time, not a single inscription from seventh- or sixth-century Judah has been found on which a goddess is mentioned by name. Olyan's

68 See above, §50.
69 Evidence for this Egyptian epithet is found only in second-millennium sources. It corresponds to the Ugaritic epithet for Anat: *b'lt šmm rmm*. Olyan has correctly questioned the value of second-millennium epithets when one seeks to identify Jeremiah's "Queen of Heaven."

discussion of Phoenician-Punic sources – in which the title "Queen of Heaven" is not found! – and his reference to the city goddess of Ashkelon, who was worshiped during the Hellenistic Period as Aphrodite Ourania (<ʿštrt šmm), could make it probable that Astarte, the partner of Baalshamem, was called the "Queen of Heaven" in Philistine and Phoenician coastal cities. This could possibly be significant for the identification of the "Naked Goddess" in illus. 331a, but it is not of further value to us for the identification of the Judahite "Queen of Heaven," because we know neither of worship of Baalshamem nor of a cult of Astarte that was widespread in Jerusalem and Judah during the seventh and sixth centuries.[70] By contrast, there is clear evidence for a Yahwistic El religion in the seventh century (see above, §§178ff.) and for the worship of the *asherah* as his female correlate.

It has been seen repeatedly that the cult of the "Queen of Heaven" is not specific to just one social class and is not limited to the *commoners* (see esp. Jer 44:17, 21for the reference to "kings and high officials"), but the description in Jeremiah 7 and 44 does point to the area of family piety, in which women played a central role (Jer 7:18; 44:15, 19, 25; cf. Winter 1983, 564; Wacker 1991b, 149f.). The aim of this cult was the transmission of blessing in the form of sufficient food, health, and security (Jer 44:17f.).[71] The "Queen of Heaven" apparently had the same area of responsibility as "Yahweh's *asherah*" at Kuntillet ʿAjrud and at Khirbet el-Qom – with the difference that the latter figure (unlike the "Queen of Heaven") did not function as an independent entity. From this perspective, the thesis advanced by K. Koch, that the Judahite "Queen of Heaven" should be identified with the *Asherah* that has been equated with the Assyrian Ishtar, has some plausibility.[72] If one remembers that the "*Sitz im Leben*" for family piety is not differentiated by social class and that the area where the "Queen of Heaven" was thought competent to function is very close to what could be effected by the *asherah*-pillar figurines,[73] a general identification that equates the "Queen of Heaven" with the "pillar goddess" and with Asherah is possible (thus, most recently, Wenning 1991b, 93f.). To be sure, nothing in Jeremiah 7 and 44 speaks about the competence of the "Queen of Heaven" in areas connected with funerary activities and the pillar figurines conversely show no celestial and astral attributes. But

---

70 Similar objections could be offered in rejecting S. Ackerman's thesis, since she uses these same sources to suggest that the "Queen of Heaven" was a syncretistic combination of Ishtar and Astarte (1989, 110–116). "Religio-historical research must still be conducted in a genuinely historical manner; one must take developments, interruptions, and regional variations into account. There is no value in offering a general overview of ancient Near Eastern sources. It is much more important to interpret the relevant texts. . . in their own historical context first. When this is done, there is nothing that suggests a presence for Astarte in preexilic Jerusalem" (Koch 1988, 109).

71 The argument of Jer 44:17f. is especially plausible if it refers to Judah's long period of prosperity under Manasseh.

72 Koch's reference to burning incense and incense priests (2 Kgs 23:4, 8; Jer 44:17–19, 25; Koch 1988, 107f.) can hardly support an identification of Asherah with the "Queen of Heaven." An astral-celestial character and worship that included incense was not limited to Asherah/Ishtar and the "Queen of Heaven" during Iron Age IIC (just see 2 Kgs 23:5!).

73 See above, §192 note 54.

the reason for this discrepancy may lie in the fact that, on the one hand, care for the deceased was traditionally one of the functions of the Palestinian goddess while, on the other hand, the specific astral form was an exclusive aspect of the image of the Assyrian Ishtar. If the Palestinian Asherah and the Assyrian Ishtar were combined in the form and cult of the "Queen of Heaven," this linkage was effected without merging all their characteristics.

The iconographic evidence corresponds to this discrepancy and to its traditio-historical interpretation insofar as it documents both extremes of the notions connected with the "Queen of Heaven." At one extreme is the Assyrian Ishtar component in the glyptic art; at the other extreme one sees the Judahite Asherah component in local terra-cotta production. The two were never merged into one divine form, unless this is shown on a unique Hebrew name seal (**illus. 331b** = Bordreuil 1986a, no. 58). The seal combines stylistic characteristics of Assyrian, Urarturian, and Phoenician glyptic art. It shows a four-winged goddess above a stylized palmetto tree. Facing her is a two-winged, bearded god on a winged, human-headed bull (**aladlammû*, often erroneously identified as *lamassu*). As in illus. 331a, this may have been an anepigraphic image seal to which an owner's name was added at a later time. A local *interpretatio judaica* by a Judahite owner could have connected this constellation of images with Yahweh (above a "cherub"; see Ps 18:11) and Asherah as "Queen of Heaven" (above a stylized tree).

Apart from this unique piece, the iconographic evidence for an Asherah with celestial features that might support her identification with the "Queen of Heaven" is sparse. This is even more frustrating since the biblical tradition concerning the "Queen of Heaven" cries out for elucidation iconographically. The Judean women who fled to Egypt, according to Jer 44:19, baked ash cakes for the "Queen of Heaven" "in order to copy her image" (*le=haᶜaṣîbāh*). Baking molds from Mari that date to the eighteenth century have been frequently cited to illustrate a cake with the picture of the goddess. They portray a "naked goddess," sitting on a bench (Winter 1983, 568f. with illus. 519; Schroer 1987a, 277 with illus. 99). A clay stamp from Ramat Rahel, found in Str. V (end of the eighth or seventh century), may offer something with a closer resemblance, since it is Judahite and approximately contemporary (**illus. 332;** see Aharoni 1962, 42). In view of the material and crude engraving, it is not possible to tell whether the piece, which has an approximately square base (41 × 43 mm) is a seal or a mold for terra-cotta appliqués or for little terra-cotta heads.[74] The piece would function especially well as a stamp for dough. It should be particularly emphasized, in conjunction with the shift in the image of the goddess mentioned above, that this stamp reproduces only the head, without the slightest attribute! This apparently sufficed to evoke the idea of the goddess, even the "Queen of Heaven." If

74 The stamp is now in the Israel Museum; the IAA catalog classifies it as Hellenistic-Roman (information from Dr. B. Sass, Jerusalem). The excavation report gives no evidence to suggest that this might have been an intrusion from a later time into Str. V. One glance at the Roman *terra sigillata* from Ramat Rahel (Aharoni 1964, pl. 7. esp. 3–4) shows that the stamp in illus. 332 could not be interpreted as being part of that later group.

this identification is correct, a methodological observation should be appended here: pictures and names or titles need not always be exactly parallel to each other but might emphasize *different* aspects of one and the same figure.

§198.   In general, throughout all periods, we find fewer terra-cotta images of male figures than figures of women or goddesses, so the appearance of male *rider figures* during Iron Age IIC is a remarkable phenomenon. We illustrate them here with two pieces from Lachish. **Illus. 333a** was found in Tomb 106. Even though the rider's head was broken off, we can see that the statuette was carefully molded and that it realistically portrays a horse and rider (note especially the reins and forehead decoration or mane). **Illustration 333b** (from Grave pit 1002) is much more schematic; the horse is a four-legged creature without clear zoological characteristics and the "rider" was simply pressed onto the back of the four-legged creature without any trace of the rider's legs.[75] The face of the "rider" is reminiscent of the "pinched nose" schematic variation of the goddess in the pillar figurines (illuss. 321c and 329). By contrast to the pillar figurines, no pieces have been found of the Iron Age IIC horse-and-rider statuettes with heads made in molds.[76]

Horse-and-rider statuettes of this type, that date to Iron Age IIC, have been found by the dozen. Holland had classified 117 clear examples some years ago already (1977, 130 Type D VI-XVI). If we count fragments of horses as part of the horse-and-rider group as well, which is probable because of the representation of reins or halter on the horse-and-rider type, the number increases to 328 examples (Holland 1977, 125). If one combines with this the simple images of a horse without reins or halter, there are at least 450 examples, a number that at present clearly surpasses the number of images of bovines or other animals. It must not be assumed that all freestanding images of horses, *pars pro toto*, once belonged to rider statuettes. It is also just as important to remember that the same holds true for these pieces as for depictions of bovines (see above, §119): one cannot assume generally that a deity is always being represented.

Holland has noted that there are large concentrations of horse-and-rider statuettes in Samaria (25), Megiddo (14), Tell en-Nasbeh (16), Gezer (21), Beth-Shemesh (13), Lachish (8), Tell Jemmeh (32), and Jerusalem (119!) (1977, 126f.; cf. 148f.). The horse-and-rider statuettes are less

75 Because there are so many slight variations in the form, it is hard to identify clear marks that would distinguish a "rider" type from the "type that shows the figure of the god on the back of the horse" (see illus. 333b), as Wenning suggests (1991b, 94). In the meantime, a letter from Wenning, dated 4 October '91, indicates that he has given up trying to differentiate these figures in this way and now thinks, as we do, that both forms represent the simple depiction of a rider. This also obviates his attempt to suggest that the second type is patterned after the Assyrian portrayals of Shamash and is "an epiphany-depiction of a god on a horse" (1991b, 94).

76 Wenning would explain this as follows: "The purely anthropomorphic representation of a god was to be avoided. No matter which god was supposedly depicted in the statuettes, the pressure not to show Yahweh in human form was in evidence here" (1991b: 96). But even with the pinched face, the rider is still always clearly anthropomorphic. During Iron Age III and the Persian Period, the face was depicted more carefully, thanks to the use of molds (see, e.g., Tufnell 1953, pl. 33.1, 5; Stern 1982, 167).

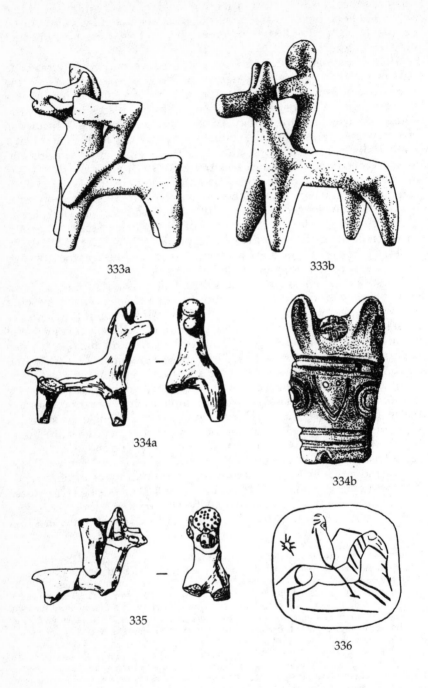

333a

333b

334a

334b

335

336

exclusively concentrated in Judah than are the pillar figurines of the goddess. But the archaeological contexts where they are found are fundamentally the same as those for the pillar figurines: houses, graves, and cultic sites (E 207 in Samaria and Cave 1 in Jerusalem; see below, §201). Here also we encounter the phenomenon of so-called "private" piety. Since the pillar figurines and the horse-and-rider statuettes are never found clearly grouped together – in cases where they are found in the same tomb they come as a rule from different burials[77] – it is hardly advisable to assume a partner relationship for the two types of statues or between the two deities that they represent (for another view, see Wenning 1991b, who regards the rider as the partner of Asherah).[78]

§199.   Ever since the discovery of a large number of horse-and-rider statuettes in Jerusalem, these figurines have been connected repeatedly with "the horses that the kings of Judah had dedicated to the sun" (or to the sun god, *la=šemeš*, 2 Kgs 23:11). In this connection, it has been pointed out that many of the horses wear a kind of disk between their ears (**illuss. 334a-b**), which some think ought to be interpreted as a solar disk (McKay 1973, 33f.; Ahlström 1984, 12f., 22f.; Schroer 1987a, 297f.; Smith 1990, 116; and many others). But a straightforward comparison between illuss. 334a-b and 333a shows that the "disk" could also be interpreted as a forelock or mane with a forehead ornament (see Holland 1977, 149–151). As a rule, crude examples of the horse-and-rider type, such as 333b, avoid showing the halter and reins, so it is noteworthy that the terra-cotta artisans expended considerable effort to show ornaments and bridles on many of the carefully shaped horse images (see Yadin 1960, 103.8–9; 1961, pl. 177.22; 216.16; Macalister 1912, II 9–11 with fig. 211; May 1935, pl. 36; and often elsewhere). Even on an older small horse head from Hazor Str. IX B (ca. 900), having a disk with a cross between the ears which the excavator related to the sun god of 2 Kgs 23:11 (**illus. 335**; see Yadin 1975, 188f.), it is easier to interpret the disk as a forehead ornament (note also the halter, reins, and triangular forehead shield).

A solar interpretation for the round head ornament cannot be rejected out of hand; nevertheless, this does not mean that the horse or rider terra-cottas represent the sun god. It is more likely that they are *intermediate* figures between the sun god (the solar Yahweh?) and human beings. According to 2 Kgs 23:11, the *"chariots* of the sun [god]" were expelled from the temple area at the same time as the horses. The horses that are mentioned appear to have been real, live horses, perhaps the animals that

---

77 "Based on the archaeological context alone, nothing can be said for sure about the grouping together of two statuettes" (Wenning 1991b, 90).

78 Wenning interprets a pillar figurine without breasts, from Grave 5 at Beth-Shemesh, as the representation of a male deity and interprets this as the partner of the goddess that was represented on a fragmentary pillar figurine with breasts from the same grave (Mackenzie 1912–1913, pl. 41; cf. Wenning, 1991b, 96f.). Nevertheless, neither the grouping of the two figures as a pair nor the interpretation of the intact figure as a male is certain. This also applies to a similar discovery in Lachish Tomb 106 (Tufnell 1953, pl. 27.1, 3; cf. Wenning, 1991b, 97 note 33). Wenning's identification of the two pillar figurines without breasts as being the riders from horse-and-rider constellations is completely hypothetical.

pulled the chariot.[79] These animals were cared for by a *sārîs*, that is, an official who had an Assyrian civil title, not a religious one. The use of horses and divine chariots is typical of Assyrian divination in the Sargon Period (end of the eighth century/seventh century), in which the all-knowing sun god Shamash played a central role (see Spieckermann 1982, 245–256). The horses served as a medium for the divination, and the chariot made the invisible deity present.

But if the presence of the horses and chariot of the sun god cause one to assume that this typically Assyrian activity was being practiced by the "kings of Judah" (Hezekiah and/or Manasseh?), possibly because *Yahweh* was regarded as a sun god, so that the horses were stationed in the temple area for use in divination, then 2 Kgs 23:11 could hardly refer to the horse figurines or to the horse-and-rider figurines. These figurines play no role in divination; they belong in the context of family piety where they, like the pillar figurines, would have transmitted divine protection or blessing.

§200.   We also find isolated rider figures on Iron Age IIC Palestinian glyptic art, as for example on a scaraboid from Beth-Shean (**illus. 336**). Behind the rider is a star and in front of him there is a branch. The astral symbol and branch do not allow us to relate this to a specific deity.[80]

In any case, the effort to try to identify the Palestinian riders by name requires one to review several possibilities. We can exclude an identification with the sun god himself (Wenning 1991b, 94f.), since this deity is not portrayed in a riding posture either in Neo-Assyrian or in local iconography, and he is never mentioned as a rider in texts. The same objection can be made when considering an identification with the warrior Baal (Stern 1989b, 27). The weather god is most often conceived of as driving a chariot (Pss 68:18; 104:3; Hab 3:8, 15; Loretz 1990, 74f.). *RKB* (Ps 68:5; Isa 19:1) is mentioned in connection with the weather god and the god of heaven, but it can mean both "ride" and "drive a chariot."[81]

---

79 The Neo-Assyrian iconography from the Sargon Period presents clear evidence that the horse was an attribute animal for the sun god. In this iconography, the sun god can be depicted at times as standing upon a horse (Schroer 1987a, esp. 288f. with illus. 107). By contrast, the idea of a solar *chariot* being drawn by horses is alien to Neo-Assyrian iconography. Literary evidence identifies mules as the animals that pull the chariot of the sun god across the heavens. Smith's reference to a ritual text from Boghazköy that mentions living mules and horses of the sun god is not very helpful (1990, 122 note 8). Since these are animals that apparently draw the processional chariot, their relation to Shamash is quite unspecific. For representations of war chariots in different media, see below, §200 note 81.

80 Scaraboids from Iron Age I-IIA, with representations of an anthropomorphic figure on a horse and one worshiper (Schroer 1987a, 294), which may be associated with the riding goddess Anat/Astarte (see above, §86), are not to be considered here; nor are the Judean seal impressions from the end of the eighth century, found on *lmlk* vessels from Jerusalem, Azekah, and Tell en-Nasbeh, that show a striding horse (Barkay 1985; Schroer 1987a, 298 with illus. 120f.; cf. McCown 1947, 154 fig. 35:6–7).

81 It is worth mentioning that models of chariots – and fragmentary at that – are rarely found in Palestinian terra-cotta production during Iron Age IIC, e.g., at Megiddo (May 1935, pl. 21 M 4724), Samaria (Crowfoot, et al., 1953, 77 fig. B:7 = 82 no. 45) and Tell Jemmeh (Petrie 1928: 18 pl. 39).

In Palestinian Iron Age IIC *glyptic art*, there are isolated images of chariots drawn by horses, e.g., with one driver on a seal impression on a pitcher handle from Hazor (Yadin 1961, pl. 196.27) and on two scaraboids, one from Gezer and one from Dan,

During the ninth and eighth centuries in Zinzirli, in northern Syria, there is mention of *rākib'il*, a protective deity for the dynasty of that time (see McKay 1973, 32f.; Olyan 1988, 52f.), who could be a chariot driver or a rider. There are no direct links from *rākib'il* to the Palestinian riders. But the form of this god at least offers an analogy to the Palestinian riders insofar as both entities perform specifically protective functions in the context of family piety, and they apparently belonged to the sphere of a high god of the El type (in Zinzirli: Baal-Hamon; in Judah: Yahweh).

The relationship between the high god and the riders, who were subordinate to him, is illustrated by a decorated tridacna mussel shell that was found in the Babylonian city of Sippar but that was produced in a Syrian workshop during the seventh century. It portrays two riders on either side of a bearded, high god who is in a lotus nimbus, pictured in an act of blessing (Stucky 1974, no. 21). Fragments of these engraved mussel shells, with Syro-Phoenician iconography that shows Assyrian influence, have also been found in Palestine, including in Jerusalem (see H. Weippert 1988, 660). We see this god in a lotus nimbus on two fragmentary pieces, one from Arad (**illus. 337a**; see Brandl 1984) and one from Bethlehem (**illus. 337b**), though without riders in these examples. Iconographically, this god unites in himself aspects of the sun god or god of heaven (see the sun symbol in the center of the nimbus) and the creator god (lotus nimbus).[82] The hybrid form, with a human upper body and a "fiery" lower body, like that of illus. 294, is reminiscent of Ezek 1:26b–27 (see Keel 1977a, 260–263). Perhaps the god in the lotus blossom is to be identified with "El, the creator of the earth" (*'lqn'rṣ*), who was also venerated in Jerusalem during the seventh century, there probably as a special aspect of Yahweh as the creator god (see above, §180).

If the Palestinian riders, like those on the tridacna shells from Sippar, belong to the sphere of that kind of El-like god of heaven and creator god, who could hardly have been anyone other than Yahweh in Judah, then the terra-cotta statuettes could possibly be understood as popular, anthropomorphic representations of the *"Host of Heaven."* Semantically, the aspect of a warlike epiphany is expressed in the iconic motif of the rider (see Jer 6:23!), as well as in the collective name *"Host of Heaven."* The fact that the designation "Host of Heaven" refers to the stars in Deut 4:19; 17:3 2 Kgs 23:5; Jer 8:2[83] should not mislead one into suppressing completely the warrior aspect of the *ṣᵉbaʾ ha=šāmayim*. "Host of Heaven" is a typical Iron Age IIC collective name for the group of assistants who surround the "Most High God" (1 Kgs 22:19), particularly in the special

with three drivers each (Macalister 1912, III pl. 209.12; Biran 1977, pl. 37C). These last pieces would have no possible connection with the chariot of the sun god in any case, whereas the impression from Hazor is too isolated to furnish evidence that would permit any conclusions to be drawn.

82 Neither this god nor the figure to which the arched pair of wings belong and above whom they are portrayed are simply identical to the Assyrian man/god in the winged sun (see above, illus. 294; contra Wenning 1991b, 95 note 26). Since the pair of wings and the lotus nimbus do not belong together anyway, the fact that they are separated cannot be blamed on the ignorance of the artist (Stucky 1974, 62).

83 See above, §184 note 38.

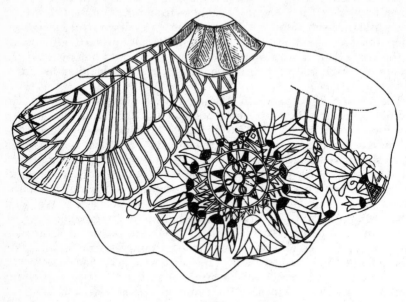

337a

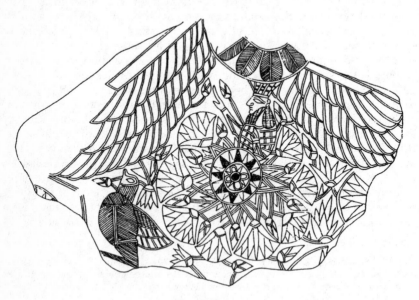

337b

aspect of their military potential. The "Host of Heaven" is the army of weapon-carrying "Holy Ones" (Deut 33:3), subordinate to the "Most High God." To this group belong the archers, the chariots, and also the riders (see 2 Kgs 6:17; 7:6; Ps 68:18; see P. D. Miller 1987, 54–64).

In contrast to the female pillar figurines, which represent a single goddess and may not be multiplied at will, the horse-and-rider statuettes appear occasionally also in small groups (see Holladay 1987, 276 for such a find at Hazor). This could relate to the fact that they were conceived of as being less individualized than the goddess. But like the "Pillar Goddess," they are found alone much more frequently. If one seeks a Judahite designation for such an individuation of the "Host of Heaven," one possibility is the title "Messengers of Yahweh" (or Yahweh's angels, *mal'ak yhwh*), as mentioned in roughly contemporary biblical texts. They function both as spiritual powers, protecting individuals (e.g., 2 Kgs 1:3, 15), and as those who defend a city against a whole army (2 Kgs 19:35). Since the rider statuettes continued to enjoy an uninterrupted popularity on into Iron Age III, they can be connected not only with the "consecrated" soldiers of the host of Yahweh in Isa 13:3f. (cf. 40:26; 45:12) but even more obviously with the riders in the first vision of Zechariah, the mounted police of Yahweh, the God of Heaven, who scour the earth (Zech 1:7–11). They apparently inherited this duty (as did the "watchers" in Dan 4:10, 14, 20 and the guardian angel of the people in Dan 10:13, 21, at a still later time) from the preexilic "Host of Heaven." The rider terra-cottas in Iron Age IIC Palestinian/Judahite homes and graves seem to have functioned, much like the personal guardian angels of a later time (see Pss 34:8; 91:11; Job 33:23; see above, illus. 308), in the context of "personal piety," as protective powers and mediators from the sphere of the "Most High God."[84]

Names such as "Queen of Heaven," and "Host of Heaven," suggest distant, astral deities, a conception of these powers that doubtless was *also* held in Iron Age IIC Judah (see above, §184). If the identification of the "Pillar Goddess" as Asherah and as "Queen of Heaven" is even somewhat close to the mark, and if the horse-and-rider statuettes are the personification of the "Host of Heaven" or of guardian angels, then the depiction of the female body of Asherah (as bringer of blessing and having a gracious countenance) and also of the rider statuettes both furnish evidence that these divine entities were present in folk or family piety during Iron Age IIC, near at hand in a popular, anthropomorphic form as bearers of blessing and protective noumena. It is all the more remarkable that there was no comparable, clearly identifiable image that would show *Yahweh* close at hand in the "personal piety" of the seventh century. Pictures of anthropomorphic figures, El as moon god (illuss. 304–307; cf. illus. 308), a winged god on a hybrid creature (illus. 331b), and a god in a lotus nimbus (illuss. 337a-b) may have shaped, in large part, the concepts of Yahweh that were entertained by the Judahite owners of the

---

84 It is obvious that the shifts in the imagery connected with the "Host of Heaven" and the messenger (or angel) can be attributed in part to the various specific types of court personnel and emissaries who served during the Assyrian, Persian, and later periods.

objects. These were not, however, *explicit* and exclusive images that depicted only Yahweh.

§201. Substantial concentrations of goddess figurines and horse-and-rider statuettes from the end of the eighth century have been found at two locations. In the area around the cultic site *E 207 in Samaria* (Crowfoot, et al., 1938, 23f.; 1957, 76–84, 137ff.), along with hundreds of cooking, eating, and drinking vessels and numerous lamps, 26 female figurines were found, including one plaque with the image of a "Naked Goddess" (Crowfoot 1957, pl. 11.6), two molds for Isis plaques (see above, illuss. 327a-b), a female tambourine player (see above, illus. 190e), and also two riders and 34 horse figurines.[85] Likewise, in the more carefully documented, so-called *Cave 1 in Jerusalem* (Holland 1977, 132–154; Franken/Steiner 1990, 44–50, 125–129) cooking, eating, and drinking vessels (well over 1,200 objects!), lamps, censers, as well as small artifacts, including 16 female figurines and five dove figurines, each with a pillar base (see above, §§189f.) and 21 horse-and/or-rider figurines were all found. Many bowls contained the remains of animal bones (cattle, sheep, and goats), which likewise suggests that the place must have been used for cultic practices. Vessels marked with personal names, apparently votive gifts, were found in both E 207 and Cave 1 (S. A. Birnbaum in Crowfoot, et al., 1957, 11–19, 21–25; Prignaud 1978). A few names are clearly Yahwistic (*ywyš*ᵉ in Samaria, *ʾlyhw* in Jerusalem) and even the non-theophoric names leave no doubt that the cult at E 207 – in spite of possible foreign influences – was practiced by men and women of Israel and that the cult at Cave 1 was practiced by men and women of Judah.

Unfortunately, the interpretation of these and other, perhaps related,[86] pieces has been made very difficult because of inadequate publication of the cultic site E 207 at Samaria. Cave 1 is a grave-like site that was not

---

85 The excavators list 83 bull figurines as well (Crowfoot, et al., 1957, 82), but most of these seem to be zoomorphic vessels and not actual figurines (see Holland 1977, 127; see above, §119 with note12!). For another vessel in the form of a horse that supposedly came from Samaria, see E. Mazar 1979, 151f.).

86 Note even smaller installations at Tell en-Nasbeh and Tell Beit Mirsim (Holladay 1987, 274f.). A recently published *intramural* discovery from Jerusalem ought to be treated separately: B. Mazar excavated several subterranean spaces that were cut into the rock southwest of the temple area. They are like Phoenician tombs in plan and execution, but, like Cave 1, show no trace of any burials (Mazar/Mazar 1989, 49–55). Particular interest has been aroused concerning what is identified as Locus 6015; two baking dishes were among the great number of objects for daily use that were found there, but 11 figurine fragments, including a roughly made female figurine, the head of a male, and the head of a horse, were discovered as well (Mazar/Mazar 1989, 108–117, esp. pl. 29:8–10; 123–127). The excavators suggest that these might be eighth-century graves that became part of the residential area during the course of the city's expansion. For that reason, they would have been cleaned out and then used as private cellars. By contrast to Cave 1, there is no evidence of any cultic activity here either. Vessels were also discovered here that used Yahwistic personal names in the inscriptions scratched on them (Mazar/Mazar 1989, 129f.). One of these vessels was written upon twice, first using Hebrew characters (*l ʾ[. . .*) and then Egyptian hieroglyphs, but both inscriptions are unfortunately only partially preserved (Mazar/Mazar 1989, 114f. pl. 28.9). No matter how one interprets the presence of the hieroglyphs (see Maeir 1990), they do show a clear acquaintance with Egyptian culture.

used as a tomb; E 207 was connected with a (grave?) cave. Both sites were located outside the city walls, which moved Holladay to suggest that they should be interpreted as "tolerated, 'nonconformist' cult areas" (1987, 257–260, 271–275).[87] Structures that were built in front of Cave 1 in Jerusalem have recently been described as "guest houses" for travelers and traders (Franken/Steiner 1990, 49, 125).

The underworld type of milieu and the massive use of cooking, eating, and drinking utensils make it probable that these sites were used for the so-called *marzēᵃḥ* sacral meals, a cultic institution deriving from Canaanite El religion (see Amos 6:7, Jer 16:5, on the whole topic, see Fabry 1984). One does not need to force the issue to detect a connection between Cave 1 and those members of the Jerusalem élite who were criticized in Isa 28:14f., 18 because, in the face of the Assyrian threat to their security, they did not put their trust exclusively in Yahweh but in a "league with death," with the god Mot, and imagined their security to be under his protection.[88]

Both sites, E 207 in Samaria and Cave 1 in Jerusalem, were no longer used in the seventh century. The factors that led to the discontinuation in the use of these two cultic sites are not known.

87 The designation "nonconformist worship" (in contrast to "established worship") is imprecise and misleading. For Holladay, it is used initially merely to identify the social setting of these cultic sites as being outside the bounds of the governmental institutions of the national religion. But Holladay then defines the social function of these cultic sites as "an attempt on the part of individuals or groups of individuals *to remedy perceived deficiencies* in the established religion" (1987, 269; emphasis ours). Such comments cause a semantic shift that assumes specific content and a decision to be nonconformist. It is just a small step further to arrive at a more or less clear antagonism between "established worship" and "nonconformist" worship, which is also implied by use of the adjective "tolerated." When Holladay ultimately suggests that "a nonconformist cult or group *might be expected* to exhibit explicit signs of 'foreign' influence" 1987, 269), and even ascribes to the foreigners a special role in the cult as "core members of the nonconformist religious group" (1987, 269), then one suspects that the archaeological evidence was used in a way that was too strongly influenced by the preliminary hypothesis and that he may therefore not be able to avoid arguing in a circle.

  One can see that Holladay's theory was influenced by quasi-deuteronomistic ideas when one observes how Braulik clearly carries the argument still further – in the context of an article on Hosea and Deuteronomy. Braulik adopts Holladay's "nonconformist cultic sites" terminology (1991, 108ff.). The cultic activity that was practiced would have imperceptibly become a "subcutaneous cult" (1991, 116), in which "much that was tolerated happened after one passed through the doorway, even though it contradicted the official Yahweh faith and was not perceived as being quite legitimate" (1991, 117). Braulik's *theological* interpretation (note the shift from Holladay's "established *religion*" to Braulik's "official Yahweh *faith*!"), which presupposes clear deuteronomistic conceptions about authentic Yahweh faith and places "nonconformity" in the twilight zone of heterodoxy, can only hinder a *religio-historical* interpretation of the archaeological evidence.

88 The divine name Mot ("Death") appears as a theophoric element in a Judean personal name even during Iron Age IIC: *mr(y)mwt* "Mot has blessed." See also a seal dated to about 700 (Bordreuil/Lemaire 1982, 29f.) and Ostracon no. 50 from Arad (Lemaire 1977, 211); cf. Ezra 8:33; 10:36; Neh 3:4, 21; 10:6; 12:3 (Pardee 1988, 127). For the cultic activity at grave sites – treated as illegitimate and taboo – see Isa 65:4.

5. Egyptian and Egyptianized Amulets and Seals and the End of Solar Symbolism

§202.   For the sake of completeness, and in connection with the iconic evidence discussed in the previous section, most of which concerns the area of so-called "personal" piety, we again refer to the Egyptian *amulets* found frequently throughout Palestine and also in Judah, especially in Iron Age IIC graves. They witness to a continued – and even increased – fascination with this genre that makes use of Egyptian religious concepts. As had been the case in earlier periods, non-anthropomorphic entities like the Horus eye or *wedjat*-eye (see above, illuss. 261a-c), along with Bes amulets (see above, illuss. 224–225), remained popular. Among the anthropomorphic deities, a number that show the nursing goddess Isis are extant (see above, illuss. 327–328). Accompanying her, one often sees images of the lion-headed Sakhmet, consort of Ptah, the Memphis creator god (**illus. 338a**; Tufnell 1953, 34.3, 18–21, 28f.; 35.36; Lamon/ Shipton 1939, pl. 74.32; McCown 1947, pl. 55.41, etc.). This raises the question of whether the popularity of these deities might not also be due to the fact that a point of contact is provided that links the lion and the goddess once again, as had been done long ago. Of the male deities, we often find images of the god Nefer-tem (Macalister 1912, III pl. 210.79; Tufnell 1953, pl. 35.38f.; Lamon/Shipton 1939, 76.3, etc.) or the dwarf-shaped pataikoi (e.g., Tufnell 1953, 34.11; 35.44f.; 36.49; Rowe 1936, no. A. 1–2). Prominent in this iconic genre are concepts of creation or regeneration, corresponding to their *"Sitz im Leben"* in "personal" piety.

Since these stepchildren of archaeological research have not so far been gathered into one catalog,[89] an exact overview of the types that have been discovered is still lacking, along with a careful articulation of the presuppositions to be used in a stylistic investigation, in an analysis of the workshops, for questions about provenance and channels of transmission, etc. For the present, it is not possible to offer anything more than a general description of what is indicated to this point. It should be expressly mentioned that the excavations in Phoenician Zarephath have yielded an absolutely identical repertoire of amulet motifs when compared with those found in Judah (Pritchard 1975, figs. 43f. and 58; 1988, figs. 13; 15.37–39; 17f.).

When one includes, along with the faience amulets, the evidence provided by the seal amulets, for which we stand on firmer ground, several other representations of Egyptian deities can be mentioned. It is not surprising that they appear especially often in Phoenician cities such as Achzib and Acre. Scaraboids need not have been imported from Egypt but could have been produced in Phoenician workshops. Egyptian and locally produced scarabs appear together. Here also we meet the lion-

---

89 See Keel/Schroer 1985, 42–45; Schroer 1987a, 414ff.; H. Weippert 1988, 649–651. Without any claim that the individual types from the Late Bronze Age were treated comprehensively, McGovern's work on Late Bronze Age amulets (1985) repeatedly cites parallels from Iron Age II. The Iron Age II amulets found in Israel/Palestine will be collected by Ch. Herrmann in the context of a dissertation project.

headed Sakhmet (**illus. 338b**,[90] two other unpublished pieces from Achzib; Giveon 1988, no. 64) and the nursing Isis (**illus. 339**).[91] A goddess in the act of blessing appears with a lance and stands behind the warlike Onuris on a scarab from Achzib (**illus. 340a**).[92] Male deities are slightly more common on seventh-century seal amulets. Remarkably, there are a number of images of warlike Montu-Onuris (**illus. 340b** from Megiddo;[93] see Giveon/Kertesz 1986, no. 130; Rowe 1936, no. SO. 48; Tufnell 1953, pl. 44/44A.109; Petrie 1928, pl. 20.16). With this so-called "striking god," whose image is related to the image of the pharaoh who strikes down (see above, illus. 279), a tradition is continued that had been interrupted during Iron Age I or else was continued in a very limited way until Iron Age IIA (see above, §82 and note 8 in that section). As for other deities, we frequently encounter the mummy-shaped creator god Ptah and a falcon-headed god with a scepter, probably Horus (e.g., Giveon/Kertesz 1986, no. 127; Yadin 1961, pl. 187.19, and an unpublished piece from Achzib). Horus also appears frequently in the onomasticon found in late Iron Age IIC inscriptions.[94] Finally, there are also scarabs from the seventh century with Amun names (e.g., McCown 1947, pl. 54.15) or *Mn-ḫpr-rˁ* cryptograms (e.g., Dothan/Porath 1982, fig. 27.7, pl. 24.11; see above, §84, note 6).

§203. We have already emphasized the strong astralization shown in the iconography during Iron Age IIC and we have thus been able to describe the Assyrian/Aramean influences as well as the particular ways in which these themes were adapted locally. In view of the dominance of the astral symbol system during Iron Age IIC, it is worth noting that a pair of clearly solar motifs appear on Judahite name seals as well. The *four-winged scarab* (see above, illuss. 275a-b and 277) can be seen on a bulla of unknown provenance with the name *dmlˀ* (Hestrin/Dayagi-Mendels 1979, no. 47) and on a seal belonging to a certain *ḥnnyhw (bn) ˀmt* (Sass 1993, fig. 106). The motif appears to have been especially popular in seventh/sixth-century Ammonite glyptic art (Aufrecht 1989, nos. 32, 42, 68, 129, 141; see Younker 1985, 175–177). The *two-winged scarab* appears on a bulla from the so-called "Burnt Archive," a collection of bullae that were supposedly found in Jerusalem and that can be dated to about 600

90 Egyptian scarab, steatite with a white coating, 15.1 × 11 × 7.7 mm; presently in Jerusalem, IAA 48–614. On the basis of the combination that takes the cartouche ("Mykerinos") together with the Horus name ˁ3-yb, the piece can be dated to the time of Psammetichos I (664–610). We are grateful to the Israel Antiquities Authority for permission to publish this piece and those that are mentioned in the following two notes (illus. 338b–340a).

91 Phoenician scaraboid, steatite or hard faience, with a bluish glaze, 13.6 × 9.8 × 5.5 mm; currently in Jerusalem, IAA 48–632).

92 Scarab, steatite(?), with remains of a light green glaze, 15.7 × 11 × 7 mm; currently in Jerusalem, IAA 48–596.

93 Phoenician scaraboid, composite material with light blue glaze, 15.5 × 10 × 5 mm; currently in Berlin, Near Eastern Museum, VA 15072b. We are grateful for permission to publish this piece.

94 See Tigay 1986, 66. In six of the seven cases, this is the popular name *pšḥr* (see Jer 20:1, 3, 6; 21:1; 38:1; and often elsewhere). It is definitely a Judean name on four of these, twice even being used with a Yahwistic patronym. But one bearer of this name was married to a woman with an Egyptian name, so he was perhaps an Egyptian himself.

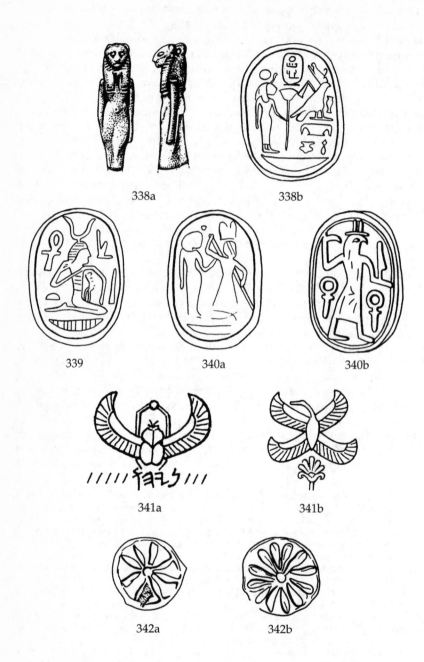

338a   338b

339   340a   340b

341a   341b

342a   342b

(**illus. 341a**; see also Avigad 1987, 200 fig. 7; 202). Two bullae from the same archive still depict the typically Judahite *four-winged uraeus* (**illus. 341b**; see above, §161). By clinging to these Egyptian solar motifs, against the general trend of the age, a tradition of conservativism manifests itself in the upper social strata in Jerusalem (see above, §162) and Ammon. This social group may have been primarily responsible for bringing the solar cultic practices mentioned in Ezek 8:10–12 to the Jerusalem Temple, for which S. Schroer is probably correct when she presumes primarily Egyptian inspiration (1987a, 71–75). But the significance of the Egyptian-inspired sun symbolism in Iron Age IIC Judah should not be overrated, in spite of Ezekiel 8. The 255 bullae from the "Burnt Archive" are from 211 different seals. Of these, only two have solar motifs. These two seals could be somewhat older than the rest, since in two other contemporary groups of bullae, one from Jerusalem (Shiloh 1986) and one from Lachish (Aharoni 1975a, 19–22), neither solar motifs nor other Egyptian motifs appear. Illustrations 294 and 337a-b show depictions of a deity that include some solar elements but which do not show Egyptian influence. This background may provide the link with the cult mentioned in Ezek 8:16.

§204. We found clearly Egyptian images of the sun god, both the four-winged scarab and the winged solar disk, on the Judahite state seals that date to the end of the eighth century. These give at least indirect evidence for the great fascination that Egypt held for Judean royalty at that time (see above, §§160–162). Impressions that date to the seventh century and that were made by the official seals of the Judean administration at the same location on the handles of storage vessels, vessels that apparently continued to be used for the same purposes, provide a very different picture, even though they were manufactured in the same workshops as the earlier *lmlk* pithoi (Mommsen, et al., 1984, 106f.). They are anepigraphic and depict only one image, usually called a *rosette*, that has anywhere from six to sixteen petals (**illuss. 342a-b**), a surprising motif that shows no connection either to Egypt or to Assyria, but appears to have been developed locally (but see the center of the lotus nimbus in illuss. 337a-b!). To date, about 160 impressions of such rosette stamps are known. They come exclusively from sites that belonged to the Kingdom of Judah at the time of Josiah. The numerically largest concentrations have appeared at Jerusalem (59 pieces), Ramat Rahel (42), and Lachish (23) (Na'aman 1991, 31–33). The impressions come from at least 28 different stamps (see Y. Nadelman in Mazar/Mazar 1989, 132). A lead seal with a twelve-petal rosette, from which these impressions could have been produced, was found at En Gedi in Str. V (ca. 630–586; Mazar/Dunayevsky 1964, 123f.).

As a result of his discoveries at Ramat Rahel, Aharoni realized that if the rosette stamps were dated earlier, contemporary with the *lmlk* stamps, they would both have served the same function – but they first appear during the last phase of Iron Age II (1964, 35). The two stamp types are never found together on the same handle. The *lmlk* stamps apparently did not continue past the reign of Hezekiah, falling out of use about the beginning of the seventh century. Whether the rosette stamps appeared immediately thereafter, or first at the time of Josiah, remains unclear at this time. But it is certain that they are more recent (Mommsen, et al., 1984, 92). They themselves, however, did not survive at all, or at least not for very long, in Iron Age III (Stern 1982, 206).

The rosettes are occasionally interpreted, on the basis of Hittite models, as sun symbols. In the absence of plausible connections, this is not very convincing (see Welten 1969, 33). It might be more likely that the "sun blossom" shown in illuss. 337a-b in the center of the lotus nimbus might illustrate a connection with a creator god who offers blessings. In support of a solar interpretation of the rosette, one might argue that solar motifs are found not only on the earlier eighth-century stamps and are apparently connected with the solar, national god, Yahweh (§162), but that the later Iron Age III stamps, that are used by the Judean administration (§§223f.), refer to Yahweh and suggest, at least to some extent (§224), that this god has solar characteristics.

6. Contours of a New Orthodoxy

§205.   The Judahite name seals of Iron Age IIC show a clear *tendency toward aniconicity*, shown in the way that iconographic decorations are limited to vegetal and ornamental elements or are avoided altogether. The shift in preference is seen clearly on the bone seals, which during Iron Age IIB were anepigraphic (see above, §§157ff.), but which developed during Iron Age IIC into pure name seals. Typical of the transition is a bone seal that combines the usual worshiper with the inscription *mtn* (Bordreuil/Lemaire 1976, 51 no. 16 = Sass 1993, fig. 128). Other aniconic pieces still keep the form of the bone seals from the ninth and eighth centuries (Bordreuil/Lemaire 1976, 47 no. 5; Hestrin/Dayagi-Mendels 1979, no. 62; Avigad 1989b, 93f. no. 10). Others have nothing in common with these except that the same material is used (Hestrin/Dayagi-Mendels 1979, nos. 91–96; Avigad 1989b, 92 no. 6).

Legal archaeological excavations have thus far produced over 80 impressions of private seals on vessel handles from the end of the eighth century and from the early seventh century, bearing a two-line name inscription without any iconographic element. With the exception of one piece from Dan, all are from Judahite sites, such as Tell Beit Mirsim, Lachish, Tell Judeidah, Beth-Shemesh, Tell en-Nasbeh, Ramat Rahel, and Jerusalem.[95] Both the site distribution and dating of the context for each find show that this is a typical phenomenon in Judah, one that began at the time of Hezekiah. For the most part, we find the aniconic impressions of name seals from the end of the eighth century right alongside impressions of royal seals (see Ussishkin 1976; Garfinkel 1984). The tendency toward aniconic name inscriptions may relate to the increasing use of seals for exclusively administrative functions and should be understood as part of an increase in bureaucracy in the Judean state. The amulet function of the seals was immaterial for administrative functions.

95 See, e.g., Bliss/Macalister 1902, pl. 56.20–24, 26–27, 30; 122 fig. 44; Grant/Wright 1939, 79–82 fig. 10a.1–5, 7–10; fig. 10b.8–11; Albright 1943, pls. 29.6, 9; 60.8; McCown 1947, pl. 57.9–12; Tufnell 1953, pls. 47A.1–11; 47B.1–7, 10; Aharoni 1962, pls. 6.1–4; 27.1–3; 1964, pl. 40.1–6; Avigad 1983, 44f. figs. 23–25.

In any case, two-line, aniconic name seals can hardly be designated as seal *amulets*.

By comparison with the number of seal impressions, very few original seals have been recovered in excavations. But more than a hundred have been purchased. Of these, at least a few might be genuine. A good dozen of them are engraved on both sides. Most often, only one side is decorated iconically, while the other side has only the name inscription. The aniconic side served primarily administrative-business purposes (as a seal) and the iconic side was primarily an amulet. This means that one should not exclude the possibility that some of the seals used to make impressions on *lmlk* vessels and later on bullae were engraved on both sides. But the two-sided seals are so much more in the minority (at most 3 – 4 per cent), in comparison with one-sided, generally aniconic Hebrew seals of Iron Age IIC, which means that they are not statistically able to influence the evidence very much. Most of the aniconic impressions on vessels or bullae may also have come from completely aniconic seals.

Both excavated impressions made by seals and seals that have been purchased corroborate the fact that there was a strong tendency for Iron Age IIC Judahite name seals to have purely ornamental images or else to be completely imageless (Sass 1993). There are also imageless seals in the neighboring cultures during the seventh and sixth centuries, but the production in those areas did not dominate the scene in quite the same way as in Judah.[96] Whoever attempts to attribute the preponderance of purely name seals in Judah to *just* one cause, that being the growing literacy of the Judean population (see H. Weippert 1988, 674), has scarcely done the issue justice.

§206.   For the seventh and sixth centuries, we find seal impressions on the so-called *bullae* much more frequently than on the handles of vessels, where they had typically appeared during the eighth century. Most of the bullae dating to Iron Age IIC bear only two-line Hebrew name inscriptions and have no iconic elements. The examples assembled from the discoveries found in hoards from archives have proved especially significant for statistical investigation. One such archive, found a few years ago at Ophel (Shiloh 1986), contained 55 bullae, one of which had been sealed with the seal of Gemaryahu ben Shafan (**illus. 343a**; cf. Jer 36:10). Four of the bullae have an iconic decoration (a bird, a griffin, a ladder-shaped motif, and the crescent moon standard shown in illus. 297a). All the rest have either rudimentary ornamentation or none at all. In each case, the decoration is limited to the space between the two lines

---

96 See, e.g., Bordreuil 1986a, nos. 39 (counterfeit?), 68, 70f., 80, 90, 116, 118, 120; Hestrin/ Dayagi-Mendels 1979, nos. 2, 28f., 102–104, 107, 109, 113, 128f., 134–135. There are 58 completely or almost completely aniconic Hebrew name seals in these two large collections, in addition to the 22 aniconic seals that are not Hebrew (among these: eleven Ammonite, seven Aramean, two Moabite, and one or two Phoenician pieces). Proportionally, the tendency for Hebrew seals to be aniconic (ca. 70% of the known seals) can be compared with the a lesser number for the Ammonite group (ca. 30%). But this observation about a general tendency ought not be confused with precise statistical evidence. For that, we would need to examine not only a much larger number of seals, but would also need much more certain criteria for classification, dating, and authenticity. Concerning most recent discussion of this issue, see the studies edited by Sass and Uehlinger, 1993.

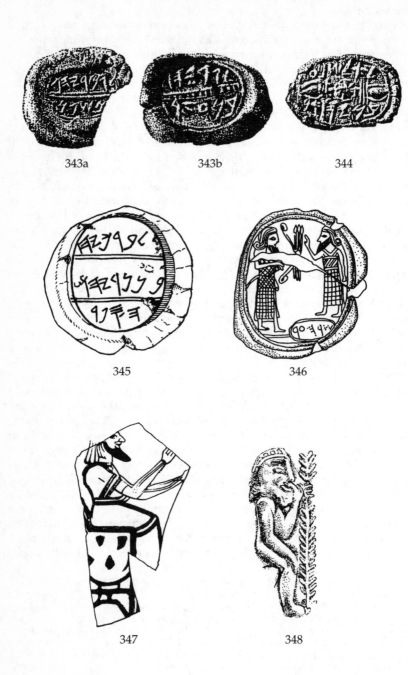

343a   343b   344

345   346

347   348

used for the owner's name, separating the lines of text by use of a double line, a ladder-shaped, notched band (**illus. 343b**), or a floral motif (rosette with two buds, **illus. 344**).

The 255 bullae from the so-called "Burnt Archive" (Avigad 1986) point in the same direction as those from Ophel. They also may have come from Jerusalem. In any case, they list such famous citizens of Jerusalem from the time of Jeremiah as his secretary Berechyahu ben Neriyahu (on one of the rarer three-register bullae, **illus. 345**), Yerachmeel, the "son of the king" (see Jer 36:26), and perhaps also the high priest Azarya ben Hilqiyahu (1 Chr 5:39, Schneider 1988; 1991). The 255 bullae from this archive, as mentioned already, were made by 211 different seals. Only 13 bullae have substantive iconographic motifs (cf. here: illuss. 200c-d, 312c, 341a-b; Avigad 1986, 118f.). The most interesting among them has a scenic composition, that being the bulla of *šr hᶜr*, the "city commandant" that includes a figurative design. It portrays an official, with hand raised in greeting, in front of a man armed with sword, arrow, and bow, who might be identified as the Judahite king, even though this man interestingly wears neither diadem nor crown (**illus. 346**; Avigad 1986, 30–33 nos. 10a-b; cf. Avigad 1976b). The interpretation of the scene as the investiture of the city commandant by the king (Barkay 1977) possibly attempts to read too much history into the picture, and Avigad is right to dispute it on such grounds (1978; 1986, 32f.). Bow and arrow are attributes of royal rule and a king would hardly hand over such items to a city commandant. The image emphasizes much more that legitimate power is in the hands of the king. By contrast, the official (identified most likely from the inscription as the city commandant) functions loyally and uses only the power that has been delegated to him by the king.

In addition to what is shown in illus. 346, a painted vessel fragment from Ramat Rahel Str. V A (end of the seventh century) depicts a bearded, enthroned figure who might be the Judahite king (**illus. 347**). The "smile" on the individual may be due to Greek influence (Geva 1981), but the clothing, posture, and especially the way the arm musculature is accentuated identifies this depiction more as Assyrian (P. Matthiae in Aharoni 1964, 85–94). Five limestone fragments in relief from Tell es-Safi (see below, note 106) and sketches in the burial cave at Khirbet Beit Lei (see above, §180; Naveh 1963, 77–80, 82; Mittmann 1989, 30f., 35–38) that depict two ships, Assyrian soldiers(?), and two military camps are somewhat older. They might also be provincial responses to Assyrian iconography. Illustrations 346–347 provide evidence for a certain fascination with the great might of Assyria and probably also show how Judean governmental iconography accommodated itself to the representations of that power (see above, illuss. 264a-b). It seems particularly noteworthy for the religious history of Judah that the Judahite monarchy could orient itself, apparently without difficulty, within the world of the Assyrian political and military symbols, without simultaneously sensing a need to adopt the religious symbols of that world power.

§207. To date, neither an anthropomorphic image of a deity nor an astral symbol has appeared on even one single bulla of the more than 300 examples from the seventh and sixth centuries. The cultic emblem of the Moon God of Haran appears on two bullae, one from Jerusalem and the other from Horvat Uza (see above, §174 with illus. 297a). As we have noted, the anthropomorphic moon god, in the form of El (see above, §178), appears on at least two Judean name seals, and for that reason we considered the *possibility* of identifying this god as Yahweh in §179. B. Sass has pointed out to us that both of these clearly Judahite name seals that bear this image are engraved on both sides. The name of the owner and the image of the moon god thus do not appear alongside each other, as on the Ammonite(?) seal shown in illus. 305a, but are separated one from the other. This would have permitted the owner to seal documents with an "orthodox" name seal but would have still enabled the owner to wear an amulet with an anthropomorphic image of the deity.

In fact, astral symbols are not only very rare on bullae but also on the actual Judahite seals themselves (see above, §§187f.). The crescent moon appears on one Judahite inscribed seal and a crescent moon with a rhomboid is seen on two such seals. Star and rhomboid appear together on the iconic side of the *špn nryhw* seal shown in illus. 317a. Even if all four of the seals mentioned here are genuine, this is a minuscule group in any case.

As mentioned above, various names of high officials from the period between Josiah and Zedekiah, who are known to us from the Bible, appear on the Jerusalem bullae as well. The bullae belong chronologically, as well as sociologically, to the milieu of the Jerusalem élite from which the *early deuteronomistic movement* also recruited its partisans and sympathizers. In view of this, it might be possible to associate the evidence seen on the bullae and name seals (especially the general lack of images of anthropomorphic deities and astral symbols) with two main concerns of the *Josianic reform* and to connect those concerns with each other (the lack of images in the Yahweh cult and the radical opposition to foreign cults, especially astral cults and astral divination, in Judah). Of course, we should not assume that the change in seal decoration to purely ornamental or even aniconic motifs is a direct consequence of the prohibition of images. First, it is debatable whether Josiah's reform was even connected with that prohibition of images. Second, the deuteronomic prohibition against images (Deut 5:8) was a specific move that prohibited portraying foreign gods and was initially related to the manufacture of cultic images, not being tied to the general area of glyptic art reproductions as a whole (see Dohmen 1985, 266–273). Third, the discontinuation of pictorial decoration on Judahite seals during the late Iron Age IIC, especially on the anepigraphic ones, was by no means total. But there were certainly *similar values* at work in the reforms of Josiah, for which there is literary documentation, and in the early deuteronomistic movement, on the one hand, and, on the other, in the emphasis among the Jerusalem élite on pure name seals, and on the avoidance of images that depicted deities and astral symbols on name seals and on the bullae that were made from such stamps. Even though Josiah's reform failed to root out astral cults in Judah entirely, as the presence of the cult of the "Queen of Heaven" shows (see above, §197), nevertheless, a religious orientation toward the heavenly bodies themselves, whether sun, moon, or stars, seems not to have been in vogue (any longer?) in Judah after the time of Josiah, at least not for the élite who carried name seals.

349a 349b

350a 350b

351a 351b

352 353a 353b

§208. The reform was not directed against astral cults alone but was also concerned with the cult for Asherah that had been introduced by Manasseh. Every indicator suggests that this cult was eliminated completely from the temple area by Josiah (2 Kgs 23:4, 6f.) To be sure, the cult of the goddess revived in the sixth century in the realm of family piety (see the discussion in §§171 and 197 regarding the "Queen of Heaven"). Nothing is known about a rehabilitation of the goddess in the official state cult in Jerusalem. A relief terra-cotta appliqué on a krater fragment from En Gedi, dated about 600, shows an enthroned figure wearing a diadem, thus probably a royal figure, worshiping before a branch (**illus. 348**). Two further appliqués on the same vessel fragment depict both a striding buck and a Bes head. There are parallels to this, known from Transjordan (Buseirah [see Stern 1978b, 13–15] and Tell Nimrin; the latter is unpublished). Since there are no other bucks in Judahite iconography but only does, the appliqués from En Gedi may possibly come from Phoenicia (see above, illus. 200a), Transjordan, or Edom.

Asherah was not permitted to have any future in Jerusalem and Judah. There are isolated representations of a *branch* on bullae that date to the end of Iron Age IIC (Avigad 1990b, 265, no. 2, pl. 28:C), below the name of the male or female owner (see below, illus. 356) or alongside it (**illuss. 349a-b**; see Avigad 1986, no. 42). By contrast to illus. 348, these can hardly be considered as survivors of the ancient traditions of "Branch Goddess," tree cult, and *asherah*. They are more likely stock elements in a repertoire of general *plant symbolism* that is both non-mythological and unrelated to the older tradition. This repertoire includes such items as the pomegranate (**illuss. 350a-b**; anepigraphic, McCown 1947, pl. 55.58), lotus buds (**illuss. 351a-b**; cf. illuss. 344c, 356) or palmetto-like blossoms (**illus. 352**). Such plant symbolism evokes ideas of continued blessing and prosperity. Nevertheless, it does not suggest specifically which underlying power grants the blessing, to say nothing of whether that power is "female."

The limited selection of vegetal ornamentation on Judahite inscribed seals and bullae from the end of Iron Age IIC may have been influenced at least in part by the *temple* and the cult. Tree fruit, palm fronds, and branches were vegetal requirements for the "female and male Israelites" who were to celebrate the Feast of Booths in the presence of Yahweh according to Lev. 23:40 (cf. Neh 8:15). Pomegranates decorate the priestly scepter and incense stand (Artzy 1990). An ivory pomegranate, which may have served as the top of a scepter, has recently received much attention because of its inscription that can be dated paleographically to the eighth century: *qdš khnm lbyt* [*yhw*]*h* "holy priestly possession from the temple of Yahweh" (see Avigad 1990c). Pomegranates appear likewise on the hem of the high priest's garments (Exod 28:33f.; 39:24–26; Sir 45:9) and are found – possibly only because of a literary addition (Görg 1991, 85) – in two rows of two hundred each on the temple pillars Jachin and Boaz (1 Kgs 7:18–20; see above, §107). Lotus buds and lotus blossoms are also part of the temple decoration (Schroer 1987a, 55–57, 60). The ornamentation on seals produced after Josiah's era apparently oriented itself toward replicating images found on the temple.

Depictions of stylized pillars with capitals tended to follow in the same direction, even though they are found only on Judahite bullae (**illuss. 353a-b**; cf. illuss. 231a, 233b). So-called "Proto-aeolian" capitals, without pillars, which appear on three Judahite name seals that were purchased, seem to be connected rather to the symbolic world of the royal palace. If the seals are genuine, two of the three owners had the title *bn hmlk* "the king's son" (Avigad 1976a, no. 3; 1987, 201 fig. 8).[97] "Proto-aeolian" capitals have also been found that date to Iron Age IIC at, among other sites, the royal palace at Ramat Rahel (Shiloh 1979, 8–10, pls. 11–14; cf. illus. 193).

These finds confirm the fact that there was a nationalistic Judahite movement that supported the Josianic reforms. It not only opposed all "Canaanite" cults and all other foreign cults, but it also consolidated the position of Jerusalem as the capital of the country and the Jerusalem Temple as the center for the Judahite national religion. Since, according to the deuteronomic-deuteronomistic conception, Yahweh was present in this temple only through his "name," the iconic symbolism on Judean name seals from the end of Iron Age IIC oriented itself toward the vegetal image symbolism of the temple and its equipment, though some who made these pieces limited themselves to a more or less symbolic representation of the male or female who owned the seal (see illuss. 200b-d and 312c) or even simply to a mere mention of the name of the seal owner. Dare we seek to find something more than an accidental relationship between the deuteronomic and deuteronomistic pathos for the divine name and the emphasis on name seals in Judah that mention only the name?

Whereas Ammonite or Moabite glyptic art of the seventh and sixth centuries still presented pictorial images that evoked a divine entity in terms of solar or lunar categories, on bullae from Jerusalem that are dated to the end of Iron Age IIC we find only inanimate temple decorations and more or less formal representations of the male and female seal owners. The break with the immediately preceding "Canaanite" renaissance in Judah, as well as with the solar religiosity of Egyptian and Phoenician inspiration and with astral religiosity of Assyrian and Aramean inspiration, could hardly have been expressed more clearly.

§209. In view of the breaks and changes just noted, it comes as no particular surprise that the impression that has been created concerning the religious concepts provided thus far from Iron Age IIC Judahite inscriptions matches well with the biblical evidence. In addition to the inscriptions from Khirbet Beit Lei and Jerusalem that have been mentioned already (see above, §180), one should take note of the *ostraca from Lachish and Arad* that are dated to the early sixth century (Lemaire 1977, 83–235; Davies 1991, 1–38). As one might expect, they include personal names that are largely Yahwistic, with many having the theophoric element *ʾl* "god," whereas the element *bʿl* "Baal" appears no

---

97 The third piece, presently in the R. and E. Hecht Museum in Haifa, which carries the inscription *lpdyhw bn hmlk*, was first published in the form of a postcard. The scholarly publication and reasons for the dating (to the beginning of the sixth century) will appear very soon, under the authorship of N. Avigad, in *Michmanim* 6 (1992).

more in either corpus (see Tigay 1986, 47ff.).[98, 99] The short formula of greeting in the letters from Arad (*brktk lyhwh* "I bless you by Yahweh"; see above, §141, note 110), by contrast to the letter prescript from Kuntillet ʿAjrud, mentions Yahweh's *asherah* no longer.[100] The longer formulas in the Lachish letters identify Yahweh exclusively as the deity responsible for the well-being of the addressee.[101] Even though Uriyahu confessed in the inscription found at Khirbet el-Qom (eighth century; see above, §141) that he had been saved by Yahweh "through his *asherah*" (Line 3: *mṣryh lʾšrth hwšʿ lh*), the writer of the slightly later Inscription C from Khirbet Beit Lei expects to be saved by Yahweh alone (*hwšʿ [y]hwh*; Naveh 1963, 86; Lemaire 1976, 561; Davies 1991, 89 no. 15.008).

At least according to Lemaire's reading (1976, 558f.; see above, §180, notes 28f.), Inscription A from Khirbet Beit Lei presents an interesting link between the local or national dimension of Yahweh (the mountains of Judah, the God of Jerusalem) and his universal dimension as the "God of the Whole Earth." A seventh-century inscription from a cave at *Nahal Yishai*, in the vicinity of En Gedi, connects personal piety and Yahweh's claim to universal authority even more impressively, if the following translation by D. Conrad (1988, 561) is correct:

Line 1   "Cursed be the one who will blot out . . .
Line 4   Blessed be Yahw[eh . . .
Line 6   May he be blessed among the people[s] as king . . .
Line 7   Blessed be my lord . . ."

Conrad cites Ps 96:3, 10 for Line 6 and Ps 68:20 for Line 7. But the point of Psalm 96 is that Yahweh's royal rule and splendor *are proclaimed*, not that Yahweh ought to be praised because of them. If the inscription from Nahal Yishai suggests that the deity is actually the object of human praise (then it would be better not to translate *brk* as "blessed"), that summons

---

98 An ostracon dated to about 600 from Mead Hashavyahu in the coastal plain supplies only questionable evidence (Tigay 1986, 14; Davies 1991, 78 no. 7.007).

99 Names with the theophoric element *qws* are found, for example, on two ostraca from Arad (12.3, 26.3) and on a seal from ʿAroer (Tigay 1986, 67), which is not surprising for the Judahite/Edomite border region.

100 In the Holy of Holies at the temple of Arad, there was a single *maṣṣebah* that was painted red. It may have represented Yahweh. No mention has been made concerning the existence of an *asherah* that would have been worshiped there as well (Keel/Küchler 1982, 231).

The stratigraphy and dating of the early phases of this temple are very much in dispute. See, most recently, Ussishkin 1988, who disputes the idea that the temple was founded by Solomon. He assigns the establishment of the temple to "Str." X-VIII, which he dates in the seventh century (i.e., at the time of Manasseh, at which time there was a thorough reurbanization of the Negev; cf. Tatum 1991). The temple would have been destroyed at the end of the period represented by "Str." VII-VI, possibly in the early sixth century (i.e, at the time that the Negev definitely slipped away from Judahite control, after which there was no longer any communication with the Jerusalem Temple, which is called *byt yhwh* in the Arad inscriptions).

101 Nos. 2.1f.; 3.2–4; 4.1–2; 5.1–3; 8.1–2; 9.1–2: *yšmʿ yhwh ʾt ʾdny šmʿt šlm/tb* "May Yahweh grant my Lord to hear a good report," and similar statements; 6.1–2: *yrʾ yhwh ʾt ʾdny ʾt hʿt hzh šlm* "May Yahweh allow my lord to see peace at this moment." See also the specific wishes expressed in the body of the letters from Arad 21.4; Lachish 2.5; 5.7–9 (on these, see Lemaire 1977, 99f., 117, 186).

would be without analogy in contemporary Northwest Semitic inscriptions. But this does not prevent the *br(w)k* formula from still referring to Yahweh in the psalter (Pss 28:6; 31:22; 41:14; 66:20; 68:20, 36; 72:18, etc.) and also in other older narrative texts (e.g., Gen 24:27; Exod 18:10; 1 Sam 25:32, 39; 2 Sam 18:28, etc.; see Scharbert 1973, 823–826). The traces of ink from the writing on the rock walls are much less clear than Conrad's translation leads one to suspect (cf. Bar-Adon 1975, 227, 229; pl. 25:B-C; Davies 1991, 91f. no. 20.002):

Line 1   *'rr. 'šr. ymḥḥ*
Line 4   *brk. yhw*[. . .
Line 6   *brk. bgy*[. . . *ẏ*]*mlk*
Line 7   *brk. 'dny*[: . . .

The spelling *gy*[*m* for *gôyîm* "peoples" in Line 6 would, in and of itself, be quite unusual (the word is otherwise never found in Hebrew inscriptions; see Davies 1991, 326). Additionally, personal names could be supplied for Lines 4 and 7 with no trouble (e.g., *yᵉhôyākîn* and *'ᵃdônîyāhû*), and a personal name, possibly with a patronym, seems likely in Line 6. The whole series of wishes for blessing is more likely being requested for the person who is named and not for Yahweh.

§210.   Inscriptions found on two pieces of thin silver, rolled up to form amulets, put us on somewhat more solid ground and bring us to the immediate vicinity of a biblical text. The amulets were found in a grave at Ketef Hinnom in Jerusalem that had once belonged to a rich family at the end of the seventh and early sixth centuries (**illuss. 354a-b**). The two inscriptions have been published recently by G. Barkay (1989, esp. 46–59; see Yardeni 1991; Davies 1991, 72f. nos. 4.301f.) and discussion of these pieces is just beginning. The following transcription and translation is limited to the more well-preserved passages.

Amulet 1 (illus. 354a)

(. . .)

Line 4   *šṁ*]*ṙ*[?][?][102] *hḃryṫ* [*w*]
Line 5   [*h*]*ḥsd l'h*[*by(w)*][??]
Line 6   [*w*]*ḃšmry*[. . .
Line 7   [. . .]
Line 8   *h 'l mš*[*k*]
Line 9   *bh* [*xx*]*h mkl* [*x'*]
Line 10   . . .] *wmhr'* [. . .
Line 11   *ky bw g'l*
Line 12   *h ky yhwh*
Line 13   [*y*]*šyḃnw* [*x'*]

Amulet 2 (illus. 354b)

Line 1   *'t*]*hḃṙw*[*k*]
Line 2   [*'/w*][??]*nyhw*
Line 3   . . .
Line 4   [*h*]*ṙ' h*[. . .[103]

---

102 Barkay reads Line 4: ['*]hb hbr* (1989, 52). But see the reference to Deut 7:9 (*šmr hbryt whḥsd l'hbyw wlšmryw mṣwtyw* "the one who keeps the covenant and graciousness with those who love him and keep his commandments") in Yardeni 1991, 178.

103 Korpel (1989, 3f.) offers another reading and interpretation of Lines 1–4 of the second amulet. This view assumes that there is a direct address to the deceased bearer of the amulet ¹*šbt* ²[*b*]*nyhw* ³[*w*]*qw. yh*[*w*] ⁴[*h*] *w'r* [*l*] ⁵[*h*], etc. "Rest, Benayahu, trust confidently in Yahweh, stay awake for him," etc. This interpretation, which

Line 14	ʾwr ybr[kʾ]	Line 5	[h] ybr[kʾ]
Line 15	k yhwh [w]	Line 6	k yhwh w
Line 16	[y]šmrk [y]	Line 7	[y]šmrk
Line 17	[ʾ]r yhwh	Line 8	yʾr yh
Line 18	[p]n̂[yw . . .	Line 9	[w]ḣ pnyẇ
[. . .]		Line 10	[ʾl]yk wẏ
		Line 11	šm lk š
		Line 12	l̇ẇ[m . . .]
		(. . .)	

Line 4   ". . . He pre]serves" the covenant and
Line 5   the grace for those who love [him]
Line 6   and with those who keep [. . .
Line 7   [his commandments"]
Line 8   . . .] in the camp " [. . .
Line 9   . . .] from all [. . .
Line 10   . . .] and from evil [. . .
Line 11   for with him is redemption,   Line 1   "[May you be"] blessed,
Line 12   for Yahweh   Line 2   [O]niyahu,
Line 13   brings us back   Line 3   . . .
Line 14   light.   Line 4   from"] evil [. . .
Lines 14/5   May blessings be
Lines 15/6   on you from Yahweh, and
Lines 16/7   may he keep you
Lines 17/8   may Yahweh cause to shine
Lines 18/9   his countenance"
[. . .]
                                            Line 10 above you and
                                            Line 11 grant you
                                            Line 12 peace."

The second part of each amulet presents a blessing formula that conforms to the so-called *Priestly benediction* in Num 6:24–26. This fact has dominated the initial discussions about the amulets: Amulet 1:14–18 corresponds to Num 6:24–25a; Amulet 2:5-12 corresponds to Num 6:24-25a, 26b. The formula contained in the canonical benediction ". . . and be gracious to you; Yahweh lift up his countenance upon you" (Num 6:25b–26a) is missing from the second amulet, while the first breaks off before it gets that far (the expansion [18]p]n̂[yw ʿly[19]k wyḥnk] for illus. 354a is pure conjecture). No matter how one might interpret the difference in the formulation,[104] it remains indisputable that Hebrew epigraphy and the biblical text coincide at this point in a way that could not be demonstrated

---

assumes that the lines were very uneven in length and which makes conjectures about the placement of words that do not match either the photographs or the drawings, has now been replaced by the much more accurate rendering by both Barkay (1989) and Yardeni (1991).

104 Varying interpretations of the evidence are found in Rösel 1986 (Num 6:25b–26a are probably secondary); Vuk 1987, 35: ". . . a free quotation from an intercessory formula, which . . . was adopted from the same common source, namely, the temple liturgy"; Haran 1989; Korpel 1989 (the amulets present a contracted version of the benediction).

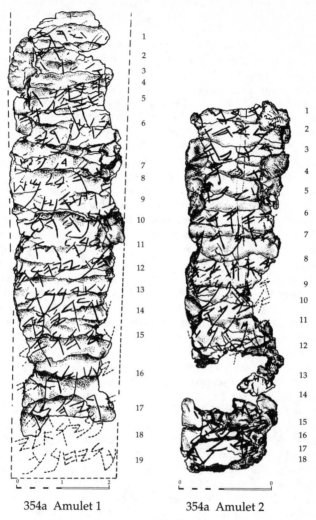

354a Amulet 1	354a Amulet 2

355

previously, especially when we consider the close relationship between the beginning of Amulet 1 and Deut 7:9 (cf. Exod 20:6), a text that speaks of Yahweh's faithfulness down to the thousandth generation.

The two silver amulets present early evidence for the practice prescribed in Exod 13:9; Deut 6:8; 11:18, which calls for wearing the words from the Torah on the body. To be sure, these are benediction formulas and not commandments. This practice of wearing inscribed amulets, known also in Egypt (see Leclant 1980; Keel 1981, 213 illus. 28), apparently started first. The didactic function, to help one remember the texts by wearing them, would have come later (see Barkay 1989, 71–76).

In the context of the issues that are important for our study, it is also very noteworthy that the amulets demonstrate a religious orientation toward the temple that parallels what happened with the name seals and bullae, as discussed above in §207, though phraseology from the temple liturgy is documented here. The seal with branch and lotus bud decorations (**illus. 355**; see above, illuss. 344, 349a-b, 351a-b) that was found in the same grave fits nicely with this observation. The combination that links Deut 7:9 and Num 6:24f. points to a link between priestly and "early deuteronomistic" thinking that appears to have left its mark on the religious practitioners among the Jerusalem élite during the early sixth century, bearing a strong resemblance to the book of Jeremiah and, with some slight differences, to Ezekiel. A glass Phoenician Bes head and a faience pendant with a picture of the Egyptian goddess Bastet (Barkay 1986, 5, 7 [Hebrew]) both show that the family who had placed their dead here had also still used small non-Judahite amulets of a kind that Ezekiel, for example, would have abhorred as "unclean crud" (Ezek 20:7f.; cf. Keel/Schroer 1985, 44f.).

Thanks to the discovery of amulets from Ketef Hinnom that can be dated precisely, we are able to place the "shining of Yahweh's countenance" within its religio-historical framework. The metaphor goes beyond the petition for blessing and protection (*ybrk[k] wyšmrk*), which we have already encountered at Kuntillet ʿAjrud (see above, §134 Inscription ᴾB 2 Line 5ʾ), and adds a new element (cf. Pss 31:17; 67:2; 80:4, 8, 15, 20; 119:135; Dan 9:17; 10:6). M. Korpel suggests deriving the words from solar concepts (1989, 6). Such concepts are known to have been in use in Jerusalem at the end of Iron Age IIC (see above, §§202–204, but see esp. illuss. 294 and 337a-b). But the very common term "shine," connected with the anthropomorphic conception of Yahweh's "countenance," may have had at least as strong a tie at the end of Iron Age IIC with the concept of Yahweh as an El with lunar connotations (see above, §§174–182), not least of all in the darkness of night and the grave, where Yahweh's own "countenance" now appears in the place of the countenance of the *asherah*.

M. Korpel suggests interpreting the opening lines of Amulet 2 as a direct address to the deceased,[105] but the preserved text does not support this interpretation. In particular, Lines 8, 11–14 from Amulet 1 point out clearly that the amulet was intended for dead people. Yahweh was to guard them with his faithfulness even in the grave and was to let his light

---

105 See above, this same §210, note 103.

shine there too. This idea would also be plausible in the context of an epoch that preferred to experience divine presence in the shining of the stars that were seen against the backdrop of the darkness of night. If we have read and translated these lines correctly, this would be eloquent testimony that the blessing of Yahweh essentially amounted to something more than social prestige even in preexilic times. It could mean hope for those who had died, for whom no further success was now possible.

In contrast to the evidence discussed in §§189ff., it is worth noting that there are no terra-cottas of doves, goddesses, or riders in the graves of Ketef Hinnom. Not Asherah, and not an "angel of Yahweh," but Yahweh himself – mediated by the presence of a text! – accompanies the deceased, with his blessing and protection, into the cold darkness of the grave. Whether as a goddess and as the "Queen of Heaven," or even as the cultic symbol that mediates the blessing of Yahweh, the motherly Asherah is far removed from the piety documented in this grave.

It remains to be considered whether the shape of the head supports in the graves of Ketef Hinnom (**illus. 356**) or – still more easily recognizable – in the graves in the garden of the École Biblique (**illus. 357a**, detail **illus. 357b**) might lead one to consider whether the Ω-shaped symbol that can characterize the shape of the womb (thus Keel, et al., 1989, 70; see above, §14 and illus. 82) might be a late remnant of the idea that the earth is symbolically the mother's womb. We find the Ω-shaped symbol twice on an unpublished seal amulet from the Middle Bronze Age Ω-group now held in a private collection in Paris. The Ω symbols on this amulet – positioned, as here, in the graves by the head and foot rests – are opened toward each other. In any case, this interpretation of the head supports would have more probability than that of Barkay and Kloner, who regard the supports in illus. 357 as stylized Hathor wigs (1986, 36). In Job 1:21, the earth is clearly called a womb and, by strict analogy, those yet unborn and those deceased are both in a womb. In contrast to this text and related texts (Ps 139:15; Isa 26:18f.; Sir 40:1; cf. Keel, et al., 1989, 70–75), it is unlikely that we have a conscious use of some mythological idea here with the use of these head supports in the Jerusalem graves. It is rather more likely that we have a dim reflection of a mythological theme, used now in the context of a piety that is decidedly unmythological in its literature and iconography. The head supports could also be understood simply as a kind of pillow, intended to guarantee the repose of the deceased.

Summary

§211. The iconographically documented symbol system of Iron Age IIC Palestine distinguishes itself fundamentally from those of preceding periods in that solar iconographic motifs of Egyptian provenance or inspiration become less important. Cylinder seals, in contrast to Iron Age IIA-B, increase perceptibly in number, marking the presence of a new world power in Palestine, that of the Assyrians. The decoration on these seals portrays cultic scenes, in the center of which the Assyrian king stands as a loyal servant of the heavenly powers, or more rarely in service of Assyrian genii and deities such as Ninurta, Adad, or Ishtar. Ishtar is found most frequently among the deities represented anthropomorphic- ally. She appears alone on stamp seals as well, accentuating her astral

356

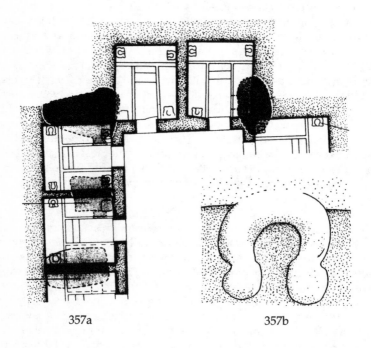

357a   357b

form in a star nimbus (illuss. 286–288). The gods Sin, Marduk, and Nabu appear only in the form of their cultic symbols.

The chief characteristic of the glyptic art of Iron Age IIC is not the generally modest presence of Assyrian deities but the general tendency toward *the astralization* of the religious symbol system. During the seventh century, preference was given to the divine powers being accepted and worshiped in their astral form, with emphasis on their *nocturnal* appearance in the starry heavens. Mediating creatures, such as winged, hybrid creatures, no longer play a significant role in Iron Age IIC iconography. Instead, there are frequent cultic scenes and representations of – almost exclusively male – worshipers. The general tendency toward astralization of the symbol system, noticeable not only on imported glyptic art but also on what was produced locally in many different formats, may have been influenced significantly by the Arameans. One of the most remarkable characteristics of the era is the appearance of the crescent moon standard, the cultic emblem of the Moon God of Haran, who appears to have been the most significant "international" god of the Assyrian Empire in the western provinces (illuss. 281, 291, 295–301). In general, the tendency toward astralization that is visible on the seals permits one to witness the same religious upheaval about which biblical texts speak, since those texts also show an awareness of the massive increase in the number of celestial-astral oriented cults in Judah during the seventh century.

§212.   On the southwestern periphery of the empire, in Judah and in northern Transjordan, the local so-called "Most High God" – in Judah: Yahweh – assumed lunar features under the influence of the Moon God of Haran. An enthroned figure, of the *El* type, appears on a typical seventh-century Palestinian seal group, in the act of blessing, as an anthropomorphic moon god (illuss. 303–307). A partially anthropomorphic El, who is giving a blessing, appears on the tridacna shells (illuss. 337a-b) as a celestial, creator god with solar connotations. Comparable changes and a *new tendency toward anthropomorphic representation* are noticeable even regarding the *asherah*. Even though the *asherah* was still thought of as a cultic symbol in the form of a stylized tree during the transition from the eighth century to the seventh century, as in earlier times (see illus. 308 for an uncommonly clear depiction of this form) and was connected with El (or Yahweh), subordinate to him and mediating his blessing, this symbol was eclipsed by another phenomenon that led in a totally different direction. In the second half of the eighth century, goddess figurines in the shape of the female body, in the form of pillar figurines (illuss. 321a-c), having been produced only rarely during Iron Age IIA-B in Israel and Judah, began to be manufactured in terra-cotta form in increasing numbers. By the turn of the century, this trend led to a widespread use of the figurines, especially in Judah, attributable to an interplay between familial or "private" piety and official state religion. This motherly goddess, whose image emphasizes especially the face (accessibility) and full breasts (blessing), appears to be none other than the (repersonalized) Asherah. According to biblical tradition, Manasseh set up a cultic image of the goddess in the Jerusalem Temple (2 Kgs 21:7; 23:6f.) that may have corresponded to the general tendency toward producing images of the female body.

Was the female form of Asherah in seventh-century Jerusalem the partner/consort of Yahweh? As attractive as such a conclusion might be, it is difficult to support. Even now, we have no clear evidence for a strict partner/consort relationship between Yahweh and Asherah. There are no pictures of a pair of deities in Judah. The rider terra-cottas and other male terra-cottas are not in a partner relationship with the goddess and cannot be connected with Yahweh. Neither biblical texts nor Iron Age IIC inscriptions offer any evidence for such a relationship. The seal in illus. 331b, with the image of a pair of deities, is not of Israelite-Judahite provenance, and it can be related only indirectly – if at all – to Yahweh and Asherah (see above, §197). *If* Yahweh did at some time have a partner, it would probably have been at the time of Manasseh. Nevertheless, we have not been able so far to find any solid evidence of any partner relationship in the sources.

§213. The terms *"Queen of Heaven"* and *"Host of Heaven"* provide evidence not only for the astral cults that flourished during the seventh century in Judah, but also for the infiltration of the Judahite religion by Assyrian cults. The evidence is too complex to justify simple generalizations that seek to attribute all the influences to any one factor alone. We have tried to explain both phenomena as part of the interplay of external and internal forces. The cult of the "Queen of Heaven" certainly did show clear Assyrian characteristics, apparently related especially to the cult of the Assyrian Ishtar, who must have been known in Palestine (§171), as one can see from the evidence provided by the seal amulets. This cult proved very influential in family piety (not being limited to any particular social stratum), but only because it could connect with indigenous traditions. The Judahite "Queen of Heaven" was probably none other than a resurrected form of the female human form of Asherah (§197). The cult of the "Host of Heaven" in Iron Age IIC appears to have been analogous to that of the "Queen of Heaven," depicted primarily as an astral cult oriented toward the stars of the night sky. At least indirectly, this might have been related to Aramean influence on the religious symbol system of Syria and Palestine, under Assyrian domination. But worship of the "Host of Heaven" need not be understood only by using the categories of the astral cult. It also found anthropomorphic-pictorial expression in family piety, in the form of horse-and-rider statuettes (§§198–200).

§214. The question about whether the Assyrian superpower exercised *religio-political coercion* in the provinces it conquered, e.g., Samaria, or in its vassal states, e.g., Judah, forcing its subjects to worship Assyrian deities, has been debated for a long time in Old Testament studies. J. McKay has recently rejected the idea of pressure; in the resurgence of the astral cult he sees a revival of old indigenous astral cults that were merely encouraged by the presence of Assyria (1973, 45–59). M. Cogan has advanced the thesis that the astral cults mentioned in the Bible are typically Syrian or Aramean (1974, 84–88). He differentiates between the religio-political treatment of peoples and districts that were brought into the Assyrian provincial system over against those that remained vassal states. In connection with the latter, among whom Judah and the Phoenician city-states were numbered, he suggests that "Assyria imposed no religious obligations upon its vassals" (1974, 85).

H. Spieckermann represents the opposite view and suggests that the Assyrians would have demanded that not only the provinces but also the vassals should demonstrate reverence, not only to the Assyrian king but also to the national deity Asshur and to the "greater deities" (*ilāni rabûti*) (1982, 322–344). The official declaration that the conquered people had been deserted by their own deities was made concrete by the deportation of their cultic statues, as, for example, from Samaria (1982, 344–354; see also Cogan 1974, esp. 22–34).

Obviously, this complex question cannot be answered simply by reference to small artifacts. Hypotheses that deal with this theme should not misuse the evidence. The small artifacts document only a marginal presence of actual Assyrian deities in Palestine, which in any case appear less frequently than the Assyrian king himself. Like the king, the Assyrian deities appear most frequently on cylinder seals that may have entered the country with the Assyrian/Aramean governmental officials, since they have been found in places that served as outposts for the Assyrian authorities. The marginal presence of Assyrian deities in the iconography of Palestine corresponds to their complete absence from local inscriptions. Unless the relation between the "Queen of Heaven" cult and the Assyrian Ishtar can be explained by means of some intermediary factors, then there is no evidence that the Assyrian administration made a deliberate attempt to propagate this cult through force. As far as the horses and chariot of the sun god mentioned in 2 Kgs 23:11 are concerned, we follow Spieckermann in associating them with typically Assyrian divination practices (§199). The fact that they were under the jurisdiction of an officer called Netanmelek ("the king has given" – a telling name?) might imply that their introduction by the "kings of Judah" could have been arranged by the Assyrians. Nevertheless, coercion regarding the *cult* was restricted. The Aramean influence, in any case, might have been stronger than the Assyrian. Even this might more likely be a concomitant of colonization and administration rather than an actual Assyrian directive.

The Assyrian conquests in Syria and Palestine, which resulted in the complete overthrow of Egypt's power during the first half of the seventh century, are certainly an important driving force for the new astral orientation of the Palestinian symbol system. The cultural pressure that a victorious power exercizes over those whom it has conquered cannot be understood by trying to find one common cause for everything, since it simultaneously operates on completely different planes: the political, the economic, the ideological, etc. The scratched drawings at Khirbet Beit Lei may give witness to a fascination with *military-political* relationships (Mittmann 1989); this is certainly true of the bulla of the "city commandant" of Jerusalem (illus. 345),[106] even though this evidence comes from at least a decade after the collapse of the Assyrian kingdom. The adoption of an iconic theme such as the killing of Humbaba by Gilgamesh and Enkidu (Keel, et al., 1990, 226–229) in the local stamp seal production of northern Palestine is evidence for the enormous *cultural* fascination that came about

---

106 The function of five limestone fragments from Tell es-Safi that are done in relief in the Assyrian style and the decoration on them, interpreted by the excavators as parts of a stele (Bliss/Macalister 1902, 41 with fig. 17; cf. Stern 1973, 13; Schroer 1987a, 189 with illus. 75), remains completely unclear.

through conquest. The cylinder seal from Beth-Shean shown in illus. 308 illustrates with extraordinary clarity how the new political reality created new plausibilities with regard to *religion* and how it demanded the accommodation of its own symbol system to brand new circumstances, while retaining its own central features. At the same time, by retaining solar motifs, Judah and Ammon expressed conservative tendencies that resisted adaptation to the Assyrian/Aramean symbolism (§§203f.).

In general, we attach more importance to the gradual, new formulation of indigenous concepts than to direct religio-political intervention by the Assyrian conquerors, which might have might have remained in force even in later times.[107] Otherwise, it would be difficult to understand why there is no evidence in the country during the time of Assyrian occupation for the ostensibly Assyrian cult of the "Queen of Heaven." That cult appears only long after the collapse of the Assyrian superpower, in the sixth century.

§215.   The design of this study makes it impossible to search within the archaeology of Israel/Palestine for proof of the historicity of the *cultic reforms of Josiah*.[108] There are other things to accomplish here. But a religio-historical study that has established, first of all, the enormous popularity of Asherah in a female human form and the so-called "Host of Heaven" in seventh-century Judah cannot help but detect *traces of an "early deuteronomistic," orthodox religious practice* that might be suggested by the artifacts that Judah left behind. We have found such evidence in Judahite name seal glyptic art from the end of the seventh century and from the beginning of the sixth century. These seals have largely abandoned iconic decoration. Where such does exist, it accentuates the imagery found in the temple (§§207f.). The fact that names that we know from the book of Jeremiah appear on bullae from Jerusalem archives of this period is no more an accident than the fact that the texts on the silver amulets from Ketef Hinnom (§210) are those we recognize from the Bible. These documents provide us with evidence for the existence of early exponents of a decidedly non-mythological movement that recognized neither Asherah nor another goddess, wanting instead to orient itself toward Yahweh and his temple alone. During the exilic and early postexilic periods, this movement gave us the Torah in its present form. The religious ambiance, documented for us by the silver amulets, name seals, and perhaps also by the bullae, points to a beginning of this effort among the élite from the capital city. The question of how the reform affected the specifics of religious practice in the country as a whole calls for separate investigation.

---

107 The deportation of Samaritan "deities" by Sargon II would belong here; see above, §136 note 99.

108 Earlier research concerning the excavations at Beer-sheba (disassembly of the squared stones from a monumental horned altar to be used in a wall of the barracks and under the glacis of Str. II, seventh century) and Arad (the con-struction of a casemate wall on top of the shrine) were readily interpreted as archaeological "evidence" for the cultic reforms that are connected with Hezekiah and Josiah in the Bible (for a discussion, see Conrad 1979, 28–33; Keel/Küchler 1982, 205–207, 227–233; H. Weippert 1988, 623f.). But as long as the shrine at Beer-sheba, to which the altar originally belonged, cannot be located exactly or dated with certainty, the reuse of the stone after the shrine was destroyed can only serve as a *terminus ante quem*. Concerning the temple at Arad, see above, §209 note 100.

IX

꧁꧂

An Era Ends:
Iron Age III

§216. A typical transition period comes once again with Iron Age III, which began in Judah in 598 and 587 with the conquest of Jerusalem by Nebuchadnezzar II and lasted until the institutional stabilization of the locally autonomous province of Yehud that began ca. 450 (Nehemiah). Politically, the loss of independent statehood for Judah, Ammon, Moab, and Edom, and their integration, first into the Babylonian and then into the Persian provincial system, are among the most important factors for an understanding of this period. From the Judean perspective, the loss of independence occurred together with the loss of territory, so that the Judean/Benjamite hill country and the northern Shephelah alone remained. The loss of territory brought about increasing cultural isolation for Judah. The Negev and southern Shephelah came into the hands of the Edomite and Arab tribes that controlled foreign trade over the so-called "incense road." The coastal plain was still controlled largely by somewhat autonomous city-states that traded throughout the entire Mediterranean world and remained open to cultural influences. Near Eastern deities, symbols, and cultic practices were transmitted through the Phoenician-Punic colonies all the way to Spain. As for the Philistine region to the south, Gaza and Ashkelon assumed a dominant position and continued to worship the goddess Astarte/Atargatis/Aphrodite (Gese 1971, 213f.). The northern region was dominated by the Phoenician city-state of Sidon. An inscription written by the king of Sidon, Eshmun-ʿazar, from the late sixth or early fifth century, tells us that the Persian emperor had transferred the cities of Dor and Jaffa, "rich lands of Dagan in the Plain of Sharon," to the Sidonian king (Butterweck 1988, 592). A votive inscription dedicated to Eshmun has been found in Jaffa (Stern 1982, 257 note 76). A fragment from a vessel from the late sixth or early fifth century has surfaced in Tel Michal. Before it was fired, an inscription was scratched into it. A. Rainey suggests that . . .]$b^clšm$ [. . . should be read as the name of the deity, Baalshamem (in Herzog 1989, 381f.).

In this chapter, we will sketch the religio-historical developments in Palestine in rough outline only. Since this is the main formative period for the writing of the Hebrew Bible and for the development of Jewish religion, it is also a most complex era and deserves an independent, far more detailed investigation. It is here that biblical texts take on even more value as sources. Nevertheless, these texts illuminate religion and history from points of view that have specific theological positions and have particular interests. They do not represent unbiased views of the religious situation, whether in Judah or in the neighboring regions. Thus we can still expect primary source material to come chiefly from archaeology. The results of efforts to integrate the fruits of such study are brought together in an exemplary fashion in the synthesis by E. Stern (1982).[1] But a diachronically arranged religio-historical study always faces the problem that it is not easy to distinguish the earlier Iron Age III, dominated by Babylon (ca. 587–539), from the later Iron Age III (i.e., the early "Postexilic Period," ca. 539–450) and from the period of the locally autonomous Persian province of Yehud (ca. 450–333). In view of the great importance of the period for the development of Judean-Jewish religion, such a differentiation is essential if one seeks to correlate the archaeological and literary-historical evidence in a plausible manner. The observations that now follow make no claim to being complete or even representative, but are intended only as a few, general, closing comments to provide perspective at the end of our overview of more than a millennium of Canaanite-Israelite religious history.

1. Symbols of Changing Foreign Domination

§217. As regards glyptic art, the cylinder seal form that had become widespread once again during the Assyrian Period fell into disuse during Iron Age III. Only a single Neo-Babylonian cylinder seal has been found in Palestine/Israel (Parker 1949, no. 7 = Ornan 1990, no. 34). It came from Tell Jemmeh and portrays a Babylonian hybrid creature of a kind not found on the local stamp seal glyptic art. It is thus a typical foreign product. More significant during Iron Age III are the more widely distributed conoids with facets, made of a hard stone (mostly agate or chalcedony). They are imports as well. These conoids have more or less carefully engraved *cultic scenes* on their bases; these depict a priest (always a man!) who worships in front of the cultic symbols of Marduk and Nabu, the two principal deities of the Babylonians (see above, illuss. 281, 291b). Above the cultic symbols one usually sees an astral symbol, which may be a star (**illus. 358a** from En Gedi; Bliss/Macalister 1902, 153 fig. 16.2; Reisner 1924, pl. 57.d7), a winged sun (Crowfoot, et al., 1953, 87 no. 19, pl. 15.19; cf. 88 no. 41), or a crescent moon (on an unpublished surface find from Midya/Modiʾim). On a bulla imprinted with a seal that was found at Tell el-Ajjul, instead of being in front of the symbols of Marduk and Nabu or before the emblem of Haran, as one might expect, the worshiper stands before a typically Babylonian cultic pedestal of the moon god Sin (**illus. 358b**). Above the worshiper there is a star. The motifs that fill the remaining space are difficult to interpret.

These seals and the seal impressions testify to a certain durability of the astral cult concepts during early Iron Age III among people who

---

1 See also H. Weippert's short summary of the "Babylonian/Persian Period" (586–333 B.C.) (1988, 697–718).

358a

358b

359

358c

360a

360b

361a

361b

361c

might have had direct contact with the Babylonian administration or who were even a part of it. Remarkably, nothing with comparable decoration has appeared thus far in the Judean heartland. A few years ago, P. Bordreuil (1986b, 305–307) published the seal of an official that can be dated on paleographic and stylistic grounds to the late sixth or early fifth century. It carries the legend *lpqd yhd*, thus appearing to have belonged to a (Persian) "Inspector of Judah/Yehud." It portrays a worshiper in front of the Aramean moon god who is positioned in a crescent moon (**illus. 358c**). A faceted conoid of this same type was discovered at el-Jib that portrays on its base nothing except an aniconic, Yahwistic name inscription (*l'nyhw bn hryhw*, **illus. 359**). The seal was apparently purchased before it was engraved and was provided with a Hebrew name inscription only later. It can hardly be by accident that the name of the female or male owner appears in place of the astral cultic scene on these and similar commercially acquired Hebrew name seals (cf. Stern 1982, 200f. with illuss. 327, 275 note 29).

§218. It is generally typical of Babylonian glyptic art that, in contrast to the Assyrians (see above, illus. 278b and §168) and the Persians, Babylon produced hardly any portrayals of the king. It is thus not surprising that no such depictions have appeared in Palestine either. This changed under the Achaemenids toward the end of the sixth century. A bulla found in Samaria portrays a *royal hero* fighting in battle against a hybrid creature that has the head and body of a lion and the wings and hindquarters of a griffin (**illus. 360a**; see Leith 1990, 398–410). On a scaraboid from Tell Keisan, the opponent is a winged bull (**illus. 360b**; see Leith 1990, 411–415). More frequently, the hero is represented in the central position in the composition as a "Lord of the Animals" who subdues two hybrid creatures, as, for example, on an agate scaraboid from Gezer (**illus. 361a**; see Leith 1990, 422–431). Seals such as this one were produced locally in Syria/Palestine at times as well, as is shown by the stylistic and iconographic characteristics on a fragmentary, typically Phoenician scarab from Samaria (**illus. 361b**), or on a scarab from Tell es-Safi (**illus. 361c**). On this last piece, the hero lacks any royal or Persian characteristics. Where he is shown wearing the royal crown, however, it may generally be assumed that the Persian king is being depicted, as in the Achaemenian palace relief that shows a warrior confronting mythical hybrid creatures (see Root 1979, 300–309).

The Syro-Phoenician seal carvers occasionally appropriated the tradition of the "Lord of the Animals," replacing the hybrid creatures with natural beasts, especially lions (Crowfoot, et al., 1957, 393 fig. 92.80; Hammond 1957; Keel-Leu 1991, nos. 106 and 167). On a bulla from Shechem, the king appears as an archer (Stern 1982, 197 fig. 317).[2] The winged sun disk (*not* Ahuramazda; see above, §172) frequently emphasizes the divine legitimation of the one who battles heroically for cosmic order.

---

2 For depictions of the hunt on horseback, on fifth-century scaraboids from Tell es-Safi and Samaria, see Bliss 1899, pl. 6.10 facing p. 332; Crowfoot, et al., 1957, pl. 15.15.

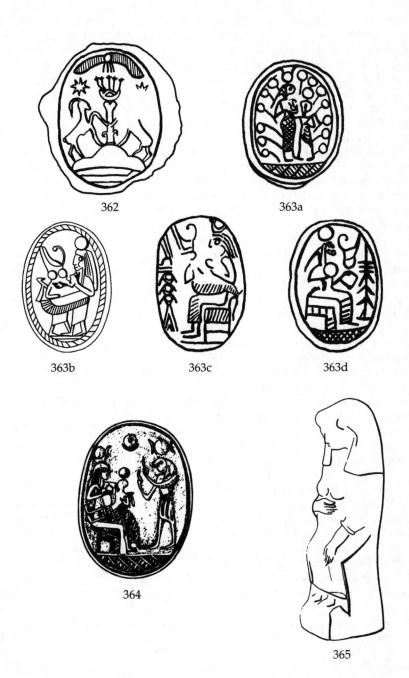

362

363a

363b

363c

363d

364

365

2. The Phoenician Economy

§219.   In the coastal plain, especially in the Sharon region and in the area around Acre, scarabs with Phoenician, Egyptian, and even Greek motifs dominate the stamp seal production of Iron Age III. As is well known, the Phoenicians and Punics are the actual heirs of the "Canaanite" culture. Representative of that culture at this point is the decoration on a seal that was pressed onto an Iron Age III bulla found in Acre. It portrays two caprids, one on either side of a stylized palmetto tree that stands on a mountain-like elevation; the constellation of the winged sun is arching overhead (**illus. 362**).

Such depictions, typical for the "Canaanite" tradition, are rather rare on Palestinian and also on Phoenician glyptic art during Iron Age III. Egyptian seal amulets and those showing Egyptian influence appear in greater numbers than either the Babylonian seals or, later, the Persian seals and are also superior in quality. With these seals, the form of the scarab again clearly becomes more dominant than the scaraboid. Cheaper pieces portray just one good luck sign, such as a striding or resting lion, but also have personal names or brief hieroglyphic formulas of personal piety (e.g., *p3 dy 3st* "given by Isis" and the like). Scarabs of higher quality portray Egyptian deities. Clearly the most commonly represented deity was *Isis*, nursing the infant Horus (see **illuss. 363a, c-d** from ʿAtlit, **illus. 363b** from Tel Megadim, **illus. 364** from Loḥame Ha-Getaʾot; on this, see Brandl 1991, 153–155). She is the goddess *par excellence* on the scarabs. It is no accident that she appears almost exclusively in her role as mother, obviously corresponding to a trend of the time. The role as mother also dominates images of the goddess in terra-cotta production much more than it did during Iron Age II. To be sure, images are still found that show the goddess naked, presenting her breasts (see below, illus. 377) or pressing on her lower body[3] (Stern 1982, 168; 272 note 53). But new types now gain in popularity, one shows a seated pregnant woman (**illus. 365**; cf. Stern 1982, 272 note 57; Culican 1986, 265–280) and one a goddess with a child (Stern 1982, 272 note 58). The great majority of the terra-cotta figures from Iron Age III come from *favissae*, meaning that they are discarded cultic and votive statuettes (Stern 1982, 158f.).

A still greater number of terra-cotta figurines were salvaged from a shipwreck near Shave Ziyyon, north of Acre (Linder 1973). Many of these figurines are on a pillar base that was stamped with the so-called Tinnit sign. This permits identification with the Phoenician-Punic goddess by name (Stieglitz 1990).

As for male images, we find a new, bearded, enthroned figure – a Greek-Cypriot-influenced Zeus figure, who can also be considered to

---

3 During Iron Age III, one sees roughly modeled, slender examples of this type that remind one of Chalcolithic ivory carvings and demonstrate impressively that this is an example of the *"longue durée"* phenomenon – "... were it not for their stratigraphic context, we would have imagined them to date hundreds or even thousands of years before this time" (Stern 1982, 168 on fig. 288, 1–2). Examples that match this from still later times are on Hellenistic bone and ivory figurines, shown in the "concubine" posture (see above, §124 note 22; for Iron Age II predecessors, see illus. 216).

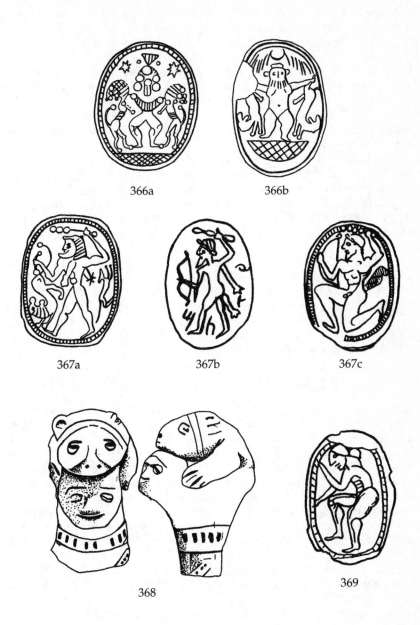

366a　　　　　　　366b

367a　　　　367b　　　　367c

368　　　　　　369

have been a descendant of El, like Baalshamem (Stern 1982, 165f.). The so-called horse-and-rider statuette type remained in production, with the rider often wearing typical Persian clothing (Stern 1982, 167f.). But the enthroned figure and the rider both seem to be absent from the seals. Instead, warrior figures are now being emphasized, analogous to the way the Persian kings were being depicted; see above, §218. A pictorial constellation shows Bes as "Lord of the Lions" in a scene that combines Egyptian and Asiatic iconographic themes (**illuss. 366a-b**; from ʿAtlit and Ashkelon; see Bisi 1980). In addition to these types, new motifs entered the Phoenician repertoire from Greece as well. We find many examples of Heracles fighting a lion or appearing as a war hero (**illus. 367a-c** from ʿAtlit; see Keel-Leu 1991, no. 108; Leith 1990, 146–176). He appears not only on scarabs but even on items from the rather conservative terra-cotta industry, as is demonstrated by a small head of Heracles that was found at Lachish (**illus. 368**). In addition to Heracles, the naked gymnast in **illus. 369** shows with absolute clarity that the increasing Greek influence resulted in the spread of a value system that recognized a clear separation of gender roles. For males, it encouraged a high valuation of the body and physical-athletic power; for females, it deified motherhood.

Toward the end of Iron Age III, new types of terra-cotta imported from regions of Greece and from Cyprus entered the "oriental" tradition (Stern 1982, 172–176). These mark the transition to a new era and can therefore be ignored here, as can the bronze figurines that appear for the first time in the fourth century. According to what has been discovered to date, they are clearly made using Egyptian themes, even though they are actually produced in Palestine (Stern 1982, 177–182).

3. Old and New in Northern Arabian and Edomite Forms

§220. *Small limestone incense boxes* were characteristic pieces of sacred ware, especially for southern Palestinian house and domestic religion, during Iron Age III and the Persian Period (Stern 1982, 182–195; O'Dwyer Shea 1983; Zwickel 1990a, 62–109). We find the same kind of incense container in the Neo-Babylonian and Persian Periods in Mesopotamia, where they were made of clay, of course, and in southern Arabia, where they were also made of limestone. Though the purely ornamental, incised decorations are typical of the Mesopotamian group and the majority of the southern Arabian boxes are characterized by name inscriptions, most of the Palestinian incense boxes are known for decorations that take the form of roughly incised drawings. The iconography of these incised drawings has not yet had the benefit of systematic, scholarly study. At first glance, these images appear to follow old "Canaanite" traditions that reach back at times to the Bronze Age, such as in the juxtaposition of a palm tree and the facade of a temple or palace (?, **illus. 370** from Lachish;[4]

---

4 The inscription that names the owner appears to identify the object as an "incense altar (*lbnt*) belonging to Iyosh, the son of Maḥalai, the king"; nevertheless, the reading and interpretation are the subject of much debate (see Zwickel 1990a, 76 with note 90).

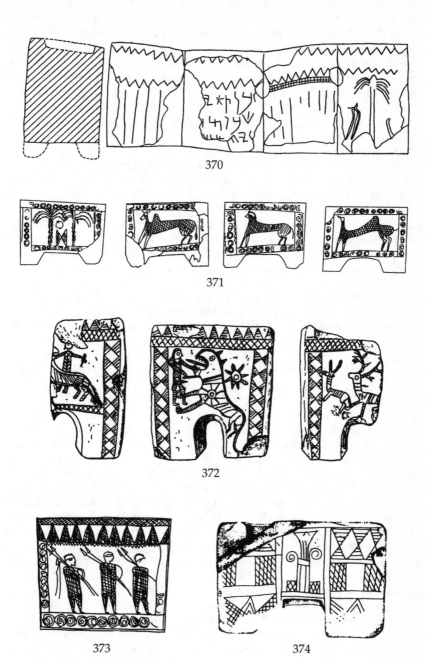

370

371

372

373   374

see above, illus. 55a) or the representation of a stylized human figure(?) between palm trees, toward which animals are moving (**illus. 371** from Tell Jemmeh; concerning dating this to the sixth century, see Zwickel 1990a, 78f.). In addition to the usual domestic and wild animals, we find some rather unusual ones represented on the small boxes, such as the oryx antelope, two addax antelope, and at least one camel. Thus we may surmise that even though there is a clear relationship to the south Arabian pieces typologically, most of the boxes were probably produced and decorated by northern Arabian craftsmen. The aromatics trade over the incense road was completely in Arab hands (see H. Weippert 1988, 717).

The battle against a lion on a piece from Gezer (**illus. 372**) is also rooted ultimately in the Bronze Age (see above, illuss. 88ff.); the close frontal combat is quite typical of Iron Age II-III (see above, illuss. 278b, 359a), and we are thus able to interpret this figure, perhaps like the terra-cotta shown in illus. 368, as a local portrayal of Heracles. Typical local aspects can also be detected in the portrayal of the warriors(?) on a small box from Tell el-Far'ah (south) that dates to the early fifth century (**illus. 373**; cf. illus. 221). Finally, a piece from Tel Sera' is especially important. It depicts a pillar with a type of "Proto-aeolian" capital (**illus. 374**; cf. illuss. 193, 352a).

§221.   A few years ago, an Edomite shrine was excavated at *Hurvat Qitmit*, in the eastern Negev, about 25 km east of Beer-sheba and about 10 km south of Arad. The smaller artifacts, especially terra-cotta figures, caused quite a sensation. Since the results of the archaeological excavation itself (Beit-Arieh 1991), as well as a description of the small finds (Beit-Arieh/Beck 1987), have been published in a very preliminary form only, we must limit ourselves to a few brief references. The site dates to the last phase of Iron Age IIC or to early Iron Age III (first half of the sixth century).

The shrine of Hurvat Qitmit was not connected to any permanent settlement but apparently served as a cultic center for the entire region, which by this time was in Edomite hands once again. The installation is comprised of two buildings, each apparently serving different cultic purposes. Building A was rectangular and consisted of three long, parallel rooms that opened toward a courtyard that was situated south of it. Building B was square and shaped like a tower. Building B contained benches or podia and an altar-like platform, constructed with uncut stones, was in the courtyard in front of it, along with a basin and a sacrificial stone(?) for the cultic functions of the site. H. Weippert (1988, 625) has noted that comparable structures have been found at Kadesh Barnea, at Idumean Lachish and Marisa for the Hellenistic Period, and even later at Nabatean temples. The three-part adyton [Tr.: innermost sanctuary] is thus most likely a characteristic feature of Edomite-Idumean sacral architecture (see also Beit-Arieh 1991, 114). The cultic interpretation of the architecture was determined by the presence of ash piles, remnants of animal bones, and especially by the numerous fragments of cultic stands and terra-cotta figurines.

Animal bones, figurine fragments, and a *maṣṣebah* at Building B all indicate that it also served a cultic function; a fragment of a vessel with

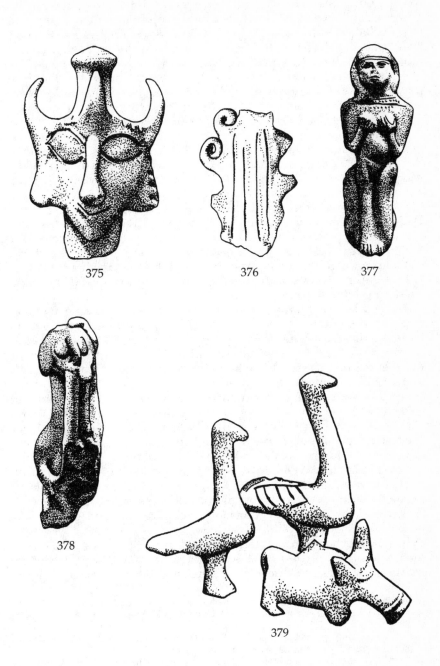

375

376

377

378

379

the incised inscription . . .]*blqwshp*[. . . was found in Building B (Beit-Arieh 1991, 108f.). The element *qws* may reproduce the name of the Edomite national god Qaus, which would support the ethnic attribution of the whole site. It is very likely that the *maṣṣebah* represents the god Qaus[5] and that Building B was used for the cult of this deity. Unfortunately, from the reports published thus far, we are not able to determine which terra-cottas came from this building. Fragments of small anthropomorphic and theriomorphic figurines and larger statuettes were apparently found scattered over the entire area (approximately 300 fragments were discovered before the excavation even began!).

The most significant terra-cotta discovery was made in the courtyard in front of Building A. It includes a hand that holds a dagger (Beit-Arieh/Beck 1987, 21), a dagger, and an arm that likewise appears to have held a weapon (Beit-Arieh/Beck 1987, 24f. [Hebrew]; Beit-Arieh 1991, 100f. fig. 7f.). These pieces probably were from a statue of a warrior deity (or a human warrior?).[6] Once again, the deity with the dagger could represent Qaus. But perhaps it is his female partner; the three-horned head from her statue is preserved as well (**illus. 375**; Beck 1986b; Beit-Arieh/Beck 1987, 27f., 32 [Hebrew]). Similar features are seen on Bronze Age metal statuettes of a goddess with a three-horned helmet (Seeden 1980, nos. 1724, 1726) that show a dagger or a fan in her left hand, while her right hand is raised to strike.

The goddess of Hurvat Qitmit cannot be identified by name. It would be premature to identify her as Astarte if the identification were based on indirect indications of her seemingly aggressive character. Another terra-cotta, in the shape of a stylized tree (**illus. 376**), poses the question of whether this might rather be an Edomite variation of Asherah. But that is a question we cannot yet answer with any certainty. There is also a statuette of a naked woman or goddess who presents her breasts, without horned helmet or any attributes of a deity (**illus. 377**; see above, §57ff., 124, 196). A double-pipe player (**illus. 378**; see above, §102) and other small anthropomorphic terra-cottas ought not be identified as deities, but are probably human male and female worshipers.[7] In general, the discoveries at Hurvat Qitmit are convincing evidence of the inertia with respect to traditional "Canaanite" religion that existed in a peripheral region like Edom. One could imagine oneself transported at this site right back into a long-past era of "Canaanite" religion, with god and goddess visibly standing side-by-side as partners.

Among the theriomorphic figurines at Hurvat Qitmit, besides a sphinx (Beit-Arieh 1987, 14) and the less surprising cattle and sheep, there are numerous images of ostriches and apparently also an image of a pig[8]

---

5 A red-painted *maṣṣebah*, in the slightly older temple of Arad (see above, §209, note 100) may have represented the Judean national god Yahweh (Keel/Küchler 1982, 231).

6 A kneeling man (Beit-Arieh/Beck 1987, 14 [Hebrew]) could be interpreted as an enemy who is being forced to assume that posture.

7 A worshiper can be seen on a stamp seal as well (Beit-Arieh/Beck 1987, 22 [Hebrew]).

8 Hübner has assembled impressive evidence on swine-herding in Iron Age Palestine (1989b). In Isa 65:4 and 66:3, 17, swine are mentioned in a cultic context as possible food offerings. Since both passages show a knowledge of the food prohibitions in

(illus. 379). The ostrich, of course, recalls the "Lord of the Ostriches." Like Qaus, and originally also like Yahweh, this deity was at home in the steppe. We have already referred to the affinity between Yahweh and the "Lord of the Ostriches" (see above, §85) and to that between Yahweh and Teman/Edom (see above, §135). The concept of Yahweh as "Lord of the Ostriches" provides the frame of reference for Job 39:13–16 (Keel 1978, 64–68, 102–108, 114f.). Job's home is not to be sought in northwestern Arabia just by chance (Knauf 1988c). Do "Yahweh of Teman," Qaus, and the "Lord of the Ostriches" all have their roots finally in one and the same figure? If the answer is "yes," for how long were they understood to be identical to one another or at least related?

From the perspective of biblical texts, Iron Age III is also the time when there was a definitive break between Judah and Edom (see Bartlett 1989, 175–186). If the discoveries at Hurvat Qitmit present an accurate picture of late Iron Age "Canaanite" religion on the southern periphery of Palestine, the archaeologically documented situation in *Judah* during Iron Age III is clearly different.

4. Judah: Exclusivity

§222.   The complexity of the religious history of Judah during Iron Age III is increased by the need to take into account the religious traditions of the groups that were dislocated when they were exiled to Babylon and Egypt, as well as for those who remained in Judah. The three groups lived in different political, social, and cultural contexts, which affected the Judean-Jewish religious concepts in different ways. Mesopotamian, Persian, and Egyptian ideas had an impact on the Judean diaspora. And yet, the contrast between their views and those of the residents of the foreign lands actually led them to justify for themselves their religious ideas and caused a conscious sharpening of their own unique identity.

Many of the religious concepts of Judaism that seem so obvious to us today were formulated explicitly for the first time in the isolation of the *Babylonian Exile*. These include the credal tenet of monotheism (the monotheism of Deutero-Isaiah is hardly to be taken as independent from the Achaemenian worship of Ahuramazda), and the concomitant, mocking polemic against the production of so-called graven images (see Schroer 1987a, 196–221) is stated explicitly for the first time. For the élite among the Judean society, who were deported to Babylon early in the sixth century, the exile provided an opportunity to collect and reformulate the religious traditions of the motherland. The criteria for the selection and transmission of the traditions, both historical and prophetic, were established by a "priestly" and a "deuteronomistic" school.

Lev 11:7 and Deut 14:8 that prohibit eating meat from pigs, such offerings are held up for scorn. These prohibitions probably would have been formulated in exilic or early postexilic times. But even if the actual observance of this prohibition was not particularly rigorous in postexilic Judah, it is hardly conceivable that a pig would be considered as a votive offering in Judah during the sixth century. The ostrich also appears among the unclean animals in Lev 11:16 and Deut 14:15.

Inhabitants of the Jewish military colony at *Elephantine* in Upper Egypt, on the other hand, demonstrated that their version of the religion had "syncretistic" tendencies. Certainly they followed the Yahwistic El-traditions of Iron Age IIC, but, apparently following the lead of some colonists from Phoenicia concerning the partner/consort issue, they recognized and acknowledged alongside Yahweh a female deity, Anat (see above, §120). This is merely a variant form of the "Late-Canaanite" religion that was common throughout the Levant and that we encounter in Hurvat Qitmit. For this religion, there was a small pantheon, with a pair of deities at its peak.

The religious situation and the conceptual world of the population that remained in *Judah* in early Iron Age III (sixth century) is more difficult to assess. The transitions between the outgoing Iron Age IIC and the early Iron Age III, on the one hand, and the transition from the Babylonian Period to the Persian Period, on the other hand, are often difficult to detect archaeologically. The biblical traditions connected with the reconstruction of the Jerusalem Temple in the last quarter of the sixth century, chiefly as reported in the books of the prophets Haggai and Zechariah, show us that the return of the exiles, with their claims on political and religious leadership, led to massive conflicts of interest, as well as social, economic, and religious tensions between the returnees and those who had remained in the country. These conflicts, the rigorous restrictions imposed by the new leadership (see Hag 2:10–14), and the fact that the temple restoration was carried out, to a large extent, under the impetus of the returning members of the Babylonian diaspora (see Zechariah 6) allow us to surmise that the Jewish women and men who had remained in Palestine had continued to follow the popular religious ideas and practices from Iron Age IIC after they emerged from under the pressure imposed by the priestly-deuteronomistic élite who had now been taken into exile.

§223. Excavations at Jerusalem, Ramat Rahel, Gibeon, Tell en-Nasbeh, Jericho, and En Gedi have thus far provided us with about 70 impressions on vessel handles that were made by anepigraphic seals, each portraying one animal. An isolated example appears at Shechem (Wright 1965, fig. 93). The vessel handles can be dated to the sixth and fifth centuries. The animal stamp, in a way that parallels the use of the royal stamp at the end of the eighth century (see above, §162) and the rosette stamp during the seventh century (see above, §204), appears to have been an instrument used by the Judean administration (Stern 1982, 209–213).

The motif we find most frequently, at least 60 times and in numerous variations, is a *lion* that stands on all four feet, with jaws either open or closed (**illus. 380a-b** from Ramat Rahel). In one case, only the forepart of the lion is shown (Aharoni 1962, pl. 8.6 = Stern 1982, 210 fig. 348.3), unless this is simply a careless, incomplete impression of the seal. It is characteristic of the lion standing in this position to have its tail raised high above its back. This detail, plus the fact that the lion is standing on a base line on seal impressions from En Gedi (Mazar/Dunayevski 1964, pl. 27E), may show that the motif is a kind of later version of the roaring lion that appeared on the seals of Israelite officials during Iron Age IIB (see above, §118). But the roaring lion has traditions of its own in Judah (see above, illuss. 206a-b).

In addition to the lion standing on all fours, there are three cases where a lion stands on its hind legs (**illus. 381a** from el-Jib; **illuss. 381b-c** from Ramat Rahel). Next to the lion, Stern has been able to identify a degenerate form of an incense stand or "fire-altar" (1982, 212). But his thesis that the upright lion conveys the idea that the animal is wounded and in agony, and that this supposedly depicts an abbreviated form of the Achaemenian king-on-a-lion-hunt, seems less plausible (1982, 212). In contrast to the parallels cited by Stern, there is no arrow sticking in the lion's body on the Jewish versions of the stamps. Late Assyrian and Late Babylonian representations show the lion being attacked but as yet unharmed by the king (see above, illus. 278b), as it stands on its hind legs and strikes with its claws (cf. Börker-Klähn 1982, nos. 259, 268). This posture is not supposed to accentuate the agony of the animal, but its rage and aggressiveness.

Stern correctly observes that Judean seal engravers may have adopted the motif of the lion standing on its hind legs from Achaemenian glyptic art themes. The major difference is that these artisans did not choose to depict a wounded animal but one that is especially aggressive. One cannot know for certain whether this lion is to be treated as a symbol for Judah (Gen 49:9; cf. Ezek 19:2–9; H. Weippert 1988, 718), a symbol which would later be replaced after 450 by an aniconic administrative seal that had the inscription *yh(w)d*, though this is certainly possible (Stern 1982, 202–206). Nor can we tell whether the royal animal represents Yahweh symbolically "roaring from Zion" (see Amos 1:2, cf. 3:8; Jer 25:30; Joel 4:16). The incense stand next to the lion suggests that the latter interpretation cannot be excluded.

§224. A few other vessel handles with seal impressions have been found in Ramat Rahel, with images that differ from those described above. A four-legged creature is on these seal impressions, with a round disk above the head of the animal (**illus. 382a**). The excavator initially spoke cautiously when the first impression was discovered (illus. 382a) and characterized this as an "animal in the usual posture" but later went on to identify the animal as a bull, wearing a solar disk between its horns (Aharoni 1962, 10; cf. 1964, 22, 45). He gained quite a following for this interpretation (P. Welten in Galling ²1977, 307; Stern 1982, 211; Ahlström 1984, 130, and many others), even though the interpretation of the iconography is not especially convincing, particularly when the image is compared with pieces found at a later time (e.g., **illus. 382b**). Bulls were usually portrayed in the ancient Near East with their tails hanging down (see above, illuss. 143, 169, 207–209; Bordreuil 1986a, nos. 69, 75, 103f., 107, etc.); the tail raised high over the back is much more typical of the way lions were represented (see above, illuss. 3, 5–6, 89, 133, 138, 145, 205, 206a, 231a, 268, 377; Bordreuil 1986a, nos. 1, 87–89, etc.; cf. a lion and a bull side by side in illuss. 169, 191). That criterion is not unequivocal (see illus. 99). Leaping bulls with tails held high were a popular motif in Ammonite glyptic art dated to the seventh century (e.g., Bordreuil 1986a, nos. 72–74; Hübner 1992). In each of those cases, however, the horns and rump are clearly engraved to depict a bovine, which we are not able to

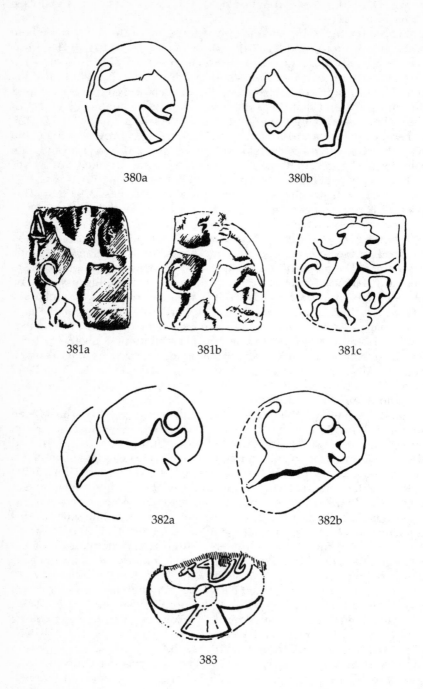

380a

380b

381a

381b

381c

382a

382b

383

say with confidence about the sketchy shapes shown in illuss. 382a-b. Since, as far as we know, there is no tradition for depicting the bull in Judean glyptic art, the leaping four-legged creature in illuss. 382a-b – in view of the general kinship with the seal impressions in illuss. 380–381 – is more likely an attacking lion, and the head of the lion, analogous to illuss. 381a-b, can be interpreted as having an open mouth.

The solar disk on the lion's head makes it probable that the aggressive animal – and consequently perhaps also those shown in illuss. 380–381 – may represent a solar connotation of Yahweh of Zion. We find even clearer sun symbolism on a bulla impression from En Gedi that might date to the sixth century, which seems to be a late variation of the royal stamp that dates to the end of the eighth century (**illus. 383**). The inscription above the solar disk, which has both wings and a tail, is likely Aramaic and is to be read *lmr'* "for the lord" or "belonging to the lord" (Mazar, et al., 1966, 34f.). We cannot identify this lord. But there can be hardly any doubt that the winged sun represents the solar god of heaven. In Isa 60:19f., the light of Yahweh transcends both sun and moon. But even in postexilic times, the God of Jerusalem was conceived primarily in terms of a "being of light," related to the sun, as Isa 60:1–3 and Mal 3:20 show very clearly. In retrospect, this solar dimension should be seen as a constant element – even though flexible and adaptable – in Israelite and Judean worship of Yahweh (see Stähli 1985; Niehr 1990, 150–161).

§225.   The discussion in the preceding chapter showed that the Judean name seals and bullae give evidence, already in Iron Age IIC, of a strong development toward aniconicity or purely ornamental design. This tendency apparently persisted into Iron Age III and even intensified. Seventy bullae, found in an admittedly illegal excavation at an early postexilic Judean site, show impressions that are exclusively simple name seals (Avigad 1976; cf. 1986, 122). The discovery contrasts sharply with that of an archive from the fourth century, found at Wadi ed-Daliyeh in Samaria, whose bullae display a colorful mixture of Greek and Persian images (Leith 1990).

§226.   How did Judahite religion develop during Iron Age III in the way it viewed the *goddess* and her relation to Yahweh? In the absence of a corpus, it is at present hard to say precisely how long the horse-and-rider figurines in terra-cotta (see above, §§198ff.) or the pillar figurines of the goddess (see above, §§190ff.) remained in use *in Judah*. One cannot assume that there is an unbroken line of continuity for pillar figurines in Judah that lasted on into the Persian Period (thus Hübner 1989a, 55). E. Stern has referred to the fact that there are hardly any terra-cotta or bronze figurines at all in *postexilic* Judah (1982, 158ff.). If isolated statuettes have been found in border areas, such as Lachish, this may be an indication that the settlement did not belong to Judah/Yehud (1989b, 53f.).

Not only figurines seem to disappear from about the fifth century on. The Egyptian, Phoenician, and Greek image seals and incense boxes discussed in this chapter are also found only infrequently in Judah. Generally, there are now "clear cultural and cultic boundaries within Palestine that coincide with those political boundaries known from historical tradition" (H. Weippert 1988, 717f.).

The contrast is striking between the discoveries on the coastal plain and in the Edomite-Arabic south (Hurvat Qitmit!). There was apparently no market for the inexpensive and once popular terra-cotta images in postexilic Judah, whether because religious development had advanced so far in the direction of monotheism that the need was no longer that great or because so-called "orthodox" circles in postexilic Judah had effectively halted the production or import of these goods. There has been too little scholarly analysis of the relevant, religio-historical material that remains from Iron Age III for us to be more precise about the control and sanction mechanisms exercised by the political authorities and about the internal shifts concerning the religious needs of the Judean population.

§227. Biblical evidence points to the fact that there was significant pressure from above and that religious control was exercised by the priestly and "deuteronomistic" returnees who were able to concentrate political and religious power under their own control after the return authorized by the Persian king Cyrus in 539. The generation that restored the temple about 520 was concerned about establishing clear lines of demarcation. The seventh vision of the prophet Zechariah, which personifies everything "evil" in the form of a woman(!) and shows her being transported in a closed vessel to southern Babylonia (Zech 5:5–11), lumps foreign cults and goddess worship together. The political-religious leadership that surrounded Zerubbabel and the high priest Joshua was vigorously oriented toward cultic orthodoxy and clearly wished to differentiate themselves from foreigners. One sees this when the leadership excludes those who had not been exiled so that they cannot help with the restoration of the temple, a practice that can be detected in the background of Hag 2:10–14. They particularly had their sights set on stopping all worship of the goddess. Since they can be seen censuring themselves, it is surprising how openly the Torah, the basic law as it was edited in the locally autonomous province of Judah ca. 450, could speak of *masṣebahs*, sacred trees, teraphim, and the like in the Genesis patriarchal traditions. In the larger context of the Pentateuch, these were nothing other than relics of a long distant past "when the Canaanites were in the land" (Gen 12:6; cf. 13:7).

The Chronicler's view of history, compiled in the fourth century, sought to eliminate all traces of the goddesses (Astarte and most especially Asherah), which had still been mentioned in the deuteronomistic history, from its own "worldview," specifically from the picture the Chronicler painted of the history of Israel and Judah. By silence or reinterpretation, even the existence of the goddess was now virtually denied (Frevel 1991). The Chronicler was less zealous about removing all mention of Baal or Dagan. This may be related to the fact that these two deities constituted no great threat in Judah. The decisive question at the time of the Chronicler was no longer about foreign cults and gods. The dangerous issues concerned the existence of the goddess, her status and function alongside Yahweh – and particularly the unimpeded continuation of the worship of goddesses in neighboring regions, goddesses such as Astarte/Atargatis/Aphrodite in Gaza, Ashkelon, and other city-states. By now, she had been promoted to equal rank with Tyche and the highest city goddess, possessing significantly more important shrines than any of her male colleagues.

But threatening as the question apparently was, the context in which the goddess could function and be worshiped in Judah was very restricted. The goddess could find no justifiable role in the legal-cultic, historical, and prophetic traditions. Only in postexilic theological speculation about wisdom was it possible, within a monotheistic-Yahwistic viewpoint about God, to think explicitly about personified wisdom as a way to show an explicitly female dimension of God. Patterned on contemporary worship of Isis, through the use of some metaphorical footprints, the heritage of the "Canaanite" Asherah lived on (see Camp 1985; Schroer 1991).

X

❧❦❧

Summary and Conclusion

1. Word and Picture

§228.   People who have never concerned themselves with the unique possibilities of words and pictures usually think that pictures are vague and ambiguous, whereas words are precise and clear. It is easy to demonstrate that this judgment is rash. An employee at the Swiss embassy in Teheran complained recently, in an oft-cited newspaper article, that if passports showed photos of women wearing heavy, black veils, they would be nearly impossible to identify. The names on the document would be no substitute for the customary photograph.

Biblical scholars also know how inadequate words are as a means of expression. They don't "trust words" (Goethe, *Faust*). One glance at a dictionary or commentary is all one needs in order to see how vague and ambiguous words can be. The word "goddess" is much more vague and ambiguous than a picture showing the goddess standing, naked, with flowers in her hand, or clothed, enthroned, with a child on her lap. Language, it is argued, gives these goddesses names and gives them their uniqueness: Anat, Asherah, Astarte. This is correct and has always been most useful for the practice of religion. The name identifies the male or female who is addressed in the cult, in hymns, and in petitions. Whoever has learned to turn to Jesus in prayer will not suddenly replace his name with "Vishnu." But, like everything linguistic, names are artificial, as a rule. Their expressivity rests upon conventions. Conventions can change easily and unilaterally. Criminals change their names like shirts.

Names give only general information, or none at all, about the essence of the deity addressed and worshiped. They can be attached to a deity much as one affixes a label. The Egyptian tree goddess who can be seen in pictures from the Eighteenth through the Twenty-first Dynasties, next to the grave of the person who has died, either has no name or she can be designated with various names (Nut, Neith, Isis, Maʿat, etc.). Yet her appearance and function are always the same. A name captures only a small part of the identity of a deity or else provides no information at all. The essence of that identity is expressed in a much more striking way by the functions of the deity and roles played by that deity. For the most part, the name can offer little more than a kind of etymology of the deity. "Yahweh" may originally have meant "he blows" (Knauf 1984). But no one would want to maintain that this etymology, itself no longer understood in preexilic Israel, expresses the dominant aspect of the God of Israel. What did "Asherah" mean? Did the term always mean the same thing? If so, what: a natural tree, an artificial tree, a pole, an anthropomorphic image? If an anthropomorphic image, what kind: a naked goddess or a clothed, enthroned lady? Or is it not an object or sculpted image at all, but rather the concept of a goddess who is perceived as a heavenly, personal being? Or does it refer not just to one *or* the other, but to various aspects and forms that are mixed together? It is quite improbable that names like "Asherah," "Baal," or "Yahweh" always referred to the same singular reality or concept.

For this reason, a good identity card *combines* evidence from both word and picture as one tries to make sense of such names. The picture reproduces the specific, physiognomic constellation. The specially coined vocabulary classifies the reflection of reality ("Portuguese female," "Romanian male," etc.), it individualizes ("born February 3, 1938", supplying a name), and it assigns value ("years as a resident," permission for permanent residency), with a power that goes beyond the picture.

Language owes this superiority to its complete artificiality – if we ignore the few onomatopoetic sounds like the "hoooot" of the owl or the "bow-wow" of the dog. It gives to language a special precision that is all its own. It is a much more flexible and pliable medium. It can be absolutely precise and yet it can provide generalizations. It is able to identify not only species and sub-species, but also can give names to each individual example, while at the same time bringing all creatures together under a single designation. But the whole art of language rests, as has been said, on conventions and codes. If these conventions are not known or accepted, precision disappears. Then what appears to be precise really is not. Apparent precision has resulted in an intellectual attraction to texts and has stimulated readers for centuries to try to clarify the meaning of the written word, with ever newer approaches being developed to try to achieve this knowledge.

Unlike speech, which is a human construct, graphic images share at least some similarity with the reality they seek to portray. If a worm has been drawn well, it can be recognized as easily by a German as by someone who is Chinese; even a fish may react to the picture. But because the picture is closer to the reality it depicts, it usually shows this reality as somewhat complex. Unlike language, it is not limited to listing a few isolated aspects of what it shows. The power of the image is in its ability to portray several aspects simultaneously; to put it another way: it represents the complexity of the reality that is portrayed in the pictorial constellation. Returning to the passport picture: words are too general and inadequate when it comes to accurately describing the relationship between the forehead and the nose, the nose and the eyes, the eyes and the cheeks, the cheeks and the mouth, the mouth and the chin, etc. When the issue concerns constellations and relationships, pictures are far more potent than words. So constellations of images depict the essence of numerous narrative structures that expand on their themes but can be reduced to the essential narrative once again (see above, §6).

§229.   Anyone who wants to reconstruct the religious symbol system of Canaan and Israel accurately, and is not content with mere supposition, cannot avoid pictures. The way a particular world appeared can be seen again and again by looking at its pictures and some important aspects are detected only in such depictions. It is a crass anachronism to continue to assert, as do those scholars who put no stock in images, that pictures are meaningless decoration. The idea that pictures and their production were important only if they measured up to some primarily or even exclusively formal and aesthetic standard is a viewpoint that is no older than the nineteenth century and is typical of so-called "enlightened," western civilization. Only modern western-thinking individuals hold such a view. The majority of ancient Near Eastern and ancient Egyptian sign systems are better described as "a valiant attempt of magic and religion at co-existence" (Goldwasser/Laor 1991, 50).

The world of Canaanite-Israelite religion is foreign to us. A deaf-mute from the western world, suddenly transported to ancient Palestine, would find it easier to adjust than would a blind person similarly transported. The blind person would be able to make sense of almost nothing; for somebody who was deaf or mute, the problem would be only partial. Many biblical scholars work their way through ancient Palestine like the blind, having learned the idiom or idioms of that world with much difficulty. Alternatively, they translate these idioms into their own world, harmonizing this alien world with their own cosmos, and they operate chiefly by setting the one at odds with the other. This approach to the biblical texts is based on a one-sided view of the Bible as the *Word* of God. It is theologically problematic and historically inappropriate, because it does not investigate the life behind the word. It understands the text in an abstract sense, not as a partial expression of a far more complex system of a whole culture.

Unfortunately, those who pay little attention to iconography are, generally speaking, less aware of their ignorance than those who are unable to read. Since pictures are less arbitrary and artificial than language, they rarely lead to complete incomprehension, as happens with writing and speech. The visual world is more cross-cultural than the verbal world. People in Europe or America can understand a Chinese film without subtitles more easily than a Chinese radio program.

2. A New Undertaking

§230. The one-sided orientation toward the world of hearing (and reading) has led to the situation that the religious history of Palestine (ca. 1800–500) has been reconstructed predominantly on the basis of two lexical corpora: the texts of Ugarit (especially the mythology) and the Hebrew Bible, and this situation continues. Recently discovered Israelite and Judean inscriptions are screened through the symbol system deduced from Ugaritic texts and then interpreted on this basis.

The problems are inescapable. The main difficulty is the distance, physical and temporal, that separates the texts of Ugarit and Palestine during the period from 1800–500. Ugarit is about 400 km (240 miles) from Jerusalem, about the same distance as Jerusalem is from Memphis, Egypt, an intellectual center of the first order. The production of the Ugaritic texts ended about 1200, thus about the mid-point of the period that concerns us here, and at a time when not a single biblical text had yet been written. Therefore, trying to make sense of the symbol system of ninth- or seventh-century Palestine with the aid of texts from Ugarit is extremely problematic. Frequently, these can offer nothing more than "parallels," a situation which increases the likelihood that someone will try to use them to fill in details. They are not primary sources for the religious history of Canaan and Israel.

The problem with biblical texts is that they were recopied, adapted, and purged over the centuries. Even if some bits from preexilic times remain amidst all the alterations, the symbol system can hardly be reconstructed convincingly to reach a consensus, given the contemporary views about the uniqueness and age of these texts.

§231.   The nature of the sources (texts from Ugarit and from the Bible) has meant that most reconstructions have been largely conjectural; the solutions that have been proposed have been filled in imaginatively with evidence from various times and places, arranged like pieces of a mosaic. The procedure is only marginally historical and is generally subject to little critical analysis.

In view of this situation, we have here for the first time, with full awareness of the limitations and deficiencies connected with an initial effort, attempted to travel a different route. With the aid of a systematic evaluation of the archaeological material, and paying strict attention to a specific geographical area and historical time period, we have attempted to reconstruct the symbol system for each of a series of periods that can be differentiated archaeologically. Emphasis has been placed upon iconography. Inscriptions have been introduced to supply supporting evidence whenever religio-historically relevant. Temple floor plans, which in our opinion are less useful, have not been treated systematically. We have ranked seal amulets as the most important images; some also have inscriptions. Because of their number, continuity, and somewhat public nature, they carry special weight, but they, particularly, have been grossly neglected. After reconstructing the symbol system of each period in this manner, we referred repeatedly, especially in the chapters devoted to the first millennium, to parallels or analogous passages in the Hebrew Bible. This is only a beginning, an initial impulse. Much work remains to be done in this field.

3. Focal Points for the Individual Periods

We began ca. 1800 with Middle Bronze Age IIB because there was a considerable gap just before that time and the reurbanization of Palestine that followed initiated a continuous development of the symbol system down to the sixth century. In this process, many concepts that no longer expressed the creative power of an idea from its original period were transferred from one age to the next (see above, §4). The following summary is intended to delineate those unique elements that seem to characterize each period. In each case, the ideas that were adopted in one period from the preceding era are noted briefly and then the actual new items are highlighted. References back to illustrations in the book are intended to help provide a quick orientation.

Interaction of the Sexes in
Middle Bronze Age IIB (ca. 1800–1550)

§231a. Middle Bronze Age IIB received impulses from Egypt and often developed such ideas in their own unique way on scarabs. For example, the heads of Egyptian goddesses were enhanced with flowers and branches (illuss. 13b, c). A "Naked Goddess," represented as mistress of the plants, is even more important (illuss. 11a–12c). The goddess also appeared as "Mistress of the Animals" (illus. 4). Goddesses are especially dominant. Their physical gender characteristics are often given special emphasis (illuss. 12a-b, 24, 26b). The interaction of a goddess with the weather god is characteristic on cylinder seals, presented in a frame of reference that accentuates the fertility of cattle (illuss. 30–31a). The weather god appears also on stamp seals as the one who provides vegetation (illuss. 32a-d). The Egyptian royal god, the falcon-headed Horus, is made to resemble the weather god as a branch or blossom is put in the Egyptian deity's hand (illuss. 33a-c).

Warlike characteristics play a subordinate role at this time (illuss. 28b–29, 34). On the human level, the prince of the city, portrayed wearing the coat with thick fringes and shown ceremoniously striding or enthroned, embodied stability and order (illuss. 35–38). People were glad to be depicted as loyal subjects of a prince or a deity (illuss. 39–40). On the human level as well, the powerfully erotic interaction between the sexes was a point of emphasis for the period (illuss. 41-43). The worship of sacred trees (illuss. 14–16) and stones (illuss. 22, 26), which can also represent goddesses (illus. 26b), strengthens the impression that a kind of religion flourished during Middle Bronze Age IIB that biblical scholars like to call *the* Canaanite religion.

Political and Warrior Aspects take the Upper Hand
in the Late Bronze Age (ca. 1550–1250/1150)

§232. The Late Bronze Age is noted for the influence of Egypt as a colonial power.[1] Thus, for example, the purely Egyptian Hathor fetish replaces the Egyptian/Canaanite head of the goddess (illuss. 73-77). In general, the Late Bronze Age is a time during which the anthropomorphic, naked, erotic goddess retreats into the background. She appears instead on various media in the form of a tree, usually flanked by caprids (illuss. 51–55b, 80–82). It is also characteristic now that she is associated with celestial (illus. 53) or warlike (illuss. 71–72, 109–110) elements and she is shown as a clothed lady (illuss. 78, 107–108).

When her portrayal is altered to give her warrior and royal connotations, the iconography that shows the goddess assumes a feature common to the era. The chariot is the chief element in this political-military symbol system (illuss. 60–65, 96). Young men in battle and heroes in military settings dominate both the sphere of the humans (illuss. 58–

---

1 The pressure exerted by Egyptian culture varied in different parts of the country and expressed itself in varying ways in the successive phases of the Late Bronze Age. It was less noticeable at Hazor than at Beth-Shean. Middle Bronze Age traditions remained for a longer time at Hazor. But it was also at Hazor that the first signs of a symbol system with astral connotations appeared, with the influences coming from northern Syria (illuss. 46–47, 83).

59; 97–98; 114–115) and the gods (illuss. 57, 85–89, 113). The weather god appears, influenced by the Egyptian Seth, no longer primarily as the bringer of fertility, but now as a warrior against any threat, whether this be the horned serpent who dwells in the sea or in the darkness of night (illuss. 87, 89) or against the lion, a figure that should probably be understood as a metaphor for summer drought (illuss. 88–90a). These warlike, close gods stand in for the distant sun god (illus. 87a, c) or for the high god Amun (illuss. 111, 116–119). Amun is also the one who gives victory to the Egyptian king (illuss. 112, 114; cf. illus. 91). The Egyptian king leads his regiment in the name of Amun and Re (illuss. 92–93). He worships the deities (illuss. 94a-d), especially Amun and Re (illuss. 94b-c), and conquers man and beast – in short, every enemy of right order (illuss. 96–101). He is revered by his subjects as the earthly representative of the divine world (illuss. 95, 120a-b).

The local princes fashion themselves as being little pharaohs (illuss. 65, 68a) and the cherub throne elevates them to a super-human status (illuss. 65, 66b). Women assume the role of servants (illuss. 65, 68a). We can verify this demotion of goddesses by observing the images; they are very rarely portrayed on metal but are shown most often on less-expensive terra-cottas. Metal is usually reserved for depicting gods during the Late Bronze Age. This reduction in status and transfer to the arena of "private" family piety, by being portrayed on the terra-cottas, resulted in the goddesses still being depicted in the attitudes that are known from Middle Bronze Age IIB (illuss. 50, 121–122), but they lose the special attributes of divinity.

The Hidden God.
Icons of Sovereignty and Blessing in Iron Age I (ca.1250/1150–1000)

§233.   On the whole, Iron Age I is a transitional period. Different political powers (Egyptians, Canaanites in the cities, proto-Israelites in the hills, Philistines) compete for dominance. Canaanite gods, depicted in bronze as warriors, or as being victoriously enthroned, survive from the Late Bronze Age or are still produced once in a while (illuss. 139, 141). Amun is no longer to be seen in pictorial form, even though the deity is still present in written form and in his cryptogram (e.g., with the lion). He is possibly promoted intensively by those who served the Amun Temple at Gaza (illuss. 130–133). He is often connected with the sun god as a highest god (Amun-Re). Deities, linked to him, that are shown in the foreground include Seth (illuss. 135–136), the winged Baal-Seth, who occasionally appears standing on a lion (illuss. 130, 134, 138), and Reshef on a gazelle (illuss. 130, 137, 138). The posture that shows the deity standing on a lion or gazelle or lifting animals up in the air (crocodiles, scorpions, illus. 140) expresses domination.

Domination is also a determinative at the human level. The ancient icon of slaughter that was used in pharaonic iconography still survives (illus. 144). But the figure that stands in a chariot or is on foot, with a bow, holding people and animals in check (illuss. 146–147) is even more popular. The bull (illus. 142) and the lion (illus. 145) also serve as metaphors for the deity or for the king in Late Bronze Age tradition (cf. illuss. 99–100, 143).

In this symbol system marked by domination, the goddess and her power to bless still appear, but – except on terra-cottas – only in the substitute symbol of the tree (illus. 153) that is occasionally flanked by caprids (illus. 154) and as a nursing mother animal (illuss. 151–152), a form that appears in this context for the first time.

Looking Back to the Traditions of the Bronze Age and Breaking Through to a New Era
Iron Age IIA (ca. 1000–925)

§234. After city culture collapsed during Iron Age I, there was a re-urbanization in Iron Age IIA. Some of the Late Bronze Age themes that disappeared completely or were found only occasionally during Iron Age I appear once again, as, for example, on the cultic stands from Taanach; one sees once again the anthropomorphic deities, such as the "Mistress of the Animals" (illus. 184), and Baal in his role as the one who subdues the serpent (illus. 122c). Apart from these relics of a former age, anthropomorphic deities are very rare. New at this time is the image of an enthroned figure, guarded by falcons, depicting the sun god or the king as his representative on earth (illuss. 158–159). As for the Egyptian gods, we find an aniconic image of Amun present in the form of his name as before. The Egyptianized "Lord of the Crocodiles" or "Lord of the Scorpions" was replaced by a local "Lord of the Ostriches," from the steppe (illus. 162). We still occasionally find the anthropomorphic Anat, riding on a horse (illus. 163a), but much more frequently the horse is depicted alone, instead of with the goddess (illuss. 163b, 164c, 184). Even in the traditional, inexpensive terra-cotta production, goddesses appear less frequently. Clothed votive figures appear in place of the naked goddesses, portraying a woman with a tambourine (illus. 190). For the first time, the enthroned, clothed mother-with-child makes her appearance; she became an extremely popular figure in Egypt and throughout the Phoenician world during the second half of the first millennium (illus. 189).

§235. The trend of the time was to discard anthropomorphic images of deities in favor of substitute figures, and this was not just for goddesses. The motif of a bull attacking a lion or lioness successfully comes from northern Syria (illus. 163). The crescent moon above bovines (illuss. 168b-c) and the crescent moon on a staff, as the emblem of the Moon God of Haran (illuss. 170–171b), are also typical of northern Syria.

We see a single "mistress" of animals between two suckling calves and caprids (illus. 165a), occasionally only in rudimentary form (illus. 166b). Most often, only the incarnated form of the blessings she was providing is portrayed (illuss. 165b, 166a, 173–175). Substitute entities, such as a horse or a suckling mother animal, can then be worshiped in her place (illuss. 164c, 168c, 172). Sometimes, only a scorpion placed with the caprid (illus. 176), or a branch (illus. 177), or a worshiping human (illus. 178) even give a hint that the goddess is really in the background behind these substitute creatures or activities.

One of the most frequently used forms for depicting the goddess in the Late Bronze Age is the tree with caprids on either side, and its use survived into Iron Age I, though it becomes rare at this time and can be identified clearly as the goddess only on large terra-cottas (illuss. 182b–184). The tree flanked by humans (illuss. 179–181) is a new image and is characteristic of Iron Age IIA glyptic art, but its association with the goddess is no longer clear. Her presence is also no longer detected on the images that show a tree flanked by lions and bulls (illus. 191) or when these creatures transport and guard the king, as do the cherubs in Solomon's temple. The tree no longer represents the goddess but stands for the kingdom (cf. illuss. 231–232). All the decoration in the Solomonic temple is predicated upon the idea that this is the place of divine order and blessing, but the motifs are not gender specific or else are associated with a "male" royal god.

The Power of Blessing in the Service of "Male" Deities and Royalty; Egyptian Royal and Sun Symbolism in Iron Age IIB (ca. 925–720/700)

§236.   Iron Age IIB is characterized politically by the coexistence of nation-states (e.g., the two kingdoms of Israel and Judah), which allowed each of them to develop somewhat independently. The warrior bull that Jeroboam I sought to give prominence in Bethel is hardly ever shown in contemporary Israelite art (cf. illuss. 207–209). It may have been, like the ark in Jerusalem, a relic of former times. The Southern Kingdom of Judah maintained its own separate ties with Egypt. Loyalty toward the sacrosanct monarchy, and the powers that protected it, was expressed on indigenous seal amulets, with worship of the name in the cartouche, with the portrayal of the winged sun above the cartouche, by the royal falcons, and by the king, striding over his enemies like a lion (illuss. 265–268, 271–272). The guardian lions, popular also in both Northern and Southern Kingdoms (illuss. 201–206), no longer have anything to do with the goddess. They, like the lions at Solomon's throne, are supposed to heighten the significance and importance of the one they are protecting.

The tree flanked by humans, typical during Iron Age IIA (illus. 179–180), is still found occasionally (illus. 233). More typical for Iron Age IIB is the tree guarded by griffins and cherubs (illuss. 230–232, 234a). The hybrid creatures may wear a royal loincloth and crown (illuss. 231–232), and the tree they guard is closely connected with kingship and with the king's rule and power to bless. As a result, even the ancient Egyptian icon of the striking down of the enemy is drawn into close proximity with this tree (illus. 262b). Direct "transparent" representations of the goddess appear only in the tree found on an ointment spoon from Hazor (illus. 214) and the vessel painting from the caravanserai of Kuntillet ʿAjrud (illus. 219), frequented by both Israelites and Phoenicians. It is at that latter site – and only there in Palestine to date – that we still find the other icon of blessing, the nursing mother animal (illus. 220) for Iron Age IIB.

§237.   Practically speaking, anthropomorphic images of the goddess are found at this time only outside Israel and Judah proper, or at most only as close as in the bordering regions like Philistia, being made in inexpensive materials such as terra-cotta or bone (illuss. 216–217). There are at best only traces of the personal, anthropomorphic goddess during Iron Age IIB. In the inscriptions at Kuntillet ʿAjrud and Khirbet el-Qom, Yahweh alone is the ultimate source of blessing and protection. If there is additional mention of "his *asherah*," this is probably not a reference to a personal deity, conceived anthropomorphically, but is rather a cultic symbol in the form of a stylized tree, an entity that serves him as an agent of blessing (cf. illuss. 181, 219, 214, 308).

And yet, anthropomorphic deities did not disappear completely in the Northern Kingdom. They appear in the form of the "Lord of the Animals," now with caprids and lions, and in the form of what is most frequently a four-winged, youthful figure (illuss. 210–211, 213) who is probably to be associated with Baal. In contrast to the Late Bronze Age, Baal is once again more strongly connected with vegetation. What is new, however, is his celestial character (indicated by wings) and that symbol's interchangeability with the four-winged scarab (a symbol for the sun god).

The Egyptian Bes is also depicted anthropomorphically at times. At Kuntillet ʿAjrud (illus. 220), among people who were less acquainted with his iconography, he was dedicated to helping anyone in great distress and was probably a protective spirit for mother and child. He was very popular in Iron Age IIB Palestine (illuss. 224–226, 228) as the one who could vanquish snakes and who was helpful in other stressful situations. Occasionally, attended by falcons and griffins, he appears in conjunction with a solar deity (illuss. 227–228).

§238. The important new theme in this period revolves around the dominance of solar elements on seal amulets and ivories. Winged creatures, such as falcons, scarabs, *uraei*, griffins, and cherubs, are virtually omnipresent (illuss. 244–257). Their celestial-solar character is often emphasized by the inclusion of additional solar disks (illuss. 250a, 251, 252, 255, 247). It was not unusual for scarabs, griffins, falcons, and winged *uraei* to be combined with winged solar disks (illuss. 258–259). Many of these pieces are typical of Phoenician-Israelite art that was influenced by Egyptian themes.

Seals with the youthful sun god, giving a blessing and kneeling on a lotus blossom, belonged – to judge by the name of the individuals who carried it – to those who were clearly Yahweh worshipers (illuss. 241a-c). What we probably have here is a further manifestation of Baal as Baalshamem. The vegetation and weather god of Middle Bronze Age IIB, the foe of all things that threaten during the entire Late Bronze Age, becomes a "Lord of Heaven" in Iron Age II. This figure was so similar to Yahweh that an intense competition was bound to occur.

The image of the solar god of heaven was characteristic not only of Israel but also of Judah during the second half of the eighth century. There is a crowned solar disk, flanked by *uraei*, on a seal that belonged to a minister of King Ahaz (illus. 273). Four-winged *uraei* were typical in Judah (illus. 274). In his vision, Isaiah saw Yahweh surrounded by six-winged *uraei* (Isaiah 6). The winged solar disks and the four-winged scarabs on the royal seals of Hezekiah may have symbolized the beaming forth (*ZRH*) of Yahweh as a sun god, and indirectly, that the Davidic Kingdom was being sanctioned by the sun god.

The Astralization of the Divine Powers; The Renaissance of the Goddess
and the Awakening of Orthodoxy in Iron Age IIC (ca. 720/700–587)

§239. Iron Age IIB was marked by a great fascination with Egypt and its symbol system. This system was assimilated selectively, with royal and solar symbols especially being the motifs of choice. In Iron Age IIC, these symbols were suppressed by the Assyrian-Aramean cultural pressure. As had not happened since the Late Bronze Age, Palestine was opened to foreign influence by the changed political and economic situation from the time when the eighth century drew to a close until about the time of the end of the seventh century. It was not Assyrian deities who first found entry: Ninurta is the only deity shown in anthropomorphic form, fighting the chaos dragon (illus. 284); Adad (closely related to Ninurta) is on a bull (illus. 285); Ishtar is found most often, as "Queen of Heaven" wreathed in light (illuss. 286–288). The nameless "Lord of the Animals" now appears in Assyrian form (illuss. 282a, 283, 308). The creator god and the god of heaven giving blessing, whose upper body protrudes in the Phoenician manner from lotus buds and blossoms that surround a disk (illus. 337), is probably not to be distinguished from the Assyrian sun god, whose upper body – upwards from the hips – rises from a winged solar disk (cf. illus. 294). At the end of Iron Age IIC, Ezekiel saw Yahweh in his splendor (*kābôd*) as this kind of figure (see Ezek 1:26f.).

The astralization of heavenly powers, transmitted by the Arameans, occurs more widely in this epoch and is characteristic of it. Deities of the night are preferred. Their astral forms, especially the crescent moon, the seven stars of the Pleiades, and the star of Venus, are omnipresent in glyptic art (illuss. 280b, 281–282, 285–292, 311–312, 314–317, 318b–319). Simultaneously, stamp seal glyptic art of the period is characterized by a preference for showing the divinities in the form of their cultic symbol rather than in anthropomorphic form or in their actual astral manifestation. Marduk and Nabu appear only in the form of their symbols (illuss. 281, 285b, 287, 291), and there is a preference for showing the moon god by using his cultic emblem from Haran: the crescent moon on a pole that is decorated with two tassels (illuss. 281, 291c, 294–301, 303). This probably expressed an awareness of the remoteness of the deity and the desire to represent the distant deities in the symbol of their cult-transmitted, accessible form.

This preference for representing cultic symbols is associated with a proclivity for depicting the worshipers themselves (nearly always male and only rarely female). The practice reached a zenith during Iron Age IIC, the likes of which had never been seen before (illuss. 280–281, 285–287, 288c–290, 291b, 293b, 299, 300, 301–303, 311–313). The portrayal of the piety of the king and especially personal piety appears to express the need to ensure attention from distant deities by means of personal effort.

§240. A typical indigenous development, running contrary to what we have just discussed, is the revival of an anthropomorphic, festally enthroned god giving a blessing. On a local Palestinian seal group from the inner region of the country, he replaces the crescent moon emblem (illuss. 303–307). These images may show El, who is also found in seventh-century inscriptions as the lord of heaven and as the moon god.

We also find the interchange of cultic symbol and anthropomorphic deity over a hundred years later, in Zechariah's vision of the lamp between two trees (Zechariah 4; cf. illus. 298b), if the lamp really signifies Yahweh, who is represented anthropomorphically elsewhere (cf. illus. 304). It is not only here that we observe that images found in Palestine appear and are assimilated into Hebrew literature and make their appearance there, following a long incubation period.

It is probably the image of El, flanked by two servants, that appears on the cylinder seal shown in illus. 308. The tree pictured in front of him, flanked by a griffin and a caprid, indirectly supports our interpretation of Yahweh's *asherah* as a cultic symbol. In Iron Age IIC, the *asherah* has an anthropomorphic shape once again. The pillar figurines shown in illuss. 321 and 329 are probably to be interpreted as depicting the goddess Asherah. The image of the "Queen of Heaven," mentioned in Jer 7:16ff. and 44:15ff., may not have been formed only by reference to the Assyrian Ishtar, with her shining crown (illuss. 287–288a-c), since she did not appear in the local glyptic art. She was shaped at least as much by these pillar figurines. In comparison with the "Branch Goddess" of Middle Bronze Age IIB, with her strongly emphasized genital features, the lower body of the pillar figurines is ignored or covered by a coat. Blessing is represented by accentuating the breasts and the face. The face appears at times either partially or completely to be representing the whole figure, *pars pro toto* (illuss. 322, 332).

Worship of the enthroned, nursing mother now begins to be more emphasized in Iron Age IIC (illuss. 327–328). Along with the figurines of the goddess, we find numerous terra-cotta horse-and-rider statuettes (illuss. 333–335), interpreting these as emissaries of El and representatives of the "Host of Heaven."

§241. In Judah, the entire, colorful world of images that had been fostered by the internationalism of the Assyrian Period appears to have come under a strong threat of elimination toward the end of the seventh century. Hebrew name seals, which still often included pictures during the eighth century, became simple name seals during the seventh century. Iconographic motifs that go much beyond pure ornamentation are very rare. Elements of temple decoration are still reproduced at times, like pomegranates (illus. 351) or palmetto capitals (illuss. 352–354); most often we find only the name of the owner and his father.

Silver lamellae [Tr.: thin plates], which replace the rider and pillar figurines, were found in a Jerusalem grave dating to this period. The writing on them betrays the strong influence of the early deuteronomistic and priestly traditions (illus. 356). Images shine only very faintly through the heavy veil of aniconic orthodoxy, as, for example, in the petition that Yahweh might cause his countenance (like the sun? . . . the moon god? . . . the pillar goddess?) to shine upon the deceased.

Regional Developments and Exclusivity in Iron Age III (ca. 587–450)

§242. The ensuing transitional period ending with the administrative reorganization to form the Persian province of Yehud about 450, presents a picture of increasing internationalization and a development of diverse cultural contacts. The seals initially mirror the changing relationships in foreign rule – showing Babylonian cultic scenes first (illus. 358) and depictions of Persian kings and heroes at a later time (illuss. 360–361). In the Phoenician glyptic art, the pictorial constellation that shows the "Lord of the Animals" expresses the internationalism of the period like no other. But side-by-side with this lord one notes the presence of an unnamed indigenous lord (illus. 361c), the Persian royal hero (illuss. 360–361a), and the Egyptian Bes (illus. 366). By the end of the period, his final companion is the Greek Heracles (illuss. 367–368). Among the female deities, the Egyptian Isis as a nursing mother is the most dominant figure in the glyptic art (illuss. 363–364). The motherly aspect of the goddess is also more prominent in terra-cotta production than during Iron Age IIC, in the form of the very popular, pregnant goddess (illus. 365). Under Greek-Cypriot influence, Baalshamem appears in terra-cotta form as well, as a bearded, enthroned Zeus. The use of hypostasized versions of these roles on images throughout the world – male forms as heroic warriors or dignified kings, females primarily as mothers – significantly affected Christianity in the latter stages of its formative period as well, and has correspondingly influenced Christian iconography for two thousand years.

§243.   The comparison of two contemporary religious symbol systems in the peripheral regions of Edom and Judah is both interesting and instructive. Architecture and terra-cottas from the double shrine at Hurvat Qitmit in the eastern Negev give evidence for the juxtaposition of a god (Qaus) and a goddess who is just as warlike and aggressive as her male partner. But, like the "Canaanite" Asherah from the Bronze Age, she appears to have been a goddess of blessing and fertility at the same time (illuss. 375–377). It is the goddess, not the god, who appears to have been the dominant figure at this shrine. The urban-élite division of roles, as one sees it when observing the Phoenician miniatures, made fewer inroads here.

The situation in Judah is quite different. Its territory was reduced by the sixth century to the hill country and the northern Shephelah. The loss of independent statehood led to a three-way split of the Judean population. The Jewish religion developed in different ways in the Judean homeland, in the Egyptian diaspora, and in the Babylonian exile. Very little is known about the religious situation in the motherland during the period of exile. Impressions of seals, which can be regarded as the successors to the royal stamp from the late eighth century and the rosette stamp from the seventh century, seem to associate Yahweh with the powerful, aggressive image of the lion (illuss. 380–381), supplementing that picture occasionally with a sun disk to express the traditional understanding of Yahweh as a solar god (illus. 382).

It is well known that political and religious authority was assumed by the returnees after they came back from the Babylonian exile in 539. These people had much clearer and more rigorous notions about Judean orthodoxy than did their forebears from the time of Josiah. A religious community that separates itself vigorously from "foreign" religions and cultic practices now rallies around the newly reconstructed temple that had been built using the resources of the diaspora community. In the vision of Zechariah, the foreign cult is personified by a woman and is dispatched to Babylon, the motherland of idol worship (Zech 5:5–11). From now on, there would be no room in Judah for a goddess alongside Yahweh.

4. Open Questions

§244. At the end of this survey, there are more open questions than answers. To say this does not diminish the value of the study. In any case, it seems to us that a look at the pictorial evidence gives the viewer a more textured awareness of the religio-historical development of Palestine/Judah than an approach that relies on texts alone. The argument of the whole book need not be repeated here. In many respects, the pictures have also helped to give a more adequate understanding of the problems involved in interpreting texts, whether they be Hebrew inscriptions or biblical texts. Naturally, there is much work to be done, in correlating texts and pictures, to complete a coherent picture.

The unanswered questions are directed more toward the sources, to which we also devoted much attention in this study: the images and the image-bearing artifacts. We were not able to do much more in this book than to sketch an overview, one which calls for supplementary studies in many directions, one that probably can be improved in many places, one that might even have to be corrected in the future. The foundational tool for this study has been the documentation for approximately 8500 stamp seals that have been found in excavations in Palestine/Israel, documentation which is now at the Biblical Institute of the University of Fribourg, Switzerland (see above, §5). This documentation has still not been studied comprehensively and additional work on the corpus of stamp seals could modify individual features of the total picture presented here. Thus, for example, the significance of the god Amun as well as his cryptographically written name in the glyptic art of the first millennium (see above, §84) has never been the subject of systematic research.

Some questions remain unanswered because of the inadequate documentation for many image-bearing artifacts and sometimes for whole genres. A systematic study of the iconographically documented religious symbol system of Canaan and Israel requires more than just a study of the corpus of stamp seals; it also calls for a full investigation of cylinder seals, amulets, large and small terra-cottas, etc. Where such genre-specific summaries exist, as in the case of the cylinder seals (Nougayrol 1939; Parker 1948) or the small terra-cottas (Pritchard 1943), they are completely antiquated and out-of-date. If basic research on various periods and benchmark groups is successful, certain conclusions will probably have to be adjusted.

§245. But unanswered questions are not only a product of inadequate work on the sources. Viewed methodologically, there are more fundamental problems. No one so far has studied the *relative importance* of the sources or their *relationship* to any particular level of religious practice and religious concept, nor thought much about how these different sources *interacted with one* other. At the moment, discussions about polytheism and monolatry in preexilic Israel and Judah have emphasized the task of distinguishing different levels of religious practice. A tripartite division, into family religion (or "family piety"), local religion ("village and city religion"), and national religion ("state cult"; see M. Weippert 1990, 150ff.; Wacker/Zenger 1991, 8) can be taken still further by setting up classifications that involve universal religion, state religion, religion in distinct regions, and family religion and personal piety on the level of how each had its own unique ideas about god (e.g., creator god, national war god, god of a place, "god of the ancestors"; see Lang 1991, 904–907). Viewed functionally, religious practice and images of deities can be differentiated: a war deity, who accompanies the military on operations carried out by a state army, has different functions and competencies than does a deity that is responsible for fertility of the fields, for the flocks, or for the increase of human posterity. As the *"Sitz im Leben"* of the deities varies in widely differing settings, so also do the interests of the females and males who worship, not just in cultic practice but also in terms of the religious concepts and "theologies." All such classifications will remain intellectual games unless work is completed on the material available for study and classification.

The differentiation that could result if one could identify each *"Sitz im Leben"* was brought into the exegetical discussion by H. Gunkel and through form-critical studies. It is no accident that this branch of research has been much more interested in religio-historical questions than in traditio-historical research, which was strongly influenced by dialectical theology. With skepticism today about traditio-historical constructs, and under the influence of general societal shifts (despite contradictory movements in the forms of fundamentalism and dogmatism), there is a growing interest in whatever influences and links religions. Exegesis is turning once more to the history of religion, and it would do well to reconsider the achievements of form criticism again as well.

§246.   This process of asking questions about the *"Sitz im Leben"* should not be limited to biblical texts. We should ask the same questions when we study archaeological inscriptions and iconographical sources. This area offers many more opportunities for reasonably reliable hypotheses, if the primary source was generally found in a (primary or secondary) *"Sitz im Leben"* (palace, temple, house, grave . . .). Interestingly, it is unusual for the *"Sitz im Leben"* of an inscription to be investigated and even more unusual for the iconographic sources to be studied. To what level of religious practice do the inscriptions on the *pithoi* of Kuntillet 'Ajrud belong? What level is to be connected with the *walls* of the caravanserai (see above, §§134ff., 144)? What levels of religious practice are represented by wall and vessel paintings, seal amulets, pendants, terra-cotta figurines, ivories, etc.?

In the context of this study, we have operated again and again with a preliminary, working hypothesis. The overwhelming majority of the sources discussed here are very small objects. This would suggest that they document, first and foremost, religious concepts from "private" piety or family religion. We have seen repeatedly that there is a kind of transfer by osmosis between the different areas, so that so-called "official" religion and "personal" piety continually influence each other. Tigay demonstrated in 1986 how proper names, which have often been understood as especially significant sources for "personal" piety, can be shown to have a close connection with "official," national religion (see §§125, 126). In addition to the valid classification into various religious levels, it is important to place more emphasis on a consideration of the permeability of the various levels, as well as their *global coherence* within each respective symbol *system*.

Finally, it remains to be stated that we are interested not only in the "*Sitz im Leben*" of the reception and use of the artifacts here discussed. We are also interested in their manufacture and distribution. What was produced where? What was the nature of the market? Egyptian faience amulets from Iron Age IIC show no influence of the astralization tendencies that affected the entire Near East during that era, even though the solarization tendencies of Iron Age IIB did appear on a wide variety of genres at that very same time. Each family and genre of image-bearing artifact has its own historical tradition because of its manufacture in a particular atelier. Hardly anyone has conducted scholarly research on these workshops and on the reciprocal influence of the iconographic repertoire on the various image-bearing artifacts.

§247. We do not believe that there was an actual Yahweh iconography in Israel and Judah. This does not mean that Israelite and Judean women and men would not have recognized an appropriate portrayal of their god in one or another of the pictures presented here. But is that enough to go on when attempting to sketch a religious history of Israel that is based not only on the epigraphic evidence but above all on the iconographic material?

Even if there is no explicit mention of a sculpted or painted image of Yahweh, the Hebrew Bible provides a wealth of information about how the people conceived Yahweh anthropomorphically, theriomorphically, in metaphors and in symbols of the widest possible variety. This process of seeing (cf. Isaiah 6, Ezekiel 1, and Zechariah 4) and imagining occurred in a context that was filled with literary and iconographic images. The world of images that fills this context was subject to constant change, sometimes dominated by internal factors and sometimes by external ones. We have tried to describe this change in the symbol system, as much as possible, on the basis of available sources. We have repeatedly correlated the pictures with the text of the Hebrew Bible. To be sure, this happened on a case-by-case basis, sometimes just by chance – for this was not the main purpose of the study. But these few biblical correlations have shown that the *external evidence* confirms neither the view that there was a fully developed Mosaic monotheism nor the popular view that late and even very late dates for the literature are justified.

5. Theological Perspectives

§248. The correlations with the Hebrew Bible have also shown that Yahweh's "essence," described by an assortment of widely varying images that have been brought together, was quite open to expansion. What Thomas Mann said in his novel *Joseph and His Brothers* about old Eliezer seems to us, *mutatis mutandis*, to apply to Yahweh. Joseph takes no offense that

> "the old man's ego was not quite clearly demarcated, that it opened at the back, as it were, and overflowed into spheres external to his own individuality both in space and time; embodying in his own experience events which, remembered and related in the clear light of day, ought actually to have been put into the third person. But then, just what do we mean by actually? And is man's ego" – and we would add here, is the deity – "a thing imprisoned in itself and sternly shut up in its boundaries of flesh and time? Do not many of the elements which make it up belong to a world before it and outside of it? The notion that each person is himself and can be no other, is that anything more than a convention, which arbitrarily leaves out of account all the transitions which bind the individual consciousness to the general?" [Knopf Edition, 1934, H. T. Lowe-Porter translation, p. 128]

Anyone who examines the pictorial world of Palestine and Israel from the Middle Bronze Age through the Iron Age will have no trouble seeing how deep the roots go, and even the little roots as well, that describe Yahweh's power, his "colorfulness," and the rich variety of the ways he shows himself.

§249.   Feminist theology, one of the few strong, green branches on the old and generally dry tree of western Christian theology in western Europe and North America, has, among many other things, renewed the discussion of anti-Judaism. On the one hand, this is because the feminists are themselves charged with anti-Judaism, since they criticize biblical patriarchalism. On the other hand, this comes because their fundamental attitude toward dominance enables them to point fearlessly to what some have called "anti-Semitic" statements in the New Testament (e.g., 1 Thess 2:15; John 8:42–44) and thus to distance themselves from these statements more easily than can the theological establishment and the ecclesiastical hierarchy (Kohn-Roelin 1991). It is an aspect of the guilt that is part of Christian history that, in its arrogance and intolerance, it has tried to secure its position and glory by devaluing and insulting Judaism. For this reason, we must constantly recall the famous metaphor in the Epistle to the Romans that calls Christians to remember their roots (Rom 11:16–18). The root, Judaism, has given birth to Christianity; it is not the other way around.

Roots, however, are only roots because of what comes later. In the words of Thomas Mann: "Very deep is the well of the past." By itself, the Jewish religion is a trunk with many branches and it has roots that also reach deeper than itself. Judean religion encountered a situation in the seventh and sixth centuries before Christ that was comparable to Christian anti-Judaism, even though its historic consequences included what was, relatively speaking, a less harmful fall into sin. It believed that it could establish its own identity only by outlawing everything

Canaanite and by calling for the destruction of such items as the holy stones (Deut 7:5; 12:5) that their ancestors had once erected (Gen 28:18, 22). What they outlawed, as Canaanite, was more than merely cultic objects. Part of the tragic history of the Judeo-Christian history of guilt is the fact that the people who later became the victims of the holocaust reported in a central passage in their own religious writings that a major preoccupation of theirs was the elimination of other groups in order to ensure the purity and sanctity of their own religious community (cf. Deut 7:2–6, 16, 24–26). Here *all* are called to humility and to change their ways.

§250.   As this study has shown repeatedly, images of god, society, and humanity are closely related. The religious symbol systems of the Middle Bronze Age and Late Bronze Age were just as marked by images of fertility and sexuality or dominating warrior-military images as were the societies in which they developed. Just as clearly as the Christian symbol system has its roots in the Israelite-Judean symbol system, the Israelite-Judean symbol system had the same relationship with the Canaanite system – one that so often is described as heathen. There is no place here for arrogant absolutism and exclusivity. Everything has its own time and importance.

Since everything has its own time, the roots – the wealth and treasure of times past – must be kept accessible or should be made accessible again. The long expected "profound change in society and community, by which both genders, that is, all people – women as well as men and children – can live together in righteousness, love, and peace, can happen only if there is a revolutionary restructuring of our symbol world." This calls for research not only into symbols connected with the areas of psychology and religious history, but also for "a detailed, historical investigation of our own iconographic and mythological heritage" (King 1991, 143). Such work will not only expose the buried feminine aspects of the Judeo-Christian image of God, with their salvific power, it can also open our eyes to the theological dignity of many images and concepts that can nourish us from the thriving Christian groups and from the encultured theologies of Asia, Africa, and Latin America. Through openness to the traditions of these peoples, the European-North American culture of subjugation, which is threatening to drive the world to destruction, can hope not only for critique and reevaluation but also for enrichment and perhaps healing. As we look at a picture of *Pachamama* ("mother earth") from the Andean Indians, can we not distinguish the features of the Bronze Age Asherah once again?

Chronological Table for Palestinian/Israelite Archaeology in the Second and First Millennia

EAEHL		Periodization Employed Here		Dominant Factors, Characteristics
MB IIA	2000–1750	Middle Bronze IIA	2000–1750	Egyptian Middle Kingdom, 12th Dynasty
MB IIB	1750–1550	Middle Bronze IIB	1750–1550	Canaanite City-states; 13–15th Dynasties
LB I	1550–1400	Late Bronze I	1550–1400	Egypt — Earlier 18th Dyn. (to Amenophis II)
LB IIA	1400–1300	Late Bronze IIA	1400–1300	New — Later 18th Dyn. (from Tuthmosis IV)
LB IIB	1300–1200	Late Bronze IIB	1300–1150	Kingdom — 19th–20th Dynasties – Ramessides
Iron IA	1200–1100	Iron IA	1250–1100	Deurbanization phase; "settlement"
Iron IB	1100–1000	Iron IB	1100–1000	Growth of settlements, regional centers
Iron IIA	1000–900	Iron IIA	1000–900	"United Monarchy" (David, Solomon)
Iron IIB	900–800	Iron IIB	925–720/700	Nation-states (Israel, Judah, Ammon . . .)
Iron IIC	800–586	Iron IIC	720/700–600	Assyria, provinces, vassal states
Babylonian-Persian Period	586–333	Iron III	600/587–450	Babylonian, early Achaemenian Periods
		Persian Period	450–333	Persian Province of Yehud, from Artaxerxes I

Source Index of Illustrations

1a Mackay/Murray 1952, pl. 10.118. **1b** Petrie 1931, pl. 13.1. **2** Keel, et al., 1989, 99 no. 41 (= Kenyon 1965, fig. 296.14). **3a** Mackay/Murray 1952, pl. 10.113. **3b** Williams 1977, 115 fig. 82.3 (= Petrie 1930, pl. 7.32). **3c** Kenyon 1965, fig. 295.23. **4** Keel, et al., 1989, 100 no. 50 (= Petrie 1933, pl. 3.89). **5a** Tufnell 1958, pl. 36.215. **5b** Keel 1984, 165 illus. 76 (= Rowe 1936, no. 69). **6** Macalister 1912, III pl. 202a.9. **7** Rowe 1936, no. 317. **8a-b** Keel, et al., 1989, 283 illuss. 9 (= Petrie 1933, pl. 28.8) and 10. **9a-b** Keel, et al., 1989, 47 illuss. 16 (= Mallett 1988, pl. 84.8) and 17. **10** Keel, et al., 51 illus. 21 (= Grant 1929, 89). **11a** Keel, et al., 1989, 97 no. 3. **11b** Keel, et al., 1989, 98 no. 16 (= Tufnell 1958, pl. 31.47). **12a** Tufnell 1958, pl. 32.99. **12b** Giveon 1985, 115 no. 16. **12c** Keel, et al., 1989, 97 no. 9 (= Giveon 1988, 51 no. 44). **13a** Kenyon 1965, fig. 293.14. **13b** Tufnell 1958, pl. 34.162. **13c** Petrie 1934, pl. 11.409. **14a** Pieper 1930, 195f. **14b** Mackay/Murray 1952, pl. 9.16. **14c** Mallet 1988, pl. 84.2. **15a** Tufnell 1958, pl. 32.100. **15b** Petrie 1931, pl. 4.136. **15c** Kenyon 1965, fig. 298.4. **16** Ziffer 1990, 11*. **17** Negbi 1976, fig. 78 no. 1532. **18a-c** Negbi 1976, 178 no. 1531; 177 no. 1525 (cf. 184 no. 1620); 183 no. 1609. **19** Loud 1948, pl. 245, 18–19. **20** Kenyon 1960, I 496 fig. 215.2. **21** Petrie 1931, pl. 21.114. **22** Galling ²1977, 207 illus. 49 (sketch by Gisela Tambour). **23** Negbi 1976, 183 no. 1601. **24** Seger 1976, 135 fig. 2a. **25a** Macalister 1912, III pl. 211.2. **25b** Negbi 1976, 183 no. 1602. **26a-b** Eisenberg 1977, 79. **27a-b** Negbi 1976, 179 nos. 1542, 1546. **28a-b** Negbi 1976, 177 no. 1519; 147 no. 58. **29** Loud 1948, pl. 269.3. **30** Loud 1948, pl. 161.21. **31a** Yadin 1961, pl. 319.1. **31b** Mallet 1974, pl. 23. **32a** Mackay/Murray 1952, pl. 9.13. **32b** Macalister 1912, III pl. 206.44. **32c** Saller 1964, 191 fig. 64.1. **32d** Keel, et al., 1989, 266 illus. 73. **33a** Petrie 1931, pl. 13.82. **33b** Petrie 1932, pl. 7.75. **33c** Petrie 1930, pl. 10.62. **34a** Kenyon 1965, fig. 303.15. **34b** Giveon 1988, 49 no. 42. **34c** Loud 1948, II pl. 151.148. **35** Yadin 1961, pl. 319.2. **36a** Gophna/Sussmann 1969, 13 figs. 10, 11. **36b** Rowe 1936, no. 154 (= Garstang 1933, pl. 26 T. 13.6). **36c** Tufnell 1958, pl. 30.64. **36d** Petrie 1930, pl. 22.235. **37** Börker-Klähn 1982, no. 282 (= Albright 1938, pls. 21a–22). **38** Böhl 1938, pl. 1 A. **39a** Giveon 1988, 21 no. 2. **39b** Rowe 1936, no. 291 (= Sellin 1927, pl. 28 Ac). **39c** Giveon 1988, 23 no. 4. **40a** Horn 1973, 293 fig. 1.62. **40b** Keel, et al., 1990, 176 fig. 5. **41** Parker 1949, no. 9 (= Petrie 1931, pl. 13.33). **42** Unpublished. **43** Loud 1948, pl. 149.52. **44** Yadin 1961, pls. 324f.). **45** Yadin 1961, pl. 341. **46** Yadin 1958, pl. 29.1–2. **47** Galling ²1977, 208 illus. 49.4. **48** Petrie 1934, pl. 13f.9. **49** Keel 1986,

165 illus. 97a. **50** Winter 1983, illus. 22. **51** Loud 1948, pl. 161.11. **52** Guy 1938, pl. 176.3 (cf. Winter 1983, illus. 143). **53** Beck 1977, pl. 21.1. **54** Guy 1938, pl. 134 (= Loud 1948, pl. 69.13). **55a** Loud 1948, pl. 251f. **55b** May 1935, pl. 40B (= Starkey/Harding 1932, pl. 58). **56** Negbi 1976, 51 fig. 59 no. 1453. **57** Pl. 24 no. 1359. **58** Loud 1948, pl. 247.7. **59** Schumacher 1908, pl. 24. **60** Keel, et al., 1990, 286 illus. 0123. **61** Keel, et al., 1990 286 illus. 0128. **62** Loud 1939, no. 36. **63** Loud 1939, no. 161. **64** Loud 1939, no. 159. **65** Loud 1939, no. 2. **66a** Keel 1977b, 139 illus. 42. **66b** Keel ⁴1984, 150 illus. 234. **66c** Zevulun 1987, 103 fig. 14. **67** Loud 1939, no. 160. **68a-b** Petrie 1930, pl. 55. **69** Winter 1983, illus. 38 (= Tufnell 1958, pl. 49.4). **70** Ben-Arie/Edelstein 1977, 29f., cover illustration. **71** Clamer 1980, 153 fig. 1. **72** H. Weippert 1988, 304 illus. 3.52.2. **73** Tufnell 1940, pl. 21.46. **74** Petrie 1932, pl. 3.27. **75a-d** Schroer 1989, 141f. no. 98 (= Tufnell 1958, pls. 37/38, 319), 99 (= Tufnell 1953, pl. 44A/45.132), 117 (= Tufnell 1958, pls. 37/38.307), 118 (= Petrie 1932, pl. 7.44). **76** Yadin 1961, pl. 323.1–3. **77** Elgavish 1975, pl. 28D. **78** Schulman 1988, 143f. fig. 52. **79a** Tufnell 1940, pl. 40.392. **79b** Tufnell 1940, pl. 32.20. **79c** Starkey/Harding 1932, pl. 48.14. **79d** Tufnell 1958, pl. 38.304. **80** Tufnell 1940, pl. 59.2. **81** Tufnell 1940, pls. 51.287; 60.3. **82** Beck 1986, pl. I 11.1. **83a-b** Petrie 1934, pl. 14.15; 18.112. **83c** Tufnell 1940, pl. 26.10. **84** Schulman 1988, 129 fig. 42. **85a** Tufnell 1940, pl. 33.47. **85b** Keel/Uehlinger 1990, 74 illus. 94c. **86** Keel, et al., 1990, 321 fig. 96. **87a** Keel, et al., 1990, 317 fig. 91 (= Tufnell 1953, pl. 43/43A.22). **87b-c** Keel, et al., 1990, 313 fig. 85; 317 fig. 92. **88a** Parker 1949, no. 142. **88b** Beck 1977, pl. 21.3. **89** Keel, et al., 1990, 311 fig. 82 (= Giveon 1978, fig. 49). **90a** Keel ⁴1984, 336 illus. 485. **90b** Rowe 1940, pl. 38A.14. **91** Keel ⁴1984, 345 illus. 495. **92a** Keel ⁴1984, illus. 496. **92b** Giveon 1985, 31 no. 26. **93** Wiese 1990, 67 illus. 86. **94a** Keel, et al., 1989, 306 illus. 93. **94b-c** Giveon 1985, 29 no. 20, 33 no. 31. **94d** Starkey/Harding 1932, pl. 57.365. **95** Wiese 1990, 73 illus. 96. **96** Dothan 1979, 44 no. 6 illus. 110. **97a-b** Tufnell 1958, pls. 36.243; 39.391. **97c** Starkey/Harding 1932, pl. 52.136. **98a-b** Starkey/Harding 1932, pl. 52.120, 139. **99** Loud 1948, pls. 152,156. **100** Starkey/Harding 1932, pl. 52.112. **101a** Ussishkin 1978, 45 fig. 11. **101b** Loud 1948, pls. 152, 154. **102** Rowe 1930, pl. 33 (cf. Rowe 1940, Frontispiece; ANEP no. 487). **103** Winter 1983, illus. 57. **104** Rowe 1940, pl. 17.1 (cf. pls. 56A.2; 57A.1–2). **105** Rowe 1940, pls. 17.3; 56A.1, 3. **106** McGovern 1985, 30 fig. 23 (= Rowe 1940, pl. 68A.5; cf. ANEP no. 478). **107** Winter 1983, illus. 241 (= Rowe 1930, pl. 48.2; cf. ANEP no. 475). **108** Rowe 1940, pl. 35.3 (= Rowe 1935, pl. 50.2). **109** Winter 1983, illus. 214 (= Rowe 1936, no. S.60A; cf. ANEP no. 468). **110** Keel, et al., 1990, 214 fig. 38 (= Keel/Uehlinger 1990, 74 fig. 94e). **111** Kruchten 1982, pl. between pp. 32 and 33. **112** Keel 1974, 178, illus. 34. **113** Keel 1974, 174 illus. 27. **114a-b** Keel/Uehlinger 1990, 19 illuss. 8a, 8b (= Rowe 1936, no. 578). **115** Rowe 1930, 34 fig. 8. **116a** Giveon 1985, 103 no. 123 (= Petrie 1933, pl. 4.193). **116b** Starkey/Harding 1932, pl. 57.389. **116c** Tufnell 1958, pl. 39.371. **117a-b** Giveon 1985, 37 no. 41 and 35 no. 36 (= Starkey/Harding 1932, pls. 52.143; 53.193). **118** Lamon/Shipton 1939, pl. 73.1. **119** Loud 1939, no. 377. **120a** James 1966, fig. 92.1. **120b** Avi-Yonah/Stern 1975, I 213. **121a-d** Winter 1983, illuss. 12, 24, 44, 55. **122a-b** Winter 1983, illuss. 28, 45. **123** Keel 1986, 175 illus. 102. **124** Mazar 1980, 83 fig. 20. **125**

Mazar 1985b, 6 fig. 2 no. 1.   **126** Potts, et al., 1985, pl. 42.   **127a** Macalister 1912, I 306 fig. 162.   **127b** Starkey/Harding 1932, pl. 47.   **128** Mazar 1980, 79 fig. 18.   **129** Keel, et al., 1990, 14 illus. 4.   **130** Keel, et al., 1990, 123 no. 1.   **131** Keel, et al., 1990, 123f. no. 2. **132a-b** Petrie 1930, pl. 35.393, 397. **133a** Tufnell 1953, pl. 44A/45.130. **133b** Pritchard 1980, figs. 22/23.8. **133c** Potts, et al. 1988, 148 pl. 24.1.   **133d** James 1966, 340 fig. 113.6.   **133e-f** Schumacher 1908, 86 illus. 124 2nd row from top, outside left; 3rd row from above, 43rd from left.   **134a** Schumacher 1908, 86, illus. 124, above right, 2nd from right.   **134b-c** Petrie 1930, pl. 22.186; pl. 31.308. **135** Keel, et al., 1990, 233 no. 22.   **136** Petrie 1930, pl. 29.247. **137a-b** Petrie 1930, 199 figs. 32b-c.   **138** Petrie 1930, 144 nos. 46–47.   **139** Seeden 1980, no. 1736 (= Negbi 1976, 165 no. 1361; pl. 24).   **140a** Keel, et al., 1990, 342 illus. 11.   **140b** Schumacher 1908, 86 illus. 124, 2nd row from top, 3rd from left (based on a photo from the Archaeological Museum in Istanbul).   **141** Negbi 1976, 50 fig. 60 no. 1454.   **142** Mazar 1982, 30 figs. 2 A-B.   **143a** Tufnell 1940, pl. 18A.   **143b** Loud 1948, pl. 204.3.   **144a** Schumacher 1908, 86 illus. 124, top row, 1st from left.   **144b-c** Keel, et al., 1990, 345 illuss. 17 and 18 (= Petrie 1930, pl. 31.319).   **145a** Schumacher 1908, 86 illus. 124, 3rd row from top, 6th piece from left.   **145b** Keel, et al., 1990, 345 illus. 19.   **146a-b** Keel, et al., 1990, 125 no. 4; 127 no. 7.   **147a-b** Keel, et al., 1990, 129 no. 11; 130 no. 14.   **148** T. Dothan 1982, 234f. fig. 9. **149a** Dothan 1971, fig. 76.1 (cf. Shuval 1990, 156f. no. 77).   **149b** Keel/ Küchler 1982, 44 illus. 29.   **149c** Keel [4]1984, 323 illus. 468.   **150** T. Dothan 1982, 239 no. 1.   **151a-b** Keel, et al., 1990, 154 nos. 72 and 70.   **152a** Keel, et al., 1990, 152 no. 64.   **152b** Grant 1934, 43 fig. 3.16.   **153** Keel, et al., 1990, 156 no. 75 = 383 illus. 81.   **154a** Starkey/Harding 1932, pl. 73.38.   **154b** Sellin 1904, 73 fig. 98.   **155a** Macalister 1912, III pl. 200.11.   **155b** Petrie 1930, pl. 43.533.   **156** Sass 1988, no. 189.   **157** Mazar 1990b, 83 fig. 4.   **158a** Keel 1982, illus. 4.   **158b** Giveon 1985, 126f. no. 53.   **158c** Keel 1982, illus. 7.   **159a-b** Keel 1982, illuss. 10, 13.   **160** Sass 1988, fig. 237.   **161** Rowe 1936, no. S 111.   **162a** Chambon 1984, 274 no. 8 (cf. pl. 80.8).   **162b-d** Keel 1978, illuss. 38, 36, 39 (corrected).   **163a-b** Keel, et al., 1990, 214 fig. 39; 210 no. 14.   **164a-d** Schroer 1987a, illuss. 115, 116, 113, 112.   **165a** Keel-Leu 1991, no. 65.   **165b-c** Unpublished.   **166a** Keel/Schroer 1985, 37 illus. 12. **166b** Keel/Schroer 1985, 36 illus. 9 (corrected).   **167a-c** Keel, et al., 1990, 368f. illuss. 64, 63 (= pl. XVIII.2, 1); pl. XXII.1.   **168a-b** Keel, et al., 1990, pl. XVIII.4; XXI.2.   **168c** Unpublished.   **169a-b** Keel, et al., 1990, 191 fig. 23; 190 no. 9.   **170** Keel, et al., 1990, pl. XX.3.   **171a** Yadin 1960, pl. 76.8.   **171b** Chambon 1984, pl. 80.7.   **172** Keel/Schroer 1985, 36 illus. 10.   **173** Keel/ Schroer 1985, illus. 11.   **174** Macalister 1912, III pl. 200.9.   **175a-b** Keel 1980a, 115f., illuss. 90-91.   **175c** Keel/Schroer 1985, 35 illus. 3.   **176a-b** Keel/Schroer 1985, 36 illuss. 6–7. **176c** Grant 1934, 43 fig. 3.18.   **177a** Chambon 1984, pl. 80.5.   **177b** Tufnell 1953, pl. 43A/44.96.   **177c** Unpublished.   **178a** Mackenzie 1912/1913, pl. 29.B2.   **178b** Stern 1978a, pl. 31.11.   **178c** Unpublished.   **179a** Keel-Leu 1991, no. 77.   **179b** Kelso 1968, pl. 119c.   **179c** Rowe 1936, no. SO.23.   **180a** Rowe 1936, no. S.72. **180b** Lamon/Shipton 1939, pl. 69f.13.   **181** McCown 1947, pl. 54.18.   **182a** Beck 1990a, 419 illus. 1.   **182b-c** Lods 1934, 141 fig. 1; 142 fig. 2.   **183** Stern 1978b, 16 fig. 6.   **184** Galling 1977, 191 illus. 45.3.   **185a-b** Schroer 1987a, illus. 44, 110 (corrected; = Rowe 1936 nos. SO. 28 and 39).   **186** Potts, et

al., 1985, pl. 41.   **187** Shiloh 1984, 59 fig. 23.   **188a** de Vaux 1955, pl. XIII.
188b Keel 1984, 145 illus. 41.   **189** Chambon 1984, pl. 63.4.   **190a** Yadin
1960, pl. 76.12.   **190b** Winter 1983, illus. 63.   **190c** Chambon 1984, pl. 63.2.
190d May 1935, pl. 27 M 65.   **190e** Barnett ²1975, 150 fig. 58 (= Crowfoot,
et al., 1953, pl. 11.8).   **190f** Schroer 1987a, illus. 90.   **191** Petrie 1930, pl.
38.232.   **192** Keel ⁴1984, 145 illlus. 226.   **193** Keel ⁴1984, 99 illus. 145.   **194**
Lamon/Shipton 1939, 60 fig. 70. **195a-b** Tufnell 1953, pl. 43A/44.84–85.
196a Biran 1982, 27 illus. 13.   **196b** Keel 1978, 93 illus. 20b.   **197a**
Unpublished.   **197b** Lapp 1964, 43 fig. 23.4.   **197c** Yadin 1960, pl. 76.11.
198a-b Tufnell 1953, pl. 43A/44.100–101.   **199a-c** Tufnell 1953, pl. 43A/
44.93–95.   **200a** Crowfoot/Crowfoot 1938, pl. 10.8a.   **200b** Keel ⁴1984, 347
illus. 498 (= Hestrin/Dayagi-Mendels 1979, no. 45).   **200c-d** Avigad 1986,
nos. 169 and 125.   **201** Albright 1938, pl. 23.   **202** Ussishkin 1974, 113 fig.
4.   **203** Schroer 1987a, 522 illus. 34 (= Crowfoot/Crowfoot 1938, pl. 10.1).
204 Schroer 1987a, 548 illus. 135 (= Crowfoot/Crowfoot 1938, pl. 9.1).
205a Davies 1986, 86 fig. 19a.   **205b** Galling 1977, 301 illus. 78.11.   **205c**
Galling 1941, no. 21.   **206a** Hachlili/Meshorer 1986, 44.   **206b** Tufnell
1953, 118 fig. 10.   **207a** Reisner 1924, II pl. 56.e4.   **207b–208** Crowfoot, et
al., 1957, pl. 15.23–24. **209** McCown 1947, pl. 55.82.   **210** Yadin 1958, pl.
151.   **211a** Macalister 1912, III pl. 208.29.   **211b** Gubel 1991b, 918 fig. 3d.
211c Keel 1977a, 202, illus. 152.   **212a** Crowfoot, et al., 1938, pl. 14.2.   **212b**
Galling 1941, pl. 7.97.   **213** Starkey/Harding 1932, pl. 73.43.   **214** Yadin
1960, pl. 167f.   **215** Crowfoot/Crowfoot 1938, pl. 13.2.   **216** Petrie 1930,
pl. 40.482–487.   **217a** Dothan/Freedman 1967, 162f. fig. 43.4.   **217b-c**
Kelm/Mazar 1990, 62f. fig. 18 C and B.   **218** H. Weippert 1988, 619 illus.
4.65.   **219** Beck 1982, 7 fig. 4.   **220** Beck 1982, 9 fig. 5 (supplemented
from Meshel 1978, fig. 12). **221** Beck 1982, 10 fig. 6.   **222a** Petrie 1928, pl.
20.14. **222b** Keel 1986, 59 illus. 9, below.   **222c** Sellin/Watzinger 1913, pl.
42.o.   **223** Tufnell 1953, pl. 50.1.   **224a-b** Tufnell 1953, pls. 34.14; 36.48.
224c Bliss/Macalister 1902, pl. 83.3.   **225a-c** Petrie 1930, pl. 40.493–495.
225d-e Macalister 1912, III pl. 210.2, 17.   **226a-b** Unpublished.   **226c**
Ussishkin 1974, 121 fig. 9.14.   **227** Keel 1982, 525 illus. 38.   **228** Yadin
1961, pl. 360.4–5 (cf. pl. 187.22; corrected).   **229** Braun 1991, 15 fig. 3a.
230 Galling 1941, pl. 7.77.   **231a** Schumacher 1908, I 142 illus. 212a.   **231b**
Lamon/Shipton 1939, pl. 67.45. **232a-b** H. Weippert 1988, 656 illuss. 4,
72.1–2. (= Crowfoot/Crowfoot 1938, pl. 5.1, 3).   **233a-b** Schroer 1987b,
213 illuss. 25 (= McCown 1947, pl. 55.63) and 26 (= Lemaire 1986b, 311).
234a Yadin 1958, pl. 155.   **234b** Yadin 1960, pls. 67.13; 162.7.   **235a** Gal
1990b, 96.   **235b** Gal 1989, [3] (unpaginated, see Gal 1990a, 94f. fig. 78.10).
235c Aharoni 1973, pl. 55.19.   **236** Hadley 1987a, 52.   **237** Beck 1982, 49
fig. 18.   **238a** Beck 1982, 54 fig. 21.   **238b** Keel 1986, 83 illus. 35b.   **239**
Crowfoot/Crowfoot 1938, pl. 11.1.   **240** H. Weippert 1988, 656 illus. 4,72
(= Crowfoot/Crowfoot 1938, pl. 1.1).   **241a** Keel/Uehlinger 1990, 84
illus. 113b (= Galling 1941, no. 84).   **241b** Bordreuil 1986a, no. 40.   **241c**
Hestrin/Dayagi-Mendels 1979, no. 39.   **242** Crowfoot/Crowfoot 1938, pl.
2.2.   **243** Crowfoot/Crowfoot 1938, pl. 3.1.   **244** McCown 1947, pl. 54.1.
245 Keel 1977a, 77 illus. 30 (= Reisner 1924, pl. 56.f).   **246** Keel 1977a, 102
illus. 84.   **247a-b** Keel 1977a, 104 illus. 86f.   **248** Unpublished.   **249**
Bartlett 1976, pl. 8.   **250a** Unpublished. **250b** Schumacher 1908, I 99 illus.
148.   **251** Unpublished.   **252** Hestrin/Dayagi-Mendels 1979, no. 41.   **253**

Hestrin/Dayagi-Mendels 1979, no. 43 (= Petrie 1930, pl. 35.427). **254a** Keel 1977a, 96 illus. 64 (= Lamon/Shipton 1939, pl. 67.43). **254b** Lamon/ Shipton 1939, pl. 67.44. **255** Crowfoot, et al., 1957, pl. 15.14. **256** Unpublished. **257a** Crowfoot, et al., 1957, p. 15.29. **257b** Macalister 1912, III pl. 209.4. **258a** Reisner 1924, pl. 56.e2. **258b** Wright 1965, fig. 82. **258c** Rowe 1936, no. SO. 3. **259a** Lamon/Shipton 1939, pl. 67.7. **259b** Unpublished, mentioned in Crowfoot, et al., 1957, 86 no. 7). **260** Crowfoot/Crowfoot 1938, pl. 3.2b. **261a-b** Lamon/Shipton 1939, pl. 75.17, 19. **261c** Tufnell 1953, pl. 36.52. **262a** Crowfoot/Crowfoot 1938, pl. 14.7. **262b** Crowfoot/Crowfoot 1938, pl. 14.1. **263a-b** Bordreuil 1986a, no. 41. **263c** Bordreuil 1986c, 55. **264a** Diringer 1934, pl. 22.12. **264b** Petrie/Ellis 1937, pl. 30.8. **265a-b** Petrie 1930, pl. 31.298 (cf. Rowe 1936, no. S. 89); 41.291. **265c** Macalister 1912, I 334 fig. 173 right (cf. Rowe 1936, no. S. 108). **266a** Unpublished. **266b** Macalister 1912, III pl. 205a.18. **267a** Tufnell 1953, pl. 44/44A.106. **267b** McCown 1947, pl. 54.56. **268a-b** Tufnell 1953, pl. 43A/44.64 and 103. **268c** Lamon/Shipton 1939, pl. 72.11. **269a-b** Dothan 1971, figs. 44.19 and 89.5. **269c** Tufnell 1953, pl. 43A/44.89 (cf. Rowe 1936, No. SO. 8). **270** Rowe 1936, no. S. 109. **271a** Tufnell 1953, pl. 43A/44.63. **271b** Lamon/Shipton 1939, pl. 67.19. **272a** Giveon/Kertesz 1986, no. 132. **272b** McCown 1947, pl. 55.73. **272c-d** Petrie 1930, pl. 35.423 and 408 (cf. Rowe 1936, nos. S. 99 and S. 96). **273** Galling 1941, 121. **274a-c** Keel 1977a, 104 illus. 85 (= Tufnell 1953, pl. 44A/45.170); 109 illus. 88; illus. 92 (= Tufnell 1953, pl. 47B.9). **274d** Sternberg 1989, 13 no. 11. **275a–276c** Galling 1977, 305 illuss. 78.27–31. **277** Tufnell 1953, pl. 45.167 (cf. Hestrin/Dayagi-Mendels 1979, no. 48). **278a** Keel/Küchler 1982, 46 illus. 33. **278b** Vignette of the series "State Archives of Assyria," Helsinki 1987ff. (drawing: Dominique Collon based on two original impressions in the British Museum, London). **279** Lamon/Shipton 1939, pl. 67.32. **280a** Wright 1962, 10f. fig. 3. **280b** Lamon/Shipton 1939, pl. 66.2. **281** Keel 1977a, 295 illus. 221. **282a** Macalister 1912, III pl. 214.22. **282b-c** Lamon/Shipton 1939, pls. 72.15; 66.11. **283** Stern 1987, 69. **284a** Parker 1949, no. 172. **284b** Macalister 1912, III pl. 214.19. **285a** Stern 1973, 13. **285b** Geva 1980, 45 fig. 1. **286** Wright 1965, fig. 82.6. **287** Parker 1949, no. 6 (cf. Winter 1983, illus. 500 = Schroer 1987a, 540 illus. 97, to be replaced by the new drawing presented here). **288a** Schroer 1987a, 540 illus. 98. **288b** Unpublished. **288c** Stern 1987, 69. **289** Schumacher 1908, 60f. illus. 72d. **290** Schumacher 1908, I/B pl. 44c. **291** Keel, et al., 1990, 238 no. 24. **292** Unpublished. **293a-b** Macalister 1912, I 293 fig. 154.14b (based on a photo of a copy in files of the Palestine Exploration Fund, London); 23 fig. 4. **294** Based on a photo of the original, BM 136202 (cf. Galling 1941, no. 82). **295a** Keel/Küchler 1982, 942 illus. 644. **295b** Keel 1977a, 295 illus. 222 (cf. Petrie 1928, 19.27). **296** Macalister 1912, I Frontispiece fig. 3 = Reich/Brandl 1985, 48 no. 3. **297a** City of David 1989, no. 9. **297b** Keel 1977a, 295 illus. 223. **298a** Keel 1977a, 288 illus. 209. **298b** Keel 1977a, 292 illus. 216 (corrected, replacing Keel, et al., 1990, 219 no. 16). **299** Giveon 1978, fig. 63 (corrected on the basis of original photos). **300** Keel, et al., 1990, 329 fig. 109. **301a** Petrie 1928, pl. 17.49 (based on a photo of the original and an impression; replacing Keel 1977a, 295 illus. 226). **301b-c** Keel 1977a, 292 illus. 219; 295 illus. 227. **302a** Keel, et al., 1990, 236 no. 23. **302b** Keel-Leu 1991, no. 135. **302c-d** Keel, et al., 1990, 329 figs. 105–106. **303** Keel 1977a, 295 illus. 220. **304** Keel 1977a, 308 illus. 238c. **305a** Avigad 1989a, 16f. no. 19. **305b** Keel-Leu 1991, no. 134. **305c** Sass 1992, fig. 137. **306a** Keel 1977a, 308 illus. 238a. **306b** Barnett 1969–1971, pl. 14.5. **306c** Keel 1977a, 308 illus. 238b. **307** Unpublished. **308** Parker 1949, no. 122. **309a-b** Briend/Humbert 1980, pl. 90.36f. **310** Sellers 1933, 59 fig. 50.5. **311a** Crowfoot, et al., 1957, pl. 15.21. **311b** Bordreuil 1986d, 284f. no. 2. **312a** Giveon 1978, fig. 66b. **312b** Ornan 1992, fig. 48. **312c** Avigad 1986a, 64 no. 77. **313** Ornan 1992, fig. 51. **314** Briend/Humbert 1980, pl. 90.34 (backwards; cf. pl. 136.34). **315a-b** Keel, et al., 1990, 325 figs. 99 and 101. **316** Keel, et al., 1990, 223 fig. 47. **317a** Bordreuil/Lemaire 1976, no. 2, pl. 4.2a. **317b** Tufnell 1953, pl. 43A/44.105. **317c** Keel 1986, 93 illus. 47a (cf. Keel-Leu 1991, no. 138). 318a Unpublished. **318b** Giveon/Kertesz 1986, no. 164. **319** Tufnell 1953, pl. 43.58. **320** Keel 1984, 152 illus. 55 (= Tufnell 1953, pl. 28.12). **321a** Tufnell 1953, pl. 28.10. **321b** Winter 1983, illus. 33. **321c** Aharoni 1973, pl. 71.1. **322a** May 1935, pl. 23 M 4117. **322b** Yadin 1960, pl. 76.15. **323** Tufnell 1953, 365 fig. 35; pl. 44/44A.124. **324** May 1935, pl. 32 M 4418. **325** Ornan 1986, 35. **326** Albright 1943, pl. 32.1. **327a-b** Crowfoot, et al., 1957, 77 fig. B.6; pl. 12.7. **328** Tufnell 1953, pl. 36.51. **329** Keel/Küchler 1982, 196 illus. 158. **330** Dothan 1971, 139 fig. 64.1. **331a-b** Sass 1992, fig. 142f. (= Bordreuil 1986a, nos. 44, 58). **332** Aharoni 1962, pl. 25.3–5. **333a-b** Tufnell 1953, pls. 27.2; 29.18. **334a-b** Holland 1977, 142 fig. 8.2; 138 fig. 7.21. **335** Yadin 1961, pl. 176.24. **336** Schroer 1987a, 543 illus. 114. **337a** Brandl 1984, 77 fig. 1. **337b** Stucky 1974, pl. 17 no. 26. **338a** Mazar/Mazar 1989, pl. 8.21. **338b–340b** Unpublished. **341a-b** Avigad 1986, 110 nos. 199 and 201. **342a-b** Aharoni 1962, fig. 15.9–10. **343a-b** Shiloh 1986, 28 fig. 8.1, 4. **344** Shiloh 1986, fig. 8.2. **345** Avigad 1986, 28 no. 9. **346** Barkay 1977, 70 (backwards). **347** Aharoni 1962, pl. 30.1. **348** Stern 1978b, 13 fig. 1a. **349a-b** Avigad 1986, nos. 20 and 34. **350a** Diringer 1934, pl. 19.24. **350b** Avigad 1986, no. 24a. **351a-b** Avigad 1986, nos. 38 and 152. **352** Avigad 1986, no. 6. **353a-b** Avigad 1986, 116 and 137. **354a-b** Barkay 1989, 52 and 58 (cf. Yardeni 1991, 179 fig. 1). **355** Barkay 1986, 34 (Hebrew). **356** Barkay 1989, 40. **357a** Barkay/Kloner 1986, 38 (detail). **357b** Keel, et al., 1989, 69 fig. 49. **358a** Keel/Küchler 1982, 424 illus. 306 (= Mazar/Dunayevski 1967, pl. 31.1). **358b** Based on a photo of the original (cf. Petrie 1933, pl. 4.197). **358c** Ornan 1992, fig. 26. **359** Pritchard 1964, fig. 51.14f. **360a** Crowfoot, et al., 1957, pl. 15.42. **360b** Keel, et al., 1990, 231 no. 21. **361a** Macalister 1912, 292 fig. 153. **361b** Crowfoot, et al., 1957, pl. 15.22. **361c** Bliss/Macalister 1902, pl. 83.5. **362** Giveon/Kertesz 1986, no. 173. **363a** Rowe 1936, no. 914 (= Johns 1933, 62 fig. 18; pl. 17.412). **363b** Stern 1982, 200 fig. 324. **363c-d** Johns 1933, 67 fig. 24, pl. 16.366; 81 fig. 52, pl. 14.649. **364** Brandl 1991, 153–155. **365** Winter 1983, illus. 381. **366a** Johns 1933, 99 fig. 85, pl. 14.935. **366b** Rahmani 1976, pl. 31.3. **367a-c** Johns 1933, 71 fig. 30, pl. 14.496; 75 fig. 41, pl. 14.552; 71 fig. 31, pl. 14.497. **368** Schroer 1987a, illus. 66 (= Tufnell 1953, pl. 31.19). **369** Johns 1933, 79 fig. 49, pl. 14.629. **370** Tufnell 1953, pl. 68.1. **371** Petrie 1928, pl. 40.1–4. **372** Macalister 1912, II 442, figs. 524.2a-c. **373** Starkey/Harding 1932, pl. 93.662. **374** Stern 1982, 184 fig. 304. 375 Beit-Arieh/Beck 1987, 32. **376** Beit-Arieh/Beck 1987, 28. **377**

Beit-Arieh/Beck 1987, 6.   **378** Beit-Arieh/Beck 1987, 14.   **379** Beit-Arieh/ Beck 1987, 15.   **380a** Aharoni 1962, fig. 9.9.   **380b** Galling ²1977, 305 illus. 78.43.   **381a-b** Stern 1982, 211 fig. 349.1–2.   **381c** Galling ²1977, 305 illus. 78.44.   **382a** Galling ²1977, illus. 78.45.   **382b** Aharoni 1962, fig. 9.11.   **383** Mazar, et al., 1966, 34 fig. 12.

Abbreviations

Abbreviations in the Text and Bibliography follow S. Schwertner, *Internationales Abkürzungsverzeichnis für Theologie und Grenzgebiete*, Berlin – New York 1984, and *idem, Theologische Realenzyklopädie: Abkürzungsverzeichnis*, Berlin – New York 1986.

AAA	Annals of Archaeology and Anthropology
AASOR	*Annual of the American Schools of Oriental Research*
ÄA	*Ägyptische Abhandlungen*
ÄAT	*Ägypten und Altes Testament*, Wiesbaden
ADAJ	*Annual of the Department of Antiquities of Jordan*
ADPV	Abhandlungen des Deutschen Palästina-Vereins
AfO	*Archiv für Orientforschung*
AHW	*Akkadisches Handwörterbuch*; ed. W. von Soden. 3 vols. Wiesbaden, 1965-1981.
AION	*Annali dell'istituto orientale di Napoli*
AIPh	*Annuaire de l'institut de philologie et d'histoire orientales et slaves*
AJSL	*American Journal of Semitic Languages and Literature*
AMI	*Archäological Mitteilungen aus Iran*
ANEP	*The Ancient Near East in Pictures Relating to the Old Testament.* 2nd edition; ed. James B. Pritchard
AnOr	Analecta Orientalia
AnSt	*Anatolian Studies*
AOAT	Alter Orient und Altes Testament
AOS	American Oriental Series
ATANT	Abhandlungen zur Theologie des Alten und Neuen Testaments
ATD	Das Alte Testament Deutsch
BA	*Biblical Archaeologist*
BAR	*Biblical Archaeology Review*, Washington D.C.
BASOR	*Bulletin of the American Schools of Oriental Research*
BASOR.S	Bulletin of the American Schools of Oriental Research. Supplements.
BBB	Bonner biblische Beiträge
BAH	Bibliothèque archéologique et historique

BETL	Bibliotheca ephemeridam theologicarum lovaniensium
BIAUL	*Bulletin of the Institute of Archaeology. University of London*
BibB	Biblische Beiträge
BIES	*Bulletin of the Israel Exploration Society (= Yediot)*
BiKi	*Bibel und Kirche*
BN	*Biblische Notizen, Bamberg – Munich*
BollS	Bollinger Series
BSAE	British School of Archaeology in Egypt, London
BTB	*Biblical Theology Bulletin*
BTS	*Bible et terre sainte*
BZAW	Beihefte zur Zeitschrift für die alttestamentliche Wissenschaft
CAD	*The Assyrian Dictionary of the Oriental Institute of the University of Chicago*
CRAI	*Computes rendus des séances de l'académie des inscriptions et belles-lettres*
CTA	A. Herdner. 1963. *Corpus des tablettes en cunéiformes alphabétiques découvertes à Ras Shamra-Ugarit de 1929 à 1939. MRS 10. Paris*
CTM	*Concordia Theological Monthly*
DFIFAO	Documents de fouilles de l'institut français d'archéologie orientale du Caire
DJD	Discoveries in the Judean Desert
DMOA	Documenta et monumenta orientis antiqui
EHS	*Einleitung in die Heilige Schrift*
ErIsr	*Eretz Israel*
FRLANT	Forschungen zur Religion und Literatur des Alten und Neuen Testaments
Ges.[18]	*Wilhelm Gesenius' Hebräisches und aramäisches Hand-wörterbuch über das Alte Testament. 18.,* completely rewritten edition, eds. H. Donner and R. Meyer, Berlin 1987ff.
GM	*Göttinger Miszellen*
HAL	*Hebräisches und aramäisches Lexikon zum Alten Testament.* 3rd edition, completely rewritten, eds. W. Baumgartner, J. J. Stamm et al., 4 vols., Leiden, etc. 1967–1990
HAT	Handbuch zum Alten Testament
HSM	Harvard Semitic Monographs
HSS	Harvard Semitic Studies
HUCA	*Hebrew Union College Annual*
IAA	Israel Antiquities Authority, Jerusalem
IEJ	*Israel Exploration Journal*
IOS	*Israel Oriental Society*
JBL	*Journal of Biblical Literature*
JCS	*Journal of Cuneiform Studies*
JdI	*Jahrbuch des (katholischen) deutschen archäologischen Instituts*

JEOL	*Jaarbericht . . . ex oriente lux*
JNES	*Journal of Near Eastern Studies*
JSOT	*Journal for the Study of the Old Testament,* Sheffield
JSOTSup	Journal for the Study of the Old Testament-- Supplement Series
KTU	M. Dietrich – O. Loretz – J. Sanmartín, *Die Keilalphabetischen Texte aus Ugarit.* Part 1: Transkription (AOAT 24/1), Kevelaer and Neukirchen-Vluyn 1976
KVR	Kleine Vandenhoeck-Reihe
LAPO	*Littératures anciennes du Proche-Orient*
LdÄ	*Lexikon der Ägyptologie,* Wiesbaden
LIMC	*Lexicon Iconographicum Mythologiae Classicae,* Zurich 1982ff.
MÄS	*Münchener ägyptologische Studien*
MDAI.A	Mitteilung des deutschen archäologischen Instituts. Athenische Abteilung
MDOG	*Mitteilungen der Deutschen Orient-Gesellschaft zu Berlin*
NBL	*Neues Bibel-Lexikon,* Zurich et al. 1988ff.
OBO	Orbis biblicus et orientalis
OIP	Oriental Institute Publications
OLP	Orientalia lovaniensia periodica
OrAnt	*Oriens Antiquus*
Or.N.S.	*Orientalia. New Series*
OrSuec	*Orientalia Suecana*
OTS	*Oudtestamentische Studiën*
PEQ	*Palestine Exploration Quarterly*
PEFQSt	*Palestine Exploration Fund Quarterly Statement*
PEFA	*Palestine Exploration Fund, Annual*
PFLUS	Publications de la faculté des lettres de l'université de Strasbourg
PJ	*Palästina-Jahrbuch des deutschen evangelischen Instituts*
PRU	*Le Palais Royal d'Ugarit,* ed. C. F. A. Schaeffer and J. Nougayrol. Paris
PSBA	*Proceedings of the Society of Biblical Archaeology*
PSBF.Ma	Pubblicazioní dello Studium biblicum franciscanum. Collectio maior
QD	Quaestiones Disputatae
QDAP	*Quarterly of the Department of Antiquities in Palestine*
RA	*Reallexikon der Assyriologie und vorderasiatischen Archäologie*
RB	*Revue Biblique*
RdE	*Revue d'égyptologie*
RHR	*Revue de l'histoire des religions*
RLA	*Reallexikon der Assyriologie*
RSF	*Rivista di Storia della Filosofia*

SBA	Studies in Biblical Archaeology
SBFLA	Studii Biblici Franciscani Liber Annuus
SBLMS	Society of Biblical Literature Monograph Series
SBS	Stuttgarter Bibelstudien
SBT	Studies in Biblical Theology
SchL	Schweich Lectures of the British Academy
ScrHier	Scripta Hierosolymitana
SMSR	*Studi e Materiali di Storia delle Religioni*
SS	Studi Semitici
SOr	Studia Orientalia
StP	Studia Pohl
TDOT	*Theological Dictionary of the Old Testament*, eds. G. Botterweck and H. Ringgren
TS	*Theological Studies*
TUAT	*Texte aus der Umwelt des Alten Testaments*, ed. O. Kaiser, Gütersloh 1982ff.
TZ	*Theologische Zeitschrift*
UAVA	Untersuchungen zur Assyriologie und vorderasiatische Archäologie
UF	*Ugarit-Forschungen*
UT	C. H. Gordon, *Ugaritic Textbook* (AnOr 38), Rome 1965
VT	*Vetus Testamentum*
VTSup	VetusTestamentum, Supplements
WMANT	Wissenschaftliche Monographien zum Alten und Neuen Testament
WO	*Die Welt des Orients*
WVDOG	Wissenschaftliche Veröffentlichungen der Deutschen Orient-Gesellschaft
WZ(H)	*Wissenschaftliche Zeitschrift der Martin-Luther-Universität Halle-Wittenberg*
ZAH	*Zeitschrift für Althebraistik*, Stuttgart, etc.
ZAW	*Zeitschrift für die alttestamentlichen Wissenschaft*
ZBK.AT	Zürcher Bibel Kommentar. Altes Testament
ZDPV	*Zeitschrift des deutschen Palästina-Vereins*

Bibliography

ABOU ASSAF, ALI (1980), "Untersuchungen zur ammonitischen Rundbildkunst," *UF* 12, 7–102.

ACKERMAN, SUSAN (1989), "'And the Women Knead Dough': the Worship of the Queen of Heaven in Sixth-Century Judah," in: Peggy L. Day, ed., *Gender and Difference in Ancient Israel*, Minneapolis, 109–124.

ACKROYD, PETER R. (1983), "Goddesses, Women and Jezebel," in: A. Cameron – Amélie Kuhrt, eds., *Images of Women in Antiquity*, London 1983, 245–259.

AHARONI, YOHANAN et al., (1962), *Excavations at Ramat Rahel: Seasons 1959 and 1960* (SS Serie Archeologica 5), Rome.

—— et al., (1964), *Excavations at Ramat Rahel: Seasons 1961 and 1962* (SS Serie Archeologica 6), Rome.

—— et al., (1973), *Beer Sheba I: Excavations at Tell Beer-Sheba, 1969–1971 Seasons* (Tel Aviv University, Publications of the Institute of Archaeology no. 2), Tel Aviv.

—— (1974a), [Notes and News] "Beer-Sheba," *IEJ* 24, 271.

—— (1974b), "Three Hebrew Seals," *Tel Aviv* 1, 157–158.

—— (1975a), *Investigations at Lachish: The Sanctuary and the Residency* (Lachish V; Tel Aviv University, Publications of the Institute of Archaeology 4), Tel Aviv.

—— (1975b), [Notes and News] "Tel Beer-Sheba," *IEJ* 25, 169–171.

—— (1984), *Das Land der Bibel: Eine historische Geographie*, Neukirchen-Vluyn. [ET: *The Land of the Bible: A Historical Geography* (1979)].

AHLSTRÖM, GÖSTA W. (1970–71), "An Israelite God Figurine from Hazor," *OrSuec* 19/20, 54–62.

—— (1975), "An Israelite Figurine, once more," *VT* 25, 106–109.

—— (1982), *Royal Administration and National Religion in Ancient Palestine* (Studies in the History of the Ancient Near East 1), Leiden.

—— (1984), "An Archaeological Picture of Iron Age Religions in Ancient Palestine," *SOr* 55.3, 117–145.

—— (1990), "The Bull Figurine from Dhahrat et-Tawileh," *BASOR* 280, 77–82.

ALBRIGHT, WILLIAM FOXWELL (1938), *The Excavation of Tell Beit Mirsim II: The Bronze Age* (AASOR 17 [1936–1937]), New Haven,Conn.

—— (1939), "Astarte Plaques and Figurines from Tell Beit Mirsim," *Mélanges syriens offerts à M. R. Dussaud* (BAH 30), Paris, T. Ier, 107–120.

ALBRIGHT, WILLIAM FOXWELL (1943), *The Excavation of Tell Beit Mirsim III: The Iron Age* (AASOR 21–22 [1941–1943]), New Haven, Conn.

ALLIOT, MAURICE (1946), "Les rites de la chasse au filet aux temples de Karnak, d'Edfou et d'Esneh," *RdE* 5, 57–118.

ALTENMÜLLER, HARTWIG (1965), *Die Apotropaia und die Götter Mittelägyptens: Eine typologische und religionsgeschichtliche Untersuchung der sog. "Zaubermesser" des Mittleren Reiches*, 2 vols., Munich.

—— (1975a), Art. "Bes," *LdÄ* I, 720–724.

—— (1975b), Art. "Beset," *LdÄ* I, 731.

AMIRAN, RUTH (1958), "A Note on Figurines with 'Disks'," *ErIsr* 8, 99–100 (hebr.). 71*.

—— (1969), *Ancient Pottery of the Holy Land: From its Beginnings in the Neolithic Period to the End of the Iron Age*, Jerusalem – Ramat Gan.

—— (1975), "The Lion Statue and the Libation Tray from Tell Beit Mirsim," *BASOR* 222, 29–40.

Archäologie zur Bibel: Kunstschätze aus den biblischen Ländern (Leihgaben der Lands of the Bible Archaeology Foundation), Mainz/Rhine.

ARTZY, MICHAL (1990), "Pomegranate Scepters and Incense Stand with Pomegranates Found in Priest's Grave," *BAR* 16/1, 48–51.

ASSMANN, JAN (1982), "Die Zeugung des Sohnes. Bild, Spiel, Erzählung und das Problem des ägyptischen Mythos," in: idem – W. Burkert – F. Stolz, *Funktionen und Leistungen des Mythos: Drei altorientalische Beispiele* (OBO 48), Fribourg, Switzerland and Göttingen, 13–61.

—— (1983), *Re und Amun: Die Krise des polytheistischen Weltbilds im Ägypten der 18.–20. Dynastie* (OBO 51), Fribourg, Switzerland and Göttingen. [ET: *Egyptian Solar Religion in the New Kingdom: Re, Amun and the Crisis of Polytheism*, trans. Anthony Alcock (London: Kegan Paul, 1995)] .

AUFRECHT, WALTER E. (1989), *A Corpus of Ammonite Inscriptions* (Ancient Near Eastern Texts & Studies 4), Lewiston, etc.

AVIGAD, NAḤMAN (1954a), "Seven Ancient Hebrew Seals," *BIES* 18, 147–153 (hebr.). IV.

—— (1954b), "Three Ornamented Hebrew Seals," *IEJ* 4, 236–238.

—— (1969), "A Group of Hebrew Seals," *ErIsr* 9, 1–9 (hebr.).134*.

—— (1976a), "New Light on the Naʿar Seals," in: F. M. Cross – W. E. Lemke – P. D. Miller, eds., *Magnalia Dei. The Mighty Acts of God: Essays on the Bible and Archaeology in Memory of G. E. Wright*, Garden City, N.Y., 294–300.

—— (1976b), "The Governor of the City," *IEJ* 26, 178–182.

—— (1976c), *Bullae and Seals from a Post-Exilic Judean Archive* (Qedem 4), Jerusalem.

—— (1977), "Two Ammonite Seals Depicting the *Dea Nutrix*," *BASOR* 225, 63–66.

—— (1978), "On 'A Second Bulla of a Sar Ha-ʿIr'," *Qadmoniot* 11 (no. 41), 34 (hebr.).

—— (1979), "A Group of Hebrew Seals from the Hecht Collection," *Festschrift Rëuben Hecht*, Jerusalem, 119–126.

—— (1983), *Discovering Jerusalem*, Nashville – Camden – New York.

—— (1986), *Hebrew Bullae from the Time of Jeremiah: Remnants of a Burnt Archive*, Jerusalem.

424   *Gods, Goddesses, and Images of God*

Avigad, Nahman (1987), "The Contribution of Hebrew Seals to an Understanding of Israelite Religion and Society," in: Miller et al., 1987, 195–208.

—— (1989a), "Another Group of West-Semitic Seals from the Hecht Collection," *Michmanim* 4, 7–21.

—— (1989b), "Two Seals of Women and other Hebrew Seals,: *ErIsr* 20, 90–96 (hebr.). 197*.

—— (1990a), "The Seal of Mefaʿah," *IEJ* 40, 42–43.

—— (1990b), "Two Hebrew 'Fiscal' Bullae," *IEJ* 40, 262–266.

—— (1990c), "The Inscribed Pomegranate from the 'House of the Lord'," *BA* 53, 157–166.

Avi-Yonah, Michael – Stern, Ephraim (1975–1978), eds., *Encyclopedia of Archaeological Excavations in the Holy Land*, 4 vols., London and Jerusalem.

Bachelot, Luc (1990), Le bassin aux femmes, in: J.-M. Durand, ed., *Tell Mohammed Diyab: Campagnes de 1987 et 1988* (Cahiers de N.A.B.U. 1), Paris, 47–50.

Bar-Adon, Pessah (1980), *The Cave of the Treasure: The Finds from the Caves in Nahal Mishmar*, Jerusalem.

—— (1985), "An Early Hebrew Inscription in a Judean Desert Cave," *IEJ* 25, 226–232.

Barkay, Gabriel (1977), "A Second Bulla of a Sar Ha-ʿIr," *Qadmoniot* 10 (nos. 38–39), 69–71.

—— (1985), "'Galloping Horse Seal Impressions' – Another Type of the 'Identical Seal Impressions'," *Cathedra* 36 (June), 197–200 (hebr.).

—— (1986), *Ketef Hinnom: A Treasure Facing Jerusalem's Walls* (Israel Museum Catalogue no. 274), Jerusalem.

—— (1989), "The Priestly Benediction on the Ketef Hinnom Plaques," *Cathedra* 52, 46–59 (hebr.).

—— (1990), "A Late Bronze Age Egyptian Temple in Jerusalem?" *ErIsr* 21, 94–106 (hebr.). 104*.

Barkay, Gabriel – Kloner, Amos (1986), "Jerusalem Tombs from the Days of the First Temple," *BAR* 12/2, 22–39.

Barnett, Richard D. (1935), "The Nimrud Ivories and the Art of the Phoenicians," *Iraq* 2, 179–210.

—— (1969), "Ezekiel and Tyre," *ErIsr* 9, 6*–13*.

—— (1969–71), "Scaraboids and Engraved Seals," *Sefunim* (Bulletin [of the National Maritime Museum Haifa]) 3, 47–48.

—— (²1975), *A Catalogue of Nimrud Ivories with Other Examples of Ancient Near Eastern Ivories in the British Museum*, London.

—— (1982), *Ancient Ivories in the Middle East and Adjacent Countries* (Qedem 14), Jerusalem.

Bartlett, John R. (1976), "The Seal of HNH from the Neighbourhood of Tell ed-Duweir," *PEQ* 108, 59–61.

—— (1989), *Edom and the Edomites* (JSOTSup 77), Sheffield.

Beck, Pirhiya (1977), "The Cylinder Seals," in: Ben-Arie/Edelstein 1977, 63–69.

—— (1982), "The Drawings from Horvat Teiman (Kuntillet ʿAjrud)," *Tel Aviv* 9, 3–68.

BECK, PIRḤIYA (1983), "The Bronze Plaque from Hazor," *IEJ* 33, 78–80.

—— (1986a), "A New Type of Female Figurine," in: Marilyn Kelly-Buccellati, ed., *Insight through Images: Studies in Honor of Edith Porada* (Bibliotheca Mesopotamica 21), Malibu, Calif., 29–34.

—— (1986b), "A Head of a Goddess from Qitmit," *Qadmoniot* 19 (nos. 75–76), 79–81 (hebr.)

—— (1989a), "Cylinder Seals from the Temple of Area H," in: Yadin 1989, 310–321.

—— (1989b), "Stone Ritual Artifacts and Statues from Areas A and H," in: ibid. 322–338.

—— (1989c), "On the Identification of the Figure on the Cult-Stand from the 'City of David'," *ErIsr* 20, 147–148 (hebr.). 199*.

—— (1990a), "The Taanach Cult Stands: Iconographic Traditions in the Iron I Cult Vessels," in: Naʾaman/Finkelstein 1990, 417–446 (hebr.).

—— (1990b), "A Figurine from Tel ʿIra," *ErIsr* 21, 87–93 (hebr.). 104*.

—— (1990c), "A Note on the "Schematic Statues" from the Stelae Temple at Hazor," *Tel Aviv* 17, 91–95.

BECKING, BOB (1983), "The Two Neo-Assyrian Documents from Gezer in their Historical Context," *JEOL* 27, 76–89.

BEIT-ARIEH, ITZHAQ (1991), "The Edomite Shrine at Ḥorvat Qitmit in the Judean Negev. Preliminary Excavation Report," *Tel Aviv* 18, 93–116.

BEIT-ARIEH, ITZHAK – BECK, PIRḤIYA (1987), *Edomite Shrine: Discoveries from Qitmit in the Negev* (Israel Museum Catalogue no. 277), Jerusalem.

BEIT-ARIEH, ITZHAQ – CRESSON, BRUCE (1985), "An Edomite Ostracon from Ḥorvat ʿUza," *Tel Aviv* 12, 96–101.

BEN-ARIE, SARA – EDELSTEIN, GERSHON (1977), *Akko: Tombs near the Persian Garden*: ʿAtiqot 12 (English Series), Jerusalem.

—— (1983), "A Mould for a Goddess Plaque," *IEJ* 33, 72–77.

BEN-DOR, IMMANUEL (1946), "A Hebrew Seal from Samaria," *QDAP* 12, 77–83.

—— (1950), "A Middle Bronze Age Temple at Nahariya," *QDAP* 14, 1–41.

BEN-TOR, AMNON – ROSENTHAL, RENATE (1978), "The First Season of Excavations at Tel Yoqneʿam. Preliminary Report," *IEJ* 28, 57–82.

BENZ, F. L. (1972), *Personal Names in the Phoenician and Punic Inscriptions* (StP 8), Rome.

BIENKOWSKI, PIOTR (1987), "The Role of Hazor in the Late Bronze Age," *PEQ* 119, 50–61.

BIRAN, AVRAHAM (1975), "Dan," in: Avi-Yonah/Stern 1975/I, 313–321.

—— (1977), "Tel Dan" [Notes and News]: *IEJ* 27, 242–246.

—— (1982), "The Temenos at Dan," *ErIsr* 16, 15–43 (hebr.). 252*–253*.

BISI, ANNA MARIA (1980), "Da Bes a Heracles. A proposito di tre scarabei del Metropolitan Museum," *RSF* 8/1, 19–42.

BITTEL, KURT (1976), *Die Hethiter: Die Kunst Anatoliens vom Ende des 3. bis zum Anfang des 1. Jahrtausends vor Christus* (Universum der Kunst), Munich.

BLISS, FREDERICK JAMES (1894), *A Mound of Many Cities or Tell el Hesy Excavated*, London.

BLISS, FREDERICK JAMES (1899), "Third Report on the Excavations at Tell Zakarîya," *PEFQSt,* 170–187.

BLISS, FREDERICK JAMES – MACALISTER, ROBERT STEWART ALEXANDER (1902) [1912?], *Excavations in Palestine During the Years 1898–1900,* London.

BÖHL, FRANZ M. TH. (1938), "Die Sichem-Plakette. Protoalphabethische Schriftzeichen der Mittelbronzezeit vom tell *balāṭa,*" *ZDPV* 61, 1–25.

BÖHM, STEPHANIE (1990), *Die "Nackte Göttin": Zur Ikonographie und Deutung unbekleideter weiblicher Figuren in der frühgriechischen Kunst,* Mainz/ Rhine.

BÖRKER-KLÄHN, JUTTA (1982), *Altvorderasiatische Bildstelen und vergleichbare Felsreliefs* (Baghdader Forschungen 4), 2 vols., Mainz.

BONNET, HANS (1952), *Reallexikon der ägyptischen Religionsgeschichte,* Berlin – New York, 2nd, unaltered edition, 1971.

BORDREUIL, PIERRE (1985), "Inscriptions sigillaires ouest-sémitiques III: Sceaux de dignitaires et de rois syro-palestiniens du VIIIᵉ et du VIIᵉ siècle av. J.-C.," *Syria* 62, 21–29.

—— (1986a), *Catalogue des sceaux ouest-sémitiques inscrits de la Bibliothèque Nationale, du Musée du Louvre et du Musée biblique de Bible et Terre Sainte,* Paris.

—— (1986b), "Charges et fonctions en Syrie-Palestine d'après quelques sceaux ouest-sémitiques du second et du premier millénaire," *CRAI* 1986, 290–307.

—— (1986c), "A Note on the Seal of Peqah the Armor-Bearer, Future King of Israel," *BA* 46, 54–55.

—— (1986d), "Perspectives nouvelles de l'épigraphie sigillaire ammonite et moabite," in: *Proceedings of the Third Conference on the History and Archaeology of Jordan,* Tübingen 283–286.

—— (1991), "Les premiers sceaux royaux phéniciens," in: *Atti del II Congresso Internazionale di Studi Fenici e Punici* (Collezione di Studi Fenici 30/II), Rome, 463–468.

BORDREUIL, PIERRE – LEMAIRE, ANDRÉ (1976), "Nouveaux sceaux hébreux, araméens et ammonites," *Semitica* 26, 45–63.

—— (1982), "Nouveau sceaux hébreux et araméens," *Semitica* 32, 21–34.

BRANDL, BARUCH (1984), "The Restoration of an Engraved Tridacna Shell from Arad," *The Israel Museum Journal* 3, 76–79.

—— (1991), "A Phoenician Scarab from Loḥamei HaGeta'ot," *'Atiqot* 20 (English Series), 153–155.

BRAULIK, GEORG (1991), "Die Ablehnung der Göttin Aschera in Israel. War sie erst deuteronomistisch, diente sie der Unterdrückung der Frauen?" in: Wacker/Zenger 1991, 106–136.

BRAUN, JOACHIM (1991), "Iron Age Seals from Ancient Israel Pertinent to Music," *Orbis Musicae* 10 (= FS Hanoch Avenary), Tel Aviv, 11–26.

BRETSCHNEIDER, JOACHIM (1991), *Architekturmodelle in Vorderasien und der östlichen Ägäis vom Neolithikum bis in das 1. Jahrtausend: Phänomene in der Kleinkunst an Beispielen aus Mesopotamien, dem Iran, Anatolien, Syrien, der Levante und dem ägäischen Raum, unter besonderer Berücksichtigung der bau – und der religionsgeschichtlichen Aspekte* (AOAT 229), Kevelaer and Neukirchen-Vluyn.

BRIEND, JACQUES – HUMBERT, JEAN-BAPTISTE (1980), eds., *Tell Keisan (1971–1976): Une cité phénicienne en Galilée* (OBO Series archaeologica 1), Fribourg, Switzerland – Göttingen – Paris.

BRUNNER-TRAUT, EMMA (1974), *Die alten Ägypter: Verborgenes Leben unter den Pharaonen*, Stuttgart, etc.

BUCHANAN, BRIGGS – MOOREY, P. ROGER S. (1988), *Catalogue of Ancient Near Eastern Seals in the Ashmolean Museum III: The Iron Age Stamp Seals (ca. 1200–350 B.C.)*, Oxford.

BUNIMOVITZ, SHLOMO (1990), "Problems in the 'Ethnic' Identification of the Philistine Material Culture," *Tel Aviv* 17, 210–222.

BUTTERWECK, CHRISTEL et al., (1988), "Phönizische Grab-, Sarg- und Votivinschriften," *TUAT* II/4, 582–605.

CAHILL, JANE – LIPTON (LIPOWITCH), G. – TARLER, T. (1987), "Tell el-Ḥammah" [Notes and News], *IEJ* 37, 280–283.

—— "Tell el-Hammeh in the Tenth Century B.C.E.," *Qadmoniot* 22 (nos. 85–86), 33–38 (hebr.).

CALMEYER, PETER (1979), "Fortuna – Tyche – Khvarnah," *JdI* 94, 347–365.

—— (1984), "'Das Zeichen der Herrschaft . . . ohne Šamaš wird es nicht gegeben'," *AMI* 17, 135–153.

CALMEYER, PETER – SEIDL, URSULA (1983), "Eine frühurartäische Siegesdarstellung," *AnSt* 33, 103–114.

CAMP, CLAUDIA V. (1985), *Wisdom and the Feminine in the Book of Proverbs* (Bible and Literature Series 11), Sheffield.

CAMP, LUDGER (1990), *Hiskija und Hiskijabild: Analyse und Interpretation von 2 Kön 18–20* (Münsteraner Theologische Abhandlungen 9), Altenberge.

CATASTINI, A. (1982), "Le iscrizioni di Kuntillet ʿAjrud e il profetismo," *AION* 42, 127–134.

CAVIGNEAUX, ANTOINE – ISMAIL, BAHIJA KHALIL (1990), "Die Statthalter von Suḫu und Mari im 8. Jh. v. Chr. anhand neuer Texte aus den irakischen Grabungen im Staugebiet des Qadissiya-Damms," *Baghdader Mitteilungen* 21, 321–456.

ČERNY, JAROSLAV (1958), "Stela of Ramesses II from Beisan," *ErIsr* 5, 75*–82*.

CHAMBON, ALAIN (1984), *Tell el-Farʿah I: L'âge du fer* (Recherche sur les civilisations, mémoire 31), Paris.

CHASE, DEBRA A. (1982), "A Note on an Inscription from KuntilletʿAjrūd," *BASOR* 246, 63–67.

CHOURAQUI, ANDRÉ (1983), ed., *L'univers de la Bible*, vol. III, Paris.

CITY OF DAVID (1989), "Discoveries from the Excavations. Exhibition in Memory of Yigal Shiloh, Institute of Archaeology of the Hebrew University, Jerusalem" (brochure).

CLAMER, CHRISTA (1980), "A Gold Plaque from Tel Lachish," *Tel Aviv* 7, 152–162.

CLIFFORD, RICHARD J. (1990), "Phoenician Religion," *BASOR* 279, 55–64.

COGAN, MORDECHAI (1974), *Imperialism and Religion: Assyria, Judah and Israel in the Eighth and Seventh Centuries B.C.E.* (SBLMS 19), Missoula.

COLLON, DOMINIQUE (1975), *The Seal Impressions from Tell Atchana/Alalakh* (AOAT 27), Kevelaer and Neukirchen-Vluyn.

COLLON, DOMINIQUE (1982), *The Alalakh Cylinder Seals: A new catalogue of the actual seals excavated by Sir Leonard Woolley at Tell Atchana, and from neighbouring sites on the Syrian-Turkish border* (BAR International Series 132), Oxford.

—— (1985), "A North Syrian Cylinder Seal Style: Evidence of North–South Links with ʿAjjul," in: J. N. Tubb, ed., *Palestine in the Bronze and Iron Ages: Papers in Honour of Olga Tufnell* (University of London, Institute of Archaeology. Occasional Publications 11), London, 57–68.

—— (1986), "The Green Jasper Cylinder Seal Workshop," in: Marilyn Kelly-Buccellati, ed., *Insight through Images: Studies in Honor of Edith Porada* (Bibliotheca Mesopotamica 21), Malibu, Calif., 57–70.

—— (1987), *First Impressions: Cylinder Seals in the Ancient Near East*, London.

CONRAD, DIETHELM (1979), "Einige (archäologische) Miszellen zur Kultgeschichte Judas in der Königszeit," in: *Textgemäß: Aufsätze und Beiträge zur Hermeneutik des Alten Testaments (FS E. Würthwein)*, Göttingen 1979, 28–32.

—— (1985), "A Note on an Astarte Plaque from Tel Akko," *Michmanim* 2, 19–24.

—— (1988), "Hebräische Bau-, Grab-, Votiv- und Siegelinschriften," *TUAT* II/4, 555–572.

—— (1991), "Ein hebräischer Segen," *TUAT* II/6, 929.

COOGAN, MICHAEL D. (1975), "A Cemetery from the Persian Period at Tell el-Hesi," *BASOR* 220, 37–46.

—— (1987a), "Canaanite Origins and Lineage: Reflections on the Religion of Ancient Israel," in: Miller et al., 1987, 115–126.

—— (1987b), "Of Cults and Cultures: Reflections on the Interpretation of Archaeological Evidence," *PEQ* 119, 1–8.

COOK, STANLEY A. (1925), *The Religion of Ancient Palestine in the Light of Archaeology* (SchL 1925), London.

COULSON, WILLIAM D. E. (1986), *Palestinian Objects at the University of Minnesota* (Monographic Journals of the Near East. Occasional Papers on the Near East 2/2), Malibu,Calif.

COUROYER, B. (1978), "*BRK* et les formules égyptiennes de salutation," *RB* 85, 575–585.

COURTOIS, JACQUES-CLAUDE – WEBB, JENNIFER M. (1987), *Les cylindres-sceaux d'Enkomi (Fouilles françaises 1957–1970)*, Nicosia.

CROSS, FRANK MOORE (1970), "The Cave Inscriptions from Khirbet Beit Lei," in: J. A. Sanders, ed., *Near Eastern Archaeology in the Twentieth Century: Essays in Honor of Nelson Glueck*, New York, 299–306.

—— (1973), *Canaanite Myth and Hebrew Epic*, Cambridge, Mass.

—— (1980), "Newly Found Inscriptions in Old Canaanite and Early Phoenician Scripts," *BASOR* 238, 1–20.

—— (1984), "An Old Canaanite Inscription Recently Found at Lachish," *Tel Aviv* 11, 71–76.

CROSS, FRANK MOORE – MILIK, JOSEPH T. (1954), "Inscribed Javelin-Heads from the Period of the Judges: a Recent Discovery in Palestine," *BASOR* 134, 5–15.

CROWFOOT, JOHN WINTER – CROWFOOT, GRACE MARY (1938), *Early Ivories from Samaria (Samaria-Sebaste: Reports of the Work of the Joint Expedition in 1931–1933 and of the British Expedition in 1935*, no. II), London.

CROWFOOT, JOHN WINTER – CROWFOOT, GRACE MARY – KENYON, KATHLEEN M. (1957), *The Objects from Samaria (Samaria-Sebaste: Reports of the Work of the Joint Expedition in 1931–1933 and of the British Expedition in 1935*, no. III), London.

CULICAN, WILLIAM (1974), "A Phoenician Seal from Khaldeh" *Levant* 6, 195–198 (= 1986, 385–390).

—— (1976), "A Terracotta Shrine from Achzib," *ZDPV* 92, 47–53 (= 1986, 481–493).

—— (1986), *Opera selecta: From Tyre to Tartessos* (Studies in Mediterranean Archaeology Pocket-book 40), Göteborg.

CURTIS, A. H. W. (1990), "Some Observations on 'Bull' Terminology in the Ugaritic Texts and the Old Testament," *OTS* 26, 17–31.

DAJANI, A. K. (1953), "An Iron Age Tomb at al-Jib," *ADAJ* 2, 66–74.

DALLEY, STEPHANIE (1990), "Yahweh in Hamath in the 8th Century B.C.: Cuneiform Material and Historical Deductions," *VT* 40, 21–32.

DALMAN, GUSTAV (1906), "Ein neu gefundenes Jahvebild," *PJ* 2, 44–50.

DAVIES, GRAHAM I. (1986), *Megiddo* (Cities of the Biblical World), Cambridge.

—— et al., (1991), *Ancient Hebrew Inscriptions: Corpus and Concordance*, Cambridge.

DAY, JOHN (1986), "Asherah in the Hebrew Bible and Northwest Semitic Literature," *JBL* 105, 385–408.

DECKER, WOLFGANG (1971), *Die physische Leistung Pharaos: Untersuchung zu Heldentum, Jagd und Leibesübungen des ägyptischen Königs*, Cologne.

—— (1978), *Annotierte Bibliographie zum Sport im alten Ägypten*, Saint Augustine.

—— (1987), *Sport und Spiel im Alten Ägypten* (Beck's Archäologische Bibliothek), Munich. [ET: *Sports and Games of Ancient Egypt*, trans. Allen Guttmann (New Haven, Conn.: Yale University Press, 1992)].

DELAPORTE, LOUIS (1910), *Catalogue des cylindres orientaux et des cachets assyro-babyloniens, perses et syro-cappadociens de la Bibliothèque Nationale*, 2 vols., Paris.

—— (1920–1923), *Musée du Louvre: Catalogue des cylindres, cachets et pierres gravées de style oriental*, 2 vols., Paris.

DELCOR, MARCEL (1974), "Astarté et la fécondité des troupeaux en Deut. 7,13 et parallèles," *UF* 6, 7–14.

DESROCHES-NOBLECOURT, CHRISTIANE (1950), "Un petit monument commémoratif du roi athlète," *RdE* 7, 37–46.

DEUTSCH, ROBERT (1989), *Ancient Coins and Antiquities* (Matsa Co. Ltd. Archaeological Center. Auction no. 60), Tel Aviv.

DEVER, WILLIAM G. (1969/70), "Iron Age Epigraphic Material from the Area of Khirbet el-Kôm," *HUCA* 40, 139–189.

—— (1974), *Gezer II: Report of the 1967–70 Seasons in Fields I and II* (Annual of the Hebrew Union College/Nelson Glueck School of Biblical Archaeology), Jerusalem.

DEVER, WILLIAM G. (1983), "Material Remains and the Cult in Ancient Israel: An Essay in Archaeological Systematics," in: Meyers – O'Connor 1983, 571–587.

—— (1984), "Asherah, Consort of Yahweh? New Evidence from Kuntillet ʿAjrûd," *BASOR* 255, 21–37.

—— et al., (1986), *Gezer IV: The 1969–1971 Seasons in Field VI, the "Acropolis"*. Parts I + II (Annual of the Hebrew Union College/Nelson Glueck School of Biblical Archaeology), Jerusalem.

—— (1987), "The Contribution of Archaeology to the Study of Canaanite and Early Israelite Religion," in: Miller et al., 1987, 209–247.

—— (1990), *Recent Archaeological Discoveries and Biblical Research*, Seattle – London.

DEVRIES, LAMOINE F. (1975), *Incense Altars from the Period of the Judges and their Significance*, University of Michigan.

DIETRICH, MANFRIED – LORETZ, OSWALD – SANMARTÍN, JOSÉ (1975), "Das Ritual RS 1.5 = CTA 33," *UF* 7, 522–528.

DIJKSTRA, MEINDERT (1991), "Response to H.-P. Müller and M. Weippert," in: Hoftijzer/van der Kooij 1991, 206–217.

DION, PAUL-E. (1979), "Les types épistolaires hébréo-araméens jusqu'au temps de Bar-Kokhbah," *RB* 86, 544–579.

—— (1991), "YHWH as Storm-God and Sun-God. The Double Legacy of Egypt and Canaan as Reflected in Ps 104," *ZAW* 103, 43–71.

DIRINGER, DAVID (1934), *Le iscrizioni antico-ebraiche palestinesi*, Florence.

DOHMEN, CHRISTOPH (1985), *Das Bilderverbot: Seine Entstehung und seine Entwicklung im Alten Testament* (BBB 62), Frankfurt/Main (^{2}1987).

DONNER, HERBERT (1982), "The Interdependence of Internal Affairs and Foreign Policy during the Davidic-Solomonic Period," in: Ishida 1982, 205–214.

—— (1986), *Geschichte des Volkes Israel und seiner Nachbarn in Grundzügen*. Part 2: *Von der Königszeit bis zu Alexander dem Großen* (Grundrisse zum Alten Testament = ATD Expanded vol. 4/2), Göttingen.

DOTHAN, MOSHE (1956), "The Excavations at Nahariya. Preliminary Report, Seasons 1954/1955," *IEJ* 6, 14–25.

—— et al., (1971), *Ashdod II-III: The Second and Third Seasons of Excavations, 1963, 1965*: ʿAtiqot 9–10 (English Series), Jerusalem.

—— (1977), "Nahariya," in: Avi-Yonah/Stern 1977/III, 908–912.

—— (1985), "A Phoenician Inscription from ʿAkko," *IEJ* 35, 81–94.

DOTHAN, MOSHE – FREEDMAN, DAVID NOEL (1967), *Ashdod I: The First Season of Excavations, 1962:* ʿAtiqot 7 (English Series), Jerusalem.

DOTHAN, MOSHE – PORATH, YOSEF (1982), *Ashdod IV: Excavations of Area M*: ʿAtiqot 15 (English Series), Jerusalem.

DOTHAN, TRUDE (1979), *The Excavation at Deir el-Balaḥ* (Qedem 10), Jerusalem.

—— (1982), *The Philistines and their Material Culture*, Jerusalem.

DUMORTIER, JEAN-BERNARD (1974), *Les scarabées de Tell el-Farʿah* (unpubl. Mémoire, École Biblique et Archéologique Française), Jerusalem.

DUNAYEVSKY, IMMANUEL – KEMPINSKI, AHARON (1973), "The Megiddo Temples," *ZDPV* 89, 161–187.

DUPONT-SOMMER, ANDRÉ (1945), "Le syncrétisme religieux des Juifs d'Éléphantine," *RHR* 130, 17–28.

EDELSTEIN, GERSHON – MILEVSKI, IANIR (1990), "Manḥat–1989," *Ḥadašot Arkeologiot* 95, 54–55 (hebr.).

EICHLER, SEYYARE et al., (1984), "Ausgrabungen in Tall Munbāqa 1983," *MDOG* 116, 65–93.

EISEN, GUSTAVUS A. (1940), *Ancient Oriental Cylinder and Other Seals with a Description of the Collection of Mrs. William H. Moore* (OIP 47), Chicago.

EISENBERG, EMMANUEL (1977), "The Temples at Tell Kittan," *BA* 40, 77–81.

EISSFELDT, OTTO (1939), "Baʿalšamēm und Jahwe," *ZAW* 57, 1–31 (= idem, *Kleine Schriften* II, Tübingen 1963, 171–198).

ELGAVISH, JOSEPH (1975), "Shiqmona 1975" [Notes and News], *IEJ* 25, 257–258.

ELLIOTT, CAROLYN (1977), "The Religious Beliefs of the Ghassulians c. 4000–3000 B.C.," *PEQ* 109, 3–25.

EMERTON, JOHN A. (1982), "New Light on Israelite Religion: The Implications of the Inscriptions from KuntilletʿAjrud," *ZAW* 94, 2–20.

ENGLE, JAMES ROBERT (1979), "Pillar Figurines of Iron Age Israel and Asherah/Asherim," Ph.D. diss. University of Pittsburgh (University Microfilms, Ann Arbor, Mich., no. 7924652).

FABRY, HEINZ-JOSEF (1984), Art. "מרזח *marzeaḥ*," *TDOT* 5,11–16.

FECHHEIMER, HEDWIG (1921), *Kleinplastik der Ägypter*, Berlin.

FINKELSTEIN, ISRAEL (1988), *The Archaeology of the Israelite Settlement*, Jerusalem.

—— (1989), "The Emergence of the Monarchy in Israel: The Environmental and Socio-Economic Aspects," *JSOT* 44, 43–74.

FITZGERALD, G. M. (1930), *Beth Shan II: The Four Canaanite Temples of Beth Shan. Part II: The Pottery*, Philadelphia.

FOWLER, JEANEANE D. (1988), *Theophoric Personal Names in Ancient Hebrew: A Comparative Study* (JSOTSup 49).

FRANKEN, HENDRICUS JACOBUS – STEINER, MARGARETE LAURA (1990), *Excavations in Jerusalem 1961–1967.* Vol. II: *The Iron Age Extramural Quarter on the South-East Hill* (British Academy Monographs in Archaeology 2), Oxford.

FREVEL, CHRISTIAN (1989), "'Dies ist der Ort, von dem geschrieben steht . . .'. Zum Verhältnis von Bibelwissenschaft und Palästinaarchäologie," *BN* 47, 35–89.

—— (1991), "Die Elimination der Göttin aus dem Weltbild des Chronisten," *ZAW* 103, 263–271.

FRITZ, VOLKMAR (1980), "Der Tempel Salomos im Licht der neueren Forschung," *MDOG* 112, 53–68.

—— (1985), *Einführung in die biblische Archäologie* (Die Archäologie. Einführungen), Darmstadt. [ET: *Introduction to Biblical Archaeology* (Sheffield: JSOT, 1993)].

—— (1986), "Vorbericht über die Ausgrabungen auf dem *Tell el-ʿOrēme* am See Genezaret in den Jahren 1982–1985," *ZDPV* 102, 1–39.

—— et al., (1990), *Kinneret: Ergebnisse der Ausgrabungen auf dem Tell el-ʿOrēme am See Gennesaret 1982–1985* (ADPV 15), Wiesbaden.

GAL, ZVI (1989), *Hurbat Rosh Zayit: Biblical Cabul* (Rëuben and Edith Hecht Museum. Catalogue no. 5), Haifa.

432   *Gods, Goddesses, and Images of God*

GAL, ZVI (1990a), *The Lower Galilee: Historical Geography in the Biblical Period*, Tel Aviv (hebr.).

—— (1990b), "Khirbet Roš Zayit – Biblical Cabul. A Historical-Geographical Case," *BA* 53, 88–97.

GALLING, KURT (1941), "Beschriftete Bildsiegel des ersten Jahrtausends v. Chr. vornehmlich aus Syrien und Palästina. Ein Beitrag zur Geschichte der phönizischen Kunst," *ZDPV* 64, 121–202.

—— (1977), ed., *Biblisches Reallexikon*. 2nd, completely rewritten, edition (HAT I/1), Tübingen.

GARBINI, GIOVANNI (1982), "I sigilli del regno di Israele," *OrAnt* 21, 163–176.

GARFINKEL, YOSEF (1984), "The Distribution of Identical Seal Impressions and the Settlement Pattern in Judea before Sennacherib's Campaign," *Cathedra* 32 (July), 35–52 (hebr.).

—— (1988), "2 Chr 11:5–10 Fortified Cities List and the *lmlk* Stamps – Reply to Nadav Na'aman," *BASOR* 271, 69–73.

GARSTANG, JOHN (1933), "Jericho: City and Necropolis. Third Report," *AAA* 20, 3–42.

GEERTZ, CLIFFORD (1973), *The Interpretation of Cultures: Selected Essays*, New York.

GERSTENBERGER, ERHARD S. (1988), *Jahwe – ein patriarchaler Gott?*, Stuttgart, etc. [ET: *Yahweh—The Patriarch: Ancient Images of God and Feminist Theology*, trans. Frederick J. Gaiser (Minneapolis, Minn.: Fortress Press, 1996)].

GESE, HARTMUT (1970), Die Religionen Altsyriens, in: idem – Maria Höfner – K. Rudolph, *Die Religionen Altsyriens, Altarabiens und der Mandäer* (Die Religionen der Menschheit 10.2), Stuttgart, etc., 1–232.

GEVA, SHULAMIT (1980), "A Neo-Assyrian Cylinder Seal from Beth Shan," *Journal of the Ancient Near Eastern Society of Columbia University* 12, 45–49.

—— (1981), "The Painted Sherd of Ramat Raḥel," *IEJ* 31, 186–189.

GILULA, MORDECHAI (1979), "To Yahweh Shomron and his Asherah," *Shnaton* 3, 129–137 (hebr.). XV-XVI (engl. summary).

GITIN, SEYMOUR (1990), "Ekron of the Philistines. Part II: Olive-Oil Suppliers to the World," *BAR* 16, 33–42, 59.

GITIN, SEYMOUR – DOTHAN, TRUDE (1987), "The Rise and Fall of Ekron of the Philistines," *BA* 50, 197–222.

GIVEON, RAPHAEL (1971), *Les bédouins Shosou des documents égyptiens* (DMOA 18), Leiden.

—— (1978), *The Impact of Egypt on Canaan: Iconographical and Related Studies* (OBO 20), Fribourg, Switzerland and Göttingen.

—— (1983), "An Inscription of Rameses III from Lachish," *Tel Aviv* 10, 176–177.

—— (1985), *Egyptian Scarabs from Western Asia from the Collections of the British Museum* (OBO Series archaeologica 3), Fribourg, Switzerland and Göttingen.

—— (1986), "Remarks on the Tel Qarnayim Goddess," *BN* 33, 7–9.

—— (1988), *Scarabs from Recent Excavations in Israel* (OBO 83), Fribourg, Switzerland and Göttingen.

GIVEON, RAPHAEL – KERTESZ, TRUDE (1986), *Egyptian Scarabs and Seals from Acco: From the Collection of the Israel Department of Antiquities and Museums*, Fribourg, Switzerland.

GLOCK, ALBERT E. (1978), "Ta'anach," in: Avi-Yonah/Stern 1978/IV, 1138–1147.

—— (1983), "Texts and Archaeology at Tell Ta'annek," *Berytus* 31, 57–66.

GLOCK, ALICE – BAILEY, VIRGINIA E. (1988), *Minuscule Monuments of Ancient Art: Catalogue of Near Eastern Stamp and Cylinder Seals Collected by Virginia E. Bailey*, Madison, N.J.

GOEDICKE, HANS (1975), *The Report of Wenamun* (The Johns Hopkins Near Eastern Studies), Baltimore – London.

GÖRG, MANFRED (1981), "Die Königstochter und die Leier," *BN* 14, 7–10.

—— (1991), "Jachin und Boas. Namen und Funktion der beiden Tempelsäulen," in: idem, *Aegyptiaca-Biblica: Notizen und Beiträge zu den Beziehungen zwischen Ägypten und Israel* (ÄAT 11), Wiesbaden, 79–98.

GOLDWASSER, ORLY (1991), "A Fragment of an Hieratic Ostracon from Tel Haror," *Qadmoniot* 24 (nos. 93–94), 19 (hebr.).

GOLDWASSER, ORLY – LAOR, NATHANIEL (1991), "The Allure of the Holy Glyfhs [*sic!*]: A Psycholinguistic Perspective on the Egyptian Script," *GM* 123, 37–51.

GOPHNA, RAM – SUSSMANN, VARDA (1969), "A Middle Bronze Age Tomb at Barqai," *'Atiqot* 5 (Hebrew Series), 1–13 (hebr.).

GRANT, ELIHU (1929), *Beth Shemesh (Palestine): Progress of the Haverford Archaeological Expedition. A Report of the Excavations Made in 1928*, Haverford.

—— (1931), *Ain Shems Excavations (Palestine)* (BKS 3), Haverford.

—— (1932), *Ain Shems Excavations (Palestine) 1928–1931, Part II* (BKS 4), Haverford.

—— (1934), *Rumeileh. Ain Shems Excavations (Palestine). Part III* (BKS 5), Haverford.

GRANT, ELIHU – WRIGHT, GEORGE ERNEST (1938), *Ain Shems Excavations (Palestine). Part IV (Pottery)* (BKS 7), Haverford.

—— (1939), *Ain Shems Excavations (Palestine). Part V (Text)* (BKS 8), Haverford.

GRESSMANN, HUGO (²1927), *Altorientalische Bilder zum Alten Testament*, Berlin – Leipzig.

GUBEL, ERIC (1985), "Notes on a Phoenician Seal in the Royal Museums for Art and History, Brussels. The Corpus Glyptica Phoenicia 1," *OLP* 16, 91–110.

—— (1986), ed., *Les Phéniciens et le monde méditerranéen*, Brussels.

—— (1987), *Phoenician Furniture: A Typology Based on Iron Age Representations with Reference to the Iconographical Context* (Studia Phoenicia 7), Louvain.

—— (1991a), "From Amathus to Zarephath and Back Again," in: Frieda Vandenabeele – R. Laffineur, eds., *Cypriote Terracottas: Proceedings of the First International Conference of Cypriote Studies [. . .]*, Brussels – Liège 131–138.

434   *Gods, Goddesses, and Images of God*

GUBEL, ERIC (1991b), "Notes sur l'iconographie royale sigillaire," in: *Atti del II Congresso Internazionale di Studi Fenici e Punici* (Collezione di Studi Fenici 30/III), Rome, 913–922.

GUNNEWEG, JAN – PERLMAN, ITZHAQ – MESHEL, ZEEV (1985), "The Origin of the Pottery of Kuntillet ʿAjrud," *IEJ* 35, 270–283.

GUY, P. L. O. (1938), *Megiddo Tombs* (OIP 33), 2 vols., Chicago.

HAAG, ERNST (1985), ed., *Gott, der einzige: Zur Entstehung des Monotheismus in Israel* (QD 104), Freiburg im Breisgau – Basel – Vienna.

HACHLILI, RACHEL – MESHORER, YAAKOV (1986), *Highlights from the Collection of the Rëuben and Edith Hecht Museum* (Catalogue no. 1), Haifa.

HACHMANN, ROLF et al., (1980), *Bericht über die Ergebnisse der Ausgrabungen in Kāmid el-Lōz in den Jahren 1968 bis 1970* (SBA 22), Bonn.

HADLEY, JUDITH M. (1987a), "The Khirbet el-Qom Inscription," *VT* 37, 50–62.

—— (1987b), "Some Drawings and Inscriptions on Two Pithoi from Kuntillet ʿAjrud," *VT* 37, 180–213.

—— (1989), "Yahweh's Asherah in the Light of Recent Discovery" (unpubl. Ph.D. diss., Cambridge University), Cambridge.

HAHN, JOACHIM (1981), *Das "Goldene Kalb": Die Jahwe-Verehrung bei Stierbildern in der Geschichte Israels* (EHS XXIII/154), Frankfurt/Main – Bern.

HAMILTON, R. W. (1935), "Excavations at Tell Abu Hawam," *QDAP* 4, 1–69.

HAMMOND P. C. (1957), "A Note on two Seal Impressions from Tell es-Sulṭan," *PEQ*, 68–69.

HARAN, MENAHEM (1989), "The Priestly Blessing on Silver Plaques: The Significance of the Discovery at Ketef Hinnom," *Cathedra* 52, July 1989, 77–89.

HELCK, WOLFGANG (1962), *Die Beziehungen Ägyptens zu Vorderasien im 3. und 2. Jahrtausend v. Chr.* (ÄA 5), Wiesbaden.

—— (1971), *Betrachtungen zur Großen Göttin und den ihr verbundenen Gottheiten* (RKAMW 2), Munich – Vienna.

—— (1975), Art. "Beischläferin," *LdÄ* I, 684–686.

HERMARY, A. (1986), Art. "Bes (Cypri et in Phoenicia)," *LIMC* II/1, 108–112.

HERR, LARRY G. (1978), *The Scripts of Ancient Northwest Semitic Seals* (HSM 18), Missoula, Mont.

HERZOG, ZEʾEV – RAPP, JR., GEORGE – NEGBI, ORA (1989), *Excavations at Tel Michal, Israel* (Tel Aviv University, Publications of the Institute of Archaeology 8), Minneapolis and Tel Aviv.

HESS, RICHARD S. (1989), "Cultural Aspects of Onomastic Distribution in the Amarna Texts," *UF* 21, 208–216.

HESTRIN, RUTH (1987a), "The Lachish Ewer and the Asherah," *IEJ* 37, 212–223.

—— (1987b), "The Cult Stand from Taʿanach and its Religious Background," in: E. Lipiński, ed., *Phoenicia and the East Mediterranean in the First Millenium B.C.* (Studia Phoenicia 5), Louvain, 61–77.

—— (1991), "Understanding Asherah – Exploring Semitic Iconography," *BAR* 17/5, 50–59.

HESTRIN, RUTH – DAYAGI-MENDELS, MICHAL (1979), *Inscribed Seals. First Temple Period: Hebrew, Ammonite, Moabite, Phoenician and Aramaic. From the Collections of the Israel Museum and the Israel Department of Antiquities and Museums* (Israel Museum Catalogue), Jerusalem.

HILLERS, DELBERT R. (1970), "The Goddess with the Tambourine. Reflections on an Object from Taanach," *CTM* 41, 94–107.

HÖLBL, GÜNTHER (1989), "Ägyptische Kunstelemente im phönikischen Kulturkreis des 1. Jahrtausends v. Chr.: Zur Methodik ihrer Verwendung," *Or.* N.S. 58, 318–325.

HOFFMANN, HANS-DETLEF (1980), *Reform und Reformen: Untersuchungen zu einem Grundthema der deuteronomistischen Geschichtsschreibung* (ATANT 66), Zurich.

HOFSTEE, WIM (1986), "The Interpretation of Religion. Some Remarks on the Work of Clifford Geertz," in: H. G. Hubbeling – H. G. Kippenberg, eds., *On Symbolic Representation of Religion*, Berlin/New York, 70–83.

HOFTIJZER, JACOB (1986), "Die Inschrift von Deir ʿAlla," *TUAT* II/1, 138–148.

HOFTIJZER, JACOB – VAN DER KOOIJ, GERRIT (1976), *Aramaic Texts from Deir ʾAllā* (DMOA 19), Leiden.

—— (1991), ed., *The Balaam Text from Deir ʿAlla Re-evaluated: Proceedings of the International Symposium held at Leiden 21–24 August 1989*, Leiden.

HOLLADAY, J. S. (1987), "Religion in Israel and Judah under the Monarchy: An Explicitly Archaeological Approach," in: Miller et al., 1987, 249–299.

HOLLAND, T. A. (1977), "A Study of Palestinian Iron Age Baked Clay Figurines, with Special Reference to Jerusalem: Cave 1," *Levant* 9, 121–155.

HOMÈS-FRÉDÉRICQ, DOMINIQUE (1987), "Possible Phoenician Influences in Jordan in the Iron Age, in," A. Hadidi, ed., *Studies in the History and Archaeology of Jordan III*, Amman, 89–96.

HORN, SIEGFRIED H. (1962), "An Early Aramaic Seal with an Unusual Design," *BASOR* 167, 16–18.

—— (1966), "Scarabs and Scarab Impressions from Shechem II," *JNES* 25, 48–65.

—— (1973), "Scarabs and Scarab Impressions from Shechem III," *JNES* 32, 281–289.

HORNUNG, ERIK (1971), *Der Eine und die Vielen: Ägyptische Gottesvorstellungen*, Darmstadt. [ET: *Conceptions of God in Ancient Egypt: The One and the Many*, trans. John Baines (Ithaca, N.Y.: Cornell University Press, 1982)].

HORNUNG, ERIK – STAEHELIN, ELISABETH (1976), *Skarabäen und andere Siegelamulette aus Basler Sammlungen* (Ägyptische Denkmäler in der Schweiz 1), Mainz.

HÜBNER, ULRICH (1986), "Aegyptiaca vom Tell el-ʿOrēme," *SBFLA* 36, 253–264.

—— (1989a), "Das Fragment einer Tonfigurine vom *Tell el-Milḥ* Überlegungen zur Funktion der sog. Pfeilerfigurinen in der israelitischen Volksreligion," *ZDPV* 105, 47–55.

—— (1989b), "Schweine, Schweineknochen und ein Speiseverbot im alten Israel," *VT* 39, 225–236.

HÜBNER, ULRICH (1993), "Das ikonographische Repertoire der ammonitischen Siegel und seine Entwicklung," in: Sass/Uehlinger 1993.

IBRAHIM, MOAWIYAH M. (1983), "Siegel und Siegelabdrücke aus Saḥab," *ZDPV* 99, 43–53.
IBRAHIM, MOAWIYAH M. – VAN DER KOOIJ, GERRIT (1991), "The Archaeology of Deir ʿAlla Phase IX," in: Hoftijzer/van der Kooij 1991, 16–29.
ISHIDA, TOMOO (1982), ed., *Studies in the Period of David and Solomon and Other Essays*, Tokyo and Winona Lake.
ISRAEL, FELICE (1990), "Note ammonite II: La religione degli Ammoniti attraverso le fonti epigrafiche," *SMSR* 56, 307–337.
ISSERLIN, B. S. J. (1957), "Israelite and pre-Israelite Place-Names in Palestine," *PEQ* 89, 133–144.

JACKSON, KENT P. (1983), "Ammonite Personal Names in the Context of the West Semitic Onomasticon," in: Meyers/O'Connor 1983, 507–521.
JAEGER, BERTRAND (1982), *Essai de classification et datation des scarabées Menkhéperrê* (OBO Series archaeologica 2), Fribourg, Switzerland and Göttingen.
JAKOB-ROST, LIANE (1975), *Die Stempelsiegel im Vorderasiatischen Museum: Staatliche Museen zu Berlin*, Berlin.
JAMES, FRANCES W. (1966), *The Iron Age at Beth Shan* (Museum Monographs), Philadelphia.
JANOWSKI, BERND (1989), *Rettungsgewißheit und Epiphanie des Heils: Das Motiv der Hilfe Gottes "am Morgen" im Alten Orient und im Alten Testament*. Vol. I: *Alter Orient* (WMANT 59), Neukirchen-Vluyn.
—— (1991), "Keruben und Zion. Thesen zur Entstehung der Zionstradition," in: D.R. Daniels – U. Gleßmer – M. Rösel, eds., *Ernten, was man sät* (FS K. Koch), Neukirchen-Vluyn, 231–264.
JAROŠ, KARL (1980), "Die Motive der Heiligen Bäume und der Schlange in Gen 2–3," *ZAW* 92, 204–215.
JOHNS, C. N. (1933), "Excavations at ʿAtlīt (1930–1931): The South-Eastern Cemetery," *QDAP* 2, 41–104.

KANTOR, HELENE J. (1962), "A Bronze Plaque with Relief Decoration from Tell Tainat," *JNES* 21, 93–117.
KEEL, OTHMAR (1973), "Das Vergraben der "fremden Götter" in Genesis XXXV, 4b," *VT* 23, 305–336.
—— (1974), *Wirkmächtige Siegeszeichen im Alten Testament: Ikonographische Studien zu Jos 8,18.26; Ex 17,8–13; 2 Kön 13,14–19 und 1 Kön 22,11* (OBO 5), Fribourg, Switzerland and Göttingen.
—— (1975), "Kanaanäische Sühneriten auf ägyptischen Tempelreliefs," *VT* 25, 413–469.
—— (1977a), *Jahwe-Visionen und Siegelkunst: Eine neue Deutung der Majestätsschilderungen in Jes 6, Ez 1 und 10 und Sach 4* (SBS 84/85), Stuttgart.

KEEL, OTHMAR (1977b), *Vögel als Boten: Studien zu Ps 68,12–14, Gen 8,6–12, Koh 10,20 und dem Aussenden von Botenvögeln in Ägypten. Mit einem Beitrag von Urs Winter zu Ps 56,1 und zur Ikonographie der Göttin mit der Taube* (OBO 14), Fribourg, Switzerland and Göttingen.

—— (1978), *Jahwes Entgegnung an Ijob: Eine Deutung von Ijob 38–41 vor dem Hintergrund der zeitgenössischen Bildkunst* (FRLANT 121), Göttingen.

—— (1979), "Wer zerstörte Sodom?" TZ 35, 10–17.

—— (1980a), *Das Böcklein in der Milch seiner Mutter und Verwandtes: Im Lichte eines altorientalischen Bildmotivs* (OBO 33), Fribourg, Switzerland and Göttingen.

—— (1980b), ed., *Monotheismus im Alten Israel und in seiner Umwelt* (BiBe 14), Fribourg.

—— (1981), "Zeichen der Verbundenheit. Zur Vorgeschichte und Bedeutung der Forderungen von Deuteronomium 6,8f. und Par.," in: P. Casetti – O. Keel – A. Schenker, eds., *Mélanges Dominique Barthélemy: Etudes bibliques offertes à l'occasion de son 60ᵉ anniversaire* (OBO 38), Fribourg, Switzerland and Göttingen, 159–240.

—— (1982), "Der Pharao als 'Vollkommene Sonne': Ein neuer ägypto-palästinischer Skarabäentyp," in: Sara Israelit-Groll, ed., *Egyptological Studies* (ScrHier 28), Jerusalem, 406–530.

—— (⁴1984), *Die Welt der altorientalischen Bildsymbolik und das Alte Testament: Am Beispiel der Psalmen*, Neukirchen-Vluyn und Zurich (¹1972). [ET: *The Symbolism of the Biblical World: Ancient Near Eastern Iconography and the Book of Psalms* (New York: Seabury, 1978)].

—— (1984), *Deine Blicke sind Tauben: Zur Metaphorik des Hohen Liedes* (SBS 114/115), Stuttgart.

—— et al., (1984) = O.K. – Max Küchler – Christoph Uehlinger, *Orte und Landschaften der Bibel: Ein Handbuch und Studienreiseführer.* Vol. 1: *Geographisch-geschichtliche Landeskunde*, Einsiedeln – Zurich – Cologne and Göttingen.

—— (1986), *Das Hohelied* (ZBK.AT 18), Zurich. [ET: *The Song of Songs*: A Continental Commentary, trans. Frederick J. Gaiser (Minneapolis, Minn.: Fortress Press, 1994)].

—— et al., (1989) = O.K. – Hildi Keel-Leu – Silvia Schroer, *Studien zu den Stempelsiegeln aus Palästina/Israel* Vol. II (OBO 88), Fribourg, Switzerland and Göttingen.

—— et al., (1990) = O.K. – Menachem Shuval – Christoph Uehlinger, *Studien zu den Stempelsiegeln aus Palästina/Israel.* Vol. III. *Die Frühe Eisenzeit: Ein Workshop* (OBO 100), Fribourg, Switzerland and Göttingen.

KEEL, OTHMAR – KÜCHLER, MAX (1982), *Orte und Landschaften der Bibel: Ein Handbuch und Studienreiseführer.* Vol. 2: *Der Süden*, Einsiedeln – Zurich – Cologne and Göttingen.

KEEL, OTHMAR – SCHROER, SILVIA (1985), *Studien zu den Stempelsiegeln aus Palästina/Israel I* (OBO 67), Fribourg, Switzerland and Göttingen.

KEEL, OTHMAR – UEHLINGER, CHRISTOPH (1990), *Altorientalische Miniatur-kunst: Die ältesten visuellen Massenkommunikationsmittel. Ein Blick in die Sammlungen des Biblischen Instituts der Universität Freiburg/Schweiz*, Mainz/Rhine.

KEEL-LEU, HILDI (1989), "Die frühesten Stempelsiegel Palästinas. Von den Anfängen bis zum Ende des 3. Jahrtausends," in: Keel et al., 1988, 1–38.

—— (1991), *Vorderasiatische Stempelsiegel: Die Sammlung des Biblischen Instituts der Universität Fribourg, Switzerland* (OBO 111), Fribourg, Switzerland and Göttingen.

KELM, GEORGE L. – MAZAR, AMIHAI (1990), "Tel Batash (Timnah) Excavations: Third Preliminary Report, 1984–1989," BASORSup 27, 47–67.

KELSO, JAMES L. et al., (1968), *The Excavation of Bethel (1934–1960)* (AASOR 39), Cambridge, Mass.

KEMPINSKI, AHARON (1975), Art. "Bet Shean," in: Avi-Yonah/Stern 1975/I, 207–215.

—— (1989a), *Megiddo: A City-State and Royal Centre in North Israel* (Materialien zur Allgemeinen und Vergleichenden Archäologie 40), Munich.

—— (1989b), "Reconstructing the Canaanite Temple Tower," *ErIsr* 20, 82–85 (hebr.). 196*–197*.

KENYON, KATHLEEN M. et al., (1960), *Excavations at Jericho.* Vol. I, Jerusalem.

—— et al., (1965), *Excavations at Jericho.* Vol. II, Jerusalem.

KING, URSULA (1991), "Der feministische Aufbruch und die Ökumene," *Orientierung* 55, 139–143.

KNAUF, ERNST AXEL (1984), "Yahwe," *VT* 34, 467–472.

—— (1988a), *Midian: Untersuchungen zur Geschichte Palästinas und Nordarabiens am Ende des 2. Jahrtausends v. Chr.* (ADPV 10), Wiesbaden.

—— (1988b), "Zur Herkunft und Sozialgeschichte Israels. 'Das Böckchen in der Milch seiner Mutter'," *Biblica* 69, 153–169.

—— (1988c), "Hiobs Heimat," *WO* 19, 65–83.

—— (1990a), "Der Staat als Männerbund – Religionsanthropologische Aspekte der politischen Evolution," in: Gisela Völger – Karin von Welck, eds., *Männerbande – Männerbünde: Zur Rolle des Mannes im Kulturvergleich*, Cologne, Vol. 1, 11–22.

—— (1990b), "War 'Biblisch-Hebräisch' eine Sprache? Empirische Gesichtspunkte zur linguistischen Annäherung an die Sprache der althebräischen Literatur," *ZAH* 3, 11–23.

—— (1991), "From History to Interpretation," in: Diana V. Edelman, ed., *The Fabric of History: Text, Artifact and Israel's Past* (JSOTSup 127), Sheffield, 26–64.

KOCH, KLAUS (1988), "Aschera als Himmelskönigin in Jerusalem," *UF* 20, 97–120.

—— (1991), "Die hebräische Sprache zwischen Polytheismus und Monotheismus," in: idem, *Spuren des hebräischen Denkens. Beiträge zur alttestamentlichen Theologie* (Gesammelte Aufsätze Vol. 1), Neukirchen-Vluyn, 25–64.

KOCHAVI, MOSHE (1972), "Tel Aphek (Ras el-ʿAin)" [Notes and News], *IEJ* 22, 238–239.

KOCHAVI, MOSHE (1989), *Aphek-Antipatris: Five Thousand Years of History*, Tel Aviv.

—— (1990), *Aphek in Canaan: The Egyptian Governor's Residency and its Finds*, Jerusalem.

KÖCKERT, MATTHIAS (1991), Art. "Gott der Väter," *NBL* I, 915–919.

KÖNIGSWEG (1987) = *Der Königsweg: 9000 Jahre Kunst und Kultur in Jordanien und Palästina,* Mainz/Rhine.

KOHN-ROELIN, JOHANNA (1991), "Antijudaismus – die Kehrseite jeder Christologie?" in: Doris Strahm – Regula Strobel, eds., *Vom Verlangen nach Heilwerden: Christologie in feministisch-theologischer Sicht,* Fribourg – Lucerne, 65–80.

KORPEL, MARJO C. A. (1989), "The Poetic Structure of the Priestly Blessing," *JSOT* 45, 3–13.

—— (1990), *A Rift in the Clouds: Ugaritic and Hebrew Descriptions of the Divine* (Ugaritisch-Biblische Literatur 8), Münster.

KOTTSIEPER, INGO (1988), "Papyrus Amherst 63 – Einführung, Text und Übersetzung von 12,11–19," in: O. Loretz, *Die Königspsalmen: Die altorientalisch-kanaanäische Königstradition in jüdischer Sicht.* Part 1: *Ps 20, 21, 72, 101 und 144. Mit einem Beitrag von I. Kottsieper zu Papyrus Amherst* (Ugaritisch-Biblische Literatur 6), Münster, 55–75.

KRUCHTEN, JEAN-MARIE (1982), "Convention et innovation dans un texte royal du début de l'époque ramesside: La stèle de l'an 1 de Séthi Ier découverte à Beith-Shan (Musée archéologique de Jérusalem, n° S. 884)," *AIPh* 26, 21–62.

KUAN, JEFFREY K. (1990), "Third Kingdoms 5.1 and Israelite-Tyrian Relations During the Reign of Solomon," *JSOT* 46, 31–46.

KÜHNE, HARTMUT (1980), "Das Nordost-Tor von Tell Mumbāqat," in: J.-C. Margueron, ed., *Le Moyen Euphrate: Zone de contacts et d'échanges* (Université des sciences humaines de Strasbourg. Travaux du Centre de recherche sur le Proche-Orient et la Grèce antiques 5), Leiden, 203–215.

KYRIELEIS, H. – RÖLLIG, WOLFGANG (1988), "Ein altorientalischer Pferdeschmuck aus dem Heraion von Samos," *MDAIA* 103, 35–75.

LAMON, ROBERT S. – SHIPTON, G. M. (1939), *Megiddo I: Seasons of 1925–34. Strata I-V* (OIP 42), Chicago.

LANG, BERNHARD (1981), "Die Jahwe-allein-Bewegung," in: idem, ed., *Der einzige Gott: Die Geburt des biblischen Monotheismus,* Munich, 47–83.

LANG, BERNHARD (1983), *Monotheism and the Prophetic Minority: An Essay in Biblical History and Sociology* (Social World of Biblical Antiquity Series 2), Sheffield and Decatur, Ga.

—— (1991), Art. "Gott," *NBL* I, 904–915.

LAPP, PAUL W. (1967), "The 1966 Excavation at Tell Ta'annek," *BASOR* 185, 2–39.

—— (1969), "The 1968 Excavations at Tell Ta'annek," *BASOR* 195, 2–49.

LECLANT, JEAN (1980), "A propos des étuis porte-amulettes égyptiens et puniques," in: *Oriental Studies presented to B.S.J. Isserlin,* Leiden 1980, 101–107.

LEGGE, G. FRANCIS (1905), "The Magic Ivories of the Middle Empire," *PSBA* 27, 130–152.

LEITH, MARY JOAN WINN (1990), "Greek and Persian Images in Pre-Alexandrine Samaria: The Wâdi ed-Dâliyeh Seal Impressions" (Ph.D. diss. Harvard University), Cambridge, Ma. (University Microfilms no. 9035612).

LEMAIRE, ANDRÉ (1976), "Prières en temps de crise: les inscriptions de Khirbet Beit Lei," *RB* 83, 558–568.

—— (1977), "Les inscriptions de Khirbet el-Qôm et l'Ashérah de Yhwh," *RB* 84, 595–608.

—— (1981), *Les écoles et la formation de la Bible dans l'ancien Israël* (OBO 39), Fribourg and Göttingen.

—— (1984a), "Date et origine des inscriptions hébraïques et phéniciennes de Kuntillet 'Ajrud," *Studi Epigrafici e Linguistici* 1, 131–143.

—— (1984b), Who or What Was Yahweh's Asherah?: *BAR* 10/6, 42–51.

—— (1985), "Les inscriptions de Deir 'Alla et la littérature araméenne antique," *CRAI* 1985, 270–285.

—— (1986a), "Divinités égyptiennes dans l'onomastique phénicienne," in: Claudine Bonnet et al., eds., *Religio Phoenicia* (Studia Phoenicia 4 = Collection d'études classiques 1), Namur, 87–98.

—— (1986b), "Nouveaux sceaux nord-ouest sémitiques," *Syria* 63, 305–325.

—— (1988), "Recherches actuelles sur les sceaux nord-ouest sémitiques," *VT* 38, 220–230.

—— (1990a), "Trois sceaux inscrits inédits avec lion rugissant," *Semitica* 39 (Hommages à Maurice Sznycer, II), 13–22.

—— (1990b), "ʾBŠʿL: Anthroponyme Hébreu fantôme?" *ZAH* 3, 212–213.

—— (1991a) "Les inscriptions sur plâtre de Deir 'Alla et leur signification historique et culturelle," in: Hoftijzer/van der Kooij, 33–57.

—— (1991b), "Notes d'épigraphie nord-ouest sémitique," *Semitica* 40, 39–54.

—— (1993), "Les critères non-iconographiques de classement des sceaux nord-ouest sémitiques inscrits," in: Sass/Uehlinger 1993.

LEVY, SHALOM – EDELMAN, GERSHON (1972), "Cinq années de fouilles à Tel 'Amal (Nir David)," *RB* 79, 325–367.

LIEBOWITZ, HAROLD A. (1977), "Bone and Ivory Inlay from Syria Palestine," *IEJ* 27, 89–97.

—— (1980), "Military and Feast Scenes on Late Bronze Palestinian Ivories," *IEJ* 30, 162–169.

—— (1987), "Late Bronze II Ivory Work: Evidence of a Cultural Highpoint," *BASOR* 265, 3–24.

LINDER, ELISHA (1973), "A Cargo of Phoenico-Punic Figurines," *Archaeology* 26, 182–187.

LIPIŃSKI, EDWARD (1972), "Aṯirat in Ancient Arabia, in Babylon and in Ugaritic: Her Relation to the Moon-God and the Sun-Goddess," OLP 3, 101–119.

—— (1986), "The Syro-Palestinian Iconography of Woman and Goddess," (Review Article): *IEJ* 36, 87–96.

LODS, M. (1934), "Autel ou réchaud? A propos du "brûle-parfums" de Taanak," *RHR* 55 (no. 109), 129–147.

LOHFINK, NORBERT (1985), "Zur Geschichte der Diskussion über den Monotheismus im Alten Israel," in: Haag 1985, 9–25.

—— (1992), *Ein Wolkenspalt: Neue Veröffentlichungen zur Religionsgeschichte Israels*: Jahrbuch für Biblische Theologie 6 [at the press].

LORETZ, OSWALD (1989), "'Anat-Aschera (Hos 14,9) und die Inschriften von Kuntillet 'Ajrud," *Studi Epigrafici e Linguistici* 6, 57–65.

—— (1990), *Ugarit und die Bibel: Kanaanäische Götter und Religion im Alten Testament*, Darmstadt.

LOUD, GEORGE (1939), *The Megiddo Ivories* (OIP 52), Chicago.

—— et al., (1948), *Megiddo II: Seasons of 1935–1939* (OIP 62), 2 vols., Chicago.

MACALISTER, ROBERT ALEXANDER STEWART (1912), *The Excavation of Gezer: 1902–1905 and 1907–1909*, 3 vols., London.

MACHULE, DITTMAR et al., (1987), "Ausgrabungen in Tall Munbāqa 1985," MDOG 119, 73–134.

—— (1989), "Ausgrabungen in Tall Munbāqa 1987," MDOG 121, 65–77.

MACKENZIE, DUNCAN (1912–1913), "Excavations at Ain Shems, April to July, 1912," *PEFA* 2, 1–100.

MAIER, III, WALTER A. (1986), *'Ašerah: Extrabiblical Evidence* (HSM 37), Atlanta, Ga.

MALAISE, MICHEL (1989), "Bès et Béset: métamorphoses d'un démon et naissance d'une démone dans l'Égypte ancienne," in: J. Ries – H. Limet, ed., *Anges et démons* (Homo religiosus 14), Louvain-la-Neuve, 53–70.

—— (1990), "Bès et les croyances solaires," in: Sarah Israelit-Groll, ed., *Studies in Egyptology: Presented to Miriam Lichtheim*, Jerusalem, 680–729.

MALLET, JOËL (1974), "Tell el-Fârʿah près de Naplouse. Remarques sur la tombe A et le cylindre-sceau F 140," *RB* 81, 423–431.

—— (1988), *Tell el-Fârʿah II,2: Le Bronze moyen. Stratigraphie des vestiges du Bronze moyen II (1ʳᵉ moitié du IIᵉ millénaire av. J.-C.) dans les chantiers principaux II nord et IV* (Ed. Recherche sur les Civilisations. Mémoire no. 66), Paris.

MARGALIT, BARUCH (1989), "Some Observations on the Inscription and Drawing from Khirbet el-Qôm," *VT* 39, 371–378.

—— (1990), "The Meaning and Significance of Asherah," *VT* 40, 264–297.

MARGUERON, JEAN (1976), "'Maquettes' architecturales de Meskéné-Emar," *Syria* 53, 193–232.

—— (1982), "Les maquettes," in: D. Beyer, ed., *Meskéné-Emar: Dix ans de travaux, 1972–1982*, Paris, 87–94.

MARKOE, GLENN (1985), *Phoenician Bronze and Silver Bowls from Cyprus and the Mediterranean* (University of California Publications. Classical Studies 26), Berkeley – Los Angeles – London.

MARTIN, GEOFFREY THORNDIKE (1971), *Egyptian Administrative and Private-Name Seals: Principally of the Middle Kingdom and Second Intermediate Period*, Oxford.

MATOUK, FOUAD SELIM (1977), *Corpus du scarabée égyptien II: Analyse thématique*, Beyrouth.

MAY, HERBERT G. (1934–1935), "An Inscribed Jar from Megiddo," *AJSL* 50, 10–14.

MAY, HERBERT G. (1935), *Material Remains of the Megiddo Cult* (OIP 26), Chicago.

MAYER-OPIFICIUS, RUTH (1984), "Die geflügelte Sonne. Himmels- und Regendarstellungen im alten Vorderasien," *UF* 16, 189–236.

Mazar, Amihai (1980), *Excavations at Tell Qasile. Part One: The Philistine Sanctuary: Architecture and Cult Objects* (Qedem 12), Jerusalem.

—— (1982), "The 'Bull Site' – An Iron Age I Open Cult Place," *BASOR* 247, 27–42.

—— (1985a) *Excavations at Tell Qasile. Part Two: The Philistine Sanctuary: Various Finds, the Pottery, Conclusions, Appendixes* (Qedem 20), Jerusalem.

—— (1985b), "Pottery Plaques Depicting Goddesses Standing in Temple Facades," *Michmanim* 2, 5–18.

—— (1986) "Excavations at Tell Qasile, 1982–1984: Preliminary Report," *IEJ* 36, 1–15.

—— (1990a), *Archaeology of the Land of the Bible: 10,000–586 B.C.E.* (The Anchor Bible Reference Library), New York, etc.

—— (1990b), "Iron Age I and II Towers at Giloh and the Israelite Settlement," *IEJ* 40, 77–101.

Mazar, Benjamin (1967), "A Philistine Seal from Tel Qasile," *BIES* 31, 64–67 (hebr.).

Mazar, Benjamin – Dunayevski, Immanuel (1964), "En-Gedi. Third Season of Excavations. Preliminary Report," *IEJ* 14, 121–130.

—— (1967), "En-Gedi: The Fourth and Fifth Seasons of Excavations (Preliminary Report)," *IEJ* 17, 133–143.

Mazar, Eilat (1979), "Archaeological Evidence for the 'Cows of Bashan who are in the Mountain of Samaria," in: *Festschrift Rëuben Hecht*, Jerusalem, 151–157.

Mazar, Eilat – Mazar, Benjamin (1989), *Excavations in the South of the Temple Mount: The Ophel of Biblical Jerusalem* (Qedem 29), Jerusalem.

McCarter, Peter Kyle (1987), "Aspects of the Religion of the Israelite Monarchy: Biblical and Epigraphic Data," in: Miller et al., 1987, 137–155.

McCown, Chester Charlton (1947), *Tell en-Naṣbeh: Excavated under the Direction of the Late William Frederic Badè. Vol. I: Archaeological and Historical Results*, Berkeley – New Haven.

McGovern, P. E. (1985), *Late Bronze Palestinian Pendants: Innovation in a Cosmopolitan Age* (JSOT/ASOR Monograph Series 1), Sheffield.

McKay, J. (1973), *Religion in Judah under the Assyrians 732–609 B.C.* (SBT II/26), London.

Menant, Joachim (1888), *Collection de Clercq: Catalogue méthodique et raisonné. I.Cylindres orientaux*, Paris.

Merhav, Rivka (1985), "The Stele of the 'Serpent Goddess' from Tell Beit Mirsim and the Plaque from Shechem Reconsidered," *The Israel Museum Journal* 4, 27–42.

Meshel, Zeev (1978), *Kuntillet 'Ajrud: A Religious Centre from the Time of the Judean Monarchy on the Border of Sinai* (Israel Museum Catalogue no. 175), Jerusalem.

—— (1979), "Did Yahweh Have a Consort? The New Religious Inscriptions from the Sinai," *BAR* 5/2, 24–35.

Mettinger, Tryggve N. D. (1982), "YHWH Sabaoth – the Heavenly King on the Cherubim Throne," in: Ishida 1982, 109–138.

METZGER, MARTIN (1985), *Königsthron und Gottesthron: Thronformen und Throndarstellungen in Ägypten und im Vorderen Orient im dritten und zweiten Jahrtausend vor Christus und deren Bedeutung für das Verständnis von Aussagen über den Thron im Alten Testament* (AOAT 15), 2 vols., Kevelaer and Neukirchen-Vluyn.

MEYERS, CAROL (1978), "Roots of Restriction: Women in Early Israel," *BA* 41, 91–103.

—— (1987), "A Terracotta at the Harvard Semitic Museum and Disc-holding Female Figures Reconsidered," *IEJ* 37, 116–122.

—— (1988), *Discovering Eve: Ancient Israelite Women in Context,* New York – Oxford.

—— (1989), "Women and the Domestic Economy of Early Israel," in: Barbara S. Lesko, ed., *Women's Earliest Records: From Ancient Egypt and Western Asia* (Brown Judaic Studies 166), Atlanta, Ga., 265–278.

—— (1991), "Of Drums and Damsels: Women's Performance in Ancient Israel," *BA* 54, 16–27.

MEYERS, CAROL L. – O'CONNOR, MICHAEL, eds., *The Word of the Lord Shall Go Forth: Essays in Honor of D. N. Freedman [. . .]* (American Schools of Oriental Research Special Volume Series 1), Winona Lake, Ind.

MILLARD, ALAN R. (1972), "An Israelite Royal Seal?," *BASOR* 208, 5–9.

—— (1980–1983), Art. "Königssiegel," *RLA* VI, 135–140.

—— (1980), *"Yw* and *yhw* Names," *VT* 30, 208–212.

—— (1985), "'BGD . . . – Magic Spell or Educational Exercise?" *ErIsr* 18, 39*–42*.

—— (1991), "Texts and Archaeology: Weighing the Evidence. The Case of King Solomon," *PEQ* 123, 19–27.

MILLER, J. MAXWELL (1991), "Solomon: International Potentate or Local King?" *PEQ* 123, 29–31.

MILLER, PATRICK D. (1970), "Animal Names as Designations in Ugaritic and Hebrew," *UF* 2, 177–186.

—— (1980), "El, The Creator of Earth," *BASOR* 239, 43–46.

—— (1981), "Psalms and Inscriptions," in: *Congress Volume Vienna, 1980* (VTSup 32), Leiden, 311–332.

—— (1986), "The Absence of the Goddess in Israelite Religion," *HAR* 10, 239–248.

—— (1987), "Cosmology and World Order in the Old Testament. The Divine Council as Cosmic-Political Symbol," *Horizons in Biblical Theology* 9, 53–78.

—— et al., (1987) = P. D. M. – P. D. Hanson – S. D. McBride, eds., *Ancient Israelite Religion: Essays in Honor of F.M. Cross,* Philadelphia.

MIRON, RENATE (1982), "Die Kleinfunde aus dem Bereich des 'spätbronzezeitlichen' Heiligtums," in: R. Hachmann et al., *Bericht über die Ergebnisse der Ausgrabungen in Kāmid el-Lōz in den Jahren 1971 bis 1974* (SBA 32), Bonn, 31–35.

MITTMANN, SIEGFRIED (1976), "Amos 3,12–15 und das Bett der Samarier," *ZDPV* 92, 149–167.

—— (1981), "Die Grabinschrift des Sängers Uriahu," *ZDPV* 97, 139–152.

MITTMANN, SIEGFRIED (1989), "A Confessional Inscription from the Year 701 B.C. Praising the Reign of Yahweh," *Acta Academica. Journal for Human Sciences Research* (Bloemfontein) 21/3, 15–38.

MOMMSEN, H./PERLMAN, I./YELLIN J. (1984), "The Provenience of the *lmlk* Jars," *IEJ* 34, 89–113.

MONTET, PIERRE (1933), *Les nouvelles fouilles de Tanis (1929–1932)* (PFLUS II/10), Paris.

DE MOOR, JOHANNES C. (1987), *An Anthology of Religious Texts from Ugarit* (Nisaba 16), Leiden.

—— (1990), *The Rise of Yahwism: The Roots of Israelite Monotheism* (BETL 91), Leuven.

MOOREY, PETER ROGER STUART – FLEMING, STUART (1984), "Problems in the Study of the Anthropomorphic Metal Statuary from Syro-Palestine before 330 B.C. (with a check-list and analyses of examples in the Ashmolean Museum, Oxford)," *Levant* 16, 67–90.

MOORTGAT, ANTON (1940), *Vorderasiatische Rollsiegel: Ein Beitrag zur Geschichte der Steinschneidekunst*, Berlin.

MOORTGAT-CORRENS, URSULA (1988), "Ein Kultbild Ninurtas aus neuassyrischer Zeit," *AfO* 35, 117–135.

MOTZKI, H. (1975), "Ein Beitrag zum Problem des Stierkultes in der Religionsgeschichte Israels," *VT* 25, 470–485.

MÜLLER, HANS-PETER (1982), "Die aramäische Inschrift von Deir ʿAllā und die älteren Bileamsprüche," *ZAW* 94, 214–244.

—— (1988), "Begriffe menschlicher Theomorphie. Zu einigen cruces interpretum in Hld 6,10," *ZAH* 1, 112–121.

—— (1989), Art. "עשתרת ʾštrt (ʿaštoræt)," *TDOT* VI, 453–463.

—— (1991), "Die Sprache der Texte von Tell Deir ʿAllā im Kontext der nordwestsemitischen Sprachen mit einigen Erwägungen zum Zusammenhang der schwachen Verbalklassen," *ZAH* 4, 1–31.

MÜLLER-WINKLER, CLAUDIA (1987), *Die ägyptischen Objekt-Amulette: Mit Publikation der Sammlung des Biblischen Instituts der Universität Freiburg/ Schweiz, formerly the collection of Fouad S. Matouk* (OBO Series archaeologica 5), Fribourg, Switzerland and Göttingen.

MULDER, M. J. (1989), "Solomon's Temple and YHWH's Exclusivity," *OTS* 25, 49–62.

MUYLDERMANS, ROBERT (1989), "Two Banquet Scenes in the Levant: A comparison between the Ahiram sarcophagus from Byblos and a North Syrian pyxis found at Nimrud," in: *Archaeologia Iranica et Orientalis: Miscellanean in Honorem L. Vanden Berghe*, Ghent, I, 393–407.

NAAG (1991) = *Ancient Art of the Mediterranean World & Ancient Coins* (Numismatic & Ancient Art Gallery. Catalogue № 7), Zurich.

NAʾAMAN, NADAV (1991), "The Kingdom of Judah under Josiah," *Tel Aviv* 18, 3–71.

NAʾAMAN, NADAV – FINKELSTEIN, ISRAEL (1990), eds., *From Nomadism to Monarchy: Archaeological and Historical Aspects of Early Israel* (FS M. Kochavi), Jerusalem (hebr.).

NAʾAMAN, NADAV – ZADOK, RAN (1988), "Sargon II's Deportations to Israel and Philistia (716–708 B.C.)," *JCS* 40,36–46.

NAUMANN, RUDOLF (1955), *Die Architektur Kleinasiens*, Tübingen.

NAVEH, JOSEPH (1963), "Old Hebrew Inscriptions in a Burial Cave," *IEJ* 13, 235–256.

—— (1979), "Graffiti and Dedications," *BASOR* 235, 27–30.

NEGBI, ORA (1970), *The Hoards of Goldwork from Tell el-ʿAjjul* (Studies in Mediterranean Archaeology 25), Göteborg.

—— (1974), "The Continuity of the Canaanite Bronzework of the Late Bronze Age into the Early Iron Age," *Tel Aviv* 1, 159–172.

—— (1976), *Canaanite Gods in Metal: An Archaeological Study of Ancient Syro-Palestinian Figurines*, Tel Aviv.

—— (1989), "The Metal Figurines," in: Yadin 1989, 348–362.

NELSON, HAROLD H. et al., (1930), *Earlier Historical Records of Ramses III: Medinet Habu I* (OIP 8), Chicago.

—— (1932), *Later Historical Records of Ramses III: Medinet Habu II* (OIP 9), Chicago.

NIEHR, HERBERT (1990), *Der höchste Gott: Alttestamentlicher JHWH-Glaube im Kontext syrisch-kanaanäischer Religion des 1. Jahrtausends v. Chr.* (BZAW 190), Berlin – New York.

NOUGAYROL, JEAN (1939), *Cylindres-sceaux et empreintes de cylindres trouvés en Palestine* (BAH 33), Paris.

NOUGAYROL, JEAN – AMIET, PIERRE (1962), "Le sceau de Sumirapa roi de Tuba," *RA* 56, 169–174.

O'DWYER SHEA, MICHAEL (1983), "The Small Cuboid Incense-Burner of the Ancient Near East," *Levant* 15, 76–109.

OHATA, KIYOSHI (1970), *Tel Zeror III: Report of the Excavation, Third Season 1966*, Tokyo.

OLYAN, SAUL M. (1987a), "Some Observations Concerning the Identity of the Queen of Heaven," *UF* 19, 161–174.

—— (1987b), "The Cultic Confessions of Jer 2,27a," *ZAW* 99, 254–259.

—— (1988), *Asherah and the Cult of Yahweh in Israel* (SBLMS 34), Atlanta, Ga.

OPIFICIUS, RUTH (1961), *Das altbabylonische Terrakottarelief* (UAVA 2), Berlin.

ORCHARD, JEREMY J. (1967), *Equestrian Bridle-Harness Ornaments: Catalogue & Plates* (Ivories from Nimrud I:2), London.

OREN, ELIEZER (1978), Art. "esh-Shariaʿa, Tell (Tel Seraʾ)," in: Avi-Yonah/Stern 1978/IV, 1059–1069.

—— et al., (1991), "Tell Haror after Six Seasons," *Qadmoniot* 24 (nos. 93–94), 2–19 (hebr.).

ORNAN, TALLAY (1986), *A Man and His Land: Highlights from the Moshe Dayan Collection* (The Israel Museum Catalogue no. 270), Jerusalem.

—— (1990), "Studies in Glyptics from the Land of Israel and Transjordan. Assyrian, Babylonian and Achaemenid Cylinder Seals from the 1st Half of the 1st Millenium B.C.E." (unpubl. M.A. thesis, Hebrew University. Institute of Archaeology), Jerusalem (hebr.).

—— (1993), "The Mesopotamian Influence on West Semitic Inscribed Seals: A Preference for the Depiction of Mortals," in: Sass/Uehlinger 1993.

ORTHMANN, WINFRIED (1989), ed., *Halawa 1980–1986: Vorläufiger Bericht über die 4.–9. Grabungskampagne* (SBA 52), Bonn.

ORY, J. (1945), "A Middle Bronze Age Tomb at el-Jisr," *QDAP* 12, 31–42.

VON DER OSTEN, HANS HENNING (1957), *Altorientalische Siegelsteine der Sammlung Hans Silvius von Aulock* (Studia Ethnographica Upsaliensia 13), Uppsala.

OTTOSSON, MAGNUS (1980), *Temples and Cult Places in Palestine* (BOREAS. Uppsala Studies in Ancient Mediterranean and Near Eastern Civilizations 22), Uppsala.

PARAYRE, DOMINIQUE (1990), "Les cachets ouest-sémitiques à travers l'image du disque solaire ailé (perspective iconographique)," *Syria* 67, 269–301.

PARDEE, DENNIS (1982), *Handbook of Ancient Hebrew Letters* (SBL Sources for Biblical Study 15), Chico, Calif.

—— (1988), "An Evaluation of the Proper Names from Ebla from a West Semitic Perspective: Pantheon Distribution According to Genre," in: A. Archi, ed., *Eblaite Personal Names and Semitic Name-Giving*, Rome, 119–151.

PARKER, BARBARA (1949), "Cylinder Seals from Palestine," *Iraq* 11, 1–42.

PARROT, ANDRÉ – CHÉHAB, MAURICE H. – MOSCATI, SABATINO (1977), *Die Phönizier: Die Entwicklung der phönizischen Kunst von den Anfängen bis zum Ende des dritten punischen Krieges* (Universum der Kunst), Munich.

PATAI, RAPHAEL (1967), *The Hebrew Goddess*, New York.

PECKHAM, B. (1987), "Phoenicia and the Religion of Israel: The Epigraphic Evidence," in: Miller et al., 1987, 79–99.

PETRIE, W. M. FLINDERS (1890), *Kahun, Gurob and Hawara*, London.

—— (1909), *Memphis I* (BSAE 15), London.

—— et al., (1923) = W.M.F.P. – Brunton, Guy – Murray, Margaret A., *Lahun II* (BSAE 33), London.

—— (1925), *Buttons and Design Scarabs: Illustrated by the Egyptian Collection in University College, London* (reprint Warminster and Encino 1974).

—— (1928), *Gerar* (BSAE 43), London.

—— (1930), *Beth-Pelet – Tell Fara I* (BSAE 48), London.

—— (1931), *Ancient Gaza I* (BSAE 53), London.

—— (1932), *Ancient Gaza II* (BSAE 54), London.

—— (1933), *Ancient Gaza III* (BSAE 55), London.

—— (1934), *Ancient Gaza IV* (BSAE 56), London.

—— (1952) = W.M.F.P. – Ernest J. H. Mackay – Margaret A. Murray, *City of Shepherd Kings. Ancient Gaza V.* (BSAE 64), London.

PETRIE, W. M. FLINDERS – ELLIS, J. C. (1937), *Anthedon (Sinai)* (BSAE 58), London.

PIEPER, MAX (1930), "Beschreibung einiger Skarabäen der Berliner Ägyptischen Sammlung," *ZDPV* 53, 195–199.

PISANO, G. (1991), "Antichità puniche nei Musei di Torino," in: *Atti del II Congresso Internazionale di Studi Fenici e Punici* (Collezione di Studi Fenici 30/III), Rome, 1143–1150.

PLATT, ELIZABETH E. (1976), "Triangular Jewelry Plaques," *BASOR* 221, 103–111.

PORADA, EDITH (1948), *Corpus of Ancient Near Eastern Seals in North American Collections: I. The Collection of the Pierpont Morgan Library* (BollS 14), Washington, D.C.

POTTS, TIMOTHY F. et al., (1985), "Preliminary Report on a Sixth Season of Excavation by the University of Sydney at Pella in Jordan 1983/84," *ADAJ* 29, 181–210.

—— et al., (1988), "Preliminary Report on the Eighth and Ninth Seasons of Excavation by the University of Sydney at Pella (Ṭabaqat Faḥl), 1986 and 1987," *ADAJ* 32, 115–149.

PRIGNAUD, JEAN (1978), "Scribes et graveurs à Jérusalem vers 700 av. J.-C.," in: P. R. S. Moorey – P. J. Parr, eds., *Archaeology in the Levant (FS K. M. Kenyon)*, Warminster, 136–148.

PRITCHARD, JAMES B. (1943), *Palestinian Figurines in Relation to Certain Goddesses Known Through Literature* (AOS 24), New Haven, Conn.

—— (1964), *Winery, Defenses, and Soundings at Gibeon* (University Museum Monograph), Philadelphia, Pa.

—— (1980), *The Cemetery at Tell es-Saʿidiyeh, Jordan* (University Museum Monograph 41), Philadelphia, Pa.

—— (1982), "The Tanit Inscription from Sarepta," in: H. G. Niemeyer, ed., *Phönizier im Westen* (Madrider Beiträge 8), 83–92.

—— (1985), *Tell es-Saʿidiyeh: Excavations on the Tell, 1964–1966* (University Museum Monographs 60), Philadelphia, Pa.

—— (1988), *Sarepta IV. The Objects from Area II, X: The University Museum of the University of Pennsylvania Excavations at Sarafand, Lebanon* (Publications de l'Université Libanaise. Section des études archéologiques II), Beyrouth.

PUECH, EMILE (1985), "L'inscription sur plâtre de Tell DeirʿAlla," in: *Biblical Archaeology Today: Proceedings of the International Congress on Biblical Archaeology, Jerusalem, April 1984*, 354–365.

—— (1986–1987), "The Canaanite Inscriptions of Lachish and their Religious Background," *Tel Aviv* 13–14, 13–25.

—— (1988), "Les écoles dans l'Israël préexilique: données épigraphiques," in: *Congress Volume Jerusalem 1986* (VTSup 40), Leiden, 189–203.

—— (1991), Review Article on: *Studien zu den Stempelsiegeln aus Palästina/Israel*, Vol. III [= Keel et al., 1990]: *RB* 98, 602–605.

RAHMANI, LEVI YIŞHAQ (1964), "Two Syrian Seals," *IEJ* 14, 180–184.

—— (1976), "A Phoenician Scarab from Ashkelon," *ʿAtiqot* (engl. Series) 11, 110–111.

RAINEY, ANSON F. (1963), "A Canaanite at Ugarit," *IEJ* 13, 43–45.

—— (1977), "Verbal Usages in the Taanach Texts," *IOS* 7, 33–64.

REICH, RONNY – BRANDL, BARUCH (1985), "Gezer under Assyrian Rule," *PEQ* 117, 41–54.

REIFENBERG, ADOLF (1938), "Some Ancient Hebrew Seals," *PEQ* 70, 113–116.

REISNER, GEORGE A. et al., (1924), *Harvard Excavations at Samaria*, 2 vols., Cambridge, Mass.

RICHARDS, FIONA V. (1992), *The Scarabs from Tomb 62 in Pella, Jordan* (OBO 117), Fribourg, Switzerland and Göttingen [at the press].

RÖSEL, HARTMUT N. (1986), "Zur Formulierung des aaronitischen Segens auf den Amuletten von Ketef Hinnom," *BN* 35, 30–36.

Roos, James-F. – Toombs, Lawrence-E. (1962), "Les découvertes effectuées au cours des dernières campagnes de fouilles à Sichem," _BTS_ 44, 6–15.

Root M. C. (1979), _The King and Kingship in Achaemenid Art: Essays on the Creation of an Iconography of Empire_ (Acta Iranica 19 = III/9), Leiden.

Rosen, B. (1988), "Early Israelite Cultic Centres in the Hill Country," _VT_ 38, 114–117.

Rothenberg, Beno (1988), _The Egyptian Mining Temple at Timna_ (Researches in the Arabah 1959–1984, Vol. 1), London.

Rowe, Alan (1929), "The Palestine Expedition. Report of the 1928 Season," _The Museum Journal_ 20, 37–88.

—— (1930), _Beth Shan I: The Topography and History of Beth Shan_, Philadelphia.

—— (1936), _A Catalogue of Egyptian Scarabs, Scaraboids, Seals and Amulets in the Palestine Archaeological Museum_, Cairo.

—— (1940), _The Four Canaanite Temples of Beth-Shan: Part I: The Temples and Cult Objects_, Philadelphia.

Rühlmann, Gerhard (1964), "Der Löwe im altägyptischen Triumphalbild," _WZ (H)_ 13, 651–658.

Rupprecht, Konrad (0000), _Der Tempel von Jerusalem: Gründung Salomos oder jebusitisches Erbe?_ (BZAW 144), Berlin – New York.

Saller, Sylvester J. (1964), _The Excavations at Dominus Flevit (Mount Olivet, Jerusalem)._ Vol. II: _The Jebusite Burial Place_ (PSBF.Ma 13), Jerusalem.

—— (1965–66), "Iron Age Tombs at Nebo, Jordan," _PSBFLA_ 16, 165–298.

Sass, Benjamin (1988), _The Genesis of the Alphabet and its Development in the Second Millenium B.C._ (ÄAT 13), Wiesbaden.

—— (1993), "The Iconography of Hebrew Seals: Iconism vs. Aniconism," in: Sass/Uehlinger 1993.

Sass, Benjamin – Uehlinger, Christoph (1993), eds., _Studies in the Iconography of Inscribed Northwest Semitic Seals_ (OBO 125), Fribourg, Switzerland and Göttingen.

Scagliarini, Fiorella (1989), "Osservazioni sulle Iscrizioni di Kuntillet ʿAjrud," _Rivista di Studi Orientali_ 63, 199–212.

Scharbert, Josef (1973), Art. BRK, "_berākāh_," _TDOT_ I, 808–841.

Schlögl, Hermann (1977), _Der Sonnengott auf der Blüte: Eine ägyptische Kosmogonie des Neuen Reiches_ (Aegyptiaca Helvetica 5), Geneva.

Schneider, Tsvi (1988), "Azariahu Son of Hilkiahu (High Priest?) on a City of David Bulla," _IEJ_ 38, 139–141.

—— (1991), "Six Biblical Signatures. Seals and Seal Impressions of Six Biblical Personages Recovered," _BAR_ 17/4, 26–33.

Schroer, Silvia (1984), "Zur Deutung der Hand unter der Grabinschrift von Chirbet el Qôm," _UF_ 15, 191–199.

—— (1987a), _In Israel gab es Bilder: Nachrichten von darstellender Kunst im Alten Testament_ (OBO 74), Fribourg, Switzerland and Göttingen.

—— (1987b), "Die Zweiggöttin in Palästina/Israel. Von der Mittelbronze II B-Zeit bis zu Jesus Sirach," in: M. Küchler/Ch. Uehlinger, eds., _Jerusalem: Texte – Bilder – Steine_ (Novum Testamentum et Orbis Antiquus 6), Fribourg, Switzerland and Göttingen, 201–225.

SCHROER, SILVIA (1989), "Die Göttin auf den Stempelsiegeln aus Palästina/ Israel," in: Keel et al., 1989, 89–207.

SCHROER, SILVIA (1991), "Die göttliche Weisheit und der nachexilische Monotheismus," in: Wacker/Zenger 1991, 151–182.

SCHULMAN, ALAN (1984), "On the Goddess Plaque Mould from Tel Qarnayim," *Journal of the Society for the Study of Egyptian Antiquities* 14, 74–80.

—— (1988), "Catalogue of the Egyptian Finds," in: Rothenberg 1988, 114–147.

SCHUMACHER, GEORG (1908), *Tell el-Mutesellim: Bericht über die 1903 bis 1905 veranstalteten Ausgrabungen I*, Leipzig.

SCHWEITZER, URSULA (1948), *Löwe und Sphinx im alten Ägypten* (Ägyptologische Forschungen 15), Glückstadt – Hamburg.

SEEDEN, HELGA (1979), "A Small Clay Shrine in the AUB Museum," *Berytus* 27, 7–25.

—— (1980), *The Standing Armed Figurines in the Levant* (Prähistorische Bronzefunde I,1), Munich.

—— (1982), "Peace Figurines from the Levant," in: *Archéologie au Levant: Recueil à la mémoire de R. Saidah* (Collection de la Maison de l'Orient méditerranéen 12 = Série archéologique 9), Lyon, 107–121.

SEGER, JOE D. (1972), *Tomb Offerings from Gezer* (The Rockefeller Museum. Catalogue no. 94), Jerusalem.

—— (1976), "Reflections on the Gold Hoard from Gezer," *BASOR* 221, 133–140.

—— et al., (1988), *Gezer V: The Field I Caves* (Annual of the Hebrew Union College/Nelson Glueck School of Biblical Archaeology), Jerusalem.

SEIDL, URSULA (1989), *Die babylonischen Kudurru-Reliefs: Symbole mesopotamischer Gottheiten* (OBO 87), Fribourg, Switzerland and Göttingen.

SELLERS, OVID ROGERS (1933), *The Citadel of Beth-Zur: A Preliminary Report on the First Excavations [. . .]*, Philadelphia.

SELLIN, ERNST (1904), *Tell Ta'annek* (DKAW.PH L/4), Berlin.

—— (1927), "Die Ausgrabungen von Sichem. Kurze vorläufige Mitteilung über die Arbeiten im Sommer 1927," *ZDPV* 50, 265–274.

SELLIN, ERNST – WATZINGER, CARL (1913), *Jericho: Die Ergebnisse der Ausgrabungen* (WVDOG 22), Leipzig (reprint, Osnabrück 1973).

SHILOH, YIGAL (1979), *The Proto-Aeolic Capital and Israelite Ashlar Masonry* (Qedem 11), Jerusalem.

—— (1984), *Excavations at the City of David I. 1978–1982: Interim Report of the First Five Seasons* (Qedem 19), Jerusalem.

—— (1985), "A Hoard of Hebrew Bullae from the City of David," *ErIsr* 18, 71–87.68*.

—— (1986), "A Group of Hebrew Bullae from the City of David," *IEJ* 36, 16–38.

SHUPAK, NILI (1989), "New Light on Shamgar ben 'Anath," *Biblica* 70, 517–525.

SHUVAL, MENAKHEM (1990), "A Catalogue of Early Iron Stamp Seals from Israel," in: Keel et al., 1990, 67–161.

SINGER, ITAMAR (1985), "The Beginning of Philistine Settlement in Canaan and the Northern Boundary of Philistia," *Tel Aviv* 12, 109–122.

SINGER, ITAMAR (1989), "The Political Status of Megiddo VII A," *Tel Aviv* 15–16, 101–112.

SINGER, ITAMAR (1990), "Egyptians, Canaanites and Philistines in the Iron I," in: Na'aman/Finkelstein 1990, 348–402 (hebr.).

SMALL, TERRY AND KATHY (1986), "A Nude Philistine Captive from Jerusalem?" *BAR* 12/2, 68–69.

SMITH, MARK S. (1987), "God Male and Female in the Old Testament: Yahweh and his asherah," *TS* 48, 333–340.

—— (1990), *The Early History of God: Yahweh and the Other Deities in Ancient Israel*, San Francisco.

SMITH, ROBERT H. – McNICOLL, ANTHONY W. – HENNESSY, J. BASIL (1981), "The 1980 Season at Pella of the Decapolis," *BASOR* 243, 1–30.

SPIECKERMANN, HERMANN (1982), *Juda unter Assur in der Sargonidenzeit* (FRLANT 129), Göttingen.

SPELEERS, LOUIS (1917), *Catalogue des intailles et empreintes orientales des Musées Royaux du Cinquantenaire*, Brussels.

SPYCKET, AGNÈS (1973), "Le culte du dieu-lune à Tell Keisan," *RB* 80, 384–395.

STADELMANN, RAINER (1967), *Syrisch-palästinische Gottheiten in Ägypten*, Leiden.

STÄHLI, HANS-PETER (1985), *Solare Elemente im Jahweglauben des Alten Testaments* (OBO 66), Fribourg, Switzerland and Göttingen.

STAGER, LAWRENCE E. (1991), "When Canaanites and Philistines Ruled Ashkelon," *BAR* 17,2, 24–43.

STARKEY, JAMES L. – HARDING, GEORGE LANKESTER (1932), *Beth-Pelet II* (BSAE 52), London.

STAUBLI, THOMAS (1991), *Das Image der Nomaden im Alten Israel und in der Ikonographie seiner sesshaften Nachbarn* (OBO 107), Fribourg, Switzerland and Göttingen.

STERN, EPHRAIM (1973), "Eretz-Israel at the End of the Period of the Monarchy," *Qadmoniot* 6 (no. 21), 2–17 (hebr.).

—— (1978a), *Excavations at Tell Mevorakh (1973–1976)*. Part 1: *From the Iron Age to the Roman Period* (Qedem 9), Jerusalem.

—— (1978b), "New Types of Phoenician Style Decorated Pottery Vases from Palestine," *PEQ* 110, 11–21.

—— (1982), *Material Culture of the Land of the Bible in the Persian Period 538–332 B.C.*, Warminster and Jerusalem.

—— (1983), "Tel Dor, 1983," *IEJ* 33, 259–261.

—— (1984), *Excavations at Tel Mevorakh (1973–1976)*. Part 2: *The Bronze Age* (Qedem 18), Jerusalem.

—— (1987), "Excavations at Tell Dor. A Canaanite-Phoenician Port-City on the Carmel Coast," *Qadmoniot* 20 (nos. 79–80), 66–81 (hebr.).

—— (1989a), "Phoenician Discoveries at Tel Dor," *Qadmoniot* 22 (nos. 87–88), 103–110 (hebr.).

—— (1989b), "What Happened to the Cult Figurines? Israelite Religion Purified After the Exile," *BAR* 15/4, 22–29, 53–54.

—— (1990), "Schumacher's Shrine in Building 338 at Megiddo: A Rejoinder," *IEJ* 40, 102–107.

STERNBERG, FRANK, ed. (1989), *Auktion XXII. Antike Münzen. Griechen, Römer, Byzantiner. Geschnittene Steine und Schmuck der Antike, etc.*, Zurich.

STIEGLITZ, ROBERT R. (1990), "Die Göttin Tanit im Orient," *Antike Welt* 21/2, 106–109.

STOLZ, FRITZ (1988), *Grundzüge der Religionswissenschaft* (KVR 1527), Göttingen.

STRANGE, JOHN (1985), "The Idea of Afterlife in Ancient Israel: Some Remarks on the Iconography in Solomon's Temple," *PEQ* 117, 35–39.

STRAUSS, ELISABETH-CHRISTINE (1974), *Die Nunschale: Eine Gefäßgruppe des Neuen Reiches* (MÄS -30), Berlin.

STUCKY, ROLF A. (1974), *The Engraved Tridacna Shells* (Dédalo X/19), Sao Paolo.

TADMOR, MIRIAM (1982), "Female Cult Figurines in Late Canaan and Early Israel: Archaeological Evidence," in: Ishida 1982, 139–173.

—— (1989), "The 'Cult Standard' from Hazor in a New Light," *ErIsr* 20, 86–89 (hebr.). 197*.

TALLQVIST, KNUT LEONARD (1938), *Akkadische Götterepitheta* (SOr 7), Helsinki.

DE TARRAGON, JEAN-MICHEL (1989), "Les rituels," in: A. Caquot – J.-M. T. – J.-L. Cunchillos, *Textes ougaritiques*. Part II: *Textes religieux et rituels: Correspondance* (LAPO 14), Paris, 125–238.

TATUM, LYNN (1991), "King Manasseh and the Royal Fortresses at Ḥorvat 'Uza," *BA* 54, 136–145.

TAYLOR, JOHN G. (1988), "The Two Earliest Known Representations of Yahweh," in: L. Eslinger – J. G. Taylor, eds., *Ascribed to the Lord: Biblical and Other Studies in Memory of P.C. Craigie* (JSOTSup 67), Sheffield, 557–566.

TEISSIER, BEATRICE (1984), *Ancient Near Eastern Cylinder Seals from the Marcopoli Collection*, Berkeley – Los Angeles – London.

THOMPSON, H. O. (1970), *Mekal, the God of Beth-Shan*, Leiden.

TIGAY, JEFFREY H. (1986), *You shall have no Other Gods: Israelite Religion in the Light of Hebrew Inscriptions* (HSS 31), Atlanta, Ga.

TIMM, STEFAN (1989), *Moab zwischen den Mächten: Studien zu historischen Denkmälern und Texten* (ÄAT 17), Wiesbaden.

TOOMBS, LARRY E. – Wright, George Ernest (1963), "The fourth Campaign at Balâṭah (Shechem)," *BASOR* 169,1–60.

TRAN TAM TINH, V. (1986a), Art. "Bes," *LIMC* II/1, 98–108.

—— (1986b), Art. "Beset," *LIMC* II/1, 112–114.

TUBB, JONATHAN N. (1977), "Three Inscribed Arrowheads from Tell el-Ajjul," *BIAUL* 14, 191–195.

—— (1980), "A Bronze Arrowhead from Gezer," *PEQ* 112, 1–6.

TUFNELL, OLGA et al., (1940), *Lachish II (Tell ed-Duweir): The Fosse Temple*, London, etc.

—— (1953), *Lachish III (Tell ed-Duweir): The Iron Age*, 2 vols., London, etc.

—— (1958), *Lachish IV (Tell ed-Duweir): The Bronze Age*, 2 vols., London, etc.

—— (1984), *Studies on Scarab Seals, II: Scarab Seals and their Contribution to the History in the Early Second Millenium* B.C., 2 vols., Warminster.

TUSHINGHAM, A. D. (1970/1971), "A Royal Israelite Seal (?) and the Royal Jar Handle Stamps," *BASOR* 200, 71–78; 201, 23–35.

Gods, Goddesses, and Images of God

Tzori, Nehemiah (1958), "Cult Figurines in the Eastern Plain of Esdraelon and Beth-Shean," *ErIsr* 5, 52–55 (hebr.).86*.

Uehlinger, Christoph (1989), "Das Zeichen des Bundes," *BiKi* (Swiss Edition) 44 (1989) 195–197.

—— (1990a), "Der Amun-Tempel Ramses' III. in Gaza, seine südpalästinischen Tempelgüter und der Übergang von der Ägypter – zur Philister-Herrschaft. Ein Hinweis auf einige wenig beachtete Skarabäen" [*ZDPV* 104 (1988) 6–25, mit Nachträgen], in: Keel et al., 1990, 3–26.

—— (1990b), "Ein ʿnḫ-ähnliches Astralkultsymbol auf Stempelsiegeln des 8./7. Jhs.," ibid., 322–330.

—— (1990c), "Leviathan und die Schiffe in Ps 104,25–26," *Biblica* 71, 499–526.

—— (1991a), Art. "Götterbild," *NBL* I, 871–892.

—— (1991b), "Der Mythos vom Drachenkampf: von Sumer nach Nicaragua. Ein biblisches Feindbild und seine Geschichte," *BiKi* 46/2, 66–77.

Ussishkin, David (1974), "Tombs from the Israelite Period at Tel ʿEton," *Tel Aviv* 1, 109–127.

—— (1976) "Royal Judean Jars and Private Seal Impressions," *BASOR* 223, 1–13.

—— (1977), "The Destruction of Lachish by Sennacherib and the Dating of the Royal Judean Storage Jars," *Tel Aviv* 4, 28–60.

—— (1978), "Excavations at Tel Lachish 1973–1977. Preliminary Report," *Tel Aviv* 5, 1–97.

—— (1983), "Excavations at Tel Lachish 1978–1983. Second Preliminary Report," *Tel Aviv* 10, 97–185.

—— (1988), "The Date of the Judaean Shrine at Arad," *IEJ* 38, 142–157.

—— (1989), "Schumacher's Shrine in Building 338 at Megiddo," *IEJ* 39, 149–172.

—— (1990), "Megiddo, Gezer, Ashdod, and Tel Batash in the Tenth to Ninth Centuries B.C.," *BASOR* 277/278, 71–91.

Van Beek, Gus (1986), "Tel Jemme – 1984," *Excavations and Surveys in Israel* 5, 54–55.

Van Buren, Elizabeth Douglas (1945), *Symbols of the Gods in Mesopotamian Art* (AnOr 23), Rome.

Vandier d'Abbadie, J. (1937), *Catalogue des ostraca figurés de Deir el Médineh (Nᵒˢ 2256 à 2722), 2ᵉᵐᵉ fascicule* (DFIFAO II/2), Le Caire.

de Vaux, Roland (1955), "Les fouilles de Tell el-Farʿah, près Naplouse," *RB* 62, 541–589.

Ventura, Raphael (1987), "Four Egyptian Funerary Stelae from Deir el-Balaḥ," *IEJ* 37, 105–115.

Vincent, Louis-Hugues (1909), "Pseudo-figure de Iahvé récemment mise en circulation," *RB* 6, 121–127.

Vuk, T. (1987), "Neue Ausgrabungen in Jerusalem-Ketef Hinnom," *BiKi* 42, 30–36.

WACKER, MARIE-THÉRÈSE (1991a), "Feministisch-theologische Blicke auf die neuere Monotheismus-Diskussion," in: Wacker/Zenger 1991, 17–48.

—— (1991b), "Aschera oder die Ambivalenz des Weiblichen. Anmerkungen zum Beitrag von Georg Braulik," in: idem, 137–150.

WACKER, MARIE-THÉRÈSE – ZENGER, ERICH (1991), eds., *Der eine Gott und die Göttin: Gottesvorstellungen des biblischen Israel im Horizont feministischer Theologie* (QD 135), Freiburg im Breisgau – Basel – Vienna.

WARD, WILLIAM A. (1972), "A Unique Beset Figurine," *Or.* N.S. 41, 149–159.

—— (1978), *Studies on Scarab Seals I: Pre–12th Dynasty Scarab Amulets*, Warminster.

WEINBERG, SAUL S. (1978), "A Moabite Shrine Group," *MUSE: Annual of the Museum of Art and Archaeology, Missouri*, 12, 30–48.

WEINFELD, MOSHE (1972), "The Worship of Molech and of the Queen of Heaven and its Background," *UF* 4, 133–154.

—— (1982), "Additions to the Inscriptions of ʿAjrud," *Shnaton* 5–6, 237–239.

—— (1984), "Kuntillet ʿAjrud Inscriptions and Their Significance," *Studi Epigrafici e Linguistici* 1, 121–130.

WEIPPERT, HELGA (1978), "Siegel mit Mondsichelstandarten aus Palästina," *BN* 5, 43–58.

—— (1985), "Amos. Seine Bilder und ihr Milieu," in: idem – K. Seybold – M. Weippert, *Beiträge zur prophetischen Bildsprache in Israel und Assyrien* (OBO 64), Fribourg, Switzerland and Göttingen, 1–29.

—— (1988), *Palästina in vorhellenistischer Zeit* (Handbuch der Archäologie. Vorderasien II/1), Munich.

—— (1990), Review Article on: Winter 1983: *ZDPV* 106, 185–188.

WEIPPERT, HELGA and MANFRED (1982), "Die 'Bileam'-Inschrift von *Tell Dēr ʿAllā*," *ZDPV* 98, 77–103.

WEIPPERT, MANFRED (1975), "Zum Präskript der hebräischen Briefe von Arad," *VT* 25, 202–212.

—— (1977), "Kanaanäische 'Gravidenflaschen'. Zur Geschichte einer ägyptischen Gefäßgattung in der asiatischen 'Provinz'," *ZDPV* 93, 268–282.

—— (1980), Art. "Israel und Juda." *RlA* V, 200–208.

—— (1982), "Zur Syrienpolitik Tiglatpilesers III.," in: H.J. Nissen – J. Renger, ed., *Mesopotamien und seine Nachbarn* (XXV. Rencontre assyriologique internationale = Berliner Beiträge zum Vorderen Orient 1), Berlin (²1987) 395–408.

—— (1990), "Synkretismus und Monotheismus. Religionsinterne Konfliktbewältigung im alten Israel," in: J. Assmann – D. Harth, eds., *Kultur und Konflikt* (edition suhrkamp 1612 = edition suhrkamp N.F. 612), Frankfurt/Main, 143–179.

—— (1991), "The Balaam Text from Deir ʿAllā and the Study of the Old Testament," in: Hoftijzer/van der Kooij 1991, 151–184.

WELTEN, PETER (1969), *Die Königs-Stempel: Ein Beitrag zur Militärpolitik Judas unter Hiskia und Josia* (ADPV 1), Wiesbaden.

WENNING, ROBERT (1981), "Griechische Importe in Palästina aus der Zeit vor Alexander d.Gr.," *Boreas* 4, 29–46.

WENNING, ROBERT (1991a), Art. "Grab," *NBL* I, 942–946.

—— (1991b), "Wer war der Paredros der Aschera? Notizen zu Terrakottastatuetten in eisenzeitlichen Gräbern," *BN* 59, 89–97.

WENNING, ROBERT – ZENGER, ERICH (1986), "Ein bäuerliches Baal-Heiligtum im samarischen Gebirge aus der Zeit der Anfänge Israels. Erwägungen zu dem von A. Mazar zwischen Dotan und Tirza entdeckten 'Bull Site'," *ZDPV* 102, 75–86.

—— (1990), "Tod und Bestattung im biblischen Israel. Eine archäologische und religionsgeschichtliche Skizze," in: *"Ihr alle aber seid Brüder"* (FS A. Th. Khoury) (Würzburger Forschungen zur Missions- und Religions-wissenschaft. Religionswissenschaftliche Studien 14), Würzburg and Altenberge, 285–303.

—— (1991), "Heiligtum ohne Stadt – Stadt ohne Heiligtum? Anmerkungen zum archäologischen Befund des *Tell Dēr 'Allā*," *ZAH* 4, 171–193.

WIESE, ANDRÉ (1990), *Zum Bild des Königs auf ägyptischen Siegelamuletten* (OBO 96), Fribourg, Switzerland and Göttingen.

WILLIAMS, ANTHONY J. (1976), "The Mythological Background of Ezekiel 28,12–19," *BTB* 6, 49–61.

WILLIAMS D. P. (1977), *The Tombs of the Middle Bronze Age II Period from the 500 Cemetery at Tell Fara (South)*, London.

WILSON, V. (1975), "The Iconography of Bes in Cyprus and the Levant," *Levant* 7, 77–103.

WIMMER, STEFAN (1990), "Egyptian Temples in Canaan and Sinai," in: Sarah Israelit-Groll, ed., *Studies in Egyptology Presented to Miriam Lichtheim*, Vol. II, Jerusalem, 1065–1106.

WINTER, IRENE J. (1976), "Phoenician and North Syrian Ivory Carving in Historical Context: Questions of Style and Distribution," *Iraq* 38, 1–22.

—— (1981), "Is there a South Syrian Style of Ivory Carving in the Early First Millenium B.C.?" *Iraq* 43, 101–130.

WINTER, URS (1983), *Frau und Göttin: Exegetische und ikonographische Studien zum weiblichen Gottesbild im Alten Israel und in dessen Umwelt* (OBO 53), Fribourg, Switzerland and Göttingen (²1987).

WRESZINSKI, WALTER (1934), *Atlas zur altägyptischen Kulturgeschichte II*, Leipzig.

WRIGHT, GEORGE ERNEST (1959), "Israelite Samaria and Iron Age Chronology," *BASOR* 155, 13–28.

—— (1962), "Selected Seals from the Excavations at Balâṭah (Shechem)," *BASOR* 167, 5–13.

—— (1965), *Shechem: The Biography of a Biblical City*, London.

WYATT, NICOLAS (1983), "The Stela of the Seated God from Ugarit," *UF* 14, 271–277.

YADIN, YIGAEL et al., (1958), *Hazor I*, Jerusalem.

—— (1959), "Note on a Proto-Canaanite Inscription from Lachish," *PEQ* 91, 130–131.

—— et al., (1960), *Hazor II*, Jerusalem.

—— et al., (1961), *Hazor III-IV. Plates*, Jerusalem.

—— (1972), *Hazor: The Head of all those Kingdoms* (SchL 1970), London.

YADIN, YIGAEL et al., (1975), *Hazor: The Rediscovery of a Great Citadel of the Bible*, London and Jerusalem.

—— (1989), *Hazor III-IV: An Account of the Third and Fourth Seasons of Excavation, 1957–1958* [ed. by A. Ben-Tor and Sh. Geva], Jerusalem.

YARDENI, ADA (1991), "Remarks on the Priestly Blessing on two Ancient Amulets from Jerusalem," *VT* 41, 176–185.

YASSINE, KHAIR – TEIXIDOR, JAVIER (1986), "Ammonite and Aramaic Inscriptions from Tell El-Mazār in Jordan," *BASOR* 264, 45–50.

YOUNKER, RANDALL W. (1985), "Israel, Judah, and Ammon and the Motifs on the Baalis Seal from Tell el-'Umeiri," *BA* 48, 173–180.

ZADOK, RAN (1985), "Samarian Notes," *BiOr* 42, 567–572.

ZEVIT, ZIONY (1984), "The Khirbet el-Qôm Inscription Mentioning a Goddess," *BASOR* 255, 33–41.

ZEVULUN, UZA (1987), "A Canaanite Ram Headed Cup," *IEJ* 37, 88–104.

ZIFFER, IRIT (1990), *At that Time the Canaanites were in the Land: Daily Life in Canaan in the Middle Bronze Age 2, 2000–1550 B.C.E.*, Tel Aviv (hebr.).

ZIMHONI, ORA (1990), "Two Ceramic Assemblages from Lachish Levels III and II," *Tel Aviv* 17, 3–52.

ZUCKERMAN, BRUCE (1987), *Puzzling out the Past: Making Sense on Ancient Inscriptions from Biblical Times [. . .]*, Wilshire Boulevard Temple.

ZWICKEL, WOLFGANG (1987), "Die Kesselwagen im salomonischen Tempel," *UF* 18, 459–461.

—— (1990a), *Räucherkult und Räuchergeräte: Exegetische und archäologische Studien zum Räucheropfer im Alten Testament* (OBO 97), Fribourg, Switzerland and Göttingen.

—— (1990b), "Die Keramikplatte aus *Tell Qasīle*. Gleichzeitig ein Beitrag zur Deutung von Jachin und Boas," *ZDPV* 106, 57–62.

Index of Subjects

The references are not exhaustive and are based on references within the text itself.
They are not coordinated with corresponding depictions in the illustrations.

The Authors

OTHMAR KEEL, born in 1937 in Einsiedeln (Switzerland), studied Theology, Biblical and Religious Studies as well as ancient Near Eastern art history in Zurich, Fribourg, Rome, Jerusalem, and Chicago. Since 1969 he has been Professor of Old Testament Exegesis and Religious History of the Biblical World at the University of Fribourg, Switzerland. His numerous publications include *The Symbolism of the Biblical World: Ancient Near Eastern Iconography and the Book of Psalms* (1978, reprint 1997); *The Song of Songs: A Continental Commentary* (1994); *Goddesses and Trees, New Moon and Yahweh: Ancient Near Eastern Art and the Hebrew Bible* (JSOT Suppl. 261, 1998). Since 1981 he has directed a long-range research program on the contribution of glyptic iconography to the religious history of the southern Levant. Publications related to this project include *Studien zu den Stempelsiegeln aus Palästina/Israel I–IV* (OBO 67, 1985; 88, 1988; 100, 1990; 135, 1994, with Hildi Keel-Leu, Silvia Schroer, Menakhem Shuval , and Christoph Uehlinger) and *Corpus der Stempelsiegel aus Palästina/Israel von den Anfägen bis zur Perserzeit: Einleitung* and *Vol. I: Abu Farağ – ʿAtlit* (OBO Series Archaeologica 10, 1995; 13, 1997), which has been awarded the 1998 Irene Levi-Sala Book Prize in the Archaeology of Israel.

CHRISTOPH UEHLINGER, born in 1958 in Zurich, studied Theology, Biblical and ancient Near Eastern studies in Fribourg, Berne, Jerusalem, and London. Since 1991 he has been a Senior Lecturer in Old Testament Exegesis and Religious History of the Biblical World at the University of Fribourg, Switzerland. His book publications include *Weltreich und «eine Rede»: Eine neue Deutung der sogenannten Turmbauerzählung (Gen 11:1–9)* (OBO 101, 1990); *Studies in the Iconography of Northwest Semitic Inscribed Seals* (OBO 125, 1993, with Benjamin Sass); *Altorientalische Miniaturkunst: Die ältesten visuellen Massenkommunikationsmittel* (1990, 2nd ed. 1996, with O. Keel).

Othmar Keel and Christoph Uehlinger are the editors of the *Orbis Biblicus et Orientalis* series and curators of the Biblical Institute's collections of ancient Near Eastern miniature art.